D1376199

DYNAMICS AND INCOME DISTRIBUTION

ECONOMISTS OF THE TWENTIETH CENTURY

General Editors: Mark Perlman, *University Professor of Economics, Emeritus, University of Pittsburgh* and Mark Blaug, *Professor Emeritus, University of London, Professor Emeritus, University of Buckingham and Visiting Professor, University of Exeter*

This innovative series comprises specially invited collections of articles and papers by economists whose work has made an important contribution to economics in the late twentieth century.

The proliferation of new journals and the ever-increasing number of new articles make it difficult for even the most assiduous economist to keep track of all the important recent advances. By focusing on those economists whose work is generally recognized to be at the forefront of the discipline, the series will be an essential reference point for the different specialisms included.

A list of published and future titles in this series is printed at the end of this volume.

Dynamics and Income Distribution

The Selected Essays of Irma Adelman
Volume II

Irma Adelman

University of California
Berkeley, US

ECONOMISTS OF THE TWENTIETH CENTURY

Edward Elgar

Published by
Edward Elgar Publishing Limited
Gower House
Croft Road
Aldershot
Hants GU11 3HR
England

Edward Elgar Publishing Company
Old Post Road
Brookfield
Vermont 05036
USA

British Library Cataloguing in Publication Data
Adelman, Irma
  Selected Essays of Irma Adelman. – Vol. II:
  Dynamics and Income Distribution. –
  (Economists of the Twentieth Century
  Series)
  I. Title II. Series
  339.2

Library of Congress Cataloguing in Publication Data
Adelman, Irma.
   Dynamics and income distribution: selected essays of Irma Adelman
/ Irma Adelman.
   v. ⟨2 ⟩ — (Economists of the twentieth century)
   1. Econometrics. 2. Business cycles. 3. Income distribution.
4. Economic development. I. Title. II. Series.
HB139.A324 1995
339.2—dc20   94–48924
                                                              CIP

ISBN 1 85898 051 8 (Volume I)
     1 85898 052 6 (Volume II)

Printed and bound in Great Britain by
Hartnolls Limited, Bodmin, Cornwall

Contents

Acknowledgements

The publishers wish to thank the following who have kindly given permission for the use of copyright material.

Academic Press for article: 'Patterns of Economic Growth, 1850–1914, or Chenery-Syrquin in Historical Perspective' (with Cynthia Taft Morris) in *Economic Structure and Performance: Essays in Honor of Hollis B. Chenery*, M. Syrquin, L. Taylor and L.E. Westphal (eds), 1984, 45–74.

American Economic Association for articles: 'Long Cycles – Fact or Artifact?', *American Economic Review*, LV(3), June 1965, 444–63; 'An Econometric Analysis of Population Growth', *American Economic Review*, LIII(3), June 1963, 314–39; 'Development Economics – A Reassessment of Goals', *American Economic Review*, 65(2), May 1975, 302–9.

Banca Nazionale del Lavoro Quarterly Review for article: 'Confessions of an Incurable Romantic', 166, September 1988, 243–62.

Blackwell Publishers for article: 'Business Cycles – Endogenous or Stochastic?', *Economic Journal*, December 1960, 783–96.

Econometric Society for article: 'The Dynamic Properties of the Klein-Goldberger Model' (with Frank L. Adelman), *Econometrica*, 27(4), October 1959, 596–625.

Economic and Political Weekly for article: 'Some Dynamic Aspects of Rural Poverty in India' (with K. Subbarao and Prem Vashishtha), XX(39), September 28, 1985, A103–A116.

Elsevier Science Inc. for articles: 'The Equalizing Role of Human Resource Intensive Growth Strategies' (with Amnon Levy), *Journal of Policy Modeling*, 6(2), May 1984, 271–87; 'Food Security Policy in a Stochastic World' (with Peter Berck), *Journal of Development Economics*, 34(1/2), 1991, 25–55.

Institute for International Development for article: 'Static and Dynamic Indices of Income Inequality' (with Peter Whitte), *Canadian Journal of Development Studies*, 1(1), 1980, 27–46.

Journal of Economic History for article: 'Institutional Influences on Poverty in the Nineteenth Century: A Quantitative Comparative Study' (with Cynthia Taft Morris), XLIII(1), March 1983, 43–55.

Kluwer Academic Publishers for article: 'Redistribution Before Growth: A Strategy for Developing Countries', Inaugural Lecture for the Cleveringa Chair, Leiden University, October 1977, Martinus Nijhoff, 1979.

McGill-Queen's University Press for article: 'What is the Evidence on Income Inequality and Development' in *Equity and Efficiency in Economic Development: Essays in Honor of Benjamin Higgins*, I. Brecher and D.J. Savoie (eds), 1992, 121–46.

Metroeconomica for article: 'The Lack of Pareto Superiority of Unegalitarian Wealth Distributions' (with L. Cheng), **XXXV**, June 1983, 105–22.

M.E. Sharpe Inc. for article: 'Strategies for Equitable Growth', *Challenge*, **17**(2), May/June 1974, 37–44.

METU Studies in Development for article: 'Development Strategies and the Size of Distribution of World Income', *METU Studies in Development*, **11**(1,2), 1984, 177–93.

OECD Development Centre for article: 'Who Benefits from Economic Development?' (with Cynthia Taft Morris) in *Planning Income Distribution, Private Foreign Investment*, 1974, 49–82.

Pergamon Press Ltd for article: 'Policies for Equitable Growth' (with Cynthia Taft Morris and Sherman Robinson), *World Development*, **4**(7), 1976, 561–82.

Transaction for article: 'A Poverty-Focused Approach to Development Policy' in *Development Strategies Reconsidered*, J.P. Lewis and V. Kallab (eds), 1986, 49–65.

Every effort has been made to trace all the copyright holders but if any have been inadvertently overlooked the publishers will be pleased to make the necessary arrangements at the first opportunity.

For permission to reprint articles co-authored with Irma Adelman we would like to thank the following:

Peter Berck, Leonard K. Cheng, Amnon Levy, Cynthia Taft Morris, Sherman Robinson, K. Subbarao, Prem Vashishtha and Peter Whittle.

INTRODUCTION

[1]

Confessions of an Incurable Romantic *

Writing my intellectual autobiography is an assignment which I have long postponed, primarily out of fear. Such a retrospective self-appraisal would inevitably make me stand naked in front of myself, influence the rest of my career and impart a sense of, hopefully premature, semi-closure. A gentle reminder by the editors has now made me grit my teeth, lay my trepidations aside, and commence.

I was born in Cernowitz, Roumania, in March, 1930. Amusingly enough, Joseph Schumpeter had played an unwitting role in my parents' marriage. My mother was a law student at the University of Cernowitz while Schumpeter was teaching there. She was being courted by my father, a businessman ten years her senior. She decided to reject his suit, took her qualifying exam in economics from Schumpeter, and returned to her home town. A few months later, she was informed that Schumpeter had lost her examination paper, and that she would have to take the exam again. She returned to Cernowitz, was met by my father who, in his sorrow at being rejected by her, had shaved his head and lost about fifteen pounds. Her heart went out to him and she reversed her decision.

Formative influences

The formative influences on my life and values were my parents, my early education, and the trauma of World War II. My mother, a very attractive, intelligent, and vivacious woman, never got to practice law. My father claimed that her working would ruin his credit rating and the

---

* Contribution to a series of recollections on professional experiences of distinguished economists. This series opened with the September 1979 issue of this *Review*.

quota on Jewish lawyers imposed by the Roumanian government in the thirties meant that by choosing to practice she would take bread out of the mouth of a Jewish male *pater familias*. So she concentrated her boundless energy and ambition on me, a single child. She was determined (poor woman) that I would be as attractive as possible given my original, rather unpropitious, endowments and that I would have the career that circumstances had conspired to rob her of. Her efforts imbued me with a view of the perfectibility of individuals and society that have dominated my teaching and research.

My father was a socialist businessman, a not unusual paradox among East European Jewish businessmen at the time. He had been studying at the University of Kiev, in the Ukraine, when the Russian Revolution broke out, and was a Zionist Menshevik, a socialist reformer. When the Bolsheviks won, he fled to Roumania. He had been scheduled to be shot, but the officer in charge of the firing squad turned out to be a friend of my uncle's and enabled him to escape. From my father I gained my commitment to social reform, my compassion for the poor, and my sense of outrage at social conditions that generate mass poverty and mass deprivation.

Despite being Jewish, my early education in Roumania was at a French Catholic nun's school, Notre Dame de Sion. The Jews are said to own "guilt" and the Catholics to have a lifetime lease on it. My early education therefore left me with a mammoth sense of primordial guilt, that was later reinforced by the guilt of the survivor of the Holocaust. The expiation of this guilt through the only mechanism it can be expiated — service to humanity — has been a primary driving force in my life.

World War II left an indelible mark, even though I escaped comparatively unscathed. My father had had the foresight and courage to leave Roumania in 1939 for Palestine, so that the entire nuclear family survived intact. The main impact of the War on me was the wrenching break in personal attachments involved in becoming a refugee, and the experience of mass religious hatred. I remember my father telling me when I was six that I might be reviled for being Jewish, but that I should be proud of this fact. Since I knew not what being Jewish was, and had been taught by the nuns that pride is sin, this talk left me totally bewildered. The War imbued me with a sense of rootlessness, a suspicion of mass ideologies, a sense of the impermanence of any state, a lack of attachment to possessions, and a sense of personal worthlessness. It also induced a sense of belonging nowhere and everywhere, that is the mark of the cosmopolitan, and a feeling of "There but for the grace of God go I" towards the less fortunate, akin to Rawl's initial state of ignorance. On the positive side, I learned that the only thing one can rely on is one's human capital — one's knowledge, skills, and character — because all else can be taken away at the bellow of a demagogue. My later fascination with stochastic shocks, with nonlinear dynamics, and socio-political view of economic development also have their roots in my World War II experience.

There was never any doubt in my mind that I had to become an intellectual. It was my only comparative advantage (I was an uncoordinated, rolly-polly and cross-eyed youngster), and my parents and world view had predisposed me to see in education my only potential for achieving a moderately stable and socially productive life. After finishing high school in Palestine and fighting in the Israeli war of independence, I enrolled in 1949 as an undergraduate at the University of California at Berkeley. I chose business administration with a minor in public administration not because of my interest in these subjects — had I let myself pursue my own inclinations I would have studied French and German literature and art history — but rather because of my perception of the primary needs of the nascent State of Israel, the furthering of whose interests I was dedicated to. But this was not to be! Shortly after coming to Berkeley, I met my husband, an American physics PhD candidate, fell in love, married, and stayed. In making the decision to marry and stay, I felt very guilty at putting my personal happiness ahead of my duty to Israel, whom I felt I was betraying by not returning there.

I sailed through undergraduate school, shifted to economics in graduate school, and obtained my PhD six years after having entered as an undergraduate. My graduate education was sadly lacking. At the time, Berkeley was very weak in economic theory and in mathematical training. Robert Dorfman was the only ray of light in the graduate program and I shudder to think what I would have become had I not been able to benefit from his tutelage. I supplemented the graduate program in economics by taking courses in statistics, mathematics, and in agricultural economics, where, together with Arnold Zellner, Zvi Griliches and Yair Mundlak, I learned my econometrics from George Kuznets. I also benefitted greatly from the influence of my husband, Frank Adelman, who taught me a view of scientific method involving a continual iterative interaction between theory and experimental or statistical "stylized facts" that is natural to applied physicists but still not to economists.

Research

From the perspective of a historian of doctrine, the research process appears planned *a priori*; from the perspective of the author, it appears as a series of unplanned choices that are guided by personal interest and a sense of the importance of the issues, and are made in response to opportunities, both external and self-generated. Although both perspectives are correct, I shall adopt the latter in this narrative.

My early research was eclectic, but there were a few common threads, arising from my values and early personal experiences: concern with dynamics, both cyclical and long run; concern with stochastic processes; and concern with aggregation procedures. "The Dynamic Properties of the Klein Goldberger Model", "Business Cycles, Endogenous or Stochastic?", "A Stochastic Analysis of the Size Distribution of Firms", my first book, and my work on hedonic index numbers (1961) were all facets of these concerns. There were also some methodological predilections, which have stayed with me throughout my entire career, and which reflect my scientific predispositions: a view of the world as an interdependent system; a view of the world as real and of scientific research as holding up a, hopefully non-distorting, mirror to it; and an inner compulsion to contribute to the elucidation of real world issues that affect the welfare of a large proportion of the world's population.

The Klein-Goldberger paper arose when my husband, a physicist, one day expressed a desire to try programming a simple problem and asked whether there was anything in economics that might be suitable. I suggested the Klein Goldberger model. This was before the days of Fortran (1955); all programming was in machine language. I remember spreading out a large sheet of paper on the floor, with a map of the computer memory, and keeping track of the location of individual variables after every operation. Nevertheless, when we ran the problem, there was only one error in the code! After we finished the computer runs, my husband taught me a valuble lesson. He said: "Now it's up to you to milk the results". The writing of the paper was excruciating: we composed it jointly and fought over every word in every sentence, finishing only one or two paragraphs per night. This paper, which confirmed the Frisch hypothesis of random origin of business cycles, has been identified as one of the best 20 articles in *Econometrica*, and achieved the status of a "classic" in business cycles and in simulation of economic systems.

My first book, *Theories of Economic Growth and Development* (Stanford Press, 1961), was originally written as the development-theory section of an undergraduate text on economic development joint with L. Mears and A. Pepelassis. The publisher, Mc Graw Hill, objected that my section was at a more advanced level than the rest of the book and insisted that it be taken out. I then revised it, making the text more lucid, but, when it came to seeking a publisher, I became racked with doubt. It seemed to me that the book contained little that was original, and that when I was describing the interactions of socio-cultural and institutional features of societies with their economic development I did not know what I was talking about. So, for a few months after finishing the revision, I held the manuscript. But this troubled me. Paul Baran, my then colleague at Stanford, noticed that I was upset and asked me why. When I blurted out my concerns, he said: "It's all very simple, Irma. Let the market decide! Send the book to a few publishers, and see whether they take it". Amusing advice from the then only Marxist economist teaching at an American university...

This book, with its associated doubts, set the stage for one of my consistent lines of research: how the economic growth of nations is affected by and, in turn, affects economic and political institutions, and socio-cultural structures and values; and how institutions and economic structures and choices affect the diffusion of benefits from economic and institutional change. I felt the need to understand these processes better and to base my understanding on empirically generated hypotheses and stylized facts. This is the line of research with which Professor Cynthia Taft Morris became associated.

I first met Cynthia Taft Morris in Washington D.C., in the summer of 1962, when we were both Research Associates at the Brookings Institution. We both had just moved to Washington, following, like the Biblical Ruth, our husbands' careers, and were both a little disoriented by the need to build new professional bases for ourselves. Our work together that summer was the beginning of a lifetime friendship and association. After the summer, Cynthia Morris combined teaching at American University with part-time work at the Agency for International Development (AID), in the research division headed by Hollis Chenery. And I started teaching at Johns Hopkins University, in Baltimore, and was brought by Hollis Chenery into his research division with a vague mandate to roam through the AID files and find something researchable. I found the AID country reports — monographs generated by AID offices in the field as annual reports on their respective

Banca Nazionale del Lavoro

countries. This was before the days of general data banks; indeed, even before the days of published comparable figures on per capita GNP! The reports were variable in quality and reliability, but had undergone some vetting before being sent to Washington, and, at least in principle, were uniform in coverage. They were treasure-troves of up to date information concerning political and socio-cultural country situations together with quantitative and descriptive information on industry, agriculture, investment and international trade. Naturally, the information had to be cross-checked, especially for political bias and lack of comparative experience with other developing countries, but nevertheless offered an invaluable starting point. I became very excited about the potential of these country reports for generating information usable in research on interactions of economic social and political facets of economic development. Also, in reading psychological literature, I had come across the use of factor analysis. This technique seemed to offer an ideal statistical vehicle for exploratory research on interactions about which there were no validated theories. I asked Cynthia Morris whether she would be interestd in collaborating with me on this project. And so, *Society, Politics, and Economic Development — A Quantitative Approach* (Johns Hopkins Press, 1967) was born.

A word about our professional collaboration may be in order: Cynthia Morris had polio as a teenager and has been on crutches ever since. As a result, her mobility has been limited. She therefore informed me early in our collaboration that she did not wish to be involved in presenting papers at conferences, professional meetings, etc.; that task would be up to me. Unfortunately, her less visible role has led the profession to underestimate her contributions to our joint work.

In 1965, when the major work on *Society, Politics, and Economic Development* was done, it occured to us that it would be interesting to see how applicable the hypotheses generated by this research on contemporary development were to the historical development process during the period of the Industrial Revolution. This research was especially appealing to Cynthia Morris, whose training was as an economic historian with a strong institutional bent. She then started working on gathering comparable information on 23 countries for the period 1850-1914. In 1972, I met Herman Wold, at a talk on the methodology of partial least squares and, more generally, on soft modelling that he gave at the World Bank. I got very excited by his philosophy and approach, rare among mainstream statisticians, to which I resonated. Ever since finishing *Society, Politics, and Economic*

Development, I had been looking for distribution-free methods of melding partial prior specification with sample information. (While my philosophy was Bayesian, there were two reasons I could not go the strict Bayesian route: I did not want to specify a specific prior distribution, especially with the type of discrete, ranked data that characterized my work on interactions between social, political, and institutional features of societies and their development patterns. I also wanted to deal with interdependent systems, and this is still difficult with present Bayesian techniques.) Herman Wold's approach seemed to be the answer. I started working with him in the early stages of the development of the partial least squares approach, and through him became aware of the work of Svante Wold, on disjoint principal components models. It is this latter approach that Cynthia Morris and I used in our historical work. Little did we know, when we started this research in 1965, that it would be 23 years before our historical work could culminate in a book describing what role institutional and political forces had played in inducing the very diverse economic responses of individual countries to the challenges and opportunities offered by the early Industrial Revolution in Great Britain! Our book, *Comparative Patterns of Economic Development, 1850-1914* (Johns Hopkins Press) appeared only in 1988. In this book, I finally succeeded in persuading Cynthia Morris to put her name as first author, both as a means of reflecting our relative contributions to this work and as a means of partially rectifying the general misconceptions about her contributions to our past joint research.

Of course, during the twenty three years that it took to complete this book, there were several detours on the way. The most important was our joint and my separate work on income distribution in developing countries. In 1969, the Agency of International Development came under fire from the US Congress for not paying enough attention to the spread of benefits from its projects. (It would appear that international junkets by Senators and Congressmen have some uses!) Cynthia and I were asked to undertake a study of the breadth of participation, both economically and politically, by developing countries' populations in the development process. The result was *Economic Growth and Social Equity in Developing Countries* (Stanford Press, 1973). While generally taken as having confirmed Kuznets' U-hypothesis, our results confirmed a J-hypothesis. We found that the share of income accruing to the poor first declines rapidly, then less rapidly, then less rapidly, and then, depending on the policy choices made, either levels off (the J) or starts increasing (the U). Politically, as the indigenous middle class and urbanization increase, and as education and communication improve, the influence on policy of non-elite groups starts extending to the middle class and to workers in the modern sector. But we found that the greater political participation of these groups does not redound to the benefit of the poor. Indeed, the middle class benefits at the expense of both the poor and the rich.

We were deeply shocked by our findings. Up to then we had believed in the benign view of economic development offered by modernization-scholars and in the trickle-down hypothesis imbuing mainstream writings on economic development. Were it not for the function-free statistical technique we adopted for our study, and were it not for our inductive empirical approach, we would have adopted an *a priori* specification confirming the modernization-cum-trickle-down theories. We would then have ascribed the poor statistical fit to poor data and small sample size. It is also fortunate that we undertook an arduous effort to obtain direct information on income distribution, despite the virtual lack of published studies. Of over 200 books and more than 1000 articles on individual countries published in the previous ten years, we found income-distribution information in only one — Samuel Barber's study of South Africa — for 1948! We found a list, prepared by the United Nations Statistical Office, of income distribution studies in developing countries that had been carried out but had not been published, and then proceeded to use the leverage or AID field offices to obtain the studies themselves. We were also fortunate to find the comparative study by Christian Morrisson, written as his PhD dissertation, with income-distribution estimates for Sub-Saharan African countries. This data, though of lesser reliability than the data for the more developed countries, played a critical role in generating the initial decline of the income share of the poorest. We submitted our report to AID and then did not publish the results for two years since we feared that our findings would be used as an argument to curtail resources for foreign-assistance rather than redirect resources to more poverty-oriented projects and programs. We felt free to publish our findings only after we were convinced they would do no harm: by 1973 the decline in foreign-assistance was already underway and new evidence concerning increasing urban unemployment despite rapid growth was making it clear that all was not well with the development process.

Our findings in this book led to the second major strand in my work: that dealing with income distribution and poverty, both descriptively and from a policy viewpoint. Two articles, "On the State of Development Economics" and "Development Economics - A Reassessment of Goals", summarize the effect my shock had on my research. In the former I argued that the fundamental failure of development economics had its roots in several methodological deficiencies: the failure to take a sufficiently broad systems-approach; the failure to monitor results adequately; the pervasive search for panaceas and for simplicity and simple guidance rules; and insufficient humility and insufficient professionalism in our approach to development. In the latter article, I argued that the goals of development should become the creation of the social and material conditions for the realization of human potential by all. This goal should replace the goal of self-sustained growth; rather, growth should be viewed as an instrument for the achievement of poverty reduction — a goal to which I referred as "depauperization". Mark Blaugh (1985) calls this paper my most readable and controversial article.

I joined the World Bank in 1971 and started a research program aimed at seeing whether an approach to economic development policy exists that would spread more of the benefits of development to the poor. This was genuinely an open question, since the history of the early phases of the Industrial Revolution in developed countries had also exhibited a decrease in the share of income accruing to the poor. It seemed to me that finding such an approach would require generating a computer-laboratory in which experiments with policies and programs could be carried out and evaluated. This laboratory should represent how economic actors interact in an actual economy, portray the governmentally set rules for markets and behavior, incorporate all the instruments for intervention and all the variables that are important in mediating the impact of the economy, of governments, and of the rest of the world on the poor. Having seen how the simple (simplistic?) *a priori* models that identified single-cause development prime-movers or bottlenecks had led the devolopment-policy formulating community into advocating a seriously flawed development process, I rejected the methodology of specifying a two or three sector model with one or two classes of actors, solving it for its comparative statics implications, and then basing policy recommendations on these findings. Rather, I argued for building a complex but realistic computer-model and then simplifying it *a posteriori*, on the basis of sensitivity experiments. This returned me to the methodology of digital simulation, introduced into economics by my first major published article, on the Klein-Goldberger model. I asked Sherman Robinson, who was then an Assistant Professor at Princeton, to join me in this research. (I had first met Sherman Robinson when, as a PhD candidate at Harvard, he asked me for the *Society, Politics, and Economic Development* data for use in his dissertation. When he finished, he sent me a copy of his dissertation, and I was impressed with him.)

We first thought that the appropriate model structure for our research on income distribution would be offered by a Johansen model. But it then became clear that, since our purpose was to model structural change and large-program interventions, a model like Johansen's, that is expressed in linear rates of growth, might miss effects that are of the same order of magnitude as the impacts of the experiments themselves. Sherman Robinson suggested that we change our formulation to solving for the levels of the endogenous variables rather than, as in the Johansen model, for their rates of change. And so, the first large-scale computable general equilibrium model (CGE) was born. The model was quite large (it contained over 3000 endogenous variables); mixed neo-classical and structuralist features; incorporated non-homogeneities in investment and government behavior; had an endogenous demand for money; two loanable funds markets (one official and one unorganized); two policy regimes (a tight-money regime with fixed money supply and rationing, and a loose-money regime with fixed interest rates); and some elements of industrial organization within sectors (four firm or farm sizes, with different behavior rules and different credit and foreign exchange access by large firms). The model was applied to South Korea, a country for which we both had a feeling. The initial reactions to our model specification were skeptical. Our critics contended that we would never be able to solve the model, and that, even if we were able to solve it, we would not be able to understand what was going on in the model. We proved them wrong, however, on both counts. Our book, *Income Distribution Policy in Developing Countries: The Case of Korea* (Stanford Press), finished in 1975, appeared in 1978. In it, we were able to identify the important policy variables, explain how the model worked, and gain a feeling for the relative importance of different policy interventions. (The first general presentation of the model was in 1973, at World Congress of the Econometric Society, in Toronto. There we met with John Whalley, then a graduate student writing his dissertation with Herbert Scarf, and he asked us many questions about solution-techniques, and about the feasibility of solving other than toy-models. The first written reports on the model were in 1973 and the first publication, giving our rather pessimistic policy conclusions based on our comparative statics experiments, was in 1975, as part of my paper calling for a shift in emphasis away from economic growth and towards poverty alleviation as the major goal of development policy.)

In the policy experiments we performed with our CGE model we found that policy interventions aimed at increasing the equality of the size distribution of income were very difficult. Of the roughly 3000 endogenous variables in the model only two, rural-urban migration and the agricultural terms of trade had a perceptible impact. The size distribution of income was exceedingly stable — even large-scale programs produced effects that altered only the second decimal of the Gini coefficient. Most interventions altered the incidence of poverty (*i.e.* the functional distribution of income), especially between the rural and urban poor and near poor, without changing the relative magnitude of poverty (*i.e.* the size distribution of income). In the absence of changes in the distribution of assets or institutions affecting the access of the poor to factor and commodity markets, only changes in development strategy, equivalent to large packages of mutually coordinated programs, could alter the relative magnitude of poverty by engendering the right kind of economic growth. Absolute poverty was easier to reduce than relative poverty. This conclusion was confirmed by our dynamic experiments and is consistent with the conclusions from models for different countries, with different closure rules, and different structural specifications (Adelman and Robinson, 1988).

After the book was finished, Sherman Robinson joined the World Bank and shifted to work on industrialization and trade with generic CGE models. He simplified the specification of the Korea-CGE model, based on the intuition gained from our sensitivity and policy experiments; improved the solution algorithm; improved the trade specification; and based the model-calibration explicitly, rather than only implicitly, on the Social Accounting Matrix (SAM) accounting framework. His work did a great deal to disseminate the use of CGE models among academic researchers and in the policy-planning community. Amusingly enough, however, with the currently renewed interest in the impact of IMF-inspired structural adjustment programs on the poor in debt-ridden developing countries, many of the monetary, macroeconomic, industrial-organization, and credit-allocation mechanisms that he ripped out of the Korea-CGE model, in an effort to arrive at a simpler generic model, are being reintroduced into CGEs of the 1980s, one by one.

I continued my work on income-distribution policy and, becoming increasingly discouraged about the potential for policy-impact on development assistance and on development policy after the two oil shocks, increasingly turned to non-policy work on institutions in development and economic history.

In 1977, I was invited to hold the Cleveringa chair at Leyden. This was a chair established by the Queen of the Netherlands to commemorate the resistance of Leyden University, led by Cleveringa, a law Professor, to the Nazi order to fire all Jewish Professors. The chair was to deal with some issue affecting human rights, be staffed by a social scientist one a one-year basis, and rotate between a Dutch and a foreign Professor. I was the fourth holder of the chair, the second economist after Tinbergen. In my inaugural address, "Redistribution Before Growth - A Strategy for Developing Countries" (Martinus Nijhof, 1978) I advocated asset redistribution before, rather than after, improvements in the asset's productivity: land reform before improvements in agricultural productivity and mass primary education before a major push on industrialization. Asset redis- tribution before improvements in productivity would enable growth-promoting measures to go hand in hand with equity-improving measures, thereby greatly enhancing the potential for improving the lot of the poor through economic development. The profession has accepted the call for increased emphasis on primary education while ignoring the call for land reform as unrealistic. In "Beyond Export-Led Growth" (World Development, 1984) I advocated a temporary shift during the low-growth-in-world-income-and-trade period of the 1980s towards agricultural development in an open trade regime as a mechanism for accelerating domestic industrialization and increasing equity (the ADLI strategy). I used the generic CGE model of Korea developed by Sherman Robinson to demonstrate the superiority of this strategy in a low-growth world environment over export-led growth.

At the same time, Cynthia Morris and I intensified our work on economic history. After finishing the historical book in 1988, we felt that we had enough insight into the complex interactions that determined the diversity of country responses to the industrial revolution in Great Britain to be able to specify a simultaneous equation partial least squares model of 19th century economic development using Herman Wold's statistical methodology (Adelman, Lohmoller, and Morris, 1988). We are now working on a monograph comparing historical and contemporary development patterns.

Policy work

My policy work started early in my career, and I have always felt that it offered both the motivation and new insights for my research. My first involvement with policy started by accident. In 1963, AID in Washington received an urgent request from its Vietnam office for a statistician who would design a rural income-expenditure survey in the Delta. I did not quite understand why this was so urgent, but was eager to travel so I volunteered. When I came to Saigon, I was struck by two things: the Vietnamese population did not seem to be committed to the war and the security situation was much worse than depicted by either military or diplomatic communications from Saigon. I reasoned that with incorrect information, correct decisions could not be made in Washington, and, with the arrogance of youth, started on a one-woman fact-finding mission. My starting point was why the Vietnamese population was not committed to the war. I soon realized that an important part of the answer was that, with existing tenurial conditions, the rural population had a large positive incentive to keep a low level of military activity going: due to the war, most of the landlords had left the rural areas, and rents had not been collected for as much as three years. At existing rents, pacification would mean an indebtedness of about 1.5 years' output! This led me to argue for a United States supported land reform of the land-to-the-tiller variety as a higher probability alternative than the military approach to ending the war. Buying all the land of the Delta at market prices from the landlords would cost only about half the then military annual budget! Upon returning from Saigon, I spent much of my effort for about three months peddling this view to the policy establishment. I gained a hearing, but, alas, the military approach prevailed. Many years later I met the director of the Saigon AID mission again and asked him why the consumption-expenditure survey had been such a high-priority item. His answer: "The country may be burning but Washington still wants to know: what's GNP?" — a sad, but accurate, comment on bureaucracies.

My work in development planning started early, has given me some insight into methods of policiy-formulation and a great deal of personal and professional satisfaction. In the 1950s and 1960s, work in economic development was by and large non-technical except in one area — that of development planning. This area, which started with Tinbergen's formulation of planning and his hierarchic view of state-economy

interactions, offered scope for the use of all techniques of econometrics
and operations-research. The technical part of my soul could therefore
find satisfaction in this branch of work. That period also offered scope
for the influential foreign adviser. Both coincided in my work on South
Korea's Second Five Year Plan, summarized in *Practical Approaches to
Development Planning - Korea's Second Five Year Plan* (John's Hopkins
Press, 1969).

My involvement in Korea started fortuitously. I was sitting in the
office of a friend at AID in the summer of 1964, and he was complaining
that his boss (Hollis Chenery) wanted him to go to South Korea,
whereas he wanted to go to Turkey. I said: "I'll go!" I went under AID
auspices in early 1965, wrote a critical report on the institutional setup
for planning in Korea, and returned home expecting never to return. To
my great surprise, my recommendations were implemented, and I was
called back to assist with the work on the plan. We wound up using all
the econometric and operations research techniques then known to
formulate investment, credit and foreign exchange allocation for the
next five year plan. The plan, initiated in 1967, involved a shift towards
export-led growth, after a 50% devaluation to realign exchange rates,
substantial reductions in tariffs and in the scope of protection to reduce
distorsions, and a doubling of interest rates to reduce inflation and
increase savings. The shift towards export-led growth was a natural
recommendation for an economy with highly developed human resources (a level of education three times the average for an economy of
its per capita income); a very small internal market (per capita income in
1965 was about $ 70); and a very poor natural resource base (hence high
import coefficients). I was not sensitive at the time to income distribution issues, but the plan worked out very well for poverty as well,
tripling the incomes of the poor in ten years, because of the very
egalitarian distribution of assets. Korea had had two major land reforms
in the early fifties, and had universal primary education. In 1972, I
received a Presidential decoration from President Park, the Order of
the Bronze Tower, for my work on the Second Five Year Plan. The
citation reads: "With deep interest in the wellbeing of the Korean
people, Mrs Irma Adelman, the professor at Northwestern University,
has devoted her efforts with superb competence to the economic
development of the Republic of Korea and thereby greatly contributed
towards attaining the goals ef economic self-sufficiency pursued by the
Government of the Republic of Korea. Her valuable donation and
service has gained for her the appreciation and admiration of the

Korean people". But when, in 1973, President Park turned from benevolent dictator to oppressive despot, torturing and jailing the opposition, I felt I had to resign from any advisory role in South Korea, after checking with my previous Korean co-workers that my resignation would not place them in jeopardy.

My final direct involvement with policy came in 1971, when I joined the World Bank. A paper summarizing the findings of my work with Cynthia Morris on income distribution and development was circulating as a working paper at the Bank. Mc Namara's speech writer, who was looking for material on this subject, came across the paper and used it as background for Mc Namara's Chile speech. This was the speech that signaled a change in Bank policy toward emphasis on poverty alleviation in lending to developing countries.

With my change of emphasis in development policy towards income distribution and poverty, I lost all popularity with planning agencies in developing countries themselves. For a while, I was popular with international agencies with a poverty orientation: the ILO and the World Bank, in particular. But as their interest shifted towards debt and trade problems, this policy involvement stopped as well. Whatever policy influence I now have is indirect: through my academic research and policy writings.

Career issues

So far, I have not touched on how the particular issues affecting professional women — discrimination; handling the multiple demands of home, child and career; and managing two careers — impinged on my life and career. I hit discrimination against women for the time when I got my PhD, in 1955. I was totally unprepared for this. I was a foreigner to the United States, and I had not realized that, like democracy in ancient Greece, the Horatio Alger myth characterizing the United States as an open, mobile society did not apply to American women. In the fifties, discrimination against women in U.S. academia was incredible. I had graduated from a top institution, at the top of my class, in a period of high demand for college teachers. Nevertheless, when it came to entering the job market, no one would waste a recommendation on a low-probability hire. At the time, openings were not advertised, and were publicised only through a network of personal contacts. When I applied for a teaching position at San Francisco State, the chairman suggested that I might look for a position in a local private high school! In the end, Berkeley hired me on a one-year appointment as a Teaching Associate — a position routinely given to third-year graduate students who have passed their field examinations. Then came six years, all on one-year, non-tenure-ladder appointments, at Berkeley, Mills College (a local private elite womens' college, where I became aware of the many phenomena described in Betty Friedan's *Feminine Mystique*), and Stanford. By then I had published my first book, the Klein-Goldberger article, two other articles on business cycles, my articles on sampling and hedonic index numbers, and my article on the use of Markov chains to predict the long-run size distribution of firms. The quantity and quality of my publications would have been sufficient to earn me a solid promotion to tenure in any first rate institution, had I been male. And still, I had no leg on the tenure ladder... The hardest thing during this period was to keep from getting bitter. I thank my lucky stars that I had the maturity to realize that, if I were to allow the process to make me bitter, the world would have won its fight against me, regardless of the ultimate professional outcome. I forbade myself the making of invidious comparisons with males, and ordered myself to consider myself as part of a Cairns-type non-competing group. And yet, had the process continued much longer, I would not have been able to hold out against being corroded by bitterness. Still, I was fortunate: I was employed continuously, at first-rate institutions, and worked with excellent colleagues, with whom I interacted on a par. My work-relationships with my colleagues and students were easier than those of males: women are used to interacting as equals with more senior males, my Assistant Professor colleagues did not consider me a threat, and the educator-maternal role with students came easily.

Then, I got a break: my husband became bored with his position at the Livermore Laboratory, and obtained a more challenging position in Washington, D.C. I used the Hungarian Connection (from Tibor Scitovsky, at Berkeley, to George Jaszy, at Johns Hopkins) to indicate my availability, and was offered a regular Associate Professorship at Hopkins, at the princely salary of $ 10,000 a year, a 60% increase on my previous salary at Stanford. We moved, I met Cynthia Morris, started being exposed to policy through Hollis Chenery at AID, and could use tenured status to engage in longer-term, riskier, research which culminated in the Adelman-Morris publications. Still, salary discrimination continued. When I complained to my chairman at Hopkins about the lack of a raise for three years despite high productivity, I was told to solicit alternative offers, as indication of my opportunity cost. Within a week, I obtained two offers, one from Maryland at 60% higher salary, and one from Northwestern, at 80% higher salary. The Northwestern position looked especially attractive, because there was an active interdisciplinary group in economic development, and because several of my would-be colleague, George Dalton, Karl de Scweinitz, and Jonathan Hughes, shared my broad-ranging institutional interests. My husband found a satisfactory position in Chicago, and, in 1966, we moved.

I was very happy at Northwestern. I liked the department, my colleagues, the size of the school, the quality of the students, the attitude of the administration, and, last but not least, the computer center. I continued my collaboration with Cynthia Morris, and would have happily stayed at Northwestern except for my husband's work-situation. His position at a research lab in Chicago proved to be unrewarding — so, again, we had to move. We spent a very happy year in 1971 at the Center for Advanced Studies in Behavioral Sciences, in Palo Alto. Influenced by Vietnam, my husband tried during this year to switch from defense-physics to work on urban social-science problems. We worked on a model of urban politics, which incorporated many novel features, but was only published in book chapters and conference proceedings. We hoped that, at the end of the year, we would be able to find joint teaching positions. But our timing was wrong: 1972 was the beginning of the academic recession, and departments were even more than usual concerned with credentialling. I tried to get us hired as a package-deal, and almost succeeded at Cornell. But, in the end, my husband's end of the deal fell through.

After the year at the Center, we moved to Washington once again. I took a job at the World Bank, my husband continued his work on the urban book, and we continued the search for joint positions. For one year, I was the major breadwinner in the family. I then learned how heavy the psychological burden of being the major breadwinner actually is. I would wake up in the middle of the night in a cold sweat, wondering what would happen to the family if I were to suffer an incapacitating accident, or be fired. I now know that what I was trying to do was wrong, even had it succeeded: my husband should have gotten a job on his own merits rather than as part of a package-deal. I felt inadequate for being unable to give him what he wanted (a professorial position in the social sciences) and he resented my efforts and support, though asking for them. When I gave up, he found a position in his old career within a week! I did not know whether to laugh or cry.

At the end of the year at the World Bank, I took a professorial position at Maryland. Maryland was a commuter campus, and this meant that both students and faculty only came there for a purpose, retreating to home or office in Washington in between. I missed the college atmosphere typical of non-urban campuses, such as Berkeley, Stanford, or Northwestern. My husband and I were both working too hard and had no energy left to build a social life. We started drifting apart, interacting only on the level of pratical problems or when going to an event at the Kennedy Center. Finally, the inevitable happened: we separated and, in 1980, divorced.

When we separated, I became a free agent, and when Berkeley's Department of Agriculture and Resource Economics enquired about my potential interest, I jumped at the opportunity. My work on poverty had made me realize the importance of agricultural development, and I was painfully aware how little I knew about agriculture, and how much more difficult agricultural development was than industrialization. I hoped that through exposure to my colleagues' work I might learn about agricultural economics, agricultural technology, and about the physical bases of agriculture. I have not been disappointed. Since joining the Department in 1979, I have learned a great deal about these issues, but I still have a great deal more to learn. Indeed, I expect agriculture-industry interactions and patterns of agricultural development to be a focus of my research in the coming years.

Thus, my response to the twin problems of discrimination against women and two careers, was high geographic mobility. I once counted that we had owned more houses than cars! We moved whenever a Pareto-optimal move was possible, and alternated in initiating moves.

My female students occasionally ask me: "When is a good time to have a child, if I want to also have a career?" My answer is: "Either in graduate school or once tenure is assured". (As a result, I wind up with a fair number of pregnant dissertation advisees...). I myself had chosen a different timing, which did not make my early career any easier. Our son was born in 1958, when I had a very precarious hold on an academic career. The most difficult parts about melding childrearing with career were the tremendous physical stamina it required, the constant guilt at not being a full-time mother, and the constant anxiety that something

might happen to him while I was at work. At the time, day care facilities
were very few and of dubious quality. Therefore, for the first ten years
of his life, I had live-in help. After that, I had day-help, at first five days
a week, then two, then one. He was an easy child, intelligent, energetic,
charming, and with a great sense of humor. Our relationship has
remained close, though there have been a few rocky patches in the last
ten years.

* * *

Like all autobiographies, my story is, fortunately, still unfinished.
However, I do not anticipate many new departures; just a deepening of
old lines of research and a continuation of my present, satisfying,
personal and professional life-style.

But then, who knows?

Berkeley

IRMA ADELMAN

BIBLIOGRAPHY

ADELMAN, IRMA, "A Stochastic Analysis of the Size Distribution of Firms", *Journal of the American Statistical Association*, pp. 839-904, 1959.

ADELMAN, IRMA and FRANK L. ADELMAN, *The Dynamic Properties of the Klein-Goldberger Model*, pp. 596-625, 1959.

ADELMAN, IRMA, "Business Cycles-Endogenous or Stochastic?", *Economic Journal*, pp. 783-796, 1960.

ADELMAN, IRMA and ZVI GRILICHES, "On an Index of Quality Change", *Journal of the American Statistical Association*, pp. 535-548, 1961.

ADELMAN, IRMA, *Theories of Economic Growth and Development*, Standford University Press, Palo Alto, 1964.

ADELMAN, IRMA and CYNTHIA TAFT MORRIS, *Society, Politics, and Economic Development: A Quantitative Approach*, Johns Hopkins Press, Baltimore, 1967.

ADELMAN, IRMA, *Practical Approaches to Development Planning: Korea's Second Five Year Plan*, Johns Hopkins Press, Baltimore, 1969.

ADELMAN, IRMA and CYNTHIA TAFT MORRIS, *Economic Growth and Social Equity in Developing Countries*, Stanford Press, Palo Alto, 1973.

ADELMAN, IRMA and SHERMAN ROBINSON, "A Non-Linear, Dynamic, Microeconomic Model of Korea: Factors Affecting the Distribution of Income in the Short Run", *Discussion Paper 36, Research Program in Economic Development*, Princeton University, 1973.

ADELMAN, IRMA and LAURA D'ANDREA TYSON, "A Regional Microeconomic Model of Jugoslavia: Factors Affecting the Distribution or Income in the Short Run", *Development Research Center*, World Bank, 1973, mimeographed.

ADELMAN, IRMA, "On the State of Development Economics", *Journal of Development Economics*, pp. 3-5, 1974.

ADELMAN, IRMA, "Development Economics-A Reassessment of Goals", *American Economic Review*, pp. 302-309, 1975.

ADELMAN, IRMA and SHERMAN ROBINSON, *Income Distribution Policy in Developing Countries: The Case of Korea*, Stanford University Press, Paolo Alto, 1978.

ADELMAN, IRMA, *Redistribution Before Growth-A Strategy for Developing Countries*, Martinus Nijhof, The Hague, 1978.

ADELMAN, IRMA, "Beyond Export Led Growth", *World Development*, vol. 12, pp. 937-949, 1984.

ADELMAN, IRMA, *A Poverty Focussed Approach to Development Policy*, pp. 49-65, Transactions Books, New Brunswick and Oxford, 1986.

ADELMAN, IRMA, JAN-BERND LOHMOLLER, and CYNTHIA TAFT MORRIS, "A Latent Variable Regression Model of Nineteenth Century Economic Development", *Giannini Foundation Working Paper No. 439*, University of California, Berkeley, 1988.

ADELMAN, IRMA and SHERMAN ROBINSON, "Macroeconomic Adjustment and Income Distribution: Alternative Models Applied to two Economies", *Journal of Development Economics*, forthcoming 1988.

BLAUG, MARK, *Great Economists since Keynes: An Introduction to the Lives and Works of one Hundred Modern Economists*, Wheatsheaf Books, 1985.

MORRIS, CYNTHIA TAFT and IRMA ADELMAN, *Comparative Patterns of Economic Development, 1850-1914*, Johns Hopkins Press, Baltimore, 1988.

PART I

DYNAMICS

[2]

THE DYNAMIC PROPERTIES OF THE KLEIN-GOLDBERGER MODEL

By Irma Adelman and Frank L. Adelman*

The authors examine the dynamic properties of the Klein-Goldberger model of the United States economy by extrapolating the exogenous variables and solving the equations on the IBM 650 for one hundred years. In this process no indication was found of oscillatory behavior. The introduction of random impulses of a reasonable order of magnitude, however, generates cycles which are comparable in their properties to those of the United States economy.

1. INTRODUCTION

ONE OF THE MOST vexing of the unsolved problems of dynamic economic analysis is that of constructing a model which will reproduce adequately the cyclical behavior of a modern industrial community. None of the schemes so far advanced have (yet) offered a satisfactory endogenous explanation of the persistent business fluctuations so characteristic of Western capitalism. It is true that there exist theories which lead to oscillatory movements, but, except under very special assumptions, these swings either die down, or else they are explosive in nature.[1] In the latter case, appeal is usually made to externally imposed constraints in order to limit the fluctuations of the system,[2] while, in the former case, exogenous shocks must be introduced from time to time to rejuvenate the cyclical movement.[3] Since recourse to either of these devices is rather artificial, it is of interest to seek a more satisfactory mechanism for the internal generation of a persistent cyclical process.

While it is desirable for an economic model (or any other model, for that matter) to be as simple as possible, it is almost certain that an adequate explanation of the business cycle cannot be found through approaches as idealized as those usually suggested. It may be of interest, therefore, to examine, from this point of view, the most complicated econometric description of the United States published in recent years—the 1955 forecast-

---

* The authors are, respectively, Acting Assistant Professor of Economics at Stanford University and physicist at the Livermore branch of the University of California Lawrence Radiation Laboratory. They are grateful to the Computation Division of the Radiation Laboratory for the use of their facilities. Also, they wish to express their appreciation to Arthur Goldberger for his helpful discussion of this paper.

[1] P. A. Samuelson, "The Interaction of the Accelerator and the Multiplier," *Review of Economic Statistics*, vol. XXI (1939), pp. 75–78.

[2] J. R. Hicks, *A Contribution to the Theory of the Trade Cycle* (Oxford, 1939.)

[3] R. Frisch, "Propagation Problems and Impulse Problems in Dynamic Economics," *Economic Essays in Honor of Gustav Cassel* (London, 1933), pp. 171–205.

596

Reprinted from ECONOMETRICA, Vol. 27, No. 4, October, 1959

ing scheme of Klein and Goldberger.[4] This structure, which consists of 25 difference equations[5] in a corresponding number of endogenous variables, is nonlinear in character, and includes lags up to the fifth order. By its very nature it constitutes a description of a dynamic world, rather than a portrayal of comparative statics. Not only are the endogenous variables in each period functions of exogenous inputs, but also of lagged endogenous quantities and of stock variables. Thus, even if all the exogenous magnitudes were held constant, the economy represented by these equations would still vary with time.

But, while this model has been applied to yearly projections of economic activity in this country with some success, its dynamic properties have been analyzed only under highly simplifying assumptions.[5a] In particular, it would be interesting to find out whether this construct really offers an endogenous explanation of a persistent cyclical process. We should like to learn whether the system is stable when subjected to single exogenous shocks, what oscillations (if any) accompany the return to the equilibrium path, and what is the reponse of the model to repeated external and internal shocks.

The purpose of this paper, then, is to investigate these issues in some detail. There are perhaps two major reasons which indicate why this work has not previously been done. First of all, the fact that Klein and Goldberger used observed quantities as inputs for their annual forecasts, rather than values generated by the model from earlier data, prevented them from studying, at the same time, the type of dynamic paths which would be traversed by the system in the absence of external interference. Secondly, the complexity of the model requires the use of modern high-speed computers for the long-run solution of the system in a reasonable length of time. Since the problem is about the right size for the IBM 650 calculator, and since the appropriate computing facilities exist at the University of California Radiation Laboratory, we programmed the equations for that machine.

2. THE MODEL

The Klein-Goldberger econometric model of the United States[6] is a system of 25 difference equations in as many endogenous variables. Some

---

[4] L. R. Klein and A. S. Goldberger, *An Econometric Model of the United States, 1929–1952* (Amsterdam, 1955).

[5] Including 5 tax equations.

[5a] In the December, 1957 meeting of the Econometric Society, A. S. Goldberger and J. Cornwall presented the results of their (independent) investigations of their respective linearized versions of the Klein-Goldberger model. (The abstracts appear in *Econometrica*, vol. 26 (1958), pp. 620, 621.) At the same meeting one of us (I.A.) gave a discussion paper on these studies, including in it the material of Sections I–V of the present paper.

[6] For an excellent, more detailed description of this model, see C. F. Christ, "Aggregate Econometric Models," *American Economic Review*, vol. XLVI (1956), pp. 385–408.

of the equations are accounting identities, while others, behavioral in nature, were derived from statistical fits to empirical data. Generally speaking, each equation describes some significant feature of the economy. The real sector of the model includes, in addition to the usual consumption and investment relationships, a production function, a corporate profits equation, and a corporate savings function. Also taken into account are private employee compensation, farm income, imports, and depreciation. The monetary sector consists of two liquid asset functions, two interest rate equations, a wage adjustment relationship, and an agricultural price equation. There are also five tax equations, which represent the impact of government tax policies upon the economy, and five accounting identities. Of the exogenous variables, the most important (aside from time) are government expenditures, population size, and the distribution of the labor force among the several sectors of the economy. All these equations are given in Appendix A, together with the definitions of the symbols used.

For this study of the Klein-Goldberger system several changes were introduced into the most recent Klein-Goldberger model, some for convenience and some for consistency or logic. First, whenever the standard error of estimate of a regression coefficient was more than twice as large as the coefficient itself, we dropped the corresponding term from the equations. The justification for so high a level of significance is that, for our purposes, we felt it less serious an error to ascribe to a zero coefficient a nonzero value than to ignore a regression coefficient which has an economic existence. The alterations made in accordance with this criterion are indicated in Appendix B, Section 1. In principle, of course, one should correct the equations for these omissions. However, since we were not interested in accurate prediction, but, rather, in the dynamic performance of the model, we felt that the required modifications were small[7] and would not add to the value of the study.

A second departure from the original system was to delete the import equation. This was done because, during the sample period, the calculated quantities of imports constituted a poor approximation to the values observed.[8] After imports had been dropped from the list of endogenous variables, it seemed reasonable also to omit both imports and exports from the model. For, since both would now be exogenous, and since their difference contributes only a small amount to GNP, it is difficult to see how their exclusion could alter the dynamic character of the system.

A modification of quite another sort was made in the form of the tax equations. Since those given by Klein and Goldberger were not intended

---

[7] Indeed, in all cases, the quantitative changes which would have been required lay within the standard errors of the constants to be altered.

[8] Cf. Klein-Goldberger, *op. cit.*, p. 95 and Figure 29, p. 102.

to be applicable for more than a few years,[9] we had to re-estimate all the tax relationships. Therefore, at the suggestion of A. Goldberger,[10] we adopted a new set of tax functions, which assumed that the tax policies of 1952, interpreted as relationships between real variables, would continue indefinitely into the future. These are incorporated into the tax equations which appear in Appendix B.1.

We were also forced to alter the interest rate equations. Since the excess bank reserves, R_t, are taken as exogenous, the short term interest rate $(i_S)_t$ and the long term rate $(i_L)_t$ can both be computed without reference to the rest of the system. With the small values of R_t typical of the postwar period, it is evident from the short-term interest rate equation [Eq. (15)] that $(i_S)_t$ will double (roughly) every decade. And yet there is no restoring force within the system to keep this quantity at a reasonable value! Similarly, $(i_L)_t$ will, ultimately, become equal to about $0.7(i_S)_t$. In view of the fact that such a projection would eventually result in economic nonsense, we decided to suppress the interest rate equations and to fix (arbitrarily) the short term rate at 2.5% and the long term rate at 3.5%.

Lastly, the agricultural price equation was re-evaluated, using only the postwar data. The reason for this alteration was the admittedly unsatisfactory behavior of the form used by Klein and Goldberger.[11]

We were still not in a position to follow the long-term development of this system, however, as it was necessary to extrapolate the exogenous variables far into the future. This was done, in some instances, by fitting a least-squares straight line to the postwar data. But, in the case of governmental expenditures, the discontinuity because of the Korean War and the subsequent intensification of military preparedness, imparted a trend to the postwar data much steeper than could reasonably be expected to continue. Therefore, we estimated the rate of increase of government expenditures by fitting a straight line to both the prewar and the postwar points, omitting only those of 1951 and 1952. The level was chosen to coincide, more or less, with that of those latter two years. With this procedure we found that our extrapolation leads to numbers which appear to be consistent with current experience.

On the other hand, agricultural subsidy income and the number of farm operators have a declining trend. For these quantities it seemed more appropriate to use a fit of the form

$$X = a + \frac{b}{t - \alpha},$$

in order that they never become negative. Finally, since there was no obvious

[9] Klein-Goldberger, *op. cit.*, pp. 96–102.
[10] Private communication.
[11] Klein-Goldberger, *op. cit.*, p. IX and Fig. 31, p. 105.

trend, during the postwar period, for the index of hours worked and the index of farm exports, both were taken as constant. The extrapolations of all the exogenous quantities appear in Appendix B. 2. The initial values of the lagged variables are listed in Appendix B. 3.

3. CALCULATIONAL PROCEDURE

The modified Klein-Goldberger model to be investigated thus consists of a set of 22 simultaneous equations in a corresponding number of endogenous variables. What we must do in order to evaluate the magnitudes of the endogenous variables for the year t is to insert into these equations the values for the $(t-1)$st and preceding years, as required, along with appropriate exogenous numbers, and solve the equations simultaneously. Using the newly found endogenous quantities for the tth year plus the required exogenous magnitudes, we can then solve the system for the endogenous variables of the $(t+1)$st period. This process is continued until we have traveled sufficiently far into the future to satisfy our curiosity.

At first glance the system we wish to analyze would appear to be highly nonlinear. The substitution of $q = 1/p$ as a variable, however, instead of the price level p itself, leaves us with only a single nonlinear equation (18), the wage and salary identity. Of course, it is much easier to solve a set of simultaneous *linear* equations than it is to evaluate a nonlinear system. For this reason it was decided to "linearize"[12] (18), and then to utilize a successive approximation procedure to find the solution of the nonlinear set to the desired degree of accuracy. Our criteria for an acceptable solution were that the value of each variable appearing in the nonlinear equation must differ from its previous approximation by less than $1/2\%$ and that the original form of that equation also be satisfied to that accuracy. Since convergence was quite rapid, even when the initial guess was poor, our criteria appear to be sufficiently stringent to assure convergence to the economically relevant solution of the system (in case there is more than one solution).

Before actually programming the equations for the IBM 650, however, it was possible, by appropriate algebraic substitutions, to reduce the 22 equations down to a set of four simultaneous equations in four unknowns. The investment relation (2) could be evaluated from exogenous and lagged data, while the equations remaining after the completion of the algebra could be solved *seriatim* as soon as the answers to the first five were available. This procedure was advantageous, if not actually necessary, because the computation time required for the solution of a simultaneous linear system by matrix inversion is proportional to the cube of the rank of the matrix.

---

[12] To do this, we wrote the equation in terms of differences from initial (extrapolated) guesses, which must be consistent with the integral form of the equation.

After all the preceding considerations were taken into account, it turned out that neither memory space nor running time was a serious limitation on the use of the IBM 650. Therefore, the problem was coded for the machine in a straightforward manner. As a matter of interest, the computations for one year could be made during an operating time of about one minute.[13]

4. THE DYNAMIC NATURE OF THE MODEL

Now, we are finally in a position to study some of the problems raised in the Introduction. First of all, what is the dynamic nature of the Klein-Goldberger model? That is, what sort of time path will these equations generate in the absence of additional external constraints or shocks? A priori, it is conceivable that the long-run extrapolation of this short-run

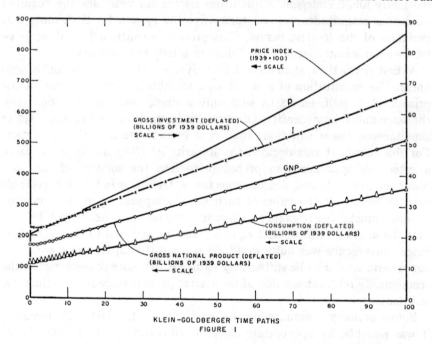

KLEIN-GOLDBERGER TIME PATHS
FIGURE I

predictive system will indicate that the economy so described is subject to a business cycle more or less analogous to that observed in modern industrialized societies. On the other hand, it is also possible that this model cannot offer even a qualitative picture of the economic growth process in the real world.

---

[13] The actual time depends on the number of iterations required for convergence; in the linear part of the time path, the first guess is adequate.

Our first machine data decided the issue unequivocally. After a brief "settling-down" period, the system is quite monotonic and essentially linear. These is no hint whatever of any internally generated business cycle, and, indeed, even in the first few years, the shock of start-up is not sufficient to induce more than a single turning point in any variable. Of course, since most of the exogenous trends are fitted by straight lines, it is not surprising that the overall character of the solution is linear, rather than, say, quadratic, but the absence of oscillations is less obvious (a priori) and more significant.

The time paths of several of the more important quantities are depicted in Figure 1. The several curves in Figure 1 represent the projections of the price index and of the real values of GNP, consumer expenditures, and gross private investment, respectively. The approximate behavior of the rest of the variables may be inferred from the information in Table I.[14]

In an attempt to see whether the qualitative properties of the solution are at all sensitive to the starting conditions, we reduced the magnitudes of all but seven[15] of the initial values of the real quantities by 10 per cent. The results of this calculation possessed the same general character as had been observed previously. As might have been anticipated, the new ordinates were invariably lower, and, except for corporate savings, the slopes of the curves tended to be the same or smaller. The linearity was even more marked with the reduced inputs; indeed, only two variables showed any turning points at all. These were corporate savings and corporate surplus, both of which were actually negative for several periods. Since, in view of these results, it was felt that small variations in our input would not lead to significant differences in the *nature* of our solution, a more detailed investigation of the influence of initial values upon the operation of the model was postponed to a future date.

The implications of these results are quite clear. Since the economic variables in the Klein-Goldberger model grow almost linearly with time, it is apparent that this scheme does not contain an intrinsic explanation of a persistent oscillatory process. That is, the complete lack of even a broad hint of cyclical behavior in the absence of shocks precludes the application of the Klein-Goldberger analysis to economies in which oscillations are presumed to develop spontaneously. The conclusions one may draw from this observation lie anywhere between the two extreme positions which follow. On the one hand, if one wishes to retain the hypothesis that periodic cumulative movements are self-generated in the course of the growth

---

[14] The authors will be happy to furnish, upon request, the detailed results of their computations.

[15] The ones excluded were N_W, h, N_E, N_F, N_G, N, N_P (for explanation of symbols, see Appendix A).

TABLE I

BEHAVIOR OF KLEIN-GOLDBERGER MODEL THROUGH TIME

Variable*	(years) 24 (first year)	30	60	90	120
$Y + T + D$	171.5	186.0	291.1	396.3	501.5
$\Delta(Y+T+D)$	.294	3.42	3.51	3.51	3.51
C	115.1	125.1	199.3	273.9	348.7
ΔC	.015	2.42	2.48	2.49	2.49
W_1	80.6	86.7	137.5	188.4	239.3
ΔW_1	—.046	1.64	1.70	1.70	1.70
A_1	9.0	9.5	12.6	15.9	19.2
ΔA_1	.008	.100	.108	.109	.110
I	22.9	24.0	37.9	51.5	64.9
ΔI	—.289	.434	.455	.450	.448
K	45.9	65.3	163.0	260.8	357.1
ΔK	3.75	3.05	3.24	3.23	3.20
D	18.5	21.0	34.6	48.2	62.2
ΔD	.396	.429	.458	.452	.448
P_C	14.9	15.4	22.5	29.6	36.8
ΔP_C	—.454	.245	.233	.237	.240
P	33.1	33.8	44.3	54.7	65.3
ΔP	—.667	.361	.343	.349	.353
S_P	.44	.57	2.17	2.85	3.16
ΔS_P	—.192	.082	.032	.015	.007
B	.63	2.96	48.80	125.71	216.51
ΔB	.250	.65	2.20	2.86	3.16
N_W	54.2	53.6	64.7	75.7	86.9
ΔN_W	—1.06	.352	.365	.370	.373
L_1	70.5	71.7	80.6	89.6	98.7
ΔL_1	.037	.288	.299	.301	.301
L_2	40.8	45.9	79.4	112.7	146.0
ΔL_2	1.40	1.00	1.12	1.11	1.11
w	344	443	1043	1817	2776
Δw	15.9	17.3	22.9	29.0	35.2
p	206	238	412	604	825
Δp	4.1	5.8	6.0	6.9	7.9
p_A	318	363	604	871	1179
Δp_A	5.7	8.1	8.3	9.6	11.0
T	14.5	15.8	25.5	35.3	45.0
ΔT	.028	.315	.324	.324	.324
T_W	7.6	9.0	19.2	29.3	39.5
ΔT_W	.069	.329	.338	.339	.339
T_A	.47	.49	.65	.82	.99
ΔT_A	.0003	.0050	.0055	.0056	.0056
T_C	9.4	9.6	12.9	16.0	19.3
ΔT_C	—.204	.110	.105	.108	.108
T_P	12.9	13.2	19.4	26.0	32.8
ΔT_P	—.268	.198	.212	.225	.231

* For any quantity Q, $\Delta Q = Q_{t+1} - Q_t$.

process in a realistic economy, one may contend that the Klein-Goldberger model is fundamentally inadequate, and hence that it is inapplicable to further business cycle theory. On the other hand, one may hold that, to the extent that the behavior of this system constitutes a valid qualitative approximation to that of a modern capitalist society, the observed solution of the Klein-Goldberger equations implies that one must look elsewhere for the origin of business fluctuations. Under the latter assumptions, cyclical analysis would be limited to an investigation of the reaction of the economic system to various perturbations. And, since the Klein-Goldberger model does present a more or less detailed description of the interactions among the various sectors of the economy, it could itself be utilized in the examination of the mechanism of response to shocks. Actually, as we shall see, exploitation of the latter alternative can prove extremely profitable.

5. STABILITY OF THE SYSTEM

It is apparent from the preceding discussion that, under ordinary conditions, the Klein-Goldberger model is non-oscillatory in nature. It remains to be seen whether the economy described by this system is stable under large exogenous displacements.

In order to study this point, we solved the equations as in the preceding section, until the system was essentially on its long-run equilibrium path (about 8 years). Then, in the ninth period, we suddenly reduced the real magnitude of federal outlays from its extrapolated level of 37.5 to the much lower figure of 10; in the succeeding years government expenditures were returned to the values they would have had in the absence of external interference.

While it is obvious that such a discontinuity in an exogenous variable is basically equivalent to a change in initial conditions, it is equally obvious that the response of a dynamic system to large displacements may be quite different from its behavior under small perturbations.[16]

Figure 2 presents some of the calculated results of this extremely severe shock to the economy.[17] As is evident from these curves, the community was immediately thrown into a very deep depression by the sudden drop in federal outlays. The restoration of a normal governmental budget during the following year alleviated the situation only slightly, but, by the second year after the dip, the business world had more than recovered. The

---

[16] E.g., consider a marble trapped in a horizontal saucer. If the disturbance is not large enough to cause the marble to cross the saucer rim, the system is stable. However, once the marble crosses the rim, it will not return to the saucer without the application of external forces. See also, P. A. Samuelson, *Foundations of Economic Analysis* (Harvard, 1953), pp. 200–262.

[17] More data are, of course, available for this case, and will be provided upon request.

next period saw the return of national income, farm receipts, and total employment to their pre-shock trends. However, it was not until the fourth year after the disturbance that real private employee compensation achieved its unperturbed level, as the price index rose more rapidly than the wage rate. Meanwhile, possibly as a result of the fact that consumer expenditures lagged yet another period, there was a mild business recession

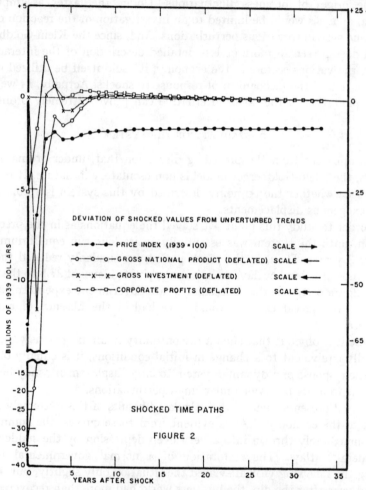

DEVIATION OF SHOCKED VALUES FROM UNPERTURBED TRENDS

- •—•—• PRICE INDEX (1939 = 100)   SCALE ——▶
- ○—○—○ GROSS NATIONAL PRODUCT (DEFLATED) SCALE ◀——
- ×—×—× GROSS INVESTMENT (DEFLATED)   SCALE ◀——
- □—□—□ CORPORATE PROFITS (DEFLATED)   SCALE ◀——

SHOCKED TIME PATHS

FIGURE 2

in the fourth year, the effects of which were felt throughout the rest of the economy for the next two periods. The subsequent boom reached its peak (with respect to its unperturbed trend) about eight years later, and then tapered off extremely slowly over an additional 22 years or so. While calculations were not continued beyond this point, it appears that, after this 34 year cycle, the economy has essentially returned to its basic equilibrium path, except for the price and wage indices[18] and for the cumulative corporate surplus (all of which remained lower).

While the details of the response of a Klein-Goldberger economy to a strong shock will depend on the nature of the perturbation, it would appear likely from this calculation that even a very strong shock will not permanently distort the long-run path of the economy. In other words, the Klein-Goldberger system is stable. Nevertheless, a sharp disturbance does suffice to create a business cycle of depth comparable to that which one would expect in an actual economy under a corresponding inpulse. And, while the duration of the cyclical movement is much longer than that normally observed in practice, it is probable that the later stages of such a cycle, if it really existed, would be obscured by the intervention of new exogenous shocks.

6. INTRODUCTION OF RANDOM SHOCKS

So far, we have studied the dynamic properties of the Klein-Goldberger system by treating it as if it were composed of a set of exact functional relationships. That is to say, we have abstracted from the random elements which are inherent in the statistical specification of the equations. Furthermore, we have used smooth extrapolation procedures for predicting the magnitudes of the exogenous variables. We saw that under those assumptions the Klein-Goldberger equations are inadequate as an explanation of the cyclical behavior of our economy.

We cannot yet assess the validity of the Klein-Goldberger equations, however, as a representation of the United States economy over a long period of time because we must still analyze the time path of their system under the impact of random shocks.[19] After all, as was pointed out by Haavelmo,[20] a model which differs from empirical fact by comparatively small and nonsystematic external factors may still be useful. It is therefore of great interest to see whether or not the introduction of relatively minor uncorrelated perturbations into the Klein-Goldberger structure will generate cyclical fluctuations analogous to those observed in practice.

With these considerations in mind, we exposed the Klein-Goldberger system to two distinct varieties of random impulses. First of all, random

---

[18] The real wage rate, however, does return to its equilibrium trend by the end of the cycle.

[19] The idea that economic fluctuations may be due to random shocks was first suggested in 1927 by E. Slutzky, "The Summation of Random Causes as the Source of Cyclical Processes," translated into English in *Econometrica*, Vol. 5 (1937), pp. 105 ff. It was also suggested independently by R. Frisch, *op. cit.*

[20] T. Haavelmo, "The Inadequacy of Testing Dynamic Theory by Comparing Theoretical Solutions and Observed Cycles," *Econometrica*, Vol. 8 (1940), p. 312.

shocks were superimposed upon the extrapolated values of the exogenous quantities (shocks of type I). Secondly, random perturbations were introduced instead into each of the empirically fitted Klein-Goldberger equations (shocks of type II). In addition we made a set of calculations in which both kinds of disturbances were present.

7. SHOCKS OF TYPE I

Shocks of type I arise logically whenever exogenous quantities are projected in a smooth manner over long periods of time, for, while it is convenient to extrapolate these variables in a continuous fashion, even a cursory glance at the data over a period of a few years shows that these magnitudes tend to jump more or less erratically with respect to any smooth curve one might draw. It is, of course, obvious that a system that incorporates such statistical fluctuations may not be completely satisfactory for quantitative purposes. On the other hand, it may still prove fruitful to compare with economic experience the frequency of occurrence and the amplitudes of whatever cycles may arise.

We shall therefore modify our method of extrapolation of the exogenous variables in order to see what effects these random perturbations may have. For this purpose we define the value of an exogenous variable y_t at time t as its trend value $\bar{y}_t$ plus the shock term δy_t, and assume that δy_t has a Gaussian distribution[21] with a mean of zero. In order that the shocks inflicted upon the system be of a more or less realistic magnitude at all times, we evaluate the standard deviation of δy_t over that portion of the data for which our least squares fit was made,[22] and, for our subsequent calculations, we maintain the ratio of the standard deviation of δy_t to y_{t-1} at a value independent of time. It is interesting to note that these standard deviations (see Appendix B. 4) are, in general, quite small; in fact, only three of them exceed 10 per cent of the trend value of the corresponding variable.

In examining the behavior of the twelve exogenous variables[23] over the sample period, it becomes evident that there exists a high degree of correlation between the long- and the short-term interest rates, and between the size of government payrolls and the number of government em-

[21] This assumption also underlies the principle of least squares fits.

[22] It will be recalled that we used data from 1946–1952 for our least squares extrapolations of all exogenous variables except government expenditures, G; for G, data for 1929–1940 and 1946–1950 were used.

[23] These variables, it will be recalled, are the short-term i_S and long term interest rates i_L, the index of hours worked h, government employee compensation W_2, government expenditures G, the index of agricultural exports F_A, agricultural subsidies A_2 and five population and labor force variables (N_P, N, N_E, N_F, and N_G).

IRMA AND FRANK ADELMAN

ployees.[24] It is therefore appropriate to assume that these pairs of variables move together and that the determination of a shock on one variable of each pair automatically sets the size of the corresponding shock on the other. Hence we are left with a set of ten random exogenous shocks, whose magnitudes and signs are to be established.

The technique employed for this purpose was to divide the normal curve of error into 100 regions of equal area. To each region we assigned both the normal deviate associated with the midpoint of its interval and a previously unassigned integer between 00 and 99, inclusive. Then selecting a two-digit random number, we effectively chose at random a specific region of the Gaussian distribution and the corresponding normal deviate. Multiplying this deviate by the standard deviation of δy_t, we found the magnitude and direction of a shock on the variable y at time t. Since the selection of an interval in this manner was thus purely random, and since all intervals defined the same area under the curve, this method produced a normally distributed[25] *random* shock upon the variable in question. By repeating this

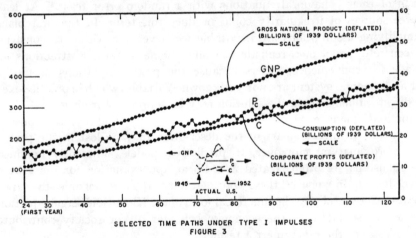

SELECTED TIME PATHS UNDER TYPE I IMPULSES
FIGURE 3

procedure for each of the exogenous variables and adding the calculated shocks to the appropriate trend values, we arrived at a set of shocked exogenous quantities to use as inputs for the tth period. The values of the endogenous variables for this period were then found, of course, as before.

Some of the results obtained with shocks of type I are summarized in Figure 3. The solid lines in this graph portray the computed time paths

[24] The correlation coefficient between government payrolls W_2 and government expenditures G for the sample years 1946–52 is 0.97 and that between the interest rates is 0.89.

[25] Since we have divided the normal curve into discrete intervals, we actually have only a (good) approximation to a normal distribution.

of GNP, consumption, and corporate profits, while the dotted lines represent actual time paths of these variables for the postwar portion of the sample period.[26] From this figure, it would seem that the introduction of forces of type I into the model generates 3 to 4 year swings in the variables of the system. However, the same graph also reveals that the average amplitude of the "cycles" induced by random shock on exogenous quantities is unrealistically small. It would appear, then, that type I perturbations of reasonable magnitude superimposed upon the Klein-Goldberger model will not produce the sort of cyclical behavior observed in the actual economy. We shall therefore proceed to see whether shocks of type II will prove more promising.

8. SHOCKS OF TYPE II

To understand the origin of shocks of type II, one should recall that, in the process of fitting their empirical data, Klein and Goldberger endowed each of their behavioral equations with a random error term.[27] At least three sources of irregularity could produce this term. In the first place, simplifying assumptions are inevitable whenever one wishes to construct a concrete model of a realistic economy. Some of these abstractions are made for convenience, others because the precise equations of motion of an economic system are not yet known. Variables which in practice exert a direct influence upon the solution may be suppressed from several of the equations, made exogenous, or omitted entirely; similarly, relationships which are an integral part of the description may be lost in the process of approximation. Moreover, in predictive models, inherently nonlinear relationships are often treated in a linear approximation for the sake of expediency. In view of these considerations, it is reasonable to expect that the inexactness of the functional form of the Klein-Goldberger equations as a representation of the economic behavior of our society contributes to the size of the random error term.

Secondly, even if the Klein-Goldberger relationships did have a functional form derived from indisputable theory, the fact that the coefficients are based upon empirical data would imply a random error term, as a result of the usual sampling fluctuations. These include, for example, the uncertainty of the degree to which the sample is representative of the universe, as well as the changes in accounting practices, coverage, and reporting techniques which generally occur in the collection of data over a long period of time.

[26] The data for the actual time paths are taken from Klein-Goldberger, *op. cit.*, pp. 131–133.

[27] This is standard econometric procedure; cf. Klein-Goldberger, *op. cit.*, pp. 42–46.

A third potential contributor to the size of shocks of type II is of quite a different character. It arises from the possibility that some of the economic relationships which compose the Klein-Goldberger system may *never* be valid as exact equations. This situation will result if the aggregation of microeconomic quantities into macroeconomic variables is not a legitimate procedure. For example, if the value of total consumption depends upon the distribution of income as well as on its magnitude, a precise macro-economic relationship between overall consumption and aggregate income will not exist. A similar effect, which will also be reflected in the size of the random error term, would occur if decision functions are probabilistic rather than single-valued.

It is therefore evident from the above discussion that the residuals of the several empirically fitted equations included in the Klein-Goldberger model can be attributed to a number of different types of irregularity. Since there would appear to be no a priori correlation among the many individual sources of fluctuation, the random error terms can be assumed for all practical purposes to be distributed in a Gaussian manner. We therefore postulate that each error term is distributed normally about a mean of zero, and we evaluate its standard deviation, just as in the case of shocks of type I, from the standard errors observed for the sample period (see Appendix B. 5).

In order to introduce perturbations of type II into the Klein-Goldberger model, we added a random error term to the right-hand side of each of the original non-definitional relationships.[28] Then the same process of algebraic substitution which was used in the simplification of the unshocked system was applied to this new group of equations. These operations left us with a set of equations in which the several error terms appear as parameters, analogous to the exogenous and the lagged variables. Once the sizes and directions of these endogenous shocks are determined (by the selection of two-digit random numbers, as in the case of type I impulses), the system is solved as before. A similar procedure can be used to investigate the behavior of the Klein-Goldberger equations when both shocks of type I and shocks of type II are present simultaneously.

Some of the results of the computation with shocks of type II are plotted in Figure 4. As in Figure 3, the solid lines represent the calculated behavior of GNP, consumption, and corporate profits, respectively, while the dotted lines depict the time paths traversed by the same quantities during the postwar period in the United States.[26] As before, we see that the shocked Klein-Goldberger system produces oscillatory movements with periods of 3 to 4 years. But, unlike the behavior of the model under the action of forces

---

[28] The equations involved are (1) – (8) and (10) – (13) of Appendix A.

of type I, the swings generated here compare favorably in magnitude with those experienced by the United States economy after World War II. Thus, the superposition of impulses of type II upon the Klein-Goldberger equations leads to cycles whose gross properties are reasonably realistic.

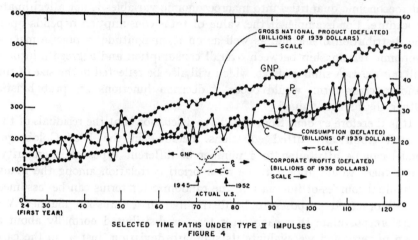

SELECTED TIME PATHS UNDER TYPE II IMPULSES
FIGURE 4

Since the effects of shocks of type II are much larger than those of type I disturbances, the same statement can be made for a system in which both kinds of perturbations are present. And, in view of the fact that, on a priori grounds, either type of shock may be present in an actual economy, it would seem appropriate to carry out our more detailed analysis for the case in which both forces are present.

9. ANALYSIS OF COMPUTED CYCLES

It is encouraging, of course, to find that the amplitudes and the periods of the oscillations observed in this model are roughly the same as those which are found in practice. But, this much agreement is merely a necessary condition for an adequate simulation of the cyclical fluctuations of a real industrial economy. We must investigate further to find out whether or not a shocked version of the Klein-Goldberger system really produces business cycles in the technical sense.[29] Specifically, how nearly all-pervasive are the cumulative movements which arise? How are the various oscillations correlated? Is there any consistent phase relationship among the

[29] R. A. Gordon, for example, defines business cycles in the following manner: "Business cycles consist of recurring alternations of expansion and contraction in aggregate economic activity, the alternating movements in each direction being self-reinforcing and pervading virtually all parts of the economy." *Business Fluctuations* (Harpers, 1952), p. 214.

several economic series? Do the time paths of the individual variables of the model correspond to those observed in the United States economy? In other words, if a business cycle analyst were asked whether or not the results of a shocked Klein-Goldberger computation could reasonably represent a United States-type economy, how would he respond?

To answer these questions we shall apply to the data techniques developed by the National Bureau of Economic Research (NBER)[30] for the analysis of business cycles.

One property of cyclical fluctuations in an industrial economy is a marked tendency for a clustering of peaks and troughs of individual economic time series about particular reference dates. It is, in fact, precisely this characteristic of business cycles that Burns and Mitchell use as their criterion for the dating of turning points in the United States economy.[31] And, inasmuch as the oscillations in the Klein-Goldberger model occur in response to random (i.e., noncorrelated) perturbations, a study of the simultaneity of occurrence of peaks (and troughs) will provide us with quite a stringent test of the validity of the model.

As in the normal NBER procedure,[32] we first date the specific cycles;[33] i.e., we determine all the turning points of each of the several time series. Then, to establish the reference dates[33] for the turning points of the *overall* business cycle, we examine the data for bunching (in time) of specific cycle peaks and troughs.[34]

Table II is a summary of some of the relevant characteristics of the business cycles observed in our shocked Klein-Goldberger economy. In examining this table, one should recall that intervals and dates can have

[30] The methods and results of the NBER work are summarized in A. F. Burns and W. C. Mitchell, *Measuring Business Cycles* (National Bureau, 1946) and in W. C. Mitchell, *What Happens During Business Cycles* (National Bureau, 1951).

[31] Mitchell, *op. cit.*, pp. 10–11.

[32] See Burns and Mitchell, *op. cit.*, Ch. 2.

[33] In the rest of this paper we will need the definitions of several quantities prevalent in the literature of business cycles. See, for example, Mitchell, *op. cit.*, pp. 9–11, or Gordon, *op. cit.*, p. 232.

(1) Reference dates are those dates which mark the turning points of overall business activity in the economy.

(2) A reference cycle of an economic variable V represents the behavior of V between the reference dates marking two consecutive minima of overall business activity.

(3) A specific cycle of V represents the behavior of V between the dates marking two consecutive minima of V itself.

[34] Our procedure corresponds to that of the NBER (cf. Mitchell, *op. cit.*, pp. 10–12). As a basis for establishing the reference dates we used all the Klein-Goldberger endogenous quantities except the 5 tax variables. A reference peak (trough) was said to occur (in our data) during any year in which the modal number of specific cycle peaks occurs, provided that at least 10 peaks (troughs) are found in a two-year period which includes the model year.

THE KLEIN-GOLDBERGER MODEL 613

TABLE II
REFERENCE DATING FOR SHOCKED KLEIN-GOLDBERGER MODEL

Reference Dates		Elapsed Time (Years)		Number of Series at Peaks Which:			Number of Series at Troughs Which:		
Trough (T)	Peak(P)	T→P	P→T	Lag One Year	Coincide	Lead One Year	Lag One Year	Coincide	Lead One Year
–	27	–	2	–	–	–	–	–	–
29	31	2	1	2	8	6	1	6	4
32	37	5	1	1	8	5	4	7	4
38	42	4	1	1	10	0	1	13	1
43	45	2	1	2	7	4	0	10	0
46	51	5	2	2	11	1	3	8	3
53	54	1	2	4	12	1	2	10	4
56	59	3	1	1	10	1	1	11	4
60	63	3	1	2	7	6	4	6	2
64	68	4	2	6	6	3	5	7	1
70	72	2	1	2	7	3	1	13	1
73	74	1	1	2	9	1	2	8	2
75	77	2	1	2	8	4	0	10	2
78	79	1	1	2	8	2	3	9	3
80	83	3	2	2	12	1	1	7	3
85	86	1	2	4	12	2	2	11	2
88	90	2	1	2	12	2	1	11	4
91	94	3	2	3	10	1	3	11	3
96	98	2	4	5	8	3	1	9	3
102	106	4	1	3	12	2	3	10	2
107	109	2	1	4	9	1	5	11	2
110	113	3	1	2	11	4	5	7	1
114	116	2	1	5	7	4	3	13	0
117	119	2	1	1	8	8	4	9	3
120	–	–	–	–	–	–	–	–	–
Totals		59	34	60	212	65	55	217	54
Average per cycle		2.56	1.48	2.61	9.22	2.82	2.39	9.43	2.34
Percent of Specific Cycles Represented		–	–	14.5	51.2	15.7	13.3	52.4	13.0

significance only to the nearest year, inasmuch as the Klein-Goldberger computation was made on a year-to-year basis. The first two columns give the reference dates for the peaks and troughs, respectively. Since one can identify 23 complete business cycles (measured either from trough to trough or from peak to peak) occurring in the 93 years included in our calculation, the average length of a cycle is 4.0 years. This result is in startling agreement with the 4 year post-World War II cycles in the United States economy, as well as with the mean length of American peacetime business cycles since 1854.[35]

The Klein-Goldberger cycles are broken down, in columns 3 and 4, to indicate the duration of the expansion and contraction phases of each cycle. The average expansion covered 2.6 years, while the normal contraction occupied only 1.5. The agreement with the observed figures for the United States (2.1 and 1.8, respectively)[36] is surprisingly good when one considers the fact that the length of a single business cycle stage in our Klein-Goldberger computation can be estimated only to an integral number of years.

The validity of this comparison of United States and Klein-Goldberger business cycles is dependent, of course, upon the degree of reliability with which the reference dates have been determined. One criterion which can be used is the extent to which specific cycle peaks (troughs) tend to cluster at times coincident with the maxima (minima) of the overall business cycles. In our Klein-Goldberger data, 51 per cent of the individual series, on the average, have maxima coincident with an upper turning point of general business activity, and 52 per cent have minima which coincide with a reference trough. The corresponding figures for the United States economy are 58 per cent and 52 per cent respectively.[36] In addition, the proportions of specific cycles which lead or lag the business cycle in our computed data is quite similar to the analogous figure[37] for the United States economy. Our numbers are given in the last line of Table II.

All in all, it would appear that there is a remarkable correspondence between the characteristics of fluctuations generated by the superposition of random shocks upon the Klein-Goldberger system and those of the business cycles which actually occur in the United States economy. The resemblance is not restricted to qualitative parallelism, but is, indeed,

[35] Computed from the NBER dating for the period 1854–1949, reproduced in Gordon, *op. cit.*, p. 216. We omitted from our averages the Civil War cycle and those corresponding to the two World Wars.

[36] These percentages were estimated from Chart 3 (pp. 16–17) of G. H. Moore, *Statistical Indicators of Cyclical Revivals and Recessions* (National Bureau Occasional Paper 31, 1950). Moore's graph was presented on a monthly basis and included the years 1885–1940.

[37] Mitchell, *op. cit.*, Table 15, pp. 154–155, Table 16, pp. 159–167, and Table 42, pp. 312–325.

TABLE III
COMPARISON OF KLEIN-GOLDBERGER AND NBER SPECIFIC CYCLES

Variable	Frequencies and Other Properties at Peaks								Frequencies and Other Properties at Troughs								Remarks
	One Year Lead	Coincide	One Year Lag	Other	K-G Classification	NBER Classification	K-G Index of Conformity (%)	NBER Index of Conformity (%)	One Year Lead	Coincide	One Year Lag	Other	K-G Classification	NBER Classification	K-G Index of Conformity (%)	NBER Index of Conformity (%)	Remarks
$Y'+T+D$	1	21	1	1	Coincident	Coincident	+100	*+100	2	21	0	1	Coincident	Coincident	+92	*+50	
Y	1	21	1	1	Coincident	Coincident	+100	*+100	1	22	0	1	Coincident	Coincident	+100	*+50	
C	1	8	3	0	Coincident	Coincident	+100	*+100	5	5	1	1	Leading-Coincident	Coincident	−17	+50	
I	4	20	0	3	Coincident	Coincident	+100	*+100	0	23	1	3	Coincident	Coincident	+100	*+100	
W_1	2	10	3	2	Coincident	Coincident	+83	*+100	1	10	3	3	Coincident	Coincident	+8	+50	
A_1	6	8	7	7	Irregular	Coincident	−4	+60	8	5	5	10	Irregular	Coincident	−33	+12	
P	4	19	0	4	Coincident	Coincident	+91	—	0	22	1	4	Coincident	Coincident	+100	—	
N_W	4	18	2	2	Coincident	Coincident	+91	+100	3	19	2	2	Coincident	Coincident	+100	+100	
P_C	4	20	0	4	Coincident	Coincident	+100	*+100	3	20	1	4	Coincident	Coincident	+92	*+100	
S_P	4	16	0	4	Coincident	Coincident	+83	+100	0	17	4	3	Coincident	Coincident	+100	+50	
B	0	5	1	1	Coincident	—	+100	—	1	5	1	0	Coincident	—	−42	—	
K	1	9	6	0	Coincident	—	+87	—	0	11	3	1	Coincident	—	+33	—	
D	10	6	3	6	Leading	—	+22	—	10	7	4	5	Leading	—	−25	—	
L_1	14	4	5	3	Leading	—	+13	—	5	6	9	5	Lagging-Irregular	—	+8	—	
L_2	4	15	0	4	Coincident	Coincident	−65	—	2	17	3	1	Coincident	Coincident	−83	+82	Inverse
p	3	17	2	0	Coincident	Coincident	+100	+64	0	20	2	0	Coincident	Coincident	+83	+60	
p_A	4	17	2	5	Coincident	Coincident	+100	+50	6	14	4	4	Coincident	Coincident	+42	−50	
w	0	1	9	1	Lagging	Lagging	+83	+100	0	4	7	0	Lagging	Coincident	−67	—	
w/p	2	17	1	5	Coincident	—	−74	—	0	21	0	4	Coincident	—	−100	—	Inverse
K/Y	4	19	1	4	Coincident	—	−100	—	5	19	1	3	Coincident	—	−100	—	Inverse

quantitative, in the sense that the duration of the cycle, the relative length of the expansion and contraction phases, and the degree of clustering of peaks and troughs are all in numerical agreement (within the accuracy of measurement) with empirical evidence. Therefore, we shall study the Klein-Goldberger cycles in more detail.

Table III summarizes, for the shocked Klein-Goldberger model, some of the significant features of the specific cycle patterns observed in the endogenous variables. As can be seen from columns 6, 7, 14, and 15, the segregation of the Klein-Goldberger economic variables into leading, coincident, and lagging series is quite similar to the division of the analogous quantities in the United States economy by the NBER. (Columns 2 – 5 and 10 – 13 give the data which lead to our grouping; the NBER separation into categories is taken from Mitchell.[37]) Of the 20 series listed, 12 are classified as coincident series at both peaks and troughs. These are gross national product $(Y + T + D)$, national income Y, gross investment I, private employee compensation W_1, non-wage non-farm income P, employment N_W, corporate profits P_C, corporate savings S_P, corporate surplus B, capital stock K, the general price index p, and the index of agricultural prices p_A. In addition, consumption C coincides at peaks, but has a tendency to lead at troughs. All of these results are in accord with NBER experience (when available), except that the United States specific cycles for consumption coincide, rather than lead at the troughs.

Three additional variables (corporate liquid assets L_2, real wages w/p, and the capital-output ratio K/Y) are in inverse coincidence with the business cycle, in the sense that their troughs tend to occur at reference peaks and vice versa. Unfortunately, we were unable to find the identical items among the NBER data; however, on both theoretical and empirical grounds, these inverse relationships are eminently reasonable. As far as L_2 is concerned, for example, both transactions demand and investment opportunities are reduced as business activity falls and therefore liquid surpluses should begin to accumulate.[38] Indeed, the NBER has some experimental data to support the proposition that the cash component of L_2, at least, tends to rise as the downturn develops (and vice versa).[39]

With respect to the capital-output ratio, it too should fall in times of expansion and climb during a contraction. From a theoretical point of view, as shown by Duesenberry,[40] a non-decreasing capital-output ratio during a business expansion would imply a rising marginal efficiency of investment. But the marginal efficiency of investment cannot increase unless

[38] An excellent description of this process can be found in Gordon, *op. cit.*, p. 270–271.
[39] Mitchell, *op. cit.*, p. 148.
[40] J. S. Duesenberry, *Business Cycles and Economic Growth* (McGraw-Hill, 1958), p. 112.

the capital-output ratio drops. Therefore, the capital-output ratio must fall during the boom phase. Furthermore, the time required for the formation and depletion of the capital stock exceeds the time lag inherent in the production of consumer goods; this too implies that the capital-output ratio will move in a direction opposite to that of the general level of economic activity.

With regard to w/p, both Marshall[41] and Keynes[42] suggested that real wages tend to vary inversely with the level of output and employment. This theorem, which has been thoroughly discussed in the literature,[43] is consistent with our observations. In addition, experimental data concerning the movement of real wages in industrial economies,[44] while somewhat inconclusive, tend to confirm the calculated inverse behavior of this variable.

Of the remaining four quantities, the NBER considers farm income A_1 to concur with the general business cycle and money wage rates w to coincide at troughs and to lag at peaks. We, on the other hand, find the former series to be irregular and the latter to lag everywhere. But, as is evident from Table III, the NBER data for agricultural incomes do not show a very high degree of conformity to the overall business cycle (especially at the troughs), and farm output itself (in real terms) tends to have a higher correlation with metereological cycles than with business cycles.[45] For wages, the disagreement between the behavior of the shocked Klein-Goldberger model at the troughs and the NBER analysis may simply be a reflection of the fact that the Klein-Goldberger equations do not appear to allow enough interaction between unemployment and wage rates.[46]

[41] A. Marshall, *Principles of Economics*, 8th ed. (Macmillan, 1947), p. 620.

[42] J. M. Keynes, *The General Theory of Employment, Interest and Money* (Harcourt Brace, 1935), p. 10.

[43] See, e.g., J. T. Dunlop, "The Movement of Real and Money Wage Rates,"*Economic Journal*, Vol. 48 (1938), pp. 413–34; L. Tarshis, "Changes in Real and Money Wages," *Economic Journal*, Vol. 49 (1939), pp. 150–154; R. Ruggles, "The Relative Movements of Real and Money Wage Rates," *Quarterly Journal of Economics*, Vol. 55 (1940), pp. 130–149; S. C. Tsiang, *The Variations of Real Wages and Profit Margins in Relation to the Trade Cycle* (London, 1947), pp. 10–12; and K. W. Rotschild, *The Theory of Wages* (New York, 1956), pp. 128–131.

[44] Roughly speaking, statistical evidence seems to support the proposition if we take account of *product wages* (i.e., money wages deflated by an index of wholesale prices) (see Tsiang, *op. cit.*, Ch. III) and to undermine it if we consider money wages deflated by a cost of living index (see Dunlop, *op. cit.*, and Tarshis, *op. cit.*). It should be noted that the deflator used for real wages in our computations is the implicit deflator for GNP, and therefore that our (w/p) is closer to the product wage rate than to the measure of real wages analyzed by Dunlop and Tarshis.

[45] Mitchell, *op. cit.*, p. 56 and Gordon, *op. cit.*, pp. 347–350.

[46] D. Creamer and M. Bernstein, *Behavior of Wage Rates During Business Cycles* (National Bureau Occasional Paper 34) applied the NBER method to British and American statistics and found an average lag of wages behind general business activity of about 7 months at the major turning points, and longer for the minor ones.

In our study personal liquid assets L_1 tend to lead at peaks and to lag somewhat irregularly at troughs. We have not encountered comparable NBER series. However, one might attribute a lead in personal liquidity at a peak to the de facto financing of the last stages of the boom by dishoarding on the part of overoptimistic consumers, and the lag at a trough to the satisfaction of pent-up demand in the light of renewed income prospects.

Finally, depreciation D leads, in our calculations, at both troughs and peaks. While Fabricant[47] has found that depreciation charges tend to show much less cyclical fluctuation than corporate gross income or physical output, our computations do not exhibit this behavior. But, it should be noted that, first of all, the Klein-Goldberger depreciation is deflated and more complicated than that of Fabricant, and, secondly, that Fabricant's data cover only the first fourteen years immediately following World War I. We feel, therefore, that existing empirical work is inconclusive on this point, especially in view of the complex nature of any realistic measure of depreciation.

Columns 8 – 9 and 16 – 17 of Table III present the indices of conformity[48] of the specific cycles to the expansions and contractions of the business cycles of both the Klein-Goldberger data and the NBER statistics.[49] These indices measure the correlation between the direction of movements in the individual series which comprise the business cycle and that of the overall economic fluctuations which result. In evaluating the data, one should note that those NBER indices which are preceded by an asterisk in the table are based upon only four complete cycles and therefore that they can assume no numerical values other than 0, $\pm$ 50, and $\pm$ 100. While, by definition, an index of $+$ 100 denotes perfect concurrence in direction of specific cycles with the general business cycle for all four cycles, an index of $+$ 50 for these data states merely that, in exactly three out of the four cases examined, the series expanded during the reference expansion (or contracted during the reference contraction).

As can be seen from this table, there is reasonably good agreement

[47] S. Fabricant, *Capital Consumption and Adjustment* (NBER, 1938), p. 197.

[48] The index of conformity of a set of specific cycles to the expansion of the overall business cycle is the percentage of conforming movements minus the percentage of non-conforming movements. A conforming movement occurs when the value of the variable at a reference peak is higher than its value at the preceding trough. If the two values are equal, the movement does not contribute to the index (although it is counted as an event in computing the percentages). A non-conforming movement is a movement opposite in direction to a conforming movement. The index of conformity to reference contractions is defined in an analogous manner.

[49] The NBER data are taken from Mitchell, *op. cit.*, Table 15, pp. 154–155, Table 16, pp. 159–167, and Table 42, pp. 312–325.

between the Klein-Goldberger indices of conformity and those of the NBER, especially during expansions.[50] A major discrepancy appears, however, in agricultural incomes A_1, where the tendency for irregular behavior of the Klein-Goldberger series observed in the classification process is confirmed by the low values of the conformity indices; the NBER conformity is somewhat higher. We also find that the Klein-Goldberger total payrolls W_1 do not conform as well to business contractions as the NBER data would suggest they should. This is probably due primarily to the failure of money wages w to contract sufficiently in the model. This tendency for rigidity in money wages during contractions, however, is confirmed in the NBER data. Finally, Klein-Goldberger consumption C appears to have little or no tendency to fall during business contractions. This behavior, which agrees with post-World War II United States experience, may be due to the fact that a strong upward trend in consumption expenditures (and in the economic variables in general) has been built into our extrapolation of the Klein-Goldberger model. It is, however, conceivable that there exists a real difference in consumption patterns since World War II, as compared with the prewar era (from which the NBER data were taken). Such a shift would be reflected, at least partially, in the Klein-Goldberger statistical fits.

Generally speaking, then, the specific cycles generated in the Klein-Goldberger model by random shocks thus bear an obvious resemblance to those of cycles found in the United States economy. The division of the Klein-Goldberger data into leading, lagging, and coincident series is almost identical to that of the NBER (when available), and is in accord with theoretical expectations. Similarly, the indices of conformity to the business cycle are reasonably consistent with those given by Mitchell[51] for the United States economy.

10. CONCLUSIONS

Our investigation into the dynamic nature of the econometric model of Klein and Goldberger suggests that their equations do not offer an immediate explanation of an internally generated cyclical process. For, in the absence of perturbations, the time paths of the economic variables are monotonic and essentially linear in character. Furthermore, the behavior of the model is remarkably stable, as evidenced by the fact that

[50] In an economy with a prevalent upward trend, conformity to expansions is more regular than conformity to contractions. Therefore, for the Klein-Goldberger data, a conformity index of +60 to expansions is fairly low. However, since the rising trend also tends to weaken the conformity to expansion of series with inverted timing, a conformity —60 to expansions is high.

[51] Mitchell, *op. cit.*, pp. 154–55, 159–167, and 312–325.

the solution resumes its unperturbed equilibrium growth trend even after a strong exogenous disturbance.

On the other hand, when random shocks of a realistic order of magnitude are superimposed upon the original form of the Klein-Goldberger equations, the cyclical fluctuations which result are remarkably similar to those described by the NBER as characterizing the United States economy. The average duration of a cycle, the mean length of the expansion and contraction phases, and the degree of clustering of individual peaks and troughs around reference dates all agree with the corresponding data for the United States economy. Furthermore, the lead-lag relationships of the endogenous variables included in the model and the indices of conformity of the specific series to the overall business cycle also resemble closely the analogous features of our society. All in all, it would appear that the shocked Klein-Goldberger model approximates the behavior of the United States economy rather well.

In view of these results, it is not unreasonable to suggest that the gross characteristics of the interactions among the real variables described in the Klein-Goldberger equations may represent good approximations to the behavioral relationships in a practical economy. There are, of course, a number of significant defects in the detailed workings of the Klein-Goldberger system. For example, the treatment of the monetary quantities and the interconnections between them and the real sector both need improvement. Nevertheless, the representation would seem to offer a good working basis for the investigation of cyclical fluctuations, especially if the deficiencies mentioned above are corrected.

But, the behavior of the Klein-Goldberger system under random perturbations is also suggestive from another point of view. Ever since the pathbreaking article of Frisch on the propagation of business cycles, the possibility that the cyclical movements observed in a capitalistic society are actually due to random shocks has been seriously considered by business cycle theorists. The results we have found in this study tend to support this possibility. For, the agreement between the data obtained by imposing uncorrelated perturbations upon a model which is otherwise non-oscillatory in character is certainly consistent with the hypothesis that the economic fluctuations experienced in modern, highly developed societies are indeed due to random impulses.

Of course, these random impulses are not necessarily synonymous with an exogenous theory of the business cycle. For, as we saw in Section 8 above, it was primarily shocks of type II which led to agreement between the cyclical behavior of the model and that of the United States economy. And, the reader will recall, these shocks may reflect inexactness in the model, statistical inaccuracies in the fits, or inherent randomness in the decision functions of the economic units themselves. While none of these factors is, strictly speaking, endogenous to the particular Klein-Goldberger system investigated, this does not imply that the type of perturbations actually responsible for the observed cyclical behavior are exogenous to economic theory in general.

In conclusion, we should like to emphasize that, while we have shown that the shocked Klein-Goldberger model offers excellent agreement with economic fact, we have not proved either that the Klein-Goldberger model itself is a good representation of the basic interactions among the several sectors of our economy or that random shocks are the prime cause of business cycles. In view of the remarkable quantitative correspondence with reality, however, we are very tempted to suggest that the second of these hypotheses is true and that, in addition, the Klein-Goldberger system is, except for the deficiencies discussed, not very far wrong.

Berkeley, California

APPENDIX A

1. Explanation of Symbols

$Y + T + D$	Gross national product, 1939 dollars
C	Consumer expenditures, 1939 dollars
I	Gross private domestic capital formation, 1939 dollars
G	Government expenditures for goods and services, 1939 dollars
p	Price index of gross national product, 1939: 100
F_E	Exports of goods and services, 1939 dollars
F_I	Imports of goods and services, 1939 dollars
W_1	Private employee compensation, deflated
W_2	Government employee compensation, deflated
D	Capital consumption charges, 1939 dollars
P_C	Corporate profits, deflated
S_P	Corporate savings, deflated
T	Indirect taxes less subsidies, deflated
T_W	Personal and payroll taxes less transfers associated with wage and salary income, deflated
T_P	Personal and corporate taxes less transfers associated with nonwage nonfarm income, deflated
T_C	Corporate income taxes, deflated
T_A	Taxes less transfers associated with farm income, deflated
K	End-of-year stock of private capital, 1939 dollars from arbitrary origin
F_A	Index of agricultural exports, 1939: 100
p_A	Index of agricultural prices, 1939: 100
p_I	Index of prices of imports, 1939: 100
N_P	Number of persons in the United States
N	Number of persons in the labor force
N_W	Number of wage-and-salary-earners
N_G	Number of government employees
N_F	Number of farm operators
N_E	Number of nonfarm entrepreneurs

IRMA AND FRANK ADELMAN

h	Index of hours worked per year, 1939: 100
w	Index of hourly wages, 1939: 122.1
P	Nonwage nonfarm income, deflated
A_1	Farm income, deflated
A_2	Government payments to farmers, deflated
i_L	Average yield on corporate bonds, per cent
i_S	Average yield on short term commercial paper, per cent
R	Excess reserves of banks as a percentage of total reserves
L_1	End-of-year liquid assets held by persons, deflated
L_2	End-of-year liquid assets held by businesses, deflated
t	Time trend, years, $t = 1$ is 1929
B	End-of-year corporate surplus, deflated, from arbitrary origin

2. Klein and Goldberger's Equations

(1)* $C_t = -22.26 + 0.55(W_1 + W_2 - T_W)_t + 0.41(P - T_P - S_P)_t$
$$+ 0.34(A_1 + A_2 - T_A)_t + 0.26C_{t-1} + 0.072(L_1)_{t-1} + 0.26(N_P)_t$$

(2)* $I_t = -16.71 + 0.78(P - T_P + A_1 + A_2 - T_A + D)_{t-1} - 0.073K_{t-1}$
$$+ 0.14(L_2)_{t-1}$$

(3)* $(S_P)_t = -3.53 + 0.72\,(P_C - T_C)_t + 0.076\,(P_C - T_C - S_P)_{t-1} - 0.028\,B_{t-1}$

(4)* $(P_C)_t = -7.60 + 0.68P_t$

(5)* $$D_t = 7.25 + 0.10\,\frac{K_t + K_{t-1}}{2} + 0.044(Y + T + D - W_2)_t$$

(6)* $(W_1)_t = -1.40 + 0.24(Y + T + D - W_2)_t + 0.24(Y + T + D - W_2)_{t-1} + 0.29t$

(7)* $(Y + T + D - W_2)_t = -26.08 + 2.17[h(N_W - N_G) + N_E + N_F]_t$
$$+ 0.16\,\frac{K_t + K_{t-1}}{2} + 2.05t$$

(8)* $w_t - w_{t-1} = 4.11 - 0.74(N - N_W - N_E - N_F)_t + 0.52(p_{t-1} - p_{t-2}) + 0.54t$

(9)* $(F_I)_t = 0.32 + 0.0060(W_1 + W_2 - T_W + P - T_P + A_1 + A_2 - T_A)_t$
$$+ 0.81(F_I)_{t-1}$$

(10)* $(A_1)_t \dfrac{p_t}{(p_A)_t} = -0.36 + 0.054(W_1 + W_2 - T_W + P - T_P - S_P)_t \dfrac{p_t}{(p_A)_t}$
$$- 0.007(W_1 + W_2 - T_W + P - T_P - S_P)_{t-1}\dfrac{p_{t-1}}{(p_A)_{t-1}} + 0.012(F_A)_t$$

(11)* $(p_A)_t = -131.17 + 2.32p_t$

(12)* $(L_1)_t = 0.14(W_1 + W_2 - T_W + P - T_P - S_P + A_1 + A_2 - T_A)_t$
$$+ 76.03(i_L - 2.0)_t^{-0.84}$$

(13)* $(L_2)_t = -0.34 + 0.26(W_1)_t - 1.02(i_S)_t - 0.26(p_t - p_{t-1}) + 0.61(L_2)_{t-1}$

(14)* $(i_L)_t = 2.58 + 0.44(i_S)_{t-3} + 0.26(i_S)_{t-5}$

(15)* $$100\,\frac{(i_S)_t - (i_S)_{t-1}}{(i_S)_{t-1}} = 11.17 - 0.67R_t$$

(16) $$C_t + I_t + G_t + (F_E)_t - (F_I)_t = Y_t + T_t + D_t$$

(17) $$(W_1)_t + (W_2)_t + P_t + (A_1)_t + (A_2)_t = Y_t$$

(18) $$h_t \frac{w_t}{p_t} (N_w)_t = (W_1)_t + (W_2)_t$$

(19) $$K_t - K_{t-1} = I_t - D_t$$

(20) $$B_t - B_{t-1} = (S_P)_t$$

(21) $$T_t = 0.0924(Y + T + D)_t - \frac{275.4}{p_t}$$

(22) $$(T_w)_t = 0.1549(W_1)_t + 0.1310(W_2)_t - \frac{1398.1}{p_t}$$

(23) $$(T_c)_t = 0.4497(P_c)_t + \frac{548.2}{p_t}$$

(24) $$(T_P)_t = 0.248(P - T_c - S_P)_t + 0.2695 \frac{p_{t-1}}{p_t} (P - T_c - S_P)_{t-1} +$$
$$+ 0.4497(P_c)_t - \frac{1162.1}{p_t}$$

(25) $$(T_A)_t = \frac{50.0}{p_t}$$

APPENDIX B

1. The equations that, for the actual calculations, replaced their counterparts of Appendix A

(3) $$(S_P)_t = -3.53 + 0.72(P_c - T_c)_t - 0.028B_{t-1}$$

(9) $$(F_I)_t = (F_E)_t$$

(10) $$(A_1)_t \frac{p_t}{(p_A)_t} = 0.054(W_1 + W_2 - T_w + P - T_P - S_P)_t \frac{p_t}{(p_A)_t} + 0.012(F_A)_t$$

(11) $$(p_A)_t = 1.39p_t + 32.0$$

(13) $$(L_2)_t = 0.26(W_1)_t - 1.02(i_S)_t - 0.26(p_t - p_{t-1}) + 0.61(L_2)_{t-1}$$

(14) $$(i_L)_t = 3.5$$

(15) $$(i_S)_t = 2.5$$

(16) $$C_t + I_t + G_t = Y_t + T_t + D_t$$

(21) $$T_t = 0.0924(Y + T + D)_t - 1.3607$$

(22) $$(T_w)_t = 0.1549(W_1)_t + 0.131(W_2)_t - 6.9076$$

(23) $$(T_c)_t = 0.4497(P_c)_t + 2.7085$$

IRMA AND FRANK ADELMAN

$$(24) \quad (T_P)_t = 0.248(P - T_C - S_P)_t + 0.2695 \frac{p_{t-1}}{p_t}(P - T_C - S_P)_{t-1}$$
$$+ 0.4497(P_C)_t - 5.7416$$

$$(25) \qquad\qquad (T_A)_t = 0.0512(A_1 + A_2)_t$$

2. Extrapolations

$$(W_2)_t = 1.82 + .578t$$

$$(N_E)_t = 3.70 + .118t$$

$$(N_F)_t = 4.01 + \frac{2.12}{t-15}$$

$$(N_G)_t = 2.01 + .321t$$

$$(N_P)_t = 97.39 + 2.589t$$

$$N_t = 44.53 + .964t$$

$$h_t = 1.062$$

$$G_t = 19.892 + .567t$$

$$(A_2)_t = .108 + \frac{.0746}{t-16}$$

$$(F_A)_t = 171.86$$

3. Initial values used in calculations

Endogenous Variables	1951 $(t-2)$	1952 $(t-1)$	Exogenous Variables	1952 $(t-1)$	1953 (t)
$Y + T + D$	—	172.0	h	—	1.062
C	—	111.4	W_2	15.12	15.70
W_1	—	78.65	G	—	33.5
A_1	—	7.3	A_2	0.1187	0.1173
I	—	24.3	F_A	—	171.86
K	—	41.5	N_P	—	159.6
D	—	19.35	N	—	67.63
P_C	—	16.51	N_E	—	6.53
P	—	35.17	N_F	—	4.25
S_P	—	1.9	N_G	—	9.71
B	—	.19	i_S	2.5	2.5
N_W	—	56.0	i_L	3.5	3.5
L_1	—	95.2			
L_2	—	38.1			
w	—	326.2			
p	197.5	202.4			
p_A	—	303.0			
T	—	14.51			
T_W	—	8.63			
T_A	—	.38			
T_C	—	10.14			
T_P	—	13.72			

4. Standard deviations used for Type I shocks (upon exogenous variables)

Variable	$\sigma_{\delta y_t}$	$\dfrac{\sigma_{\delta y_t}}{y_{t-1}}$
i_S	.512	.20
i_L	.146	.0423
h	.0185	.018
W_2	1.77	.123
G	.88	.026
A_2	.0192	.16
F_A	12.2	.071
N_P	.086	.00054
N	.125	.0018
N_E	.114	.017
N_F	.234	.055
N_G	.975	.10

5. Standard deviations used for Type II shocks (upon equations)

Variable	Equation	$\sigma_{\delta y_t}$	$\dfrac{\sigma_{\delta y_t}}{y_{t-1}}$
C	(1)*	.958	.0086
I	(2)*	2.946	.12
S_P	(3)	5.428	.29
P_C	(4)*	.700	.044
D	(5)*	.699	.036
W_1	(6)*	1.0325	.013
$Y + T + D$	(7)*	2.319	.013
w	(8)*	4.861	.015
A_1	(10)	.955	.13
L_1	(12)*	.017575	.00059
L_2	(13)	1.2911	.034
p_A†	(11)	15.716	.052

† Based on residuals from our re-estimated equation for p_A for the years 1946–52.

[3]

BUSINESS CYCLES—ENDOGENOUS OR STOCHASTIC?[1]

I. INTRODUCTION

THE idea that the cyclical fluctuations observed in advanced industrial economies may be due to the effect of erratic, uncorrelated shocks upon an otherwise interrelated system was first suggested by Ragnar Frisch in 1933.[2] This hypothesis received a rather mixed reception. For, on the one hand, an appeal to unexplained random perturbations in order to account for a fundamental feature of the dynamics of a capitalistic economy is not particularly satisfying. This is evidently the position taken by Hicks, who states categorically in discussing Frisch's theory, " this particular hypothesis will not do." [3]

On the other hand, several studies [4] have indicated that Frisch's explanation of cyclical behaviour provides us with an extremely good approximation to the qualitative features of the actual motion of economic time series. One of the most recent of these, and the most detailed, was part of an investigation into the dynamic nature of the Klein–Goldberger econometric model of the United States economy, undertaken in 1956–58 by my husband and myself and published in the October 1959 issue of *Econometrica*.[5] In this paper we found that, in the absence of external perturbations, the time paths of the economic variables of the Klein–Goldberger equations were monotonic and essentially linear in character. Thus, their model does not offer an immediate explanation of an internally generated cyclical process. However, when random shocks of a realistic order of magnitude were superimposed upon the Klein–Goldberger system the cyclical fluctuations which resulted were remarkably similar to those described by the N.B.E.R. as characterising the United States economy. The average duration of a cycle, the mean length of the expansion and contraction phases, and the degree of clustering of individual peaks and troughs around the turning points of the general business cycle all agreed with the corre-

---

[1] This paper was presented at the December 1959 meeting of the Econometric Society. I am indebted to F. L. Adelman and K. J. Arrow for their valuable suggestions.

[2] R. Frisch, " Propagation and Impulse Problems in Dynamic Economics," *Economic Essays in Honour of Gustav Cassel* (London, 1933), pp. 171–205.

[3] J. R. Hicks, *A Contribution to the Theory of the Trade Cycle* (Oxford, 1950), p. 90. See also, pp. 193–195.

[4] Cf., *e.g.*, R. M. Goodwin, " Econometrics in Business Cycle Analysis," in A. H. Hansen's *Business Cycles and National Income* (New York, 1951), p. 421; E. Slutzky, " The Summation of Random Causes as the Source of the Cyclic Processes," *Econometrica*, Vol. 5 (April 1937), pp. 105–46; M. G. Kendall, *The Advanced Theory of Statistics* (London, 1946), Vol. II, pp. 400–37; and G. H. Fisher, " Some Comments on Stochastic Macro-Economic Models," *American Economic Review*, Vol. 42, June, December 1952, pp. 528–39.

[5] I. Adelman and F. L. Adelman, " The Dynamic Properties of the Klein–Goldberger Model," *Econometrica*, Vol. 27, October 1959, pp. 596–625.

sponding data for the United States.   Furthermore, the lead–lag relationships of the endogenous variables included in the model and the indices of
conformity of the specific series to the overall business cycle also resembled
closely the analogous features of our society.   All in all, the shocked Klein–
Goldberger model approximated the cyclical behaviour of the United States
economy extremely well.

But the fact that the shocked Klein–Goldberger model corresponds so
well to economic experience does not prove either that the model itself is a
good representation of the fundamental interactions among the several
sectors of our economy or that random shocks are the prime cause of business
cycles.   For the close agreement with reality is, *a priori*, a consequence of
both the model and the shocks.   How much of this agreement is due to the
basic structure of the underlying economic relations, and how much to the
stochastic features superimposed upon the model remains to be determined.

This study is designed to shed some light upon this question.   We shall
proceed in the following way: First of all, in a manner analogous to that
used in the previous study, we impose random, uncorrelated shocks upon
a set of economic time series related only by accounting definitions, and
study the oscillations which result.   The degree to which these fluctuations
approximate the business cycle observed in the United States economy will
then be compared with the corresponding results of our Klein–Goldberger
study.   We will see that the superposition of shocks upon a model with
minimal economic content leads to a reasonable facsimile of a business cycle.
However, the approximation will be seen to be distinctly inferior to that
derived from the shocked Klein–Goldberger system.

II. The Naïve Model

The simplest model of an expanding economy that one can generate is
to extrapolate all the endogenous variables of the system linearly, having
regard only for the accounting identities inherent in the choice of variables.
To facilitate comparison with the Klein–Goldberger model, our " naïve "
model was derived in the following fashion.   All the variables and the
accounting identities of the Klein–Goldberger model were retained.   However, all the behavioural equations of the system were replaced by simple
extrapolations based on least-squares fits to the post-war (1946–52) data.
For consumption (C), investment (I), government expenditures (G),
corporate savings (S_P), corporate profits (P_C), indirect taxes less subsidies
(T), depreciation (D), private (W_1) and government (W_2) employee
compensation, the number of wage and salary earners (N_W), the index of
hourly wages (w) and the price index (p), simple linear fits were used.
Since the short (i_S) and long-term (i_L) interest rates and the index of hours
worked per year (h) exhibited no obvious trends during this period, they
were taken to be constant.   On the other hand, farm income (A_1), government payments to farmers (A_2) and private (L_1) and business (L_2) liquid

assets all had declining trends during the sample period. For these quantities it therefore seemed more appropriate to use a fit of the form

$$X = a + \frac{b}{t - \alpha}$$

in order that they never become negative. This procedure yielded a basic set of twenty-five equations in an equal number of variables. Five of these equations are accounting definitions, while the rest express each variable as a function only of time.

In order to see what effects random perturbations may have upon this "naïve" model, a random term δy_t was then inserted into those extrapolations which replace *behavioural* equations of the Klein–Goldberger model. For this purpose the value of a variable y_t at time t was defined as its trend value, $\bar{y}_t$, plus a shock term δy_t. And y_t was assumed to have a Gaussian distribution with a mean of zero. (The resulting system of equations appears in Appendix A2.) In order that the shocks inflicted upon the system be of a realistic order of magnitude at all times, the standard deviation of δy_t was evaluated over that portion of the data for which the least-squares fit was made. And, for the subsequent calculations, the ratio of the standard deviation of δy_t to $\bar{y}_{t-1}$ was maintained at a value independent of time. It is interesting to note that these standard deviations (see Appendix A3) are, in general, quite small; in fact, only four of them exceed 10% of the trend value of the corresponding variable.

Given the size of the standard deviation, the technique employed to determine the magnitude and sign of the exogenous shock upon each variable was to divide the normal curve of error into 100 regions of equal area. To each region was assigned both the normal deviate associated with the mid-point of its interval and a previously unassigned integer between 00 and 99, inclusive. Then the selection of a two-digit random number effectively specified at random a particular region of the Gaussian distribution and its corresponding normal deviate. Multiplying this deviate by the standard deviation of δy_t, the magnitude and direction of a shock upon the variable y at time t were established. Since the selection of an interval in this manner was thus purely random, and since all intervals define the same area under the curve, this method produced a normally distributed *random* shock upon the variable in question. The repetition of this procedure for each of the variables of equations (1)–(14) yielded a series of random, normally distributed, uncorrelated shocks of realistic size.

Using this technique for the evaluation of the magnitudes and signs of the random terms, the shocked "naïve" model was solved for 100 years with the aid of an I.B.M. 650 calculator. The typical behaviour of the time series generated by this process is portrayed in Fig. 1. The solid lines in this graph describe the computed time paths of national income, investment and corporate profits, while the dotted lines represent the actual time

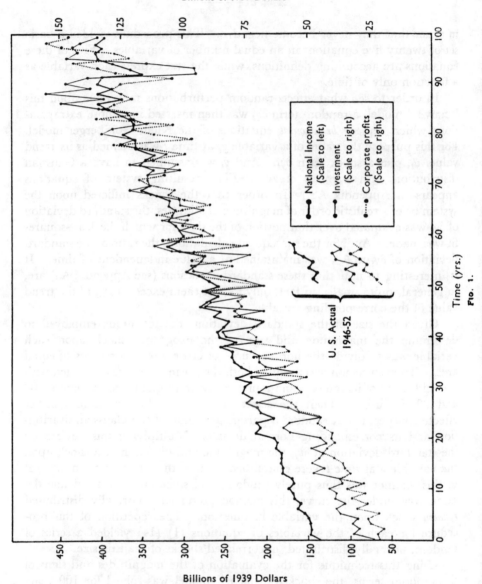

Billions of 1939 Dollars

Fig. 1.

paths of the same variables during the post-war period in the United States. As apparent from this figure, under the impact of random shocks the individual variables of the system exhibit cyclical swings of more or less realistic durations and amplitudes.

The presence of qualitatively correct oscillatory movements in the individual variables of this system is but to be expected, however. This much agreement with reality is merely a *necessary* condition of an adequate simulation of the cyclical fluctuations of a real industrial economy. We must investigate further to find out whether or not the shocked version of this " naïve " model really produces business cycles in the technical sense. Specifically, how nearly all-pervasive are the cumulative movements which arise? Are the various oscillations correlated? Is there any consistent phase relationship among the several economic series? Do the time-paths of the individual variables of the model correspond to those observed in the United States economy? To answer these questions, the techniques developed by the N.B.E.R. for the analysis of business cycles were applied to the data.

One property of cyclical fluctuations in an industrial economy is a marked tendency for a clustering of peaks and troughs of individual economic time series about particular reference dates. It is, in fact, precisely this characteristic of business cycles that Burns and Mitchell[1] use as their criterion for the dating of turning-points in the United States economy. And, inasmuch as the oscillations in our model occur in response to random non-correlated perturbations, a study of the simultaneity of occurrence of peaks (and troughs) provides us with quite stringent a test of the realism of this system.

As in the normal N.B.E.R.[2] procedure, the specific cycles were dated first; *i.e.*, all the turning-points of each of the time series were determined. Then, to establish reference dates for the turning-points of the *overall* business cycles, the data were examined for bunching (in time) of specific cycle peaks and troughs. A reference peak (trough) was said to occur in our data during any year in which the modal number of specific cycle peaks occurs, provided that at least 10 peaks (troughs) are found in a 2-year period which includes the modal year.

Table I is a summary of some of the relevant characteristics observed in the shocked naïve model. The first two columns give the reference dates for the peaks and troughs, respectively. Since one can identify 20 complete business cycles (measured either from trough to trough or from peak to peak) occurring in the 90 years included in the calculation, the average length of a cycle is 4·5 years. This result is in startling agreement with the

[1] A. F. Burns and W. C. Mitchell, *Measuring Business Cycles* (National Bureau, 1946), and W. C. Mitchell, *What Happens During Business Cycles* (National Bureau, 1951), pp. 10–11.

[2] The methods and results of the N.B.E.R. are summarised in Burns and Mitchell, *op. cit.*, and in Mitchell, *op. cit.*

4-year post-Second World War cycles in the United States economy, as well as with the mean length of American peace-time business cycles since 1864.[1] The longest cycle in our data as measured from trough to trough was

TABLE I

Reference Dating for the Shocked Naïve Model

Reference dates.		Elapsed time, years.		Number of series at peaks which:			Number of series at troughs which:		
Peaks (P).	Trough (T).	$T - P.$	$P - T.$	Lead, one year.	Co-incide.	Lag, one year.	Lead, one year.	Co-incide.	Lag, one year.
11	8	3	1	4	5	2	4	6	1
22	12	10	3	1	8	3	2	7	3
28	25	3	2	0	8	3	3	8	1
33	30	3	1	4	8	3	5	6	2
39	34	5	1	3	7	2	5	7	3
41	40	1	3	2	5	5	3	7	2
47	44	3	2	3	7	2	2	8	2
50	49	1	2	3	9	2	3	7	3
53	52	1	4	1	8	2	5	7	1
61	57	4	1	3	7	2	3	8	1
63	62	1	1	2	8	8	5	8	2
72	66	6	3	5	6	1	4	7	4
75	73	2	2	4	7	4	4	5	4
78	77	1	2	2	6	5	6	7	2
82	80	2	1	4	8	1	2	8	2
85	83	2	1	4	7	3	2	10	0
87	86	1	1	3	5	5	5	6	3
89	88	1	1	5	5	5	3	6	4
91	90	1	1	6	5	3	4	7	4
96	92	4	2	2	7	4	2	8	4
—	98	—	—	—	—	—	2	7	4
TOTALS		56	34	61	137	65	74.	150	57
Average per cycle		2·80	1·70	3·05	6·85	3·25	3·70	7·50	2·85
% of specific cycles represented		—	—	17·9	40·2	19·1	21·8	44·1	16·8

13 years in duration; the shortest lasted 2 years. The corresponding figures for the United States economy were 9·2 and 2·2 years respectively.

The computed cycles are broken down, in columns 3 and 4, to indicate the duration of the expansion and contraction phases of each cycle. The average expansion covered 2·8 years, while the normal contraction took 1·7. The agreement with the observed figures for the United States (2·0 and 1·8 respectively) is surprisingly good, considering the fact that, in our computations, the length of a single business-cycle stage can be estimated only to an integral number of years.

The validity of this comparison of United States and computed business cycles is dependent, of course, upon the degree of reliability with which the

[1] Computed from the N.B.E.R. dating for the period 1854–1949. We omitted from our averages the Civil War cycle and those corresponding to the two World Wars.

reference dates have been determined.   One criterion which can be used is the extent to which specific cycle peaks (troughs) tend to cluster at times coincident with the turning-points of the overall business cycles.   In our results 40% of the individual series, on the average, have maxima coincident with an upper turning-point of general business activity, and 44% have minima which coincide with a reference trough.   The corresponding figures for the United States economy are 58 and 52%, respectively.[1]   In addition, the percentage of specific cycles which lead or lag the business cycle in our computed data are 17·9 and 19·1% at the peaks, and 21·8 and 16·8% at the troughs.   The analogous numbers for the United States economy lie between 13 and 16%.[1]   Thus, while the computed specific cycles definitely tend to cluster at business-cycle turning-points, the degree of bunching is significantly less in the shocked naïve model than in the United States economy.

All in all, it would appear that there is a fair correspondence between the characteristics of the fluctuations generated by the superposition of random shocks upon economic time series related only through accounting definitions and the nature of the business cycles which actually occur in the United States economy.   The mean duration of the cycles and the relative length of their expansion and contraction phases are in close numerical agreement with empirical evidence.   The degree of bunching of peaks and troughs, however, while significant, does not approximate actual experience as closely as might be desired.   We must therefore study the computed cycles in greater detail.

Table II summarises some of the significant features of the specific cycle patterns observed in the variables of the perturbed naïve model.   Columns 2–5 and 10–13 give the data which lead to our grouping of the economic variables into leading, coincident and lagging series.   As apparent from these columns, the number of turning-points of the specific cycles which occur in the " other " column is generally comparable to the modal number of events in the leading, coincident or lagging columns.   As a result, it was generally impossible to classify the variables of the model unambiguously according to the timing of their turning-points relative to those of the reference cycle.   Of the twenty variables listed in Table II, five were completely irregular in their behaviour at the turning-points of the general business cycle (see columns 6 and 14 of this table).   Twelve series were classified as coincident-irregular, and one (consumption) as coincident-lagging.   Only a single variable, national income (Y), tended to have peaks and troughs which coincided consistently with those of the overall reference cycle.   It should be noted, though, that, as can be seen by comparing columns 6 and 14 with 7 and 15, except for the tendency towards more erratic behaviour in the computed series, the classification of the variables of

---

[1] These percentages were estimated from Chart 3 (pp. 16–17) of G. H. Moore, *Statistical Indicators of Cyclical Revivals and Recessions* (National Bureau Occasional Paper 31, 1950).

TABLE II
Comparison of Computed and N.B.E.R. Specific Cycles

Variable	Properties at peaks.								Properties at troughs.								Remarks.
	One-year lead.	Co-incide	One-year lag.	Other.	Our classification.	N.B.E.R. classification.	Our index of conformity, %.	N.B.E.R. index of conformity.	One-year lead.	Co-incide.	One-year lag.	Other.	Our classification.	N.B.E.R. classification.	Our index of conformity, %.	N.B.E.R. index of conformity.	
C	3	5	5	3	Coinc.-Lag	Coinc.	+70	+100	3	3	3	7	Irreg.	Coinc.	−80	+50	
I	1	11	5	12	Coinc.-Irreg.	Coinc.	+90	+100	3	14	3	7	Coinc.	Coinc.	+60	+100	
Sp	3	11	2	12	Coinc.-Irreg.	Coinc.	+40	+100	4	7	4	9	Irreg.	Coinc.	+30	+50	
Po	4	6	6	15	Irreg.	Coinc.	+30	+100	1	12	1	13	Coinc.-Irreg.	Coinc.	+30	+100	
D	3	8	8	9	Lag-Irreg.	—	+40	—	8	4	8	5	Lag	—	−70	—	
W_1	1	8	4	9	Coinc.-Irreg.	Coinc.	+60	+100	6	7	6	8	Coinc.-Irreg.	Coinc.	0	+50	
Nw	6	6	3	10	Coinc.-Irreg.	Coinc.	+80	+100	3	8	3	12	Coinc.-Irreg.	Coinc.	−50	+100	
w	2	12	2	5	Coinc.-Irreg.	Lagging	+50	+50	1	6	1	1	Coinc.-Irreg.	Coinc.	−70	+60	
PA	3	3	4	9	Irreg.	—	+10	—	6	11	6	9	Irreg.	—	+20	—	
iS, iL	3	9	6	13	Coinc.-Irreg.	Coinc.	+50	+60	4	4	4	10	Coinc.-Irreg.	Coinc.	+5	+12	
A_1	4	7	5	15	Irreg.	—	+30	—	1	11	1	14	Irreg.	—	+40	—	
L_1	2	12	8	13	Coinc.-Irreg.	—	+100	—	3	10	3	12	Coinc.-Irreg.	Coinc.	+60	+50	
L_2	−1	13	2	14	Coinc.	Coinc.	+60	+100	2	13	2	14	Coinc.-Irreg.	Coinc.	+60	—	
Y	1	7	3	6	Irreg.	Coinc.	+70	—	4	11	4	4	Coinc.-Irreg.	Coinc.	+60	+82	
P	6	5	3	12	Coinc.-Irreg.	—	+100	+100	3	8	3	9	Coinc.-Irreg.	Coinc.	−50	—	
p	0	1	3	11	Irreg.	—	+60	—	6	1	6	11	Coinc.	—	−20	—	
K	−1	13	−1	6	Coinc.-Irreg.	—	+70	+64	4	13	4	3	Coinc.	—	−90	—	
B	2	12	2	0	Irreg.	—	+100	—	1	13	1	0	Coinc.-	—	−80	—	
K/r	2	12	2	10	Coinc.-Irreg.	—	+60	—	0	2	0	5	Coinc.-	—	−80	—	
w/p	3	9	4	12	Coinc.-Irreg.	—	+20	—	4	9	4	9	Coinc.-Irreg.	—	−10	—	Inverse

the model into leading, coincident and lagging quantities is generally similar to that of the N.B.E.R.

Columns 8–9 and 16–17 of Table II present the indices of conformity of the specific cycles to the expansions and contractions of the business cycles for both the computed time series and the N.B.E.R. statistics. These indices measure the correlation between the direction of movement in the individual series and that of the overall business fluctuations. As can be seen from this table, there is fairly poor agreement between the indices of conformity of the computed series and those of the N.B.E.R., especially during contractions.

Generally speaking, then, the cycles generated by random uncorrelated shocks upon a system in which the only relationships among the variables are due to accounting procedures bear a certain amount of resemblance to the cycles found in the United States economy. The mean length of the cycles, and the average duration of prosperity and recession, agree fairly well with United States experience. On the other hand, the tendency towards a clustering of turning-points of specific cycles at reference peaks and troughs is significantly weaker in the computed cycles than it is in practice. And, in addition, the computed time series were much more erratic in their lead–lag behaviour than their counterparts in the United States economy.

III. The Klein–Goldberger Model

To help us assess these results, let us see how they compare with those obtained when the dynamic behaviour of the shocked 1954 Klein–Goldberger econometric model of the United States economy was studied in the same manner. The details of the Klein–Goldberger investigation are discussed in the October 1959 issue of *Econometrica*, and will not be given here.

Table III summarises the characteristics of the reference cycles in the shocked Klein–Goldberger economy in a form similar to that of Table I. As before, the mean duration of the computed cyclical swings (4·0 years) and the relative length of the average expansion and contraction (2·6 and 1·5 years respectively) are in close agreement with the actual data for the United States. Unlike in the shocked naïve model, however, the specific cycle peaks and troughs of the Klein–Goldberger system tend to cluster more markedly at reference turning dates: In the Klein–Goldberger calculations 51% of the specific cycle peaks and 52% of specific cycle troughs occurred at reference extrema, as compared to only 40 and 44% for the naïve model. Thus, the substitution of the economic interactions of the Klein–Goldberger system for the simple extrapolations of the naïve scheme leads to a decided improvement in the characteristics of the reference cycle.

However, for an adequate description of actual experience we must require, in addition, that the specific cycle patterns observed be realistic as

64 *Dynamics and Income Distribution*

TABLE III
Reference Dating for Shocked Klein–Goldberger Model

Reference dates.		Elapsed time, years.		Number of series at peaks which:			Number of series at troughs which:		
Trough (T).	Peak (P).	$T - P$.	$P - T$.	Lag, one year.	Co-incide.	Lead, one year.	Lag, one year.	Co-incide.	Lead, one year.
—	27	—	2	—	—	—	—	—	—
29	31	2	1	2	8	6	1	6	4
32	37	5	1	1	8	5	4	7	4
38	42	4	1	1	10	0	1	13	1
43	45	2	1	2	7	4	0	10	0
46	51	5	2	2	11	1	3	8	3
53	54	1	2	4	12	1	2	10	4
56	59	3	1	1	10	1	1	11	4
60	63	3	1	2	7	6	4	6	2
64	68	4	2	6	6	3	5	7	1
70	72	2	1	2	7	3	1	13	1
73	74	1	1	2	9	1	2	8	2
75	77	2	1	2	8	4	0	10	2
78	79	1	1	2	8	2	3	9	3
80	83	3	2	2	12	1	1	7	3
85	86	1	2	4	12	2	2	11	2
88	90	2	1	2	12	2	1	11	4
91	94	3	2	3	10	1	3	11	3
96	98	2	4	5	8	3	1	9	3
102	106	4	1	3	12	2	3	10	2
107	109	2	1	4	9	1	5	11	2
110	113	3	1	2	11	4	5	7	1
114	116	2	1	5	7	4	3	13	0
117	119	2	1	1	8	8	4	9	3
120	—	—	—	—	—	—	—	—	—
TOTALS . .		59	34	60	212	65	55	217	54
Average per cycle .		2·56	1·48	2·61	9·22	2·82	2·39	9·43	2·34
% of specific cycles represented .		—	—	14·5	51·2	15·7	13·3	52·4	13·0

well. Table IV presents a comparison of the Klein–Goldberger and N.B.E.R. specific cycles, in a form analogous to that of Table II. As can be seen by comparing columns 6 and 14 of the two tables, the Klein–Goldberger model succeeds in removing the indeterminacy present in the naïve system. Only agricultural incomes (A_1) remain irregular in their pattern of behavior in the Klein–Goldberger data. But, in view of the low index of conformity reported by the N.B.E.R. for this variable, this may not be unrealistic. In addition, there is also extremely close agreement between the N.B.E.R. and the Klein–Goldberger classification of variables into leading, lagging and coincident series. Eleven Klein–Goldberger variables are classified as coincident at both peaks and troughs. These are: national income (Y), gross investment (I), private employee compensation (W_1), non-wage, non-farm income (P), employment (N_W), corporate profits (P_C), corporate savings (S_P), corporate surplus (B), capital stock (K), the

TABLE IV

Comparison of Klein–Goldberger and N.B.E.R. Specific Cycles

Variable	Properties at peaks.								Properties at troughs.								Remarks.
	One-year lead.	Co-incide.	One-year lag.	Other.	K.-G. classifi-cation.	N.B.E.R. classifi-cation.	K.-G. index of con-formity, %.	N.B.E.R. index of con-formity, %.	One-year lead.	Co-incide.	One-year lag.	Other.	K.-G. classifi-cation.	N.B.E.R. classifi-cation.	K.-G. index of con-formity, %.	N.B.E.R. index of con-formity, %.	
$Y + T \div D$	1	21	1	1	Coinc.	Coinc.	+100	+100	2	21	0	1	Coinc.	Coinc.	+92	+50	
Y	1	21	1	1	Coinc.	Coinc.	+100	+100	1	22	0	1	Coinc.	Coinc.	+100	+50	
C	1	8	3	0	Coinc.	Coinc.	+100	+100	5	5	1	1	Leading	Coinc.	−17	+50	
I	4	20	0	3	Coinc.	Coinc.	+100	+100	0	23	1	3	Coinc.	Coinc.	+100	+100	
W_1	2	10	3	2	Coinc.	Coinc.	+83	+100	1	10	3	3	Coinc.	Coinc.	+8	+50	
A_1	6	8	7	7	Irreg.	Coinc.	+4	+60	8	5	5	10	Irreg.	Coinc.	+33	+12	
P	4	19	0	4	Coinc.	Coinc.	+91	—	3	22	1	4	Coinc.	Coinc.	+100	+100	
Nw	4	18	2	2	Coinc.	Coinc.	+100	+100	3	19	2	2	Coinc.	Coinc.	+92	+100	
Pc	4	20	0	4	Coinc.	Coinc.	+83	+100	3	20	1	4	Coinc.	Coinc.	+100	+50	
Sp	0	16	0	1	Coinc.	Coinc.	+100	+100	0	17	4	3	Coinc.	Coinc.	+42	—	
B	0	5	6	0	Coinc.	—	+87	—	1	5	1	0	Coinc.	—	+33	—	
K	10	9	3	6	Coinc.	—	+22	—	0	11	3	1	Leading	—	+25	—	
D	0	6	3	3	Leading	—	+13	—	10	7	4	5	Lagging	—	+8	—	
L_1	14	4	5	—	Leading	—	—	—	5	6	9	5	Irreg.	—	—	—	
L_s	4	15	0	4	Coinc.	Coinc.	+65	+64	2	17	3	1	Coinc.	Coinc.	+83	+82	Inverse
p	3	17	2	0	Coinc.	Coinc.	+100	+50	0	20	2	0	Coinc.	Coinc.	+83	+60	
p_A	4	1	9	5	Coinc.	Lagging	+100	+100	6	14	4	4	Coinc.	Coinc.	+42	+50	
w	0	17	1	1	Lagging	—	+83	—	0	4	7	0	Lagging	—	+67	—	
u/p	2	17	—	5	Coinc.	—	+74	—	0	21	0	4	Coinc.	—	−100	—	Inverse
K/r	4	19	1	4	Coinc.	—	−100	—	5	19	1	3	Coinc.	—	−100	—	Inverse

general price index (p) and the index of agricultural prices (p_A). Consumption (C) coincides at peaks, but has a tendency to lead at troughs. And corporate liquid assets (L_2), real wages (w/p) and the capital/output ratio (K/Y) are in inverse coincidence with the business cycle in the sense that their troughs tend to occur at reference peaks, and vice versa. All of these results are in accord with N.B.E.R. experience (when available), except that United States specific cycles for consumption coincide, rather than lead, at the troughs. In addition, as evident from columns 8–9 and 16–17 of this table, the indices of conformity calculated for the Klein–Goldberger statistics are quite consistent with those given by Mitchell for the United States economy.

Generally speaking, then, it would appear that the specific cycles generated in the Klein–Goldberger model by random shocks resemble the cycles found in the United States economy much more closely than do those of the naïve model. Since, in addition, the characteristics of the reference cycles of the Klein–Goldberger model are also more satisfactory, we conclude that the shocked Klein–Goldberger equations offer a better approximation to United States cyclical experience than does the shocked naïve model.

IV. Discussion

When the work described in this paper on a minimal stochastic model of a complex industrial economy is compared with the earlier investigation on the Klein–Goldberger system three facts stand out:

(1) a minimal stochastic model is reasonably satisfactory in simulating business fluctuations in the United States;

(2) the Klein–Goldberger equations by themselves describe a non-oscillatory economy;

(3) the superposition of random shocks upon the Klein–Goldberger system leads to an extremely close representation of the cyclical fluctuations of American business activity.

These results suggest that it is the stochastic features of the shocked Klein–Goldberger model, rather than the interactions described directly by the Klein–Goldberger equations themselves, which are responsible for the excellent agreement with reality mentioned above. We have not, of course, proved that business cycles are stochastic in origin, but it is my belief that the evidence presented here creates a strong presumption in favour of this hypothesis. This is especially significant in view of the absence (to date) of a completely satisfactory endogenous theory of business cycles.

It would also appear that there is some validity to the Klein–Goldberger description of the interactions which take place among the several sectors of the economy. That is to say, the interrelations which exist among economic units must be incorporated in a reasonable manner into any rational description of the dynamic behaviour of an industrial complex. A purely stochastic theory of cyclical fluctuations constitutes merely a first approximation to reality.

The implications for the student of business cycles are quite clear. The theorist need not explain a determinate economic path with observable oscillations at predetermined points of time. If he accepts the stochastic hypothesis he knows how and why business cycles arise: the normal perturbations upon the day-to-day operation of an economy suffice to generate a persistent oscillatory process of the observed magnitude. The primary task of the business-cycle analyst is to investigate the reaction patterns of an economic system to various shocks, for it is in this sphere of activity that his efforts are likely to be most significant.

IRMA ADELMAN

Stanford University.

APPENDIX A

1. *Explanation of Symbols*

$Y + T + D$	Gross national product, 1939 dollars
C	Consumer expenditures, 1939 dollars
I	Gross private domestic capital formation, 1939 dollars
G	Government expenditures for goods and services, 1939 dollars
p	Price index of gross national product, 1939 : 100
W_1	Private employee compensation, deflated
W_2	Government employee compensation, deflated
D	Capital consumption charges, 1939 dollars
P_C	Corporate profits, deflated
S_P	Corporate savings, deflated
T	Indirect taxes less subsidies, deflated
K	End-of-year stock of private capital, 1939 dollars from arbitrary origin
p_A	Index of agricultural prices, 1939 = 100
p_1	Index of prices of imports, 1939 = 100
N_p	Number of persons in the United States
N	Number of persons in the labor force
N_w	Number of wage-and-salary-earners
N_g	Number of government employees
N_f	Number of farm operators
N_e	Number of non-farm entrepreneurs
h	Index of hours worked per year, 1939 = 100
w	Index of hourly wages, 1939 = 122·1
P	Non-wage, non-farm income, deflated
A_1	Farm income deflated
A_2	Government payments to farmers, deflated
i_L	Average yield on corporate bonds, %
i_S	Average yield on short term commercial paper, %
L_1	End-of-year liquid assets held by persons, deflated
L_2	End-of-year liquid assets held by businesses, deflated
t	Time trend, years, $t = 2$ in 1952
B	End-of-year corporate surplus, deflated, from arbitrary origin

2. *The Naïve Model*

(1) $\quad C_t = 111 \cdot 9 + 2 \cdot 72t + \delta_c$

(2) $\quad I_t = 26 \cdot 2 + 1 \cdot 17t + \delta_I$

(3) $\quad S_{Pt} = 2 \cdot 85 + 0 \cdot 20t + \delta_{Sp}$

(4) $\quad P_{Ct} = 18 \cdot 53 + 1 \cdot 23t + \delta_{p_c}$

(5) $\quad D_t = 18 \cdot 76 + 1 \cdot 21t + \delta_D$

(6) $\quad (W_1)_t = 77 \cdot 25 + 2 \cdot 69t + \delta_{W_1}$

(7) $\quad (Nw)_t = 54 \cdot 68 + 1 \cdot 13t + \delta_{Nw}$

(8) $\quad W_t = 326 \cdot 8 + 17 \cdot 92t + \delta_W$

(9) $\quad (p_A)_t = 305 + 7 \cdot 07t + \delta_{p_a}$

(10) $\quad i_S = 2 \cdot 5 + \delta_{iS}$

(11) $\quad i_t = 3 \cdot 5 + \delta_{iS}$

(12) $\quad (A_1)_t = 7 \cdot 3 + \dfrac{2 \cdot 5}{t + 7} + \delta_A$

(13) $\quad (L_1)_t = 92 \cdot 44 + \dfrac{16 \cdot 76}{t + 7} + \delta_{L_1}$

(14) $\quad (L_2)_t = 35 \cdot 88 + \dfrac{6 \cdot 69}{t + 7} + \delta_{L2}$

(15) $\quad G_t = 32 \cdot 933 + 0 \cdot 567t$

(16) $\quad (W_2)_t = 15 \cdot 114 + 0 \cdot 578t$

(17) $\quad T_t = 14 \cdot 146 + 0 \cdot 514t$

(18) $\quad (A_2)_t = 0 \cdot 108 + \dfrac{0 \cdot 0746}{t + 7}$

(19) $\quad h_t = 1 \cdot 062$

(20) $\quad Y_t = C_t + I_t + G_t - T_t - D_t$

(21) $\quad P_t = Y_t - (W_1)_t - (W_2)_t - (A_2)_t - (A_1)_t$

(22) $\quad p_t = \dfrac{h_t \, w_t \, (Nw)_t}{(W_1)_t + (W_2)_t}$

(23) $\quad K_t = K_{t-1} + I_t - D_t$

(24) $\quad B_t = B_{t-1} + S_p$

3. *Standard Errors Used for Shocks*

Variable	% Standard deviation
C	1·07
I	9·79
S_P	61·4
P_C	9·43
D	3·97
W_1	2·41
N_w	2·89
w	1·49
p_A	7·29
i_S	20·00
i_L	14·28
A_1	10·2
L_1	3·0
L_2	3·57

4

LONG CYCLES—FACT OR ARTIFACT?

By IRMA ADELMAN*

Both economists and economic historians generally agree that the economic growth of advanced capitalist economies did not proceed in a completely smooth, monotonic fashion. On the contrary, the evolution of industrial societies appears to have been characterized by recurrent waves of acceleration and deceleration in the levels and in the rates of growth of output and of other measures of economic performance. These waves, which vary between 10 and 20 years in duration, seem to emerge from the historical record after the effects of primary trends and short cycles have been largely eliminated by the use of various smoothing procedures.

Long swings of this nature have been isolated in many economic variables, including, among others, the outputs and prices of individual commodities [4]; the rates of growth of production in major industries and industrial groups [4]; the rate of growth of total industrial production and GNP [1]; construction activity [10]; immigration [14]; the rates of growth of the labor force and of population [14]; total gross and net investment [1]; and the rate of increase of productivity per man-hour and per unit of resources employed [1].

Nevertheless, the question of whether or not these longer movements constitute a class of economic phenomena independent of (though perhaps interacting with) the shorter cyclical fluctuations is not yet settled. Indeed, this issue has plagued every serious student of the longer swings ever since their existence was first recognized.

The answer to this question hinges upon two issues: (1) the nature of the forces which are responsible for the generation of the longer swings; and (2) the extent to which the smoothing procedures themselves are responsible for the apparent cyclical movements.

With respect to the first issue, one extreme point of view is that the

* The author, associate professor of economics at The Johns Hopkins University, would like to express her deep appreciation to M. Hatanaka for his generous assistance in all stages of this work, as well as for the use of his computer program with which the present calculations were made. She is grateful also to E. Parzen for a very fruitful discussion, in the course of which he suggested the filtering formula used in this work, and to R. H. Jones for calculating the transfer function of this filter. Marc Nerlove, in the course of refereeing the paper, made some basic criticisms which led to a fundamental change in conclusions. Helpful suggestions were also made by D. Brillinger, R. Easterlin, M. Godfrey, E. J. Hannan, J. Jarem, and H. Rosenblatt. Finally, as always, the author is also indebted to F. L. Adelman for his helpful comments on both logic and style.

amplitudes and durations of the longer swings have nothing to do with the structure of the economy, but are merely reflections of more or less randomly generated runs of abnormally severe recessions and unusually vigorous booms. If this position is correct, the detailed analysis of the longer waves from an economic point of view would appear to be of dubious value. At the other extreme, the existence of the longer swings is attributed solely to the operation of *economic* forces upon an interrelated economic mechanism constrained by certain physical and sociocultural factors which tend to delay and stretch out some types of economic response over extended periods of time. Under these circumstances, the analysis of long cycles would obviously constitute an important branch of both economic theory and economic history.

Actually, the position adopted by most writers lies somewhere in between the two extreme points of view just sketched. For example, Abramovitz concludes that:

> Although many features of the long swings in economic development can now be described, the cause of these fluctuations is still to be determined. It is not known whether they are the result of some stable mechanism inherent in the structure of the U.S. economy, or whether they are set in motion by the episodic occurrence of wars, financial panics or other unsystematic disturbances. Their pronounced uniformities, however, make it likely that continued study of long swings will shed light on the process of economic growth and on the origins of serious depressions [1, p. 412].

In an earlier paper [2] the author attempted to look into the question of the origin (and hence, indirectly, the significance) of the long swings. Specifically, in a simulation of the ordinary business cycles of the U.S. economy by a randomly shocked Klein-Goldberger model [13], long swings were generated which corresponded in all important respects to the extended waves observed in the U.S. economy.

The only major discrepancies found were the smaller absolute amplitudes of the Klein-Goldberger long cycles and the failure in the model economy of the retardation phase of the reference cycle to exceed the duration of the acceleration phase. The primary cause of the first of these differences is probably the omission of unusually strong shocks, such as that of World War II, from our data. And the second reflects either deficiencies of the Klein-Goldberger model, structural changes in the behavior of the system since 1929, or both.

One interpretation of the remarkable agreement between Klein-Goldberger long cycles and those of the U.S. economy is that the *purely* random explanation of the long cycle is not valid, and that the interactions among the several economic variables, as represented by, say, the Klein-Goldberger model, are necessary in order to explain the observed lead-lag relationships and other properties of the long swings. On the other hand, in view of the paucity of data, both the U.S. long swings and those of our model are usually consistent with a random distribution of long-cycle durations.

An alternative point of view, therefore, is that the long swings *are* random in origin and that the observed lead-lag relationships are either accidental or else they merely reflect the lead-lag relationships found in the ordinary business cycles (regardless of their origin). An additional argument in favor of this conclusion is the fact that the smoothing procedures employed for the elimination of the effects of the shorter business cycles are common to both the empirical investigation of U.S. historical experience and to the Klein-Goldberger simulation experiment. The possibility therefore remains that the apparent longer swings are merely the combined results of the effects of shorter cycles and of the systematic biases induced by the smoothing practices.

The purpose of the present investigation is to determine whether the smoothing biases constitute in themselves a sufficient explanation for the existence of the long cycles. In this paper, the statistical technique of spectral analysis[1] is applied to historical data in an effort to investigate the existence and nature of the longer cycles. Since the spectral-density technique leads to the *simultaneous* determination of cycles of all durations, it does not require the elimination of shorter cycles from the series before cycles of longer duration can be studied. This feature of the present analysis is a consequence of the powerful statistical tools employed and represents an important advance over traditional economic procedures for time-series decomposition.

Since the theory of spectral analysis has been developed almost exclusively for stationary processes, one might expect, at first sight, that it could not be applied to economic time series. There exist schemes, however, to transform an economic time series, which represents a nonstationary stochastic process, into an equivalent series which is approximately stationary. The transformed series can then be analyzed by the usual spectral techniques.

In any event, the very fact that the time-series-analysis practices employed in the present investigation are very different in nature from the ones traditionally used by economic historians and business-cycle analysts offers an independent check upon the validity of their respective results.

---

[1] Good general discussions of the techniques of spectral analysis are to be found in references [3] [23]. Since most of these references require a certain degree of mathematical sophistication, a wholly nonmathematical exposition is presented in Section II.

I. *Traditional Techniques for the Analysis of Long Swings*

As has been indicated above, the techniques which have been utilized in the past for the analysis of long swings employ some sort of
smoothing procedure to mask the effects of the short cycles. Kuznets,
in his pioneering work on production and price series in the United
States [16], used simple moving averages to eliminate trend and to
smooth out the short cycles. His subsequent work on the national
product [15] is based upon rates of change between overlapping decade averages. Both of these procedures are open to the charge that, unless the period chosen for the moving average corresponds precisely to
the frequency of the short cycles, they will tend to introduce spurious
cyclical fluctuations into the basic series.[2]

Burns's technique is open to similar objections. In his study of a
large number of production series [4, p. 175], he first calculated ten-
year growth rates at five-year intervals. The deviations of these rates
of growth from the trend rate of growth formed the raw material for
his study of "trend cycles."

The most sophisticated smoothing methods which have so far been
applied are those introduced by Abramovitz [1]. He first calculates
the average value of each series during successive reference cycles
measured both from trough to trough and from peak to peak. The
trend is then removed by computing the annual percentage rates of
growth of each variable between average reference cycle standings.
The trough-to-trough percentages are intermingled with the peak-to-
peak percentages to yield a series of rates of growth between overlapping business-cycle periods. Oscillations in these rates of growth are
taken to indicate the existence of alternating phases of acceleration
and retardation in the rates of expansion of economic quantities. Inci-
dentally, the Abramovitz technique was utilized in the Klein-Goldberger simulation experiment referred to above.

While the Abramovitz analysis exhibits no obvious systematic bias,
the approach is too complex to permit ready analytic evaluation. Indeed, no a priori formula for his approach can be written down, and
hence a direct assessment of the effects of his technique is not possible.
Since, however, it has not been demonstrated that the method does not
introduce spurious long cycles to a greater or lesser extent, it would be
highly desirable to provide an independent check on the existence of
such oscillations.

[2] In spectral terms, one can interpret the moving-average approach used by both Kuznets
and Burns as a filtering process. (See Section II.D.4 below.) The effects of their smoothing
procedures can therefore be evaluated by computing the transfer functions of the respective
filters. It is not necessary to do this, however, since the difference equations implied by their
smoothing processes have been solved exactly [20] and yield a ten-year cycle.

II. *The Technique of Spectral Analysis*

A. *Time Series and Fourier Series*[3]

Before we discuss the philosophy and techniques of spectral analysis, it may prove worthwhile to spend a few moments on another method of time-series analysis. Basically, there are two ways of looking at a time series. The more obvious one is that the series is a sequence of values of the variable as a function of time. The other is that the value of a time series at each time is the summation of a particular set of sinusoidal waves with frequencies which are integral multiples of some fundamental frequency. Each of these waves is characterized by an amplitude (the maximum value of the oscillation), a frequency (the fraction of a cycle completed in one time period), and a phase (the fraction of cycle of a given frequency through which the sinusoidal wave must be displaced in order to have the value zero and positive slope at a particular point of time). For each frequency component it is possible to combine the amplitude and phase information into a single complex number, whose absolute value represents the amplitude, and the ratio of whose components determines the phase of that wave. Thus, if one specifies for a given fundamental frequency the complex amplitude $C(n)$ of the wave for each mutiple of the fundamental frequency, one has determined completely the time series $X(t)$. The values $C(n)$ are called the complex Fourier coefficients and are a representation of $X(t)$ in terms of frequency. The $C(n)$ constitute the complex spectrum of $X(t)$. The absolute values of the squares of $C(n)$ form the power spectrum of $X(t)$.

The Fourier-series approach has proved to be an extremely useful technique for the analysis of periodic time series. Attempts to apply these methods to economic time series, however, have met with a notable lack of success, most likely because actual economic time series are not strictly periodic in nature. Rather, after the removal of trend effects, they appear to consist of periodic functions upon which are superimposed strong stochastic variations. The reason that spectral analysis offers hope of being more appropriate for economics than Fourier series is that spectral analysis has been developed specifically for the study of functions of precisely this character.

B. *Basic Postulates*

The fundamental assumption underlying the development of spectral analysis, as contrasted with Fourier analysis, is that a time series is merely a single realization of a random function [23, Ch. 1, p. 2].

---

[3] A good exposition of Fourier analysis is given in [6].

That is, the variable $X(t)$ is probabilistic in nature, and the observed value of X at a particular time t is a sample chosen in some way from a universe containing all permissible values of X at time t. As t varies from the beginning to the end of the time interval in question, the sequence of values assumed by the variable X traces the observed time series, which is one sample function out of a whole ensemble of possible time sequences. Given the random function from which $X(t)$ is derived, then, the probability of occurrence (or the probability density) of any particular realization can be determined.

From a purely statistical point of view, however, the task of the time-series analyst is just the opposite—to infer from a single sample realization the relevant features of the random function from which this particular realization originated. Clearly, if the nature of the random process which gives rise to the sequence X (t) is not constrained in some manner, the reconstruction of the random function is a hopeless task. In order to bypass this difficulty, the theory of spectral analysis specifies that the random function must be stationary and ergodic in time. In other words, it is assumed that the expectation value of all possible values of $X(t)$ at time t is independent of time and that the expectation value of the covariance[4] of $X(t)$ and $X(t + T)$ is a function only of the time difference T.

Under these circumstances it can be demonstrated that the mean value of a particular realization of $X(t)$ approaches, as the number of observations becomes large, the ensemble average at any point of time t. Similarly, the corresponding statement is valid for the covariance function of $X(t)$. This theorem, which is known as the ergodic theorem, has important practical implications, as it permits one to estimate from a single realization of the random process the mean and covariance functions of the stationary random function $X(t)$. If it is assumed also that the stationary random function is normally distributed, the mean value and the covariance function suffice to specify $X(t)$ completely.

C. Spectral Representation of the Random Time Series

Spectral-density analysis constitutes, in essence, an extension of Fourier analysis to the treatment of probabilistic processes. Basically, this approach assumes that a time series can be represented as a sum of individual sinusoidal waves whose frequencies are all multiples of a given fundamental frequency, and that the amplitudes and the phase displacements associated with each multiple of the fundamental frequency are random variables. The main purpose of spectral-density analysis is to determine the average value of the amplitude associated

[4] The covariance function of $X(t)$ and $X(t+T)$ is $R(T) = E[X(t) \cdot X(t+T)]$.

with each frequency of oscillation, and thereby to separate important cyclical components from insignificant ones.

As in the case of Fourier analysis, the power spectrum of a series is a function which specifies, for each cyclical frequency, the absolute value of the square of the complex amplitude. Since the expression for the power at a particular frequency is identical to the equation for the variance of that frequency component, the power spectrum might equally well be called the "variance spectrum." Furthermore, in view of the fact that each component of the spectrum is linearly independent of every other component, the power spectrum also specifies the contribution of each frequency component to the total variance. Spectral analysis is thus, in essence, an analysis of the variance of a time series in terms of frequency [21].

One may therefore define a spectral function which indicates, for each frequency, the percentage of the over-all variance of a series which is attributable to cycles of that frequency. This spectral function is known as the spectral density of a time series. For stationary random processes the spectral density of a time series can, in principle, be obtained from the original time series simply by means of a Fourier-series transformation of the normalized autocovariance function of $X(t)$.

Since spectral-density analysis is based upon an explicitly formulated probabilistic model, it permits us to apply statistical significance tests to the individual spectral components.[5] That is, it enables us to answer the question: Is the contribution of cycles of a particular duration significantly different from zero?

D. Some Practical Considerations[6]

1. *Nonstationarity*. A crucial problem which arises whenever one attempts to apply the spectral-density approach to economic time series is that the statistical model has been developed only for stationary random processes. Since processes whose expected value and covariance are time-dependent cannot be treated in the usual formulation of this model, the analysis of economic activities, which are generally characterized by a secular trend in both mean and variance, requires some modification of the theory. The obvious technique for handling this difficulty, which is to operate upon first differences of the data, reduces the signal-to-noise ratio and therefore does not always lead to useful results. An alternative method that has been used to eliminate trend, which is the one adopted in the calculations that follow, is to fit a least-square linear trend to the logarithms of the original data. The

[5] Some relevant statistical tests are given in [3, pp. 22-23].
[6] The organization of the exposition of this section is patterned after that in [18].

deviations from this fitted trend are then used as input data to the spectral-density analysis. Although both approaches have advantages, the second method was chosen because it was felt to be closer to the basic purpose of this analysis—to decompose oscillations around a trend. The logarithmic transformation is used to make the autocovariance functions more nearly independent of time.

2. *The Sample Size.* A second difficulty which almost always arises in the application of spectral analysis to economic time series is a very severe limitation on the number of observations available for study. This problem is particularly serious in the context of the investigation of long cycles. Continuous aggregative yearly economic statistics of reasonable reliability are available only from 1889 on. Since the cycles with which we are concerned in this paper are typically 10 to 20 years in length, the effective number of cycles available would appear to be at most seven. This number of cycles is far too small for an accurate statistical analysis of the cycle length. However, to the extent that business cycles constitute movements which affect the entire economy, as distinct from the summation of unrelated oscillatory movements in individual economic time series, they represent fluctuations "occurring at about the same time in many economic activities" [20, p. 3]. That is, they pervade virtually all parts of the economy and exhibit more or less systematic lead-lag patterns. We would therefore expect the qualitative characteristics of the power spectra of the observed variation around the trend of each of the several indicators of economic performance to be similar in nature. The existence of such a family resemblance, while not increasing the effective number of cycles available, will tend to reinforce the extent of one's belief in the qualitative validity of the results. Even this reinforcement one must accept with caution, however, as the existence of common procedural biases in the several series and/or in the estimation of their spectra would also account for at least some of the similarity in parallel series.

3. *Spectral Averages and Spectral Windows.* The technique for the derivation of the power spectrum based upon a Fourier transformation of the autocovariance function is appropriate only for the investigation of time series whose components have frequencies, amplitudes, and relative phases which do not vary statistically. In order to obtain statistically consistent results when the time series under consideration are not strictly periodic, it is necessary to estimate the *average* power in a frequency band centered around the frequency in question, rather than the power associated with a precise frequency. In principle, one would like to minimize the width of the frequency band. However, it can be shown [19, p. 180] that, no matter how many observations are taken, the variance of any estimate of the average power increases as

the width of the frequency band over which the power is measured is reduced.

This fundamental indeterminancy principle implies that, in practice, a compromise must be made between the accuracy with which the average spectrum is estimated and the accuracy with which the frequency interval to which the spectral estimate applies is specified. The nature of this compromise depends, to some extent, upon the precise average chosen [11, pp. 145-48]. In practice, the averaging is accomplished by weighting the covariances before deriving the spectral estimates by Fourier transformation. The weighting function selected for this purpose is called the *lag window* in the time domain; its Fourier transform, the representation of the lag window in the frequency domain, is known as the spectral window.

An ideal spectral window would (1) assign equal weight to power at all frequencies in a band of width equal to the fundamental frequency centered about a particular frequency, and (2) assign zero weight to power outside that frequency interval. While it is mathematically impossible to devise a lag window of such a shape with a finite amount of data, several approximations to this ideal have been proposed.

In order to discuss the properties and effects of the lag window profitably, we must first define what is meant by the term "number of lags." The autocovariance function, as defined in footnote 4, is calculated by multiplying the value of a series at one time by its value some number of periods later, and then summing over all points of time for which both factors are defined. In principle, the maximum possible difference in time between the two factors is one less than the number of data points for which the series is specified. However, with a finite amount of data, the smaller the time difference between the two factors, the larger the number of points which can be included in the summation. On the other hand, the larger the time difference, the better the lag window approximates the ideal. The largest value of the time difference actually used in the calculation of the autocovariance function is called the number of lags.

The number of lags is a crucial parameter, as it determines, among other things, the bandwidth of the lag window and the number of degrees of freedom of the estimate, both of which are inversely proportional to the number of lags. Since the effective number of data points increases as the number of lags is reduced, the choice of the number of lags represents a compromise between the reliability with which one can specify the general shape of the power spectrum and the accuracy to which one can determine the frequencies at which the power is concentrated. A relatively small number of lags (15) was chosen for the

present work, because it was felt that, in the investigation of the existence of long swings, the localization of the precise periods of the cycles involved is far less important than the determination of the relative amounts of power in the long and short cycles. For purposes of
comparison, preliminary calculations were also made with other
choices of the number of lags.

The lag window used in the present investigation was suggested by
Parzen.[7] It was selected because, for a given number of data points
and a given number of lags, this window has the property of having
the smallest variance and the largest bandwidth of all the windows
which have been suggested so far. It also introduces the smallest dis-

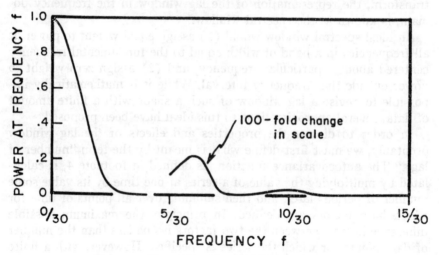

FIGURE 1. NORMALIZED PARZEN WINDOW (15 lags)

tortion of spectral estimates at distant frequencies. This choice of window is, of course, consistent with the criteria given in the previous paragraph.

Figure 1 shows the Parzen spectral window with 15 lags, which is
the window used in the present analysis.[8] The window is symmetrical
about the origin. On the horizontal axis is measured the distance in
fractions of cycles per year from the frequency about which the esti-

[7] Specifically, if m is the number of lags for which the autocovariance function is computed, the weight assigned to the autocovariance computed with a lag of k is given by

$$1 - 6k^2/m^2(1 - k/m), \qquad 0 \leq k \leq m/2$$
$$2(1 - k/m)^3, \qquad m/2 \leq k \leq m.$$
$$0, \qquad k \geq m$$

[8] The formula for the computation of the spectral windows appears in [19, p. 146].

mate is centered to the frequency of interest. The vertical axis indicates the relative weight accorded to power at the latter frequency. Thus, if the true power were concentrated in a small frequency interval Δf about some particular frequency f_1, the lag window of Figure 1 would produce an apparent spectrum consisting of a set of lines (of finite widths) whose relative amplitudes can be determined from the figure. In Table 1 several of the numerical values are given. True power at any other frequency, of course, would be distributed among its neighboring frequencies in a similar (additive) manner.

4. *Filtering.* As was mentioned earlier, all lag windows devised for use with a finite amount of data must inevitably assign some nonzero weight to frequencies outside the desired interval. This deficiency is

TABLE 1

Frequency	Amplitude
f_1	1.0
$f_1 \pm \dfrac{1}{30}$	0.658
$f_1 \pm \dfrac{2}{30}$	0.165
etc.	

particularly serious in the case of economic time series, as a failure to remove trend completely (which is not unlikely in the case of real world data) will be reflected in the existence of apparent high power at frequencies close to zero. In the context of the present investigation of the long-cycle (low frequency) components of economic series, this difficulty is exacerbated.

To reduce the distortion of the spectrum due to leakage of power from frequencies below those of interest it is desirable to base the spectral analysis upon series from which most of the low-frequency power has been removed. This can be accomplished by subjecting the input data to a mathematical filtering process, which selectively reduces the power in the undesired portion of the frequency range.[9] The spectral analysis is then applied to the filtered data. Various filters have been devised for this purpose. Common to all of these is the disadvantage that some, usually significant, portion of the original data is removed

[9] Mathematical filters, just like electrical filters, can be designed to pass or exclude arbitrary finite or infinite portions of the spectrum.

in the filtering process. The filter used in the present investigation, which was suggested by Parzen,[10] is designed to filter out most of the power at frequencies lower than 1/18 of a cycle per year.

In Figure 2, the filtered (solid line) and the unfiltered (dashed line) power spectra of GNP are plotted for comparison. The vertical scale is the logarithm of the power associated with the frequency given on the horizontal axis. A glance at the two curves suggests that the filter used has indeed accomplished its purpose. At the first two frequencies, the

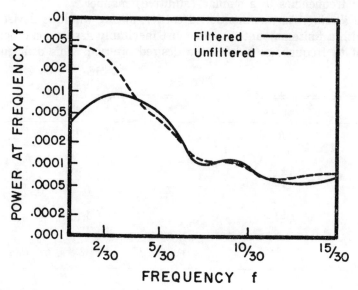

FIGURE 2. POWER SPECTRUM OF NATURAL LOGS OF DEVIATIONS FROM TREND OF GNP

power of the filtered spectrum is much smaller than that of the unfiltered one; in the 10-15 year cycle range the filtered spectrum is significantly lower than the unfiltered, primarily because the distortion from leakage of power from the lower frequencies through the window has been greatly reduced. This should lead to a fairly conservative estimate of the power in the 10-15 year region. The relatively minor differences between the two spectra at high frequencies are probably due mostly to sampling fluctuations, as the filtered series is based on 18 fewer data points than the unfiltered series.

[10] The filtered series $Z(t)$ is formed from the original data $X(t)$ by setting

$$Z(t) = X(t) - \sum_{T=-9}^{T=9} \frac{\text{Sin } \pi T/9}{\pi T} X(t+T).$$

The term $(\text{Sin } \pi T/9)/\pi T$ is a typical term of the Fourier transform of a rectangular frequency function which has an amplitude of $+1$ in the open interval $\pm 1/9$ cycle/year and is zero outside that interval. See [3, p. 68].

Some additional insight into the effects of the filtering process may be gained by looking at the graph of the transfer function of the filter (i.e., the squared modulus of the frequency response function of the filter). It can be shown that the power spectrum of the output from a linear filter is the product of its input spectrum and the transfer function of the filter. Division of the filtered spectrum by the transfer function of the filter therefore results in an estimate of the power spectrum of the original (unfiltered) series.

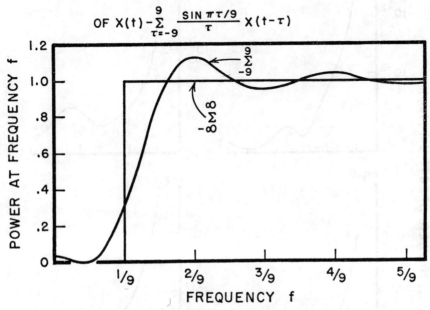

$$\text{OF } X(t) - \sum_{\tau=-9}^{9} \frac{\text{SIN } \pi\tau/9}{\tau} X(t-\tau)$$

FIGURE 3. POWER TRANSFER FUNCTION

The dashed line in Figure 3 represents the transfer function of an ideal filter, while the solid line indicates the transfer function of the filter used in the present investigation. One can see that, in contrast to an ideal filter, the filter used in this work permits some power to pass through at the very low frequencies and multiplies the power just above the "cutoff" frequency by a factor close to unity.

III. *Empirical Results*

Figures 4 to 11 portray typical power spectra calculated for output, investment, consumption, employment, capital stock, productivity of labor, productivity of capital, and the wholesale price index. Many series pertaining to each economic variable were used (see the Appendix for the data sources and precise identification of each series). However, since all the power spectra were qualitatively quite similar, only a single representative spectrum is plotted for each type of series. The power spectra plotted in Figures 4 to 11 were derived by first calculating the filtered spectrum of each individual time series and then dividing the filtered spectra by the transfer function of the filter.

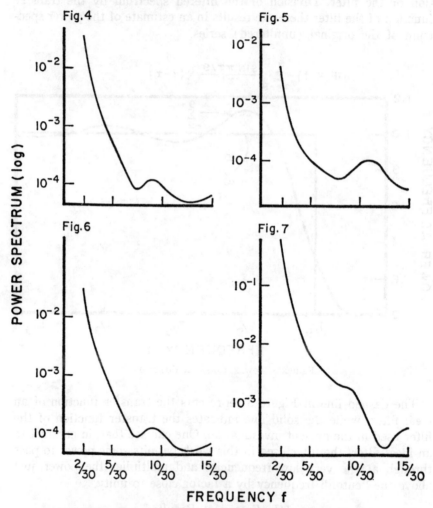

FIGURE 4. POWER SPECTRUM OF NATURAL LOG OF DEVIATIONS FROM TREND OF OUTPUT SERIES

FIGURE 5. POWER SPECTRUM OF NATURAL LOG OF DEVIATIONS FROM TREND OF PRODUCTIVITY OF LABOR

FIGURE 6. POWER SPECTRUM OF NATURAL LOG OF DEVIATIONS FROM TREND OF PRODUCTIVITY OF CAPITAL

FIGURE 7. POWER SPECTRUM OF NATURAL LOG OF DEVIATIONS FROM TREND OF INVESTMENT

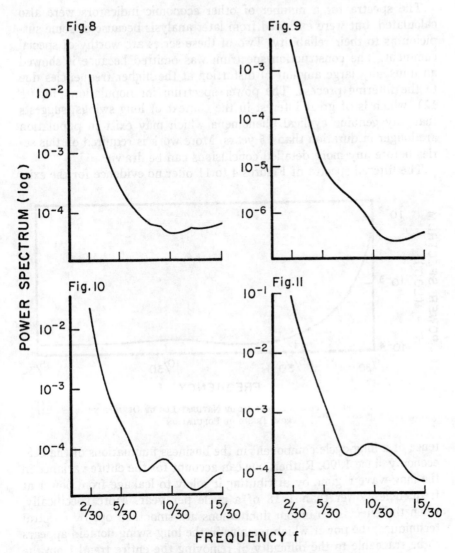

FIGURE 8. POWER SPECTRUM OF NATURAL LOG OF DEVIATIONS
FROM TREND OF CONSUMPTION

FIGURE 9. POWER SPECTRUM OF NATURAL LOG OF DEVIATIONS
FROM TREND OF CAPITAL STOCK

FIGURE 10. POWER SPECTRUM OF NATURAL LOG OF DEVIATIONS
FROM TREND OF EMPLOYMENT

FIGURE 11. POWER SPECTRUM OF NATURAL LOG OF DEVIATIONS
FROM TREND OF WHOLESALE PRICE INDEX

The spectra for a number of other economic indicators were also calculated, but were excluded from later analysis because of some suspicion as to their reliability. Two of these series are worthy of special comment. The construction spectrum was omitted because it showed an unusually large amount of distortion at the higher frequencies due to the filtering process. The power spectrum for population (Figure 12), which is of great interest in the context of long swings, suggests that any genuine cyclical phenomena which may exist in population are longer in duration than 15 years. More work is required on this series before any more detailed conclusions can be drawn.

The filtered spectra of Figures 4 to 11 offer no evidence for the exis-

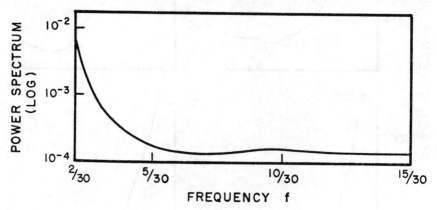

FIGURE 12. POWER SPECTRUM OF NATURAL LOG OF DEVIATIONS
FROM TREND OF POPULATION

tence of a long-cycle component in the business fluctuations of the U.S. economy since 1890. Rather, one can account for the entire variance in the long-wave regime by attributing it solely to leakage from power at frequencies lower than 1/18 of a cycle per year. More specifically, when the effects of random fluctuations are smoothed out by spectral techniques, the power which remains in the long-swing domain appears to be traceable to the difficulty of removing the entire trend from the data which were analyzed. In view of this result, it is likely that the long swings which have been observed in the U.S. economy since 1890 are due in part to the introduction of spurious long cycles by the smoothing process, and in part to the necessity for averaging over a statistically small number of random shocks.

The evidence of the present spectral analysis is not at all inconsistent with certain other observations on the existence of long cycles:

1. The distribution of long-cycle durations found by Abramovitz

and others is consistent with a random distribution of frequencies [2, p. 175].

2. The beginning of the long cycles is, in almost all instances, directly associated with a strong exogenous shock, such as a war or a financial crisis [1, p. 412].

3. Despite the fact that most of the economic interactions which have been considered necessary for the generation of long cycles in the U.S. economy are absent in the Klein-Goldberger model, it has proved possible, by imposing a series of random shocks upon that model, to generate fluctuations which reproduce, in almost all important respects, the characteristics of the long swings observed in the U.S. economy [2].

These considerations together with the results of the present spectral analysis suggest that, unlike the case of the usual business cycle, the apparent frequencies of response of the economy to a large shock depend upon the nature, magnitude, and timing of the shock. One is therefore strongly tempted to conclude that the economic mechanisms inherent in the modern U.S. economy do not tend to generate long cycles.

Appendix

Output Series[a]
(Indices, 1929 = 100)

1. Net National Product, Kuznets
2. Gross National Product, Kuznets
3. Net National Product, Department of Commerce
*4. Gross National Product, Department of Commerce
5. Real Gross Product, Private Domestic Economy, Nonfarm
6. Output in Mining
7. Net Output in Agriculture
8. Output in Manufacturing

Employment Series
(Indices, 1929 = 100)

1. Number of Persons Employed in the Production of the Net National Product, Kuznets
2. Number of Man-hours Worked for the Production of the Net National Product, Kuznets
3. Number of Persons Employed in the Production of the Real Gross Product, Private Domestic Economy, Department of Commerce
*4. Number of Man-hours Worked for the Production of the Real Gross Product, Private Domestic Economy, Department of Commerce

* Starred series are those for which the power spectrum is reproduced in Figures 4 to 12.

5. Number of Persons Employed in the Production of Nonfarm Real Gross Output, Department of Commerce
6. Number of Man-hours Worked for the Production of Nonfarm Real Gross Output, Department of Commerce
7. Number of Persons Employed in Manufacturing
8. Number of Man-hours Worked in Manufacturing

Capital Stock Series[a]
(Hundreds of millions of 1929 dollars)

1. Capital Stock, National Economy
*2. Capital Stock, Domestic Economy
3. Capital Stock, Total Structures

Productivity of Labor[a]
(Indices, 1929 = 100)

1. Output per Person, Private Domestic Nonfarm, Department of Commerce
2. Output per Man-hour, Private Domestic Nonfarm, Department of Commerce
*3. Output per Unit of Labor Input, Private Domestic Nonfarm, Department of Commerce
4. Output per Person, Gross National Product, Department of Commerce
5. Output per Man-hour, Gross National Product, Department of Commerce
6. Output per Unit of Labor Input, Gross National Product, Department of Commerce
7. Output per Person, Net National Product, Kuznets
8. Output per Man-hour, Net National Product, Kuznets
9. Output per Unit of Labor Input, Kuznets
10. Output per Man-hour, Manufacturing
11. Output per Unit of Labor Input, Manufacturing

Productivity of Capital[a]
(Indices, 1929 = 100)

1. Output per Unit of Capital, Net National Product, Kuznets
*2. Output per Unit of Capital, Gross National Product, Department of Commerce
3. Output per Unit of Capital, Private Domestic Nonfarm Gross Product, Department of Commerce

Investment Series[a]
(Hundreds of millions of 1929 dollars)

1. Gross Private Domestic Investment, New Construction and Equipment, Kuznets

Sources:
[a] [5]; period 1889-1957.

*2. Gross Private Domestic Investment, New Construction and Equipment, Department of Commerce

Consumption Series[a]
(Hundreds of millions of 1929 dollars)

*1. Total Consumption Expenditures, Kuznets

Wholesale Price Series,[b] Bureau of Labor Statistics
(Indices, 1926 = 100)

*1. All Commodities
 2. Hides and Leather
 3. Textiles
 4. Fuel and Lighting
 5. Metal and Metal Products
 6. Building Materials
 7. Chemicals and Allied Products
 8. House Furnishings
 9. Farm Products
10. Foods

Population[c]
(Thousands of people)

*1. Total Population Residing in the United States

REFERENCES

1. M. ABRAMOVITZ, Statement in *Hearings before the Joint Economic Committee of the Congress of the United States*, 86th Cong., 1st sess., Pt. 2, pp. 411-66.
2. I. ADELMAN, "Long Swings—A Simulation Experiment," in F. Balderston and A. Hoggatt ed., *Proceedings of a Conference on Simulation*, Cincinnati 1964.
3. R. B. BLACKMAN AND J. W. TUKEY, *The Measurement of Power Spectra.* New York and Dover 1958.
4. A. F. BURNS, *Production Trends in the United States since 1870.* New York (NBER) 1934.
5. ——— and W. C. MITCHELL, *Measuring Business Cycles.* New York (NBER) 1934.
6. R. V. CHURCHILL, *Fourier Series and Boundary Value Problems.* New York 1941.
7. J. CUNNYNGHAM, *Spectral Analysis of Economic Time Series.* Unpublished doctoral dissertation, Univ. Chicago, 1964.
8. C. W. GRANGER AND M. HATANAKA, *Spectral Analysis of Economic Time Series.* Princeton 1964.
9. W. GRENANDER AND M. ROSENBLATT, *Statistical Analysis of Stationary Time Series.* New York 1957.

 [b] [12]; period 1890-1951.
 [c] [12]; period 1790-1957.

10. W. IZARD, "A Neglected Cycle: The Transport-Building Cycle," *Rev. Econ. Stat.*, Nov. 1942, 149-58.
11. G. M. JENKINS, "General Considerations in the Analysis of Spectra," *Technometrics*, Vol. 3, 1961, pp. 133-66.
12. J. W. KENDRICK WITH M. R. PECH, *Productivity Trends in the United States*. Princeton (NBER) 1961.
13. L. R. KLEIN AND A. S. GOLDBERGER, *An Econometric Model of the United States, 1929-1952*. Amsterdam 1955.
14. S. S. KUZNETS, "Long Swings in the Growth of Population and in Related Economic Variables," *Am. Philos. Soc., Proc.*, Feb. 1958, *102*, 25-52.
15. ———, "Long Term Changes in National Income of the United States since 1870," *Income and Wealth*, Ser. II, Cambridge 1952.
16. ———, *Secular Movements in Production and Prices*. New York 1930.
17. Y. W. LEE, *Statistical Theory of Communication*. New York 1960.
18. M. NERLOVE, "Spectral Analysis of Seasonal Adjustment Procedures," *Econometrica*, July 1964, *32*, 241-86.
19. E. PARZEN, "Mathematical Considerations in the Estimation of Spectra," *Technometrics*, Vol. 3, 1961, pp. 167-90.
20. P. J. TAUBMAN, "On the Existence of Long Cycles," Discussion Paper No. 2, Econ. Research Services Unit, Univ. of Pennsylvania.
21. J. W. TUKEY, "Discussion, Emphasizing the Connection Between Analysis of Variance and Spectrum Analysis," *Technometrics*, Vol. 3, 1961, pp. 191-219.
22. H. WOLD, *A Study in the Analysis of Stationary Time Series*, 2nd ed. Stockholm 1954.
23. A. M. YAGLOM, *An Introduction to the Theory of Stationary Random Functions*. Englewood Cliffs, N.J. 1962.
24. BUREAU OF THE CENSUS, *Historical Statistics of the United States— Colonial Times to 1957*. Washington, D.C. 1960.

5

AN ECONOMETRIC ANALYSIS OF POPULATION GROWTH

IRMA ADELMAN*

There has been remarkably little theoretical or empirical analysis of the effects of economic development upon population change.[1] While the existence of an interaction between the economic and the demographic evolution of a society has long been acknowledged by authorities in both fields, only the impact of population growth on economic development has received any significant amount of attention in the economic literature.

The present paper attempts to illuminate the other side of the coin. Specifically, this manuscript constitutes an economic analysis of fertility and mortality patterns as they are affected by economic and social forces. First, age specific birth and death rates in various countries are correlated with several economic and sociocultural indicators. As a partial test of the validity of this approach, the derived relations are then used to estimate crude birth and death rates in 1953 in the various continents. Finally, a quantitative feeling for the relative impact of changes in economic and social variables upon the demographic features of a society is obtained by calculating the changes in the equilibrium age distribution and in the equilibrium rate of population growth which would result *(ceteris paribus)* from a permanent change in each of the socioeconomic variables.

I. *The Statistical Approach*

In principle, long-run relationships between demographic and socioeconomic factors can be investigated statistically from either of two points of view [4, pp. 629-630]. One possibility is to study one or more geographical units over time and determine the variations in fertility and mortality which are, on the average, associated with changes in

* The author is associate professor of economics, Johns Hopkins University. This paper was written while the author was the recipient of a Social Science Research Council Faculty Research Grant. In addition, the author is indebted to the Stanford University Research Center in Economic Growth for financial assistance. She would like to thank J. J. Spengler, K. Davies, and R. A. Easterlin for their helpful suggestions during early stages of this work, and George Fishman, Mildred Mikelson, and George Guy for their computational assistance.

[1] Some notable exceptions to this statement are to be found in the work of G. S. Becker [24, pp. 209-31], R. A. Easterlin [4], E. E. Hagen [6], H. Leibenstein [9], B. Okun [12], and G. H. Orcutt, M. Greenberger, J. Korbel, and A. M. Rivlin [13].

the per capita income, degree of industrialization, education, and other relevant characteristics of each unit. For conclusions of general validity to be drawn from this approach, a similar analysis must be repeated for several countries over long periods of time.

Alternatively, a number of geographical units can be investigated at the same point in time. The influence of income, industrial development, and other socioeconomic indicators upon fertility and mortality can then be established quantitatively, in some average sense. One advantage of this approach is that the greater range of variation in characteristics among countries and the lesser degree of interaction among the explanatory variables permit a much more accurate determination of regression coefficients than does time-series analysis. However, there is a fundamental difficulty inherent in this cross-section technique: in order to draw any conclusions from the data it must be assumed that, regardless of any differences in environmental and historical conditions, each human population, from a demographic point of view, responds to a small number of more or less quantifiable socioeconomic variables as if it were drawn from a homogeneous environment. In view of the tremendous variations in values, outlook, and other sociocultural imponderables throughout the world, this condition is a very severe one; fortunately, it is open to empirical test. For, whenever specific cultural factors lead to systematic deviations in demographic behavior in different countries, low correlation coefficients, large standard errors, and significant differences in regression coefficients among individual subsamples will be observed.

In choosing between the techniques it must also be recognized that variations in the over-all (or crude) birth and death rates reflect not only changes in fertility and mortality conditions, but also differences in the age and sex distribution of the populations. In order to isolate the impact of socioeconomic forces upon fertility and mortality patterns, therefore, one must eliminate those variations in general birth and death rates which occur for purely demographic reasons; for it is the response of *age specific* birth and death rates to changes in economic and social factors that constitutes the focus of our study.

Since extended time series for age specific birth and death rates are unavailable even for the United States [4, p. 876], the time-series approach cannot effectively be used. The present study must therefore rely upon cross-country analysis to establish long-term effects of economic and sociocultural factors on age specific birth and death rates.

II. *Input Data*

The data upon which this study is based are primarily the result of a concerted effort by the United Nations to maximize the number of countries for which good demographic and other statistical information would exist. All countries for which roughly comparable demographic and economic data were available at some date in the period from 1947-57 were included in the study.

For each country in our sample the most recent year for which age specific demographic statistics could be found was determined, and the values of the independent (economic and sociocultural) variables were centered on or around that date. The sample used for the fertility study consists of 37 countries, whose annual per capita incomes range from $125 (Morocco) to $1900 (United States), with about half the incomes below $350. The geographic distribution of the observations is also wide, even though Africa and Asia are relatively underrepresented. The mortality study was performed on a similar sample of 34 nations. The list of countries included in the fertility and mortality samples, the data used for each study, and the sources and methods of computation are given in detail in tables available upon request from the author.

III. *Fertility Analysis*

A. *Determinants of Fertility*

Effects of economic conditions upon birth rates, at least in the short run, have often been observed by demographers. For example, Yule [15] found a weak-lagged positive correlation between the course of the business cycle in Great Britain during the latter half of the 19th century and the deviation of birth rates from their secular trend. Similar results were obtained by Ogburn and Thomas [11] for the United States for 1870-1920. From the years 1920-41, Kirk and Nortman [8], working with percentage deviations from the trend, found a correlation coefficient of + .77 between birth per thousand women of childbearing age and real per capita income. Their results were confirmed by Galbraith and Thomas [5], and, more recently, by Becker [24, pp. 209-231].

The long-run relationship between fertility and economic conditions is less clearly established. On the one hand, the normal pattern of fertility differentials among social and economic classes is that of negative association between socioeconomic status and fertility [20, pp. 86-88] [24, p. 5]. Moreover, casual empiricism suggests that, at least up to World War II, differences in fertility among countries were negatively correlated with their levels of economic development. On the other hand, the postwar baby boom experienced by the high-income Anglo-Saxon countries in sparsely populated areas argues in the opposite direction. In addition, Easterlin [4] has adduced strong evidence for the existence of a positive long-run relationship between births and economic conditions in the United States from 1890 to the present. Since the direction and extent of long-run association between child-bearing and living standards is unclear, it would appear that one of the socioeconomic variables whose long-run effects upon fertility ought to be analyzed in this study is the level of real per capita national income (or some similar indicator).

A second set of factors commonly credited with responsibility for the continued decline in fertility which occurred prior to 1930 in north-western Europe is the social and economic transformation brought about by the Industrial Revolution [17, pp. 76-80]. The resulting urbanization and industrialization process appears to have led to persistent changes in fundamental attitudes towards family limitation. Indeed, in all countries, the historical decline in fertility has been preceded by or accompanied by a great shift of the population from country to city. And both the urban-rural differential in fertility and the agricultural-industrial differential have persisted through time [24, pp. 77-87].

A logical indicator of urbanization is, of course, the percentage of the total population living in cities. Similarly, it is reasonable to choose as an indicator of industrialization the percentage of nonagricultural employment of the labor force. From preliminary tests on our sample data, however, it became apparent that there is a very high degree of correlation between these two indicators. Since, in addition, data on urban and rural populations are not internationally comparable because of national differences in the definitions of "urban" residents [23, pp. 1-2], it was decided to use the nonagricultural employment figures alone to represent the variety of socioeconomic forces related to the urbanization-industrialization complex.

Another major influence upon childbearing behavior is the mother's level of education [17, p. 89]. While the net direction of the effect of education upon fertility for college graduates is somewhat uncertain, at lower education levels a clear inverse correlation between the number of years of schooling of the wife and family size is well established from cross-sectional studies [24, pp. 155-70]. Unfortunately, there exist no international data on education for the female population alone; instead, an educational index for the over-all population is included in our regression analysis. This index was constructed by computing the unweighted arithmetic average of the literacy index and an index of newspaper circulation (tons per year) per capita, each based on U.S. = 100. These particular indicators of the educational level of a population were chosen primarily because of their ready availability. The averaging procedure was adopted in order to gain some discrimination among high-income countries, since the literacy index reported for most developed nations is 100.

A measure of population density is also included in the analysis. This was done because, ever since the days of Malthus, the concept of a stable optimum population size which maximizes the per capita income of a nation for a given set of techniques, resources, tastes, and institutions has played a central role in demographic theories.[2] For smaller than optimal populations the extent of the market is too limited to permit full benefits to be derived from division of labor and economies of scale. With too large a population diminishing returns set in, since fewer cooperating resources are available per worker. There exists, therefore, an intermediate population density which optimizes the average real income per capita.

Obviously, these more or less static considerations are not completely appropriate in a dynamic setting. However, in many underdeveloped regions, actual population numbers are so far out of balance with existing arable land resources, given their almost static techniques and their essentially fixed endowments of other cooperating factors, that the population-resource ratio may actually exert some practical influence upon reproductive behavior. Admittedly, population density is only a very crude index of the extent of population pressure upon available resources. In and of itself, a high (or low) ratio of people to land is not synonymous with over- (or under-) population. For it fails to take account of nonland resources and makes no allowance for differences in natural soil fertility, climate, crops and techniques, and the related institutional arrangements. A more refined measure of the population-land ratio, such as the number of people per square mile of cultivable or of arable land, would still be very far from the mark. Nonetheless, some indication of the influence of the population-resource ratio upon fertility may be obtained by including the average population density in the regression equations.

The decline in mortality among infants and young children has sometimes been advanced as another factor responsible for the decrease in fertility [17, pp. 81]. To the extent that families strive towards some optimal size, a greater rate of survival among the young may cause couples to limit the number of children born. In addition, the level of infant mortality may also serve as an index of the general social situation, insofar as the latter bears upon attitudes and practices related to childbearing. For these reasons infant mortality was incorporated into our preliminary regression analysis. Moreover, since infant mortality is highly correlated with per capita income, the partial regression coefficient of age specific birth rates upon infant mortality

[2] For a more detailed discussion of this point, see [9, pp. 171-91].

was not statistically significant and fluctuated in direction. This variable was therefore eliminated from the ultimate set of equations.

The final factor whose influence upon fertility was tested in our investigation is the percentage rate of growth of real per capita income. Leibenstein [9, pp. 173-75] argues that this variable has a direct effect upon the rate of population growth since, at a given level of per capita income, a higher rate of growth implies a higher percentage of investment goods and a lower percentage of consumer products. According to his theory, this shift in the composition of output leads to higher mortality and (perhaps) lower birth rates than would otherwise prevail. This variable, however, was ultimately dropped from the fertility study, as some of the earlier calculations indicated that it would not be statistically significant in the form of the regression equations chosen for our analysis.[3]

B. *The Regression Model*

From preliminary least-squares regression calculations using the indicators suggested by the discussion of the last section, it was found that the highest coefficients of determination and most consistent regression coefficients were obtained by using regression equations of the form:

$$(1) \quad \log_e b_i = a_{0i} + a_{1i} \log_e Y + a_{2i} \log_e I + a_{3i} \log_e E + a_{4i} \log_e P + u_i.$$

In these equations, b represents the number of live births per 1000 females in the ith age group, Y stands for the level of real national income per capita in 1953 U.S. dollars, I indicates the per cent of the labor force employed outside of agriculture, E is the index of education, P is the number of inhabitants per square mile, and u_i is a random disturbance term. Since, in (1), all the socioeconomic variables are expressed in logarithmic terms, the regression coefficients a_{ji} ($j = 1, 2, 3, 4$) measure the elasticities of the birth rate in the ith age group with respect to the jth variable.

In the computation of the regression coefficients from the cross-section data, it was recognized that there are significant differences in the statistical accuracy of the information available from each country. For this reason the data from each country were weighted; the weights were computed from information published in the 1956 *Demographic Yearbook* [19, pp. 9-23, 26-28]. Each weight is the product of three quantities:

1. The reciprocals of the Whipple Index. This index represents a measure of the inaccuracy of the age statistics [19, pp. 26-28].

---

[3] The percentage rate of growth of real per capita income was sometimes statistically significant in some of the nonlogarithmic forms of the regression equations.

2. A measure of the birth registration procedure. This factor is 100 if births and deaths are recorded as they occur (continuous register) and 70 otherwise.

3. A measure of the completeness of the data. This factor is 100 if the data are based on a census covering more than 90 per cent of the population and is taken as 80 otherwise.

The resulting weights (available upon request from the author) vary from 28 for El Salvador and the Dominican Republic to 100 for Morocco, Algeria, and most of the European countries.

It was assumed in the calculations that the u_i, corrected by weighting for intercountry differentials in the quality of the statistics, are normally distributed around the regression surface defined by equation (1) with zero mean and constant variance. Therefore a_{ji} are unbiased estimates of the regression coefficients.

The validity of the cross-country approach was tested by computing separate regression equations—one for the developed lands and one for the undeveloped ones. No statistically significant differences in regression coefficients emerged, a result which indicates that the basic postulate of the cross-section technique—homogeneity of population response—is satisfied.

C. *The Regression Results*

The regression results derived with the aid of the statistical model described in the previous section are summarized in Table 1. The upper entry in the ith row and the jth column of this table is an unbiased estimate of the regression coefficient a_{ji}. The standard error of this estimate is listed in parentheses below the corresponding coefficient.

It is apparent from the last two columns of this table that our regression model accounts for roughly 50 to 70 per cent of the total variance in age specific birth rates among countries. The values of R^2 are all statistically significant, and the standard errors of estimate (column 6) are satisfactorily small. In addition, the signs of the individual regression coefficients are all internally consistent and in accord with a priori expectations.

A closer look at the table reveals that our results support the hypothesis that, *ceteris paribus,* age specific birth rates tend to vary directly with per capita income in the long run. Since the sign of the partial regression coefficient of births upon income is consistently positive, this conclusion appears to be valid even though the income coefficient is significantly different from zero for only the first two age groups. The dependence of births upon income, however, is not very strong even in the two lowest age groups; in fact, the calculated income elasticity never exceeds .55.

ADELMAN: POPULATION GROWTH

TABLE 1—AGE SPECIFIC BIRTH RATE REGRESSIONS

Age of Mother	ln Y	ln I	ln E	ln P	Constant	S	R^2	$\bar{R}^2$
15–19	.553 (.207)	−.209* (.366)	−1.229 (.315)	−.180 (.057)	6.896	.094	.497	.434
20–24	.202 (.086)	−.086* (.152)	−.533 (.125)	−.079 (.024)	6.782	.040	.527	.468
25–29	.075* (.065)	−.110* (.116)	−.332 (.100)	−.044 (.018)	6.765	.030	.480	.415
30–34	.061* (.074)	−.150* (.130)	−.380 (.112)	−.045 (.020)	6.892	.034	.513	.452
35–39	.089* (.092)	−.284 (.163)	−.490 (.141)	−.047 (.025)	7.213	.042	.530	.472
40–44	.084* (.130)	−.559 (.230)	−.540 (.198)	−.070 (.036)	7.622	.060	.507	.445
45–49	.268* (.197)	−1.182 (.350)	−1.472 (.301)	−.057 (.054)	10.816	.091	.700	.663

* Not significant at the 5 per cent level.
Symbols:
 Y=per capita income, converted into U.S. dollars at purchasing parity exchange rate.
 I=per cent of labor force employed outside of agriculture
 E=an index of education
 P=population density
 Dependent variable is the natural log of the number of live births per 1000 females in age group specified.

These results of our regression analysis are consistent with the findings of Easterlin [4] for the United States from 1870 to 1960. Easterlin observed a positive correlation between long swings in white urban births and Kuznetz cycles in nonagricultural economic activity. He also found that the amplitude of the long waves in birth rates is much smaller than that of the corresponding long cycles in economic indicators.

Our findings are also consistent with the short-run results of Becker, whose estimates of average income elasticities for the short business cycles for first- and second-order births were .56 and .42, respectively [24, pp. 224-25].

There appears to be a systematic variation in income effects with age. The impact of income upon births, which tends to be strongest for women between 15 and 19, declines with age for a while and then rises again from age 35. This pattern of variation suggests the hypothesis that both desired family size and the timing of childbearing tend to react to economic factors. At the early ages, there is a strong tendency to adjust the family size to short-run variations in family income by temporarily postponing or accelerating childbearing in response to changes in economic conditions. As would-be mothers age, however, the strength of the timing effect diminishes, leading to a declining income elasticity to about age 34. The rising income elasticity at higher ages, on the other hand, represents primarily the increasing influence of the "permanent" effect of changes in per capita income.

As expected, the socioeconomic phenomena associated with the urbanization process tend to reduce birth rates in the long run. It is apparent from column 2 of Table 1 that the age specific elasticity of birth rates with respect to nonagricultural employment is negative throughout. It is not statistically significant up to age 35. The calculated values, however, decline to age 25 and then begin to rise; the elasticity is greater than unity for the 45-49 age group. The progressively stronger impact of industrialization upon age specific birth rates is thus quite marked. A reasonable interpretation of this pattern is that the reduction in crude birth rates which has historically accompanied the process of urbanization has been achieved, in part, by a shortening of that portion of the life span devoted to childbearing activities by an average woman. Further, the strongest effect appears among the older women.

The well-known negative correlation of birth rates with the level of education is also apparent in our results. The regression coefficient of birth rates with respect to the educational index is always negative and statistically significant. Furthermore, as indicated by the analogous age specific pattern of variation of the relevant elasticities, the impact of the level of education upon fertility is qualitatively similar to that of the degree of industrialization. Quantitatively, among all the variables, a 1 per cent change in the index of education appears to exert the largest absolute influence upon age specific birth rates.

In view of the rough degree of approximation to which the population density figure represents the theoretical concept of the population-resource ratio, the unequivocal significance of P in the regression analysis is somewhat surprising. To a certain extent, as indicated by the negative sign of the regression coefficient in column 4, overpopulation tends to generate its own antidote. However, the over-all elasticity of birth rates with respect to population density is rather small.

The regression equations for age specific birth rates for the subsample of developed countries taken by themselves are reproduced in Table 2 for comparison purposes. Since for this subsample the correlation coefficient between the logarithms of per capita income and of the degree of industrialization was quite high ($r = .81$), the latter variable had to be omitted from the regression equations. As stated above, the

ADELMAN: POPULATION GROWTH   323

TABLE 2—AGE SPECIFIC BIRTH RATE REGRESSIONS
DEVELOPED COUNTRIES

Age of Mother	ln Y	ln E	ln P	Constant	S	R^2
15–19	.703 (.224)	−.965 (.523)	−.127* (.077)	3.502	.099	.617
20–24	.179* (.112)	−.227* (.262)	−.809 (.038)	5.179	.050	.519
25–29	.175 (.090)	−.121* (.210)	−.050* (.030)	4.678	.040	.216
30–34	−.0051* (.094)	−.282* (.219)	−.045* (.032)	6.519	.042	.206
35–39	−.0015* (.104)	−.519 (.243)	−.042* (.136)	6.651	.046	.284
40–44	−.0392* (.148)	−.735 (.345)	−.060* (.051)	6.799	.065	.286
45–49	−.0923* (.214)	−1.212 (.501)	−.081* (.074)	6.897	.095	.327

* Not significant at the 5 per cent level.
Symbols:
  Y=per capita income, converted into U.S. dollars at purchasing parity exchange rates
  E=an index of education
  P=population density
  Dependent variable is the natural log of the number of live births per 1000 females in age group specified.

results of the regression for the developed subsample are consistent with those for the combined group of countries. Indeed, in no case is the difference in regression coefficients significant at the 5 per cent level. In developed countries, the influence of income levels upon births seems to decline more rapidly with age, and becomes negative from the age of 30 onward. The educational level exercises its primary impact at early ages and from 30 onwards, as before. And the impact of population density is statistically less significant for the developed subgroup than for all countries combined. In addition, R^2 declines more rapidly with age in the developed subsample than for the entire group of countries.

IV. *The Analysis of Mortality*

A. *Determinants of Mortality*

There is general agreement among demographers that the determinants of changes in mortality in both developed and underdeveloped areas are of two kinds: (1) those related to the standard of living of the population, and (2) those associated with public health programs for the control of epidemic and endemic diseases. The relative importance of these two classes of factors in both the short and the long run, however, and the extent to which they are interdependent are still unclear.

For example, in discussing recent trends and determinants of mortality in developed countries Stolnitz argues that, "To a significant degree, the great mortality movements of the West appear to have been initiated by medical advances, particularly as applied to governments. Improving economic conditions were important, but much more as permissive elements than as precipitating factors" [16, p. 34]. Similarly, with respect to underdeveloped areas, Bourgeois-Pichat and Chia-Liu Pau point out that, "In the short run the steep mortality decline during the postwar period in, for example, Ceylon, Formosa and Japan stressed that the drop was attributable more to the development of public health programs with a wide use of new drugs than to any possible rising level of living of the people" [16, p. 25].

Clearly, the immediate impact upon death rates in underdeveloped countries of such public health measures as the control and purification of the water supply, the disposal of sewage, the use of new drugs, large-scale innoculations against communicable diseases, and progress in environmental sanitation is bound to be dramatic. On the other hand, once the major benefits from these improvements have been reaped, it may well be that economic conditions play the primary role in determining the subsequent rate of progress in mortality. For it stands to reason that such factors as better nutrition, improved housing, healthier and more humane working conditions, and a somewhat more secure and less careworn mode of life, all of which accompany economic growth, must contribute to improvements in life expectancy. In addition, as pointed out by Spiegelman, "Fundamentally, health progress depends upon economic progress. By the rapid advance in their economies in the postwar period, the highly developed countries have produced wealth for the development of health programs. Also, more efficient technologies in industry are releasing the manpower needed for an extension of medical care and public health services. The intangible contribution of economic progress to lower mortality is derived from the advantage of a high standard of living—more abundant, better and more varied food—a more healthful work and home environment—and more time for healthful recreation" [16, p. 59].

In our study of mortality, the indicator of public health conditions used was the number of physicians per thousand inhabitants. It might be argued that the sum of real per capita expenditures on public health and social security would have been a preferable criterion. However, as pointed out by the United Nations [18, p. 489], the significance of this item in the total health picture varies from country to country depending upon the type of state organization and the scope of the government's share in economic activity. In socialist economies and in centralized states, for example, the national government is almost completely responsible for the health of the public. In private enterprise economies, on the other hand, the degree of public responsibility for health assumed by the government varies significantly from country to country and, in some, constitutes only a minor share of the total. The number of physicians per capita was therefore considered to be a more satisfactory indicator.

As before, economic conditions were represented in our mortality analysis by the level of real per capita income. The percentage of non-agricultural employment of the labor force was used as a measure of the degree of industrialization and urbanization. And the percentage rate of growth of real per capita income was introduced in order to investigate the empirical relevance of one of Leibenstein's population theories [9, pp. 173-75].

The same considerations which suggested the incorporation of population density into the birth rate analysis also led us to test the effects of this variable upon mortality. To our surprise, however, the partial regression coefficient of age specific death rates upon population density was never statistically significant in either the logarithmic or the non-logarithmic forms of the equations calculated. This variable was therefore dropped.

The influence of the degree of education upon mortality patterns was also investigated by means of an index of education analogous to that used in the fertility study. This factor might be expected to affect especially postneonatal mortality for infants and of young children because survival probabilities at early ages are largely affected by the socially and educationally conditioned techniques which mothers employ in the feeding and care of babies. Indeed, our regression results indicate that, in the logarithmic form of the equations, the partial regression coefficient of death rates with respect to the educational index E was statistically significant up to the age of 25. Moreover, in accord with expectations, the effect of educational forces upon mortality after the first five years was found to diminish steadily with age. It was observed in the preliminary calculations that E and the health indicator H were never both statistically significant for the same regression surface, except in the case of infant mortality. Since H is the better indicator for most of the age groups, and since it was felt desirable to have a uniform set of explanatory variables for mortality at all ages, the number of physicians per capita (H) was used instead of the educational index (E) throughout the entire mortality calculation.

B. *The Regression Model*

The regression equations fitted by least squares to the data were of the form:

$$(2) \quad \log_e m_i = c_{0i} + c_{1i} \log_e Y + c_{2i} \frac{\Delta Y}{Y} + c_{3i} \log_e I + c_{4i} \log_e H + \delta_i.$$

In (2) m_i represents the number of deaths per 1000 people in the ith age group; Y and I have the same meanings as in the birth rate equations; $\Delta Y/Y$ is the percentage rate of growth of per capita real income; H is our health indicator—the number of physicians per 10,000 inhabitants; and δ_i is a random error term. The variable $\Delta Y/Y$ was not represented in logarithmic form since, for some countries, it takes on zero or negative values.

As before, in order to achieve a homoscedastic distribution of the δ_i, the least-square fits were computed with country weights derived in the same manner as in the birth rate analysis.

Nonlogarithmic forms of the regression equations with nonlinear terms in income were also fitted to the data. The nonlogarithmic alternatives resulted in slightly poorer fits than (2) up to the age of 40 and somewhat better fits afterwards. The decision to adopt the logarithmic version was made primarily for consistency with the birth rate study.

Disaggregation of the sample into developed and underdeveloped subgroups led to no significant differences in regression coefficients. This time, however, the values of R^2 for the underdeveloped countries were significantly higher than for the developed ones. This observation tends to bear out the contention of Ansley Coale that, "The course of mortality in *industrialized* areas can safely be discussed without reference to prospective variation in strictly economic forces" [24, p. 9].

C. *The Regression Results*

Table 3 presents a summary of the regression results derived with the statistical model just described. As before, the upper entry in the ith row and the jth column of this table is an estimate of the regression coefficient a_{ji}. The standard error of this estimate is listed in parentheses below the corresponding coefficient.

It is evident from the last 2 columns of the table that, up to the age of 50, medical and socioeconomic forces account for something like 50 to 85 per cent of the total variance among countries in age specific death rates. Up to the age of 70, the values of R^2 are all statistically significant. In addition, the signs of the individual regression coefficients are all internally consistent.

TABLE 3—AGE SPECIFIC DEATH RATE REGRESSIONS

Age Group	ln Y	$\Delta Y/Y$	ln I	ln H	Constant	S	R^2	$\bar{R}^2$
0–1	−.275 (.116)	+.025* (.030)	−.664 (.255)	−.149* (.129)	8.417	.0571	.686	.643
1–4	−.583 (.034)	−.035 (.008)	1.284 (.074)	−.311 (.037)	10.681	.0166	.857	.838
5–9	−.420 (.138)	−.033* (.035)	−.610 (.303)	−.336 (.153)	5.776	0679	.721	.683
10–14	−.304 (.089)	−.065 (.023)	−.713 (.196)	−1.57* (.099)	4.916	.0437	.771	.740
15–19	−.433 (.092)	−.093 (.024)	−.476 (.203)	+.044* (.103)	5.014	.0455	.653	.606
20–24	−.372 (.105)	−.043 (.026)	−.362* (.231)	−.203 (.117)	4.808	.0519	.702	.661
25–29	−.341 (.103)	−.045 (.026)	−.637 (.225)	−.135* (.114)	5.738	.0504	.717	.678
30–34	−.274 (.100)	−.045 (.026)	−.615 (.220)	−.178* (.111)	5.470	.0493	.699	.658
35–39	−.240 (.098)	−.050 (.025)	−.514 (.214)	−.198 (.108)	5.175	.0481	.670	.625
40–44	−.137 (.098)	−.047 (.025)	−.528 (.214)	−.175* (.109)	4.878	.0484	.562	.502
45–49	−.207 (.097)	−.038* (.025)	−.185* (.211)	−.185 (.106)	4.252	.0472	.478	.372
50–54	−.065* (.090)	−.031* (.023)	−0.220* (.198)	−.198 (.100)	3.976	.0448	.444	.368
55–59	−.017* (.080)	−.016* (.020)	−.144* (.175)	−.194 (.088)	3.717	.0393	.358	.270
60–64	−.031* (.066)	−.015* (.016)	−.114* (.146)	−.170 (.072)	4.074	.0324	.410	.329
65–69	−.0008* (.085)	−.004* (.022)	−.060* (.187)	−.170 (.095)	4.082	.0422	.255	.153
70–74	−.048* (.066)	−.002* (.016)	+.008* (.146)	−.098 (.072)	4.409	.0323	.199	.089*

* Not significant at 5 per cent level.

Symbols:

Y = per capita income, converted into U.S. 1953 dollars at purchasing parity exchange rates

$\Delta Y/Y$ = the percentage rate of growth of per capita real income

I = the percentage of the labor force employed outside agriculture

H = health indicator, the number of physicians per 10,000 inhabitants

Dependent variable is the number of deaths per 1000 people in the appropriate age group.

One interesting feature of our calculations is the steadily diminishing importance of economic, social, and medical factors in explaining inter-country death rate differentials at higher ages. (From the age of 35 onwards, the values of R^2 decrease continuously.) Similar results were obtained by Moriyama and Guralnick [16, pp. 61-73] in a cross-sectional study of differences in mortality between occupational and social strata in the United States; they found that the gap in mortality rates between socioeconomic classes narrows with age, especially after 55. This observation may be related to some suggestions from recent medical research that the physiological quality of human organisms is largely determined at a very early stage in life. Economic and social conditions during early childhood, therefore, may well play a more significant role in determining differences in mortality rates after age 55 than do current variations in socioeconomic and medical factors.

A more detailed examination of our regression results leads to the following generalizations:

1. *Ceteris paribus*, there exists a negative long-run association between death rates and economic conditions. Column 1 of Table 3 indicates that the regression coefficient of deaths upon income is negative throughout and statistically significant up to the age of 50. The elasticity of death rates with respect to income is considerably below unity, however. These results are in accord with the conclusions of Moriyama and Guralnick in the study previously cited.

2. Urbanization and industrialization seem to play a significant direct role in the reduction of mortality (col. 3). Much of the apparent effect of urbanization may be due to differences between city and country in environmental sanitation (water supply, sewage, etc.), type of housing, and availability of professional (as opposed to traditional) medical care and the willingness of the population to utilize it. In addition, differences in occupational structure and in per capita income between urban and rural communities may also contribute to the negative correlation between mortality rates and the percentage of non-agricultural employment.

3. As expected, mortality is negatively associated with differentials in medical care (col. 4). Indeed, from the age of 50 onwards, variations in mortality are largely accounted for by differences in medical services. None of the other socioeconomic factors is statistically significant after that age.

4. Finally, our results also indicate the existence of a negative partial correlation between the rate of growth of real per capita income and death rates (col. 2). This finding is in direct conflict with that theory of Leibenstein which suggests that, *ceteris paribus*, a more rapid rate of economic growth will, on the average, be correlated with an *increase* in mortality [9, pp. 173-75].

The explanation of the latter phenomenon may be much more classical in nature than Leibenstein's argument would indicate. As pointed out by Adam Smith, "It is not the actual greatness of national wealth, but its continual increase, which occasions a rise in the wages of labour. It is not, accordingly, in the richest countries, but in the most thriving or in those which are growing rich the fastest that the wages of labour are highest" [14, p. 69]. Now, at a given level of income and within a given sociocultural context, the over-all death rate of the population might be expected to vary with the distribution of income between classes. Even when the over-all average standard of living is low, the per capita income of profit receivers is so high that mortality rates within the entrepreneurial classes are not particularly sensitive to changes in income. In contrast, at low levels of income, a higher wage rate reduces mortality among the laboring population through the better nutritional, health, and sanitation standards that accompany improved wages. As a result, an increase in the rate of growth of income, which augments the relative share of wages in the total product by increasing demand for labor, diminishes death rates. By the same token, by increasing the share of profit receivers, a decline in the rate of economic expansion leads to an increase in mortality.[4]

The flaw in Leibenstein's contention would appear to be that, even though a higher rate of growth of per capita income is associated with a decrease in over-all consumption, it is also associated with an increase in the amount of consumer products accruing to the lower income groups. This decreases mortality among the laboring classes without a corresponding increase in the mortality rate of upper income groups. The result is, of course, a net reduction in mortality for the community as a whole.

V. *Estimates for 1953*

To obtain a partial indication of the usefulness of the above regression approach to natality and mortality phenomena, the regression coefficients of Tables 1 and 3 were used to estimate the crude birth and death rates in 1953 in the six inhabited continents. The year 1953 was used as a bench-mark date because good estimates of per capita income were available for that year and because empirical demographic data for 1950-55 have been published by the United Nations. In addition, for this period, the socioeconomic regression estimates can also be compared with estimates of crude birth and death rates computed by the United Nations Population Division on the basis of purely demo-

[4] A similar argument is made in I. Adelman [1, pp. 110-11].

graphic phenomenological models of population growth [20] [21] [22].

Before our regression analysis can be used for this purpose, however, the values of the independent variables in our equations have to be estimated. For North America, Oceania, and Europe, our estimates are the arithmetic averages of the single country data for 1953, weighted by population; but for Latin America, Asia, and Africa, statistics are notoriously scanty. Our estimates for these regions were therefore necessarily based upon fragmentary data, and are consequently much less reliable. Also, in the absence of better information, a uniform figure of 2 per cent was chosen for the rate of growth of real per capita income in order to avoid a suggestion of spurious accuracy. The values of the independent variables assumed for the 1953 estimates are given in Table 4.

TABLE 4—VALUES OF INDEPENDENT VARIABLES ASSUMED FOR 1953 ESTIMATES

Region	Population Density P^a	Per Capita Income Y	% Rate of Growth of Per-Cap. Income $\Delta Y^c/Y$	Physicians per 10,000 Population H	Educational Index E	% of Labor Force Outside Agriculture I
North America	7.8	1800[c]	2.0	12.5[c]	94[c]	87[c]
Latin America	8.1	265[d]	2.0	2.0[f]	30[f]	40[f]
Asia	51[b]	75[d]	2.0	1.0[f]	20[f]	30[f]
Europe	59	770[c]	2.0	11.0[c]	95[c]	78[c]
Oceania	1.3	1120[c]	2.0	12.7[c]	100[c]	84[c]
Africa	6.5	105[d]	2.0	0.5[e]	20[f]	35[f]

Sources: a *Demographic Yearbook* 1956, p. 151. Population per km² in 1950.
b Corrected in the light of later estimates, back to 1950.
c Averages, weighted by population, of data for 1953 for countries in the region.
d Estimates taken from T. Kristensen and Associates, *The World Economic Balance* (North Holland, 1960), p. 250.
e Hypothetical figure.
f Estimate based on fragmentary data.

The resulting age specific birth and death rates are indicated in Tables 5 and 6 respectively. Since, from the age of 70 onwards, our death regressions were not statistically significant, the United Nations model mortality tables were used to estimate death rates for the uppermost age groups [22, pp. 72-73]. The pattern of birth and death rates estimated is consistent with later empirical data and a priori expectations. In our estimates, birth rates are lowest in Europe, higher and fairly similar in North America and Oceania, and higher still in Asia, Latin America, and Africa. Death rates in North America and in Oceania are somewhat lower than those in Europe. They are high in both Africa and Asia, and intermediate in Latin America. In accord with observation, Europe, in our estimates, appears to be in a low-birth-and-low-death-rate demographic state; North America and Oceania are of a low-death-rate and intermediate-birth-rate type; and Latin America is in a transition phase, with both mortality and natality intermediate between those of the Asian and African continents and the much lower birth and death rates of the more developed continents. In addition, the age specific pattern of variation of both birth and death rates in each continent is consistent with that found in the real world.

TABLE 5—AGE SPECIFIC BIRTH RATES ESTIMATED FOR 1953

Age of Mother	Asia	Africa	Latin America	North America	Oceania	Europe
15–19	66	111	106	64	63	28
20–24	234	291	274	206	209	149
25–29	256	283	259	188	193	163
30–34	206	226	199	129	133	113
35–39	145	158	134	73	74	63
40–44	66	72	57	23	25	20
45–49	28	28	17	2	2	2

TABLE 6—ESTIMATED AGE SPECIFIC DEATH RATES (1953)

Age Groups	North America	Africa	Latin America	Asia	Europe	Oceania
0–1	21.4	138	120.0[a]	152	29.6	24.9
1–4	.76	34.8	11.1	41.5	1.49	1.04
5–9	.36	6.17	2.42	6.19	.58	.45
10–14	.34	2.57	1.42	2.85	.49	.40
15–19	.65	2.98	1.99	3.82	.98	.81
20–24	.82	6.32	3.22	6.58	1.20	.99
25–29	.91	6.62	3.68	7.45	1.33	1.09
30–34	1.14	7.69	4.30	8.20	1.57	1.32
34–39	1.62	9.65	5.49	9.88	2.15	1.84
40–44	2.59	10.90	7.03	11.0	3.16	2.82
45–49	3.78	14.60	9.12	14.2	4.71	4.19
50–54	6.98	19.40	13.50	17.9	7.76	7.24
55–59	11.30	25.20	18.60	22.8	11.90	11.40
60–64	17.70	37.10	28.00	33.9	18.88	18.0
65–69	27.2	49.75	39.00	44.6	30.00	27.2
70–74	46.10	72.10	65.00	68.4	48.6	47.0
75–79[a]	74	118	99	108	77	75
80–84[a]	118	176	152	163	122	118
85[a]	232	277	255	265	234	232

[a] Estimated on the basis of U.N. model mortality tables, *Methods for Population Projection by Sex and Age, Manual III;* U.N. 1956, pp. 72–73.

Our estimates of the crude birth and death rates for each continent in 1953 are summarized in Table 7. These estimates are based upon population age distributions derived by interpolation from the actual data for age groups 0-14, 15-64, 65 and over listed in the 1956 *Demographic Yearbook*. The ratio of females to total population used for these estimates was calculated from individual country data on sex distribution by age given in the 1957 *Demographic Yearbook*. From Table 7 one can see that our birth rate estimates are close to the actual figures and compare very favorably with those of the United Nations. Our death rate estimates are less satisfactory. They are still considerably better than the U.N. estimates, but they tend to be low. Since crude death rates are quite sensitive to the details of the age distribution of the population, especially at ages above 45, a large part of the discrepancy between our calculations and empirical observations can be ascribed to inaccuracies and approximations in our assumed age structure. This hypothesis is supported by the fact that life expectancy at birth (see Table 8), which is independent of age structure, is consistent with observation.

One would expect, of course, that even better agreement with real world birth and death rates could be achieved if crude vital statistics were estimated from the regression equations country by country and averaged (using relative populations as weights) for each continent. Unfortunately, however, the scarcity of data, especially in the underdeveloped regions, precluded this approach.

TABLE 7—COMPARISON OF BIRTH AND DEATH RATE ESTIMATES 1950–55

Continent	Crude Birth Rate			Crude Death Rate			Natural Increase		
	Actual*	Our Estimate	U.N.** Estimate	Actual*	Our Estimate	U.N.** Estimate	Actual*	Our Estimate	U.N.** Estimate
	1951–55	1953	1950	1951–55	1953	1950	1951–55	1953	1950
Africa	45	43	47	25	20	33	20	23	14
North America	25	23	22	9	9	0	16[a]	14	13
Latin America	42	41	40	18	13	19	24[a]	28	21
Asia	39	39	46	22	19	33	17	20	13
Europe[b]	20	21	20	11	9	9	9[a]	12	11
Oceania	25	23	26	8	9	12	17	14	14

* Source: *Demographic Yearbook* 1956, Table A, p. 2.
Rates are estimated on annual averages for 1951–55.
[a] This rate excludes the effect of migration.
[b] Excluding USSR.
** Source: *The Future Growth of World Population*, U.N. 1958, Table 11, p. 32.

TABLE 8—COMPARISONS OF LIFE EXPECTANCY AND REPRODUCTION
RATE ESTIMATES, U.N. AND OURS

Continent	Life Expectancy at Birth			Gross Reproduction Rate			NRR
	U.N. Estimate 1950	Our Estimate 1953[i]	Actual[a]	U.N. Estimate 1950	Our Estimate 1953[i]	Actual[a]	Our Estimate[1]
Africa	31.5[a]	46.5	49	3.0[a]	2.89	h	2.33
North America	68.2[b]	71.9	71	1.5[b]	1.70	1.74	1.66
Latin America	46.8[c]	56.7	50	2.75[c]	2.59	3.08	2.31
Asia	32.2[d]	45.2	h	2.92[d]	2.47	h	1.95
Europe	68.2[e]	69.9	66	1.29[e]	1.33	1.22	1.29
Oceania	68.2[f]	71.2	69	1.5[f]	1.73	1.59	1.69

[a] Source: *The Future Growth of World Population* (p. 12), Model AB for Middle Africa and Models CG and DH for Northern and Southern Africa.
[b] *Loc. cit.*, Model LMS.
[c] *Loc. cit.*, Model DH for Central, Tropical and Southern America and Model LMS for Temperate America.
[d] *Loc. cit.*, Model CG for Asia excluding Japan and Model LRVW for Japan.
[e] *Loc. cit.*, Model QRS for Northern and Central Europe and average QRS and LRS Models for Southern Europe.
[f] *Loc. cit.*, Model LMN.
[g] Estimated from available country data on or about 1953 in *Demographic Yearbook*. Averages weighted by population. Figures are rounded to nearest year.
[h] Sample available too unrepresentative to use.
[i] For this computation the regression death rates were converted into life table mortality rates with the aid of the Reed & Merrell Tables reproduced in [7, pp. 19–26].
[1] In this computation it is assumed that .495 of all births are females.

VI. *Equilibrium Distributions and Demographic Multipliers*

A. *Some General Considerations*

One important problem which our regression analysis enables us to attack is: how sensitive is the rate of population growth to changes in each of the socioeconomic variables? In attempting to answer this question, one cannot simply compare elasticities. For a given percentage change in one of the independent variables does not, in general, have the same a priori probability as the same percentage change in another independent variable. One must instead compute the effect on population growth of each of a set of equiprobable percentage changes in the independent variables in order to achieve a more or less objective intervariable comparison.

A more basic difficulty arises when one tries to determine the relevant whole-population elasticities (elasticities averaged over all age groups), as the averaging process depends of necessity on the age distribution assumed for the population. One can bypass this problem by rephrasing the question in a manner similar to that used in comparative statics analysis. Thus we shall not ask: what changes in the *actual* demographic features of a community will be brought about by a given percentage variation in a particular socioeconomic quantity? Instead, we shall compare the *equilibrium* configurations which correspond to the age specific birth and death rates of the society before and after the change.

This alternative approach leads us to the calculation of demographic multipliers, conceptually analogous to the more familiar multipliers of modern economics. These demographic multipliers indicate the differences in the equilibrium demographic features of a society before and after a change in the value of some particular social or economic variable. A demographic multiplier is derived by (1) calculating the equilibrium age distribution corresponding to a certain set of initial

TABLE 9—EQUILIBRIUM DEMOGRAPHIC FEATURES BY CONTINENT

Continent	Conditions	Age Distribution %			Depend-ency	Crude Birth Rate	Crude Death Rate[c]	Natural In-crease[d]
		0–14	15–60	>60				
Africa	Actual '53[a]	42	52	6	.92	45	25	20
	Equilibrium	46	50	4	1.00	42	11	30
	Regression Est. 1953	—	—	—	—	43	20	23
Asia	Actual '53[a]	38	56	6	.78	39	22	17
	Equilibrium	41	53	5	.86	36	13	23
	Regression Est. 1953	—	—	—	—	39	19	20
Latin America	Actual '53[a]	40	55	5	.82	42	18	24
	Equilibrium	44	51	5	.94	38	8	30
	Regression Est. 1953	—	—	—	—	41	13	28
North America	Actual '53[a]	27	61	12	.64	25	9	16
	Equilibrium	33	57	10	.75	25	7	19
	Regression Est. 1953	—	—	—	—	22	9	14
Oceania	Actual '53[a]	30	59	11	.69	25	8	17
	Equilibrium	34	56	10	.78	26	7	19
	Regression Est. 1953	—	—	—	—	23	9	14
Europe[b]	Actual '53[a]	25	62	13	.61	20	11	9
	Equilibrium	27	59	15	.70	19	10	9
	Regression Est. 1953	—	—	—	—	21	9	12

[a] Source: *Demographic Yearbook* 1956, p. 8, Table B.
[b] Excluding USSR.
[c] Calculated by the method given in [25, p. 32].
[d] Excluding the effect of migration.

values of those socioeconomic variables which determine the age specific birth and death rates; (2) changing one of our independent variables, such as per capita income, by a certain percentage; (3) calculating the new age specific birth and death rates; (4) calculating the new equilibrium age distribution; and (5) comparing the demographic characteristics of the two equilibria.

Before these demographic multipliers can be calculated, therefore, we must derive the equilibrium configuration implied by a given pattern of age specific birth and death rates. The equilibrium age distribution of a society is that age distribution which would ultimately tend to establish itself under unchanging birth and death conditions [3, pp. 236-51].[5] It can be shown that, if the fertility of women at each age were to remain constant for a sufficient length of time, the age structure of the population would assume a definite pattern which is independent of the initial age distribution of the population. In addition, it can also be proved that, given a set of fertility and mortality rates, the equilibrium configuration is stable with respect to large displacements as well as to small. The nature of the implied equilibrium age distribution is therefore of demographic interest both intrinsically and as a means of obtaining a better representation of the inherent power for growth of a population. From an economic point of view, the equilibrium age distribution is also of interest, as such important features of an economy as its consumption pattern, the savings tendencies of the community, the attitudes of the society towards risk, the labor-force participation rate, and the average productivity of the employed are all age-dependent phenomena [24, pp. 287-522].

B. *Equilibrium Distributions and Multipliers*

Some of the significant demographic features of the calculated equilibrium distributions are given in Table 9 for the six continents. For each continent the predicted age configuration in equilibrium consists of a larger proportion of younger people than was observed in 1953, and, except possibly for Europe, it implies a reversal of the current tendencies towards an older population. Since the decrease in the aged is more than counterbalanced by the increase in the proportion of children, the economic burden upon the working population rises in equilibrium. In Table 9 this effect is measured by the dependency ratio, an indicator which is obtained by dividing the proportion of the population under 15 and over 59 by the working age population. These

---

[5] This equilibrium age distribution is identical with the "stable age distribution" first introduced by Lotka in 1911 [10]. The approximation technique suggested [3, pp. 240-42] was used for its calculation.

projected changes are obviously related to the dramatic difference in death rates between the actual and the predicted populations.

The demographic multiplier calculations summarized in Tables 10 and 11 were carried out for four continents, chosen to represent four different demographic situations. North America is an example of a high-birth-rate and low-death-rate society. Asia represents a community with both birth and death rates high. Europe is more or less typical of a low-death-rate and low-birth-rate region; and Latin America has an intermediate death rate and a high birth rate. The changes for which the multiplier calculations were carried out were of a magnitude which might be expected to result from a reasonably successful 5-year development program. Inasmuch as neither the literacy index nor the degree of nonagricultural employment in Europe and North America is likely to change very much, no educational or industrialization multipliers were calculated for these continents. In addition, it was not obvious what assumption could reasonably be made about changes in the number of physicians per capita and changes in population density. Therefore, no multipliers were calculated for these variables.

From Tables 10 and 11 it would appear that the demographic characteristics of a society are most sensitive to changes in the educational level of the population. Some of the demographic indicators, such as the rate of natural increase, also respond noticeably to changes in per capita income. The net effect of changes in industrialization per se or in the rate of increase of per capita income is, in general, quite small. On the other hand, the degree of industrialization has a significant influ-

TABLE 10—DEMOGRAPHIC MULTIPLIERS BY CONTINENT

Continent	Demographic Quantity	Equilibrium Value Based on 1953 Data	Effect of 25% Increase in			Effect of Change in $\Delta Y/Y$ from 2% to 4%
			Y	I	E	
North America	Birth Rate (%)	2.55	+.12	•	•	0
	Death Rate (%)	.69	−.04	•	•	0
	Rate of Natural Increase (%)	1.86	+.16	•	•	0
	Doubling Period (years)	37.61	−2.95	•	•	0
	Life expectancy (years)	71.88	+.34	•	•	+.31
Europe	Birth Rate (%)	1.92	+.08	•	•	0
	Death Rate (%)	1.03	−.05	•	•	−.01
	Rate of Natural Increase (%)	.89	+.14	•	•	+.01
	Doubling Period (years)	78.23	−10.59	•	•	−.87
	Life Expectancy (years)	69.94	+.43	•	•	+.35
Latin America	Birth Rate (%)	3.82	+.15	−.14	−.47	0
	Death Rate (%)	.78	−.05	−.05	+.09	−.02
	Rate of Natural Increase (%)	+3.03	+.21	−.08	−.55	+.02
	Doubling Period (years)	23.22	−1.48	+.62	+5.07	+.15
	Life Expectancy (years)	56.72	+1.08	+2.45	•	+.47
Asia	Birth Rate (%)	3.60	+.12	−.14	−.41	0
	Death Rate (%)	1.27	−.09	−.12	+.20	−.05
	Rate of Natural Increase (%)	+2.33	+.22	−.02	−.20	+.05
	Doubling Period (years)	30.09	−2.56	+.26	+8.13	−.62
	Life Expectancy (years)	45.17	+1.83	+4.04	•	+.97

• Not calculated.

TABLE 11— EQUILIBRIUM AGE STRUCTURE AND DEPENDENCY RATIOS BY CONTINENT[a]

Continent	Age Group	Equilibrium Value	Effect of 25% Increase in			Effect of Change in $\Delta Y/Y$ from 2% to 4%
			Y	I	E	
North America	0–14 (%)	33.14	+1.12	•	•	−.06
	15–35 (%)	31.65	+.19	•	•	−.04
	35–60 (%)	24.92	−.69	•	•	+.02
	>60 (%)	10.29	−.63	•	•	+.09
	Dependency ratio	.75	+.04	•	•	0
Europe	0–14 (%)	26.70	+.85	•	•	−.08
	15–35 (%)	29.96	+.29	•	•	−.06
	35–60 (%)	28.84	−.49	•	•	+.02
	>60 (%)	14.50	−.65	•	•	+.11
	Dependency ratio	.70	+.01	•	•	0
Latin America	0–14 (%)	43.79	+1.24	−.94	−3.86	−.08
	15–35 (%)	32.94	−.10	+.01	+.08	−.05
	35–60 (%)	18.51	−.73	+.63	+2.42	+.09
	>60 (%)	4.76	−.41	+.30	+1.36	+.04
	Dependency ratio	.94	+.03	−.02	−.09	0
Asia	0–14 (%)	41.33	+1.12	−.79	−3.46	−.05
	15–36 (%)	33.29	−.02	−.02	−.07	−.03
	35–60 (%)	19.99	−.68	+.55	+2.20	+.03
	>60 (%)	5.39	−.42	+.25	+1.32	+.05
	Dependency ratio	.86	+.04	−.003	−.06	0

[a] Percentages may not add up to 100 due to rounding.

ence upon life expectancy. Perhaps the major surprise in the results is the apparently paradoxical observation that the crude death rate increases as the educational level of the society is raised. The explanation of this effect is that, in the long run, the decreased birth rate accompanying an improvement in education leads to an older population, with its associated higher mortality rates.

VII *Conclusions*

The results of this study suggest that there is a systematic dependence of age specific birth and death rates upon some of the important socioeconomic variables. This relationship can be utilized to estimate the potential demographic changes which may be induced by national development programs. The demographic effects of changes in per capita income and in its rate of growth, however, do not appear to be very dramatic.

For economic development, the implications of this study are therefore rather encouraging. They indicate, for example, that the increase induced in the ratio of population growth by a 25 per cent improvement in per capita income would not raise the population by more than 1 per cent over a 5-year period. Furthermore, if the development program were accompanied by an effective educational effort, the rate of population expansion might actually decline.

All in all, it would seem that the influence of socioeconomic variables upon the demographic features of a society is very much smaller than the effect of population growth upon economic development.

REFERENCES

[1] I. ADELMAN, *Theories of Economic Growth and Development.* Stanford 1961.

[2] H. B. CHENERY, "Patterns of Industrial Growth," *Amer. Econ. Rev.,* Sept. 1960, *50,* 624-54.

[3] L. I. DUBLIN, A. J. LOTKA, AND M. SPIEGELMAN, *Length of Life.* New York 1949.

[4] R. A. EASTERLIN, "The Baby Boom in Perspective," *Amer. Econ. Rev.,* Dec. 1961, *51,* 869-911.

[5] V. L. GALBRAITH AND D. S. THOMAS, "Birth Rates and the Interwar Business Cycles, *Jour. Amer. Stat. Assoc.,* Dec. 1941, *36,* 465.

[6] E. E. HAGEN, "Population and Economic Growth," *Am. Econ. Rev.,* June 1959, *49,* 310-27.

[7] A. J. JAFFE, *Handbook of Statistical Methods for Demographers.* U.S. Department of Commerce, Washington 1951.

[8] D. KIRK AND D. L. NORTMAN, "Business and Babies: The Influence of the Business Cycle on Birth Rates," *Proc. Am. Stat. Assoc.,* Soc. Stat. Sec., 1958, pp. 151-60.

[9] H. LEIBENSTEIN, *Economic Backwardness and Economic Growth.* New York 1957.

[10] A. J. LOTKA, *Analyse demographique avec application particulère à l'espèce humaine.* Paris 1939.

[11] W. F. OGBURN AND D. S. THOMAS, "The Influence of the Business Cycle on Certain Social Conditions," *Jour. Amer. Stat. Assoc.,* 1922, *18,* 324-40.

[12] B. OKUN, *Trends in Birth Rates in the United States Since 1870.* Baltimore 1958.

[13] G. H. ORCUTT, M. GREENBERGER, J. KORBEL AND A. M. RIVLIN, *Microanalysis of Socio-Economic Systems: A Simulation Study.* New York 1961.

[14] ADAM SMITH, *The Wealth of Nations.* New York 1937.

[15] G. U. YULE, "On the Changes in the Marriage and Birth Rates in England and Wales during the Past Half Century with an Inquiry as to Their Probable Causes," *Jour. Roy. Stat. Soc.,* 1906, *69,* 88-132.

[16] MILLBANK MEMORIAL FUND. *Trends and Differentials in Mortality.* New York 1956.

[17] UNITED NATIONS, Department of Social Affairs, *The Determinants and Consequences of Population Trends,* Population Studies 17. New York 1953.

[18] ——, Department of Economic and Social Affairs, *Statistical Yearbook.* New York 1959.

[19] ——, Department of Economic and Social Affairs, *Demographic Yearbook.* New York, various years.

[20] ——, Department of Social Affairs, *Age and Sex Patterns of Mortality Model Life Tables for Underdeveloped Countries,* Population Studies 22. New York 1955.

[21] ———, Department of Economic and Social Affairs, *The Future Growth of World Population*, Population Studies 28. New York 1958.

[22] ———, Department of Economic and Social Affairs, *Methods for Population Projections by Sex and Age*, Manual III, Population Studies 25. New York 1956.

[23] ———, Department of Social Affairs. *Data on Urban and Rural Population in Recent Censuses*. New York 1950.

[24] *Universities-National Bureau*, Committee for Economic Research, *Demographic and Econmic Change in Developed Countries*, Spec. Conf. 11. Princeton 1960.

6

3

Patterns of Economic Growth, 1850–1914, or Chenery–Syrquin in Historical Perspective*

IRMA ADELMAN
CYNTHIA TAFT MORRIS

Introduction

Much of Hollis Chenery's work during the past quarter century has been devoted to elucidating the regularities in growth patterns of developing countries by systematic econometric analyses of cross-section and time series data. Following Kuznets (1957), Chenery applied slightly more sophisticated techniques and an intuition educated by policy-oriented, contemporary experience with developing countries to statistical analyses of typical changes in the pace and structure of economic growth of newly industrializing nations. Over the past 25 years, he studied and restudied the subject, bringing to it ever more disaggregated, longer, more comprehensive, and conceptually clearer data bases. The result, which culminated in *Structural Change and Development Policy* (Chenery, 1979), is as sharp and comprehensive a summary chronicle of the transition processes that developing countries are undergoing as can be produced while relying solely on continuous quantitative economic data.

The purpose of this chapter is to restudy economic history using the Chenery cross-country method. It perhaps is appropriate that we do so since one of us (Adelman) was the first in a long line of Chenery coauthors—a line that includes two of the three editors of this *Festschrift*—to repeat the study of patterns using a conceptually better data base.

* This essay was first presented as a paper at a conference at the University of the South, Sewanee, Tennessee.

45

This chapter is part of a comparative study of institutional change and economic growth in the nineteenth century (Morris and Adelman, in press). We focus here only on the impact of trade and investment on the pace and structure of economic change. Our data, developed over 20 years of research especially for the larger study, are classifactory indicators summarizing 35 socioeconomic and political traits of 23 countries for three sub-periods between 1850 and 1914.

In spirit, our approach is akin to that of contemporary economic historians who focus on a broad spectrum of determinants of institutional change and on the relationships between institutional transformations, on the one hand, and quantitative changes stressed in theories of optimizing behavior on the other hand. The approach provides a quantitative counterpart to the analyses of such noneconometric economic historians as Gerschenkron (1962), Polanyi (1957), Landes (1969), Hughes (1970), and Jones (1967), for whom the processes of empirical research and theorizing on causes of economic growth are intertwined. The merit of our approach is that, like Chenery and Kuznets, we apply quantitative methods to many countries and many aspects of economic change. By contrast, most empirically oriented economic historians base their generalizations on non-systematic comparisons of, at most, two or three countries selected to shed light on some specific set of issues.

In this chapter our major interest lies in the interactions between quantitative economic growth and the structural transformations that typically accompany long-term economic growth. We define *economic growth* in the same way as Kuznets: as a rise in per capita gross national product (GNP) and population accompanied by a shift of labor and resources from agricultural to nonagricultural sectors and from rural to urban locations. By *economic development* we mean the process of institutional transformation by which structural change is achieved and the gains and losses are distributed. Thus, we deal here only with quantitative historical economic growth, not with economic development as we understand it.

During the period under study, 1850–1914, the expansion of foreign trade and investment was spectacular, and the increase in colonial empires, striking. The economically more advanced nations of Western Europe industrialized rapidly and expanded their trade and investment throughout the world. Sharp declines in shipping costs, with the introduction of steamships and the development of refrigeration, contributed to an unprecedented increase in the flow of food and raw materials from the far corners of the world to European markets, with striking consequences for the pace and structure of European growth. Other countries—in Europe and elsewhere—expanded more unevenly, usually as a result of primary export expansion. The transfer overseas of European manpower and capital was unprecedented. Resources flowed mainly to other European countries or to countries of European settlement. But the relatively small flow to economically backward peasant economies usually had far-reaching and sometimes disastrous consequences for indigenous preindustrial systems.

Method

We attempted to replicate the Chenery–Syrquin (1975) analysis as far as our data would permit. The conceptual framework of the Chenery–Syrquin statistical analysis is based on a reduced-form model of the interactions between structural changes in the composition of demand, on the one hand, and supply responses on the other. In reduced form, the changes in both demand and supply can be represented as functions of per capita income[1] and population. One can then estimate regressions of the form:

$$X = \alpha + \beta_1 \ln Y + \beta_2 (\ln Y)^2 + \gamma_1 \ln N + \gamma_2 (\ln N)^2 + \sum \delta_i T_i + \varepsilon F,$$

where X is the dependent variable, Y the per capita GNP in constant U.S. dollars, N the population in millions, T_i the time period, and F the net resource inflow as a share of GNP.

The resulting regressions portray the average transformation pattern for an average country. The impact, good or bad, of development strategy is analyzed by looking at the pattern of deviations of countries from the typical pattern. The influence of comparative advantage is captured by grouping countries by their resource endowments. The result is a simple but relatively comprehensive picture of the regularities involved in economic growth.

We follow the same method, departing only to the extent that our data do not permit exact replication, to compare historical with contemporary patterns.

Data

The sample consists of 23 countries whose GNP increased substantially between 1850 and 1914. Each country enters the statistical analysis as three observations: once for its characteristics in 1850 to 1869, once for those in 1870 to 1889, and once for those in 1890 to 1914, giving 69 observations in all.

The data are classifications representing diverse facets of social and economic structure. The data were developed as part of a large quantitative study of interactions between economic and political institutions, initial conditions, and patterns of economic transformation during the second part of the nineteenth and early twentieth centuries (Morris and Adelman, 1983). Appendix A gives brief definitions of the classifications of dependent variables used here. Fuller definitions and the set of references used in classifying countries are in Adelman and Morris (1980) and in Morris and Ademan (in press).

In constructing the variables, we started with a priori definitions of categories based on specific features for which descriptive or quantitative information was likely to be available. For instance, we judged the development of industrial technology mostly by mechanization in the major industry of the nineteenth century—textiles. For each variable, the definitions of the categories were constructed to provide as differentiated, comprehensive, and reliable an overview of the process of change during the period under study described by the variable as the information permits. Information on the relevant country characteristics was then used to classify the observations. The number of categories varied from one indicator to another, depending on the coverage and reliability of the basic information.

The classifications provide partial rankings of the observations to which we apply an arbitrary linear scoring scheme that preserves ranks. The data are thus ordinal, a property they share with all economic indices that represent concepts of interest to economists. Statistically, a form of multinomial logit or of mixed continuous–discrete estimation would have been more appropriate to our data. But these techniques would not have maintained comparability with Chenery–Syrquin (1975). Moreover, experiments with other data comparing ordinary least squares with logit indicate that, when correlations are moderate to high, the alternative techniques all yield similar results.

Of necessity, the comparability of the historical and Chenery–Syrquin studies is limited by the data. On the one hand, it is impossible to develop detailed structural estimates on, say, the composition of national income and structure of demand for the nineteenth century, except for a handful of countries. This leads to the omission of some variables from our study included in the Chenery–Syrquin (1975) study. It also leads us to use categorized data, in which we can have some confidence, rather than point estimates with large margins of error. On the other hand, the use of categorized data enables us to include broader and more comprehensive measures of economic change that Chenery–Syrquin exclude: special measures of levels of technological development in both agriculture and industry and their rates of change, an index of levels of development of transportation, and a measure of international migration. These are introduced because we believe that the forces they represent might be significant in the nineteenth century.

Statistical Results: All Countries

The results of the regression analysis, which summarize the historical transformation processes, are in Table 3.1. In Table 3.2 those results are used to infer the dimensions of the transition of an average country during 1850 to 1914.

THE HISTORICAL PATTERN

The Average Structure. The first three columns of Table 3.2 paint pictures of the economic structure of an average nineteenth-century country during the transition process.[2] The description that follows is based on a verbal interpretation of the average scores for each variable in a given period. The average country in the sample during 1850 to 1870 was predominantly rural. There were only a few factories of small horsepower in some consumer-goods industries. Power spinning of cotton was established but did not predominate over hand spinning. Cotton weaving was generally done by hand, and the production of other textiles was not mechanized. In agriculture, the biological and organizational breakthroughs, which characterized the advanced countries at that time, had not become predominant in the average country. In the average country in 1850 to 1870, stockbreeding of animals and improved crop rotations were not in general practice. But there was some large-scale agriculture using substantial division of labor and improved crop rotations, and diversification of commercial crops was practiced in some regions. Over 60% of the population in the average country was illiterate. Net immigration accounted for substantially less than one-tenth of the population change plus net emigration.

Between 1850 and 1870 the average country in the sample was fairly dynamic even though the average annual growth rate of per capita income was only between $\frac{1}{2}$ and 1%. There was rapid industrialization involving mainly the introduction of factory production of consumer goods. A mixture of labor-saving and land-saving agricultural innovations were being initiated on large farms. The rate of growth of exports, starting from a small base, probably exceeded 4%. And in the average country, there was

TABLE 3.1

Combined Cross-Section, Time Series Regressions, 1850–1914[a]

Process	Constant	$\ln Y$	$\ln Y^2$	$\ln N$	$\ln N^2$	T_1	T_2	R^2	F ratio
Socioeconomic structure									
Percentage of labor force in agriculture	-89.22* (57.17)[b]	113.94 (23.98)	-19.75 (3.57)	-.92 (27.70)	1.09* (3.91)	-3.53* (3.72)	-4.22* (3.92)	.70	23.89
Level of technology in industry	-2.83* (57.02)	-64.40 (23.93)	12.75 (3.56)	41.42* (27.65)	-4.28* (3.90)	3.27* (3.70)	10.80 (3.91)	.69	23.00
Level of technology in agriculture	-235.66 (90.00)	1.57* (37.76)	3.48* (5.62)	125.47 (43.64)	-16.89 (6.16)	.48* (5.85)	10.45 (6.17)	.54	12.35
Urbanization	-77.62* (73.72)	-134.30 (30.92)	23.42 (4.60)	66.42 (35.75)	-8.87 (5.04)	2.30* (4.79)	8.36 (5.05)	.65	19.10
Capital stock and accumulation									
Development of inland transportation	-95.37* (97.18)	-71.61 (40.78)	14.47 (6.07)	90.97 (47.13)	-10.57* (6.65)	2.46* (6.32)	19.45 (6.67)	.57	14.05
Literacy	106.80* (88.45)	10.56 (3.71)	5.82 (.55)	-20.38* (42.89)	4.22 (.60)	.43* (5.75)	-5.43* (6.06)	.63	17.35
Immigration	408.85 (110.59)	-56.23 (23.39)	7.48 (2.90)	-138.12 (53.63)	17.58 (7.57)	0.82 (7.19)	3.00 (7.58)	.52	12.61
Dynamism									
Growth of GNP per capita	42.84* (129.80)	62.20* (54.45)	-7.68* (8.10)	-64.75* (62.94)	8.40* (8.89)	-6.83* (8.44)	12.06* (8.90)	.18	2.22
Growth of exports	41.99* (135.66)	-36.26* (56.91)	6.69* (8.47)	39.27* (65.79)	-6.11* (9.28)	-19.05 (8.82)	-6.36* (9.30)	.13	1.59
Change of export structure	-247.33 (103.30)	56.08* (43.34)	-5.39* (6.45)	74.75* (50.09)	-9.02* (7.07)	3.64* (6.72)	7.31* (7.08)	.34	5.39
Improvement of technology in industry	-35.84* (67.65)	-20.80* (28.38)	6.14* (4.22)	31.28* (32.80)	-2.68* (4.62)	1.49* (4.40)	5.95* (4.64)	.54	12.24
Improvement of technology in agriculture	-22.74* (81.17)	-24.82* (34.05)	6.60* (5.06)	31.39* (39.36)	-4.48* (5.55)	4.36* (5.28)	23.03 (5.57)	.56	13.60

[a] Statistically insignificant coefficients are asterisked; T_1 and T_2 are dummy variables for 1870 to 1890 and for 1890 to 1914, respectively.
[b] Figures in parentheses are standard errors.

a slight shift in the structure of exports from primary to processed primary and manufactured consumer goods. In the most advanced countries in the sample, railroads were becoming the predominant mode of internal transport.

By 1870 to 1890 the use of inanimate power in the industrial sector had spread to several consumer-goods industries, and cotton spinning had become predominantly mechanized in the average country in the sample. In agriculture, improved crop rotation and animal breeding had spread to smaller farms but were still limited to a few regions or a few crops. The use of machinery was starting to spread to a small proportion of large holdings. Urbanization had increased to between 10 and 20%. Adult illiteracy had fallen to about 50%. Immigration and the average rate of growth of per capita GNP remained at their earlier modest average levels. The rate of growth of exports had fallen from above 4 to between 2 and 4% but on a larger base. The shift in export structure was continuing. Industrialization was proceeding rapidly but still from a very narrow base. The major dynamic breakthroughs were in transport, with all the induced institutional, locational, and relative cost transformations. In most continental European countries, railroads linked towns and cities in all populated sections of the country, and the agricultural sector was served by a system of publicly maintained waterways and all-weather roads. The telegraph was being introduced in the most advanced countries.

By 1890 to 1914 there had been considerable progress in industrialization in the average country in the sample: both cotton spinning and weaving had become predominantly mechanized; factories existed in many consumer goods industries; and a few specialized machines were being produced. But industry was still less than 20% of GNP. Irrigation, improved crop rotation, and some use of natural fertilizer had become widespread. The rate of growth of per capital GNP had risen to between 1 and 2%. Average annual rates of industrial growth were very high, averaging over 5% from a narrow base. Factory production of consumer goods was becoming predominant in the average country. In agriculture, productivity improved significantly through mechanization of large holdings. The rate of growth of exports rose to above 4%. Exports were diversifying into intermediate goods. The period was thus characterized by considerable dynamism.

THE HISTORICAL TRANSITION PROCESS: ALL
COUNTRIES

To arrive at a picture of how these transformations were achieved, we now follow Chenery (1979) in imparting a dynamic interpretation to cross-

TABLE 3.2
Dimensions of the Transition, 1850–1914

Process	Mean score			Δ 1870 (column 2 minus column 1) (4)	Δ 1890 (column 3 minus column 2) (5)	Elasticity 1870–1890 @ Y = $250 (6)	Score at income[b]				Income[b] level at		
	1850–1870[a] (1)	1870–1890[a] (2)	1890–1914[a] (3)				$70 (7)	$200 (8)	$400 (9)	$800 (10)	One-quarter point (11)	One-half point (12)	Three-quarter point (13)
Socioeconomic structure													
Percentage of labor force in agriculture	71	61	55	−10	−6	−.63	76	64	46	24	275	365	550
Level of technology in industry	24	35	47	11	12	.92	13	31	51	68	220	300	550
Level of technology in agriculture	40	48	59	8	11	.52	20	51	67	79	130	200	350
Urbanization	24	36	48	12	12	1.32	20	28	56	83	275	300	550

Capital stock and accumulation										
Level of development of inland transport	22	13	21	1.05	10	31	55	75	220	300	550
Literacy	47	7	7	.81	18	52	72	87	140	230	400
Immigration	42	8	−4	.07	57	34	37	40	70	100	170
Dynamism										
Growth of GNP per capita	41	−4	19	.06	20	43	43	41	115	130	190
Growth of exports	59	−15	14	.35	37	43	52	59	220	300	550
Change of export structure	29	9	3	.33	9	42	50	53	100	150	230
Improvement of technology in industry	45	8	7	.47	29	60	66	78	170	275	400
Improvement of technology in agriculture	27	10	21	.66	15	35	50	62	200	215	480

a Computed.
b In 1960 U.S. dollars.

sectional results and in inferring the speed and timing of individual transformations from comparisons based on the combined cross-section time-
series regressions. There is no rigorous basis for these interpretations and
procedures. But since our aim here is to draw out comparisons between
contemporary and nineteenth-century economic development, the use of
a uniform method for both periods is essential.

In principle, various procedures can be used to infer probable time rates
and time sequences of change from combined cross-section time-series
regressions:

1. One can compute regression elasticities with respect to GNP at various levels of GNP. If one assumes an average growth rate for GNP,
   one can calculate the time scale for change implicit in the elasticities.
2. One can compare the relative levels of per capita GNP at which
   individual processes complete a given fraction of their ultimate
   transformation. This is the Chenery approach; conceptually it is a
   variant of procedure 1.
3. One can compare changes in appropriately normalized means over
   time.
4. One can use discretion and eschew the subject.

We follow Chenery (1979) in using procedures 1, 2, and 3. Procedures 1
and 3 indicate speed of change; procedure 2 can be used to infer lead–lag
relationships.

The change elasticities for 1870 to 1890 are in Table 3.2, column 6,
centered at levels of per capita GNP of about US$250 in 1960 prices (GNP
score of 50).[3] At this GNP level, the average country in the sample completed one-quarter of the transformation by an average country during the
second half of the nineteenth century and the first quarter of the twentieth
century.[4] The processes with the highest growth elasticities—which in a
sense were the processes that exhibited the most dynamism—were urbanization, transport, and industrial technology (see Landes, 1969;
Kuznets, 1957; and Hughes, 1970, for discussions that stress the overwhelming importance of these factors in nineteenth-century development).[5] Those with the lowest elasticities were immigration and the rate of
growth of per capita GNP; regressions for both suggest that they fluctuated around almost constant average levels. On the basis of careful comparisons of turning points, Thomas (1973) argued that in the nineteenth
century there were long swings in immigration that induced similar swings
in GNP growth rates with a lag.

The relative ranking of forces by their extent of dynamism obtained
from the elasticities is confirmed by a comparison of sample means for

1870 to 1890 with 1850 to 1870, and for 1890 to 1914 with 1870 to 1890 (see Table 3.1, columns 1–5). A comparison of changes over time in the means of our variables has meaning since, by our method of scoring, each variable is in essence standardized. For each process, the lowest value observed in the sample between 1850 and 1914 was assigned a score of zero, the highest a score of 100; variations in between were scored by reference to the gradations in the change of the process during the entire period.[6]

Between 1850 and 1870, and 1870 and 1890,[7] the largest increases in means occurred in transport, urbanization, and industrial technology, followed by reorientation in the structure of exports and by declines in the agricultural labor force. At the other extreme, the average rate of growth of GNP was slightly lower in the later period and the average rate of growth of exports was significantly lower than in the earlier period.

Comparison of 1870 to 1890 with 1890 to 1914 changes the ordering of the processes by their dynamism somewhat.[8] Transport still heads the list of dymanic forces. But the rate of improvement in agricultural technology appears to have accelerated to second position. The rates of growth of per capita GNP and of exports both accelerated. Immigration is the only process, other than agricultural employment and illiteracy, whose level declines.

The Timing.   Consider the levels of per capita GNP at which the various transformations are one-quarter, one-half, and three-quarters complete as indicating lead–lag relationships in the timing of structural change (Table 3.1, columns 11–13). The picture of the transformation process which emerges from our regressions is then the following:[9] the leading process during the early phase of the second half of the nineteenth century was net immigration,[10] which reached its quarter marker at a very much lower per capita income ($70 in 1960 prices) than the other processes. A change in the structure of exports toward manufacturing followed; it attained a quarter of its transformation at a per capita income of $100. Next came an increase in the rate of growth of per capita GNP, a higher level of agricultural technology, and a drop in illiteracy—all of which achieved a quarter of their total change at per capita incomes below $150.[11] Improvements in industrial and agricultural technology reached their quarter marks at per capita incomes below $200. A rise in industrial technology, achievements in inland transport, and an acceleration of exports came next—at per capita incomes of about $220, the average per capita income for a country in our sample in 1850 to 1870. Decreases in agricultural employment and urbanization came last, reaching their quarter marks at a per capita income of $275. Thus, a quarter of the ultimate economic transformation during the second half of the nineteenth century and first quarter of the twentieth century was completed in one generation by the average country in the sample.

Half the economic transformation in the average country growth patterns was completed at a per capita income of about $365. This implies a time scale of about two generations for a country with the average per capita income in the sample for 1850 to 1870 traveling at the average rate of growth for the period. Both the quarter and the half mark snapshots of the process of economic development reveal similar clusters of forces in similar relative positions.

Three-quarters of the transformation is complete at a per capita GNP of $550. Comparisons of GNP per capita at the half mark of each process with its level at the three-quarter mark indicate lower elasticities of change at the later phases of the transformation.[12]

Comparison of Historical with Contemporary Patterns

Before turning to a discussion of how the historical and the contemporary patterns compare, we summarize the major stylized features of the Chenery–Syrquin (1975) results for the post–World War II development patterns of developing countries. These will serve as a background for the comparison.

THE CONTEMPORARY PATTERN

If one follows Chenery (1979) in interpreting combined cross-section and time-series regressions as portraying the dynamics of the transition in an average developing country, the story that emerges from the Chenery–Syrquin (1975) regressions is the following. The earliest phase in the transition process, at per capita incomes of about $200 (in 1964 prices), involves a substantial rise in exports, mostly of primary exports, accompanied by a gradual but steady shift in their structure toward manufacturing exports. The expansion and transformation in exports are accompanied by a substantial increase in investment in human and physical capital (in that order) and by a sharp drop in the share of primary production in total output, all of which occur in the early phases of the transition.

Next come shifts in the composition of consumption—from food to nonfood—which generate increases in demand for manufactured consumer goods. The share of manufacturing in total domestic output rises, reaching the midpoint of its eventual value at a per capita income of $300. But the shift of labor from primary production lags substantially behind the transformation in the structure of production, and the relative productivity of labor in agriculture declines to about half that in manufacturing. Partly as a result of the ensuing dualistic character of growth, the distribution of income worsens as well. When countries reach per capita incomes of $800, the transition is complete in most respects: manufactured exports are about equal in value to primary exports, industrial output is about three times primary output, industrial employment is about the same as primary employment, relative productivities have almost converged, and the distribution of income has started to recover.

HISTORICAL COMPARISON

By comparison with the contemporary pattern, the transformation of the *average*[13] country in the historical sample appears to have started at lower levels of per capita GNP. But its subsequent turning points are spaced at similar levels of GNP, implying a lengthier transition. In addition, the historical sequence that emerges from the regressions assigns a greater role to human capital, agriculture, technology, and transport in the nineteenth-century transformation than does the contemporary analysis.

International migration appears to have led other phases of the transformation in the second half of the nineteenth century even when lags in some variables are taken into account.[14] It reached its halfway mark at a much lower income than did the other processes (Table 3.1, column 12), a finding consistent with the contention of Thomas (1973) that international migration played an initiating role in the long swings in economic activity that characterized the economies of the Atlantic community during that period. This contrasts with the contemporary developing country story that assigns to exports the initiating role. In Thomas's theory, Malthusian pressures, coupled with labor-saving innovations in agriculture, generated a push toward emigration in parts of the Old World.[15] The pull was the wage difference.

Immigration provided an inducement to increase infrastructure investment in railways, roads, ports, land clearing, and houses. By lowering the cost of transport and unifying the internal market, the infrastructure investment increased the international competitiveness of exports (i.e., lowered the factorial terms of trade). An increase in exports followed with a lag due to the long gestation period of infrastructure investment. The

Thomas sequence appears to be consistent with the regression results for 1850 to 1914, in which immigration led changes in transport and in the rate of growth of exports (Table 3.1, columns 11–13). But there appear to have been other intervening variables not brought out by Thomas.

In particular, just as in the Chenery–Syrquin (1975) results for contemporary developing countries, a change in the structure of exports toward a greater share of manufactured exports seems to have occurred at a very early phase in the transition for the average country (Table 3.1, column 11).

In addition, our results suggest that historically productive agriculture seems to have been a prerequisite for the increases in exports. (The agricultural variables, representing levels and improvements in agricultural technology, reach their benchmark levels early in the transition.) This latter feature of nineteenth-century development is consistent with the writings of most historians. For example, Jones (1967) stresses the significant economic role of the major biological and organizational innovations in agriculture in seventeenth- and eighteenth-century England, innovations that spread to Europe in the later eighteenth century, and were of sufficient scope to be characterized as an agricultural revolution.

These breakthroughs in agricultural productivity provided the agricultural surpluses to feed the urban agglomerations that manned the factory system of the industrial revolution. The increases in rural incomes attendant on the spread of scientific crop rotations and enclosures, which occurred despite falling grain prices in the later nineteenth century, helped generate the demand for urban manufactures. And as the labor-intensive agricultural revolution in mixed farming was gradually replaced by selective mechanization in the advanced countries during the latter part of the period, agricultural labor was released for urban expansion. Both historically and contemporarily, the release of labor from agriculture lagged behind the other transformation processes. In today's underdeveloped countries this lag implies lower agricultural productivity, but in the average country in the historical sample it implied a substantial increase in agricultural production.

Our results suggest that the agricultural revolution interacted with the transport revolution in a positive feedback loop. During the early phases of the agricultural revolution, some transport investments—e.g., the canals of eighteenth-century England—were financed, in part, from the agricultural surplus. The later phases of the agricultural revolution, in turn, received a strong impetus from railroads and steamships, which made national and international markets for agricultural commodities feasible by lowering the cost of bulk transport and increasing the speed of long-distance cartage. Transport thus made possible the creation of the Atlantic community and accelerated Great Britain's specialization in manufacturing while drawing on the land resources of the rest of the world. So important was this process that Marshall (1920, pp. 674–675) assigned to the transport revolution a primary role in the Industrial Revolution and a secondary role to the development of manufacturing.

The transport revolution consisted of a combination of technological innovations in iron rails and mobile steam engines (Hawke and Higgins, 1981, p. 235). The impact of technology is reflected not only in the technology and productivity variables but in transport as well. Not surprisingly, Landes (1969) views the Industrial Revolution as consisting of an interrelated complex of technological change whose culmination was the transformation from an agrarian economy to one dominated by industry and machine power. Our results confirm the importance of technological change as a prime mover in the nineteenth-century transformation: the variable representing improvements in industrial technology is a leading variable.

In general, the changes in technology needed to make the application of the new technology productive were clusters of inventions rather than single innovations. Sometimes the lags between the first invention and its follow-up were substantial. In Great Britain, for example, the lag between the invention of the first steam engine and its final forms was as long as 40 years (Landes, 1969). This lag is reflected in our results: the variable representing the *level* of development of industrial technology reaches its benchmark points relatively late (Table 3.1, columns 11–13).

The implementation of the new technologies required institutional change and the transformation of production systems (Hughes, 1970; Landes, 1969). The new technologies were the first to engender substantial economies of scale that required the agglomeration of the work force in large-scale mills, factories, and industrial towns. The urbanization variable, whose turning points are almost concurrent with those of the level of industrial technology, confirms this point. In addition, the new technologies implied major changes in industrial organization, in financial markets, and in property rights. Combined, these changes remade industrial and production relations and (eventually) transformed the basis and structure of political systems. Omitted from this study, these institutional facets of economic growth form the core of our larger study (Morris and Adelman, in press).

The improvements in productivity, achieved by the technological revolution, were phenomenal. Landes (1969, p. 4) cites factors of 1000 to 1 in spinning and energy and 100 to 1 in weaving, iron smelting, and shoe production. Furthermore, by contrast with most developing countries, the innovations started a dynamic process in which innovation induced innovation rather than culminate in a once-and-for-all change.

The diffusion of technology from Great Britain to continental Europe in the early part of the Industrial Revolution was slow and uneven. Its spread depended on the political and institutional readiness of each country and on its sociocultural attitudes (Landes, 1969, pp. 124–230). On the average, it took about 50 years (Landes, 1969). It was slow because the export of technology from Great Britain was illegal and occurred mainly through international migration of workers and entrepreneurs (Hughes, 1970, pp. 73–75).

Thus, migration, technological change, and institutional development interacted to spread the Industrial Revolution. This pattern contrasts strongly with the process in developing countries, in which exports are the prime mover; technological change plays a limited role and consists mostly of technology transfer rather than absorption, adaptation, and innovation; and institutional development is at best uneven and dualistic.

Typologies of Industrialization

Srinivasan is reputed to have said of the Chenery–Syrquin (1975) regressions that "the average pattern is the country's Karma, and the deviations are the country's policy." We now turn to a discussion of the more specific patterns resulting from the interaction of differing policies with differing initial conditions and with constraints not responsive to policy.

The Chenery–Syrquin (1975) typologies by country size and trade strategies do not seem to have great force in the historical context. Instead, we construct typologies based on the dynamics of the countries' industrialization patterns. The historical validity of these typologies was confirmed by the statistical analyses summarized in Adelman and Morris (1980).

We distinguish four patterns of industrialization and analyze their deviations from the typical pattern:

1. Early substantial industrialization through fairly autonomous growth of market systems.
2. Later substantial industrialization promoted by national government intervention.
3. Later modest industrialization in response to primary export expansion of fairly land-abundant countries.
4. Negligible industrialization in export-oriented densely populated peasant economies.

We have not run separate regressions for each typology because, for some subgroups, the number of degrees of freedom would have been small. Instead, we study the pattern of deviations of each country from the all-country regressions and base our discussion of group patterns in the following sections on the group and country deviations. The description of each group is based on its average scores for the characteristics discussed and is supplemented by the underlying information used to classify the countries.

GROUP 1: EARLY SUBSTANTIAL INDUSTRIALIZATION THROUGH FAIRLY AUTONOMOUS GROWTH OF MARKET SYSTEMS

The early substantial industrializers (Great Britain. Belgium. France, Switzerland, and the United States) began their industrialization early in the nineteenth century, favored by socioeconomic and political institutions conducive to the growth of markets, internal mobility, capital accumulation, and investment. Their take-offs, where identifiable, occurred before 1850. They underwent widespread industrialization and, by the early twentieth century, became major producers and exporters of diverse manufactured goods, including machinery.

In this group, institutional restrictions on factor and commodity markets were, in general, modest for the time; and agricultural reorganization, including the distribution of common lands and rearrangements of fields, was well under way. Commercial capital and entrepreneurial skills had accumulated during the eighteenth century, substantial population growth had enlarged the labor force, and the use of land for profit had become common. The government played a modest direct role in their industrialization. Indirectly, governments were important—aiding transportation, regulating capital markets, setting tariff policies, and establishing political frameworks that permitted the growth of markets.

This group performed consistently above average in most aspects of growth and change after 1850. On the average,[16] rapid industrialization was associated with more rapid growth in per capita income.[17] More extensive and more rapid mechanization in industry[18] interacted with better agricultural technology and more rapid improvement in agricultural productivity[19]—with greater investment in transport networks[20] and in human resources[21]—to generate higher than average rates of economic growth and more rapid structural transformation of the economy out of agriculture.[22] But during 1890 to 1914, there is evidence of regression toward the mean in all processes. Although generally still ahead of the average pattern, the early industrializers were much less so during 1890 to

1914 than during 1850 to 1870. Indeed, by then their rates of growth of per capita GNP[23] and the rates of growth of exports[24] were on the average below the regression average. The roles of international trade in stimulating growth varied. Most of the countries in this group followed an export-led strategy, although in the larger countries domestic markets accounted for a significant share of demand, and the relative timing of industrialization and trade expansion varied. Export diversification was less rapid than average in Great Britain, France, and Belgium, and more rapid than average in Switzerland and the United States.

The timing, structure, and path of industrialization varied considerably. Great Britain, the earliest industrializer, had few tariffs and the least government aid and maintained its industrial leadership only into the last quarter of the nineteenth century. France underwent industrial change early but gradually; the lack of mineral resources, a more direct role by the government at times, and high tariffs marked a more agrarian development pattern and a somewhat slower growth of manufacturing. Belgium alternated spurts of industrialization and economic stagnation until strong international markets for industrial goods helped overcome the constraints of a small internal market. In Switzerland, textiles were mechanized early despite the lack of iron, coal, and internal markets; the industrial sector proved adaptable in developing specialized skill-intensive exports. In the United States, mechanization also began early, and the major exports were still primary goods. But by 1870, the United States had become a major industrial power exporting a wide range of industrial products.

GROUP 2: LATER SUBSTANTIAL INDUSTRIALIZATION
PROMOTED BY NATIONAL GOVERNMENTS

The second group of countries—Germany, Italy, Japan, and Russia—used government intervention to overcome less-favorable initial conditions by removing market restrictions and promoting industry in the face of the challenge of the early industrializers. Although these countries were at least moderately backward in 1815, they later experienced major surges of industrial development. But their paths of industrialization were considerably more dualistic than those of the early industrializers, and only Germany became a leading exporter of manufactures by 1914.

This group of countries is more analogous to the current-day developing countries than is the first group for several reasons. Like most developing countries, it had unfavorable initial conditions to contend with: institutions were not designed to allow maximum scope for the operation of market incentives and for the internal mobilization of factors of production, especially capital. When ready to enter international markets for industrial exports, this group had to face stiff competition from the first industrializers. But like today's newly industrialized nations, starting in 1850 its rates of economic growth and export growth rose above those for the first industrializers.

Legal and political constraints on the movement of factors and commodities were much greater in these countries in the early nineteenth century than for the early industrializers. Restrictions on labor migration and remnants of servitude persisted in most of them until at least the third quarter of the century. National unification was not effective, nor did parliamentary systems consistently favorable to business and commercial interests evolve before the last few decades of the nineteenth century.

Government drives toward industrialization were a characteristic of the countries in this group. Only in Italy were government efforts to promote particular industries possibly unfavorable to general industrial expansion. Foreign capital inflows were, on occasion, significant but nowhere did foreign influences predominate. In general, the path of industrialization in this group was uneven and dualistic during the later nineteenth century. The larger-scale technologies available in the last decades of the century and the government policies of attracting skills and capital to selected sectors of national importance increased the contrasts between advanced and backward sectors. And severe international competition in the last quarter of the nineteenth century raised the capital requirements of industrial expansion, spurring government intervention to promote selective industrial advances.

The study of the deviations from the regression for this group of countries stresses the key role that governments can play in promoting economic growth and structural change by removing rural institutional restrictions on market growth and by directly promoting industrialization. Major efforts by governments to overcome the unfavorable initial conditions posed by traditional land systems, the underdevelopment of capitalist enterprise, political constraints, and transport networks were undertaken between 1870 and 1890.[25] During this major restructuring period, Russia and Italy (but not Germany or Japan) performed below the all-country average in all respects except the movement of population out of agriculture.[26] On the average, about two decades of major political, institutional, and investment efforts by governments paid off later: in economic growth, export growth, and improvements in industrial technology and agricultural productivity. By 1890 the countries in this group were, on the average, substantially surpassing the early industrializers in their rates of change, though having started from a narrow base.

The average masks substantial intercountry differences in the timing and success of industrialization. Germany, the least backward at midcentury, made great strides toward economic unification and started its industrial expansion before national unification in 1871; it then industrialized at a spectacular rate to become a world power by 1914. In Japan, institutional reforms and government promotion of development starting in the 1870s led, with a lag, to a major spurt of industrialization that transformed only selected sectors before 1914. In Russia and Italy, economic stagnation, erratic growth, and severe setbacks were interspersed with periods of sustained industrial advances starting in the 1880s.

GROUP 3: LATER MODEST INDUSTRIALIZATION IN
RESPONSE TO PRIMARY EXPORT EXPANSION OF
FAIRLY LAND-ABUNDANT COUNTRIES

In the third group of countries, a surge of primary-export expansion in the last quarter of the nineteenth century eventually led to the growth of domestic markets and modest industrial development. The class includes three Scandinavian countries (Norway, Sweden. and Denmark); three colonies settled by the British (Canada, Australia. and New Zealand); and Argentina and Brazil. Until 1850, their economies were characterized either by considerable local self-sufficiency or, if newly settled, by dependence on imports. Lack of transportation was the critical barrier to domestic market expansion.[27] Institutional restrictions on commodity markets were few, but restrictions on labor markets remained in 1850—feudal remnants in Scandinavia, convict labor in Australia, and slavery in Brazil. After railroads led to major transport breakthroughs in the 1870s or 1880s,[28] domestic farming and primary export production accelerated. Import substitution proceeded slowly because of a lack of domestic markets and critical inputs. With favorable export markets late in the century and the consequent acceleration of exports, rates of growth of per capita GNP became high in almost all these countries; only Australia experienced high growth rates as early as the 1870s and 1880s.

The pace and structure of industrialization varied in response to, among other influences, natural resource constraints, ocean and domestic transport, the distribution of export proceeds, and the progress in the farming sector. On the average, the interaction of land settlement or internal migration and commercialization with pastoral and agricultural production for the export market proceeded more rapidly where political conditions were reasonably secure, freehold tenure predominated, and major institutional impediments to the development of labor markets had been removed. As exports to Europe expanded, domestic processing increased and formed the nucleus of small manufacturing sectors: iron (Sweden); wool (Australia, Argentina, and New Zealand); wheat (Argentina and, later, Canada); dairy products (Denmark and, later, New Zealand); meat (Australia, Argentina, and New Zealand); and coffee (Brazil). The stimulus to domestic markets varied with the character of export proceeds and the size of population. Populations were mostly small, usually not over 5 million until the last quarter of the century, if then. Only Brazil had a larger population, but poverty constrained market size. Large-scale immigration marked land settlement in Australia, New Zealand, Argentina, and later Canada; by contrast, emigration from Scandinavia increased land availability there. Where export proceeds were widely distributed (Denmark, Sweden, Canada, and, later, Australia), export expansion favored domestic manufactures more; where proceeds were concentrated, as in Brazil and Argentina, it contributed less. The expansion of domestic farming for urban areas contributed to wider distribution of proceeds and thus to the growth of domestic industry in Scandinavia and, ultimately, in the British colonies.

Industrialization in this class was modest in 1914. Only in Sweden was it somewhat greater because of iron manufactures based on the domestic mining sector. Industrial technology was above that for their income and population in Brazil, Sweden, Denmark, and New Zealand. It was and remained substantially below the regression average in Norway, Canada, Australia, and Argentina. Consumer goods were produced where international competition was less effective. Domestic production of intermediate goods was mainly limited to machinery for the export sector, except in Sweden, with some beginnings of production of textile and agricultural machinery.

The African countries today are, by and large, attempting to follow the development strategies of this third group of countries. Like this group of countries, they are not constrained by land scarcity; they have small populations; they no longer have major institutional constraints on land, labor, and commodity markets; they have very limited internal transport and human resources; and they are using expatriates to initiate the industrialization process. And like them, they are relying on primary exports to provide the surplus and foreign exchange for a modest industrialization effort centering on the import substitution of consumer goods. As in some countries in this group in the third quarter of the century (Brazil, Argentina, and New Zealand), major political conflicts have impeded their economic expansion. Success to date has been modest and limited to enclaves.

Latin America, under the influence of the examples of Brazil and Argentina and the Economic Commission for Latin America, used this development model during the 1950s and 1960s with the aid of heavy tariffs and carried import substitution beyond the modest levels of the African countries. During the 1970s, it started switching from the Group 3 development model to the industrial export-oriented model of the countries in Group 2.

GROUP 4: NEGLIGIBLE INDUSTRIALIZATION IN
EXPORT-ORIENTED, DENSELY POPULATED PEASANT
ECONOMIES

Group 4 consists of four peasant economies in which little modern industrial growth took place before 1914—Burma, China, Egypt, and India. Mechanized production using inanimate power was restricted largely to some processing of primary products for export. Local mechanized industry was limited to producing some foods, beverages, and building materials.

The failure of domestic markets to develop in these countries was associated with the poverty of their peasants, the backwardness of their agriculture, and the course of colonial exploitation, among other influences. Foreign capital flowed into cotton in Egypt; rice in Burma; cotton, rice, and jute in India; and silk in China. But cash-cropping for export generated little income above subsistence for the average cultivator. In the three British colonies, traditional handicraft industries declined under the impact of free trade and the decline of indigenous luxury demand. In China, where foreign dominance extended little beyond the treaty ports, the expansion of domestic handicrafts persisted into the twentieth century.

In 1850 subsistence production predominated in this group of countries. Except in Burma, the ratio of population to land was sufficiently unfavorable to be a major cause of poverty. In many areas, farms had become too small to support a family. The introduction of Western legal conditions for sale and mortgaging of land contributed to the rapid spread of commercialization and production for export. Indebtedness also increased greatly, with the consequent transfer of much land to nonagriculturalists. In all four countries domestic savings went into land and traditional valuables, domestic entrepreneurship was mainly in trading, agriculture used primitive tools, and political systems were autocratic or unstable.

This group of countries resembled the Group 3 countries in that the main force for economic change was export expansion. But they differed in the (extremely small) linkages between export expansion and the growth of domestic market systems. The limited impact of foreign capital inflows was associated with a relatively small inflow of settlers so that the consumption linkages flowing from export expansion were almost absent.

The comparison of deviations from the regressions indicates a narrow range of variation around a low average level of achievement. Even allowing for the low per capita GNPs, this group of countries was predominantly below the regression line in the development of agricultural and industrial technology and of transport (except Egypt, because of the Nile); the group had slower GNP growth and slower growth in exports (except India to 1890); and exports remained primary despite a more diversified export structure than was consistent with the GNP per capita before 1870.

This is the classic profile of Asian underdevelopment. In a class defined by foreign-stimulated export expansion, unfavorable land–population ratios, and a negligible spread of mechanization, none of the economic changes summarized by the variables led systematically to either significant industrial advances or agricultural development. The conditions perpetuating their predominantly traditional agricultural structures were land institutions, resource constraints, the absence of domestic demand linkages, and demographic characteristics.

Conclusions

The historical process reveals a diversity in patterns and outcomes similar to the contemporary process. But, just as with the contemporary process, the Chenery (1979) method appears to offer a powerful tool for portraying the average historical pattern and for describing the typologies of the major alternative patterns of economic growth. Theory, and a knowledge of the economic histories of individual countries, can then be used to analyze, interpret, and qualify the results.

The average per capita income in 1850 of the countries that achieved substantial degrees of industrialization by 1914 (Group 1 and Germany) was substantially above that of the average middle-income developing country in 1957 in the Chenery–Syrquin sample: $360 compared with $286. Indeed, it was above that of all but the three top-income middle-income countries (Israel, Venezuela, and Argentina). The institutional development of these countries in 1870 was much superior to that of the average middle-income country in the 1950s. Despite this, the pace of economic growth of the successful industrializers was quite slow by contemporary developing-country standards.[29]

The nineteenth-century pattern of economic growth of the successful industrializers was more balanced than that of the average developing country: agricultural technology and productivity improved before or with industrial technology and productivity. Industrialization after 1850 was not accompanied by major spurts in population growth. On the contrary, migration helped balance the distribution of population and resources internationally.

Then, as now, the most successful industrializers shifted to a manufacturing export-oriented development strategy early in their development process. But migration, international capital flows, and technological dynamism played a more significant role during the Industrial Revolution than they have in even the newly industrializing countries. Then, as now, the result was a marked change in international comparative advantage—a change that required major adaptations in trade and capital flows as well as in trade regimes and payments systems.

Appendix A: Summary Definitions of Classificatory Indicators

The following paragraphs give a general idea of the character of the classification scheme used in the analyses. Only leading traits of the schemes and a few key sources of comparative information are indicated. They will be presented in detail with the sources on which they are based in Morris and Adelman (in press).

Per Capita GNP. The difficulties in comparing per capita income figures across countries are multiplied when incommensurabilities of the magnitude involved in contrasting the nineteenth century with the present are involved. Fortunately, Bairoch (1976) and Maddison (1979) have attempted the improbable for most of the OECD countries, and other references could be found for the other countries in the sample. Our classification is based on indices of per capita income relative to that of Great Britain in 1890. To reduce spurious accuracy and increase validity, scores are assigned to income ranges rather than to point estimates.

Population. The 69 observations are grouped in seven classes by the size of their total population. Since population data in the nineteenth century were generally poor, margins of error were assumed to be large and the point estimates were categorized in population classes with wide ranges.

LEVEL OF TECHNOLOGY IN INDUSTRY: 1850, 1870, AND 1890

The indicator classifies countries in seven categories by the use of several criteria for judging mechanization of the factory sector. The principal criteria used were the degree of mechanization of textile production, the range of consumer goods produced mainly in factories, the extent of factory production of machinery, and the overall weight of factory employment. The top three categories differentiate among countries in which both cotton spinning and weaving were largely mechanized; the middle category included countries where in 1850 it was mainly cotton spinning that was fully mechanized, together with those that in 1870 or 1890 had a few factories in many industries. The bottom three categories were for countries where hand methods prevailed.

IMPROVEMENT OF TECHNOLOGY IN INDUSTRY: 1850–1869, 1870–1889, AND 1890–1914

This classification groups the observations in seven categories by the breadth and pace of the expansion and increased mechanization of their factory sectors. The top two categories distinguish among countries where industrialization was widespread. The next two categories include countries where a major spurt of industrialization occurred from a limited base. Next down the line were countries where industrial expansion affected mainly processing of natural products for internal or foreign markets. In the bottom categories were cases where expansion was mainly in hand manufactures or where the growth of industry was negligible.

LEVEL OF TECHNOLOGY IN AGRICULTURE: 1850, 1870, AND 1890

This classification is based on four types of agricultural improvements: the use of animal-driven iron or steel machinery in crop production; the use of enclosures, stock breeding, and supplementary feeding in animal farming; the use of improved crop rotations, irrigation systems, and fertilizer; and the development in individual enterprises of mixed crop and animal farming. Rough weights for different types of improvements are provided according to their likely impact on output per person. The observations are grouped in seven categories: in the top two, machinery use was widespread; in the third, little machinery was used but improved crop rotations and natural fertilizers were widespread; in the fourth and fifth, improvements were either in limited regions or in a narrow range of crops; and in the lowest two categories were countries with few improvements.

IMPROVEMENTS IN AGRICULTURAL PRODUCTIVITY:
1850–1869, 1870–1889, AND 1890–1914

This classification is based on the same four types of improvements considered in the indicator of levels of agricultural productivity and uses the same types of weights. Two categories of widespread improvements are differentiated with the highest marked by a widespread increase in the use of machinery; the third category involves use of machinery on large farms only; the fourth entails improved rotations and drainage on large farms only; the fifth includes fairly widespread and varied small improvements; and in the bottom two there were only minimal improvements.

LEVEL OF DEVELOPMENT OF INLAND TRANSPORT:
1850, 1870, AND 1890

This indicator classifies observations in four categories by the extent and effectiveness of the transportation system, including railways, waterways, and roads. At the top of the spectrum are countries where large cities and towns were linked by railways, waterways, or all-weather roads and where the agricultural sector was served by a system of feeder roads. In the two middle categories, railways and first-class waterways existed only between major cities and in major populated regions. At the lower end of the spectrum were cases where important populated regions were not served by railways or first-class waterways and transportation by pack animals on dirt roads was widespread.

GROWTH RATE OF GNP PER CAPITA: 1850–1869,
1870–1889, AND 1890–1914

The observations are grouped in only four categories with the break points between them selected to minimize variations based on different measurement procedures. The small number of categories made possible the assignment of countries lacking national income data on the basis of similarities of economic structure and information on rates of change in particular sectors. The top category includes countries for which national income rose by an average annual rate of over 2%. The second category includes countries where annual average rates of growth were probably between 1 and 2%. The third category includes all other countries for which varied statistical or qualitative information in country studies indicated a likelihood that rates of growth were positive but not substantial. The lowest category was reserved for countries where similar information suggested that rates of growth were negligible, with a minus for cases where per capita income appears to have declined.

URBANIZATION: 1850, 1870, AND 1890

This classification groups observations in four categories by the percentage of the population living in towns having more than 10,000 inhabitants.

ILLITERACY: 1850, 1870, AND 1890

The observations are grouped in 10 categories by the extent of adult illiteracy. Although point estimates were available for many countries, we grouped them because of the variation in the concept of *illiteracy* and because it facilitated the assignment of countries for which illiteracy had to be inferred from past school enrollment data of doubtful quality.

IMMIGRATION: 1850–1869, 1870–1889, AND 1890–1914

This indicator classifies countries in six categories: major net immigration probably equivalent to at least one-third of the population increase; moderate net immigration probably between one-tenth and one-third of the population increase; net immigration clearly positive but probably less than one-tenth of the population increase; net emigration positive but probably less than one-tenth of the sum of population increase plus net emigration; major net emigration probably increase plus net emigration; and major net emigration probably more than one-third of the sum of the population increase plus net emigration.

PERCENTAGE OF LABOR FORCE IN AGRICULTURE: 1850,
1870, AND 1890

The classification scheme groups the 69 observations in seven categories. Estimates of the percentage of the population in agriculture were adjusted in some cases to bring them closer to estimates of the labor force in agriculture. Since almost all estimates (particularly for the earlier period) were affected by the lack of a clear dividing line between industry and agriculture, the data were grouped. Breakpoints between categories were selected to minimize variations arising from doubtful data.

Notes

[1] We recognize the deficiencies of per capita income as a proxy for economic growth because of its failure to take account of distributional composition and structural change, among other things.

[2] The "average" country characteristics are estimated from means for a sample that includes both relatively advanced and very underdeveloped countries; the means are based on classificatory indicators that group data in intervals.

[3] The correspondence between our income scores and the per capita income figures in the text and tables is only approximate. Since our scores represent income ranges, the per capita income estimates in Maddison (1979, p. 425) for countries with scores corresponding to the desired score were averaged and converted from 1970 prices to 1960 prices to arrive at the correspondence.

[4] The numbers in Table 3.2 are approximations since the data for all dependent variables are categorized and an arbitrary linear scoring scheme that preserves ranks was applied.

[5] The elasticities for the transport and urbanization variables are between 1850 and 1870, since these variables were measured at the beginning year of each period. The other variables are averages over two decades, 1850–1869 and 1870–1890.

[6] Since our data are ordinal, the comparisons of changes over time pose the same measurement problems as do such comparisons with conventional ordinal economic indices.

[7] While the comparisons for dynamic variables here refer to 1870 to 1890 compared with 1850 to 1870, the comparisons for "level" variables are for 1870 compared with 1850.

[8] Here, the level variables refer to 1870 and 1890.

[9] The following generalizations represent a considerable abstraction from the diversity of country experience: for example, whereas the average pattern shows net immigration reaching its quarter mark at a relatively lower per capita income than other processes, some countries were characterized by emigration throughout the century.

[10] The notion of average is particularly difficult for this variable since some countries were consistently characterized by emigration while others were characterized by immigration.

[11] A rise of $50 in per capita income was achieved in about two decades by an average country moving at the average rate of growth in 1850 to 1870.

[12] The elasticities that are not lower are constant.

[13] The average is over all countries in the sample and includes those where GNP grew without raising per capita incomes. The average GNP per capita in 1850 for countries that were industrialized by 1914 was considerably above the 1950 developing-country average.

[14] The transport and urbanization variables are for the beginning year of the period; net immigration is an average over a 20-year period. In effect, the transport and urbanization variables are lagged by 10 years. For an average nineteenth-century country whose per capita GNP is growing at the average rate, 10 years' change in per capita GNP would correspond to $25. The difference between the per capita GNP corresponding to one quarter of the transformation for net immigration and transport is $150 per capita(!).

[15] The timing varied among countries depending on when their population cycles peaked. Our time periods overlap Thomas's cycle peaks and troughs, but when his data are plotted against our dates, the same lead–lag relationships emerge.

[16] There are exceptions to all the generalizations that follow. To make the text less cumbersome, these are put in footnotes; and if an aspect of growth is not discussed in the average pattern for the particular group, the reason is that the diversity of country experiences makes the average meaningless. This procedure is followed in the rest of the chapter.

[17] The exceptions are Switzerland thoughout the whole period and Great Britain between 1890 and 1914.

[18] Great Britain from 1870 to 1914 is an exception.

[19] Exceptions are Great Britain after 1870 and France and Switzerland between 1890 and 1914.

[20] Switzerland is an exception.

[21] Belgium is a consistent exception.

[22] Employment in agriculture declined less rapidly than the average in the United States and Switzerland.

[23] The United States is a notable exception.

[24] The exceptions are the United States and Belgium.

[25] Earlier in Germany.

[26] The exceptions are Russia, for the level of industrial technology and immigration, and Italy, for the diversification of exports.

[27] New Zealand is the only exception.

[28] The spurt in railroads still left the countries below average in transport development for their per capita GNP and population.

[29] The average annual rate of growth of per capita GNP was 2.6% for OECD countries during 1870 to 1914 and 1.5% for Groups 1 and 2 during 1870 to 1976 (Maddison, 1979). The average rate of growth of current developing countries during 1950 to 1980 has been over 5%.

References

Adelman, I., and C. T. Morris (1980). "Patterns of Industrialization in the Nineteenth and Early Twentieth Centuries: A Cross-Sectional Quantitative Study." In *Research in Economic History* (vol. 5, pp. 1–83). P. Uselding (ed.). Greenwich, CT: JAI Press.

Bairoch, P. (1976). "Europe's Gross National Products: 1800–1975." *Journal of European Economic History*, vol. 5, pp. 273–340.

Chenery, H. (1979). *Structural Change and Development Policy*. London: Oxford University Press.

Chenery, H., and M. Syrquin (1975). *Patterns of Development, 1950–1970*. London: Oxford University Press.

Gerschenkron, A. (1962). *Economic Backwardness in Historical Perspective*. Cambridge: Harvard University Press.

Hawke, G. R., and J. P. P. Higgins (1981). "Transport and Social Overhead Capital." In *The Economic History of Britain Since 1700* (vol. 1, pp. 227–252). R. Floud and D. McCloskey (eds.). Cambridge: Cambridge University Press.

Hughes, J. R. T. (1970). *Industrialization and Economic Growth*. New York: McGraw-Hill.

Jones, E. L. (1967). *Agriculture and Economic Growth in England: 1650–1815*. London: Methuen.

Kuznets, S. (1957). "Quantitative Aspects of the Economic Growth of Nations." *Economic Development and Cultural Change* 6, Supplement.

Landes, D. S. (1969). *The Unbound Prometheus: Technological Change and Industrial Development in Western Europe from 1750 to Present.* London: Cambridge University Press.

Maddison, A. (1979). "Per Capita Output in the Long Run." *Kyklos* 32, pp. 412–429.

Marshall, A. (1920). *Principles of Economics.* London: Macmillan.

Morris, C. T. and I. Adelman (in press). *Where Angels Fear to Tread.* Stanford: Stanford University Press.

Polanyi, K. (1957). *The Great Transformation.* Boston: Beacon Press.

Thomas, B. (1973). *Migration and Economic Growth.* London: Cambridge University Press.

PART II

POVERTY AND INCOME DISTRIBUTION

A REASSESSMENT OF DEVELOPMENT ECONOMICS

Development Economics—A Reassessment of Goals

By Irma Adelman*

The theme of this paper is the need to be more specific on the goals of economic development and the interdependence between values and goals. This theme is not original; Gunnar Myrdal has argued for many years the importance of values in determining the orientation of development economics. Implicitly, by concentrating on growth, development economists have assumed that other goals, such as greater equity, need not be considered because they are positively correlated with growth. There has been some discontent with this view, but convincing scientific evidence refuting it has not become available until recently. Given that the relationships among the goals of distribution, welfare, and development are by no means simple, it is clearly necessary to examine the purposes of development and to state explicitly the value premises underlying the basic goals. In this paper I shall first review some recent work which bears on these relationships. I shall then propose a minimum humanistic goal for development and, finally, shall suggest development strategies that may permit achievement of that goal.

I. The Evidence

In this section I shall draw primarily on two recent efforts: my latest book with

* Professor of economics, University of Maryland. With the usual disclaimer of their responsibility, I am indebted to F. L. Adelman, J. L. Joy, C. Taft Morris, S. Robinson, and P. P. Streeten for their most helpful comments.

Cynthia Taft Morris and the results of comparative statics experiments performed with a detailed, instrument-specific, general equilibrium model of the South Korean economy, constructed by Sherman Robinson and me.

A. A Review of the Adelman-Morris Findings

Using 1950–63 cross-section data for forty-three underdeveloped countries, Adelman and Morris studied the relationships between the shares of income accruing to the poorest 60 percent of households on the one hand and various broad aspects of a nation's economic, social, and political performance on the other. We found that for the longest part of the development process—corresponding to the transition from the state of development of sub-Saharan Africa to that of the least developed Latin American countries—the primary impact of economic development on income distribution is, on the average, to decrease both the absolute and the relative incomes of the poor. Not only is there no automatic trickle-down of the benefits of development; on the contrary, the development process leads typically to a trickle-up in favor of the middle classes and the rich. The absolute incomes of the poor begin to rise with development only when the nation moves well into the "intermediate" level of development. Further, even here improvement is not automatic: "the poorest segments of the population typically benefit from economic growth only when the government plays an important economic role and when widespread efforts are made to improve the human resource base ... " (Adelman-Morris, p. 181).

These results imply that, for a lengthy portion of the process of economic development, there is a conflict between the growth of overall national income and an increase in the welfare of the poor. Equally important, there is an analogous conflict with respect to policy instruments for systematic intervention.

It follows then that, in the formulation of development planning models and development policy, it is necessary to decide in advance the extent to which increases in the welfare of the poor are to be weighed against simple growth of *GNP*. In addition, traditional economic instruments of policy appear to have only a weak, or at most a nonsystematic, effect on the relative share of income accruing to the poor. Indeed, our study "reinforces the view that the policy instruments that are most effective in improving income distributions are different from those that are best for raising economic growth rates" (p. 185). It also supports the view that "economic structure, not level or rate of economic growth, is the basic determinant of patterns of income distribution" (p. 186).

Implicit in these conclusions is the suggestion that the price of economic equity is high: a necessary condition for its achievement is radical structural change.

B. The Adelman-Robinson Model

In order to test the validity of this last hypothesis, an income distribution-oriented planning model of an ambitious and novel variety was formulated.[1] The results of comparative statics experiments

[1] Work on this model has been supported by the International Bank for Reconstruction and Development.

with the model reinforce the conclusions of the Adelman-Morris book. Dynamic experiments are now in process.

The model is designed to investigate the impact of a variety of traditional economic instruments on income distribution: relative factor prices, product prices (influenced directly through price fixing, taxes, subsidies, and/or world prices, and degree of monopoly), rationing of products and services, rationing of credit, government taxes and transfers, trade policy, labor market policy, technology, and inflation. The model is dynamic and instrument-specific. It captures the effect of various policy instruments on distribution through a modified general equilibrium approach in which both factor prices and product prices are endogenous. Given the initial ownership of assets and the institutional rules of the game, the short-run income distribution derives from the interaction of production and consumption decisions.

The model is capable of portraying a large variety of economic and institutional rules of the game. One can vary the degree of monopoly, the principles of operation of credit markets, the clearing principles for labor markets and for commodity markets, and the permissible degrees of disequilibrium in individual markets. The model combines Keynesian and Walrasian analysis (it can operate in either mode, depending on the labor market specification). It portrays a monetary economy (combining Schumpeter-Wicksell with Walras) open to foreign trade. It can be run in an equilibrium or in a disequilibrium mode. The model is rich in sectoral detail (twenty-nine sectors), is disaggregated by firm size (four per sector), and has fifteen factors of production and twelve socioeconomic consumer (= saver) household categories.

Solution for each time step is by tatonnement in a two-stage process. In the first stage an allocation of investible funds is made across sectors and firm sizes by making firm demand (based on production functions and anticipated sales, rates of return, and capital cost) consistent with a given interest rate, a target credit expansion, or a direct rationing program. The second stage of the model is a microeconomic market model rich in institutional, sectoral, firm size, and household category detail. A series of markets must clear—a process that determines production, employment, prices, wages, and income distribution. Before the next period the model updates the variables, sets expectations, and selects credit and trade regimes for the first stage of the next period.

This model has been implemented for South Korea. Some indication of the validity of the model may be inferred from the fact that the base period solution for the model reproduces the 1968 data to within less than 1 percent for every one of

the approximately 2,000 endogenous variables.

Some of the comparative statics experiments performed to date are listed in Table 1. The results of these experiments are summarized in Tables 2 and 3. Each column of Table 2 indicates the distribution of household income after the model is solved under the conditions of the corresponding experiment, indicated at the top of the column. There appears to be a remarkable insensitivity of relative income distribution to the experiments performed. Table 3 indicates the composition by socioeconomic group of the lowest decile for each of the experiments. The bottom row of the table gives the average real household income of the decile. An examination of this table suggests, by contrast, that economic policy, by changing the functional distribution of income, can play a major role in determining who are the poor

TABLE 1—DESCRIPTION OF COMPARATIVE STATICS EXPERIMENTS
Adelman-Robinson Model

Experiment	
A-1	Peg agricultural prices at 1.25 of base price.
A-2	Increase agricultural capital stock by 50 percent.
A-3	Increase agricultural productivity 25 percent in cereals and 15 percent in other agriculture. Peg both prices at .90 of base price, and allow free trade in agricultural products.
A-4	Increase productivity in cereals by 25 percent and give cereals a price subsidy of 25 percent.
B-1	Double all direct taxes on households and transfer the proceeds to skilled labor, apprentices, and workers.
B-2	Give price subsidy of 20 percent to labor intensive sectors. Increase their capital stock by 20 percent. Peg their prices to world prices, allowing unlimited exports.
B-3	Same as B-2 but, in addition, increase agricultural productivity by 25 percent.
C-1	Increase entire capital stock by 50 percent.
C-2	Increase capital stocks by 50 percent for nonagricultural firms with less than 50 employees (two smallest sizes).
D-1	Increase all exports by 25 percent.
D-2	Devalue by 30 percent. Peg prices of traded goods to world prices. Increase capital stocks of trading sectors by 20 percent.
E-1	Increase supply of engineers, technicians, skilled workers, and clericals by 10 percent, reducing the number of unskilled workers correspondingly. *CES* functions.
E-2	Increase elasticity of substitution between capital and labor in manufacturing.
E-3	Set minimum wage at 125 percent of unskilled wage rate.

TABLE 2—DISTRIBUTION OF HOUSEHOLD INCOME (PERCENT) AFTER TAXES AND TRANSFERS

Deciles (in percent)	Experiments														
	A-1	A-2	A-3	A-4	B-1	B-2	B-3	C-1	C-2	D-1	D-2	E-1	E-2	E-3	Base
Bottom 10	2.41	2.31	2.39	2.40	2.50	2.42	2.06	2.33	2.44	2.45	2.45	2.27	2.10	2.19	2.50
20	3.88	3.63	3.75	3.79	3.99	3.89	3.29	3.76	3.88	3.90	3.89	3.70	3.42	3.60	3.90
30	4.91	4.63	4.75	4.80	5.04	4.93	4.24	4.79	4.90	4.92	4.90	4.75	4.44	4.67	4.90
40	5.93	5.63	5.75	5.81	6.07	5.95	5.23	5.82	5.91	5.92	5.91	5.78	5.49	5.75	5.90
50	7.04	6.74	6.85	6.92	7.18	7.10	6.34	6.96	7.01	7.02	7.01	6.93	6.68	6.92	6.97
60	8.34	8.06	8.15	8.24	8.47	8.38	7.69	8.31	8.32	8.30	8.30	8.28	8.11	8.29	8.24
70	10.00	9.77	9.83	9.92	10.08	10.04	9.47	10.03	9.99	9.93	9.95	10.01	9.97	10.03	9.86
80	12.33	12.20	12.23	12.30	12.32	12.38	12.10	12.45	12.34	12.24	12.28	12.44	12.58	12.45	12.15
90	16.24	16.40	16.34	16.34	16.07	16.30	16.81	16.51	16.31	16.17	16.24	16.46	16.89	16.46	16.08
100	28.93	30.62	29.97	29.47	28.27	28.66	32.78	29.03	28.90	29.14	29.07	29.36	30.33	29.63	29.49
Gini Coefficient	.38	.40	.39	.39	.37	.38	.43	.39	.38	.38	.38	.39	.41	.40	.38

and, in particular, whether they are primarily urban or rural. There is also somewhat more scope for affecting the absolute level of poverty through economic intervention than for changing the overall distribution of incomes.

The remarkable insensitivity of the relative shares of national income accruing to households by deciles to the wide array of economic policy packages represented in

the model suggests that, while one can make small gains in the welfare of the poor through large changes within the system, the goal of equity cannot be achieved without radical reform. This result is consistent with the Adelman-Morris findings.

C. A Major Conclusion

The two studies just described attack the issue of income distribution and de-

TABLE 3—PERCENT OF HOUSEHOLDS IN THE BOTTOM DECILE

Who are the Poor?

Socioeconomic Groups	Experiments														
	A-1	A-2	A-3	A-4	B-1	B-2	B-3	C-1	C-2	D-1	D-2	E-1	E-2	E-3	Base
Engineers	0.0	0.0	0.0	0.0	0.0	0.0	0.0	0.0	0.0	0.0	0.0	0.0	0.0	0.0	0.0
Technicians	0.1	0.0	0.0	0.0	0.1	0.0	0.0	0.0	0.1	0.0	0.0	1.0	1.0	0.5	0.8
Skilled	14.2	3.9	1.5	6.5	3.7	9.5	2.2	17.7	14.4	7.6	6.9	9.0	16.8	3.9	8.8
Apprentices	0.4	0.2	7.6	0.3	0.2	0.5	0.2	0.0	0.5	0.3	0.3	0.5	0.6	0.2	0.3
Workers	4.3	12.4	7.9	13.8	13.5	17.0	5.4	15.2	16.8	19.1	15.1	5.6	28.6	10.5	19.4
White Collar	4.6	1.7	0.4	2.2	4.4	2.2	0.2	2.1	2.5	3.4	2.2	6.2	3.5	2.7	3.2
Government	8.6	6.4	3.0	9.4	11.1	13.0	8.0	11.0	10.3	9.2	11.8	6.9	4.6	6.5	7.4
Self-Employed 1	9.5	5.3	3.3	7.4	10.1	10.6	5.5	13.4	10.4	8.8	8.8	3.6	5.7	3.0	7.6
Self-Employed 2	11.1	7.1	3.1	9.7	12.3	15.9	7.7	18.7	14.2	9.8	12.7	5.4	4.9	5.2	9.8
Capitalists	0.0	0.0	0.0	0.0	0.0	0.0	0.0	0.0	0.0	0.0	0.0	0.0	0.0	0.0	0.0
Agric. Labor	5.6	11.2	5.7	9.2	8.9	6.1	13.4	4.4	6.4	8.4	8.5	33.0	22.9	34.2	8.4
Agric. 1 (Tiny)	13.4	30.6	36.1	26.6	20.9	17.1	34.4	11.6	14.9	19.7	20.3	18.6	8.0	21.1	20.2
Agric. 2 (Small)	7.8	19.6	22.8	14.2	13.8	7.7	21.3	5.8	9.0	12.8	12.6	10.0	3.5	11.8	13.2
Agric. 3 (Medium)	0.4	1.4	8.5	0.7	0.9	0.3	1.8	0.2	0.4	0.8	0.7	0.3	0.0	0.3	0.9
Agric. 4 (Large)	0.0	0.0	0.2	0.0	0.0	0.0	0.0	0.0	0.0	0.0	0.0	0.0	0.0	0.0	0.0
Average HH Income[a]	46.	47.	31.	51.	48.	52.	52.	52.	49.	47.	48.	46.	43.	42.	47.

[a] Average income is in thousands of real (1968) Won.

velopment with two very different techniques and bodies of data. The general conclusions they reach are very similar and therefore strongly reinforcing. Both studies show quite clearly that, in approaching the subject of economic development, whether theoretically or in terms of policy formulation, one cannot duck the issue of the purpose of development. This is a result of extreme importance: very different models, policy instruments, and disciplinary mixes are implicit in the choice of objectives. It is not simply a matter of tradeoffs; the optimal time sequences of dynamic strategies are almost certainly quite sensitive to the choice of goals. The conclusion is inescapable that, in setting the directions for the future of the field of economic development, we must be very clear, much clearer than we have been in the past, in our choice of development goals.

II. Development Objectives

The currently accepted definition of development focuses upon the creation of conditions for self-sustained growth in per capita *GNP* and the requisite modernization of economic, social, and political structures implicit in the achievement of this goal. To the extent that growth in *GNP* and concomitant changes, on the one hand, and improvements in the welfare of the poor, on the other, are monotonically and positively related (except possibly for short-term startup problems), this definition of development could offer an acceptable working definition. If, however, as is suggested by the work described above, a *U*-shaped relation exists, then the accepted definition of the development is, at the very least, badly misleading as a focus for thought and practice in the field. Since trickle-down does not work, basing the definition of the process of economic development upon a faulty analogy with modern industrial nations has led to the use of incorrect performance criteria, the

selection of largely incorrect development strategies, and the use of inappropriately framed models and inappropriately focused planning methodologies.

On a moral basis, it seems to me that in each nation the proper long-term goal of national development policy must be the successive relaxation of the systemic obstacles to the full realization of the human potential of its members. The goals of *economic* development are then twofold: to provide the material basis for achieving these objectives and to establish the economic conditions for relaxing the other barriers to self-realization (access to education, work satisfaction, status, security, self-expression, and power). The proper balance between these two economic goals is a dynamic one and will depend on the state of welfare of the poorest segments of the population at each decision point.

This definition of the purpose of development, which I shall call *depauperization*, is humanistic, largely spiritual, and highly dynamic. It is focused upon individual welfare, as perceived by the individual himself, with full recognition of the nonmaterial, human relations, and intergenerational aspects of personal welfare.

Depauperization has both economic and noneconomic dimensions and stresses the removal not only of material but equally importantly of social, political, and spiritual forms of deprivation. It involves not only equity but more significantly the creation of conditions conducive to continuing improvements in equity. It may require temporary sacrifices in national economic growth and involves major social, political and institutional change. In addition, the optimization of some of the components of this overall objective may, in the short run, necessitate sacrifices in some of the others, so that the ultimate realization of depauperization is likely to require appropriately phased sequences of dynamic strategies, each aimed at optimizing some subset of the total goal package.

In order to develop appropriate criteria, strategies, models, and methodologies for future development decisions, it is important to distinguish among four conceptual goals: equity, growth, equitable growth, and depauperization. Equity, growth, and depauperization are all special cases of equitable growth. Equity lies at one extreme. Equity alone as a goal, with growth given a subsidiary role, implies that the most important objectives are justice and fairness in some sense, rather than absolute welfare. Growth alone as a goal lies at the opposite extreme and has been discredited, as indicated above, in the minds of most of us. Depauperization, like equitable growth, involves some weighted combination of equity and growth, but in view of its explicit emphasis on the dynamic and nonmaterial aspects of individual welfare, depauperization lies well towards the side of equity. It implies that a primary objective of development is not only to help the poor to achieve a decent standard of living but in addition to create the conditions, economic and otherwise, that will allow them and their children continuing equal access to opportunities for self-realization. The achievement of depauperization, therefore, requires institutional change, a measure of economic, social, and political equity, and economic growth, not as goals in themselves but as instruments for the achievement of permanent self-perpetuating gains in the welfare of the poor.

A normative judgment implicit in depauperization is that no societal process can be morally acceptable which imposes, maintains, or intensifies the objective and perceptual barriers to self-realization of major segments of that society. To my mind, the major crime of humanity—practiced on an appalling scale—is to create and enforce, by means of institutional barriers and structural dynamics, conditions which lead to the waste of as

much as 90 percent of its potential for fulfilled life, creativity, and personal growth. Empirical evidence shows that the natural historical process of modern economic growth works systematically to perpetuate those conditions for most of the period from the beginning of economic modernization. To counteract this social distortion should be a basic purpose of all national social policy and a prime objective of international assistance; to show how this might be done should be a major objective of all social scientists concerned with development.

III. Strategies for Depauperization

Most of the discussion concerning development strategies has been in terms of contemporary tradeoffs among major policy packages, rather than in terms of sequences of more or less pure strategies. A cursory survey of the dynamic processes that have led to the development of the currently industrialized nations suggests, however, that the development process has in fact proceeded as a sequence of pure strategies, rather than in a progression of mutually balanced strategy mixes. Emphasis on strategies that focus on a single major objective (such as the creation of a viable political system, or industrialization, or social development), largely unaccompanied by concomitant changes in the rest of the system, has in general created strategic imbalances which set conditions for the next phase. It is only at the beginning and the end of the entire process that there appears to be a balance among the various features of economic, social, and political development.

An examination of the development process of those non-Communist countries which have recently successfully combined improvements in the incomes of the poor with accelerated growth (Israel, Japan, South Korea, Singapore, and Taiwan) shows that they all have followed a similar dynamic sequence of strategies, varying only in the extent and consciousness with which it has been pursued. Aided by large infusions of foreign capital, all of these have followed the following dynamic sequence:

Stage I: Radical asset redistribution, focusing primarily on land;[2] but also imposing (at the very minimum) curbs upon the use and further accumulation of financial capital. This stage may involve negative growth rates, but is necessary to set the economic and political conditions to ensure that subsequent economic growth is not highly unequalizing.

Stage II: Massive accumulation of human capital, far in excess of current demand for skills. In this stage ownership of human capital is redistributed, the human resource base is vastly enlarged, and both the economic opportunities and the political pressures for the next stage are generated. In all five countries, this stage was accompanied by relatively slow rates of economic growth and, at later times, by political instability, social tension, and unrest.

Stage III: Rapid, human-resource-intensive growth. After the investment in human resources has been made, continuing depauperization requires that subsequent increases in growth rate be achieved through strategies that stress rapid labor-intensive growth. This implies that sufficient attention must be paid to the formulation of economic policy. In the smaller nations development will have to be oriented towards export markets. In large countries, on the other hand, industrialization can be oriented more towards satisfying domestic demand, particularly when a more equitable growth pattern generates a mass consumer market and when a more appropriate import-substitution technology is found.

To achieve depauperization, two extreme strategies are theoretically possible: grow now, redistribute and educate later; or redistribute and educate now, grow later.[3] The former strategy is the one that has typically been followed historically in developed non-Communist economies, except for the United States and Japan. The redistribute-first strategy is the one followed by the successful equitable-growth countries in the past two decades.

I am convinced that for rapid depauperization there must be a deliberate application of the redistribute-and-educate-first strategy on a wide scale. My argument is a practical one: there is selective but consistent evidence that this strategy can work and significant evidence that the opposite strategy does not work on anything resembling an acceptable time scale. Once the slower growth phase of Stages I and II is passed, the transition to a stage of relatively high development can be accomplished in short order. In the five countries considered, the first phase lasted about a decade. In another decade and a half, once economic incentives were restructured to permit an export-oriented industrialization that employed the new skills of the population, both depauperization and rapid economic growth became self-sustaining.

Some may dismiss the success stories as special cases, asserting that these are all

---

[2] Except in Singapore, which is entirely urban. A major welfare program, however, accomplished some of the same redistributive objectives.

[3] The remainder of this section is a minor reediting of Adelman (1974). While originally written as a prescription for equitable growth, I have since recognized that the prescription is more precisely one for depauperization. The recommendations for achieving a weaker form of equitable growth would differ primarily in the relative emphasis on growth and equity and the relative emphasis on social, political, and institutional changes compared with purely economic actions. The specific policies associated with achieving the respective goals would differ considerably more than the goals themselves.

small nations with nonrepresentative cultural traditions and attitudes, helped by unusually large per capita infusions of foreign aid and subjected to exceptional challenges that strengthened the legitimacy of their governments and made economic viability a major condition for national survival. Special cases they may be, but five successful cases are certainly more encouraging than none, and the consistency of their experiences surely weakens the "uniqueness" argument.

There is also evidence that the entire package—resource redistribution, massive education, and labor-intensive growth policies—must be adopted in that sequence to achieve rapid success. Incomplete versions of this program, such as land reform alone or education without labor-intensive growth, have not worked. For the advanced countries which followed a grow-first pattern, economic development did eventually benefit the poor, but the time it took to do so was much longer (roughly two or more generations) than in our five successful cases.

The traditional strategy for economic development—rapid economic moderniza-tion involving trade and investment policies aimed at the fast expansion of the industrial sector—has not been so much wrong as premature for most developing countries. When applied *at the proper time in the proper strategic sequence* (i.e., *after* the equalizing preconditions of Stage I and Stage II), labor-intensive rapid industrialization phased in with appropriately paced agricultural development appears to be the key to realizing the full economic value of the redistributed assets and, hence, to *actual* depauperization, rather than to merely potential depauperization, as in Stages I and II.

REFERENCES

I. Adelman, "Strategies for Equitable Growth," *Challenge*, June 1974, 37–44.
——— and C. T. Morris, *Economic Growth and Social Equity in Developing Countries*, Stanford 1973.
——— and S. Robinson, "A Non-Linear, Dynamic, Micro-Economic Model of Korea: Factors Affecting the Distribution of Income in the Short Run," Woodrow Wilson School dis. pap. no. 36, July 1973.
G. Myrdal, *Value in Social Theory*, New York 1958.

Reprinted from

THE AMERICAN ECONOMIC REVIEW

[8]

REDISTRIBUTION BEFORE GROWTH

A strategy for developing countries

I

The liberal assumption, on which policies of developing countries and attitudes towards them were based, was that economic growth and social modernization would take care of poverty. That, with perhaps a slight delay, the benefits of economic growth would trickle down to the poorest segments of society. This growth optimism seems to have been invalidated by the recent Third World experience. Average income per head in the Third World has grown more rapidly in the last two decades than ever before. But so have unemployment, famines, malnutrition, abject poverty, and hunger. The income gap between the richest members of developing societies and the poorest has in most developing countries risen and, not infrequently, the absolute real income of the poorest has actually dropped in these decades of accelerated growth. The implications are clear – they require major rethinking of development theory and policy.

I should like to take this occasion to propose such a rethinking and provide a theory of development strategy for growth with equity in developing countries. That theory is offered as a hypothesis but is, I believe, well grounded in both the historical experience of currently developed countries and in the contemporary experience of developing ones.

Our starting point is the classical theory of distribution. We assume with the classics that households derive their income from selling the services of the factors of production which they own, and that they are paid roughly in accordance with the productivity of those factors. When the amount of factors or their productivity goes up, so does the household's income.

To transform this theory into a theory of equitable growth, one needs to inject a dynamic dimension into the analysis. The dynamics must take account of the dynamic changes in the patterns of production as they impinge upon the productivity, accumulation, and ownership of the factors of production.

To dynamize the theory of production and accumulation, we assume that countries engage in international trade and specialize in accordance with their dynamic comparative advantage. We also assume that part of the economic surplus is reinvested in the accumulation of further amounts of factors of production and that the reinvestment occurs in accordance with the prospective rates of return from various potential assets. That is, primary emphasis is given to the further accumulation of that factor from which the rate of return is the highest.

The dynamics of managed growth in developing countries follow a process aimed at changing their patterns of comparative advantage dynamically, through a process of institutional change, innovation, and accumulation, so as to enable the economic transformation of agrarian economies into modern industrial states. Thus, as economies develop, the composition of production changes, with the share of manufacturing output increasing at the expense of primary, agricultural and mining production. In this process, both the critical factor of production, as indicated by its functional share and/or by the size of economic rent from its use, and the productivity of that factor change over time. In the agrarian economy, the critical factor of production is land and the institutional and technological innovations which take place are aimed at raising its productivity. Then, as economies commercialize, the critical factor becomes financial capital. Finally, as economies industrialize, the critical factors become physical and human capital, and the major technological and institutional innovations are aimed at raising their productivity.

Our theory of economic policy states that, for equitable growth, *at each stage of the development process,* access to the critical factor of production should be redistributed *before* its productivity is improved. This policy prescription precisely reverses the time sequence of the historical process in most currently developed countries. By doing so, I would claim, it greatly foreshortens the time scale to the achievement of growth with equity and substantially reduces the degree of human suffering required historically for the implementation of the necessary economic, social and political transformations.

We now turn to a brief, broadbrush overview of the historical process in a few currently developed European economies. Next, we state our thesis in more detail and examine the experience of the last two decades in the small number of currently developing countries that have successfully combined accelerated growth with non-deteriorating relative incomes for the poorest 40% of their populations. We then look at the domestic political implications of the proposed programme, particularly as they impinge on the equity vs. democracy dilemma. We end by examining the implications for foreign assistance and for the international economic order.

4

II

The historical growth process of currently developed countries involved a set of transformations – from purely agrarian, to agrarian and commercial, to primarily manufacturing and industrial economies. As part of this process the nature of the critical factor of production involved in the major economic activity changed over time, from land to financial capital, to physical and human capital. Whenever the critical factor of production changed, as part of that change, the productivity of the critical factor of production involved in the major economic activity was improved. With each change, a two-step sequence was initiated which entailed initial improvements in the productivity of the critical factor of production, followed, with a longish – one or two generation – delay, by an equalizing redistribution in the ownership of that factor.

At each step, this sequence proceeded as follows. The productivity of the most important factor of production was increased, through technological innovations and/or through institutional change. The increase generated augmented returns for some and decreased returns for others. Increased returns were experienced directly by: (1) those owners of the critical factor who could take advantage of the productivity increase; (2) those owners of other factors which could be transformed into the critical factor at the new technology level; (3) owners of factors co-operating with the critical factor under the new technology: the co-operating factors include intermediate inputs, other primary factors, and factors required for marketing services; (4) producers of goods and services complementary in use with the output produced under the new technology. Decreased returns were experienced by (1) those owners of the critical factor who could not take advantage of the productivity increasing innovation; (2) owners of substitute factors replaced by the productivity increasing innovation; (3) owners of factors co-operating with the critical factor under the old technology; (4) producers of goods and services which are substitutes for the output produced under the new technology. The latter experienced displacement (or 'backwash effects') since the more productive uses reduced the rates of return from the old technologies, and from ways of satisfying wants. The increases in overall product supply due to the augmented factor productivity led to declines in output prices, at the same time that the inputs for the traditional processes became more expensive and less available, and the markets for traditionally produced

5

output shrank because profits from marketing them dropped. Displacement effects were also experienced by owners of substitute factors and by producers of substitute products. Institutional change making access to the factor whose productivity was increased, more restricted or more expensive, also contributed to marginalization and eventual dispossession. Unfortunately, in general it was the few who owned large amounts of the factor whose productivity was improved [2] or large amounts of factors that could be transformed into it who could adapt to the new technologies, while the many whose initial endowments of the factor were meagre could not. The latter could not gain access to the finance required to adapt production processes; they could not bear the greater risk involved in trying new processes; they could not gain access to the new knowledge, the new inputs, and the networks for marketing the improved outputs. As a result, for the many who owned only small amounts of the factor whose productivity was improved or of substitutes for it, displacement effects tended to dominate expansion effects and therefore their incomes dropped. For the relatively few who owned larger quantities of that factor, or of factors that could be transformed into that factor, expansion effects dominated displacement effects and their incomes rose. Thus, as a result of the changes in productivity, even in the absence of further reinforcing institutional change, for a relatively long time after the innovation the rich as a group grew richer and the poor poorer. The distribution of income from the ownership of the factor whose productivity was increased became more skewed, and those who owned only small amounts of the critical factor became more impoverished. This combination of simultaneous enrichment and impoverishment is typical of the first step in the historical income effect of a productivity-increasing innovation in the medium run.

After several decades, some of those initially marginalized by the innovation were able to change occupation (sometimes through migration). Others could adapt, with a lag, to the new technologies or find ways of cashing-in on the profit-inducing effects of the innovation. But the process was quite slow and its speed depended both on the overall rate of economic growth, and on the nature of the institutions surrounding factor markets and commodity markets.

The relative and absolute impoverishment induced by the increase in productivity and by the dispossession and displacement of owners of the

2. This section draws upon references 5, 6, 7.

6

inferior factor as a result of its comparative disadvantage, led to political pressures in the form of demonstrations, strikes, revolts, and revolutions, for the redistribution of ownership or access to the utilization of the critical factor. In the wake of the revolts, a certain amount of redistribution was carried out and, for a while, improvements in both growth and in relative and absolute incomes of the poorest occurred. However, eventually the dynamics of comparative advantage, innovation and accumulation, led to a shift in the patterns of production and to a new factor of production becoming the critical factor. And the process of productivity increase followed by eventual redistributive revolt was then repeated.

Thus the first European revolutions were agrarian, aimed at redistributing land and at generating the institutional conditions for wider participation in the fruits of its exploitation.

The Industrial Revolution increased the rates of return from both raw, unskilled labour and from physical capital. At the same time, it displaced cottage industry, created sweatshops, and made young, able-bodied men an obsolescent resource as the 'man-power' of the factory became largely women and children. After the Industrial Revolution, therefore, the major economic revolts were aimed at gaining wider access to the productive use of labour services, and more humane and equitable conditions for the employment and remuneration of unskilled labour (strikes, unionization, etc). Two to three generations later came the revolutions aimed at changing the institutions for the ownership of capital both *per se* and in relation to labour. In the countries that did not undergo communist revolutions, reforms to redistribute financial wealth were introduced through gift and death duties.

Subsequently, technological innovations have made processes of production both more capital- and more skill-intensive. The post-World War II period has therefore seen major clamour for wider access to the accumulation of middle and higher levels of human capital as well as confrontations in the labour-management field. As a result, educational pyramids have become (and are continuing to become) wider, as both secondary and university education are becoming less elitist in nature. The result of these quiet revolutions has been again an improvement in both the growth and distribution performance of most Western European countries.

Thus, the currently successful marriage of growth and social justice in the currently developed world has involved a sequence of changes in the

7

critical factor of production, increases in its productivity, followed by redistribution of the factor's ownership combined with changes in the institutions for its monetization. The redistribution phase has usually involved varying degrees of violent confrontation. From a distribution point of view, the innovations led first to a deterioration in economic equity, and then, after the redistribution was effected, an improvement. From a growth point of view, the productivity-improving innovation phase led to an acceleration of growth. Then, depending on the degree of violent restructuring of economic networks and institutions entailed by the social-economic confrontation which followed, economic stagnation may or may not have been the result. Sometimes, as in the USSR, the stagnation in the year following the Revolution may even have been quite prolonged. But once redistribution was implemented, growth and equity went hand in hand, as all segments of society benefitted from the higher rates of economic growth. With each change in the critical factor the whole process, from increases in productivity, through increases in poverty, to subsequent reductions in poverty as both growth and distribution improved, took, in a typical European country, somewhere between one and two generations and was quite costly in terms of human suffering both before and during the violent redistribution confrontations.

III

My proposed theory of economic strategy for equitable economic development in developing countries is quite simple. As indicated earlier, what I would urge is that, at each step in the growth process, the historical time sequence of productivity improvement followed by redistribution, be reversed. First, the critical asset whose productivity will subsequently be improved should be redistributed. Then, and only then, its productivity should be improved.

The rationale for the proposed sequence is threefold. First, with a better distribution of the major asset and with better access to opportunities for its monetization and for improvements in its productivity, most of the backwash effects of the innovation upon the asset-poor can be avoided. Secondly, before improvement in its productivity the redistributed asset is not as valuable as it is thereafter. Redistribution with compensation, and redistribution requiring a lesser degree of violence, would therefore be possible, at least in principle. Thirdly, the time scale for

8

achieving equitable growth can be greatly foreshortened as demonstrated by the experience of the currently developing countries that have followed the proposed sequence, largely as a result of historical accidents. Instead of the historical two or three generations before improvements in the incomes of the poorest can take place, only one generation need elapse. Thus, if the need for redistribution is *anticipated* and acted upon, the social suffering involved in the developed country process can be greatly reduced in developing nations and the time scale before equitable growth can take place can be greatly accelerated. For the equitable development of developing countries, I would therefore argue that the slogan should be redistribute first – improve productivity later.

The experiences of the recently developed non-communist developing countries which have successfully combined no-deterioration-in-the-relative-incomes-of-the poorest with accelerated growth (Israel, Japan, South Korea, Singapore and Taiwan) show that they all have followed a dynamic sequence of strategies similar to the one recommended by me for equitable growth. The sequence varied in the consciousness of its design and in the political mechanism used to implement it, but was universally characterized by the following dynamic sequence.

Stage I: Radical Asset Redistribution, focussing primarily on land, but also imposing (at the very minimum) curbs upon the use and further accumulation of financial capital to avoid excessive centralization in industry and in political power. This stage may involve negative growth rates, but is necessary to set the economic and political conditions to ensure that subsequent improvements in agricultural productivity are not highly unequalizing.

Stage II: Improvements in Agricultural Productivity. These are necessary to generate an economic surplus for accumulation of industrial capital and to a lesser extent to release the labour force required for industrialization. The productivity improvements are generated not only by technological change but also through changes in price incentives, markets and marketing mechanisms and, more generally, economic and institutional infrastructure for rural development. This phase involves an acceleration of economic growth, and its timing not infrequently overlaps the beginning of the next step.

Stage III: Massive Accumulation of Human Capital, far in excess of the current demand for skills. In this stage ownership of human capital is redistributed, the human resource base is vastly enlarged, and both the

9

economic opportunities and the political pressures for the next stage are generated. In all five countries, this stage was accompanied by relatively slow rates of economic growth and, at later times, by political instability, social tension, and unrest.

Stage IV: Rapid Human Resource Intensive Growth. After the investment in human resources has been made, continuing the equitable growth requires that subsequent increases in growth rate be achieved through strategies that stress rapid labour intensive growth. This implies that sufficient attention is paid to the formulation of economic policy. In the smaller nations development will have to be oriented towards export markets. In large countries, on the other hand, industrialization can be oriented more towards satisfying domestic demand, particularly when a more appropriate import-substitution technology is found. This stage, of course, is the equivalent of the human and physical capital productivity improving stage.

I shall illustrate this sequence by reference to the experience of Mainland China, Taiwan and South Korea.

China[2] followed a path of redistribution through institutional restructuring preceding growth. But its development has been marked by radical shifts and by rapid changes in overall development strategies.

1949 to 1952: The Land Reform and Economic Recovery Phase
A land reform redistributed land and other assets to individual farmers in small-scale privately owned plots and eliminated the economic and political power of the landlords from the countryside. The land reform was a traumatic event, involving over 2 million deaths. Nevertheless, despite little state investment in rural development, agricultural output recovered rapidly within the framework of traditional agriculture. In the rest of the economy, the focus was upon the control of hyperinflation, which was halted by mid-1950, and industrial reconstruction within a traditional institutional framework without major nationalizations. Industrial output grew quite rapidly because idle plant capacity was brought back into production.

1952 to 1959: Educational Expansion and Accelerated Socialization of Both Agriculture and Industry
In agriculture, the socialization took the form of, first, cooperativistation, then, collectivisation of land and major capital goods in a cooperative

framework, and finally reorganization into Communes. 1952 witnessed the first campaign for agricultural collectivisation; by 1956 over 90 percent of Chinese peasants were in cooperatives; by 1959, 99 percent were in rural Communes. During this period, it was hoped that increases in agricultural output could be obtained without major investments of state resources in agriculture – the First Five-Year Plan devoted only 23 percent of total investment to agriculture – within the *technological* framework of traditional agriculture. Increases in productivity were to be obtained mostly through reorganization of asset ownership and through ideologically induced increases in motivation, without major reliance on market incentives. The policy was successful – grain output rose by 4.4 percent annually – but it eventually ran into technologically diminishing returns as well as into incentive problems.

Till 1952, private enterprise was quite important in both small-scale and large-scale industry and modern trade. From 1952 to 1955 the scope of the government sector in modern industry and trade was increased by a mixture of inducements and economic pressures. In mid-1955, a nationalisation campaign was launched, which by 1956 resulted in two-thirds of modern industrial enterprises owned by the state and one-third joint public-private. From the point of view of policy and management there was no difference between the two forms; both involved control by a cyclically fluctuating combination of the Party committee and the operational management of the enterprise. In the public-private enterprises, however, private shareholders received dividends; in 1960, there were still reported to be one-quarter of a million ex-capitalists receiving dividends in Shanghai. In the handicrafts industry sector, till 1955, private ownership was predominant; by 1956, only 8 percent of persons engaged in handicrafts, small-scale industry, native transport and native trade were privately employed and 92 percent were working in cooperatives.

In 1957, a decentralization decree was issued to encourage local initiative, especially in small-scale industry and local self-sufficiency. Starting with 1958 a vast number of small-scale labor intensive establishments were built up in the cities and throughout the countryside. They focused on alternative technologies, and on a intelligent system of subcontracting of components for large-scale enterprises to small labor-intensive workshops.

As a result of more intensive utilization of capacity, and, later, of the maturing of heavy industrial investments, overall industrial output grew

11

quite rapidly (20 percent annually) during this period.

This period also saw major investments in human capital, both rural and urban, through vast expansion of primary education, health care, and social welfare expenditures. Primary school enrollment rates rose in the countryside from about one-tenth to over two-thirds, and to virtually 100 percent in the cities. Before the Cultural Revolution the educational pyramid was quite steep – with 76 percent of young children in primary school and only 7 percent in middle school.

Thus, this period was devoted mostly to simultaneous redistribution of all types of assets – land, physical and human capital – and to institutional restructuring. Despite this, however, unlike the experiences of South Korea and Taiwan, this period also involved an acceleration in economic growth. But the strain was too much.

1959-1961: The Great Crises

The combination of major restructuring, major redistribution, major reorientation of economic policy, administrative confusion, economic blunders, sheer human exhaustion, withdrawal of Soviet aid, and natural disaster, led to a temporary virtual collapse of all sectors of the economy.

1962-1966: Reorientation and Recovery

The response was a major readjustment of economic policy, evolving from the Soviet style of development in the fifties towards an 'Agriculture First' policy. A commitment to the technical modernization of agriculture was implemented by increased investment, rural electrification, use of chemical fertilizer, as well as by increasing farm incentives through improvements in the agricultural terms of trade and by raising rural consumption. As a result, grain output rose quite rapidly (over 4 percent annually) during this period.

Industrial policy shifted as well, in support of a 'self-sufficiency' policy. This involved a shift in the composition of output towards defense-oriented and agriculture-oriented industries; producer and intermediate goods – oil, machinery, and fertilizer – were stressed at the expense of light consumer goods. The rate of growth of industrial output slowed down compared to the fifties, in part due to a disastrous decline during the Culture Revolution.

12

1966-1968: The Cultural Revolution

The Cultural Revolution was motivated by political/ideological considerations. But it had marked, still persisting effects on the accumulation and distribution of ownership of human capital. Prior to the Cultural Revolution, the educational pyramid was quite narrow, with three-quarters of school-age children in primary school, and only 2 percent in senior middle-level schools and higher. During the Cultural Revolution, middle-level schools and universities were closed, reopening gradually since 1969, and changing in character. The educational reforms since have served to widen and redistribute access to middle and higher level education, to make education more 'practical' and more adapted to the needs of rural development and to low-level industrial-technical development at the expense of building up human resources for more sophisticated industrial technology and for research and development. Linking education to production became a major emphasis in education. Factory-run universities, worker colleges, part-time colleges giving crash courses on specific technical problems, mushroomed in the early 1970s. Regular colleges and secondary schools, which reopened, established ongoing relationships with factories by having exchange of students and faculty between themselves and factories.

1970-1977: Egalitarian Growth

Agricultural expansion, largely untouched by the Cultural Revolution, continued at a moderate rate. The recovery from the effects of the Cultural Revolution led to accelerated industrial growth and to increased foreign trade. An interlocked, complementary, highly dualistic development pattern evolved in industry. Small-scale, appropriate-technology industry, and rural industry support of modernization of agriculture continued to expand, but, at the same time, highly modern, large-scale plants based on imported, capital-intensive, large-scale technology, were also being established.

In assessing China's economic performance, one must always bear in mind its vast size and the massive levels of destitution which were characteristic of the great majority of its people. Viewed in this perspective, China's performance has been spectacular. It attained a high growth rate – 7 percent annually if one starts with 1949 and 5.6 percent if one starts from 1952 – though significantly below that of South Korea and Taiwan.

13

It has also met the basic needs of *all* its people, setting an adequate floor on the consumption standard of its poor. 'It has fed, clothed, and housed everyone, has kept them healthy, and has educated most. Millions were not starved; sidewalks and streets have not been covered with multitudes of sleeping, begging, hungry and illiterate human beings; millions are not disease-ridden. To find such deplorable conditions, one does not look to China these days but, rather, to India, Pakistan, and anywhere else in the underdeveloped world' (Reference 7, p. 13). But inequality, though narrowing, is still surprisingly large. Urban wages range from ratios of 5 to 1 to 3 to 1 within the same factory. The income gap between urban and rural, though steadily narrowing, is still quite substantial (of the order of 1.5-1.7). And within the rural sector, there is still large variation in incomes among provinces, within them, and even within villages and between families in villages.

In *Taiwan*,[3] in 1950, a major land reform was carried out in which tenancy was virtually abolished, a ceiling of 7.5 acres per farm was established and land redistributed to about 10 million small farmers with just over 2 acres. At the same time, the agricultural support system, taken over from Japanese colonial rule, was strengthened so as to provide access to credit, fertilizer, seed, technology and agricultural extension to the small farmer. Management systems for agriculture and rural industry based on a cooperative structure built around the township and village farmers' association were established. Education, health services and electrification were extended to rural areas. The result was spectacular increases in agricultural productivity, which started at the rate of 5% annually and has continued to increase over the past 20 years, leading to far more productive, and both more labour- and land-intensive agriculture than in most developing countries. This, in turn, led not only to a high growth rate and a quite equitable income distribution within agriculture, but also to a steadily narrowing rural-urban income gap and to a stimulus of rapid growth of non-agricultural output. The latter occured through exports which generated foreign exchange for the import of industrial inputs and machinery, and through the formation of an agricultural surplus. The next decade saw major extensions of the educational system to effective universal primary education, publicly supported, and large increases in secondary and university education, mostly privately paid for. Taiwan's level of education rose to about four times the norm

3. This section draws primarily on reference [9].

14

for a country with its level of per capita GNP. Industrial output increased as well, using, however, capital-intensive technology and centered upon import substitution. Labour absorption in urban employment, and overall growth rates, while high by international developing country standards, were therefore not as high as in the decade of the sixties, which marked a shift of industrial policy towards labour-intensive exports. During the 1960s, non-agricultural employment grew at 6.6 percent, exports at 35 percent, and GNP at 10 percent annually. Agricultural productivity growth actually accelerated, and rural incomes rose to a level comparable and currently even exceeding urban ones. Unlike the experience of most developing countries, income distribution in Taiwan actually improved markedly: the ratio of the income share of the top 20 percent to that of the bottom 20 percent of income recipients fell from 15 to 1 in 1953, to 5 to 1 in 1969, and the income of the poorest 20 percent *tripled*.

The experience of *South Korea* and its policies were quite similar. The partition of Korea and the Korean War both resulted in wholesale re-distribution of physical capital and a levelling of wealth – property damage from the fighting was estimated at $ 2 billion. Land reform pro-ceeded in two stages. Under American auspices in 1947, land once held by the Japanese was redistributed, reducing the full-time tenancy rate from 70 percent to 33 percent and reducing rent ceilings to 33 percent from 50 percent and higher. A second, purely domestic land reform in 1950 redistributed Korean landlord holdings, with nominal compensation, and eliminated tenancy altogether. Most of the farms were quite small – 70 percent below one hectare of paddy land – thus exacerbating the problems of low income and low productivity on the farm.

The next phase – from 1953 to 1963 – saw moderate increases in agricultural productivity as institutions much like those in Taiwan but less effective were created to serve the small farmers; an import-substitution industrialization program centered on consumer non-durables, which led to economic stagnation, substantial investment in social overhead, and a major education explosion. From 1953 to 1963, the literacy rate rose from 30 percent to more than 80 percent. Universal primary education became the rule in the countryside as well as in the cities, and secondary and higher education also grew extremely rapidly. By 1965 South Korea had a level of human resource development which exceeded the norm of a country with three times its median per capita GNP. At the same time,

15

due to economic stagnation unemployment of college graduates was about 50 percent and student unrest was at its height. In 1963 there were about 2,000 student political demonstrations!

The first two phases of Korean post-World War II development, by redistributing assets and opportunities for asset accumulation, set the stage not only for economic growth but, if desired, for egalitarian economic growth as well. What was required next, to achieve equitable growth, was a set of policies which would create favorable markets for the re-distributed assets, or for their services, or for both – in other words, a set of policies which would lead to rapid labor and skill-intensive growth.

Such a set of policies was initiated during the redistributed-asset-value realization phase in 1964 by applying standard economic tools to create an appropriate system of incentives and by reorienting the overall development strategy from one of import substitution to one of export expansion. Korean development strategy was chosen primarily on purely economic growth considerations; the favorable equity consequences, while now welcomed, were not recognized at the time.

The major results of policy changes were (a) a phenomenally rapid expansion of exports and GNP (at average annual rates of 38 and 11 percent in constant prices, respectively, between 1964 and 1970) and (b) a rise in non-farm employment of 1.6 million accompanied by a drop in unemployment from 7.7 percent to 4.5 percent of the labor force (over the same period). The increases in exports were almost exclusively in labor-intensive industries resulting in the absorption of nearly one-half of the overall increase in the labor force between 1966 and 1970 absorbed into export-related employment.

The distributional impact of these policies was that income distribution in South Korea became and remained one of the most equal in the developing world, comparing favorably with that of Sweden and the Netherlands. The poorest 40 percent received a much larger share (18 percent as compared with about 14 percent) in South Korea than in Sweden and the Netherlands, while the top 20 percent received about the same as in Sweden (44 percent) and significantly less than in the Netherlands. The absolute incomes of the poorest 20 percent doubled between 1955 and 1975.

Thus, the recent historical experience of the successful developing equitable-growth countries confirms our thesis. In addition, however, there is also evidence that rapidly growing developing countries which have

16

skipped part of the sequence, or reversed it, or become stuck in one phase of the sequence, have all not been successful in accomplishing the equitable growth objective in the one generation since 1950. Thus, for example, Brazil, in which the distribution of income worsened markedly during its accelerated growth phase in the 1960s, skipped Stages I and III. Mexico, in which rapid growth was also unequalizing, *de facto* retreated from its land reform of several decades earlier and did not markedly expand its educational base before embarking on its rapid industrialization programme. Sri Lanka has passed through the redistributive Stages I and III, but not through the productivity improving Stages II and IV, with deleterious consequences for both growth and the absolute income levels of the poor.

The less successful Communist countries in terms of the combined criterion of productivity and distribution, have in the last phase, stressed capital-intensive rather than labor-intensive growth, and the production of investment rather than of consumer goods. They have also been less successful in early attempts at improving agricultural productivity in Stage II and have not done much to generalize access to education, especially higher education, in Stage III. Other Communist countries, such as Cuba, have not yet entered Stage IV.

Thus, there is selective but consistent evidence that the proposed programme does lead to equitable growth and significant evidence that the opposite strategy does not work on anything resembling an acceptable time scale.

It might be argued that the successful cases all (except for Mainland China) involve small countries, countries with a Chinese or Judaic cultural tradition favouring education, entrepreneurship, and talent for organization, countries under threat, and countries which have benefitted from major infusions of foreign capital. Also, it might be said that the international environment was more favourable to foreign trade during the 1960s than it is likely to be during the 1970s. All that is true. However, the experience of the successful countries *does* offer a proof of feasibility – a powerful counter argument to those who would say that there is no escape for developing countries except to repeat the travail of those already developed. In addition, the conscious design of the process, and the mobilization of the climate of international opinion in favour of its pursuit, together with reforms in the international system designed to support developing countries wanting to engage in the process outlined,

17

can all contribute greatly to the feasibility of wider replication by more developing nations of the process just outlined.

IV

What are the political implications within developing countries of the proposed sequence of strategies? [4] Here we must distinguish between the implementation of the redistribution and its effects, and between early and later stages in the development process. Unfortunately, at the early stages in the development process, there would appear to be definite conflict between broadening political participation and economic redistribution, particularly land reform. At that step, broadening participation involves including middle-class groups in the political process. Both historical and contemporary experience indicate that if participation has increased to the point at which medium size landowners exercise influence on political decision making, then land reform through parliamentary means becomes virtually impossible. The contemporary evidence is overwhelming that most successful land reform results from action by non-democratic governments – domestic, or as in Korea, Taiwan and post-World War II Japan, foreign.[8] Land reform, implemented as recommended here at very early stages in the development process, would therefore regrettably appear to require restriction of participation and concentration of power in an autocratic ruler.

Once the land reform is carried out, however (in Stage II), especially if the administration of the programme is decentralized, participation, in the form of greatly enhanced political strength of the former tenant farmers, tends to increase. Thus, in Stage II, the proposed programme can contribute to both greater *political participation* and to more equitable growth.

The next redistribution phase, that of Stage III, if implemented, usually involves both a broadening of political participation, in the form of enhanced political consciousness and political activism, and increases in equity. Education promotes a greater sense of political efficacy at the individual level, and hence greater levels of individual political participation. Our strategy of stressing education in Stage III beyond the levels required for current economic expansion, would tend to lead to a society with more equal but lower average levels of educationally conferred

4. This section draws primarily on references [8] and [10].

18

status. There is some evidence that political participation in communities of the latter type is greater than in those of the former. In Stage III, therefore, there is likely to be a participation explosion. At that stage, elites have the choice of either stressing faster economic growth and less equality, both economic and political, or slower growth and more participation on both the economic and political fronts. In those countries that stress equity, increases in participation in Stage III can lead, with a relatively short time lag, to politically stable, prosperous, equitable economic growth in Stage IV, thus permitting increases in both economic and political participation. Not infrequently, however, the participation explosion of Stage III, accompanied as it is by less political stability, frightens political elites into a return to the autocratic models of political development, which may be maintained well into Stage IV. At some point, however, once both faster economic growth and the conditions for establishment-channelled, peaceful political participation have been created, more democratic and more equitable development are likely to go hand in hand. The *long run* association of greater economic development and more politically participant institutions at higher levels of economic development is well established, both in contemporary cross-country studies and historically. The political history of Western societies in the 19th century is largely one of broadening suffrage to the lower classes preceded by a trend towards greater economic equality and followed by an acceleration of that trend.

To summarize, politically, within nations, it must be admitted that regrettably the first phase of the strategy recommended for developing nations (land reform), will most likely require autocratic, non-democratic systems for its implementation. But the very implementation of the proposed programme will result in widening political participation – first to the peasants who benefit from the reform, and then, eventually, as the massive educational programme is carried out, to the population as a whole. The increased political participation will first take the form of greater political commitment and activism. This could result in a backlash, in favour of oppression, and to a retreat from equity enhancing programmes in favour of the pursuit of economic growth. Or it could lead to adoption of labour-intensive growth strategies which, by increasing the employment of unskilled, semi-skilled and skilled labour, validate its economic value. If the last strategy is adopted, conditions are created for a growth process which combines both equity and democracy.

19

V

What are the implications of the proposed strategy for the international community? [5] In particular, what are the modifications desirable in the international economic order, and in foreign assistance?

In small countries, the changes in the structure of domestic production implicit in the dynamic process of equitable transition from an under-developed state to a developed one can be greatly facilitated by a supportive international environment. International trade offers a mechanism for decoupling domestic production from domestic consumption and accumulation. Once the first stages of import substitution are accomplished further labour-intensive industrialization is most easily carried out, with the least disruption in domestic socio-cultural consumption patterns, if the labour-intensive industrialization is export-oriented. Otherwise, changes in domestic patterns of consumption and production towards greater use of goods with a high labour-capital ratio are required to support future expansion in labour-intensive industries. Alternatively, import substitution can be carried into the next stage (that of capital-intensive production), which involves high capital-labour and lower labour-output ratios, and has deleterious effects for both growth and the relative and absolute incomes of the poorest.

An international order receptive to the expansion of exports by LDCs at favourable prices is therefore highly desirable. This implies, at a minimum, high growth rates in developed countries, coupled with no import quotas, no licensing and with low tariffs for imports from all LDCs.

Receptivity in developed countries to competition from developing countries should include especially imports from those countries that take steps to redistribute domestic wealth, even if they nationalize foreign-owned firms, or curb multinationals in the process. Some developed countries, especially the United States and Germany, tend to discriminate currently against such countries, thereby providing powerful incentives against domestic reform.

We must now turn to the role of foreign assistance in the proposed programme. The selection of countries receiving foreign aid should emphasize those commited to egalitarian growth and support them in pursuit of that programme.

5. A fuel discussion of NIEO can be found in [11].

The redistributive phases of the recommended strategy are likely to induce reductions in household savings, in private domestic investment and capital flight. This is because they increase risk and uncertainty, both in and of themselves, and because of fear of expropriation. They also disrupt economic networks, reduce production, lower actual rates of return, and decrease rates of economic growth. At that stage, foreign assistance, both financial and technical, in programme design, can help substantially in reducing or even avoiding the lower investment and growth rate consequences of redistribution. It can also ease the transition politically by reducing disaffection, alienation, strikes, etc.

The influx of foreign aid can substitute for lost domestic savings. It can reduce the need for inflationary finance of investment by forced savings and hence for domestic inflation. It can increase domestic investors' confidence in the future of the economy and in the safety of their investment from further expropriation; private savings may be larger as a result. It can bolster a reform-oriented government, thereby enabling it to carry through its reform programme with more confidence and with less need for oppression of personal and political freedoms. It can increase the rationality and appropriateness of the design of institutions for more egalitarian ownership and more egalitarian access to productivity-improving innovations. And it can increase the probability of quick, intelligent follow-up with appropriate productivity-improving technological and institutional innovations and with well-designed development strategies. Thus, during the redistributive phases of the strategy, foreign assistance can be extremely helpful. Indeed, it is then that foreign assistance, especially of a balance of payments, programme support variety, is most needed.

But foreign aid can be quite helpful at the beginning of the productivity-improving stage as well. At that stage, foreign aid can help with appropriate technology, with the design of participant productivity-improving institutions, and with the supply of investment capital, particularly for infrastructural projects involving egalitarian-access to building up of both human and physical capital. At that stage, foreign aid appears in its traditional role, but with greater emphasis on benefitting small producers and increasing the availability of opportunities to the poor.

VII

The liberal model of economic development posited a three-way, long-term positive association between economic development, economic and social equity, and political participation. Both current and historical experience demonstrate that the presumed positive association holds only when quite high levels of economic and social development have been reached. In between, both economically and politically, things tend to get substantially worse before they get better. With historical policies, the period of worsening tends to be quite prolonged. The composite strategy proposed here is likely to reduce both the severity and duration of the deterioration.

BIBLIOGRAPHY

1. Irma Adelman and Cynthia Taft Morris, *Social Equity and Economic Growth in Developing Countries* (Stanford University Press, 1973).
2. Irma Adelman and S. Robinson, *Income Distribution Policy in Developing Countries: A Case Study of Korea* (Stanford University Press, 1978).
3. Irma Adelman, 'South Korea', in H. Chenery et al., *Redistribution with Growth* (Oxford, 1974), 280-285.
4. H. Chenery et al., *Redistribution with Growth* (Oxford University Press, 1974).
5. Alexander Eckstein, *China's Economic Revolution* (Cambridge Press, 1977).
6. John G. Gurley, *China's Economy and the Maoist Strategy* (Monthly Review Press, 1976).
7. Christopher Howe, *China's Economy* (Ecale, 1978).
8. Samuel P. Huntington and Joan N. Nelson, *No Easy Choice: Political Participation in Developing Countries* (Harvard University Press, 1976).
9. Gustav Ranis, 'Taiwan', in H. Chenery et al., *Redistribution with Growth* (Oxford, 1974), 285-290.
10. Hung-chao Tai, *Land Reform and Politics* (University of California Press, 1974).
11. J. Tinbergen et. al., *Reshaping the International order* (RIO Report Dutton, 1976).

[9]

THE LACK OF PARETO SUPERIORITY
OF UNEGALITARIAN WEALTH DISTRIBUTIONS

I. Adelman

University of California, Berkeley

L. Cheng

University of Florida

1. INTRODUCTION

In a recent paper, Bourguignon [4] has shown that, when one or more unegalitarian wealth distributions exist within the «stability interval» of a stable egalitarian distribution, they are Pareto superior to the egalitarian one. This result, if applicable to a real economy, would have profound implications for social policy. In particular, it would imply that social policies aimed at achieving more egalitarian income and wealth distributions could end up making everyone worse off. However, since Bourguignon's result is obtained in a one-sector model and is not consistent with empirical evidence in some of the less-developed countries (for example, South Korea, Taiwan, and Singapore [3]), one may question its validity in a more general framework.

The purpose of this note is to demonstrate that Bourguignon's results do not generalize to a two-sector model of wealth distribution. It is shown that, in a two-sector model, there are no *a priori* reasons why less egalitarian distributions should be Pareto superior to more egalitarian ones. Indeed, the converse is equally likely. Conditions are given under which every equilibrium among the set of multiple equilibria associated with a given set of parameters is Pareto efficient and no equilibrium is Pareto superior.

Existing theoretical works on the dynamic relationship between wealth distribution, factor income and personal income distribution are few in

175

number and are an outgrowth of Stiglitz's contributions [9, 10]. While Bourguignon's paper [4] represents an extension of Stiglitz's one-sector n-class model [10], this note is based on a generalization of Stiglitz's two-sector two-class model [9]([1]). These generalizations are introduced to make it more compatible with empirical evidence on developing economies.

Before we present our model formally, let us point out three major differences between it and [9]. First, Stiglitz [9] assumed that each class saves a constant fraction of its total income. Along with the other standard features of the model in [9], this assumption was responsible for the uniqueness of a two-class equilibrium (stationary distribution). We will instead assume, more realistically, that the saving ratio is an increasing function of wealth holding. Second, capitalists and workers were assumed in [9] to consume the same good, or, equivalently, the technology for producing workers' consumption good and capitalists' consumption good was assumed to be the same. There is a great deal of empirical literature suggesting that the factor intensities of consumption of various classes differ and that the difference has important implications for the dynamic paths of different initial wealth distributions. We therefore assume that the consumption goods for capitalists and workers differ. Third, in proving stability of the equilibrium of wealth distributions, Stiglitz assumed that the consumption good was more capital intensive than the investment good. Although sufficient, this assumption is not necessary for the stability of his equilibrium (see [5, 9]). More important, it runs counter to empirical evidence. We assume that the wage good is less capital intensive than the investment good. This capital intensity assumption is especially appropriate for less developed economies.

The next section presents the formal structure of our model. Section 3 is devoted to a characterization of its equilibrium properties while Section 4 discusses the welfare implications for redistributive policies and demonstrates the nonexistence of Pareto-superior distributions. Section 5 compares our model with that of Bourguignon.

2. THE MODEL

Throughout this note, all variables are expressed as per laborer ratios unless otherwise specified, and the subscripts c and w refer to capitalists and workers respectively.

([1]) Other works based on [10] include Holländer [6] and Schlicht [8]; Adelman and Cheng [1, 2] follow the lines of [9].

In the model economy, there are two goods and two classes. Good 1 is both a consumption good for capitalists and an investment good for capital accumulation. Good 2 is the wage good. Both capitalists and workers own capital, the only form of wealth. Assume further that both the number of workers L and capitalists C grows exogenously at the same rate ([2]) with $L > C$; that capital depreciates at the rate u; that there is no interclass marriage; and, finally, that wealth is bequeathed equally among all descendants. Define the ratios to total labor of total capital owned by capitalists and by workers as k_c and k_w, respectively. Let y_w and y_c be similarly defined as the income/labor ratios for workers and capitalists and S_w and S_c be the saving/income ratios of workers and capitalists.

Under these conditions and by adopting good 1 as the numeraire, the differential equations describing the behavior of wealth ownership over time is given by

$$\frac{\dot{k}_c(t)}{k_c(t)} = S_c(t)R(t) - \eta - u \tag{1a}$$

$$\frac{\dot{k}_w(t)}{k_w(t)} = S_w(t)\left[R(t) + \frac{W(t)}{k_w(t)}\right] - \eta - u \tag{1b}$$

$$k_c(0) = k_c^0 > 0 \, ; \qquad k_w(0) = k_w^0 > 0 \tag{1c}$$

where k_c^0 and k_w^0 are given initial wealth holdings; $R(t)$ is the rental rate and $W(t)$ is the wage rate at time t amd a dot $(\cdot)$ over a variable denotes the derivative of that variable with respect to time. In writing down (1) we have made use of the definition of $y_w(t)$ and $y_c(t)$, namely, $y_w(t) = R(t)k_w(t) + W(t)$ and $y_c(t) = R(t)k_c(t)$.

At any moment in time, $k_c(t)$ and $k_w(t)$ are given; the other variables, in particular $R(t)$, $W(t)$, $S_c(t)$ and $S_w(t)$, are determined endogenously by the equilibrium conditions defining a momentary equilibrium. These specify that supply equals respectively demand in both factor and output markets. The equilibrium values of these variables are then used in (1a), (1b) to generate new values of $k_c(t + \Delta)$, $k_w(t + \Delta)$, $\Delta \to 0$, and the process repeats itself *ad infinitum*. It is clear that the differential equations in (1a), (1b), (1c) plus the conditions of momentary equilibrium fully

---

([2]) To write down (1), it is not necessary to assume anything about the growth rate of the capitalists. However, if the growth rate of the capitalists differs from that of the workers, the relationship between k_c and average personal wealth for the capitalists will change over time, and our analysis would be more complicated.

describe the possible dynamic paths of the economy, including the dynamics of wealth ownership.

2.1. *The momentary equilibrium*

Since our interest is primarily in the long-run dynamics of the wealth distribution, we assume that the momentary equilibrium is unique and stable[3]. For the sake of notational simplicity, dependence on t is suppressed.

There are two factors of production—labor, L, and capital, K. Let Y_i be the total output of good i. Assume that the production functions exhibit constant returns to scale so that they can be written in the conventional intensive form:

$$y_i = f_i(k_i) \quad (i = 1, 2) \tag{2}$$

where

$y_i = Y_i/L_i$,   output/labor ratio in industry i ;

$k_i = K_i/L_i$,   capital/labor ratio in industry i .

We also assume that the Inada [7] conditions hold[4]:

$$f_i' > 0; \ f_i'' < 0; \ f_i'(0) = \infty; \ f_i'(\infty) = 0; \ f_i(0) = 0 \quad (i = 1, 2) \tag{3}$$

where f_i' and f_i'' are the first- and second-order derivatives of f_i respectively.

---

[3] It can be shown that stability of the momentary equilibrium requires that the expression

$$\Delta = \left\{ \left(\eta_2 + \frac{k_2}{k_1 - k_2} \right) \sigma_2 + k_1 \sigma_1 \left(\frac{1}{k_1 - k} - \frac{1}{k_1 - k_2} \right) + (1 - \eta_2) - \frac{w}{w + k_w} \right\}$$

be positive, where

$$\eta_i = \frac{d \log f_i}{d \log k_i} ; \qquad \sigma_i = \frac{d \log k_i}{d \log w} \qquad (i = 1, 2)$$

and k_i, f_i $(i = 1, 2)$, w, k_w, and k are as defined in the text. It can be shown that the following two conditions are sufficient to guarantee stability:

$$\sigma_2 > \eta_1 - \eta_2(1 - \eta_1)/(1 - \eta_2) \tag{a}$$

and

$$k_w > k_2 . \tag{b}$$

[4] For a generalization of such conditions and the necessary modifications of our subsequent analysis, see [5].

Assume further that both the factor markets and the product markets are competitive, so that the usual marginal product conditions are satisfied. Then

$$w \equiv \frac{W}{R} = \frac{f_i}{f_i'} - k_i \qquad (i = 1, 2) \tag{4}$$

Since $\partial w/\partial k_i > 0$ for all $k_i \in [0, \infty)$, we may invert (4) to obtain the optimal capital/labor ratio k_i as a function of the wage/rental ratio w, i.e., $k_i(w)$, $i = 1, 2$. Let us assume that the capital goods and capitalist consumption industry (the first industry) is more capital intensive than the wage good industry (the second industry) for all positive wage/rental ratios:

$$k_1(w) > k_2(w) \quad \text{for all } w > 0. \tag{5}$$

Let λ be the fraction of the labor force in industry 1. Then the assumption of full employment of both factors amounts algebraically to (6).

$$\lambda k_1 + (1 - \lambda) k_2 = k \equiv k_w + k_c. \tag{6}$$

We have now completely specified the supply conditions in the economy. To close the model of momentary equilibrium, let us bring in the demand conditions. Since good 2 is a consumption good for the workers only, the total demand/labor ratio for good 2 is given by (7).

$$D_2 = [1 - S_w(k_w)](Rk_w + W)/p \tag{7}$$

where the relative price of good 2

$$p = f_1'(k_1)/f_2'(k_2)$$

under the competitive condition.

Since the supply of good 2 (per laborer) is given by $(1 - \lambda)y_2$, momentary equilibrium is determined by the following condition:

$$(1 - \lambda)y_2 = [1 - S_w(k_w)](Rk_w + W)/p. \tag{9}$$

We need not specify either the demand or supply of good 1 since, thanks to Walras' Law, the market clearing condition for good 1 follows from that of good 2.

If S_w is a given constant fraction, then (9) is a special case of Stiglitz's [9] momentary equilibrium. As indicated earlier, we assume, more realistically, that S_w and S_c are increasing functions of k_w and k_c respectively. Despite this, however, if the sum of the Hicksian elasticities of substitution equals or exceeds unity, momentary equilibrium is unique because our model is functionally identical to the Uzawa model as extended by Inada (1963) (see [9]).

Let us summarize the model of momentary equilibrium. It is represented by a system of six equations in six variables (R, W, k_1, k_2, p, and λ) and two parameters (k_c, k_w):

$$R = f_1'(k_1) \tag{10a}$$

$$W = f_1(k_1) - k_1 f_1'(k_1) \tag{10b}$$

$$k_2 = k_2(w) = k_2\left(\frac{W}{R}\right) \tag{10c}$$

$$\lambda = \frac{k_w + k_c - k_2}{k_1 - k_2} \tag{10d}$$

$$(1-\lambda)f_2(k_2) = [1 - S_w(k_w)](k_w \cdot R + W)/p \tag{10e}$$

$$p = \frac{f_1'(k_1)}{f_2'(k_2)} \tag{10f}$$

where k_2 is obtained by inverting (4) and (10d) is obtained by solving (6).

2.2. *The long-run equilibrium*

From (10a, b, c, d, e, and f), we may solve the six variables in terms of the two parameters. In particular, we may express R and W as functions of k_c and k_w. If the Hicksian elasticity conditions holds, then the functional relationship is unique so that we can write $R(k_c, k_w)$ and $W(k_c, k_w)$. We may substitute these expressions into (1a) and (1b) and solve for the long-run stationary states.

$$S_c(k_c) R(k_c, k_w) = \eta + u \tag{11a}$$

$$S_w(k_w)\left[R(k_c, k_w) + \frac{W(k_c, k_w)}{k_w}\right] = \eta + u. \tag{11b}$$

Thus, we have completely specified our basic model of wealth and income determination. In the subsequent sections, we will look into the

— 111 —

question of multiple long-run equilibria and the welfare implications of egalitarian social policies.

3. MULTIPLICITY AND STABILITY OF EQUILIBRIA

Stiglitz [9] showed that the long-run equilibrium (steady state) is unique if S_w and S_c are constants. However, if the latter are functions of k_w and k_c, respectively, the proof of uniqueness of the long-run equilibrium would no longer go through. There may be multiple long-run equilibria despite the uniqueness of the momentary equilibrium.

To study the dynamics implied by (1) taking note of the depencence of R and W on k_c and k_w, we will construct a phase diagram in the (k_w, k_c) space.

3.1. *The accumulation of wealth by workers*

Let us define H as the graph of positive k_w and k_c satisfying (11*b*), i.e.,

$$H = \{(k_w, k_c) | k_w > 0; k_c > 0; S_w(k_w)[R(k_c, k_w) + W(k_c, k_w)/k_w] = \eta + u\}.$$

H can be thought of as the dividing line between two subspaces, one in which k_w is positive and the other in which k_w is negative. Denote the mapping of $\{k_w > 0\}$ into $\{k_c > 0\}$ on the graph H by h, i.e. $k_c = h(k_w)$ for all $(k_w, k_c) \in H$. Under fairly general conditions h would be continuous and differentiable, although it may be multi-valued in the general case. To study the dynamics implied by (1*b*), let us take derivative of (1*b*) with respect to k_c.

$$\frac{\partial}{\partial k_c} \left(\frac{k_w}{k_w} \right)\bigg|_{h(k_w)} = S_w(k_w) \left(\frac{\partial R}{\partial k_c} + \frac{1}{k_w} \frac{\partial W}{\partial k_c} \right) \tag{12}$$

where

$$\frac{\partial W}{\partial k_c} = \frac{\partial W}{\partial R} \frac{\partial R}{\partial k_c} = \frac{\partial R}{\partial k_c} \left(\frac{\partial W/\partial k_1}{\partial R/\partial k_1} \right) = -\frac{\partial R}{\partial k_c} k_1. \tag{13}$$

In (13) the factor employment conditions in the first industry, namely, $R = f_1'$ and $W = f_1 - k_1 f_1'$ are used to obtain the last equality. Using (13) we can rewrite (12) as

$$\frac{\partial}{\partial k_c}\left(\frac{k_w}{k_w}\right)\bigg|_{h(k_w)} = S_w(k_w)\frac{\partial R}{\partial k_c}\left(1-\frac{k_1}{k_w}\right) > 0 . \tag{14}$$

It can be shown that $\partial R/\partial k_c < 0$. Because of (5) $k_1 > k_2$. But $k = k_w + k_c$ must lie strictly between k_1 and k_2, it follows that $k_1 > k_w$, and hence the positivity of the expression in (14). The meaning of (14) is that, for any k_w and k_c, $\dot{k}_w \gtreqless 0$ if and only if $k_c \gtreqless \tilde{k}_c$ where $(k_w, \tilde{k}_c) \in H$. From this we may also infer that $h(k_w)$ must be a single-valued function or else the set $\{k_c|k_c = h(k_w)\}$ must be connected for every k_w at which h is multi-valued [5]. An example of a permissible h is given in fig. 1a.

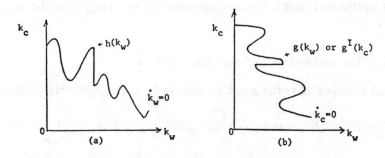

Figure 1. Permissible stationary loci

To obtain the slope of $h(k_w)$, we apply the implicit function rule to (11b).

$$\frac{dh}{dk_w} = -\frac{\partial s_w/\partial k_w}{S_w(k_w)(\partial R/\partial k_c)\cdot(1-k_1/k_w)} \tag{15}$$

where s_w is defined as the workers' saving/wealth ratio, i.e., $s_w = S_w \cdot (k_w)\,y_w/k_w$.

From (14) we know that the denominator in (15) is positive so that the sign of dh/dk_w is opposite to that of $\partial s_w/\partial k_w$. It can be shown that y_w is increasing in k_w if the wage good (good 2) is wealth normal, i.e.,

---

[5] If h were multi-valued for some $\hat{k}_w$ and if the set $\{k\,/k_c = h(\hat{k}_w)\}$ were not connected, then under the assumption that h is continuous, there must exist different k_c's corresponding to $\hat{k}_w$ such that (14) is violated. This is so because H divides the (k_w, k_c) space into two sub-spaces which have opposite signs for $\dot{k}_w$.

if $\partial/\partial k_w\{[1 - S_w(k_w)]y_w\} > 0$. That is to say, under this condition s_w is the product of two increasing functions of k_w ($S_w(k_w)$ and $y_w(k_w)$) and a rectangular hyperbola of k_w. This implies that in the general case $\partial s_w/\partial k_w$ may change sign for different values of k_w, which in turn implies that in the general case $h(k_w)$ may wiggle as in fig. 1a.

3.2. *The accumulation of wealth by capitalists*

As in the previous sub-section, let us define G as the graph of positive k_w and k_c satisfying (11a), i.e.

$$G = \{(k_w, k_c) | k_w > 0; \; k_c > 0; \; S_c(k_c)R(k_c, k_w) = \eta + u\} .$$

G can be thought of as the dividing line between two subspaces, one in which k_c is positive and the other in which k_c is negative. Denote the mapping of $\{k_w > 0\}$ into $\{k_c > 0\}$ on the graph G by g and the inverse mapping by $g^I(k_c)$ for all $(k_w, k_c) \in G$.

To study the dynamics implied by (1a), let us take derivative of (1a) with respect to k_w.

$$\frac{\partial}{\partial k_w}\left(\frac{k_c}{k_c}\right)\bigg|_{g(k_w)} = S_c(k_c)\frac{\partial R}{\partial k_w} . \tag{16}$$

It can be shown that $\partial R/\partial k_w$ is negative if good 2 is wealth normal. Under this condition (16) says that, for any k_w and k_c, $k_c \gtreqless 0$ if and only if $k_w \lesseqgtr \tilde{k}_w$, where $(\tilde{k}_w, k_c) \in G$. From this we may also infer that $g^I(k_c)$ must be a single-valued function or else the set $\{k_w | k_w = g^I(k_c)\}$ must be connected for every k_c at which g^I is multi-valued [6]. An example of a permissible g^I is given in fig. 1b.

The slope of $g(k_w)$ can be derived rather easily by applying the implicit function rule to (11a).

$$\frac{dg}{dk_w} = -\frac{S_c(\partial R/\partial k_w)}{((\partial S_c/\partial k_c)R + S_c(\partial R/\partial k_c))} = -\frac{S_c(\partial R/\partial k_w)}{(S_c R/k_c)(\varepsilon_{S_c} - \varepsilon_R)} \tag{17}$$

where $\varepsilon_{S_c} = (\partial S_c/\partial k_c)(k_c/S_c)$ is the elasticity of the capitalist's saving ratio and $\varepsilon_R \equiv -(\partial R/\partial k_c)(k_c/R)$ is the absolute value of the elasticity of rental rate with respect to k_c.

---

[6] Similar arguments as in footnote [5].

If good 2 is wealth normal, $\partial R/\partial k_w$ is negative and, hence, the sign of dg/dk_w depends on the relative magnitudes of ε_{S_e} and ε_R. More specifically, $dg/dk_w \gtreqless 0$ if and only if $\varepsilon_{S_e} \gtreqless \varepsilon_R$. If S_c is sufficiently inelastic with respect to k_c, $\varepsilon_{S_e} < \varepsilon_R$ and, therefore, $dg/dk_w < 0$. Otherwise, $g(k_w)$ may also wiggle as in fig. 1*b*.

3.3. *The long-run equilibrium*

Combining (14), (15), (16), and (17) we may determine the long-run equilibria and the dynamics outside of the equilibria. An example consistent with fig. 1 is given in fig. 2, where four equilibria of wealth distribution (*A*, *B*, *C*, and *D*) are shown. While equilibria *B* and *D* are unstable, equilibria *A* and *C* are locally stable and could possibly be surrounded by limit cycles.

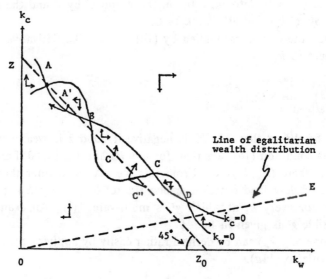

Figure 2. Phase diagram of wealth accumulation.

4. THE WELFARE IMPLICATIONS FOR REDISTRIBUTIVE POLICIES AND THE NON-EXISTENCE OF PARETO SUPERIOR DISTRIBUTIONS

We are now in a position to consider some welfare implications for redistributive policies aiming at more egalitarian distributions. To this end, let us assume that the limit cycles, when they exist, are sufficiently close to A and C, respectively, so that we may simply broaden the concept of equilibrium to include the regions covered by the cycles. Under this assumption, we may use fig. 2 as an example to study the welfare impacts of redistributive policies.

Let us define the wealth egalitarian line as the locus in the (k_c, k_w) space of equal personal wealth distribution, i.e., $k_c = Ck_w/L$. This is given by the line OE in fig. 2.

We say that a wealth distribution is more egalitarian than another if it is closer to the egalitarian line OE. From fig. 2, it is clear that equilibrium C is more egalitarian than equilibrium A. The line ZAZ_0 is an iso-aggregate-wealth line and represents all the possibilities of wealth redistribution given the initial equilibrium A in the absence of redistribution costs. As can be seen in the diagram, a moderate redistribution policy such as the movement to A' would not have any long-run effect. In the short run, the economy is more egalitarian than at A. But, in the long run, it returns to A. It is also shown that, as a result of wealth redistribution to A', the aggregate capital/labor ratio in the economy falls in the short run. On the other hand, if the redistribution is more drastic—for instance, to C' or C''—the economy will converge to equilibrium C in the long run, although in the short run there is also an adverse effect on aggregate capital at C''. As the diagram is drawn, the aggregate capital/labor ratio in position C is higher than that in position A, implying that the long-run effect of a redistribution may be opposite to its short-run impact.

Let us now offer some intuitive reasons why in the long run a more egalitarian equilibrium such as C may be possible. If wealth is redistributed in favour of the workers and away from the capitalists, then the workers' average income y_w would go up if good 2 is wealth normal. Because the savings ratio of the workers S_w is an increasing function of k_w, the total savings out of y_w would also go up making it possible for the new wealth position of the workers to be sustained. On the other hand, the capitalists' average income y_c and savings would go down. Similarly, this makes it possible for the capitalists' wealth to be sustained at a lower level. While the above argument is no proof for the existence of a long-run equilibrium like C, it does indicate its possibility and why it may exist. Let us also note that the argument is not necessarily invalidated when the savings ratios are decreasing functions of wealth.

One might object that a more egalitarian wealth distribution does not mean much unless it leads to a more egalitarian distribution of consumption. It is easy however to demonstrate that under certain conditions it does. The average consumption of the capitalists is equal to

$$[1 - S_c(k_c)]y_c C/L$$

and that of the workers is equal to

$$[1 - S_w(k_w)]y_w/p.$$

If the wage good is wealth normal and if the Hicksian elasticities are sufficiently large, p, W and R would change very little, and therefore the workers' average consumption (of good 2) would move in the same direction as k_w. Similarly, if we also assume that the consumption good for the capitalists is wealth normal, i.e., if

$$\frac{\partial}{\partial k_c}\{[1 - S_c(k_c)]y_c\} > 0,$$

then the capitalists' average consumption (of good 1) would move in the same direction as k_c. Therefore, when the consumption goods for both classes are wealth normal and the elasticities of factor substitution are sufficiently large, an increase (a decrease) in wealth leads to an increase (a decrease) in consumption. Hence a more egalitarian wealth distribution implies a more egalitarian distribution of consumption.

Let us now turn to the question of Pareto superior distributions with reference to fig. 2. If A lies to the northeast of C, but above the line connecting C to the origin, then A is less egalitarian than C but is Pareto superior to C. On the other hand, if C lies to the northeast of A but below the line connecting A to the origin, then C is both more egalitarian and Pareto superior to A. While the first case lends support to Bourguignon's conclusion, the second case contradicts it.

Although it is difficult to see which case would hold under what assumptions, it is possible to specify conditions which rule out the existence of any Pareto superior distributions. From (17) we see that $dg/dk_w < 0$ if the wage good is wealth normal and if S_c is sufficiently inelastic so that $\varepsilon_{S_e} < \varepsilon_R$. Under these conditions, each of the multiple equilibria associated with a given set of parameters is Pareto efficient and no equilibrium is Pareto superior.

5. COMPARISON WITH BOURGUIGNON'S MODEL

Let us summarize the differences between our model and [4] very briefly. First, [4] is a one-sector model whereas ours is a two-sector model. Second, one of the classes in our model (the capitalists) do not work but in [4] everybody works. Third, workers and capitalists consume different goods in our model but in [4] they consume the same good because of the one-sector assumption.

Two features were deemed by Bourguignon as essential for his result: that (*a*) total saving is an increasing, convex function of income and (*b*) « all individuals have a positive wealth » [4, p. 1470]. It is straight-forward to see that (*b*) is implicit in our equation (1). Since we assume that the savings ratios, S_c and S_w, are increasing functions of k_c and k_w, respectively, it is clear that total saving for each class is increasing and convex in the income of that class if y_w is increasing in k_w and y_c in k_c. It can be shown that y_w is increasing in k_w if the wage good is wealth normal and that y_c is increasing in k_c if the Hicksian elasticities are suffi-ciently large.

It can be shown that under the above assumptions the marginal rate of saving for the workers is less than unity as in [4, p. 1470], i.e.,

$$\frac{\partial}{\partial y_w}[S_w(k_w)y_w(k_w, k_c)] < 1 \ (^7).$$

We may also show that the marginal rate of saving for the capitalists is less than unity if the capitalists' consumption good (good 1) is wealth normal (^{8}).

(^{7}) To see this let us notice that y_w and k_w are uniquely related if $\sigma_1 + \sigma_2 \geqslant 1$. As a result we may determine the workers' marginal rate of saving.

$$\frac{\partial}{\partial y_w}[S_w(k_w)\,y_w(k_w, k_c)] = S_w\left[1 + \frac{\partial S_w/\partial k_w \cdot k_w}{S_w \cdot \partial \log y_w/\partial \log k_w}\right]$$

$$= S_w\left[1 + \frac{\partial S_w/\partial k_w \cdot k_w}{(S_w(k_w/(k_w + w)) + X)}\right]$$

where

$$X = \{S_w(1 - \eta_1)\eta_1(k_1 - k_w)[k_w/(k_1 - k) + k_w/(w + k_w) - S_w\varepsilon_{S_w}/(1 - S_w)\}/$$
$$/\{\Delta[\eta_1 k_w + k_1(1 - \eta_1)]\}.$$

It can be shown that X is positive if good 2 is wealth normal. Moreover, if good 2 is normal

$$\frac{1}{w + k_w} > \frac{\partial S_w/\partial k_w}{(1 - S_w)},$$

which implies that

$$\frac{\partial}{\partial y_w}[S_w(k_w)\,y_w(k_w, k_c)] < 1.$$

(^{8}) First let us notice that from the definition of wealth normality for the capi-talist consumption good in Section 4 we can derive the following inequality:

$$\frac{1}{k_c} > \frac{\partial S_c}{\partial k_c}\Big/(1 - S_c).$$

Although the above conditions guarantee that the saving functions in our model have the same properties as postulated in [4], these conditions do not guarantee that they are identical.

6. CONCLUDING REMARKS

In a two-sector two-class model along the lines of Stiglitz [9] we have shown that Bourguignon's result about wealth distribution do not hold in the general case. The nature of consumption goods and production technology, in particular the ease of factor substitution, appear to have important bearing on the relative optimality of egalitarian vs. nonegalitarian wealth and income distributions. Thus, there is no *a priori* presumption that, in a multiclass, multisector world, egalitarianism necessarily makes every one worse off.

APPENDIX

Formal proofs of some assertions in the paper.

In the paper a number of assertions have been made without formal proof. These include

(1) $\partial R/\partial k_c < 0$ (Subsection 3.1, p. 112);

(2) $\partial R/\partial k_w < 0$ if good 2 is wealth normal (Subsection 3.2, p. 113);

(3) $\partial y_w/\partial k_w > 0$ if good 2 is wealth normal (Subsection 3.1, p. 112, Section 5, p. 117);

(4) $\partial y_c/\partial k_c > 0$ if the Hicksian elasticities are sufficiently large (Section 5, p. 117);

(5) The changes in p, W, and R are sufficiently close to zero if the Hicksian elasticities are sufficiently large (Section 4, p. 116);

(6) Necessary and sufficient conditions for the momentary equilibrium to be stable (footnote (^{2})), and

(7) The expression X in footnote (^{7}) is positive if good 2 is wealth normal.

To determine the marginal rate of capitalist saving let us perform the following simple derivation, knowing that there is a unique relationship between y_c and k_c when $\sigma_1 + \sigma_2 > 1$.

$$\frac{\partial}{\partial y_c} [S_c(k_c) y_c(k_c, k_w)] = S_c + k_c \frac{\partial S_c}{\partial k_c} \left[\frac{1}{\partial \log y_c/\partial \log k_c} \right] = S_c + k_c \frac{\partial S_c}{\partial k_c} \left[\frac{1}{1 - Y/\Delta} \right]$$

where $Y = [(1 - \eta_1) k_c]/(k_1 - k)] > 0$ because of (5).

If σ_1 and σ_2 are sufficiently large Y/Δ is sufficiently small and hence $\partial/\partial y_c \cdot [S_c(k_c) y_c(k_c, k_w)]$ is sufficiently close to $S_c + k_c(\partial S_c/\partial k_c)$, which is less than unity if the capitalist consumption good is wealth normal.

The purpose of this Appendix is to provide the technical details which are omitted in the main body of our note. Before we proceed, it is useful to note some implications of profit maximization on the part of the producers—more specifically, some implications of (4).

Fact 1.

$$\varepsilon_i \sigma_i + 1 - n_i = 0 \quad (i = 1, 2);$$

where σ_i and η_i are as defined in footnote (^{3}) and $\varepsilon_i \equiv (f_i'')/(f_i') \cdot k_i$ is negative in view of (3).

Fact 1 is obtained by taking total derivative of (4) with respect to w and rearranging terms.

Fact 2.

$$k_i(1 - \eta_i)/(\eta_i) = w \quad (i = 1, 2).$$

This is just a different way of writing (4). Notice that under (5) $\eta_1 > \eta_2$. Using Fact 1, we may derive (A.1) from (10a):

$$d \log R = \varepsilon_1 \sigma_1 d \log w = (\eta_1 - 1) d \log w. \tag{A.1}$$

By definition, $W = Rw$. We may derive (A.2) by making use of (A.1):

$$d \log W = d \log R + d \log w = \eta_1 d \log w. \tag{A.2}$$

From (10c), the following is straightforward:

$$d \log k_2 = \sigma_2 d \log w. \tag{A.3}$$

Using (10f), we may derive (A.4):

$$d \log p = (\varepsilon_1 \sigma_1 - \varepsilon_2 \sigma_2) d \log w$$

$$= [(\eta_1 - 1) - (\eta_2 - 1)] d \log w = (\eta_1 - \eta_2) d \log w. \tag{A.4}$$

Finally, substituting (10d) into (10e), taking total derivatives logarithmically of (10e) with respect to w, and making use of (A.1) through (A.4), we obtain:

$$\left[\frac{k_1}{k_1 - k} \sigma_1 + \eta_2 \sigma_2 - \frac{k_1 \sigma_1}{k_1 - k_2} + \frac{k_2 \sigma_2}{k_1 - k_2} - \frac{k_w}{w + k_w} \varepsilon_1 \sigma_1 \right.$$

$$\left. - \frac{w}{w + k_w} \eta_1 + \eta_1 - \eta_2 \right] d \log w = Z_1 d \log k_c + Z_2 d \log k_w \tag{A.5}$$

where

$$Z_1 = k_c/(k_1 - k) > 0,$$

$$Z_2 = [k_w/(k_1 - k) + k_w/(w + k_w) - S_w \varepsilon_{S_w}/(1 - S_w)]$$

and

$$\varepsilon_{S_w} = (\partial S_w/\partial k_w)(k_w/S_w).$$

Equation (A.5) may be further simplified by using Fact 1.

$$\Delta \cdot d \log w = Z_1 d \log k_c + Z_2 d \log k_w \tag{A.6}$$

where Δ is defined in footnote ([3]).

Since

$$\frac{\partial}{\partial k_w} \{[1 - S_w(k_w)] y_w\} = (1 - S_w) R - \frac{\partial S_w}{\partial k_w} (W + R k_w),$$

the hypothesis of wealth normality implies that:

$$\frac{1}{w + k_w} > \frac{\partial S_w}{\partial k_w} \Big/ (1 - S_w). \tag{A.7}$$

Therefore

$$Z_2 = \left(\frac{k_w}{k_1 - k} + \frac{k_w}{w + k_w} - \frac{S_w}{1 - S_w} \varepsilon_{S_w} \right)$$

$$= k_w \left(\frac{1}{k_1 - k} + \frac{1}{w + k_w} - \frac{\partial S_w / \partial k_w}{1 - S_w} \right) > 0 \tag{A.8}$$

for any $k_w > 0$ if good 2 is wealth normal.

The left-hand side of (10e) represents the supply of, and the right-hand side represents the demand for, good 2, i.e.,

$$S_2 = (1 - \lambda) f_2(k_2)$$

$$D_2 = [1 - S_w(k_w)](k_w \cdot R + W)/p. \tag{A.9}$$

Mathematically, the momentary equilibrium is stable if and only if

$$(\partial \log S_2)/(\partial \log p) > (\partial \log D_2)/(\partial \log p).$$

But, we know from (A.4) that p and w are positively related. Thus, the good markets are stable if and only if

$$(\partial \log S_2)/(\partial \log w) > (\partial \log D_2)/(\partial \log w).$$

Substituting the definition of λ into (A.9), taking derivatives logarithmically, and using (A.4), we obtain the stability condition: the good markets are stable if and only if $\Delta > 0$.

For given k_c and k_w, our model is equivalent to Uzawa's (1962) model in which the saving ratio out of wages is S_w and the saving ratio out of profit is S_c (see Inada (1963)) if we define S_c as follows:

$$S_c = S_w + (1 - S_w) \frac{k_c}{k} > S_w. \tag{A.10}$$

The total demand for investment good is then given by:

$$S_c k + S_w w. \tag{A.11}$$

By hypothesis, the factor markets are in equilibrium; hence, k can be expressed as the following (see Drandakis (1963), p. 220):

$$k = \frac{k_1 k_2 [S_w k_1 + (1 - S_w) k_2] w}{(1 - \bar{S}_c) k_1 + \bar{S}_c k_2 + w} = \frac{k_1 k_2 + [S_w k_1 + (1 - S_w) k_2] w}{\delta} \tag{A.12}$$

where $\delta = (1 - S_w) k_w k_1/k + [S_w + (1 - S_w) k_c/k] k_2 + w$.

Substitute (A.12) into the definition of Δ, we may express the stability condition as

$$\Delta \equiv \left(\eta_2 + \frac{k_2}{k_1 - k_2}\right)\sigma_2 + \frac{k_1}{k_1 - k_2}\left\{\frac{[S_w + (1 - S_w)(k_c/k)]k_2 + S_w w}{(1 - S_w)[k_1(k_w/k) + w]}\right\}\sigma_1$$

$$+ (1 - \eta_2) - \frac{w}{w - k_w} > 0. \tag{A.13}$$

Making use of the relationship, $k_i(1 - \eta_i)/\eta_i = w$, $i = 1, 2$, and after some tedious substitution and cancellation, we may rewrite (A.13) as

$$\frac{\Delta}{\eta_2} = \frac{(1 - \eta_2)}{m}\sigma_2 + \frac{(1 - \eta_1)}{m}\frac{[S_w/\eta_2 + (1 - S_w)(k_c/k)]}{(1 - S_w)[1/\eta_1 - k_c/k]}\sigma_1$$

$$- (1 - \eta_2)\left[\frac{(1 - (k_w/k_2))}{(1 - \eta_2) + (k_w/k_2)\eta_2}\right] > 0 \tag{A.14}$$

where $m = (1 - \eta_2)\eta_1 - (1 - \eta_1)\eta_2 > 0$ because of (5).

Condition (A.14) is the necessary and sufficient condition for the good markets to be stable. From the definition of m and the restrictions imposed on η_1 and η_2, it is clear that the coefficient of σ_2 exceeds 1. A sufficient condition for stability is $\sigma_2 > m/(1 - \eta_2) = \eta_1 - \eta_2(1 - \eta_1)/(1 - \eta_2)$ because

$$(1 - \eta_2)\left[\frac{1 - k_w/k_2}{(1 - \eta_2) + (k_w/k_2)\eta_2}\right]$$

is always smaller than 1 algebraically and equal to 1 only when $k_w = 0$. Should k_w equal 0, it is easy to show that the coefficient of σ_1 also exceeds 1. Under this condition, $\sigma_1 + \sigma_2 > 1$ is sufficient for stability. Furthermore, because the coefficients of σ_1 and σ_2 are always positive, $(A.14)$ is satisfied automatically if $k_w > k_2(k_w, k_c)$ where $k_2(k_w, k_c)$ is determined by (10). This proves Assertion (6).

Under the stability conditions let us validate the other assertions. Using (A.1) and (A.6) we may derive $\partial \log R / \partial \log k_c$

$$\frac{\partial \log R}{\partial \log k_c} = (\eta_1 - 1) Z_1/\Delta < 0 \tag{A.15}$$

This proves Assertion (1) because log represents a monotone increasing transformation. Similarly we may derive $\partial \log R / \partial \log k_w$.

$$\frac{\partial \log R}{\partial \log k_w} = (\eta_1 - 1) Z_2/\Delta, \tag{A.16}$$

— 122 —

which is negative if good 2 is wealth normal (A.8). This proves Assertion (2).

It can be verified that

$$\frac{\partial \log y_w}{\partial \log k_c} = (1 - \eta_1)\eta_1 \frac{Z_1}{\Delta}\left(\frac{k_1 - k_w}{\eta_1 k_w + k_1(1 - \eta_1)}\right) > 0 \tag{A.17}$$

because $k_1 > k > k_w$. This proves Assertion (3).

Assertion (4) is true because

$$\frac{\partial \log y_c}{\partial \log k_c} = 1 - (1 - \eta_1)\frac{Z_1}{\Delta} , \tag{A.18}$$

which is positive if Δ is sufficiently large. But Δ is sufficiently large if σ_1 and σ_2 are sufficiently large.

From (A.1), (A.2) and (A.4), we see that the changes in R, W, and p depend on the changes in w. But from (A.6) we see that the changes in w induced by a change in k_c or k_w or both is sufficiently close to zero if Δ is sufficiently large, which holds if σ_1 and σ_2 are sufficiently large. This proves Assertion (5).

Using (A.8) in the expression for X in footnote [7], we see that $X > 0$. Using the same condition in the expression for $\partial[S_w(k_w)\,y_w(k_w, k_c)]/\partial y_w$, we see that it is less than unity. This proves Assertion (7).

REFERENCES

[1] Adelman I. and Cheng L.: *A Dynamic Model of Personal Wealth and Income Distribution in a Growing Closed Economy*, Jahrbücher für Nationalökonomie, 198/6 (1983), pp. 481-504.

[2] Adelman I. and Cheng L.: *Redistribution before Growth: A Theoretical Model*, Working paper, Division of Agricultural Sciences, University of California, July 1981.

[3] Adelman I. and Robinson S.: *Income Distribution Policy in Developing Countries: A Case Study of Korea*, Stanford University Press, Stanford, California, 1978.

[4] Bourguignon F.: « Pareto Superiority of Unegalitarian Equilibria in Stiglitz' Model of Wealth Distribution with Convex Saving Function », *Econometrica*, 49 (1981), 1469-1475.

[5] Drandakis E.M.: « Factor Substitution in the Two Sector Growth Model », *Review of Economic Studies*, 30 (1963), 217-228.

[6] Holländer H.: *Capital Accumulation and Distribution of Productive Wealth*, Working paper, Universität Dortmund, July 1978.

[7] Inada K.: « On a Two-Sector Model of Economic Growth: Comments and a Generalization », *Review of Economic Studies*, 30 (1963), 119-127.

[8] Schlicht V.E.: « A Neoclassical Theory of Wealth Distribution », *Jahrbücher für Nationalökonomie und Statistik*, 189 (1975), 78-96.

[9] Stiglitz J.E.: « A Two-Sector Two-Class Model of Economic Growth », *Review of Economic Studies*, 34 (1967), 227-238.

[10] Stiglitz J.E.: « Distribution of Income and Wealth Among Individuals », *Econometrica*, 37 (1969), 382-397.

The Equalizing Role of Human Resource Intensive Growth Strategies: A Theoretical Model

Irma Adelman, *University of California, Berkeley*
and
Amnon Levy, *Ben Gurion University*

Empirical evidence concerning the relationship between education-intensive development strategies and income distribution is used to formulate a growth model in which the variance of the dispersion rate of income is linked to the human and physical capital intensity of production. It is shown that, under plausible assumptions, the growth trajectory does not have a unique steady state. Of the possible steady states, for any two steady states characterized by equal per capita output and by different combinations of physical capital-labor ratio and average human capital, the income distribution associated with the steady state with the higher level of average human capital is Lorenz superior.

1. INTRODUCTION

Much of Jan Tinbergen's work throughout his entire life has centered on the reduction of inequality in the distribution of income. In his analysis of distributional issues, he has stressed the role of inequality in the ownership and rewards to human capital as the most important determinant of income inequality in developed countries. He has explored this problem from both a normative (Tinbergen 1970, 1980) and a positive point of view (Tinbergen 1973, 1974, 1975a, 1977a, 1977b). In his policy recommendations, he consistently urged increasing the stock of high-level manpower as a method for lessening income inequality (see, for example, Tinbergen 1975a, 1975b, 1977).

From a technical point of view, Tinbergen's analysis has bridged the gap between the human capital school, which emphasizes the determinants of the supply of skills using household decision models, and the manpower-planning school, which focuses on the pattern of demand for educated labor, deriving it from a projection of the production profile of the economy. His models typically offer both demand and supply functions for educated labor and derive the returns to labor from equating

Journal of Policy Modeling 6(2):271–287(1984)   271
© Society for Policy Modeling, 1984   0161-8938/84/$3.00

the two. His analysis has been insightful, innovative, and powerful in its simplicity.

The literature on the economics of education is voluminous, and will not be surveyed here in view of the existence of several recent surveys. Analytic surveys of the human capital school approach to education and income distribution are provided in Blaugh (1976), Cain (1976), and Rosen (1976). Their relationship to theories of personal income distribution is appraised in Sahota (1978), and the culminating statement of models linking household choice to the acquisition of human capital is spelled out in Becker (1981) and discussed in Ben-Porath (1982) and Hannan (1982). Multisector macroeconomic models of educational planning are summarized in Fox (1972). An important contribution to the literature on education and income distribution is contained in Ritzen (1977).

In this paper, we proceed in the spirit of Tinbergen to extend his demand-supply framework from the medium term to the long run. Our main focus is on the interaction of parametric variations in the dynamic accumulation strategies for the accumulation of education with the production-income-generation processes of a growing economy. The rest of this paper develops a macroeconomic dynamic growth model aimed at investigating the long-run relationship between human and physical capital accumulation strategies and income distribution. Section 2 describes how changes in the average level of human capital and in the physical capital-labor ratio affect income distribution. Section 3 presents a system of differential equations describing the evolution of the physical capital-labor ratio and of the average stock of human capital. Section 4 derives the system's steady state and its stability properties. Section 5 discusses the optimal choice of steady state in a multiequilibrium case. We conclude that the Pareto optimal development strategies are human-capital intensive.

2. EFFECTS OF PHYSICAL AND HUMAN CAPITAL ON POVERTY AND INCOME DISTRIBUTION

In this section, we present a static macroeconomic model for studying the effects of physical and human capital endowments on the distribution of income. We assume that the distribution of income within the population is log-normal. In particular, we assume that the income of person i, y_i, is a product of the median income, y_m, and an exponential dispersion factor, e^{u_i}:

$$y_i = y_m e^{u_i}. \tag{1}$$

The dispersion rate, u, is assumed to be normally distributed within the population with zero mean and constant variance

$$u \sim N(0, \sigma^2).$$

The variance of the dispersion rate reflects the degree of income inequality; the greater σ^2, the higher income inequality.

We hypothesize that the variance of the dispersion rate always increases in the physical capital-labor ratio, k, and decreases in the average level of human capital, α, in the population, i.e.,

$$\sigma^2 = \sigma^2(k, \alpha) \tag{2}$$

and

$$\frac{\partial \sigma^2}{\partial k} > 0, \qquad \frac{\partial \sigma^2}{\partial \alpha} < 0.$$

These assumptions are supported by empirical evidence. In a similar model, Tinbergen (1973) found that doubling the number of people with secondary and tertiary schooling will halve inequality in earnings. Adelman and Morris (1973) found that, of 35 variables tested, the educational variable ranked first in terms of its ability to explain differences in income distribution. In their study, greater education was associated with lower inequality. Their findings were confirmed by Ahluwalia (1974) and by Chenery and Syrquin (1975) using somewhat different educational indices. Ahluwalia found that primary education is associated with an increase in the share of income accruing to the poorest 40 percent of the population and that more prevalent secondary education is associated with greater shares of income accruing to the middle income groups. Chenery and Syrquin found that an increase in a combination of primary plus secondary enrollment ratios shifts the distribution of income away from the richest 20 percent of the population in favor of the poorest 40 percent. Psacharopoulos (1977) constructed an index of educational inequality[1] and found an association between increases in this index and greater inequality in the distribution of income.

---

[1]The index (I) is defined as the coefficient of variation of enrollment by school level:

$$I = \frac{\dfrac{\sqrt{\Sigma_i^3 (S_i - \bar{S})^2}}{3}}{\bar{S}},$$

where S_i is the school enrollment ratio by school level and $\bar{S}$ the average overall school enrollment ratio.

Our assumptions are also in accord with what can be expected on theoretical grounds. With marginal propensities to save which are nondeclining functions of income levels, a given mean income will generate higher savings (and accumulation) rates with more unequal distributions of income. Thus, a higher dispersion of income will yield a higher capital-labor ratio. In addition, if rates of return on physical capital are nondecreasing functions of the amount of capital, a higher physical-capital to labor ratio will give rise to a more unequal distribution of income.

By contrast, a higher average level of human capital can only be achieved if access to education is more widespread. This is so because formal education has a maximum. If returns to education are non-decreasing functions of the variance of education (Psacharopoulos 1977), a higher average level of human capital must correspond to a lower variance of income.

The personal income mean in the population, μ_y, is given by

$$\mu_y = \xi(y) = \int_0^{\infty} y_i\, g_1(y_i)\, dy_i. \tag{3}$$

where ξ is the expectation operator, and g_1 is the probability density function of y.

Substituting equation (1) into equation (3) implies

$$\mu_y = y_m \int_{-\infty}^{+\infty} e^{u_i} g_2(u_i)\, du_i, \tag{4}$$

where g_2 is the probability density function of u. The integral in equation (4) is the moment generating function of g_2; and, since g_2 is assumed to be normal with zero mean and $\sigma^2(k,\,\alpha)$ variance, then

$$\mu_y = y_m e^{0.5\, \sigma^2(k,\,\alpha)}. \tag{5}$$

That is, the mean of the personal income in the population is equal to the median income times an exponential function of half the variance of the dispersion rate.

The variance of personal income in the population is given by

$$\begin{aligned}
\mathrm{Var}(y) &= \int_{-\infty}^{+\infty} [y_m e^{u_i} - y_m e^{0.5\, \sigma^2(k,\,\alpha)}]^2\, g_2(u_i)\, du_i \\
&= y_m^2 \left[\int_{-\infty}^{\infty} e^{2u_i} g_2(u_i)\, du_i + e^{\sigma^2(k,\,\alpha)} \right. \\
&\quad \left. - 2e^{0.5\, \sigma^2(k,\,\alpha)} \int_{-\infty}^{+\infty} e^{u_i} g_2(u_i)\, du_i \right].
\end{aligned} \tag{6}$$

Again, using the definition of the moment generating function, we get

$$\text{Var}(y) = y_m^2 [e^{2\sigma^2(k,\alpha)} - e^{\sigma^2(k,\alpha)}]. \tag{7}$$

Under the above assumptions, the distribution of income within the population is lognormal with mean and variance being functions of k, α, and/or the median income, y_m. Note that writing $\sigma^2(k, \alpha)$ in this general form allows for covariances among holdings of physical and human capital.

To find the median income, note the accounting identity between national income and national product

$$L\, y_m e^{0.5\, \sigma^2(k,\alpha)} = F(K, L, \alpha), \tag{8}$$

where F is an aggregate production function of quite general shape, L is the labor force (including owners of physical capital), and K is the amount of physical capital. A more usual treatment of F would be to disaggregate its labor arguments into several labor qualities differentiated by their educational characteristics rather than as in (8), making F( ) a function of the general amount of raw labor, L, and of its educational quality, α. The two specifications differ in terms of the educational policies they imply and, hence, in the distributional consequences of those policies. The differentiated labor-quality approach corresponds to increasing medium-to high-level manpower, while leaving the amount and quality of unskilled labor unchanged. By contrast, our specification corresponds to an across-the-board improvement of the educational content of raw labor. The contrast between the two kinds of educational policies is quite real. The first policy represents a Brazil-type policy, while the second represents a Korea–Taiwan–Hong Kong–Singapore policy. [For a discussion of the income distribution implications of the respective educational policies, see Fishlow (1972) on Brazil and Adelman (1978) and Fei, Ranis, and Kuo (1978) on the far eastern economies.]

Equation (8) implies

$$y_m = f(k, \alpha)\, e^{-0.5\, \sigma^2(k,\alpha)}, \tag{9}$$

where $f(k, \alpha)$ is defined as per capita output. We assume $f(k, \alpha)$ to be increasing in both k and α. As long as the variance of the dispersion rate of income is greater than zero, the median income is smaller than the per capita income.

Although per capita income always increases in k and α, the median income might not. The distinction is important since, unlike the mean, the median is a good indication of the percentage of the population in poverty.

Proposition 1. If both per capita income and the variance of the dispersion rate are increasing in k, then the effect of accumulation of physical capital on the extent of population in poverty depends on whether the productivity increasing effects of accumulation outweigh the inequality increasing effects. Specifically, the median income increases, remains the same, or decreases with the rising physical-capital labor ratios according to whether the effect of an increment in the capital-labor ratio on per capita output is greater, equal, or smaller than its effect on the variance of the dispersion rate of income. (For proof, see Appendix A, Proposition 1).

Proposition 2. If per capita income increases in α and the variance of the dispersion rates decreases in α, then the median income will increase in α. (For proof, see Appendix A, Proposition 2.)

This proposition states that, at the margin, the accumulation of human capital reduces the population in poverty. The underlying reason is that both the productivity effect and the inequality effect reduce poverty.

Using eq. (9), we can also write the moments of the distribution of income (within the population) as functions of the physical capital-labor ratio and average human capital in the population

$$y \sim \log N\{f(k, \alpha), f(k, \alpha)^2[e^{1.5\,\sigma^2(k,\alpha)} - e^{0.5\,\sigma^2(k,\alpha)}]\}.$$

This result and the assumptions about the signs of the first derivatives of $f(k, \alpha)$ and $\sigma^2(k, \alpha)$ imply that the mean income increases with k and α and that the income variance increases with k but not necessarily with α. Rather,

$$\frac{\partial \operatorname{Var} y}{\partial \alpha} \gtreqless 0$$

as

$$\eta_\alpha \gtreqless -\frac{\alpha[\frac{3}{2} e^{1.5\,\sigma^2(k,\alpha)} - \frac{1}{2} e^{0.5\,\sigma^2(k,\alpha)}]}{e^{1.5\,\sigma^2(k,\alpha)} - e^{0.5\,\sigma^2(k,\alpha)}} \frac{\partial \sigma^2(k, \alpha)}{\partial \alpha} \; (> 0),$$

where η_α is the elasticity of per capita output with respect to average human capital.

3. EVOLUTION OF THE PHYSICAL CAPITAL-LABOR RATIO AND AVERAGE HUMAN CAPITAL

We assume that the motion equation of physical capital, K, is

$$\dot{K}_t = I(k_t, \alpha_t, \sigma_t^2) + G_t - \delta(\alpha_t, \dot{\alpha}_t) K_t, \tag{10}$$

where I is private investment in physical capital, G is governmental investment in physical capital, and δ is rate of depreciation on physical capital at time t (t is a continuous variable).

We further assume that

$$\frac{\partial I}{\partial k}\bigg|_{\sigma^2 = \text{constant}} > 0 \quad \text{and} \quad \frac{\partial I}{\partial \alpha}\bigg|_{\sigma^2 = \text{constant}} > 0$$

at every t, and that the level of private saving and, hence, investment increases with the variance of the dispersion rate of income (see, for example, Kaldor 1955). Since the variance increases in k and decreases in α we get

$$\frac{\partial I}{\partial \sigma^2} \frac{\partial \sigma^2}{\partial k} > 0 \quad \text{and} \quad \frac{\partial I}{\partial \sigma^2} \frac{\partial \sigma^2}{\partial \alpha} < 0.$$

Combining the two previous assumptions implies that the total effect of an increment in the physical capital-labor ratio on the level of private investment is positive; but, the total effect of an increment in average human capital on the level of private investment in physical capital is positive, zero, or negative according to whether the productivity-increasing effect embedded in $\partial I/\partial \alpha$ outweighs the savings-decreasing effect.

The rate of depreciation on physical capital stock is assumed to decrease in the average human capital and increase in the rate of change of the average human capital (i.e., $\partial \delta/\partial \alpha < 0$ and $\partial \dot{\delta}/\partial \alpha > 0$). The first effect is due to better maintenance. The second effect can be interpreted as the obsolescence effect—increments in the population's average human capital lead to the adoption of newer technologies which require machinery and equipment which are different from the currently existing ones. The larger the increments in average human capital, the stronger the replacement effect and, hence, the greater the obsolescence of physical capital of earlier vintages.

The motion equation of the economically active, L, is assumed to be

$$\dot{L}_t = n(R_t, k_t, \alpha_t) L_t, \tag{11}$$

where n is the rate of growth of the labor force, and R is the per capita governmental expenditures on health services, family planning programs, etc. We assume that $\partial n/\partial k < 0$ and $\partial n/\partial \alpha < 0$. However, the total effect of governmental expenditures, R, on L is unpredictable. Improved health services act to increase survival rates; but fertility may decline because of family planning programs.

Finally, we assume that the motion equation of the average quality of the labor force is

$$\dot{\alpha}_t = h(E_t, k_t, \alpha_t), \tag{12}$$

where E_t is the per capita governmental expenditure on education at time t. We assume that the population's capacity to learn and private investment in education both increase with the economy's level of industrialization and modernization (i.e., $\partial h/\partial k > 0$ and $\partial h/\partial \alpha > 0$). The supply side of educated labor embodied in (11) and (12) could have been modeled more explicitly, say, by using a household decision model a la Becker (1981). However, to do so would have detracted from the main thrust of the model.

The evolution of per capita material wealth, k, is given by

$$\dot{k}_t = \frac{\dot{K}_t}{L_t} - k_t \frac{\dot{L}_t}{L_t}. \tag{13}$$

Substituting equations (12), (13), and (14) into (15) implies

$$\dot{k}_t = \frac{I(k_t, \alpha_t, \sigma_t^2) + G_t}{L_t} - \{\delta[\alpha_t, h(E_t, k_t, \alpha_t)] + n(R_t, k_t, \alpha_t)\} k_t. \tag{14}$$

The first term on the right-hand side of eq. (14) is the per capita investment in physical capital. The second term is the total depreciation on per capita physical capital. Since k and α appear in this equation in several places, their effects on the accumulation of per capita physical capital are not obvious. Their effects will be explored in the next section.

4. SYSTEM DYNAMICS

Our dynamic system consists of eqs. (12) and (14). This sytem's potential steady state(s) are found by the intersection of the isoclines $\dot{\alpha} = 0$ and $\dot{k} = 0$. The isocline $\dot{\alpha} = 0$ is downward sloped[2] in the phase plane (k, α).

---

[2]Setting $\dot{\alpha} = 0$ implies

$$h(E, k, \alpha) = 0.$$

(The subscript t is omitted for convenience.) The total differential of this equation with E and L held constant implies

$$\frac{d\alpha}{dk}\bigg|_{\dot{\alpha}=0} = -\frac{\partial h/\partial k}{\partial h/\partial \alpha},$$

which by our assumptions is negative.

HUMAN RESOURCES GROWTH STRATEGIES 279

The slope of the isocline $\dot{k} = 0$ is not unambiguous, however.[3] If the private investment (saving) effect is positive and dominates the total depreciation effect on the accumulation of per capita physical capital when α or k increase, then the isocline $\dot{k} = 0$ is downward sloped.[4] These conditions must be satisfied in a growing economy.

In that case, both the $\dot{\alpha} = 0$ curve and the $\dot{k} = 0$ curve are downward sloping in the (k, α) plane. The existence of a steady state, which we assume, requires that these curves intersect in the interior of the first orthant. However, since the slopes of the isoclines vary, they might intersect more than once and, hence, the case of a multiple equilibria cannot be ruled out.

Theorem 1. If the $\dot{\alpha} = 0$ curve crosses the $\dot{k} = 0$ curve from above (below), then the system's steady state is a saddle point (unstable node).

Proof: By our assumptions, the isoclines $\dot{\alpha} = 0$ and $\dot{k} = 0$ are downward sloping and

$$\frac{d\dot{\alpha}}{dk} = \frac{\partial h}{\partial k} > 0, \quad \frac{d\dot{k}}{k\alpha} = \frac{1}{L}\left(\frac{\partial I}{\partial\alpha} + \frac{\partial I}{\partial\sigma^2}\frac{\partial\sigma^2}{\partial\alpha}\right) - \left(\frac{\partial\delta}{\partial\alpha} + \frac{\partial\delta}{\partial h}\frac{\partial h}{\partial\alpha} + \frac{\partial n}{\partial\alpha}\right). k > 0.$$

Therefore, when the $\alpha = 0$ curve crosses the $\dot{k} = 0$ curve from above, the directions of the dynamic trajectories are as shown by the arrows in Figure 1 around 0_1; they indicate that the steady state, 0_1, is a saddle

---

[3] Setting $\dot{k} = 0$ implies

$$\frac{I(k, \alpha, \sigma^2) + G}{L} - \{\delta[\alpha, h(E, k, \alpha)] + n(R, k, \alpha)\}k = 0.$$

The total differential of this equation with $G, E, R,$ and L held constant, implies

$$\frac{d\alpha}{dk}\bigg|_k = 0 = -\frac{\dfrac{1}{L}\left(\dfrac{\partial I}{\partial k} + \dfrac{\partial I}{\partial\sigma^2}\dfrac{\partial\sigma^2}{\partial k}\right) - \left[(\delta + n) + \left(\dfrac{\partial\delta}{\partial h}\dfrac{\partial h}{\partial k} + \dfrac{\partial n}{\partial k}\right)k\right]}{\left(\dfrac{1}{L}\dfrac{\partial I}{\partial\alpha} + \dfrac{\partial I}{\partial\sigma^2}\dfrac{\partial\sigma^2}{\partial\alpha}\right) - \left(\dfrac{\partial\delta}{\partial\alpha} + \dfrac{\partial\delta}{\partial h}\dfrac{\partial h}{\partial\alpha} + \dfrac{\partial n}{\partial\alpha}\right)k}. \quad \text{(ii)}$$

[4] *Proof.* In this case, both the numerator (the effect of an infinitesimal increment in k on $\dot{k}$) and denominator (the effect of infinitesimal increment in α on $\dot{k}$) on the right-hand side of eq. (ii) are positive. And since their ratio is multiplied by -1 then

$$\frac{d\alpha}{dk}\bigg|_{\dot{k}=0} < 0. \quad \blacksquare$$

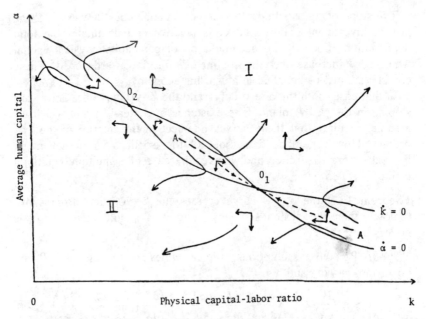

Figure 1. Phase plane diagram.

point. When the $\dot{\alpha} = 0$ curve crosses the $\dot{k} = 0$ curve from below (point 0_2 in Figure 1), the directions of the dynamic trajectories show that the equilibrium point, 0_2, is an unstable node. ∎

A saddle point is an unstable equilibrium; but, unlike at the unstable node, 0_2, two stable trajectories do converge to the equilibrium point in the case of the saddle point, 0_1. This implies that a steady state can be gradually reached if and only if the system is initially on the convergent arm to 0_1 (the broken line AA in Figure 1). If initially the system is neither on the convergent arm nor in equilibrium, only a policy of shocks might cause it to arrive at a steady state.

A growth path which is not characterized by a steady state is not necessarily undesirable. Along the dynamic trajectories in Region I (the area above the upper contour of the isoclines in Figure 1), private investment in physical capital and in human capital exceed depreciation; and, hence, both the physical capital-labor ratio and average human capital increase as time progresses. Per capita income increases, and income inequality might be lessened provided that the rate of growth of the average human capital is sufficiently high relative to the rate of growth of the physical capital-labor ratio, the elasticity of per capita output with respect to average human capital is sufficiently low, and the variance of the dispersion rate is sufficiently sensitive to changes in average human capital. If this is the case, governmental intervention to bring the system into a steady state will not be advisable.

By contrast, being in Region II (the area below the lower contour of the isoclines in Figure 1) is undesirable. Once the system is in this region, private investments in physical capital and in human capital fall below the total depreciation levels. In this case, adequate governmental investments in education, physical capital, health, and family planning are required to stop and reverse the catastrophic process in which the physical capital-labor ratio and the average level of human capital converge to zero.

5. THE OPTIMAL CHOICE OF STEADY STATE IN A MULTIPLE EQUILIBRIUM CASE

When two or more steady states are possible, the question of relative social desirability arises. Income distribution as well as efficiency of production should be considered when choosing the socially most desirable steady state. But one can make unambigous statements about the ranking of alternative steady states only when the means of the associated income distributions are the same. Otherwise, more specific assumptions about social trade-offs between per capita income and inequality are required. For an elegant optimizing approach to this issue based on an explicit welfare function which trades off mean income versus its variance, see Ritzen (1977). We here limit our results only to Pareto optimal statements concerning welfare comparisons among alternative dynamic paths which are valid independently of the shape of the social welfare function. Our results are, therefore, quite general.

Theorem 2. Under our assumptions, for any two steady states characterized by equal per capita output but by different combinations of physical capital-labor ratio and average human capital, the income distribution associated with the steady state with the higher level of average human capital is Lorenz superior to the other. (Appendix A, Theorem 2.)

The above theorem follows from the fact that the variance of income is smaller for the case with higher level of average human capital and from the symmetry property of the Lorenz curve for lognormal income distributions. Since individual utility functions are concave, the result that the income distribution associated with the steady state with the higher level of average human capital is Lorenz superior is equivalent to saying that this steady state is socially preferred for any social welfare function which is increasing, symmetric, and quasi-concave in individual utilities.[5]

Loosely speaking, this theorem states that human capital intensive strategies are preferred, provided they can yield the same levels of per capita output. The relevance of this theorem depends critically on whether the assumption that one can achieve the same mean output with either human-capital or physical-capital intensive technologies is an empirically valid one. Straight comparisons of per capita GNPs of countries that have followed the appropriate strategies cannot be used directly to shed light on this issue since countries adopting the two strategies have differed quite drastically in their natural resource endowments. Generally, countries with poor natural resources have tended to adopt human resource intensive strategies, while countries with good man-land ratios and large mineral and fossil resources have tended to adopt physical-capital intensive strategies. The average GNPs per capita (weighted by population) in 1978 were 1,154 for the physical-capital-intensive group[6] and 905 for the human-resource-intensive group, in 1978 U.S. dollars.[7] However, the physical-capital-intensive group had about nine times (!) the amount of land per capita (39.9 versus 4.4 in thousands of square kilometers). Thus, considering the magnitude of the natural resource endowment handicap which the human-resource-intensive strategy had to compensate for, the comparison of levels of GNP per capita is quite encouraging for our postulate.

Theoretically, whether alternative accumulation strategies leading to equivalent per capita GNPs can exist depends on the degree of substitutability of human and physical capital in production. Since our theorem is based on a "one-commodity" economy, the necessary substitutability can be achieved not only by varying technology in the production of a single commodity, but also by changing the production profile of the economy to favor either human-resource intensive or physical-capital intensive products. Furthermore, in deciding upon the resource-intensity of GNP countries are not bound by the composition of their domestic demand since they can use international trade to acquire the commodities in which their accumulation pattern has led to low comparative advantage. Empirical evidence that countries actually use the combination of accumulation and international trade in this way is

---

[5]For the proof of this equivalence, see Dasgupta, Sen, and Starrett (1973).

[6]The countries included in this average are Brazil, Mexico, Colombia, Pakistan, and Spain.

[7]The countries included in this average are Israel, South Korea, Taiwan, Philippines, and Sri Lanka.

provided in Balassa (1979). It, therefore, seems to us that, by appropriate choice of accumulation, specialization, and trade patterns countries can meet the conditions of the above theorem.

6. CONCLUSIONS

In this paper, we have examined, by means of a theoretical model, the income distribution and poverty implications of alternative accumulation strategies. The model results refer to comparative dynamics. They represent the dynamic analogs of comparative statics experiments concerning the long run consequences of alternative time paths of different long-run human and physical capital accumulation strategies. They are not statements concerning one-time marginal changes in accumulation strategies and adjustments to them in a given economy.

In principle, countries can stress either the accumulation of physical capital or the accumulation of human capital or they can pursue a balanced long-term strategy of accumulation. Our model suggests that appropriately designed and implemented human-resource intensive accumulation strategies are socially preferable.

This conclusion is very much in the spirit of Tinbergen's work. Indeed, in summarizing the policy implications of our results, we can do no better than to quote him:

Educational policies deserve to be programmed not only with a view to improving education in the widest sense, but also in order to influence income distribution. In most of our results ... the equalizing consequences of extended education are reflected. Since the heart of the matter is to approach, as much as possible, equality between the demand for and the supply of the manifold types of labor, our recommendation is not simply a quantitative one, but requires many qualitative changes in education as well .... An interdependence and mutual impact of cultural elements on both the demand and the supply side may considerably enrich this complex of policies" [Tinbergen (1975b, p. 148)].

In the last two decades, developing countries have invested quite heavily in education. In the 1970s, educational expenditures absorbed an average of 4 percent of overall Less Developed Countries (LDC) GNP [World Development Report (1980, p. 46)]. Between 1960 and 1977, secondary enrollment ratios in LDCs doubled and primary education ratios increased by one-third. The decade closed with an overall LDC average of 30 percent of secondary-age students and 80 percent of primary-age students in school [World Development Report (1980, p. 46)].

However, the results of the education explosion have been considered by some to be somewhat disappointing especially in regard to the contribution of education to improving the lot and prospects of the poor (Simmons 1970). In part, the disappointment stems from the fact that investment in education was supposed to do too much: it was expected by itself to solve the problems of poverty and discrimination in environments which produced too small a supply of productive jobs and in which access to both jobs and education was rationed by ascriptive, status, and inequality-perpetuating criteria. The problems of the unemployed high school graduates and the political and social unrest associated with them have led to a revision in attitudes of politicians and planners toward investment in education. Our theoretical results suggest that the general education-pessimism is most likely premature and support Tinbergen's educational optimism. Empirically, developing countries that have pursued human-resource intensive strategies have had both better income distributions and a better growth performance. In the group of developing countries that have stressed the physical-capital-intensive strategy during 1950–1978, the average share of income accruing to the poorest 40 percent was only 11 percent while in the group that emphasized the human resource-intensive strategy the average was 16 percent.[8] The growth consequences of the two strategies have also been more favorable for the group of countries that emphasized the accumulation of human resources. From 1960 to 1978, this group achieved an average (weighted by population) real per capita GNP growth rate of 4.68 percent per year; the comparable number for the physical-capital-intensive group was 3.86 percent.

Currently, under the impact of budgeting deficits and inflation, all of the Organization for Economic Cooperation Development countries except Japan are decreasing their commitments to higher education. Our results suggest that, if allowed to persist to the long run, the current policies are tragically misguided from both a growth and an equity perspective.

APPENDIX A

Proposition 1. If both per capita income and the variance of the dispersion rate are increasing in k, then

$$\frac{\partial y_m}{\partial k} \gtreqless 0 \qquad as \qquad \eta_k \gtreqless \frac{1}{2} k \frac{\partial \sigma^2(k, \alpha)}{\partial k}$$

Proof. Differentiating eq. (9) with respect to k implies

---

[8]The countries included in the averages in this paragraph are those listed in footnotes 6 and 7, respectively.

HUMAN RESOURCES GROWTH STRATEGIES

$$\frac{\partial y_m}{\partial k} = \left[\frac{\partial f(k,\,\alpha)}{\partial k} - \frac{1}{2} \frac{\partial \sigma^2(k,\,\alpha)}{\partial k} f(k,\,\alpha) \right] e^{-0.5\,\sigma^2(k,\alpha)}.$$

Clearly,

$$\frac{\partial y_m}{\partial k} \gtreqless 0 \quad \text{as} \quad \left[\frac{\partial f(k,\,\alpha)}{\partial k} - \frac{1}{2} \frac{\partial \sigma^2(k,\,\alpha)}{\partial k} f(k,\,\alpha) \right] \gtreqless 0.$$

Since $\partial \sigma^2/\partial k > 0$, then

$$\frac{\partial y_m}{\partial k} \gtreqless 0 \quad \text{as} \quad \frac{\partial f(k,\,\alpha)}{\partial k} \gtreqless \frac{1}{2} \frac{\partial \sigma^2(k,\,\alpha)}{\partial k} f(k,\,\alpha).$$

Multiplying both sides of the last inequality by $k/f(k,\,\alpha)$ changes nothing and, hence,

$$\frac{\partial y_m}{\partial k} \gtreqless 0 \quad \text{as} \quad \eta_k \gtreqless \frac{1}{2} k \frac{\partial \sigma^2(k,\,\alpha)}{\partial k}. \quad \blacksquare$$

Proposition 2. If per capita income increases in α and variance of the dispersion rates decreases in α, then the median income will increase in α.

Proof. Differentiating eq. (9) with respect to α implies

$$\frac{\partial y_m}{\partial \alpha} = \left[\frac{\partial f(k,\,\alpha)}{\partial \alpha} - \frac{1}{2} \frac{\partial \sigma^2(k,\,\alpha)}{\partial \alpha} f(k,\,\alpha) \right] e^{-0.5\,\sigma^2(k,\alpha)}$$

which is positive provided that $\partial f(k,\,\alpha)/\partial \alpha > 0$ and $\partial \sigma^2(k,\,\alpha)/\partial \alpha < 0$.

Theorem 2. For any two steady states, $0_1 = (k_1,\,\alpha_1)$ and $0_2 = (k_2,\,\alpha_2)$ satisfying $k_1 > k_2$, $\alpha_1 < \alpha_2$, and $f(k_1,\,\alpha_1) = f(k_2,\,\alpha_2)$, the income distribution in 0_2, $G_2(y \mid k_2,\,\alpha_2)$, is Lorenz superior to the income distribution in 0_1, $G_1(y \mid k_1,\,\alpha_1)$ if, as assumed throughout,

(i)
$$\frac{\partial \sigma^2(k,\,\alpha)}{\partial k} > 0,$$

(ii)
$$\frac{\partial \sigma^2(k,\,\alpha)}{\partial \alpha} < 0,$$

for all $k_2 \leq k \leq k_1$ and $\alpha_1 \leq \alpha \leq \alpha_2$.

Proof: It was shown in Section 3 that

$$\mathrm{Var}(y \mid k,\,\alpha) = f(k,\,\alpha)^2 \left[e^{1.5\,\sigma^2(k,\alpha)} - e^{0.5\sigma^2(k,\alpha)} \right].$$

Define

$$A(k,\,\alpha) = e^{1.5\,\sigma^2(k,\alpha)} - e^{0.5\,\sigma^2(k,\alpha)}.$$

Since

$$f(k_1,\,\alpha_1) = f(k_2,\,\alpha_2), \quad \mathrm{Var}(y \mid k_1,\,\alpha_1) > \mathrm{Var}(y \mid k_2,\,\alpha_2)$$

when

$$A(k_1,\,\alpha_1) > A(k_2,\,\alpha_2).$$

The partial derivatives of A are:

$$\frac{\partial A}{Mk} = \frac{\partial \sigma^2(k, \alpha)}{\partial \kappa} \left[\frac{3}{2} e^{1.5 \, \sigma^2(k,\alpha)} - \frac{1}{2} e^{0.5 \, \sigma^2(k,\alpha)} \right],$$

$$\frac{\partial A}{\partial \alpha} = \frac{\partial \sigma^2(k, \alpha)}{\partial \alpha} \left[\frac{3}{2} e^{1.5 \, \sigma^2(k,\alpha)} - \frac{1}{2} e^{0.5 \, \sigma^2(k,\alpha)} \right].$$

$|\frac{3}{2} e^{1.5 \, \sigma^2(k,\alpha)} - \frac{1}{2} e^{0.5 \, \sigma^2(k,\alpha)}|$ is always positive, and given that conditions (i) and (ii) hold $A(k_1, \alpha_1) > A(k_2, \alpha_2)$ and, hence, $\mathrm{Var}(y|k_1, \alpha_1) > \mathrm{Var}(y|k_2, \alpha_2)$.

The distribution functions, G_1 and G_2, are lognormal. Therefore, their Lorenz curves, L_1 and L_2 (respectively), are symmetric.[9] i.e., L_1 and L_2 do not intersect. Since G_1 and G_2 have the same mean $|f(k_1, \alpha_1) = f(k_2, \alpha_2)|$ and G_1 has a greater variance, L_1 lies below L_2; and, hence, G_2 is Lorenz superior to G_1. ∎

REFERENCES

Adelman, I. (1980) Redistribution Before Growth—A Strategy for Developing Countries. Inaugural Lecture for the Cleveringa Chair, Leiden University, The Netherlands, October, 1977. The Hague: Martinus Nijhof.

Adelman, I., and Morris, C. T. (1973) *Economic Growth and Social Equity in Developing Countries.* Stanford: Stanford University Press.

Ahluwalia, M. S. (1974) Income Inequality: Some Dimensions of the Problem, in *Redistribution With Growth* (H. Chenery et al., Eds.). New York: Oxford University Press.

Balassa, B. (1979) A Stages Approach to Comparative Advantage, *Economic Growth and Resources: National and International Issues* (I. Adelman, ed.). New York: The Macmillan Company.

Becker, G. S. (1981) *A Treatise on the Family.* Cambridge: Harvard University Press.

Ben-Porath, Y. (1982) Economics and the Family—Match or Mismatch," *Journal of Economic Literature,* 20(1), 52–64.

Blaugh, Mark (1976) The Empirical Status of Human Capital Theory: A Slightly Jaundiced Survey, *Journal of Economic Literature,* 14(3), 827–55.

Cain, G. G. (1976) The Challenge of Segmented Labor Market Theories to Orthodox Theory: A Survey, *Journal of Economic Literature,* 14(4), 1215–57.

Chenery, H., and Syrquin, M. (1975) *Patterns of Development, 1950–1970.* New York: Oxford University Press.

Dasgupta, P., Sen, A. K., and Starrett, D. (1973) Notes on the Measurement of Inequality, *Journal of Economic Theory,* 6, 180–187.

Fei, J., Ranis, G., and Kuo, S. (1978) Growth and the Family Distribution of Income by Factor Components, *Quarterly Journal of Economics,* XCII, 17–53.

Fishlow, A. (1972) Brazilian Size Distribution of Income. *American Economic Review,* LXII, 391–402.

Fox, K. A. (1972) *Economic Analysis for Educational Planning,* Baltimore: Johns Hopkins Press.

Hannan, M. T. (1982) Families, Markets, and Social Structures: An Essay on Becker's *A Treatise on the Family, Journal of Economic Literature,* 20(1), 65–72.

---

[9]See Lemma 3.6 in Kakwani (1980).

Kakwani, N. C. (1980) *Income Inequality and Poverty: Methods of Estimation and Policy Applications.* New York: Oxford University Press.

Kaldor, N. (1955) Alternative Theories of Distribution, *Review of Economic Studies,* 23, 83–100.

Psacharopoulos, G. (1977) Unequal Access to Education and Income Distribution: An International Comparison, *De Economist,* 125, 383–392.

Rosen, S. (1975) Human Capital: A Survey of Empirical Research, paper presented at the Third World Congress of the Econometric Society, Toronto, 1975.

Ritzen, J. M. (1977) *Education, Economic Growth, and Income Distribution.* Amsterdam: North Holland.

Sahota, G. S. (1978) Theories of Personal Income Distribution: A Survey, *Journal of Economic Literature,* 14(1), 1–55.

Simmons, J. (1979) Education for Development Reconsidered, *World Development,* 7, 1005–1016.

Tinbergen, J., A Positive and a Normative Theory of Income Distribution, *Review of Income Wealth,* 16, 221–234.

Tinbergen, J. (1978) Labor with Different Types of Skills and Jobs as Production Factors, *De Economist,* 121, 213–224.

Tinbergen, J. (1974) Substitution of Graduate by Other Labour, *Kyklos,* 27, 217–226.

Tinbergen, J. (1975a) Substitution of Academically Trained by Other Manpower, *Weltwirtsch. Arch.,* 111, 466–476.

Tinbergen, J. (1975b) *Income Distribution.* Amsterdam: North Holland.

Tinbergen, J. (1977a) How to Reduce the Incomes of the Two Labour Elites? *European Economic Review,* 10, 115–124.

Tinbergen, J. (1977b) Income Distribution: Second Thoughts, *De Economist,* 125, 315–339.

Tinbergen, J. (1980) Two Approaches to Quantify the Concept of Equitable Income Distribution, *Kyklos,* 33, 3–15.

World Bank (1980) *World Development Report, 1980,* Washington, D.C.

[11]

INCOME DISTRIBUTION AND EMPLOYMENT

GENERAL INTRODUCTION

WHO BENEFITS FROM ECONOMIC DEVELOPMENT ?

by Mrs. Irma ADELMAN
Development Research Centre,
International Bank for Reconstruction and Development,
Washington D.C., U.S.A.

and Mrs. Cynthia TAFT MORRIS
The American University, Washington D.C., U.S.A.

INTRODUCTION

The equitable distribution of income among individuals and households is central to
a nation's welfare and has become a major public concern in both developed and underdeveloped countries. Egalitarian philosophies stimulated by the industrial revolutions of Western
Europe have produced widespread expectations that economic growth will equalize wealth and
earnings opportunities as well as raise the average level of economic welfare (1). These
expectations have not been borne out. Even in econmically advanced countries, the persis-
tence of significant hardcore poverty for large minorities in the midst of growing afflu-
ence for the majority has contributed to serious social tensions and political conflict (2).
Public concern over income inequality has been heightened both by Marxian and contemporary
radical stress on forces in capitalist societies that tend to increase the concentration of
wealth and income, (3) and by more orthodox studies of conflicts between distributional
justice and economic efficiency (4).

---

1) See R.H. Tawney, Equality (London, Unwin-Books, 1964), for a well-known statement of
   egalitarian philosophy. See Herman P. Milller, Rich Man, Poor Man (New York, Thomas Y.
   Crowell, 1964), Chap. 4, for a discussion of the common "myth" that recent economic
   growth in the United States has led to more equal income distribution. For an excellent
   discussion of the various rationales for income equality, see Michael Lipton, Assessing
   Economic Performance (London, Staples Press, 1968), pp. 85ff.

2) See, for example, Michael Harrington, The Other America : Poverty in the United States,
   rev. ed. (Baltimore, Md.. Pelican Books, 1971), passim.

3) See, For instance, Stephan Michelson, "The Economics of Real Income Distribution",
   Review of Radical Political Economics, Spring 1970, pp. 35-48.

4) James E. Meade, Efficiency, Equality, and the Ownership of Property (London, 1964).
   There is relatively little disagreement over the proposition that the total economic
   welfare of a community with marked income inequality can be increased significantly by
   income transfers from wealthier to substantially poorer persons, given the presence of
   eventually diminishing marginal utility of commodities as a whole to individuals. This
   is so even without the assumption that interpersonal comparisons of utility are possible
   for all persons in an income distribution. The proposition only requires the weaker
   assumption that the marginal utility of commodities as a whole for persons at the extremes of the income distribution can be ranked. For a defense of comparing marginal
   utilities for the purpose of measuring the effects on welfare of distributional changes,

49

Theories of income distribution usually emphasize explanations of functional income shares (5). They also vary greatly in the distributional patterns they imply. Classical economists combined a subsistence wage theory, a competitive profit model, and the Ricardian rent theory to developed a dynamic analysis of growth and distribution. On this basis they predicted that, as a rule, landlords would benefit at the expense of both capitalists and workers in the course of economic development (6). Marx, in his model of capitalist accumulation, assumed that continuous labor-saving technical advances would increase the industrial reserve army of unemployed and depress wage levels, resulting in a falling share of wages in total output (7). In neoclassical theory, relative factor shares are governed by relative marginal productivities that, given the technology, are determined by the relative amounts of factors employed. In this model, relative shares change with both technical changes affecting marginal productivities and changes in the relative amounts of factors employed (8). More recently, Keynesian behavioral assumptions have produced distributional theories in which differences in the propensity to save between wage earners and capitalists and variations in the rate of investment interact to determine the distribution of income between wages and profits (9). The implicit assumption of all these theories with respect to the size distribution of income is that individuals possess various quantities of primary factors of production (capital, labor, land, or entrepreneurship) which determine their income shares and that these functional shares determine the distribution of personal incomes.

Little explicit theorizing has been done about the determinants of the size distribution of income among individuals except for a few elegant models in which income distribution is determined by stochastic processes marginally related to basic economic forces(10). In contrast, empirical studies of income variation have yielded a variety of hypotheses and some sketchy evidence on the impact of such influences as industrialization, level of

---

(Note 4, continued from previous page.)

see James E. Meade, <u>Trade and Welfare</u> (London, Oxford University Press, 1955), chap.5. A now classic discussion of interrelationships between economic welfare and income distribution can be found in I.M.D. Little, A Critique of Welfare Economics, 2d ed. (Oxford, Clarendon Press, 1957).

5) For a survey of recent theories of the functional income distribution, see Tibor Scitovsky, "A Survey of Some Theories of Income Distribution", in National Bureau of Economic Research, <u>The Behavior of Income Shares : Selected Theoretical and Empirical Issues</u> (Princeton, N.J., University Press, 1964), pp. 15FF. See also Martin Bronfenbrenner, <u>Income Distribution Theory</u> (Chicago, Aldine-Atherton, 1971).

6) John Stuart Mill, <u>Principles of Political Economy</u>, new ed., Ed. W.J. Ashley (New York, Augustus M. Kelley, 1961), Book 4, chap. 3, especially pp. 720-724.

7) Karl Marx, <u>Das Capital, The Communist Manifesto, and Other Writings,</u> Max Eastman (New York, Modern Library, 1932), especially pp. 141-146 and 161-182.

8) See, for example, John Bates Clark, <u>The Distribution of Wealth</u> (New York, Kelley and Millman, 1956), esp. chap. 2; and J.R. Hicks, <u>The Theory of Wages</u>, 2d ed. (London, MacMillan, 1964), chap. 6.

9) See Nicholas Kaldor, "Alternative Theories of Distribution","<u>Review of Economic Studies</u>, 23, 2 (1956) : 83-100.

10) See D.G. Champernowne, "A Model of Income Distribution", <u>Economic Journal</u>, 63 (1953) : 318-351; and B. Mandelbrot, "Stable Paretian Random Functions and the Multiplicative Variation of Income", <u>Econometrica</u>, 29 (1961) : 517-543. An exception is J.E. Stiglitz, "Distribution of Income Wealth Among Individuals", <u>Econometrica</u>, 37 (1969) : 382-397, in which the impact of alternative assumptions about savings, reproduction, inheritance policies, and labor homogeneity are analyzed within the framework of a simple model of capital accumulation. For a summary of a variety of hypotheses that have been put forth to explain the skewedness in the size distribution of income, see Stanley Lebergott, "The Shape of the Income Distribution", <u>American Economic Review</u>, 49 (1959) :328-347.

education, distribution of wealth, and taxation, and of such personal characteristics as age, sex, race, family size, and occupation, to mention a few (11). The results, while interesting, have been scanty and have generally been based on observations over relatively short time periods in a few advanced countries. Comparisons between countries have been few because of insufficient data and conceptual difficulties (12).

In recent years, interest in the process of economic development has stimulated empirical analyses of the interrelationship between economic growth and distribution of income. Kuznets's work on currently advanced nations indicates that "the relative distribution of income, as measured by annual incidence in rather broad classes, has been moving toward equality -- with these trends particularly noticeable since the 1920's but beginning perhaps in the period before the first world war." (13) But other evidence suggests that at low levels of development economic growth tends to induce greater inequality in the distribution of income. Studies of the early years of industrialization in several European countries indicate a relative worsening of the position of low-income groups with, at best, stability in their absolute position (14). Little work has been done on growth and distribution in today's underdeveloped countries, but such evidence as there is suggests that in many of

---

11) See Simon Kuznets, "Economic Growth and Income Inequality", American Economic Review, 65 (1955): 1-28; Gary S. Becker and Barry R. Chiswick, "Education and the Distribution of Earnings", American Economic Association Papers and Proceedings, 56 (1966): 358-69; Robert J. Lampman, The Share of Top Wealth-Holders in National Wealth (Princeton, N.J., 1962); Roger A. Herriot and Herman P. Miller, "Who Paid the Taxes in 1968 ?", (Paper prepared for a meeting of the National Industrial Conference Board, New York, March 18, 1971, mimeo.) for an attempt to measure the total tax burden (federal, state, and local) by income levels. The result in this latter study indicate very little progressivity in the U.S. tax structure below the very highest income levels. For an interesting application of the technique used in this chapter to "explain" differential changes in money income for a sample of 1,274 family units in terms of the characteristics of heads of families, see James D. Smith and James N. Morgan, "Variability of Economic Well-being and Its Determinants", American Economic Association Papers and Proceedings, 60 (1970): 286-95.

12) See, however, H.T. Oshima, "The International Comparison of Size Distribution of Family Incomes with Special Reference to Asia", Review of Economics and Statistics, 44 (1962): 439-445, and Irving B. Kravis, "International Differences in the Distribution of Incomes", Review of Economics and Statistics, 42 (1960): 408-416.

13) Simon Kuznets, "Economic Growth and Income Inequality", American Economic Review, 65 (1955): 4. This generalization is based on data for the United States, Great Britain and Germany; data on Norway and Sweden also show the same broad pattern, according to the same author in Modern Economic Growth : Rate, Structure, and Spread (New Haven; Yale University Press, 1966), pp. 206ff. For further data supporting this generalization see Irving Kravis, The Structure of Income : Some Quantitative Essays (Philadelphia, University of Pennsylvia, 1962), chap. 7; and Simon Kuznets, assisted by Elizabeth Jenks, Shares of Upper Income Groups in Income and Savings (New York : National Bureau of Economic Research, 1953). A recent study indicating a slight positive effect of growth in equalizing incomes is Andrew F. Brimmer, "Inflation and Income Distribution in the United States", Review of Economics and Statistics, 53 (1971), esp. pp. 40-41.

14) Kuznets suggests that relative income inequality may well have widened in England between about 1780 and 1850 and in the United States and Germany between 1840 and 1890. "Economic Growth and Income Inequality", pp. 18-19. Even the most optimistic estimates for Great Britain during the industrial revolution conclude that little, if any, absolute betterment in workers' standards of living occurred before the 1820's at the earliest. See E.J. Hobsbaum (Part A) and R.M. Hartwell (Part B), "The Standard of Living During the Industrial Revolution : A discussion", Economic History Review, 16 (1963), reprinted in The Economic Development of Western Europe : The Eighteenth and Early Nineteenth Centuries, eds. Warren C. Scoville and J. Clayburn LaForce (Lexington, Mass., 1969), pp. 135-169. A recent note on "Trends in Wealth Concentration Before 1860" by Jackson Turner Main indicates that a striking increase in the concentration of wealth took place in the United States between 1780 and 1860 (Journal of Economic History, 31 (1971): 445-447); it may be presumed that greater inequality of income resulted.

them economic growth has led to increased inequality in the distribution of income (15).

The study of income distribution in currently underdeveloped countries is handicapped by inadequacies of both theory and data, and by the importance of nonmarket influences rarely allowed for in theories of distribution. The application of neoclassical functional theories to very-low-income countries, for example, is greatly complicated by the impact upon earnings differentials of such nonmarket forces as norms set by powerful traditional or expatriate elites, semiarbitrary wage scales for government employees, minimum wage laws that are inconsistent with labor availabilities, and the degree of often premature unionization. Keynesian theories are also not very relevant because nonmarket forces restrict the operation of presumed links among savings, investment, and income. While Marxian theories stressing the impact of property ownership on income distribution have greater relevance, they are (like non-Marxian theories) simplistic in their two-class view of society and in their assumption that materialistic motives dominate economic activity. In underdeveloped countries, it is to be expected that a variety of historical and political influences that are difficult to measure will interact with classical economic considerations in determining the distribution of personal incomes.

This study investigates the source of variations in the distribution of income among contemporary, noncommunist, low-income developing countries. Income distribution data on 43 underdeveloped countries, ranging from those with subsistence economies to those rapidly approaching a developed economy, are used to construct crude measures of various facets of income distribution. The independent variables used are indices of economic, political, and social forces that could be expected a priori to influence the distribution of income. These data are analyzed by a stepwise analysis-of-variance technique (described below) that permits highly nonlinear interactions in order to obtain a "best fitting" statistical representation of the empirical regularities underlying the data.

The methodology is thus overtly empirical rather than theoretical. This approach seems appropriate at present, since theorizing about the subject to date has produced a variety of equally plausible but poorly vali ated hypotheses that do not provide an adequate basis for the construction of a priori specified models (16). This is not to say, of course, that we have shunned the use of theory. Theory, as well as historical and comparative evidence, guided our choice of variables and was a major input in the construction of the socioeconomic and political typologies employed as independent variables. It also played an important role in our interpretations of the statistical results. Since the use of crosssectional data to gain insights into dynamic processes poses well-known problems (17), interpreting these data as representing changes over time requires major use of theoretical

---

15) Kuznets conjectured in 1955 that in contemporary underdeveloped countries the cumulative effect of concentration of past savings, combined with the absence of dynamic forces for equalization and of government policies to improve the conditions of the poor, had created "a possibility that inequality in the secular income structure of underdeveloped countries may have widened in recent decades". ("Economic Growth and Income Inequality", p. 24). A recent study by Richard Weisskoff indicates that in Puerto Rico, Argentina, and Mexico between 1950 and 1963, the income share of lower income groups declined while per capita GNP was rising. "Income Distribution and Economic Growth in Puerto Rico, Argentina and Mexico", *Review of Income and Wealth*, 16 (Dec. 1970).

16) For a more detailed discussion of empirical approaches to the use of quantitative techniques, see Irma Adelman and Cynthia Taft Morris, "Analysis-of-Variance Technique for the Study of Economic Development", *Journal of Development Studies*, 8 (1971): 99-106.

17) For an analysis of the biases of cross-sectional statistical analyses, see Edwin Kuh, "The Validity of Cross-Sectionally Estimated Behavior Equations in Time Series Applications", *Econometrica*, 27 (1959): 197-214.

reasoning and historical evidence regarding both the progressions over time suggested by the data and the direction of relationship between closely associated variables.

It should be stressed that this study is exploratory and offers only preliminary and tentative insights into the varied interactions affecting the distribution of income in underdeveloped countries (18). Both the income distribution variables and the independent variables are crude indices appropriate only for the early stages of exploration of the relevant relationships. Nevertheless, this type of exploratory effort is essential both to further research into the conceptualization and measurement of the influences involved and to the design of research in depth on their interrelationships. Indeed, without the kind of preliminary insights provided by exploratory studies such as this one, any major investment of resources in research on the determinants of variations in the distribution of income in underdeveloped countries is likely to be wasted.

II. THE ANALYSIS OF HIERARCHICAL INTERACTIONS

Our choice of analytic technique was guided by the need for a statistical method that did not assume linear relationships and that placed as few restrictions as possible on the forms of interactions among variables. Such a flexible technique is desirable because the complex processes influencing income distribution affect different strata of the population in different ways and because the forces inducing changes in income distribution may interact quite differently in countries having different characteristics. For example, one might expect that in heavily agricultural countries, industrialization will decrease the share in total income of the lower 60 percent of the population and increase the income share of the upper 20 percent, while in countries with sizable industrial sectors, further industrialization may shift income distribution in favor of the middle 40 to 60 percent of the population.

The statistical method used here is based on an analysis of variance. As with other analysis-of-variance techniques, the focus is on "explaining" variations in the dependent variable (19). The analysis selects from a set of independent variables the one that splits the parent sample into two subgroups having the smallest possible combined dependent-variable variance within the subgroups or, alternatively, for which the sum of the squared deviations of the subgroup means from the parent-sample mean is at a maximum. Each of the two subgroups thus obtained is then treated as a new parent sample for which the analysis again selects the independent variable providing the "best" split -- that is, the one that gives the largest total variance of subgroup means from the parent-sample mean. Each of these subgroups is again treated as a parent sample, and the process is continued through a series of binary splits. The result is an asymmetrical branching process that subdivides the original parent sample into subgroups constructed to facilitate prediction of the value of the dependent variable with the least error.

---

18) We might say with Kuznets ("Economic Growth and Income Inequality", p. 4) that "the trends in the income structure can be discerned but dimly, and the results considered as preliminary informed guesses".

19) For a description of the technique, see John A. Sonquist and James N. Morgan, The Detection of Interaction Effects (Ann Arbor, Mich., Institute for Social Research, University of Michigan, 1964). The only applications of the technique which have come to our attention are two papers by James N. Morgan and James D. Smith : "Measures of Economic Well-offness and Their Correlates", American Economic Association Papers and Proceedings, 59 (1969): 450-62; and "Variability of Economic Well-being".

More specifically, at each step in the analysis, and for each candidate <u>independent</u> variable, all possible mutually exclusive partitions of the parent group into subgroups are examined, each of which includes particular (usually successive) values of the <u>independent</u> variable. For each possible partition of the relevant independent variable, the variance of the subgroup means from the grand mean is calculated for the dependent variable. The "best" partition is one that maximizes the fraction of the total variance of the dependent variable accounted for by the means of the subgroups -- that is in other words, that maximizes the sum of the squared deviations of the subgroup means from the grand mean weighted by the sample size. The proportion of parent-sample variance thus "explained" by the best partition for the relevant independent variable is compared with the best partition for all other candidate independent variables. At each step in the analysis, that independent variable is selected for which the best partition accounts for the largest proportion of the overall variance of the dependent variable. The corresponding partition is then carried aout and each subgroup is treated as a new parent sample (20).

To ensure statistical significance, groups are candidates for splits only (1) if they contain a number of observations greater than $\overline{N}$ (set equal to 10), and (2) if they include at least a specified proportion of the overall variance (set equal to 10 percent). In addition, splits that are not statistically significant at the 5 percent level (by an $\underline{F}$ test) and splits that produce splinter groups (i.e. that contain less than 5 observations) are not carried out in the present analysis.

If the independent variables are ordinal (i.e., are ranked in either ascending or descending order so that X_{r+1} is either greater than or less than X_r), only those splits are permissible that place all values of X_r that are less than or equal to a certain value, say W_m, in a given group. If an independent variable is only nominal (i.e., is assumed to have no natural order), then the analysis forms the partitions that correspond to all possible combinations of values of X_r taken 2, 3, 4,..., r-1 at a time, and selects the partition that performs best. The analysis can therefore accomodate dummy variables, or variables for which the investigator does not wish to specify a ranking beforehand.

It is evident that this particular form of analysis of variance is extremely flexible. In spirit, it is akin to a highly nonlinear type of stepwise multiple regression analysis. Like stepwise regression, this technique finds, at each step, those combinations of values of the independent variables that permit prediction of the value of the dependent variable

---

20) For example, if the independent variable $\underline{X}$ assumes $\underline{r}$ distinct values X_r then the parent group is arranged initially so that all observations that have values $X_r < X_1$ are in group 1, and all observations that have values $X_2,..., X_r$ are in group 2. The means of the two subgroups are then calculated, as well as the variance from the overall sample means that is due to the group means (the "regression" sum of squares); this latter variance is equivalent to the variance attributable to (or "explained" by) the partition. Next, the partition that places the values of $X_r < X_2$ in group 1 and the remaining data in the parent group in group 2 is tried and the same calculations are carried out. The process is repeated then for $X_r < X_3$, $X_r < X_4$, etc. For each independent variable, that binary partition of the parent group which provides the largest reduction in the unexplained sum of squares becomes a candidate for splitting the parent group. The same analysis is carried out for each of the independent variables in turn, and the reductions in the variance provided by the best partitions associated with each independent variable are then compared with one another. At each step of the analysis, that split of the parent group is chosen which maximizes the sum of squares explained by the partition over all possible binary, nonoverlapping partitions and over all the independent variables included in the analysis.

with the least error. But, unlike regression analysis, this branching process admits highly nonlinear interactions. For high values of the dependent variable, the variables, interactions, and coefficients that best "explain" a difference of ΔY in the values of the dependent variable can be quite different from those that are required to account for the same difference at low or intermediate values. Furthermore, unlike regression analysis, the independent variables need not be assumed to be uncorrelated with one another. That is, this statistical technique can accomodate interactions among independent variables. (These interactions, of course, constitute a particular type of nonlinearity.)

This analytical technique is ideally suited, therefore, to studying systematic interactions between a dependent variable and a set of independent variables, when the phenomenon to be analyzed may affect different parts of the data differently and when the best principles for stratifying the original sample into subsamples are not known in advance. Indeed, this technique of analysis is very well adapted to indicating the best principles for stratifications.

III. THE VARIABLES

The Dependent Variables : Measuring the Distribution of Income

Since the concept of income distribution is multidimensional, it is susceptible to measurement by a variety of methods, no one of which is valid for all purposes (21). Summary indices, such as the Gini coefficient, can be suitable for broad comparisons of distributions with very different degrees of inequality, but they are not adequate for comparing distributions with quite different forms of inequality. For investigations differential impacts of distributional changes on various segments of the population, measures of the relative income shares received by particular quantiles of income recipients can be more appropriate. Yet indices of relative income shares also have their drawbacks : the choice of appropriate quantile is arbitrary, and variations in the incidence of characteristics of income receivers both within given quantiles in different distributions and between different quantiles in a given distribution complicate comparisons over time and across countries (22). Finally, it should be stressed that all measures of income distribution provide at best only an ordinal ranking of observations with respect to the underlying aspect of incoe distribution measured (23).

Overwhelming data deficiencies greatly complicate any efforts to measure variations in the distribution of income. It would be desirable, for example, to have income data for family expenditure units adjusted for the number of persons in the family and their stage of participation in the labor force; in addition, income distribution data ideally should refer to secular income levels and should take account of movements of individuals between

---

21) For discussions of various measures of income distribution, see, among others, James N. Morgan, "The Anatomy of Income Distributions", Review of Economics and Statistics, 44 (1962) : 270-283; Kuznets, "Economic Growth and Income Inequality", esp. pp. 12-16; and Anthony B. Atkinson, "On the Measurement of Inequality", Journal of Economic Theory, 2 (1970) : 244-263.

22) See Irving Kravis, The Structure of Income (Philadelphia, 1962).

23) Strictly speaking, it is not correct to use ordinal data with statistical techniques requiring the calculation of means and variances. Sensitivity studies are needed to justify the arbitrary assumption of cardinality. In our treatment of the dependent variable we follow the general practice among econometricians of using index numbers in statistical analyses as if they were cardinal. It should be noted, however, that with respect to the independent variables their ordinality is appropriate to the technique of hierarchical interactions.

different income groups over time (24). Yet, income distribution data almost invariably relate to income in a single year, are seldom available by appropriate expenditure units, are frequently unadjusted for number of persons, and rarely take account of mobility between income groups. Furthermore, except for recent years in a few countries, data are usually available for only a small number of broad income groups. Finally, the raw data on incomes received, even in many developed countries, are notoriously unreliable (25).

The raw data on incomes in the 43 underdeveloped countries studied here have all the deficiencies just described. In addition they pose several special problems regarding comparability, and adjustments could be made for only a few of them. Three types of sources were used : budget (income and expenditure) studies that sample different strata of the population, income information compiled from national censuses, and tax returns. For some countries, budget data referring to particular segments of the population (e.g., only urban or wage earners) were used in conjunction with national accounts and other income data in order to construct an overall picture of income distribution. For some countries for which basic information was exceedingly coarse, a finer breakdown by class intervals was achieved by fitting the available data to an appropriate empirical or theoretical distribution. If the lowest end of the lowest income class was not available, the minimum income was estimated by fitting with an appropriate curve. And if the average income in the highest class interval was not available, the figure was estimated by selecting a value that would equate the average per capita (or per household) income estimated from the income distribution to the corresponding value estimated from the national accounts (i.e., to per capita national income).

There were other sources of incompatibility in the basic data. Some of the information referred to households, some to individuals, and some to active population. When more than one type of information was available, information on households was preferred because they most closely approximate expenditure units. No adjustments of distribution relating to individuals or active population were made because of the difficulties in estimating the appropriate adjustments.

Some of the data are, strictly speaking, not comparable in that they refer to different years in the late 1950's and 1960's. But, this source of variation is not of great import since the broad lines of income distribution do not, as a rule, change very rapidly over time. More serious as a cause of incompatibility are differences in the extent of breakdown in the raw data by class intervals. Twenty-eight class intervals are available for example, but only five for Zambia, for other African and some Latin American nations. Other things being equal, a greater amount of detail provides a larger estimate of income concentration.

The basic income distribution data for the study are summarized in Table 1. Three dependent variables were constructed from these data (26).

24) For a detailed discussion of desiderata for income distribution data, see Kuznets, "Economic Growth and Income Inequality", pp. 1-3.

25) For an opinion to the contrary with respect to U.S.data, see Miller, <u>Rich Man, Poor Man</u>, chap. 3. The deficiency often cited is that the basic income data are usually derived from information supplied by the income recipients themselves, the accuracy of which is a function of the recall of the respondent, his perception of the use to which the information will be put, his veracity about a sensitive subject, etc. Only when income data are based on information reported on tax returns can they be regarded as somewhat more reliable.

26) Initially, four additional dependent variables were used : the concentration (Gini) coefficient, the income share of the poorest 20 percent of the population, the income share of the upper 20 percent of the population, and an index of the point at which the income distribution shifts its slope from less than unity to greater than unity. The results of the three analyses presented here are quite representative of the full range of results for the original seven dependent variables.

Table I

INCOME DISTRIBUTION ESTIMATES (1)

(Percentage shares by population groups)

Country	0-40	40-60	0-60	60-80	80-100	95-100
1. Argentina	17.30	13.10	30.40	17.60	52.00	29.40
2. Bolivia	12.90	13.70	26.60	14.30	59.10	35.70
3. Brazil	12.50	10.20	22.70	15.80	61.50	38.40
4. Burma	23.00	13.00	36.00	15.50	48.50	28.21
5. Ceylon	13.66	13.81	27.47	20.22	52.31	18.38
6. Chad	23.00	12.00	35.00	22.00	43.00	23.00
7. Chile	15.00	12.00	27.00	20.70	52.30	22.60
8. Colombia	7.30	9.70	17.00	16.06	68.06	40.36
9. Costa Rica	13.30	12.10	25.40	14.60	60.00	35.00
10. Dahomey	18.00	12.00	30.00	20.00	50.00	32.00
11. Ecuador	16.90	13.50	30.40	15.60	54.00	33.70
12. El Salvador	12.30	11.30	23.60	15.00	61.40	33.00
13. Gabon	8.00	7.00	15.00	14.00	71.00	47.00
14. Greece	21.30	12.30	34.10	16.40	49.50	23.00
15. India	20.00	16.00	36.00	22.00	42.00	20.00
16. Iraq	8.00	8.00	16.00	16.00	68.00	34.00
17. Israel	16.00	17.00	33.00	23.90	43.10	14.80
18. Ivory Coast	18.00	12.00	30.00	15.00	55.00	29.00
19. Jamaica	8.20	10.80	19.00	19.50	61.50	31.20
20. Japan	15.30	15.80	31.10	22.90	46.00	14.80
21. Lebanon	7.20	15.80	23.00	16.00	61.00	34.00
22. Lybia	.50	1.28	1.78	8.72	89.50	46.20
23. Malagasy	14.00	9.00	23.00	18.00	59.00	37.00
24. Mexico	10.50	11.25	21.75	20.21	58.04	28.52
25. Morocco	14.50	7.70	22.20	12.40	65.40	20.60
26. Niger	23.00	12.00	35.00	23.00	42.00	23.00
27. Nigeria	14.00	9.00	23.00	16.10	60.90	38.38
28. Pakistan	17.50	15.50	33.00	22.00	45.00	20.00
29. Panama	14.30	13.80	28.10	15.20	56.70	34.50
30. Peru	8.80	8.30	17.10	15.30	67.60	48.30
31. Philippines	12.70	12.00	24.70	19.50	55.80	27.50
32. Rhodesia	12.00	8.00	20.00	15.00	65.00	40.00
33. Senegal	10.00	10.00	20.00	16.00	64.00	36.00
34. Sierra Leone	10.10	9.10	19.20	16.70	64.10	33.80
35. South Africa	6.11	10.16	16.27	26.37	57.36	39.38
36. Sudan	15.00	14.30	29.30	22.60	48.10	17.10
37. Surinam	22.26	14.74	37.00	20.60	42.40	15.10
38. Taiwan	14.20	14.80	29.00	19.00	52.00	24.10
39. Tanzania	19.50	9.75	29.25	9.75	61.00	42.90
40. Trinidad & Tobago	9.42	9.10	18.52	24.48	57.00	26.60
41. Tunisia	10.62	9.95	20.57	14.43	65.00	22.44
42. Venezuela	13.40	16.60	30.00	22.90	47.10	23.20
43. Zambia	15.85	11.10	26.95	15.95	57.10	37.50

1) Data sources and interpolation techniques are given in : I. Adelman & Cynthia Taft Morriss, Economic Growth and Social Equity in Developing Countries (Stanford Press, July 1973).

1. The income share of the lowest 60 percent of the population.

2. The income share of the middle quintile of the population (i.e., the 10 percent above and the 10 percent below the median income).

3. The income share of the wealthiest 5 percent of the population.

The Independent Variables

The independent variables used in this study consist of 31 indicators of economic, social, and political influences that could be expected, on theoretical grounds, to affect income distribution. For the most part, they describe country characteristics for the period 1957-62; only the measures of rates of change refer to the longer period 1950/51 to 1962/63.

With respect to economic influences, four variables represent, directly or indirectly, the extent of factor endowments : natural resource abundance, adequacy of physical overhead capital, effectiveness of financial institutions, and rate of improvement in human resources. Variables indicative of sectoral productivity in agriculture are level of modernization of agricultural techniques, degree of improvement in agricultural productivity, and an index of the institutional structure of agriculture, which combines information on land tenure patterns and the size and viability of farming units. The influences on sectoral productivity in industry are represented by indicators of level of industrial modernization and change in degree of industrialization. Several variables summarize various aspects of the allocation of resources between sectors likely to influence economy-wide productivity : subsistence farming (the size of the traditional agricultural sector), an index of the intersectoral pattern of development (the extent of socioeconomic dualism), and the composition of exports (the structure of foreign trade). A population variable is included to suggest the influence on resource productivity of external economies associated with the size of the market. Finally, two direct measures of overall economy-wide resource productivity were introduced into the analysis-indicators of per capita GNP and of level of socioeconomic development, as well as a measure of broad rates of change in total productivity which indicates the potential for economic development (27). These economic measures were supplemented by a variable suggestive of the extent of income redistribution through taxation, or level of effectiveness of the tax system, and a measure of country size and orientation of development strategy.

Socio-cultural influences likely to affect income distribution are represented by indicators of urbanization and of literacy as well as of the importance of the indigenous middle class and of social mobility (measured by a composite of educational opportunity, access to membership in the middle class, and racial and cultural barriers to mobility). Also included is a measure of cultural and ethnic homogeneity based on the proportion of the population speaking the predominant language as well as on the extent of ethnic and religious homogeneity.

The political indicators include measures descriptive both of political institutions and of characteristics of political leadership likely to influence the distribution of income. Indicators of the extent of political participation and the strength of the labor movement represent the importance of participant political institutions. Two variables represent selected aspects of colonial experience of possible relevance to the current type of government : a nominal indicator of type of colonial experience (British, French, or other) and a variable scoring countries by the number of years they have been self-governing. (Neither of these variables entered the analysis.) Finally, four measures summarize key characteristics of political leadership : the political strength of traditional elites, the political strength of the military, the leadership commitment to promoting economic development, and direct government economic activity.

---

27) For a description of this measure, see Irman Adelman and Cynthia Taft Morris, "Performance Criteria for Evaluating Economic Development Potential : An Operational Approach, "Quarterly Journal of Economics, 82 (1968) : 261-262. For individual country scores, see Table 5 of that article, pp. 278-279.

The coverage of these independent variables is quite broad. They include most of the political, social, and economic institutional influences stressed in social science literature as important to the shape of the income distribution. The coverage of conventional, purely economic variables, however, is noticeably incomplete. There are no measures, for example, of relative abundance or relative prices of capital and labor or of relative propensities to save by different classes. While these omissions were necessary because of inadequate data, we do not regard them as seriously hampering our investigation. Our main interest, after all, is in underlying economic and noneconomic institutional influences that are usually taken as given in economic analyses of income distribution. More serious is the absence of measures of the distribution of property. Another omission is any measure of variations in the incidence of such household characteristics as age, sex, occupation and stage of participation in the labor force. It should be noted, however, that the broader the classes of income considered, the more likely it is that variations in the incidence of household characteristics will cancel out and the less likely it is that they will affect the results systematically (28).

Validity of Data

In view of the crudeness of our independent variables, the substantial margin of error, and several sources of incompatibility in our income distribution data, the validity of our data for the present investigation needs to be considered.

A basic characteristic of a valid measure is that it "measures what it purports to measure (29). Whether it does so or not can be established in two fundamentally different ways; one is a matter of definition (30) and the other (more relevant for the social sciences) is a matter of empirical connections. "Here", says Kaplan, "the validity of a measurement is a matter of the success with which the measures obtained in particular cases allow us to predict the measures that would be arrived at by other procedures and in other contexts." (31) Valid measurements also requires, of course, that a measure be relatively free of error in its several senses.

Several considerations suggest that our crude data are reasonably valid for the purpose of exploring broad interrelationships between income distribution and the various factors we investigate. With respect to our dependent variables, the consistency of the empirical connections obtained with alternative specifications of income distribution, together with the interpretability of the variation among subsets of results, suggests their validity for the present analysis. As for our independent variables, earlier statistical studies indicate their relative insensitivity to reasonable alternative specifications of the

---

28) For example, the lowest quintile usually includes a high incidence of both one-person households and large-family households. It seems likely that a predominance of the latter will slightly bias the results, since data unadjusted for size of family tend to overstate the share of the lowest income group and understate the share of higher income groups.

29) Kaplan, The Conduct of Inquiry, p. 198.

30) The meaning of a variable may be specified by the measurement procedure itself, as when "national product" is specified by the rules for estimating GNP. There is then no question that, for example, GNP measures "national product." This does not, however, validate the use of GNP to represent theoretical concepts of economic welfare or productive capacity.

31) Kaplan, Conduct of Inquiry, p. 199. To illustrate, the use of GNP as a measure of national productive capacity might be validated by the extent to which it can be used to predict other aspects of productive capacity such as constraints revealed by input-output studies or constraints on consumption revealed by budget studies.

concepts measured; in addition, the statistical interconnections obtained are interpretable and are broadly consistent with other knowledge and evidence. Specific empirical associations between measures that are conceptually close yet were obtained by independent procedures also suggest that our methods are reasonably appropriate. For example, our indicator of socioeconomic dualism close conceptually to extent of socioeconomic inequalities, and based on qualitative evidence shows a close empirical connection to independent estimates of degree of income inequality. Nevertheless it is evident that the empirical connections obtained and our limited experimentation with alternative specifications of indicators do not fully demonstrate that our data measure what they purport to measure. Extensive testing with alternative specifications using different measurement procedures and other bodies of data would be necessary to evaluate them fully.

Validity of measurement also requires reasonable freedom from error (32). That is, a measure should be sufficiently <u>reliable</u> or invariant under repreated measurement; sufficiently sensitive, or able to discriminate between different amounts of the property measured; and sufficiently <u>accurate</u>, or free of systematic error resulting from omitted influences included, <u>for the purpose at hand</u>. With respect to reliability, our resources have not permitted the kind of fieldwork necessary to establish invariance under repeated measurement. Nevertheless our procedures in the construction of the independent variables appear to assure a reasonable degree of reliability for our purpose (33). We tried to obtain a variability under repeated measurement that was small enough so that variations in country rankings due to unreliability would be small relative to the broad systematic variations that provide the substance of our statistic 1 results. With respect to sensitivity, it is clear that the degree of discrimination provided by our income distribution data and by our independent variables is not great absolutely. It would not be sufficient, for example, for the use of much of our data as inputs to policy-planning models. Nevertheless, the nature of our results suggests that the degree of discrimination is adequate for exploring the broad interractions we are interested in (34). In order to test the impact on our results of the lack of sensitivity of our data, we made test runs replacing the income distribution variables with a set of scores computed by assigning countries to categories having arbitrary numbers that preserved the ordering of countries in the original data (except that partial ordering replaced full ordering). The results were identical for two of the analyses and substantially similar for the third. With respect to the independent variables, it should be stressed that our technique of analysis requires only ranking of observations. These data need not be as sensitive, therefore, as would be desirable with other statistical techniques.

With respect to accuracy, our independent variables do not seem to pose major problems of systematic error due to influences that are omitted through <u>presumed included</u>. With our income distribution data, the major possibility for systematic error would seem to be a possible tendency to overstate the share of the lowest income groups and to understate that

---

32) This discussion follows Kaplan, <u>Conduct of Inquiry</u>, pp. 199-201.

33) The application of the method of successive definition together with the use of expert opinion to eliminate inconsistencies between preliminary operational definitions and actual observations, seems to have reduced variability to a scale not likely to alter the broad picture of interactions obtained in our statistical results.

34) In selecting the number of categories for our qualitative indicators, we compromised between two desiderata : to obtain sufficient discrimination between our observations and to obtain categories sufficiently broad so that judgmental information could be used reliably to classify countries for which point information was unavailable. The extent of discrimination in the income distribution data was dictated by the data that were available.

of the highest ones because of lack of adjustments for variations in the size of households, which tend to be greater at the lower end of the income distribution (35).

The major problems with our data are the interrelated ones of conceptualization and of the availability of primary data. That is, while the operational definitions do indicate reasonably well what is included and what is omitted from the measures, they suffer from the inadequacy of links between the measures themselves and the often vague and ill-defined social science concepts they are intended to represent. It is for this reason, for example, that we have chosen a battery of income distribution variables to measure income inequality; any one taken alone cannot be presumed to represent adequately the rather imprecise multidimensional concept of income inequality.

Thus, in summary, the variables included in our study provide rough measures of an unusually wide range of potential influences on the distribution of income. While very crude, these measures appear to provide reasonably valid country rankings for exploratory investigations into the broad interrelationships involved in changes in the distribution of income in underdeveloped nations.

IV. THE STATISTICAL RESULTS

Each analysis for the three dependent variables presented here is discussed as follows. First, a diagram of the successive splits obtained by the analysis shows, for each split, (a) the independent variable that "best" splits the sample at that step, (b) the size of the subgroups obtained, (c) the dependent variable means for each of the resultant subgroups, and (d) the percent of the dependent variable variance "explained" by the differences between subgroup means and parent sample mean. Notes to the diagrams list the "next best" independent variables (that are significant at the 1 percent level) with the percentages of dependent variable variance they account for. Summaries follow of the characteristics (as of about 1961) of the countries in the different subgroups obtained in each analysis.

In interpreting our results, we apply theoretical reasoning, together with historical and comparative evidence, to gain semiquantitative insights into dynamic interactions between the shape of the income distribution and a wide range of socioeconomic and political characteristics summarized by our data. The pitfalls in using statistical relationships to shed light on causal forces are well known : empirical associations may represent causality in either direction or may result from common forces; an included variable may represent closely related influences not explicitly measured by it, and so forth. In addition, cross-sectional data typically violate the assumption of statistical models that, given correctly specified relationships, the behavior patterns of cross-sectional units are homogeneous except for random diversity and the systematic differences in objective opportunities expressed in the included variables. Nor would time-series data give a better view of underlying dynamic relationships, for they violate (again, given correctly specified relationships) the assumption required by statistical models that behavior patterns over time are unchanging except for random variations. Given the respective biases of cross-sectional and time series approaches, it is clearly desirable to make complementary use of both.

---

35) While a number of biases may be present in our basic data, <u>systematic</u> bias due to our use of expert opinion and qualitative evidence appears to be <u>absent</u>. We obtained marked differences in simple correlations for subsamples representing different levels of development (subsamples were constructed after data preparation was complete); to maintain that there is systematic bias in expert opinions requires the assumption that such bias varies systematically with level of development - a somewhat implausible contention.

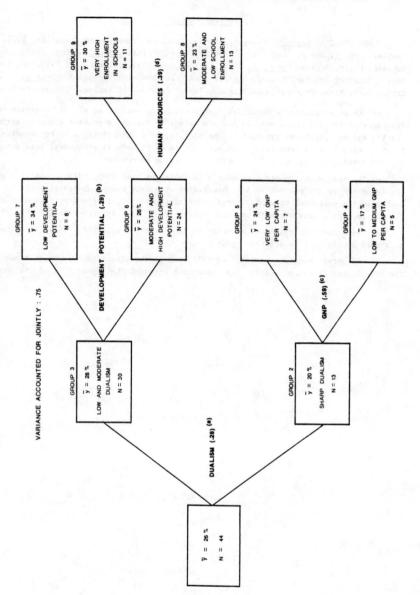

Figure 1

ANALYSIS OF SHARE OF INCOME OF THE POOREST 60 PERCENT OF THE POPULATION

Notes to Figure 1

GROUP MEMBERS. Group 5, Malagasy, Morocco, Sierra Leone, Sudan, Tanzania, Tunisia, Zambia. Group 4, Gabon, Iraq, Peru, Senegal, South Africa. Group 7, Burma, Chad, Dahomey, Ecuador, Niger, Surinam. Group 8, Bolivia, Brazil, Ceylon, Colombia, El Salvador, Ivory Coast, Jamaica, Lebanon, Mexico, Nigeria, Pakistan, Rhodesia, Trinidad. Group 9, Argentina, Chile, Costa Rica, Greece, India, Israel, Japan, Panama, Philippines, Taiwan, Venezuela.

a) The other candidate variables that distinguish well among all 43 Countries are the abundance of natural resources (23 %), the extent of direct government economic activity (20 %), and the political strength of the traditional elite (18 %). A higher average share to the lowest 60 % is associated with more abundance of natural resources, less strength of the traditional elite, and a larger role for the government.

b) The nest most important candidate variables at this step indicate that a higher average share to the poorest 60 % is associated with less ethnic homogeneity (28 %), lower scores on the character of agricultural organization (27 %), less modernization of industry (23 %), less political strength of labor unions (21 %), and lower per capita GNP (21 %).

c) There are no significant alternative candidates at this step. Libya is omited at this step by reason of a splinter split.

d) The other important variable at this step is the structure of foreign trade (35 %). The more diversified are exports, the higher the share of the lowest 60 % of the population.

It is obvious that any firm validation of our findings will require testing our conclusions against other bodies of cross-sectional data and against time series studies of individual countries having different characteristics.

Analysis of Share of Income Accruing to Poorest 60 Percent of Population

On the average, over the entire set of 43 countries, the poorest 60 percent of the population receives 26 percent of total income. This is a little over 40 percent of the share they would receive were income evenly distributed throughout the economy. The standard deviation of their income share is 7 percent; the range is from 2 percent (Libya) to 38 percent (Israel).

The results summarized in Figure 1 show that the allocation of income to the poorest 60 percent of the population is "explained", broadly speaking, by the extent of socio-economic dualism, the level of social and economic modernization, and the expansion of secondary and higher level education. The poorest 60 percent received a relatively large share of total income -- on the average, between 30 and 34 percent -- under two quite different sets of circumstances : quite pervasive underdevelopment marked by the predominance of small-scale or communal subsistence agriculture (group 7), and substantial development associated with major efforts to improve human resources (group 9). Their income share was smallest where a sharply dualistic development process had been initiated by well-entrenched expatriate or military elites ideologically oriented to receive most of the benefits of economic development (group 4). The remaining subgroups of countries, in which the income share of the poorest 60 percent ranged from 23 to 26 percent, include both fairly well-developed, moderately dualistic countries (group 8) and sharply dualistic countries that had less dynamic modern sectors and were not under the political control of tradition-oriented expatriate elites (group 5).*

In general, the results do not support the hypothesis that economic growth raises the share of income of the poorer segments of the population. On the contrary, the contrast between the sharply dualistic economies in groups 4 and 5 suggests that economic dynamism at at low levels of development worked to the relative disadvantage of lower income groups. In the countries in group 4, per capita money incomes significantly higher than those in group 5 were associated with an income share of only 17 percent to the poorest 60 percent. Thus rising money incomes per capita originating in the rapid growth of narrow modern sectors benefited small, usually expatriate, elites. Inequality in both groups of sharply dualistic economies was in turn greater than in the low-income, less dualistic countries in group 7, in which economic growth, even narrowly based, had not yet been effectively initiated during the period studied here. As for countries at higher levels of development (group 6), the significant overlap in levels of socioeconomic development between subgroups 8 and 9 suggests that even here economic growth did not necessarily result in benefits to the very poor. Our results suggest rather that this group benefited only when there were also broad-based efforts to improve the economy's human resource base.

---

* The source for these three summaries is chap. 2 of Irma Adelman and Cynthia Taft Morris, *Society, Politics, and Economic Development* (Baltimore, 1971).

Summary of Characteristics (about 1961) of Subgroups in
Analysis of Share of Income of Poorest 60 % of the Population

<u>Group 2</u> ($\bar{y}$ = 20 %) : 13 sharply dualistic countries
 - Rich in natural resources (except Senegal and Sudan).
 - Characterized by sharp sectoral and/or geographic cleavage between an important exchange sector and a predominant, traditional, nonmonetized agricultural sector.
 - Handicraft production more important than modern techniques in the manufacture of consumer goods (except South Africa).
 - School enrollment ratios less than 40 %.
 - Literacy rates less than 35 % (except Peru and South Africa).

<u>Group 4</u> ($\bar{y}$ = 17 %) : 5 sharply dualistic countries with per capita GNP in 1961 ranging from $175 to $200 (except South Africa, $427).
 - Income share of upper 20 % of population ranges from 64 to 71 % (except South Africa, 57 %).
 - Tradition-oriented elites politically strong (except Gabon and Iraq).
 - At best, moderate development potential (except South Africa).
 - At best, moderate factor scores on socioeconomic development.

<u>Group 5</u> ($\bar{y}$ = 24 %) : 7 sharply dualistic countries with per capita GNP in 1961 below $171.
 - Income share of upper 20 % of population ranged from 48 to 65 %.
 - Tradition-oriented elites <u>not</u> politically strong (except Morocco).
 - Low development potential and low factor scores on socioeconomic development (except Tunisia).

<u>Group 3</u> ($\bar{y}$ = 28 %) : 30 countries that at most were moderately dualistic (except Bolivia and Burma).
 - Includes two types of countries : those that were not dualistic because there was almost no modern sector, and those that, despite some cleavage between traditional and modern sectors, were characterized by significant interaction between the two.

<u>Group 6</u> ($\bar{y}$ = 26 %) : 24 moderately dualistic countries (except Bolivia) with moderate or high development potential.

<u>Group 8</u> ($\bar{y}$ = 23 %) : 13 countries with low or moderate rates of improvement in human resources.
 - Factor scores in the middle two quartiles for the full sample (except Lebanon and Trinidad in upper quartile and Nigeria and Ivory Coast in lower quartile).
 - Literacy rates less than 55 % (except Trinidad, Jamaica, Colombia and Ceylon).
 - Per capita GNP under $340 in 1961 (except Trinidad, Lebanon, and Jamaica).

<u>Group 9</u> ($\bar{y}$ = 30 %) : 11 countries with <u>exceptionally</u> high rates of improvement in human resources.
 - Factor scores on socioeconomic development in the upper third for the full sample (except India and the Philippines).

- Literacy rates over 55 % (except India and Taiwan).
- Per capita GNP over $340 in 1961 (except India, the Philippines, and Taiwan).

Group 7 ($\overline{y}$ = 34 %) : 6 little or moderately dualistic countries (except Burma) with low
development potential.
- Characterized by predominance of either small subsistence farms in which marketing
of output was of marginal importance or communally owned and operated lands.
- Limited industrial sectors in which a narrow range of goods was produced in small-
scale factories and rare large-scale production was foreign financed and managed.
- Manufactured commodities less than 10 % of exports; marked concentration of exports
with more than 75 % of exports from 4 landing commodities.

Analysis of Share or Income Accruing to Wealthiest 5 Percent of the Population

In our sample the average share of income received by the top 5 percent of the population is 30 percent -- six times as large as their share would be with an even distribution pattern. The standard deviation of this share is quite large, 9 percent. The lowest
share is 15 percent, in Japan; the highest is 48 percent, in Peru.

The results presented in Figure 2 indicate that the extent of natural resource abundance and the extent of direct government economic activity account statistically for a
substantial part of the variations among countries in the share of income received by the
wealthiest 5 percent of the population. The extreme concentration of income, however, is
accounted for by the political and economic dominance of expatriate and other ethnically
and culturally distinct subgroups in the population.

The average share of the top 5 percent in resource-rich countries (group 3) is almost
50 percent greater than in less well-endowed countries (group 2). Within both resource-rich
and resource-poor countries, the best differentiator for degrees of income concentration is
the extent of the direct economic role of the government : the average share of the upper
5 percent is significantly smaller in countries with large public sectors and important
government net investment (groups 8 and 6) than in predominantly private enterprise economies (groups 9 and 7). The wealthiest 5 percent receives the smallest share for the entire
sample in countries with relatively poor resource endowments in which the government economic role is very important (group 8).

Extreme income concentration at the top is found only in underdeveloped countries
with an abundance of natural resources. Group 7 with the highest average share to the
wealthiest 5 percent has rather special characteristics. It combines low-level African
countries with countries at the Latin American level of development. The major common
characteristics of the group other than resource abundance and income inequality was that
the direct economic role of the government was not of major importance.

The African countries in group 7 all in the lowest quartile on socioeconomic development, had either traditional elites that were politically influential or expatriate domination of the middle class, and political participation was very restricted. Their economies
were characterized by sharply dualistic growth of a small modern sector and a large relatively backward subsistence agricultural sector.

The special traits of these countries suggest that,historically, colonial powers have
sought the firmest entrenchment in those poor countries best endowed with natural resources
and, further, that the more firmly entrenched the expatriate financial, commercial, and

technical elites, the greater the concentration of income in the hands of the top 5 percent. Our results are thus consistent with the view of economic backwardness under colonialism held by such political economists as Paul A. Baran, according to which very uneven income distribution is a typical outcome of a narrowly based growth process where natural resources are exploited for the primary benefit of a small class of wealthy, usually expatriate, businessmen (36).

The remaining countries in group 7 were in the middle third of the full example on socioeconomic development. In most of them during the the period studied, traditional elites were politically influential and major groups in the population were effectively barred from the political process. In addition, their agricultural sectors were characterized by a combination of subsistence agriculture and absentee-owned commercial plantations. These characteristics are also consistent with Baran's thesis that the concentration of control over resources in the hands of a coalition of feudal-type land owners and politically entrenched business elites is a major factor contributing to income concentration at the top.

Concentration was least for resource abundant nations in those at relatively high levels of development where broad-based social and economic advances and intensive efforts to improve human resources were accompanied by the expansion of political participation to include all major groups in the population. Six countries with these characteristics split off from the mainstream of the analysis into group 4 by reason of their large indigenous middle classes. In the remaining resource abundant countries spanning the full range of development levels, the share of the top 5 percent varies systematically with the importance of the government sector. Where the government sector was of major importance their share was 31 percent compared with 39 percent for the group having greatest concentration. This mild average degree of redistribution appears to be the best that can be achieved without either successful expansion of political participation or broad-based socioeconomic development.

The relationship suggested by our results between economic growth and the income share of the top income group is nonlinear. The only way typically available for very low-income countries to reduce income concentration at the top appears to be direct economic action on the part of the government. Where either the political influence of traditional elites or the economic dominance of an expatriate middle class prevents an expansion of the government economic role, extreme income concentration usually results. For moderated-developed countries, broad based economic growth provides a way to achieve redistribution only where accompanied by social and educational development as well as substantial broadening of political participation. Where these conditions are not met, it is the extent of a country's resource endowment and the size of the government role rather than economic growth per se that are the primary forces for redistribution away from the top.

---

36) See Paul A. Baran, "On the Political Economy of Backwardness", in The Economics of Underdevelopment, ed. A. N. Agarwala and S. P. Singh (New York, Oxford University Press, 1958), pp. 75-92.

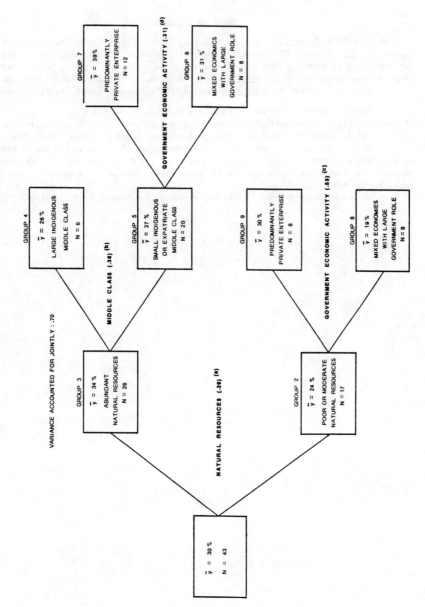

Figure 2

ANALYSIS OF SHARE OF INCOME OF WEALTHIEST 5 % OF THE POPULATION

<u>Notes to Figure 2</u>

GROUP MEMBERS. <u>Group 8</u>, Ceylon, Chad, India, Israel, Japan, Niger, Pakistan, Sudan, Taiwan. <u>Group 9</u>, Dahomey, El Salvador, Ivory Coast, Jamaica, Lebanon, Philippines, Senegal, Surinam. <u>Group 7</u>, Brazil, Colombia, Gabon, Iraq, Libya, Malagasy, Nigeria, Panama, Peru, Sierra Leone, Tanzania, Zambia. <u>Group 6</u>, Burma, Bolivia, Costa Rica, Ecuador, Morocco, Tunisia, Rhodesia, S. Africa. <u>Group 4</u>, Argentina, Chile, Greece, Mexico, Trinidad, Venezuela.

a) The two important alternative candidate variables show that a lower share of income of the top families is associated with greater direct government participation in economic activity (28 %) and broader popular participation in political processes (20 %). The remaining significant variables indicate that less concentration of income at the top is associated with more political strength of the labor movement (17 %), a less powerful traditional elite (17 %), higher per capita GNP (16 %), and a higher rate of improvement of human resources (16 %).

b), c) and d) There are no significant alternative variables at this split.

Summary of Characteristics (About 1961) of Subgroups in
Analysis of Share of Income of Wealthiest 5 % of the Population

Group 2 ($\bar{y}$ = 23 %) : 18 countries not very well endowed with natural resources.
- Had at best either fairly abundant agricultural resources (1 acre or more of agricultural land per capita) with no significant mineral resources or limited agricultural resources (less than 1 acre of agricultural land per capita) with some but not abundant mineral resources.
- Spanned entire range of levels of socioeconomic development and of development policies covered by the sample.

Group 8 ($\bar{y}$ = 18 %) : 9 countries with government-private enterprise economies.
- Had economies in which the government's direct role was of major importance as indicated by substantial government investment in infrastructure, health and education, and by the shares of net investment undertaken by the government, often greater than the share of private industry.
- Spanned all levels of development and development policies.

Group 9 ($\bar{y}$ = 28 %) : 9 countries with predominantly private enterprise economies.
- Had small public sectors and relatively small contributions of government to net investment (except Senegal and Kenya, in which direct role of government was moderately important).
- Spanned all levels of development and development policies.

Group 3 ($\bar{y}$ = 34 %) : 26 countries that are very well endowed with natural resources.
- Were rich in agricultural resources as well as in either fuel or nonfuel resources (or both).
- Spanned entire range of levels of socioeconomic development and of development policies covered by the sample.

Group 4 ($\bar{y}$ = 26 %) : 6 resource-abundant countries with large indigenous middle classes.
- Upper quartile on factor scores on socioeconomic development.
- All but Trinidad in top category on political participation and efforts to improve human resources.
- Were in top category on social mobility.
- Had per capita GNP greater than $312 in 1961.

Group 5 ($\bar{y}$ = 37 %) : 20 resource-abundant countries with small indigenous or expatriate middle classes.
- Spanned lowest three quartiles on factor scores on socioeconomic development.
- None except Costá Rica and Colombia scored in top two categories on political participation.
- None except South Africa and Brazil was in the highest group of discriminant scores on development potential.

70

Group 6 ($\overline{y}$ = 31 %) : 8 resource-abundant countries with small indigenous or expatriate
middle classes where the direct economic role of the government was
of major importance.
- All had important public sectors and large shares of government in net investment.
- Spanned the middle two quartiles on factor scores on socioeconomic development.

Group 7 ($\overline{y}$ = 39 %) : 12 resource-abundant countries with small indigenous or expatriate
middle classes where the direct economic role of the government was
at most moderately important.
- In most the direct economic role of the government was not important; while in the
remainder it was only moderately important.
- In all except Colombia political participation was very restricted.
- In all except Iraq either the traditional elite was influential politically or the
middle class was dominated by expatriates.
- The 7 African countries were characterized by sharp dualism (except Nigeria); while
the remaining countries had agricultural sectors marked by a combination of subsistence and absentee-owner commercial plantation agriculture (except Panama).

Analysis of Shares of Income Accruing to the Middle 20 Percent of the Population

The average share of income accruing to the middle 20 percent of the population in
our sample (i.e. the two deciles clustered around the median income) is 12 percent, with
a standard deviation of 3 percent. The share ranges from 1 percent for Libya to 17 percent
for Israel (37). In no country in the sample do middle-income families get as much as they
would with a uniform income distribution.

The portion of income allocated to the middle groups in the income distribution according to Figure 3, is the only share that appears to vary systematically with level of development. The countries with the highest average share to the middle quintile (groups 6 and 8)
are among the more developed in the sample socially and economically, while countries in
the group with the smallest average share (group 3) are among the least developed. However,
the relationship is nonlinear since more rapid short-term economic change in the middle
range of countries is associated with a smaller share to the middle quintile (group 9) than
that received by somewhat lower-level countries undergoing less rapid economic change
(group 10).

The primary influence differentiating among countries with respect to the income share
of the middle quintile is the extent of socioeconomic dualism (38). Thirteen countries with

---

37) The next highest figures are, respectively, 7 percent for Kenya and 15.8 percent for
Japan.

38) In earlier runs with provisional income distribution data, the primary variable was
the importance of the indegenous middle class - an important next-best candidate
variable in the present analysis. Not unexpectedly, the results for the middle 20 percent of the population proved more sensitive to final data revisions than did those
for the poorest 60 percent or the richest 5 percent (the latter results were substantially unchanged). The reasons are that the range of values is narrower and the cumulation
of estimating errors usually greater. Nevertheless, neither the general import of the
middle quintile results nor the full set of significant variables has been greatly
affected by income-data revisions. But the particular primary variables at successive
splits are different.

The only independent variable to be revised was the structure of foreign trade. This
variable was redefined to give greater differentiation among countries at the upper
(continued on p. 74)

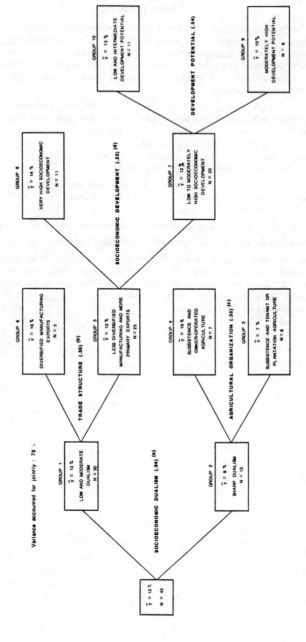

Figure 3

ANALYSIS OF SHARE OF INCOME OF MIDDLE INCOME GROUPS (40-60 %)

Notes to Figure 3

GROUP MEMBERS. Group 3, Gabon, Iraq, Libya, Morocco, Malagasy, Tanzania. Group 4, Peru, Senegal, Sudan, Sierra Leone, South Africa, Tunisia, Zambia. Group 6, India, Israel, Japan, Taiwan, Pakistan. Group 8, Argentina, Chile, Greece, Lebanon, Venezuela. Group 9, Brazil, Colombia, Costa Rica, Jamaica, Mexico, Nigeria, Philippines, Rhodesia, Trinidad and Tobago. Group 10, Bolivia, Burma, Ceylon, Chad, Dahomey, Ecuador, El Salvador, Ivory Coast, Niger, Panama, Surinam.

a) Other candidate variables of importance indicate that a higher share of income for the middle quintile is associated with higher development potential (26 % of the variance), a higher rate of improvement in human resources (25 %), a larger indigenous middle class (24 %), a greater extent of political participation (21 %), a higher degree of urbanization (20 %), greater strength of the labor movement (20 %), a higher level of modernization of industry (19 %), and a higher literacy rate (17 %).

b) The next best candidate variables indicate that the middle sector receives a larger income share when the rate of improvement in human resources is higher (26 %), and when the level of socioeconomic development is higher (23 %).

c) There are no significant alternative candidate variables at this step.

d) There are no significant alternative candidate variables at this step.

e) The next most important candidate variables are the level of development of financial institutions (34 %) and the extent of leadership commitment to economic development (31 %). The share of income of the middle twenty percent of the population is higher when the level of development of financial institutions is lower and leadership commitment to economic development is less.

sharp cleavages between a small exchange sector and a large subsistence sector (group 2) had an average share for the middle group of only 9 percent. The remaining countries with an average share of 13 percent (group 1) include those that were less dualistic because of the wider spread of economic growth achieved with higher development levels and those that were dualistic by reason of relative stagnation at low levels of development. The importance of this split is not surprising since rapid dualistic growth of a narrow modern enclave in countries at low levels of development typically benefited a small expatriate group of a culturally distinct indigenous oligarchy. Furthermore, the carryover of economic growth to the remainder of the economy was usually so restricted that the middle 20 % of the population counted among the agricultural poor.

Given the narrow spread of economic change in sharply dualistic countries, it is not surprising that the variable best accounting for variations among them in the income share of the middle quintile is the nature of institutional arrangements in agriculture. Specifically, the share of the middle income group is heavily influenced by the character of commercialized agriculture. A larger share went to the middle quintile in countries where small-scale owner-operated cash cropping prevailed in the small commercialized sector (group 4). The smallest average share for the entire sample went to those dualistic countries where tenant farming, plantation agriculture or absentee-landownership predominated (group 3).

The influences differentiating best among countries that are at most moderately dualistic are the structure of foreign trade, the level of socioeconomic development, and potential for short-term economic performance. The first two of these splits suggest that two rather different paths of change tend to benefit the middle income groups in countries that are moderately developed for low-income nations, neither possible where the middle class is dominated by expatriates. One path is representend by the countries in group 6.

These countries had rather sparse natural resources, a diversified trade structure based on the export of manufacturing goods, and ranked high on the direct economic role of the government, improvements in financial institutions, and leadership commitment to economic development. These associations suggest that in countries at this level where natural resources are not abundant, the diversification of trade structure supported by an active direct role of the government and the growth of financial institutions provides an effective path for increasing the income share of the middle sector. The alternative path available to countries with more generous resource endowments involves broad based social and economic development simultaneous with quite widespread political participation. This path is represented by the countries in group 8 that rank very high for low-income nations on socioeconomic development, political participation, and efforts to improve human resources.

In interpreting the final split for moderately dualistic countries, it is important to bear in mind that since the countries in group 7 span the lower three quartiles on socioeconomic development, most of their "middle class" falls in the upper, not the middle, 20 percent of the population. These countries have not selected either trade diversification supported by government policy nor exceptional efforts to improve human resources as their

---

(Note 38, continued from p. 71)

end of the spectrum. It is undoubtedly for this reason that it gains importance in the present analysis.

For the earlier results see Irma Adelman and Cynthia Taft Morris, "An Anatomy of Income Distribution in Developing Nations", <u>Development Digest</u>, IX (October, 1971), pp. 24-37.

development strategies. The variable accounting best for difference among them in the middle income share is their development potential (measured by past advances along a broad front), with an inverse relationship between the middle income share and development potential. The average share is lower in the group with greater development potential and a higher level of socioeconomic development (group 9). Furthermore, the consistently higher levels of industrial and financial development and the higher rates of economic change in this group suggest strongly that a development strategy stressing even quite broad based economic change does not, as a rule, improve the relative position of the middle 20 % of the population unless accompanied by an intensive effort to improve human resources. Rather, in these countries the usual beneficiaries of economic growth appear to have been the upper 20 percent of the income spectrum. This generalization is supported by the fact that the average income of the top 20 percent for this group is 61 percent compared with 51 percent for the lower level group with a higher share for the middle quintile (group 10).

Summary of Characteristics (About 1961) of Subgroups
in Analysis of Share of Middle 20 Percent of the Population

Group 1 ($\overline{y}$ = 13 %) : 30 countries that at most were moderately dualistic (except Bolivia
and Burma).
- Includes two types of countries : those that were not dualistic because there was
almost no modern sector, and those that, despite some cleavage between traditional
and modern sectors, were characterized by significant interaction between the two.

Group 6 ($\overline{y}$ = 16 %) : 5 countries that were no more than moderately dualistic with trade
structures marked by a share of manufactured goods in total exports
of more than 20 % and significant diversification of exports.
- All had sparse natural resources. None had an abundance of minerals : at most, they
had some fuel or some nonfuel resources (but not both).
- All gave the government an important direct economic role, as indicated by large
public sectors and important shares of government in net investment.
- All except Taiwan had leadership showing sustained and reasonably effective commitment to promoting economic development during the period 1957-62.
- All demonstrated a marked improvement in the effectiveness of their financial institutions during the period 1950-63.
- All had significant indigenous middle classes, although those of India and Pakistan
were fairly small.

Group 5 ($\overline{y}$ = 12 %) : 25 countries that were no more than moderately dualistic (except
Bolivia and Burma) with trade structures in most instances marked by
a share of manufactured goods in total exports of less than 10 % and
at most moderate diversification of exports.
- In all but five, the share of manufactured goods in total exports was less than 10 %;
in the majority over 75 % of exports came from the four leading commodities.
- These countries spanned the full range of levels of socioeconomic development and
of short-term economic performance.

Group 8 ($\overline{y}$ = 14 %) : 5 nondualistic countries, having trade structures not marked by significant diversification of exports, that were at very high levels of
socioeconomic development for low-income nations.
- All had factor scores on socioeconomic development in the upper quartile for the
full sample.
- All ranked in the highest category on importance of the indigenous middle class.
- All but Lebanon ranked in the highest category on rate of improvement of human
resources, modernization of industry, and political participation, and all but
Chile in the highest category on level of effectiveness of financial institutions.

Group 7 ($\overline{y}$ = 12 %) : 20 countries that were at most moderately dualistic (except Burma and
Bolivia) and were characterized by neither significant diversification
of exports nor very high levels of socioeconomic development.

76

- All but three (Jamaica, Trinidad, and Panama) had factor scores on socioeconomic development in the lower three quartiles for the full sample.
- Spanned the full range of scores on most measures of short-term economic performance.

Group 9 ($\bar{y}$ = 10 %) : 9 at most moderately dualistic countries (characterized by neither significant diversification of exports nor very high levels of socioeconomic development) that had fairly high development potential.

- Discriminant scores on development potential in the upper half for the full sample.
- All but Jamaica and the Philippines had fairly abundant natural resources.
- All except Nigeria had industrial sectors that were producing at least a fair variety of consumer and/or exports goods by means of power-driven factory production methods.
- Local financial institutions that were sufficiently developed to attract at least a small and significant volume of indigenous savings.
- 6 out of 9 had average annual rates of growth of per capita GNP of over 2 % during the period 1950/51-1963/64, while the remainder had rates of growth of between 1 and 2 %.

Group 10 ($\bar{y}$ = 13 %) : 11 moderately dualistic countries (except Bolivia and Burma), characterized by neither significant diversification of exports nor very high levels of socioeconomic development, that had low and intermediate development potential.

- 6 out of 11 had relatively sparse natural resources.
- Industrial sectors where handicraft industry was more important in the production of domestic consumers goods than modern methods and where the majority of modern production units were foreign managed and financed.
- Local financial institutions that attracted a negligible volume of private savings.
- All except Burma and Ecuador had average annual rates of growth of per capita GNP of less than 2 % for the period 1950/51-1963/64; 6 out 11 had rates of growth of less than 1 %.

Group 2 ($\bar{y}$ = 9 %) : 13 sharply dualistic countries.

- Rich in natural resources (except Senegal and Sudan).
- Characterized by sharp sectoral or geographic cleavage between an important exchange sector and a predominant, traditional, nonmonetized agricultural sector.
- Handicraft production more important than modern techniques in the manufacture of consumer goods (except South Africa).
- School enrollment ratios less than 40 %.
- Literacy rates le-s than 35 % (except Peru and South Africa).

Group 3 ($\bar{y}$ = 7 %) : 6 sharply dualistic countries where the predominance of subsistence agriculture was combined with a small commercialized agricultural sector dominated tenantry, plantation agriculture, or absentee landownership.

Group 4 ($\bar{y}$ = 10 %) : 7 sharply dualistic countries where the predominance of subsistence agriculture was combined with a small commercialized agricultural sector characterized by owner-operated farms (except Peru where plantation agriculture dominated a large commercialized sector).

V. ECONOMIC DEVELOPMENT AND THE DISTRIBUTION OF INCOME

The three cross-sectional analyses of income distribution discussed here suggest a group of multifaceted and highly nonlinear interactions over time between the dynamic process of economic development and changes in the distribution of income. When economic growth begins in a subsistence agrarian economy through the expansion of a narrow modern sector, inequality in the distribution of income typically increases greatly, particularly where expatriate exploitation of rich natural resources provides the motivating force for growth. The income share of the poorest 60 percent declines significantly, as does that of the middle 20 percent (39), and the income share of the top 5 percent increases strikingly.

The gains of the top 5 percent are particularly great in very low income countries where a sharply dualistic structure is associated with political and economic domination by traditional or expatriate elites. Once countries move successfully beyond the stage of sharply dualistic growth, further development as such generates no systematic advantage or disadvantage for the top 5 percent until they reach the very highest level for underdeveloped countries when broad based social and economic advances operate to their disadvantage. Instead, their share increases with greater natural resources available for exploitation and decreases with greater government action to improve infrastructure and to raise the level of human resource development.

As developing nations become less dualistic, the middle income group is the primary beneficiary under two possible development strategies available to countries which are at least moderately developed. Widely based social and economic advances combined with consistent efforts to improve human resources and expand political participation and facilitated by a reasonable abundance of natural resources typically favor the middle sector. Where resources are sparse, the middle sector may nevertheless benefit through the development of a diversified manufacturing export sector supported by an active government economic role and expanding financial institutions. In contrast, when neither of these strategies is followed but rapid and quite widespread economic growth under moderate dualism nevertheless takes place, the relative position of the middle quintile worsens with the benefits of economic change going rather to the upper 20 percent of the population.

The position of the poorest 60 percent typically worsens, both relatively and absolutely, when an initial spurt of narrowly based dualistic growth is imposed upon an agrarian subsistence economy. Our study suggests that, in an average country going through the earliest phases of economic development, it takes at least a generation for the poorest 60 percent to recover the loss in absolute income associated with the typical spurt in growth. This hypothesis is strongly suggested by a study of Fig. 1 (analysis for the poorest 60 percent of the population). In the relatively less dualistic subsistence economies of group 5, an average growth rate of per capita GNP in the neighborhood of zero percent is associated with an average share to the poorest 60 percent of the population of 34 percent. In the more sharply dualistic economies of group 2, an average growth rate of per capita GNP of about 3 percent is associated with an average income share to the poorest 60 percent of 20

---

39) There is obviously an overlap between the income share of the poorest 60 percent and that of the middle 20 %. The former measure is of interest when one is concerned with the position of the poorer "majority" of the population. The latter is of most interest to those concerned with the middle groups, which are assumed by political and economic historians to play key roles in national development.

percent. If we hypothesize that the typical path of change is represented by a movement from group 7 to group 2 and assume that the income share of the poorest 60 percent drops from 34 percent to 20 percent, it follows that about a generation would be needed for the poorest 60 percent in a country with a hypothesized increase in growth rate of 3 percentage points to recover the absolute loss associated with a decline in income share of 14 percentage points.

Even when growth changes from the sharply dualistic form to one that is more broadly based, the middle sector usually benefits and the poorest 60 percent typically continues to lose both absolutely and relatively. To predict by how much the income position of the poor worsens with given increases in economic growth rates requires assumptions about the nature and the time path of development of a typical country in this transitional phase of economic growth. The most likely transitional path appears to be represented by a move from the less extreme sharply dualistic African countries of group 5 to the moderately dualistic intermediate level countries of group 8 in the analysis for the poorest 60 percent of the population. This move implies a drop of between 2 and 3 percentage points in the share of the poorest 40 percent associated, on the average, with an increment in average per capita economic growth rates of less than 1 percentage point. These comparisons suggest that close to two generations would be required before the poorest two quintiles recovered their absolute position (40). Even in the last phase of the stage before takeoff, with relatively high levels of development and capacity for more broadly based economic growth, the poorest segments of the population typically benefit from economic growth only when the government plays an important economic role and when widespread efforts are made to improve the human resource base. These hypotheses are suggested by both the implied gains to the poor in group 9 in Fig. 1 (analysis for the poorest 60 percent) and the major losses to the richest 5 percent implied by the characteristics of group 10 in Fig. 2 (analysis for the richest 5 percent).

Our analysis provides some grounds for speculating about the mechanisms that operate before the takeoff point to depress the standard of living of the poorest 40 percent. In the very earliest stage of dualistic growth, increased wage payments to indigenous workers in modern plantation, extractive, and industrial enterprises tend to be more than offset by concurrent changes in population, relative prices, tastes, and product availability. The lowering of death rates through the introduction of modern health measures such as malaria control, accelerates population growth and thus tends to depress the per capita income of the indigenous population. Since increased cash wages are not immediately matched by increased availability of consumers'goods, higher prices erode gains in money income. Subsistence farmers shifting to cash crops are particularly hard hit by rising prices. Typically they suffer both declines in real income and nutritional deficiencies as they become dependent on the market for major necessities previously produced at home.

---

40) Computations from data for countries in groups 5 and 8 give an average share to the poorest 40 % of 15.7 % for group 5 and 13.0 % for group 8, the average growth rate of per capita GNP for group 8 is about 2.0 %, compared with approximately 1.5 % for group 5. To regain the implied absolute loss in income share of 2.5 percentage points with an increment in average growth rates of per capita GNP of only 0.5 percentage point requires almost 35 years. It should be stressed that this jump is from countries at the African level of development to countries at the lower end of the Latin American spectrum of development. Our results do not imply an absolute worsening in the position of the poorest 40 percent for, say, a jump from the lower to the upper end of the Latin American range of development levels.

As the process of economic growth spreads beyond the narrow expatriate enclave, the factors at work to erode the relative and even the absolute positions of the poorest 40 percent appear to be changes in product mix and technology within both agricultural and nonagricultural sectors, rapid expansion of the urban industrial sectors, continued rapid population increases, migration to the cities, lack of social mobility, and inflation.

Regional income inequality typically increases as the concentration of rapidly growing, technologically advanced enterprises in cities widens the gap between rural and urban per capita income. Income inequality also intensifies in the urban sector with the accumulation of assets in the hands of a relatively small number of owners (usually expatriate) of modern enterprises. This concentration is accelerated by the spread of capital intensive industrial technology through at least three factors - the ease with which owners of modern enterprises obtain capital abroad, the inability of small-scale enterprise to obtain financing, and a growing preference of medium and large entrepreneurs for advanced modern technologies. This labor-saving bias of technological advance, the rapidity of urban population growth, the migration to cities of unemployed rural workers, and the lack of social mobility all tend to swell the numbers of urban impoverished and to decrease the income share of the poorest segments of the urban population.

Several concomitants of the growth process characteristic of the period before economic takeoff also operate to worsen the absolute position of the poor. As agricultural output expands, the inelasticity of international and domestic demand for many agricultural products tends to reduce the real income of agricultural producers. Import substitution policies can raise the prices of consumers' goods above international levels. Simultaneously, mechanization in industry tends to preempt markets formerly supplied by large numbers of artisans and cottage workers : The destruction of handicraft industries acts to reduce incomes and increase unemployment among rural and urban poor. Finally, inflation, the product of investment efforts typically well beyond capacities to save, drives up prices faster than the wages of low-income workers, who have meager bargaining power. At the same time profits tend to rise both absolutely and relatively. Thus, to summarize, inflation, population growth, technological change, the commercialisation of the traditional sector, and urbanisation all combine to reduce the real income of the poorest 40 percent of the population in very low-income countries in the before-takeoff stage of development. Those middle and upper income groups benefit, that are better able to finance the application of more advanced capital intensive techniques of production.

These findings and speculations are, broadly speaking, consistent with other studies, both cross-sectional and time series. Sketchy evidence cited by Kuznets on the early stages of economic growth in currently advanced nations suggests a relative worsening of the position of the poor. Cross-sectional and time series studies of contemporary underdeveloped countries also lend support to the hypothesis that the initial phases of economic growth increase the inequality of income distribution (41). It is only very recently, however, that evidence has been brought forward of absolute declines in the average income of the poorest 40 to 60 percent of the population as a consequence of economic growth in these countries.

41) For time series studies, see Subramanian Swamy, "Structural Changes and the Distribution of Incomes by Size : The Case of India", Review of Income and Wealth, Series 2 (June 1967), pp. 155-174; Weisskoff, "Income Distribution and Economic Growth"; and the references cited on p. 305 of the latter article. For examples of cross-sectional studies, see T. Morgan, "Distribution of Income in Ceylon, Puerto Rico, the United States and the United Kingdom", Economic Journal, 43 (1953) : 825-835 and Oshima, "International Comparison".

VI. SUMMARY

The most important variables affecting income distribution are ecological, socio-economic, and political. Table II lists them in the order of the frequency with which they are significant candidates for splitting parent groups into subgroups. The number of times each variable appears as the primary variable in binary splits is also given. The six most important variables associated with intercountry differences in patterns of income distribution, as judged by frequency of significance, are rate of improvement in human resources, direct government economic activity, socioeconomic dualism, potential for economic development, per capita GNP, and strength of the labor movement.

Of the variables of greatest significance in this analysis, the most reliable for increasing the quality of income distribution appear to be the rate of improvement in human resources and direct governmental economic activity. Increased access to the acquisition of middle-level skills and professional training appears, from our results, to be quite predictable in equalizing effects on the income distribution. The distributional effects of increasing the proportion of government investment in total investment also appear to be favorable to lower and middle-income recipients. As policy instruments, measures to increase political participation through stronger labor unions, are probably less reliable because of their unpredictable impact upon the stability of social and political institutions.

Table II

SUMMARY OF SIGNIFICANT VARIABLES

Variable	Frequency of significance	Frequency of appearance as primary variable
Rate of improvement in human resources	4	1
Direct government economic activity	4	2
Socioeconomic dualism	3	2
Potential for economic development	3	2
Per capita GNP	3	1
Strength of labor movement	3	0
Abundance of natural resources	2	1
Factor scores of level of socioeconomic development	2	1
Structure of foreign trade	2	1
Importance of indigenous middle class	2	1
Character of agricultural organization	2	1
Political participation	2	0
Political strength of traditional elite	2	0
Level of modernization of industry	2	0
Literacy	1	0
Degree of cultural and ethnic homogeneity	1	0
Leadership commitment to economic development	1	0
Effectiveness of financial institutions	1	0
Urbanization	1	0

While the extent of socioeconomic dualisme cannot itself be considered a policy instrument, our results suggest strongly that policies tending to reduce dualism by widening the base for economic growth can be very important for increasing income equality and particularly for improving the position of the middle-income groups. Instruments having this effect might include providing credit to small, indigenous rural and urban entrepreneurs and expanding-technical services to promote the spread of new seeds throughout agriculture.

The consequences for income distribution of increasing the rate of economic growth and improving economic institutions (represented by the development potential variable) are not fully predictable, probably because of the unfavorable effects discussed above. Nevertheless, our results suggest that, once some minimum level of development is reached, a wider coverage of improvements in economic institutions accompanied by either social advances or a shift in trade structure toward more diversified manufacturing exports supported by government policy are likely to increase the share in total income of middle income groups. Increase in per capita GNP are associated with worsening of the income distribution at low levels of development; only at very high levels for low income nations is higher per capita GNP associated with a more equal income distribution.

It is quite striking that several variables most closely associated with variations in patterns of income distribution proved to have little importance in our earlier studies of influences on short-term growth rates of per capita GNP. These variables include natural resource abundance, structure of foreign trade, direct economic role of the government, political participation, and even rates of improvement in middle and higher-level human resources (42). Yet, this study underlines their relevance to differences in the extent of income inequality and thus reinforces the view that the policy instruments that are most effective in improving income distributions are different from those that are best for raising economic growth rates.

---

42) See Adelman and Morris, Society, Politics,and Economic Development.

[12]

Institutional Influences on Poverty in the Nineteenth Century: A Quantitative Comparative Study

CYNTHIA TAFT MORRIS AND IRMA ADELMAN

We apply disjoint principal components analysis to study institutional influences on the course of poverty in the nineteenth century. Classificatory data summarize varied facets of economic and noneconomic institutional structure and change. Four sets of countries are distinguished by characteristics of the course of poverty. The components models show that the impact of economic and demographic changes (export expansion, marketization, industrial expansion, immigration) have consequences for poverty that vary greatly between and within country sets, depending on the character of institutions: above all, land systems, dependence relationships, and political institutions.

FOR our study of long-term institutional influences on poverty between 1850 and 1914, our data are 35 classification systems, our method is comparative, and our techniques are quantitative. We have studied 17 countries. The paper is part of a larger study of long-term growth and development in which we focus successively on the expansion and character of market institutions, patterns of industrialization, the role of agricultural development, the dynamics of foreign dependence, and the course of poverty. Together these studies form the quantitative core of our forthcoming book.[1]

The thesis here is that the consequences for poverty of dynamic economic or demographic change were very different depending on the character of fundamental institutions, above all, land systems, market institutions, dependence relationships, political institutions, and initial economic conditions. Major theories about growth and development make only crude distinctions among types of countries in their key propositions about poverty.[2]

Journal of Economic History, Vol. XLIII, No. 1 (March 1983). © The Economic History Association. All rights reserved. ISSN 0022-0507.

Cynthia Taft Morris is Professor of Economics at The American University, Washington, D.C. 20016. Irma Adelman is Professor of Economics at the University of California, Berkeley, California 94720. They are deeply indebted to the National Science Foundation for support over the years for the work that has gone into this project (NSF Grants GS2272, GS3258, and SES79-14243 to The American University). Only one of the long list of their other debts can be cited here: without the superb research assistance of Frances Summe-Smith, Ph.D. candidate at The American University, the classification systems for per capita income, wages, and exports could not have been completed within a reasonable time.

[1] Cynthia Taft Morris and Irma Adelman, *Where Angels Fear to Tread: Quantitative Studies in History and Development* (Stanford, California, forthcoming).

[2] Our selection and definition of variables and our typology are nevertheless heavily dependent on this literature—a literature rich in "partial" hypotheses about institutional influences on poverty with a few "grand" theories. Because of space constraints, we omit our discussion of this literature.

43

Our approach is comparative and inductive, with theory playing a role in the choice and definition of variables and the construction of subsamples. The comparative approach permits including slowly changing institutions that escape quantitative analysis in individual country studies. Applied to larger samples it demonstrates the wide range of ways in which economic changes and institutional influences interact in different contexts. The inductive approach is particularly appropriate for the study of institutional influences on development and poverty since there is little consensus on the causes of contrasting experiences.

Our classificatory data include such institutional influences as the structure and stability of political power, landholding and tenure arrangements, the extent of foreign economic dependence, the predominant scale of landholdings, and the legal institutional characteristics of market development. We also include indicators of land availability, population size and growth, immigration, transportation development, the percent of labor in agriculture, human resource development, and levels and rates of adoption of new techniques in industry and agriculture, among others. (See Tables 2–5 for the full list.[3]) Our measures of poverty are quite aggregate: classifications by per capita income and its growth and classifications for decadal changes in average wages in agriculture and industry. (The deficiencies of these measures are well known.) The final dimension of poverty we include is the proportion of the population in poverty and its course between 1850 and 1914. Here we apply judgments partially ranking countries and periods for the limited purpose of grouping countries into subsamples by the course of poverty. The concept of "poverty line" that we use is not rigorous, lying below a rigorously determined level of adequacy of diet and above the level of near starvation and destitution. Fragmentary and descriptive data and wage series are used to infer the outlines of what happened to the poor.

Each country enters as three observations: once for each of the periods 1850–1870, 1870–1890, and 1890–1914. For each period indicators of levels of development or structure refer to the initial year of the period (for example, the literacy rate); characteristics of change and political characteristics refer to the entire period (for example, political stability); and lagged variables refer to the two decades prior to the initial year (for example, population growth). Some classifications are based primarily on quantitative data, some on a mixture of statistical

[3] John Coatsworth's comments remind us to explain that the set of variables in this paper differs in two respects from our earlier published sets: we have added foreign economic dependence, export expansion, shift in export structure, changes in real agricultural wages, and changes in real industrial wages. Since excessive proliferation of variables appears to reduce the stability of components results, we have offset these additions by forming three composite indicators of market institutional development out of the previous 12 market variables. Turkey was omitted when we could not classify it on the new variables.

and qualitative data, and some primarily on descriptive information. Even where the data are mainly quantitative, variables are categorized—categorization permitting the more reliable use of indirect information where point estimates are lacking.[4]

We group the 17 countries into four classes by what happened to poverty during 1850 to 1914. (See the typology in Table 1.) Class One consists of Western European countries with significant industrial sectors and favorable institutional conditions in 1850 where widespread industrialization after 1850 led to a substantial reduction in poverty (Belgium, France, Germany, Great Britain, Switzerland). Class Two consists of three Scandinavian countries, overwhelmingly agricultural with large labor surpluses at midcentury but with favorable institutions, where agricultural expansion, a start on industrialization, and heavy emigration combined to reduce poverty greatly by 1914. Class Three consists of low productivity agricultural economies where aggregate export expansion promoted by foreign penetration neither raised average standards of living nor significantly reduced the proportion in poverty (Burma, China, Egypt, India, Russia). Class Four consists of very land-abundant countries settled by Europeans where foreign penetration usually contributed with a long lag to modest rises in standards of living. Six countries from our full sample of 23 were excluded from the typology either because their experience represented an individual mix already incorporated in the typology (United States, Spain, and Italy) or because their paths of change were otherwise strongly individual (Netherlands, Japan, and Brazil).[5]

A few words about our technique. It is a variant of principal components analysis developed in Sweden by Svante Wold for the chemical and botanical sciences.[6] It starts with the principle that the observations fall into different classes within which observations are somehow similar (for example, different species of flowers or, in the present application, classes of countries with different courses of poverty). Measures describing the observations are selected by their presumed *a priori* relevance to the phenomenon studied. The method yields principal components models for each class and measures of (1) the similarity between all pairs of classes; (2) the relevance of each

---

[4] Brief descriptions of most of the classification systems may be found in Irma Adelman and Cynthia Taft Morris, "Patterns of Industrialization in the Nineteenth and Early Twentieth Centuries: A Cross-Sectional Quantitative Study," *Research in Economic History*, 5 (1980), 1–83.

[5] John Coatsworth's comments remind us of a more important reason than those mentioned in the text for unclassified countries. Our experience with the disjoint technique has indicated that a minimum of three countries (yielding nine observations) is required in a class in order to obtain reliable results of general interest. Among the unclassified countries, the courses of poverty were too diverse either to form a group of three having reasonably similar courses of poverty or to add any of these countries to Classes One through Four.

[6] Svante Wold, "Pattern Recognition by Means of Disjoint Principal Components Models," *Pattern Recognition*, 8 (1976), 127–137.

TABLE 1
A TYPOLOGY OF THE COURSE OF POVERTY IN THE NINETEENTH CENTURY
(TO 1914)

Description of Class	Country
1. Countries that began industrializing substantially at latest toward the middle of the nineteenth century where poverty during the first half of the century was increasingly concentrated among casual or unemployed urban workers, handicraft workers, the landless or near landless in agricultural areas of labor surplus. In all but Britain the numbers in extreme poverty increased early in the century. In the latter half of the century widely based economic growth and industrialization resulted in reductions in poverty, the absorption of labor, and fairly steady rises in average wages.	Belgium France Germany Great Britain[a] Switzerland
2. Agricultural economies dominated by family farming where increases in extreme poverty among the landless occurred during the first half of the nineteenth century alongside surges in population growth and with negligible industralization; at the same time, among those with land, gradually rising productivity was associated with improving living standards. The latter half of the nineteenth century was marked by major emigration abroad from areas of surplus agricultural population, and specialized agriculture and small-scale industry expanded greatly.	Denmark Norway Sweden
3. Densely populated low-productivity predominantly peasant economies where there was no marked long-term trend in the extent of extreme poverty in the early nineteenth century; fluctuations in poverty were associated primarily with variation in harvests. During the latter half of the century regional increases in extreme poverty were most often associated with increased dependence on the market for subsistence, land parcelization, indebtedness, and loss of land to nonagriculturalists.	Burma China Egypt India Russia
4. Sparsely settled land-abundant countries where extreme poverty during the first half of the nineteenth century was largely among urban families of immigrants or in regions of subsistence farming. Fluctuations in extreme poverty during the latter half of the nineteenth century were mainly associated with waves of immigration and cyclical fluctuations in primary product markets; where domestic markets expanded significantly as independent farms spread and small-scale industry grew, most of the poor were eventually absorbed in quite widely based growth.	Argentina Australia Canada New Zealand
Unclassified	Brazil Italy Japan Netherlands Spain United States

[a] In Great Britain the processes of reduction in extreme poverty and rises in average wages began already in the first half of the nineteenth century. There is considerable controversy over the timing and extent of these developments.
Sources: See the sources cited for each country in the table by this title in Morris and Adelman, *Where Angels Fear to Tread.*

variable in explaining total within-class variations; (3) the relevance of each variable in discriminating between classes; and (4) the fit of each observation to every class.[7] The method is thus very suitable to studying relationships among country characteristics that vary from one set of countries to another.[8] Components analysis identifies clusters of indicators that vary most closely together. The first cluster captures the most variance in the data; we interpret it to represent the processes of change most typical of the class. The second cluster summarizes best the variations not captured by the first cluster, representing processes that complement or substitute for those of the first cluster. Country scores on each component identify countries that we interpret to have moved farthest or least far along the spectrum of change summarized by the component. We stress the usual caveat of those using statistical analyses to infer causal relationships: there is no *statistical* justification for doing so.

THE RESULTS

Class One: Western European Industrializers (Table 2)

The indicators varying most closely together in the first component are levels of per capita income, agricultural productivity, industrial development; the character of land systems, the level of development of market systems, leading traits of political systems; the rates of industrialization, agricultural improvements, transportation improvements (lagged), export expansion; and changes in industrial and agricultural wages.[9] We interpret these in the context of the class characteristics of widespread industrialization and substantial reduction in poverty. The inclusion of institutional influences yields nothing surprising here; the

---

[7] Because of space constraints we discuss only (1) in this paper. (See footnote 12.)

[8] Because the samples are not random, conventional tests of differences among samples are not applicable.

[9] The inclusion of the land variables shows higher levels and rates of economic change associated with the predominance of cultivator-owned holdings rather than tenant holdings and with the predominance of neither very large nor very small holdings. The inclusion of the classification by socioeconomic character of political leadership shows higher levels and rates of economic change associated with greater political influence in national leaderships of rising industrial, commercial, and working classes. We limit our discussion to variables with weights or "loadings" rounding to at least .17. This ad hoc cut-off was selected on the basis of sensible interpretations across all six chapters of final results for our book; it is less restrictive than our earlier cut-off based on only a few sets of results. We simplify the discussion in the text by not distinguishing between primary and secondary high loadings. Comparison of the whole set of our earlier published results with the current final set indicates substantial stability in the composition of components, allowing for differences due to our new variables; however, the division of variables between primary and secondary high loadings is less stable. John Coatsworth's comments remind us to mention that the choice of number of components is based on the sensibleness and theoretical interest of associations in additional components. We think the presence of three rather than two interesting components in the present results has occurred because of the new variables we added.

TABLE 2
PRINCIPAL COMPONENTS ANALYSIS FOR CLASS ONE

Classification Scheme	Principal Components[a]		
	One	Two	Three
Level of per capita income	.20	.19*	.20*
Level of development of techniques in agriculture	.23	.11	.04
Rate of improvement in technique in industry	.24	−.01	−.06
Rate of improvement in technique in industry (lagged)	.23	.08	−.01
Predominant form of land tenure and holding	.23	−.22*	−.02
Favorableness of land institutions to improvements	.21	−.06	−.09
Direction of change in real wages in industry	.22	−.10	.05
Level of development of techniques in industry	.18*	.20	.15
Level of development of inland transportation	.22*	.34	−.13
Percent of labor force in agriculture	.13	−.36	−.16
Extent of urbanization	.16	.46	−.03
Degree of shift in export structure	.15	−.20	.12
Direction of change in real wages in agriculture	.22*	−.30	.23*
Level of development of market system (composite)	.13	.19	−.14
Total population	.14	.02	−.24
Rate of change in per capita income	.15	.03	−.29
Rate of improvement in techniques in agriculture	.17*	−.05	.18
Rate of improvement in inland transportation (lagged)	.18*	.13	−.29
Extent of illiteracy	.07	.07	−.24
Rate of spread of primary education (lagged)	.15	−.22*	−.30
Favorableness of attitudes toward entrepreneurship	.21*	.10	.23
Rate of growth of exports	.18*	−.23*	−.28
Socioeconomic character of political leadership	.18*	.09	.24
Strength of national representative institutions	.20*	−.04	.25
Extent of political stability	.19*	−.12	.29
Relative abundance of agricultural resources	.09	−.06	−.09
Rate of improvement in techniques in agriculture (lagged)	.13	−.03	.04
Rate of population growth (lagged)	.12	.05	−.02
Net immigration	.09	−.02	.00
Concentration of landholdings	.13	.03	−.14
Colonial status	.07	−.16	.05
Degree of foreign economic dependence	.03	−.03	−.05
Extent of domestic economic role of government	.14	−.05	.03
Rate of spread of market system (composite)	.15	−.07	−.06
Rate of spread of market system, lagged (composite)	.10	.12	−.05

[a] Numbers in boxes indicate the highest loading for each variable rounding to at least .17, reading across rows.
* "Secondary" high loadings. They include all other loadings rounding to at least .17, reading down a component column.
Source: See text.

well-known importance of land systems, political systems open to rising business influence, and well-developed market systems to the quantitative success of Western European countries in transforming their economies is confirmed. Component Two summarizes a highly urbanized and industrialized pattern typical of Great Britain in the 1870s and 1880s: slowing export expansion, slowing agricultural improvements, and slowing agricultural wage increases expressing the unfavorable impact of the forces of international competition on agricultural wage earners. Component Three points to an alternative pattern typical of Switzerland where radical agricultural transformations were favorable with a considerable lag to small agriculturalists, and ultimately per capita income growth. It must be stressed that all three patterns describe countries with land systems, market institutions, and political conditions favorable to widespread industrialization.

Class Two: Scandinavia (Table 3)

This class is much less industrialized, more literate, with a great deal of agricultural poverty in 1850 and class characteristics of a successful start on industrial growth by 1914, moderately aided by foreign capital. Component One shows a complex of favorable institutional conditions, agricultural achievements, export expansion, rising industrial wages, and rising per capita income similar to that in the first class but without any indication of systematic benefits to agriculturalists. Components Two and Three point to two complementary processes for raising agricultural wages in these less advanced, labor surplus, institutionally favored countries. Component Two underlines the great importance of railways in eliminating transportation bottlenecks to improving agricultural productivity and wages; Component Three points to the best known Scandinavian pattern: the strong impact of emigration from areas of labor surplus in raising both agricultural and industrial wages.[10]

Class Three: Low Productivity Agricultural Economies (Table 4)

In the primary pattern for this class, neither strong foreign economic penetration, nor dramatic export expansion, nor the freeing of land from communal restrictions, nor increased marketization, nor more rapid population growth brought systematic benefits to standards of living.[11] In the secondary cluster agricultural commercialization and population growth went with rising per capita income, but with faster income growth went slower or negative agricultural wage changes. Given the class characteristic of land systems with problems of insecure cultivator titles and parcelized holdings, the pattern suggests a set of interrelated

[10] In the interpretation of a component as a process of change, the signs may be reversed for convenience since it is only the relationship among signs within a component that matters. The continuum for "net immigration" extends from high net immigration at the top of the scale to high net emigration at the bottom of the scale. Since all Scandinavian countries were at the lower end of the scale, then a negative association between agricultural wage movements and net immigration means faster wage increases with more net emigration.

[11] The indicator of foreign economic dependence is a composite of seven dimensions of foreign dependence with heavier weights for those listed first: foreign control of trade and distribution, foreign ownership and control of modern industry, dependence on foreign skills, locus of entrepreneurial initiative, share of foreign capital in domestic investment, reliance of governments on foreign loans, and dependence of production structure on trade.

The freeing of land from communal restrictions is a major element of our composite measure of the development of market systems at the lower end of the spectrum.

Morris and Adelman

TABLE 3
PRINCIPAL COMPONENTS ANALYSIS FOR CLASS TWO

Classification Scheme	Principal Components[a]		
	One	Two	Three
Level of per capita income	.17	.01	.00
Level of development of techniques in agriculture	.22	−.13	.09
Relative abundance of agricultural resources	.21	.16	−.18*
Predominant form of land tenure and holding	.29	.02	.08
Favorableness of attitudes toward entrepreneurship	.23	−.05	−.08
Degree of foreign economic dependence	.17	.09	−.02
Strength of national representative institutions	.19	−.11	−.08
Rate of spread of market system, lagged (composite)	.21*	.20	.12
Level of development of inland transportation	.09	−.27	.04
Percent of labor force in agriculture	.23*	.27	−.02
Rate of change in per capita income	.21*	−.24	.01
Rate of improvement in inland transportation (lagged)	.13	−.38	−.04
Rate of spread of primary education (lagged)	.20*	.44	−.07
Colonial status	.13	.18	−.02
Level of development of market system (composite)	.23*	.28	−.05
Rate of improvement in techniques in agriculture	.16	−.17*	.21
Net immigration	.07	.09	.18
Concentration of landholdings	.13	−.01	.20
Favorableness of land institutions to improvements	.22*	−.09	.39
Rate of growth of exports	.17*	−.01	.27
Degree of shift in export structure	.16	−.10	.22
Extent of political stability	.15	−.14	−.34
Direction of change in real wages in industry	.22*	.07	−.40
Direction of change in real wages in agriculture	.12	−.26*	−.43
Level of development of techniques in industry	.12	−.14	.01
Total population	.08	.05	.00
Rate of improvement in techniques in industry	.16	−.03	−.08
Rate of improvement in techniques in industry (lagged)	.14	−.01	−.03
Rate of improvement in techniques in agriculture (lagged)	.12	−.09	.14
Rate of population growth (lagged)	.16	.13	.07
Extent of illiteracy	.04	.05	−.01
Extent of urbanization	.09	−.08	−.06
Extent of domestic economic role of government	.15	−.15	.05
Socioeconomic character of political leadership	.15	−.07	−.03
Rate of spread of market system (composite)	.09	−.04	−.11

[a] Numbers in boxes indicate the highest loading for each variable rounding to at least .17, reading across rows.

* "Secondary" high loadings. They include all other loadings rounding to at least .17, reading down a component column.

Source: See text.

features of impoverishment accelerated by colonial policies: the rise of indebtedness and land alienation as peasant market dependence increased (promoted by land and tax policies) and, in colonies, the reduction of alternative employments with the destruction of handicrafts. Component Three gives an alternative pattern typical of Russia. Here is the only path to reduction of poverty apparent in this set of countries. The achievement of a small modern industrial sector brought rising per capita income and higher industrial wages for a tiny fraction of

Institutional Influences on Poverty 51

TABLE 4
PRINCIPAL COMPONENTS ANALYSIS FOR CLASS THREE

Classification Scheme	Principal Components[a]		
	One	Two	Three
Percent of labor force in agriculture	.32	−.09	.13
Net immigration	.20	.02	−.02
Extent of illiteracy	.33	−.03	.07
Degree of foreign economic dependence	.30	.09	−.19*
Level of development of market system (composite)	.32	−.11	−.18*
Rate of spread of market system, lagged (composite)	.17	.00	.00
Total population	.26*	−.40	.38*
Rate of change in per capita income	.09	.26	.23*
Rate of population growth (lagged)	.20*	.23	−.10
Predominant form of land tenure and holding	.21*	−.51	−.06
Concentration of landholdings	.19*	.40	.18*
Extent of domestic economic role of government	.14	.19	.10
Direction of change in real wages in agriculture	.07	−.19	.05
Level of development of techniques in industry	.08	.03	.22
Relative abundance of agricultural resources	.17*	.09	.25
Colonial status	.25*	−.14	−.40
Socioeconomic character of political leadership	.05	.07	.23
Direction of change in real wages in industry	.07	−.04	.26
Rate of spread of market system (composite)	.27*	.22*	−.43
Level of per capita income	.07	.08	.07
Level of development of techniques in agriculture	.07	.14	−.04
Level of development of inland transportation	.08	.11	−.06
Rate of improvement in techniques in industry	.15	.03	.14
Rate of improvement in techniques in industry (lagged)	.12	.04	.11
Rate of improvement in techniques in agriculture	.07	.04	.01
Rate of improvement in techniques in agriculture (lagged)	.05	.02	.01
Rate of improvement in inland transportation (lagged)	.10	.13	−.00
Favorableness of land institutions to improvements	.12	−.15	.08
Rate of spread of primary education (lagged)	.05	.00	.13
Extent of urbanization	.06	.01	−.02
Favorableness of attitudes toward entrepreneurship	.06	.07	.09
Rate of growth of exports	.14	.15	.02
Degree of shift in export structure	.04	−.01	.00
Strength of national representative institutions	.07	−.06	.06
Extent of political stability	.09	−.01	−.02

[a] Numbers in boxes indicate the highest loading for each variable rounding to at least .17, reading across rows.

* "Secondary" high loadings. They include all other loadings rounding to at least .17, reading down a component column.

Source: See text.

the population, but no systematic benefits in agricultural wages. The favorable conditions for this modest success suggested by the component were a large population forming a potential home market, greater land concentration favoring staple export expansion, and political conditions limiting foreign penetration, such as freedom from colonial domination and heavy foreign dependence and the political dominance of indigenous landed elites.

Class Four: Land-Abundant and Dependent European Settled Countries (Table 5)

In the primary pattern for this class colonialism and foreign dependence promoted immigration, export expansion, market institutional development, and population growth all proceeding more rapidly as higher levels of per capita income were achieved. We interpret the associations to reflect the positive role of foreign penetration on economic growth—an interpretation strengthened by the inclusion of political conditions and attitudes favoring the rising indigenous commercial and industrial groups. This primary pattern, however, shows no systematic benefits from export-based growth for standards of living—a marked contrast to Western Europe. Components Two and Three point to two special conjunctions of influences that determined improvements in the standard of living. Component Two points to the favorable conjunction of several influences in raising agricultural productivity and wages: transportation breakthroughs, urbanization, the spread of literacy into agriculture, and the shift of political power away from the landed elite. Component Three points to the unfavorable impact of extremely heavy immigration on per capita income growth, as in Australia where striking increases in exports and total GNP promoted by heavy immigration did not succeed in raising per capita income.

SUMMARY AND CONCLUSION

In summary our results show the strong force of industrialization for long-term rises in standards of living where industrial and agricultural advances went hand in hand in a favorable institutional setting.[12] The crucial institutional conditions suggested by our results were developed transportation and market institutions, agricultural systems providing a fairly wide distribution of a significant aggregate agricultural surplus above subsistence, and reasonably open political systems dominated by indigenous groups. While almost all the variance in industrial wages for both Classes One and Two is explained by this pattern, the influences governing the course of agricultural real wages were considerably more complex. In the industrialized countries of Class One, the crucial secondary force was success in transforming agriculture and maintaining momentum in manufacturing exports when international competi-

---

[12] Because of space constraints, we have omitted the section in our paper on measures of statistical fit (including Table 6). In pair-wise comparisons among Classes One, Three, and Four, the own-class variance of each class is substantially lower than the variance obtained by fitting each class's observations to the components models of the other two classes (a comparison indicative of the distance between pairs of classes). Similar calculations for Class Two, however, show it to be fairly close to both Classes One and Four. This reflects the similarity of the Scandinavian primary pattern to that of Class One and the similarity of its secondary patterns to those of Class Four.

Institutional Influences on Poverty   53

TABLE 5
PRINCIPAL COMPONENTS ANALYSIS FOR CLASS FOUR

Classification Scheme	Principal Components[a]		
	One	Two	Three
Level of per capita income	.19	.09	.14
Relative abundance of agricultural resources	.28	−.19*	−.06
Rate of population growth (lagged)	.24	−.07	.17*
Net immigration	.24	−.21*	.20*
Favorableness of attitudes toward entrepreneurship	.20	.05	−.09
Colonial status	.23	−.05	−.09
Degree of foreign economic dependence	.21	−.17*	−.12
Rate of growth of exports	.22	−.12	.04
Rate of spread of market system, lagged (composite)	.27	−.24*	−.07
Level of development of inland transportation	.08	.23	−.09
Percent of labor force in agriculture	.14	−.24	−.16
Rate of improvement in techniques in agriculture	.16	.31	−.01
Rate of improvement in inland transportation (lagged)	.14	.30	.08
Extent of illiteracy	.11	−.39	.05
Rate of spread of primary education (lagged)	.16	.19	−.06
Socioeconomic character of political leadership	.17*	.20	−.08
Direction of change in real wages in agriculture	.10	.21	.14
Rate of change in per capita income	.15	−.09	−.39
Predominant form of land tenure and holding	.20*	.14	−.31
Concentration of landholdings	.23*	−.10	.40
Favorableness of land institutions to improvements	.17*	.03	−.29
Extent of urbanization	.14	.19*	.29
Degree of shift in export structure	.08	.07	−.35
Strength of national representative institutions	.20*	−.08	.21
Level of development of techniques in industry	.08	.15	.04
Level of development of techniques in agriculture	.12	.12	−.06
Total population	.06	−.03	−.02
Rate of improvement in techniques in industry	.15	.05	−.00
Rate of improvement in techniques in industry (lagged)	.12	.13	−.01
Rate of improvement in techniques in agriculture (lagged)	.08	.14	−.10
Extent of domestic economic role of government	.16	.16	.03
Extent of political stability	.11	.16	.10
Direction of change in real wages in industry	.13	.07	.12
Level of development of market system (composite)	.15	−.09	−.22
Rate of spread of market system (composite)	.07	.03	.10

[a] Numbers in boxes indicate the highest loading for each variable rounding to at least .17, reading across rows.

* "Secondary" high loadings. They include all other loadings rounding to at least .17, reading down a component column.

Source: See text.

tion intensified greatly in the last quarter of the nineteenth century. A critical influence on agriculture in the less industrialized countries of Classes Two and Four, the Scandinavian and the land-abundant countries, was transportation breakthroughs that substantially raised real wages in agriculture; where they had not yet taken place, agricultural wages systematically lagged behind the wages of the very small industrial labor forces. The third influence on the strength of long-term upward movements in agricultural wages evident in our results was international

54   Morris and Adelman

migration. Emigration from Scandinavia in the latter part of the century contributed with little delay to the elimination of regional labor surpluses and rising wages. In the land-abundant countries to which labor and capital flowed together, heavy immigration tended to relieve labor shortages and thereby to dampen the forces for wage increases created by rapid primary export expansion.[13]

Our results show striking variations in the impact of export expansion in reducing poverty. The manufacturing export expansion typical of successful industrializers as well as the primary export expansion characteristic of Scandinavia proved to be systematically favorable to the reduction of poverty. In the land-abundant settler countries, however, institutions were considerably less favorable to a wide spread of the benefits from export expansion. Access to land was less, landholding and tenure systems were less propitious, and the structure of economic and political power depended much more on foreigners. Our results suggest that while foreign economic penetration was nevertheless on the average favorable to export-based, long-term economic growth, this growth systematically raised living standards only where governments succeeded in both overcoming the transportation bottleneck and making land available for the growth of family farming serving urban markets. Operating against such success were political and economic alliances among expatriate exporting interests, the indigenous landed elite, and merchant capitalists. Country data suggest that this negative force retarded the cheapening of food production and biased transportation systems toward exporting interests rather than the growth of a domestic market.

Nowhere in our results for overwhelmingly agricultural low productivity peasant economies do we find the processes of foreign penetration, export expansion, marketization, and population growth in general benefiting the poor. Whether colony or not, the more rapid the pace of marketization, the more negative the effect on the real incomes of the agricultural poor, even where per capita income grew faster as a result. Country data portray processes of land alienation and increased landlessness that in colonial economies were accelerated by tax and tariff policies. Where indigenous governments dominated management and banking, and population was large enough to form a domestic market for factory goods, marketization did produce systematic benefits for workers in a handful of modern factories, but even here the mass of agricultural workers did not benefit significantly.

Political influences are important throughout our results, both between and within classes. In Classes One and Two at midcentury

---

[13] Because of space constraints we have omitted Table 7 giving statistical measures of the importance of individual variables in "explaining" within-class variations and in discriminating between classes.

political systems already had characteristics favorable to widely based growth and thus indirectly to the reduction of poverty: relatively moderate exercise of arbitrary power over private economic initiatives and sufficient beginnings of representative government to permit the incorporation into the political process of rising business and commercial groups. Given these and other favorable conditions, economic growth induced a generally peaceful process of increasing participation by diverse economic groups in leaderships and parliaments. Two features of these results suggest a positive role of literacy in this political process. In Scandinavia greater literacy favored peasant political power that in turn contributed to tax and land policies conducive to stronger spread effects of growth within agriculture. A similar process is suggested by the Class One pattern of agricultural improvements on which Switzerland scores high.

Political influences were also crucial in Classes Three and Four where heavy foreign economic dependence and colonialism were common. In the low productivity peasant economies of Class Three, indigenous rather than expatriate leaderships dominated politically in the only pattern favoring increased standards of living for even a few of the poor. Negative effects of colonial tax, tariff, and transportation policies have been noted, but similar policies also operated in politically independent Argentina (Class Four) where political alliances among indigenous elites and expatriate exporting interests dominated the political process. In general, the results for Class Four's land-abundant countries indicate that greater political clout for rising commercial, business, and labor groups interacted with higher literacy to promote more widely based export-led growth. It appears that declining political power of landed elites, induced by the changing structure of economic power, led to both educational developments and land policies favoring a wider spread of growth, while greater literacy and the increased political power of rising groups including commercial family farmers in turn accelerated political changes favorable to more dispersed domestic growth beneficial to the poor.

5 What Is the Evidence on Income Inequality and Development?

IRMA ADELMAN

INTRODUCTION

The long-term relationship between income distribution and development has been one of the most closely investigated issues in development economics. In his path-breaking article "Economic Growth and Income Inequality," Kuznets[1] formulated the hypothesis that early economic growth increases inequality, while later economic development narrows it. He based this hypothesis on an analytic model, on data for developed countries since the 1930s that showed a narrowing of inequality, and on cross-country comparisons between inequality in developed countries and inequality in two developing countries, comparisons that showed considerably greater inequality in the latter. This paper formulated the U-hypothesis and posed the research agenda for subsequent studies of the relationship between income distribution and development.

Nevertheless, the first twenty years of economic development immediately following the Second World War proceeded on the basis of an optimistic view of the relationship between economic development and inequality. In the design of development policy and of foreign assistance, it was assumed that the growth of the modern sector, if sustained, would eventually spread the benefits of economic growth to all, including the poorest. Economic growth and industrialization were proceeding at an unprecedented rate. The benefits to newly prosperous urban groups, to the workers in the modern sector, and to an expanding middle class of merchants, professionals, and civil servants were easily apparent, while data on unemployment, poverty, and income distribution were not available to cast doubt on the rosy picture of the effects of development. The U-hypothesis was ignored by all but a few radical critics, such as Baran[2] and Myrdal.[3]

The first identification of development failures by mainstream Western economists came in the late 1960s, when, as a result of the work of the International Labour Organization (ILO), it was realized that despite rapid industrialization and increasing gross national product (GNP), unemployment was rising to alarming proportions of the urban labour force. Slow labour absorption in the modern sector, rapid population growth, an education explosion, and the exploitation of agriculture had combined to transform disguised rural unemployment into disguised urban unemployment in the informal sector and increased open unemployment of recent secondary and university graduates. The realization of these trends revived interest in the Kuznets U-hypothesis. Distributional and poverty issues came to the centre of the development agenda.

In the early 1970s, initiatives were taken to conduct research on the distribution of benefits of growth in developing countries. Data on income distribution in developing countries, however, were (and remain) scant. The first major study of the relationship between income distribution and economic development was by Adelman and Morris.[4] Completed in 1971 as a report to the Agency for International Development and based on unpublished income-distribution studies in forty-four developing countries, their study confirmed the increase in inequality inherent in the Kuznets U-hypothesis while indicating that the subsequent decrease in inequality with continued development was dependent on specific policy choices made in the course of the development process. With policies stressing the reduction of economic dualism and increases in primary and secondary education, the later stages of development would reduce inequality; with a continuation of dualistic growth involving neglect of the agricultural sector and a narrow educational pyramid, inequality would not decrease, even at the latest stages of development. The Adelman-Morris study did not use regression analysis to establish the relationships between income distribution and development. The authors argued that the heterogeneity of the data and the state of ignorance about the appropriate functional form made the use of regression analysis a dangerous research tool. Instead they relied on the use of analysis of variance (the analysis of hierarchic interactions), which was relatively robust to data quality and did not require the prior specification of functional forms.

Following their analysis, a large number of investigators used cross-section regressions to study the relationship between inequality and development.[5] These studies generally used a functional form that is quadratic in the log of per capita GNP. They also added some conditioning or policy variables to the regressions, such as education, population, or a socialism dummy. The samples of countries varied, sometimes including and sometimes excluding developed and Communist countries. The regressions all confirmed the exist-

123 Income Inequality and Development

ence of the Kuznets curve. Anand and Kanbur,[6] however, argue that the location of the minimum point of the U is sensitive to sample composition and to the specific functional form. Such sensitivity is to be expected if, as claimed by Adelman and Morris,[7] the underlying relationship is either U-shaped or J-shaped, depending on policy choices made at higher levels of development for developing countries. Papanek and Kyn[8] contradict the Anand and Kanbur contention, and find the relationship to be stable and insensitive to the inclusion or exclusion of specific countries. The conditioning variables they include, however, capture the very policy choices that affect whether the relationship is U- or J-shaped. They also find the Kuznets curve to be quite flat.

In this chapter, we investigate the issue of whether there is a trade-off between inequality and economic growth, using changes over time in the shares of income accruing to the poor and rich deciles as dependent variables and the rate of growth of per capita GNP together with conditioning variables as independent variables. Our procedure provides a more direct test than previous studies of the policy issues raised by the Kuznets curve.

THE STATISTICAL ANALYSIS

The estimation of trends in the size distribution of income within countries requires a consistent series of calculations of income distribution within countries over time. Unfortunately, there are very few countries with more than a single estimate of the size distribution of income. Of those for which estimates of the size distribution of income are available for more than one point of time, differences in coverage and differences in the definition of the basic income-recipient units make for lack of comparability of income shares over time. In addition, cross-country comparisons of income-share changes require comparability across countries as well. To mitigate these difficulties, we adopt a three-step estimation procedure.

In the first step, we use cross-country regressions to estimate how the within-country distribution of income varies in response to changes in a set of independent variables. In the second step, we use these regressions together with data on the independent variables to estimate decile income shares for all non-Communist developing countries with populations of more than two million in 1960. In the third step, we regress the changes in the estimated shares between 1960 and 1970 and 1970 and 1980 on the rates of growth of per capita gross domestic product (GDP) and other conditioning variables to see whether the Kuznets U-hypothesis holds over time. Conceptually, this three-step approach is the equivalent of two-stage least squares. The primary statistical differences between the present approach and classical two-stage least squares are that (1) the sample coverages for the two stages of the estimation procedure are different and (2) the regressions in both stages are non-linear.

The advantages of this approach are twofold: it provides for consistent estimates of income distribution over time and across countries, and it enables the use of a large sample. Generally, the data sources for the estimation of income distribution are consumer household budget surveys, blown up to mimic national coverage. In these surveys, the definitions of response units, the income concepts, and the procedures used to blow up the sample surveys to national coverage vary across countries. Because our approach to estimating income distributions involves using regressions, this study's basic response unit, income concept, and blow-up procedures are "standardized averages" of a constant and consistent, but undefined, nature. The procedure used enabled us to extend the sample of countries from about thirty to about seventy.

ESTIMATING INCOME DISTRIBUTIONS WITHIN COUNTRIES

To estimate the decile distributions of income, we must first assume a one- or two-parameter distribution function for incomes. We experimented with two alternatives, the log normal distribution and the Pareto distribution, and found that the latter gave closer overall fits. We decomposed the economy into two sectors, rural and urban, and assumed that each sector has its own Pareto distribution. The Pareto distribution used in this study is a one-parameter function of the form $Y = X^{-\alpha}$ where Y is the relative frequency of people having income greater or equal to X and α is a parameter indicating the degree of inequality of the distribution of income. (Other forms of the Pareto distribution exist.) The dependent variables in our cross-country regressions are the exponents α for income inequality in each country's rural and urban sectors. To estimate α, we fitted the Pareto distribution to the decile distributions for the rural and urban sectors of those countries for which we had data.

The next step involved estimating polynomial regression functions relating α to set of independent variables that were deemed on *a priori* grounds to be potentially relevant to within-sector inequality. Since the ultimate purpose of the regressions is projection, we limited ourselves to candidate variables for which time series are available from international statistical compendia, such as the World Bank's World Tables. The variables were in logs and entered in polynomial form. Whether sectoral inequality increases or decreases with an increase in the level of a particular variable therefore varies with the level of the variable. The regressions are summarized in Table 5.1. The column labelled "Power" in the table indicates the degree of the polynomial.

For the rural sector, the statistically significant variables were the share of agricultural exports in agricultural gross domestic product, the agricultural terms of trade, and the school enrolment ratio. R-squared for the regression

125 Income Inequality and Development

TABLE 5.1
Pareto Coefficient Regression Equations

RURAL PARETO COEFFICIENT

$R^2 = .578$; degrees of freedom = 28	Power	Coefficient	Standard Error
Intercept		1.943	
Independent variables (log)			
Share of agricultural exports			
in agricultural output	1	1.054	.355
	2	1.656	.644
	3	1.151	.480
	4	.365	.155
	5	.425	.018
Agricultural terms of trade	1	−.297	.126
School enrolment ratio	2	−.246	.113
	3	.040	.019

URBAN PARETO COEFFICIENT

$R^2 = .561$; degrees of freedom = 30	Power	Coefficient	Standard Error
Intercept		-318.512	
Independent variables (log)			
School enrolment ratio	1	277.886	143.520
	2	−111.254	56.234
	3	19.681	9.754
	4	−1.29	8.632
GDP per capita	1	42.634	17.645
	2	−11.245	4.644
	3	1.304	.539
	4	−.056	.023
Share of non-agricultural			
exports in non-agricultural output	1	−.226	.123
	2	−.071	.041
	3	−.006	.004
Ratio of productivity in non-agricultural			
activity to productivity in agriculture	1	−.029	.019

was .59. The estimated relationship indicates that a larger share of agricultural exports increases rural inequality, presumably because agricultural exports are produced mostly in large commercial farms and plantations. It suggests that higher agricultural terms of trade reduce rural inequality, probably because they increase the employment of landless labour and raise the marketed surplus and off-farm employment of small, semi-commercial farmers. The estimated regression suggests that the impact on inequality of increases in the national school enrolment ratio varies with the school

126   Irma Adelman

enrolment ratio, but is mostly negative; it is usually only at quite high levels of national schooling that mass education spreads to rural areas.

For the urban sector, the statistically significant explanatory variables were per capita GDP, non-primary exports as a ratio to non-primary GDP, and the ratio of the productivity in agriculture to productivity in the primary sector. R-squared for the regression was .56. Both school enrolment and per capita GDP have a U-shaped effect on urban inequality, increasing it at low levels of education and GDP and then reducing it. Increases in the share of non-agricultural exports in non-agricultural output unambiguously reduce urban inequality, presumably because manufacturing exports from less-developed countries (LDCs) tend to be labour intensive. Similarly, when the ratio of productivity in non-agricultural activities to productivity in agriculture increases, urban (but not, as we shall see below, national) inequality is reduced.

These estimated regression functions were used in conjunction with time series for the independent variables in the regressions to derive sectoral-size distributions of income for each non-Communist developing country in each of three years: 1960, 1970, and 1980. For each year, the sectoral distributions were then aggregated numerically in each country to derive within-country decile distributions of income. These deciles formed the basis for our subsequent exploration of the Kuznets hypothesis.

The results of these computations were used to estimate the changes in the average decile distributions within developing countries. Table 5.2 indicates that, for an average non-Communist developing country, there was a steady increase in within-country inequality over two decades. The share of income of the poorest 20 percent fell from 7.3 percent in 1960 to 6.8 percent in 1970 and to 6.7 percent in 1980, while the share of the richest 5 percent rose from 37.5 percent in 1960 to 39.4 percent in 1970 and to 40.1 percent in 1980. The most substantial increases in inequality occurred between 1960 and 1970, as might be expected from the Kuznets hypothesis.

The decline in income share of the poorest over the first quarter century of development is also consistent with the historical experience of currently developed countries. Typically, the historical increase in inequality in currently developed countries during the early stages of their industrialization lasted about half a century or more. Lindert and Williamson[9] display evidence for income inequality rising steadily during the Industrial Revolution in Great Britain and levelling in the last quarter of the nineteenth century. Morris and Adelman[10] find that Belgium, France, Germany, Great Britain, and Switzerland all underwent an industrialization process that followed the Kuznets curve: the numbers in extreme poverty increased early in the nineteenth century in all but Great Britain, where the increase occurred earlier; and in the latter half of the nineteenth century, widely based economic growth and industrialization resulted in reductions in poverty, labour absorption, and

127 Income Inequality and Development

TABLE 5.2
Mean Income Shares for 1960, 1970, and 1980, Non-Communist LDCs

Group	1960	1970	1980
Poorest 20%	7.3	6.8	6.7
Poorest 40%	15.8	14.9	14.7
Poorest 60%	26.4	25.1	24.7
Middle 40%*	25.6	24.4	24.4
Top 20%	58.6	60.3	60.9
Top 10%	46.8	48.7	49.4
Top 5%	37.5	39.4	40.1
Top 1%	22.8	24.4	25.0

Source: Estimated, see text.
* The middle 40 percent group is the fifth through eighth deciles, inclusive.

steadily rising average wages. Denmark, Norway, and Sweden also displayed a Kuznets curve, but the dynamics of the curve were somewhat different: increases in extreme poverty occurred during the first half of the nineteenth century, especially among the landless, as a result of surges in population growth and negligible industrialization; and the subsequent reductions in poverty occurred in the second half of the century as a result of major emigration of surplus agricultural population and the expansion of specialized agriculture and small-scale industrialization.

We now turn to an examination of the systematic connections between growth and inequality. This is a particularly important issue because it is relevant to development policy. In particular, the dynamic version of the Kuznets curve elucidates whether there is a policy trade-off between the speed of economic growth and the extent of inequality.

DOES FASTER GROWTH INCREASE INCOME INEQUALITY?

Most tests of the Kuznets hypothesis have been based on cross-section data. As indicated earlier, all these cross-section studies trace out a Kuznets curve, showing that income inequality first increases with development and then declines. But how is income inequality related to the process of transition from one development level to another? There is no time dimension to cross-sections. And special assumptions, amounting to acts of faith, are required to enable one to take the cross-section curve, which traces out average relationships among economic states, as indicative of processes of change between neighbouring economic states. For this, time series of change in individual countries are required.

128 Irma Adelman

There are two recent combined cross-section time-series analyses, both of which support the Kuznets hypothesis. Papanek and Kyn[11] used the income share of various income deciles as dependent variables, and the log of per capita income, its square, time, socio-political dummy variables, education, and the structure of exports as independent variables. They confirmed the Kuznets U-hypothesis in their regressions but found the Kuznets curve to be quite flat. They also investigated the hypothesis that faster growth is associated with a greater deterioration in the share of income accruing to the poorest deciles. They confirmed the hypothesis but again found that the deterioration in income share with more rapid growth is small.

In the present paper, we test the hypothesis that faster growth is negatively correlated with the share of income accruing to the poor more directly than has been done in previous studies. We take as our dependent variable not the income shares of the poor (and rich) deciles, but rather the changes in these shares over time. And we do not use per capita income as an explanatory variable, but rather the rate of growth of per capita income. Thus, our cross-section analysis is based on the dynamic variables that are directly related to the policy issue of whether there exists a trade-off between economic growth and the equality of the distribution of income.

The results of our analysis are summarized in tables 5.3 and 5.4, for 1960 to 1970, and in tables 5.5 and 5.6, for 1970 to 1980. In fitting the regressions, we started with a set of uniform independent variables and then omitted from the regression set for each period those variables that were not statistically significant, on the basis of either a t-test for individual significance or on an F-test for the specific subgroup, for any of the regressions for the particular period. As a result, the list of independent variables is larger for the 1970–80 period than for 1960–70. The values of R-squared for the regressions range from between about .4 and .5 for the 1960–70 period and between about .71 and .73 for 1970–80. These values of R-squared are very high when one considers that both our dependent variables and most of our independent variables are expressed in rates of change rather than in levels. The F-tests for the entire regression and for particular subgroups of variables are all high.

In selecting the list of candidate variables, we did not include variables that are directly related to the derivation of the national income shares from the sectoral distributions. For example, we did not include changes in the share of population in non-agricultural employment; rather, we included changes in the share of population in industry. We were also limited to variables for which time series exist for a large number of developing countries. Some candidate variables were not significant in any of our regressions and therefore do not appear in the summary of results. For example, we tested for the significance of regional dummies on all regions, for all classes of independent variables, and found that only a Latin America dummy for rates of growth of per capita GNP and an Asia dummy for the debt-service ratio

TABLE 5.3
Change in Income Shares of the Poorest Groups, 1960–70, Regression Results

Variable	Poorest 20%* Coefficient	t-value	Poorest 40%* Coefficient	t-value	Poorest 60%* Coefficient	t-value	Middle** 40%* Coefficient	t-value
1. Base income share	-3.94	-4.17	-1.84	-4.24	-1.1	-4.21	-1.09	-3.94
2. GDP per capita growth rate (G)	-0.857	-0.60	-0.849	-0.62	-0.765	-0.60	-.490	-0.47
3. Square of G	-14.5	-1.08	-13.9	-1.07	-13.7	-1.13	-13.1	-1.33
$F_{(2,57)}$***		5.21		5.31		5.47		6.02
4. Lat. Am. dummy X G	-25.1	-4.16	-23.8	-4.10	-22.3	-4.09	-17.7	-3.98
5. Lat. Am. dummy X sq. of G	1050	4.75	992	4.69	931	4.67	737	4.54
$F_{(2,57)}$***		12.1		11.8		11.8		11.1
6. Change in share labour in ind.	-0.136	-2.02	-0.133	-2.03	-0.124	-2.02	-0.0964	-1.92
7. Constant	0.327	3.92	0.332	4.02	0.328	4.03	0.309	3.87
R-squared	0.495		0.495		0.496		0.484	
R-squared adjusted for degrees of freedom	0.442		0.442		0.443		0.429	
F on full regression (6,57)	9.32		9.32		9.34		8.90	

Note: See Table 5.7 for a description of variables and sources.

* The dependent variable is the ratio of the change in income share to the base income share.

** The middle 40 percent group is the fifth through eighth deciles, inclusive.

*** Joint F-statistic for variables and their squares. Values in parentheses are degrees of freedom in the numerator and denominator.

TABLE 5.4
Change in Income Shares of the Richest Groups, 1960–70, Regression Results

Variable	Top 20%*		Top 10%*		Top 5%*		Top 1%*	
	Coefficient	t-value	Coefficient	t-value	Coefficient	t-value	Coefficient	t-value
1. Base income share	-0.564	-4.44	-0.715	-4.26	-0.903	-4.06	-1.52	-3.55
2. GDP per capita growth rate (G)	0.628	0.72	0.896	0.68	1.17	0.64	1.69	0.51
3. Square of G	4.74	0.57	7.11	0.57	9.68	0.56	16.8	0.54
$F_{(2,57)}$**		*3.05*		*2.83*		*2.61*		*2.00*
4. Lat. Am. dummy X G	12.2	3.27	17.8	3.16	23.9	3.05	40.2	2.83
5. Lat. Am. dummy X sq. of G	-497.0	-3.66	-726	-3.53	-967	-3.39	-1610	-3.12
$F_{(2,57)}$**		*6.98*		*6.48*		*5.95*		*5.00*
6. Change in share labour in ind.	0.0581	1.38	0.0775	1.22	0.0955	1.08	0.123	0.77
7. Constant	0.325	4.43	0.331	4.17	0.339	3.85	0.366	3.11
R-squared	0.419		0.398		0.375		0.321	
R-squared adjusted for degrees of freedom	0.358		0.335		0.309		0.249	
F on full regression (6,57)	6.85		6.29		5.70		4.48	

Note: See Table 5.7 for a description of variables and sources.

* The dependent variable is the ratio of the change in income share to the base income share.

** Joint F-statistic for variables and their squares. Values in parentheses are degrees of freedom in the numerator and denominator.

TABLE 5.5 Change in Income Shares of the Poorest Groups, 1970–80, Regression Results

Variable	Poorest 20%*		Poorest 40%*		Poorest 60%*		Middle** 40%***	
	Coefficient	t-value	Coefficient	t-value	Coefficient	t-value	Coefficient	t-value
1. Base income share	-6.15	-5.77	-2.79	-5.70	-1.64	-5.65	-1.64	-5.70
2. GDP per capita growth rate (G)	-2.00	-2.27	-1.87	-2.21	-1.74	-2.18	-1.31	-2.08
3. Square of G	53.8	2.76	50.4	2.68	47.5	2.69	36.9	2.65
F(2,44)***		3.89		3.69		3.68		3.55
4. Lat. Am. dummy X G	2.46	0.87	2.27	0.83	2.18	0.85	1.92	0.94
5. Lat. Am. dummy X sq. of G	147	1.67	140	1.65	130	1.63	92	1.45
F(2,44)***		9.44		9.05		9.02		8.42
6. Debt service/export ratio (D)	5.32	2.98	5.2	3.02	4.88	3.02	3.93	3.07
7. Square of D	-41.1	-2.81	-40.0	-2.84	-37.5	-2.83	-30.0	-2.86
8. Cube of D	89.2	02.7	86.6	02.7	80.8	02.7	64.3	02.7
F(3,44)***		3.70		3.27		3.27		3.38
9. Asia dummy X D	3.37	0.67	2.98	0.61	2.80	0.61	2.17	0.60
10. Asia dummy X sq. of D	-17.3	-0.22	-13.5	-0.18	-12.8	-0.18	-10.3	-0.19
11. Asia dummy X cu. of D	32.4	0.12	21.4	0.08	20.7	0.08	18.7	0.09
F(3,44)***		3.98		3.83		3.79		3.79
12. Change in Non-ag/AG inc. ratio	-0.248	-4.14	-.233	-4.03	-0.22	-4.05	-0.18	-4.19
13. Change in literacy rate	0.0173	1.65	0.0161	1.59	0.0152	1.60	0.012	1.61
14. Constant	0.174	1.78	0.178	1.85	0.185	1.98	0.221	2.64
R-squared	0.717		0.711		0.711		0.716	
R-squared adjusted for degrees of freedom	0.634		0.625		0.626		0.632	
F on full regression (13,44)		8.58		8.30		8.32		8.53

Note: See Table 5.7 for a description of variables and sources.

* The dependent variable is the ratio of the change in income share to the base income share.

** The middle 40 percent group is the fifth through eighth deciles, inclusive.

*** Joint F-statistic for variables and their powers. Values in parentheses are degrees of freedom in the numerator and denominator.

TABLE 5.6 Change in Income Shares of the Richest Groups, 1970–80, Regression Results

Variable	Top 20%*		Top 10%*		Top 5%*		Top 1%*	
	Coefficient	t-value	Coefficient	t-value	Coefficient	t-value	Coefficient	t-value
1. Base Income Share	-0.554	-4.70	-0.686	-4.67	-0.850	-4.63	-1.39	-4.48
2. GDP per capita growth rate (G)	1.44	2.75	2.02	2.66	2.56	2.55	3.8	2.31
3. Square of G	-28.7	-2.68	-40.3	-2.60	-51.5	-2.50	-76.1	-2.27
$F_{(2,41)}$**		4.16		3.91		3.61		2.96
4. Lat. Am. dummy X G	0.122	0.08	0.230	0.11	0.360	0.13	0.857	0.19
5. Lat. Am. dummy X sq. of G	-69.4	1.56	-96.5	-1.50	122	-1.43	-176	-1.27
$F_{(2,41)}$**		3.65		3.26		2.86		2.05
6. Debt service/export ratio (D)	-3.17	-3.50	-4.68	-3.56	-6.31	-3.61	-10.5	-3.67
7. Square of D	25.1	3.41	37.0	3.46	49.6	3.49	82.2	3.53
8. Cube of D	-54.8	-03.3	-81.0	-03.3	-108.0	-03.3	-178.0	-03.4
$F_{(3,41)}$**		4.27		4.41		4.51		4.65
9. Asia dummy X D	9.10	2.13	14.2	2.29	19.7	2.40	34.8	2.61
10. Asia dummy X sq. of D	-184	-2.39	-283	-2.55	-392	-2.66	-683	-2.85
11. Asia dummy X cu. of D	790	2.50	1220	2.66	1680	2.76	2930	2.96
$F_{(3,41)}$**		2.58		2.81		2.94		3.26
12. Change in non-ag/AG inc. ratio	0.0939	3.06	0.133	2.98	0.172	2.90	0.265	2.73
13. Change in sec. educ. rate	0.0311	2.93	0.0462	3.00	0.0620	3.02	0.105	3.13
14. Constant	0.428	5.30	0.473	5.26	0.523	5.14	0.653	4.74
R-squared	0.732		0.732		0.729		0.721	
R-squared adjusted for degrees of freedom	0.648		0.647		0.643		0.633	
F on full regression (13,41)		8.63		8.62		8.49		8.16

Note: See Table 5.7 for a description of variables and sources.

* The dependent variable is the ratio of the change in income share to the base income share.

** Joint F-statistic for variables and their powers. Values in parentheses are degrees of freedom in the numerator and denominator.

133 Income Inequality and Development

TABLE 5.7
Description of Variables

Dependent Variable

1. Change in income share of poorest and richest groups – For group x and period $t1$–$t2$ this is

Income share of group x in $t2$ – income share of group x in $t1$

$$\overline{\text{income share of group } x \text{ in } t1}$$

Explanatory Variables

2. Base income share – Income share in 1960 for 1960–70 results and 1970 for 1970–80 results
3. GDP per capita growth rt (G) – Growth rate of per capita GDP from $t1$ to $t2$ in Kravis dollars for each period.
4. Debt service/export ratio (D) – Ratio of external public debt service to exports of goods and services, average of 1970 and 1980 values.
5. Change in non-ag/ag inc. ratio – For period $t1$–$t2$ this variable is

$$\frac{\text{NAR2-NAR1}}{\text{NAR1}}$$

where NAR# is the ratio of non-agricultural income per capita to agricultural income per capita in period #.
6. Change in literacy rate – For period $t1$–$t2$ this variable is

$$\frac{\text{LIT2-LIT1}}{\text{LIT1}}$$

where LIT# is the number of literate adults as a percentage of the population 15 years or older in period #.
7. Change in sec. educ. rate – For period $t1$–$t2$ this variable is

$$\frac{\text{SER2-SER1}}{\text{SER1}}$$

where SER# is the number enrolled in secondary school as a percentage of 12-17-years-olds.
8. Change in share of labour in ind. – For the period $t1$–$t2$ this variable is

$$\frac{\text{IND2-IND1}}{\text{IND1}}$$

where IND# is the share of labour in industry as a percentage of the total labour force in period #.

Sources: 1, 2, Estimated, see text; 3, 5–8, World Bank, *World Tables*, 3rd ed., 1983; Kravis conversions from Irving B. Kravis, *World Product and Income: International Comparison of Real Gross Domestic Product* (Baltimore: Johns Hopkins University Press, 1975); and 4, World Bank, *World Development Report*, various years.

survived the significance test. The rate of population growth was never statistically significant, confirming recent studies of other authors on the ambiguity of the effects of rapid population growth on poverty and income distribution.[12] Also, none of the purely political variables survived the

134   Irma Adelman

significance test. A variable characterizing the extent of political participation[13] and a variable characterizing the extent of a country's foreign dependence[14] were found to be statistically insignificant for both time periods. Since we excluded Communist countries from the analysis, we could not use a socialism dummy, as in other studies.

VARIATIONS WITH THE RATE OF GROWTH OF PER CAPITA GNP

Results

For the 1960–70 period, our regressions indicate that faster GNP growth was associated with a steadily increasing deterioration in the shares of income of the poorest 20 percent, the poorest 40 percent, the poorest 60 percent, and the middle 40 to 80 percent of the population. In our regressions, on the average for all developing countries, both the rate of growth of per capita GNP and the square of the rate of growth are negatively associated with the shares of income accruing to the poorest deciles during this period. The regressions in Table 5.3 thus suggest that, on the average over all countries, the shares of the poor could increase but only with negative growth rates. By contrast, on the average for all developing countries, the shares of the richest 20, 10, 5, and 1 percent of the population all rose steadily with faster growth in per capita GNP for this period (Table 5.4). For the rich, the signs of the coefficients of the rate of growth of per capita GNP and its square were both positive in the regressions for this period. Thus, our results for 1960 to 1970 indicate that during this period, in an average LDC, the benefits of faster growth were distributed in a very skewed manner. The rich not only captured their proportional share of benefits from growth but also benefited from a trickle-up from the poorest 80 percent of the population.

Our regressions suggest that in Latin American countries in the 1960s, the trade-offs were not quite as stark as for the average LDC. The coefficients in our regression for the product of the Latin America dummy variables and the rate of economic growth indicate that in Latin American countries in the 1960s, the changes in the income shares of both poor and rich traced a U-shaped relationship with growth rates, as they do for all LDCs during the 1970s. In Latin America, the income shares of the poor first decline and then rise, with faster growth and the shares of the rich first rise and then decline. Our estimates suggest that the rate of growth of per capita income up to which the shares of the poor decline in Latin America is about the same as the rate up to which the shares of the rich rise – 2.5 percent. However, this rate was exceeded by only three Latin American countries in this period.

For the 1970–80 period, our results are less stark. As in Latin America of the 1960s, we now find a U-shaped relationship for changes in the income

135 Income Inequality and Development

share of each decile with the rate of growth of per capita GNP for all developing countries, on the average. For the poor, on the average, the signs of the
regression coefficients of the income shares are negative on the growth rate
and positive on its square (Table 5.5). This suggests that, up to a point, the
shares of the poor decline with increases in the growth rates and after that
they rise with higher growth rates. Our regression estimates indicate that, on
the average for all developing countries, the positive GNP growth rate at
which no change in the income share of the poorest occurred in the 1970s
was 4.2 percent per capita. At positive growth rates lower than 4.2 percent
per capita, the shares of the poor declined with more rapid growth; at rates
above 4.2 percent, they rose. Since the average rate of population growth in
LDCs was about 2.2 percent, the constant-income-share growth rate of total
GNP was about 6.5 percent. A similar U-shaped relationship held for the
income shares of the rich (Table 5.6). The positive constant-income-share
growth rate for the rich was about 6 percent. At slower growth rates, on the
average for all LDCs, the income shares of the rich rose with faster growth; at
more rapid growth rates, the income shares declined.

Taken together, the results of our regressions for both periods indicate that
growth, up to a point, tends not to benefit the poor, in relative terms, except
with a substantial delay, and then only if growth is quite rapid. These results
support the notion of a trade-off between growth and distribution up to quite
high growth rates posited in the Adelman-Morris 1973 study.

Discussion

Relating these results to the Kuznets hypothesis requires that there be a
significant association between development levels and growth rates, since
the Kuznets' hypothesis relates to systematic variations in income shares of
the poor with *levels* of development. Our data indicate that there was a statistically significant correlation between development levels and growth rates
in both periods. Fourteen out of 16 countries with growth rates of per capita
GNP in Kravis dollars less than 1 percent were at the lowest level of development, by the Adelman-Morris index of level of socio-economic development,[15] in the 1960–70 period. The analogous number for 1970–80 was 12
out of 17. At the other extreme, of the non-oil–exporting countries that had
growth rates exceeding 3 percent per capita in Kravis dollars, 8 out of 11 in
1960–70 and 9 out of 10 in 1970–80 were at high or intermediate levels of
development. Our results, which associate declines in the shares of income of
the poor with increasing growth rates up to quite high rates of economic
growth followed by a turnaround, may therefore be taken as confirming a dynamic version of the Kuznets hypothesis. The U-shaped relationship posited
by Kuznets between the share of income of the poor and development levels
extends also to the speed of transition between levels of per capita GNP. Not

136   Irma Adelman

only development levels, but also the speed of transition among levels of per capita GNP, exhibit a U-shaped relationship with rates of economic growth.

There are many *a priori* reasons why one might expect more rapid growth to be associated with decreases in the share of income accruing to the poor. More rapid growth requires higher rates of savings and investment. Therefore, if more rapid growth is to materialize, income must be shifted from low savers (the poor) to high savers (the rich). This hypothesis was first advanced by Kalecki[16] and later taken up by Kaldor[17] and the Latin American structuralist school. But this hypothesis offers a closed-economy argument that does not incorporate the possibility of foreign aid and foreign borrowing as sources of investment funds and assumes that the government is neutral in the mobilization of savings. It also imparts the major role in the mobilization of savings to transfers among classes of savers rather than, as in the Lewis model, to transfers of savings between sectors, especially between agriculture and industry. The latter is probably a more significant mechanism for mobilizing savings than the former.[18]

Intersectoral transfers of resources affect the relationship between the distribution of income and the rate of economic growth indirectly, through the structure of growth, rather than directly, through savings requirements. Many Kuznets U-generating models of the relationships between income distribution and development rely on intersectoral transfers of population and income to provide the income-inequality-generating mechanisms. The course of income inequality with development is then explained by the technological and income-distribution characteristics within sectors and by how the development strategy and the strategy for mobilizing savings affect the income and productivity gaps between sectors and their relative rates of growth. This was the mechanism on which Kuznets himself relied to generate the U-hypothesis. More mathematical exposition was given by Fields.[19]

Lewis's 1957 model of development through industrialization is also in this spirit. It also implies the generation of a U-shaped income distribution through intersectoral transfers. The acceleration of growth in the early stages of industrialization implies increasing the income (and productivity) gap between industry and agriculture by transferring savings (and hence investment) and labour from the low-productivity, even distribution, traditional sector to the high-productivity, unequal distribution modern sector. Up to a point, this process will generate an increase in inequality. The per capita income and productivity gaps between sectors will start closing in the Lewis model only when a rising wage rate is required to attract increased labour into the modern sector. Numerical simulations and individual-country studies suggest that, in a given country, the association of decreased inequality with further growth will start after more than half the labour force is employed in the modern sector.[20]

A more dynamic explanation of the relationship between inequality and the speed of growth points to the contrast in initial conditions faced by the

137 Income Inequality and Development

poor and the rich when responding to the new economic opportunities inherent in economic growth.[21] Fundamentally, all processes of economic change give rise to both increased absorption of some individuals and displacement and marginalization of others. Those who own (or have access) to factors used disproportionately in the expanding sectors or in the new technologies, or to complementary factors, are enriched by the change. Those who own factors used in producing substitute commodities or less productive technologies lose relatively from the change. How more rapid growth affects different deciles depends on the net balance between the two forces for each decile. Those with assets – including not only financial capital and land but also human capital, information, and networks facilitating migration and access to high-productivity jobs – are better positioned to take immediate advantage of the opening up of any set of new economic opportunities. The poor are slower to respond to increased opportunities because they have less assets, in the more general sense. Furthermore, since the poor use traditional technologies and combine them with small amounts of low-productivity complementary factors, they are more likely to be marginalized by new technological opportunities, to which they require more time to adapt. Slower growth also allows more opportunity for social adaptation by the poor (through demographic change, migration, and schooling) and hence is likely to affect them less unfavourably. The contrast between the extent to which economic growth marginalized the poor in the nineteenth century in France, a slow-growing country, and the extent to which it marginalized the poor in Germany and Great Britain, fast-growing countries, illustrates this point. During the early stages of the Industrial Revolution, poverty increased faster with growth in Great Britain and Germany than in France.

These considerations suggest not only reasons for the dynamic version of the Kuznets curve but also for the contrast between our results for the 1960s and 1970s. The average picture sketched by the regression results for the 1960s associated continued declines in the income shares of the poor with more rapid growth at even the highest growth rates. It is only during the 1970s that we found that at growth rates exceeding 6.5 percent in total GDP, higher growth rates led to improvements in the shares of income of the poorest. Both the Lewis model[22] and the "initial conditions of poverty" explanation of the previous paragraph are consistent with these findings. The initial-conditions explanation suggests why, in the face of structural change, delays as long as a decade may occur before a high rate of economic growth would benefit the poor. Historically, during the Industrial Revolution, periods as long as two generations passed before economic growth benefited the poor.[23]

The Lewis[24] turning-point is consistent both with the delayed reaction to high growth rates and with the specific 6.5 percent growth rate of aggregate GDP for a turnaround to be attained. At a minimum, the turnaround requires that the growth rate of employment in the modern sector exceed the growth rate of supply of labour to the modern sector. The growth rate of supply is the

138   Irma Adelman

sum of the rate of population growth in urban areas from urban fertility and from rural–urban migration. In the 1970s, this sum, which equals the rate of urbanization, averaged 5 percent per year. This is the rate of growth of industrial employment that would just match the rate of increase in labour supply. However, the rate of growth of industrial employment must also be sufficient to absorb existing urban unemployment, before industrialization can result in increases in wages. In the early 1970s, the World Employment Missions of the ILO put the urban unemployment rate at about 20 percent in many middle-income developing countries. A rate of growth of 1.5 percent, maintained over a decade, would therefore be required to mop up the initial urban unemployment of 20 percent of the urban labour force. The sum of the two rates – 6.5 percent – just equals our estimate of the minimum rate of growth of GDP before growth increases the income shares of the poorest. These rates were attained by only eleven countries in our sample. Fei and Ranis[25] estimated that Japan, Korea, and Taiwan had reached the Lewis turning-point by the 1970s.

Papanek and Kyn's[26] study indicated that the Kuznets curve was quite flat and so was the relationship of income shares to growth rates. Our results do not support this finding for this period. Figure 5.1 portrays the relationship between the income share of the poorest 40 percent and the growth rate of per capita GNP in Kravis dollars estimated by our regression. We find that, for the 1970–80 period, the share decreased from 0.19 percent at a growth rate of –2 percent to about 0.12 at 2 percent, and that a one percentage point change in growth rate around the minimum income share produces an 9.5 percent change in the income share of the poorest 40 percent.

VARIATION WITH THE DEBT-SERVICE RATIO

Results

The debt-service ratio became a serious constraint on economic growth only during the 1970s. After the first oil shock in 1973, developing countries shifted from trade-and-aid-led growth to debt-led growth. The average debt-service ratio to exports rose from 8.9 percent in 1970 to 13.7 percent in 1980. After the second oil shock in 1980, the debt-service problem became a debt crisis, affecting growth and income distribution in all developing countries. Our time period, however, covers only the debt-accumulation phase.

A large literature on the incidence of adjustment to the debt crisis points to the fact that the poor have borne the brunt of the cost of adjustment.[27] We find, in our regressions of Table 5.5, that the impact of debt accumulation on the share of national income accruing to the poor was non-linear. For the poorest groups, there is a positive coefficient on the debt share to exports, a negative coefficient on the square of the debt share, and a small positive co-

139 Income Inequality and Development

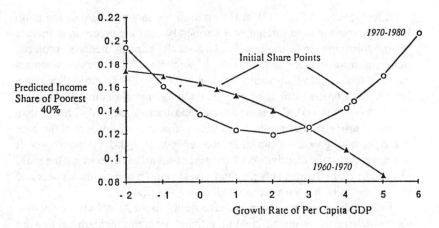

Source: Regressions, tables 5.3–5.6.

Figure 5.1
Income Shares versus Growth Rate, 1960–70 and 1970–80

efficient on the cube of the debt. For the rich (Table 5.6), the pattern of signs is the mirror image of that for the poor. The Asia dummy intensifies the quantitative impact of the basic pattern for both poor and rich deciles.

Discussion

The effects of debt accumulation on the poor and rich obviously depend on the projects and policies the new debt finances. If there is a correlation between the uses to which indebtedness is put and the relative size of the debt, changes in the share of debt to exports would have non-linear effects on the income shares of both poor and rich.

Higher debt ratios may benefit the poor when the debt is used to finance social programs and to subsidize consumption of food and public services by the poor, especially the urban poor. A large number of countries used foreign debt to maintain a dual price policy in agriculture, paying higher prices to rural producers than they charged to consumers. The dual price policy benefits the rural poor, especially agricultural workers and semi-commercial farmers, raising their marginal product. Also, after the food crisis of 1973, many developing countries borrowed for agricultural development projects. These investments decrease the productivity gap between sectors, thereby reducing overall inequality. Depending on the design of the agricultural projects (e.g., what types of irrigation were expanded and how the productivity-increasing measures were distributed between large commercial farms and small owner-operated farms), the investments could either increase or decrease income inequality within the agricultural sector.[28]

Alternatively, increased debt may reduce the income share of the poor. Countries that incurred foreign debt frequently used the proceeds to finance import-substitute industrialization, large-scale capital-intensive projects, industrial infrastructure, and armaments purchases. All of these investment patterns tend to have unequalizing effects on the distribution of income. Import substitution turns the terms of trade against agriculture, where the poor are concentrated. Capital-intensive industrialization is skill rather than labour intensive, and therefore does little to raise the employment of the poor while generating excess demand for the services of high-level manpower. It therefore makes the distribution of wages less equal, while reducing the share of wages in GNP. Armaments purchases have small domestic multipliers and indirect benefits that are concentrated among the rich.

Thus, debt accumulation may have quite disparate effects on income shares, depending on the different investment programs and policies that are financed by the debt. If social and agricultural programs predominate at both small and large levels of indebtedness while investments in import substitution, armaments, and heavy industry predominate at middling levels, one would expect to find the particular non-linear association between the income shares of the poor and debt accumulation that is present in our regression results.

VARIATIONS WITH OTHER ECONOMIC VARIABLES

Technological Dualism among Sectors

The rise and fall in sectoral imbalances in total-factor-productivity change may be expected to be a prime mover of income inequality. According to Kuznets[29] and the Chenery-Syrquin[30] studies, early development is characterized by an increase in the imbalance in productivity among sectors, followed by a levelling in productivity differentials, and finally by a movement towards more-balanced productivity growth, quite late in the development process. Even without population movement from the low-productivity to the high-productivity sector, the U-shaped movement in the productivity gap would by itself suffice to generate a Kuznets curve.

We experimented with several measures of changes in technological dualism: (1) changes in per capita income gaps between agriculture and non-agriculture (these also represent measures of productivity differentials between sectors); (2) total income gaps between the agricultural and non-agricultural sectors; and (3) relative changes in the composition of production. Of the three, the first measure was the most significant statistically. It also comes closest to the factor-productivity-differentials explanation of the Kuznets curve.

Our results indicate that the share of income of the poor decreases with greater relative neglect of agricultural productivity. Since the poor are

141 Income Inequality and Development

concentrated in the agricultural sector, emphasis on industrial development at
the expense of agricultural development decreases the share of the poorest 80
percent of the population. But the magnitude of the decrease becomes
steadily smaller the higher the income of the poorest deciles, starting at an
elasticity of –0.25 for the income share of the poorest 20 percent and decreasing to an elasticity of –0.18 for the share of the fourth to eighth deciles. By
the same token, since the top 20 percent of the population derive their
incomes from the non-agricultural sector, either as workers in modern
industry or as owners of industrial enterprises, a decrease in the relative share
of agriculture in total output benefits the upper-income groups. For the rich, a
sectoral bias in development against agriculture is increasingly more beneficial the higher their income level, rising from an elasticity of 0.09 for the top
two deciles to an elasticity of 0.27 for the richest 1 percent of the population.

The 1970s witnessed a renewed emphasis on agricultural development in
many developing countries. Fuelled by the food crisis of 1973 and by the
need to substitute for increasing imports of basic grains to feed the urban
population, many semi-industrial LDCs and several low-income LDCs turned
to agricultural development. Agricultural development has beneficial effects
on the income share of the poorest[31] and on their food security[32] provided it is
coupled with agricultural terms-of-trade policies that do not take away all the
benefits of agricultural output increases from the farmers. Gaiha[33] finds a
negative correlation between agricultural productivity and rural poverty in a
cross-country analysis. Simulations by Adelman[34] of the income-distribution
consequences of adopting an agricultural development strategy that combines
increases in agricultural productivity on small- and medium-sized firms with
increases in exports and in agricultural terms of trade in all developing
countries[35] indicated that this strategy is likely to result in a substantial
improvement in the distribution of income within LDCs, among all groups of
LDCs except East Asia, among all non-Communist LDCs, and in the world as
a whole. These agricultural development strategies also reduced worldwide
absolute poverty by 30 percent relative to the base case.

Labour Absorption into the Modern Sector

Factor movements among markets with different pay structures are another
potential major source of inequality. Even without changes in the relative
magnitude of the productivity and income gaps among sectors in the course
of development, transfer of labour from the low-paying sector with a low-
income variance to the high-paying sector with a high-income variance would
suffice to generate the Kuznets U.[36]

We could not use changes in the share of labour outside agriculture in our
regressions, despite high correlations of income shares with this variable,
because it comes too close to one of the variables we had used to derive
national income shares from sectoral shares. Instead, we used the more

restricted concept of changes in the share of the labour force employed in industry. This measure is indicative of labour absorption into the modern sector. We found that, during the 1960–70 period, increases in the share of labour force in industry reduced the share of the poor and raised the share of the rich. This finding is consistent with the early stages of the Lewis[37] model, when labour is transferred from the low-inequality to the high-inequality sector and the income gap between the sectors increases. In the 1970–80 period this variable was not statistically significant and therefore does not appear in the regressions despite its theoretical appeal.

The Distribution of Wealth

One would expect both land distribution and the distribution of physical capital to affect the distribution of income. Indeed, many revolutions (1848 in France and 1917 in Russia, in particular) have been based on this theory. Unfortunately, there are no time series we could construct to test this hypothesis. Also, as Lindert and Williamson point out,[38] major wealth redistributions such as land reform, slave emancipation, war, and losses from economic crises are too sporadic to offer a systematic explanation of the course of the Kuznets curve. They are likely to lead to important shifts in the Kuznets curve, however. Elsewhere, I have argued that land reform needs to be an important precursor to productivity improvement in agriculture, if technology change, such as the Green Revolution, is not to deteriorate the distribution of income rather than provide for egalitarian growth.[39]

What about the distribution of human capital? One policy prescription on which both conservative and progressive economists agree is that improving the educational attainments of the masses will make the distribution of income more equal. The "human capital" school[40] sees education as a means of improving the earnings capacity of individuals. The "redistribution with growth"[41] and the "redistribution before growth"[42] schools see the broadening of the educational pyramid as a redistribution of wealth. Chenery et al. argue for increasing the education of the poor as part of a strategy to redirect a larger share of investment towards increasing the assets of the poor. Adelman argues for increasing the education of the poor as part of a strategy to equalize the distribution of wealth of the major productive asset before its productivity is improved, as a means of setting the stage for more egalitarian subsequent growth. Previous regression studies all support the equalizing role of increases in primary education.[43]

We used two different educational variables to represent the educational continuum relevant for the particular income group – literacy for the poor and secondary schooling for the rich. We find (tables 5.5 and 5.6) that the elasticity of the income shares of the poor with respect to literacy is of the order of 0.02 and that the elasticity of the income shares of the rich with

143 Income Inequality and Development

respect to the secondary schooling rate increases from 0.03 for the richest 20 percent to 0.10 for the top 1 percent. Our results thus indicate that the type of education that is improved has a bearing on income distribution. Increases in secondary (and presumably university) education will favour the rich and increase inequality, while increases in literacy (and presumably primary) education will decrease inequality.

SUMMARY AND CONCLUSION

Even in the absence of the debt crisis, the prospects for the poor in developing countries can hardly be considered satisfactory. For the 1960–70 period, our results indicate that the trade-off between the speed of economic growth and the share of income of the poor was unmitigated and that the deterioration in the share of income of the poor with growth was quite substantial. For the 1970–80 period, our results suggest the existence of an even stronger trade-off between the speed of growth and the equality of the distribution of income. At rates of growth less than 1 percent per capita, a levelling between 1 and 2 percent is followed by possibilities for a turnaround. However, our results also suggest that, in the typical LDC of the 1970s, the decline in the share of the poor with growth at low growth rates was sufficiently large to ensure that the poor would not recover their 1970 income share unless the LDC could attain quite high rates of growth for the period and reach at least moderate levels of development. These results hardly give much hope for attaining the goal of poverty eradication in LDCs through economic growth in the foreseeable future.

Our results do suggest policies that might mitigate the growth-equality trade-off somewhat. Foremost among those are rural development policies designed to close the agricultural/non-agricultural productivity and income gaps and massive primary education. I have advocated both approaches to the design of development strategies in earlier writings and found theoretical and empirical arguments to bolster these recommendations.[44]

In short, our findings support the view that the primary hope of the poor in the current low-growth world lies not in accelerating their country's growth rate, but rather in changing the structure of growth and the assets of the poor.

NOTES

1 S. Kuznets, "Economic Growth and Income Inequality," *American Economic Review* 45 (1955): 1–28.
2 P. Baran, *The Political Economy of Growth* (New York: Monthly Review Press, 1957).
3 G. Myrdal, *The Asian Drama* (New York: Pantheon Press, 1968).

144 Irma Adelman

4   I. Adelman and C. Taft Morris, *Economic Growth and Social Equity in Developing Countries* (Stanford, CA: Stanford University Press, 1973).

5   F. Paukert, "Income Distribution at Different Levels of Development: A Study of Evidence," *International Labor Review* 108 (1973): 97–125; H.S. Chenery et al., *Redistribution with Growth* (Oxford: Oxford University Press, 1974); M.S. Ahluwalia, "Inequality, Poverty and Development," *Journal of Development Economics* 6 (1976): 307–42; M.S. Ahluwalia, "Income Distribution and Development: Some Stylized Facts," *American Economic Review* 66 (1976): 128–35; J. Cronwell, "The Size Distribution of Income: An International Comparison," *Review of Income and Wealth* 23 (1977): 291–308; M.S. Ahluwalia, N.G. Carter, and H.B. Chenery, "Growth and Poverty in Developing Countries," *Journal of Development Economics* 6 (1979): 299–341; E. Bacha, "The Kuznets Curve and Beyond: Growth and Change in Inequalities," in E. Malinvaud ed., *Economic Growth and Resources* (New York: St Martin's Press, 1979), 52–73; and Papanek and Kyn 1986 (see note 8); Papanek and Kyn 1987 (see note 11).

6   S. Anand and S.M.R. Kanbur, "Inequality and Development: A Critique," paper presented to the 25th Anniversary Symposium, Yale Growth Center, 11–13 April 1986.

7   Adelman and Morris, *Economic Growth and Social Equity.*

8   G.S. Papanek and O. Kyn, "The Effect of Income Distribution on Development: The Growth Rate, and Economic Strategy," *Journal of Development Economics* 23 (1986): 55–66.

9   P.H. Lindert and J.G. Williamson, "Growth, Equality and History," *Explorations in Economic History* 22 (1985): 341–77.

10   C. Taft Morris and I. Adelman, *Comparative Patterns of Economic Development, 1850–1914* (Baltimore: Johns Hopkins University Press, 1988).

11   G.S. Papanek and O. Kyn, "Flattening the Kuznets Curve: The Consequences for Income Distribution of Development Strategy, Government Intervention, Income and the Rate of Growth," *Pakistan Development Review* 26 (1987): 1–54.

12   N. Birdsall and C.C. Griffin, "Fertility and Poverty in Developing Countries," *Journal of Policy Modelling* 10 (1988): 30–55; and C.Y.C. Chu, "The Dynamics of Population Growth," *American Economic Review* 77 (1987): 1054–6.

13   Adelman and Morris, *Economic Growth and Social Equity.*

14   I. Adelman, J.B. Lohmoller, and C. Taft Morris, "A Latent Variable Regression Model of Nineteenth Century Economic Development," Giannini Foundation Working Paper 439, University of California, Berkeley, 1988.

15   I. Adelman and C. Taft Morris, *Society, Politics, and Economic Development – A Quantitative Approach* (Stanford, CA: Stanford University Press, 1967).

16   M. Kalecki, *Studies in Economic Dynamics* (London: Allen and Unwin, 1943).

17   N. Kaldor, "Alternative Theories of Distribution," *Review of Economic Studies* 23 (1955): 83–100.

145 Income Inequality and Development

18 W.R. Cline, *Potential Effects of Income Redistribution on Economic Growth: Latin American Cases* (New York: Praeger, 1972); and I. Adelman and S. Robinson, "Macroeconomic Adjustment and Income Distribution in Two Economies: Alternative Models Applied to Two Economies," *Journal of Development Economics* 29 (1988): 23–44.

19 G.S. Fields, *Poverty, Inequality and Development* (New York: Cambridge University Press, 1980).

20 S. Robinson, "A Note on the U-hypothesis Relating Income Inequality and Economic Development," *American Economic Review* 66 (1976): 437–40; J.C. Fei and G. Ranis, *Development of the Surplus Labor Economy* (Homewood, IL: Irwin, 1964); and G. Ranis, "Equity and Growth in Taiwan: How 'Special' is the 'Special Case'?" *World Development* 6 (1978): 397–409.

21 Adelman and Morris, *Economic Growth and Social Equity*; C. Taft Morris and I. Adelman, "Institutional Influences on Poverty," *Journal of Economic History* 43 (1983): 43–55.

22 W.A. Lewis, "Reflections on Unlimited Labor," in L.E. Marco, ed., *International Economics and Economic Development* (New York: Academic Press, 1972).

23 Morris and Adelman, "Institutional Influences"; Lindert and Williamson, "Growth, Equality and History."

24 W.A. Lewis, "Economic Development with Unlimited Supplies of Labor," *Manchester School* 22 (1954): 139–91.

25 Fei and Ranis, *Development of the Surplus Labor Economy*.

26 Papanek and Kyn, "Flattening the Kuznets Curve."

27 P. Pinstrup-Anderson, "Macroeconomic Adjustment Policies and Human Nutrition: Available Evidence and Research Needs" (Washington, DC: International Food Research Institute, 1986); and L. Taylor, *Varieties of Stabilization Experience. WIDER Studies in Development* (Oxford: Clarendon, 1988).

28 I. Adelman, "Beyond Export Led Growth," *World Development* 12 (1984): 937–50; E. Yeldan, "Turkish Economy in Transition: A General Equilibrium Analysis of Export-Led versus Domestic Demand Led Strategies of Development," unpublished doctoral dissertation, University of Minnesota, Minnesota, 1988.

29 S. Kuznets, *Modern Economic Growth* (New Haven: Yale University Press, 1966).

30 H.B. Chenery and Syrquin, M. *Patterns of Development, 1950–1970* (London: Oxford University Press, 1975).

31 I. Adelman and S. Robinson, *Income Distribution Policy in Developing Countries: A Case Study of Korea* (Stanford, CA: Stanford University Press, 1978); I. Adelman, "Beyond Export Led Growth"; and Yeldan, "Turkish Economy in Transition."

32 I. Adelman and P. Berck, "Food Security in a Stochastic World," *Journal of Development Economics* 34 (1991): 25–55.

146 Irma Adelman

33 R. Gaiha, "Rural Poverty: Dimensions and Trends," Food and Agriculture Organization (FAO), Mimeo, 1987.

34 I. Adelman, "The World Distribution of Income," *Weltwirtschaftliches Archiv* 121 (1985): 110–20.

35 Ibid.

36 Robinson, "A Note on the U-hypothesis."

37 Lewis, "Reflections on Unlimited Labor."

38 Lindert and Williamson, "Growth, Equality and History."

39 I. Adelman, *Redistribution before Growth – A Strategy for Developing Countries* (The Hague: Martinus Nijhof, 1978).

40 T.W. Schultz, *Investment in Human Capital: The Role of Education and Research* (New York: Free Press, 1971); and G.S. Becker, *Human Capital and the Personal Distribution of Income: An Analytic Approach* (Ann Arbor, MI: Institute of Public Administration, 1967).

41 H.S. Chenery, M.S. Ahluwalia and C.G. Bell et al., *Redistribution with Growth* (Oxford: Oxford University Press, 1974).

42 Adelman, "Redistribution before Growth – A Strategy."

43 Adelman and Morris, *Economic Growth and Social Equity*; Ahluwalia, "Inequality, Poverty and Development"; Ahluwalia, "Income Distribution and Development"; and Papanek and Kyn, "Flattening the Kuznets Curve."

44 Adelman, "Beyond Export Led Growth"; and Adelman, "Redistribution before Growth – A Strategy."

[14]

METU Studies in Development 11 (1–2) 1984, 177-193

DEVELOPMENT STRATEGIES AND THE SIZE
DISTRIBUTION OF WORLD INCOME

Irma ADELMAN*

1) Introduction

The current orthodoxy in development strategy is that of export-led growth. It argues for trade liberalization in developing countries and a shift toward an incentive system which is neutral between foreign and domestic markets. Basing their recommendations on the experience of the "Gang of Four" countries (South Korea, Taiwan, Singapore, and Hong Kong) once they shifted from import substitution toward export-led growth, the proponents of this strategy argue that its generalization to all less developed countries (LDC) will result in a replication of the "Gang of Four" economic miracle. They admit that, in the current low-growth-in-world-trade environment, the pursuit of such a strategy may prove more difficult but they maintain (correctly) that this strategy is still preferable to import substitution.

The purpose of this paper is to argue in favor of a third strategy which is different from both export-led growth and from import substitution in manufacturing.

The impetus for arguing in favor of an alternative strategy to export-led growth stems, in part, from the change in the world environment since 1973. The two global recessions in the Organization for Economic Cooperation and Development (OECD) countries during the 1970s and the early 1980s induced a slowdown in the volume of world trade. This slowdown had depressing effects on the prices and

---

Professor of Agricultural and Resource Economics, University of California, Berkeley, USA.

export volumes of nonoil-exporting developing countries and lowered
their ability to import. The second oil-shock recession hit developing
countries particularly hard. Between 1980 and 1982, total merchandise LDC exports fell by 0.5 percent; the average annual rate of growth
of manufacturing exports fell from 12.4 percent in the previous seven
years to 4.1 percent; protectionist sentiment and protectionist legis-
lation were introduced in the OECD countries, thus, leading to lower
import elasticities out of stagnant incomes; and the access of LDCs
to commercial credit to support exports was severely decreased.

These developments indicate the need to revise downward projections for the growth in world demand for nonfuel merchandise
exports from LDCs. This, in turn, calls for a reassessment of the feasibility of continuing to rely on manufacturing export-led growth
as the major development dynamic for most LDCs during the next
decade. Most LDCs which are not already newly industrialized countries (NICs) with established export markets -the second-tier co-
untries- are unlikely to be able to break into international markets
for nontraditional exports in the next decade. For them, the need to
search for an alternative strategy is acute.

The development strategy advocated in this paper consists of a
public investment program designed to induce a progressive downward shift in the supply curve of domestic agriculture. The arguments
in favor of this strategy, which I shall call an agricultural-demand-
led-industrialization (ADLI) program, are twofold. The strategy
creates a domestic mass market for industrial products through intermediate and final demand linkages. It also has a favorable distributional impact through increasing the supply of wage goods and
the incomes of the poorer members of society. The proposed strategy
is simultaneously a growth program; an employment program since
agriculture is considerably more labor intensive than even labor-
intensive manufacturing; a basic needs, food security and income distribution program; and an industrialization program. It also constitutes a foreign-exchange-saving program by reducing the need for
food imports which, in the 1970s, have accounted for an average of
13 percent of total LDC imports. Finally, the proposed strategy is
also a risk-reducing program since some of the investments required
for its implementation (e.g., investments in water control and pesti-
cides) reduce weather dependence and decrease environmentally induced fluctuations in agricultural yields and since the strategy sub-

stitutes a development dynamic based on the more controllable increases in domestic demand for one based on exogenously fluctuating
world demand.

Discussions concerning the relative merit of agricultural versus
industrial development strategies are not new. They were central to
the debate between the physiocrats and the mercantilists in the nineteenth century and, more recently, to the controversy concerning
balanced versus unbalanced growth. They were also reflected in the
debates surrounding the early five-year plans of India (Mellor et al,
1968; Mellor, 1976) and the Soviet Union (Domar, 1957). In the
main, the wrong views favoring emphasis on capital-intensive import-
substitution industrialization prevailed, fueled by export, primary
terms of trade and domestic linkage pessimism. The results were
highly dualistic development patterns, slow gross national product
(GNP) growth, serious balance-of-payments problems, high capital-
output and capital-labor ratios, slow growth in food production and
in employment, and deteriorating distributions of income. The response, once these failures became apparent, was to urge a shift by
LDCs toward industrial export-led growth and toward "basic needs"
oriented strategies. The adoption of the export-led strategies during
the high world-demand growth era of the mid-1960s led to success in
GNP growth, in labor absorption, and in industrialization. But it
was also accompanied by increasing international indebtedness and
by rapidly rising food imports. As a result, the debate is now starting
anew, fueled, in part, by renewed export pessimism, as well as by increased awareness of the vulnerability to shocks arising from export
markets, and by the serious liquidity and foreign-exchange constraints
faced by LDCs. A body of economists (Streeten, 1982; Mellor, 1976;
Singer, 1979; Hirschman, 1981; de Janvry, 1984) is urging the adoption of agrarian, wage-goods strategies.

Pro-agricultural strategies have usually been associated with self-
sufficiency and closed-economy ideologies. It should be emphasized
that this is not the ideology underlying the present proposal. This
is not an argument for a closed development strategy. The last 30
years of development experience have clearly demonstrated the infe-
riority of import substitution strategies. It is rather a call for a shift
in sectoral emphasis for public investment toward agriculture while
maintaining or even, if necessary, switching to an open development
strategy.

The present paper provides a quantitative basis for assessing the relative merits of the proposed strategy. The next section summarizes merits of the proposed strategy. The next section summarizes the results of a simulation experiment in which export-led growth and ADLI were compared within a CGE model of South Korea. The next two sections explore the results of the two strategies for the size distribution of World income. The paper concludes with a general discussion.

2) Within Country Effects of Alternative Strategies

In a previous paper (Adelman, 1984) the relative merits of the ADLI strategy were explored by means of a computable general equilibrium (CGE) model of a small, semi-industrial, low income, open economy that is a stylization of South Korea in 1963. The model was used to perform simulation experiments with alternative development strategies. Two alternative strategies were compared in a low world demand regime typical of the prospects for the next 15 years: a strategy of export-led growth and a strategy of agricultural development-led growth.

The CGE model consists of an economy-wide, simultaneous, multisectoral model that solves endogenously not only for quantities but also for prices (for detailed descriptions of the model, see Adelman and Robinson, 1978; Derviş, de Melo and Robinson, 1982). The core of the model consists of the reconciliation of potential demand and supply imbalances in the factor and commodity markets by price adjustments which simulate the workings of the markets for labor, commodities, and foreign exchange. The model solves for: wages, profits, product prices, and the exchange rate; sectoral production, import, export, employment, consumption and investment; the flow of funds, GNP and the balance-of-payments accounts; and for the functional and personal distributions of income.

The simulations with the CGE model indicate that both the export-led growth and the ADLI strategies are an improvement over the no strategy, low-world-demand-growth trajectory. However, the simulations also indicate that the agricultural strategy is superior (see Table 1). It generates the same rate of industrialization as does export-led growth but leads to a better distribution of income, higher rate of growth of per capita GNP, better balance of payments, hig-

TABLE 1 Experiment Results

Terminal year (1978)	High demand	Low demand base	Export promotion (low demand)	ADLI (low demand)
Real gross domestic product[a]	2,706	2,305	2,397	2,666
Merchandise exports[a]	775	162	208	387
Merchandise imports[a]	457	392	473	242
Foreign capital inflow[a]	310	230	248	− 120
Domestic savings ratio (percent)	19	16	16	16
Foreign savings total (percent)	− 64	60	38	− 30
Gross domestic product ICOR	2.9	3.1	2.6	2.2
Agricultural terms of trade	.91	.89	1.05	1.00
International terms of trade	85	85	85	85
Exchange rate[b]	.130	.141	.120	.130
Domestic resource costs				
Exports	.118	.119	.122	.124
Imports	.146	.165	.122	.124
Tariffs[a]	92	78	0	0
Subsidies[a]	0	0	95	0
Total unemployment (percent)	0	7.0	4.0	3.0
Structure of value added (percent)				
Primary	29	32	34	44
Consumer manufacturing	19	10	9	11
Producer manufacturing	17	14	18	16
Infrastructure	8	9	9	7
Services	27	35	30	22
Structure of exports (percent)				
Primary	1	28	11	83
Consumer manufacturing	80	42	53	9
Intermediate manufacturing	15	25	30	7
Capital goods	4	5	6	1
Share of exports in domestic production (percent)				
Primary	3.6	2.6	1.9	6.6
Consumer manufacturing	3.1	3.6	7.5	3.4
Producer manufacturing	1.5	4.2	7.9	3.9
Infrastructure	4.6	4.4	3.4	5.5
Services	6.6	3.6	2.7	3.8
Total share of exports	15.2	3.5	5.0	4.8
Structure of imports (percent)				
Primary	20	22	27	1
Consumer manufacturing	10	8	7	10
Intermediate manufacturing	42	42	41	54
Capital goods	28	28	25	35
Growth rates to terminal year (annual percent)				
	5.8	4.7	5.0	5.7
Agriculture	4.0	3.4	3.5	5.5
Manufacturing	9.1	6.6	7.6	5.3
Construction	6.1	5.2	5.1	4.8
Social overhead	4.7	4.6	4.8	8.3

Continued overleaf

(TABLE 1 continued.)

Terminal year (1978)	High demand	Low demand base	Export promotion (low demand)	ADLI (low demand
Services	4.7	4.3	4.4	4.7
Private consumption	3.9	4.7	5.2	5.2
Investment	7.2	6.0	6.0	6.0
Exports	18.0	5.5	8.0	15.5
Imports	7.0	5.3	7.3	5.0
	3.0	2.5	2.6	2.8
Primary	2.4	2.5	2.6	2.8
Consumer manufacturing	4.3	– .1	– .1	.9
Producer manufacturing	7.0	5.1	6.3	5.2
Infrastructure	1.0	1.4	1.2	2.1
Services	3.0	3.0	3.0	2.8
	3.8	2.2	3.8	2.8
Primary	.3	– .1	.9	2.0
Manufacturing	4.0	4.0	5.0	5.0
Services	2.5	3.5	4.5	2.0
Distribution, terminal year real per capita incomes[c]				
Farmers	11	10	12	16
Marginal labor	29	24	26	27
Organized labor	64	42	51	48
Service labor	33	38	37	29
Agricultural capital	2,629	3,683	4,203	4,411
Industrial capital	1,035	2,849	3,207	1,152
Service capital	1,476	2,913	2,778	1,672
Gini[d]	.501	.508	.494	.438
Share of income (percent)				
Bottom 40 percent	8.9	7.1	7.9	10.1
Next 40 percent	27.9	21.8	21.3	23.8
Next 20 percent	63.2	71.1	70.8	65.1
Top 10 percent	50.8	61.3	61.6	56.4
Mean income of bottom 40 percent[d]	6.5	9	10	2.5
Ratio of top 10 percent to bottom 40	5.7	8.6	7.8	5.6
Ratio of bottom 40 percent to mean income	.21	.22	.23	.31

a In 100,000 won of 1963.

b In 1.000 won per U.S. dollar.

c In 10,000 won of 1963.

d Calculated assuming log normality.

her rate of labor absorption, and less poverty than does export-led growth.

The more favorable results of the agricultural strategy are due to several factors: The final demand linkages that arise when agricultural production and agricultural incomes increase are quite substantial; the increase in total factor productivity that results from an increase in agricultural productivity is larger than that resulting from a similar increase in the productivity of manufacturing because agriculture is by far the most important sector of the economy in most developing countries; the improvement in agricultural productivity leads to a larger reduction in unemployment than that which would result from an expansion of manufacturing because agriculture is considerably more labor intensive than even the most labor-intensive sector of manufacturing; and, finally, agriculture is less import intensive than is industry, and farmer consumption is less import intensive than is urban consumption.

It may be appropriate to speculate on the political conjuncture which would be favorable to the implementation of the ADLI strategies. Assuming rational self-interest, a comparison of the differences between the functional distributions of income under the export-led and the ADLI strategies in the terminal year should provide a clue. The gainers from the strategy are, in order: farmers (30 percent higher income under ADLI), and marginal labor (7 percent income improvement). The losers are: industrial capitalists (63 percent lower income), service capital (39 percent less income) and service labor (16 percent lower income). Thus, an agrarian landlord and / or farmer-dominated political scene would strongly favor the ADLI strategy. However, the political coalition supporting the ADLI strategy could also include some urban workers as well as those industrial interests producing investment and intermediate goods for agriculture and the producers of industrial wage goods for domestic consumption. The opposition would come mainly from industrial capitalists producing industrial export goods inappropriate for domestic consumption and luxury goods and services purchased by high-income urban consumers.

3) Agricultural-Demand-Led-Industrialization and the World-Wide Size Distribution of Income

We now turn to an examination of the implications of the two strategy options in LDCs for the size distribution of World income. The calculations assume that all LDCs pursue either an export-led growth strategy or an ADLI strategy. They are based on partial equilibrium analyses of the effects of the strategies and do not take account of the interactions in world markets among the strategies. It is assumed that the implicit expansions and contractions in overall LDC exports and imports are compensated for by corresponding adjustments in OECD imports and exports.

The Methodology

The estimation of size distribution of income within countries is plagued by conceptual problems and by problems of lack of comparability in estimation procedures among countries. The data sources for the estimation of income distributions are mostly consumer household budget surveys, which tend to vary across countries in their definitions of response unit (the individual, the household, or the household per capita) and income concepts. Because our approach to estimating income distributions involves using regressions, the basic response unit in our study is a "standardized average" unit of constant but undefined nature.

Performing counterfactual experiments and devising policy scenarios requires estimating variations in decile distributions of income as functions of policy variables. For this purpose, we follow Braulke (1983) in decomposing the overall economy into two sectors-rural and urban-each with its own Pareto distribution. We estimate the parameters of the rural and urban Pareto distributions statistically as functions of structural and policy variables. We then use the approximation developed by Braulke (1983) to derive the aggregate Gini coefficient for the country as a whole as a function of the two Pareto distribution parameters, the ratio of sectoral mean incomes, and the population shares. Tests performed by Braulke using data given in Jain (1975) indicate that, for ten developing countries for which the necessary data were available, the average absolute error involved in estimating the overall Gini coefficient following this procedure was .004.

Polynomial regression functions relating the Pareto exponents for the rural and urban sectors to a set of independent variables were estimated using stepwise ordinary least squares. The independent variables chosen as explanatory variables for each regression were those that were deemed on a priori grounds to be potentially relevant to within sector inequality in each sector and for which time series could be constructed. For the rural sector, the significant variables were: the share of agricultural exports in the agricultural gross domestic product (GDP); the agricultural terms of trade; and the school enrollment ratio ($R^2 = .60$). For the urban sector, the relevant variables were: per capita GNP; nonprimary exports as a ratio to the non-primary GDP; the school enrollment ratio; nonagricultural employment (percent); and the ratio of productivity in agriculture to productivity in the primary sector ($R^2 = .56$). The variables were logs and entered in polynomial form so that whether sectoral inequality increases or decreases with an increase in the level of a particular independent variable varies with the level of the variable. The regressions are summarized in Table 2.

TABLE 2 Regression Equations

Rural Pareto coefficient $R^2 = .578$; degrees of freedom = 28	Power	Coefficient	Standard error
Intercept		1.943	
Independent variables (log): Share of agricultural exports in agricultural output			
	1	1.054	.355
	2	1.656	.644
	3	1.151	.480
	4	.365	.155
	5	.425	.108
Agricultural terms of trade School enrollment ratio			
	1	– .297	.126
	2	– .246	.113
	3	.040	.019

Urban Pareto coefficient $R^2 = .561$; degrees of freedom = 30	Power	Coefficient	Standard error
Intercept		–318.512	
Independent variables (log):			
	1	277.886	143.52
School enrollment ratio			
	2	–111.254	56.234
	3	19.681	9.754
	4	– 1.298	.632
GDP per capita			
	1	42.634	17.645
	2	– 11.245	4.644
	3	1.304	.539
	4	– .056	.023
Share of nonagricultural exports in nonagricultural output			
	1	– .226	.123
	2	– .071	.041
	3	– .006	.004
Ratio of productivity in non-agricultural activity to productivity in agriculture			
	1	– .029	.019

The estimated regression functions were used to derive sectoral and aggregate Gini coefficients and size distributions of income for each nonsocialist developing country in each of two years: 1980 and 2000. For each year the distributions were then aggregated numerically across countries within a given geo-economic region to derive within-region inequalities. Finally, the regions were aggregated numerically into a World distribution of income. The Gini coefficients for the regions and for the world as a whole were also estimated numerically.

As our regressions do not cover developed and socialist countries, the distributions for these countries were taken from Berry **et al.** (1984) and kept constant over time. For China we used the distributions given in the World Bank report on China for 1980 (World Bank, 1983a).

The Data

To estimate changes in the overall distribution of income within countries, we require time series on the independent variables used to explain the Pareto coefficients as well as time series for the sectoral income levels and the sectoral populations by country. These come largely from the World Bank World Tables 1983 (World Bank, 1983b).

Two time series are required at the national level: population and GNP per capita in purchasing-power-parity-converted constant dollars. The population and GNP per capita in dollars come from World Tables 1983 (World Bank, 1983b); 1970 dollar values were converted to purchasing power parity dollars using the exchange rate adjustment ratios in Kravis **et al.** (1978).

Alternative Scenarios

Column 1 of Table 3 summarizes the size distribution of income in 1980 for major geo-political regions. Columns 2 and 3 present forecasts for the year 2000 under two alternative scenarios, one high growth and one low growth.

The forecasts were generated by looking at the performance of countries on the independent variables during the period 1970–1980. For all variables other than per capita GNP and population, it was assumed that the trends from 1970 to 1980 would continue unchanged to the year 2000. For per capita GNP and population, the extrapolations were constructed from the World Bank World Development Reports for 1982 and 1983 (World Bank, 1982, 1983c). Two extrapolations were used-a high and a low one. It was assumed that there is a Malthusian relationship between the rate of population growth and the rate of growth of income such that when GNP growth is high so is the rate of growth of population.

The forecasts indicate that, under the "high" scenario, the distribution of income to the year 2000 is virtually the same as in 1980 (a Gini coefficient of .656). Under the "low" forecast, there is a substantial improvement in the distribution of world income but there is also an increase of about 30 percent in the proportion of the world population that is below the poverty line.

Column 4 of Table 3 portrays the calculated results of an export-led growth strategy in LDC from 1980 to 2000. This strategy is implemented in the present analysis by performing a composite experiment. It is assumed that the share of nonagricultural exports in non-agricultural output is increased by 2 percent by year; that, as a result, the rate of growth of the GNP rises by 2 percent by year; that

TABLE 3 Forecast and Scenario Analysis, Year 2000 (Gini Coefficients)

Country grouping	1980	Year 2000			
		High	Low	Export-led growth	ADLI
Low income nonsocialist LDC					
Sub-Saharan Africa	.598	.576	.576	.605	.564
Asia and Pacific	.420	.464	.461	.509	.478
Middle income nonoil exporters					
Sub-Saharan Africa	.692	.656	.659	.668	.647
Middle East and North Africa	.559	.586	.589	.604	.567
Latin America and Caribbean	.499	.562	.511	.524	.554
East Asia and Pacific	.572	.552	.559	.569	.564
Southern Europe	.525	.538	.538	.538	.538
Oil exporters	.633	.674	.655	.690	.668
Nonsocialist LDC	.602	.647	.633	.657	.645
Market economies	.409	.409	.409	.409	.409
Nonmarket economies	.312	.312	.312	.312	.312
China	.339	.339	.339	.339	.339
World	.658	.656	.647	.645	.636
World poverty ratio	.228	.0972	.123	.080	.066
Ratio of share of world's richest 20 percent to poorest 20 percent	37.1	40.8	38.1	38.9	35.7

the exposure to world markets leads to an increase in manufacturing productivity that, with unchanged agricultural productivity, results in a decrease of 2 percent per year in the ratio of agricultural to nonagricultural productivity; that the increase in urban productivity and income induces a rise in the demand for agricultural output that results in an improvement in agricultural terms of trade of 1 percent per year; and that this increase in agricultural terms of trade leads to an improvement of 1 percent per year in agricultural income.

The experiment results in a deterioration in the distribution of income among LDC as the dispersion in growth rates between them is increased and the distribution of income inside individual countries deteriorates. The deterioration in distribution is most marked within the rural sectors of LDC as the improvement in the agricultural terms of trade widens the gap between rich and poor farmers. In addition, although both rural and urban incomes rise as a results of the export-led growth strategy, urban incomes (which are much higher to begin with) rise even faster. The ratio of rural to urban incomes, there fore, falls; and this leads to an increase in country-wide inequality. Nevertheless, there is a lessening in worldwide inequality (the worldwide Gini coefficient falls from. 656 to. 645), and there is also a substantial decrease in overall poverty as the export-led growth strategy reduces the income gap between the LDC as a group and the industrialized economies.

The ADLI strategy is summarized in the last column of Table 3. It, too is modeled by means of a composite experiment: Agricultural productivity is increased by 2 percent annually; under conditions of unchanging urban productivity, this leads to a corresponding rise in the ratio of agricultural to nonagricultural productivity. Agricultural terms of trade are increased by 2 percent annually to provide incentives for the rise in agricultural productivity. The increase in agricultural productivity leads to an increase in agricultural exports that augments the share of agricultural exports in agricultural production by 2 percent annually. Agricultural incomes are increased by the sum of the rate of increase in agricultural productivity and agricultural terms of trade. Finally, the rate of growth of GNP per capita is increased by 2 peccent per year - the same rate as in the export -led growth experiment- despite the fact that the simulations with the CGE model of South Korea indicated that the ADLI strategy leads to a higher rate of growth than does the export-led strategy.

The current experiment confirms the results of my earlier simulations with the CGE model of South Korea. The ADLI strategy results in a substantial improvement in the distribution of income within LDC, among all groups of LDC expect East Asia, among all nonsocialist LDC, and in the world as a whole. It also leads to very substantial reduction in worldwide poverty: Worldwide poverty is about 30 percent less than in the base case and about 20 percent less than with the export-led growth strategy.

These results reinforce the major conclusion of the previous analysis, i.e., that for most LDCs which are not already newly industrialized countires with established export markets, an agriculture–driven, open-development strategy is preferable to an industrial-export driven strategy. A reallocation of investment resources away from industrial export sectors and toward agriculture, coupled with a price policy that allows farmer incomes to rise, will lead to a superior performance in both income distribution and economic growth.

4) Discussion

The simulations reported in this paper lend strong support to the desirability of taking a hard look at agricultural options in the design of development strategies. Various pessimistic attitudes have dominated the design of development strategy. The initial implementation of import substitution strategies was born out of export pessimism and of a desire for a more controllable development strategy. The export pessimism proved unjustified for economies that have attained certain levels of industrialization and for countries facing favorable demand conditions for their exports, and the adverse balance-of-payments effects of the import-substitution strategy led to less rather than more control over the growth path of the economy. The current stress on the need for export-led growth as the major means of capitalizing on economies of scale, competition, and (more dubiously) capturing allocative efficiency is born partly out of agricultural pessimism on both the output and the savings fronts.

Agricultural pessimism on the output side is not warranted. During the decade of the 1970s, agricultural output rose at an average annual rate of 2.3 percent in low-income economies and 3 percent in middle-income economies. Between 1960 and 1980, agricultural output in developing countries rose by 70 percent. The 1982 World Bank study of **Agriculture in Developing Countries** confirms the view of agriculture as a potentially dynamic sector. The report notes that:

> ... where prices have not been kept artificially low, and where other conditions for growth have been favorable, farmers have responded by increasing output. The responsiveness of farmers to incentives - in contrast to the outmoded and mistaken view that peasants are set in traditional ways- has been observed in societies with diverse social systems and levels of development (pp. 46–47).

How is the productivity improvement in agriculture to be accomplished? The strategy should focus on the implementation of land augmenting innovations especially on small and medium scale farms. The focus on land augmenting innovations is dictated by the fact that land is the limiting resource for agricultural households. And the emphasis on small and medium size farms is dictated by both equity and efficiency considerations. Small farms have higher total factor productivity than do large farms, and the linkage effects with domestic industry are larger since the marginal propensity to consume domestic manufactures by small farmers is higher.

The land augmenting innovations can be implemented by improving the physical and institutional infrastructure of agriculture in order to effect shifts in the agricultural production functions. In the Southeast Asian sub-continent, the primary requisite is water control. Increasing irrigation, improving the management, maintenance, and design of existing irrigation systems, and investing in tube wells, hand pumps, and irrigation ditch maintenance could all play a role. Other partial steps toward the goal of improving agricultural productivity would include roads and terracing, selective mechanization, technological improvements, easing credit terms for the small-holder, the development of institutions for marketing and for the distribution of improved seed and fertilizer, and developing institutions for the effective dissemination of knowledge.

In implementing an ADLI strategy, particular attention would have to be paid to the system of incentives facing the farmers. Land augmenting innovations increase agricultural output; if there is no corresponding increase in demand for agricultural products, agricultural prices will fall. There will, therefore, be a natural tendency for the agricultural terms of trade to turn against farmers as a result of the ADLI strategy. It is, therefore, important to combine the implementation of ADLI with an appropriate price policy. The dynamic incentives of ADLI will not materialize if shifts in domestic terms of trade against agriculture are allowed to negate the income benefits of productivity improvement. Therefore, what is required as part of the productivity-improving package is a terms-of-trade policy which allows farmers to improve their incomes while improving output. The incentive effects of the ADLI strategy will also not materialize if tenurial conditions in agriculture are sufficiently unfavorable. Land augmenting innovations will increase the price of land. Under unregulated conditions, rents paid by tenant farmers will, therefore, have a tendency to rise as a result of the ADLI strategy. Both tenancy arrangements and terms-of-trade policies must, therefore, be adjusted so that they more than compensate for the adverse income effects upon the innovator-farmer which could arise under free-market conditions. Otherwise, the ADLI strategy will turn out not to have been implemented since agricultural incomes will not rise and linkages into industrial demand will, therefore, not materialize.

The ADLI strategy is not suggested as a strategy for all time and for all places, nor is it inconsistent with a system of neutral trade incentives (the definition of export-led growth of some economists). Indeed, the Korea simulations were performed with just such a system of neutral trade incentives. The ADLI strategy should be considered primarily by countries which, during a given period, are not anticipating rapidly expanding growth in world demand for their nontraditional exports. In addition, the ADLI strategy is most promising for countries with potentially large domestic markets and in which there already exists a large industrial base with the institutional flexibility to generate supply responsiveness. In practice, this means most second-tier counties and those large low-income countries which do not yet have proven export potential.

The ADLI strategy is recommended primarily as a strategy for the 1980s and early 1990 s to allow time for implementing the structural changes which must be introduced in industrial countries. Technological change, the growth of the NICs and differential rates of adoption of industrial innovations during the 1960s and 1970s in the various OECD countries have vastly altered the comparative advantage of the industrial nations. The OECD countries must adapt to their altered patterns of comparative advantage. If the OECD countries succeed in making the appropriate structural changes through industrial policies aimed at creating economic conditions propitious for the expansion of industrial "winners" rather than by protecting "losers", the appropriate industrialization strategy for the LDCs in the latter part of the 1990s may well again become one of export -led growth.

Meanwhile, it is important to point out that potentially productive alternatives to export-led growth and export-led industrialization exist, that these alternatives do not consist solely of import substitution, and that the arsenal of policy options currently open to developing countries for adjusting to their current crisis can profitably be enlarged by adding the option of agricultural-demand-led industrialization.

REFERENCES

ADELMAN, I. (1984), "Beyond Export Led Growth." World Development September.

ADELMAN, I. and ROBINSON, S. (1978), Income Distribution Policies in Developing Countries. Stanford, CA: Stanford University Press.

BRAULKE, M. (1983), "An Approximation to the Gini Coefficient for a Population Based on Sparse Information for Subgroups". Journal of Development Economics (12) April, 75 - 83.

DERVIŞ, K, de MELO, J. and ROBINSON, S. (1982), General Equilibrium Models for Development Policy. Cambridge: Cambridge University Press.

De JANVRY, A. (1984), "The Search for Styles of Development: Lessons from Latin America and Implications for India", mimeo. Berkeley, California: March.

DOMAR, E.D. (1957), Essays in the Theory of Economic Growth. Oxford, U. K.: Oxford University Press.

HIRSCHMAN, A. (1981), "A Generalized Linkage Approach to Development with Special Reference to Staples," in Hirschman, ed., Essays in Tresspassing. Cambridge, U. K.: Cambridge University Press, 1981 (pp. 59–97).

JAIN, S. (1975).Size Distribution of Income. The World Bank. Washington, D.C.

KRAVIS, I.B. (1978), "Real GDP Per Capita for More Than One Hunderd Countries" Economic Journal (88) June, 215–42.

MELLOR, J.W., WEAVER, T.F., LELE, U.J., and SMITH, S.R. (1968), Developing Rural India: Plan and Practice, Ithaca, Cornell University Press.

MELLOR, J.W. (1976), The New Economics of Growth: A Strategy for India and the Developing World, New York: Twentieth Century Fund, Cornell University Press.

SINGER, H. (1979), "Policy Implications of the Lima Target", Industry and Development, (3), 17–32.

STREETEN, P. (1982), "A Cool Look at 'Outward-Looking' Strategies for Development". **The World Economy** (5), September, 159–69.

WORLD BANK, (1982), **World Development Report,** 1982. Oxford: Oxford University Press.

WORLD BANK (1983a) **China, Socialist Economic Development.** The World Bank. Washington, D.C.

WORLD BANK, (1983b), **World Tables.** The World Bank. Washington, D.C.

WORLD BANK (1983c), **World Development Report,** 1983. Oxford: Oxford University Press.

[15]

Static and Dynamic Indices of
Income Inequality

IRMA ADELMAN

College of Natural Resources
University of California, Berkeley

PETER WHITTE

Statistical Laboratory
Cambridge University, England

ABSTRACT

   The present paper proposes a combined measure of static and dynamic inequality to be used in cross-country and historical comparisons. The measure proposed generalises any static index of inequality whether based upon some social welfare function or not. The measure is applied, in an illustrative fashion, to data from Great Britain and the United States. The results shed light on potential tradeoffs by indicating the upper limits on welfare gains to society attainable through redistribution. They suggest that this tradeoff is likely to be quite small since differences in social stratification and economic performance as large as those between the United States and Great Britain in the sixties led to quite similar social welfare gains through dynamic income prospect equalisation.

RÉSUMÉ

   Cette étude présente la nouvelle formulation d'une mesure qui rend compte de la perspective tant statique que dynamique de l'inégalité, pouvant ultérieurement s'utiliser lors d'analyses comparatives et historiques. La nouvelle mesure généralise les indices statiques d'inégalité qu'ils soient fondés ou non sur des fonctions de bien-être collectif. De plus, elle s'applique de manière explicite à des données en provenance des États-Unis et de Grande-Bretagne. Les résultats obtenus précisent les arbitrages possibles en tenant compte des gains sociaux optimaux attribuables à la redistribution. L'étude conclue que ces échanges sont plutôt minimes étant donné les grands écarts entre la stratification sociale et les performances économiques existant entre les États-Unis et la Grande-Bretagne. Ce type d'analyse pourrait s'utiliser avec pertinence dans un contexte

   * This paper has been prepared under the auspices of the Income Distribution Division of the International Labour Office.

d'études dans les pays en voie de développement car il indique de façon adéquate les problèmes des inégalités dans la distribution du revenu.

INTRODUCTION

Economists have generally concentrated on the static aspects of income inequality, or on the end product of such inequality, the distribution of wealth. Sociologists, on the other hand, have stressed both the static and the dynamic aspects of inequality in the their analyses of, respectively, social stratification and social mobility.

In their measures of static inequality economists focus primarily on income, or, sometimes, directly on utility. By contrast, sociologists frame their static analyses in terms of occupational categories, and their dynamic studies in terms of occupational mobility. These latter studies refer especially to the mechanism of the transfer of inequality from one generation to another. Only recently have sociologists begun to construct income-mobility matrices, a concept natural to the economist.

In normative discussions there tends to be an analogous static/ dynamic division among social analysts. There are those whose vision of a just society would emphasize equality in the distribution of the fruits of economic development. There are also those who would stress equality only in the distribution of *access* to the fruits of economic development. Such equality would be achieved by evening out opportunities for both the accumulation of marketable assets and their transformation into income-earning assets.

Clearly, both the static and the dynamic aspects of inequality are important characteristics of social performance, to which different societies and individuals give differing relative values. There is more tolerance of inequality in the distribution of income when social mobility is substantial. Indeed, Hirschmann[1] has argued that increases in inequality which occur when middle and upper income groups find a prosperity which the bottom stratum does not share may actually have the immediate effect of raising the welfare of the bottom stratum. The poor will take improvements in the incomes of the middle groups as signals for improved income prospects of their own. However, if the increase in static inequality is not matched by an increase in social mobility, they will soon feel disaffected, and even cheated, by the social process. The result will be social and political unrest. Proper understanding of the interactions of economic and political processes, and so of politics, thus requires that economic inequality be considered in both its static and dynamic manifestations. Measures of both are therefore needed.

The present paper proposes a combined measure of static and dynamic inequality, to be used in cross-country and historical comparisons. The measure proposed generalizes any static index of inequality, whether based upon some social welfare function or not. It incorporates a discount

[1] A. HIRSHMAN, "On the Changing Tolerance for Income Inequality" (mimeographed, 1976).

factor, whose variation permits one to change the relative weighting of the static and dynamic aspects of inequality. For the sake of specifity, computations are carried out for the case of a particular index based upon a particular welfare function. The measure is applied, in an illustrative fashion, to data from two countries: Great Britain and the United States. The comparison is an interesting one, since these two countries differ quite markedly in their relative valuations of static and dynamic inequality. The United States has a more unequal distribution of income, but much greater social mobility than Great Britain.

STATIC MEASURES OF INEQUALITY

We shall assume that income as measured is *real* income, and denote it by y. A typical index of income inequality will be denoted by I(y). Of course, the index is actually a function of the frequency distribution of the variable y, not of y itself, but the notation is a convenient one.

As will be apparent, our procedure supplies a dynamic version of any static index. However, one is ultimately faced with the necessity of choosing a particular index. This choice is a matter of some interest in itself, and raises a number of issues which we discuss in this section.

In seeking an index of income inequality which will extend naturally to the dynamic case one looks for a definition which is theoretically appealing, and which leads to amenable calculations. Since the ultimate aim of national policy is, presumably, to increase social welfare, the most natural definition would rest on the concept of a social welfare function. Even indices not obviously based upon such a concept in fact imply a partial specification of a social welfare function.

Of the several static indices of inequality which have been used, only two, Dalton's[2] and Atkinson's[3] now appear to recommend themselves as being both consistent with a socially acceptable welfare function and easily computable. As indicated by these authors, all other previously proposed indices imply social welfare functions which are inconsistent with egalitarian values. Indeed, as shown by Newbery[4], there exists no additive utility function which ranks income distributions in the same order as the Gini coefficient.

We consider, then, indices based on a social welfare function. A welfare-based criterion for the efficiency of the distribution of income would rest on a comparison of two different quantities: (i) the social welfare level actually achieved with the existing distribution of income, and (ii) the maximal social welfare level achievable with the same resources. Under egalitarian assumptions, which imply equal weighting of individuals' util-

---

[2] H. DALTON, "The Measurement of Inequality of Incomes", *Economic Journal*, 30 (1920), pp. 348-61.

[3] A. B. ATKINSON, "On the Measurement of Inequality", *Journal of Economic Theory*, 2 (1970), 244-263.

[4] D. NEWBERY, "A Theorem on the Measurement of Inequality", *Journal of Economic Theory*, 2, 1970, pp. 264-266.

ities, and utility independence among individuals, one can identify social welfare with the average utility in the economy. In symbols, the criterion would then be

$$F = \frac{EU(y)}{\max EU(y)} \tag{1}$$

Here $U(y)$ is the utility of income y to an individual and E is the operation of averaging over the population (giving different individuals equal weighting). The quantity $\max EU(y)$ is the social welfare maximised over income distributions achievable with the same resources. In carrying out this maximisation we shall neglect the price and production effects induced by a redistribution of income. The assumption is, then, that the maximisation $\max EU(y)$, is carried out subject to holding total income fixed, i.e. holding $E(y)$ fixed. Strictly speaking, the index therefore accurately reflects the initial definition only when "efficiency" is near maximal.

We could regard a quantity such as F as a measure of efficiency, or of equality. It decreases from 1 to 0 as the situation changes from one of equality to one extreme inequality. The conventional measure of *inequality* will be

$$I = 1 - F$$

which increases from 0 to 1 as one moves away from complete inequality. There are good reasons for rather taking $-\log F$ as a measure of inequality. For one thing, extreme inequality then appears more realistically, as an infinitely remote condition, which can be approached, but not normally attained. But, more importantly, if heterogeneity in distribution of income or wealth can be decomposed, in that components of it can be attributed to several causes, then F has a corresponding multiplicative decomposition (see later). The index $-\log F$ then has a corresponding additive decomposition, whereas the analogous decomposition for $1 - F$ has a clumsy, unnatural form.

In order to be able to exploit simplicity of decomposition and yet avoid outright conflict with convention we shall work principally in terms of the *equality* index F. Readers who wish to translate this into the corresponding inequality index $1 - F$ may do so.

If U is concave then, by Jensen's inequality,

$$EU(y) \leqslant U(Ey)$$

which implies that average utility is maximal when available income is distributed uniformly over the entire population. The index of equality is then

$$F_D = \frac{EU(y)}{U(Ey)} \tag{2}$$

This is effectively the index proposed by Dalton in 1920, and used by Aigner and Heins[5] to compare indices of inequality in the 51 states of the United States.

[5] D. J. AIGNER and A. J. HEINS, "A Social Welfare View of the Measurement of Income Inequality", *Review of Income and Wealth*, 13 (1967), pp. 12-25.

More generally, since there is no natural unique form for the utility function, one could take as index

$$F = \frac{\phi\,[EU(y)]}{\phi\,[U(Ey)]} \qquad (3)$$

where ϕ is a transformation function with the properties:

(i) ϕ non-negative
(ii) ϕ non-decreasing
(iii) ϕ such that the index (2) is invariant under a scaling of utility, $U \to kU$ and, *arguably,*
(iv) ϕ such that the index is also invariant under a change of utility-origin (a translation), $U \to a + U$.

Conditions (i)-(iii) reflect the fact that utility is ordinal. One would impose condition (iv) if there were no natural utility-origin.

The Dalton index (2) is naturally a special case of (3), and satisfies conditions (i)-(iii).

The modified Dalton index

$$F_D = \frac{EU(y) - U(o)}{U(Ey) - U(o)} \qquad (4)$$

couched in terms of utility *increases,* satisfies all four conditions. We shall consider only utility functions for which $U(o)$ is zero, so that the two versions, (2) and (4), of the Dalton index coincide.

Another special case of (3), which also satisfies all four conditions, is the Atkinson index, defined as

$$F_A = \frac{U^{-1}\,[EU(y)]}{Ey} = \frac{Y_A}{Ey} \qquad (5)$$

Here U^{-1} is the function inverse to U, which maps utility onto income. The quantity $y_A = U^{-1}\,[EU(y)]$ is thus the fixed income that would give the same utility as the average utility achieved in the population (the "equivalent" or "certainty equivalent" income).

Indices (2), (4) and (5) are all of the form (3), with $\phi(\xi)$ equal to $\xi, \xi - U(o)$ and $U_{-1}(\xi)$ respectively.

CHOICE OF A UTILITY FUNCTION

Indices of type (3) require the use of an explicit utility function for their evaluation. Natural conditions on such a function are that it be non-negative, non-decreasing and concave. These constraints still leave much room for arbitrariness in the specific choice of a utility function.

One common choice is a power law

$$U(y) = y^{1-\epsilon} \qquad (6)$$

$(0 \leq \epsilon < 1)$. For such a choice, any index satisfying condition (iii) has the property of being invariant under a fixed rescaling of income

$$I(vy) = I(y) \tag{7}$$

The Atkinson index (4) tends to be coupled with this particular choice of utility function.

The choice

$$U(y) = 1 - e^{-\gamma y} \tag{8}$$

proves, however, considerably more convenient computationally. This can be modified to

$$U(y) = 1 - e^{-\gamma y} + \lambda y$$

if it is desired that utility not satiate with increasing income. As indicated in Aigner and Heins, who use Dalton's index with utility function (8), the ranking of observations by degrees of inequality is not very sensitive to the specific nature of the utility function used.

COMPARISON OF THE DALTON AND ATKINSON INDICES

The major contenders for empirical application of the efficiency criterion (1) are Dalton's and Atkinson's indices. Both are special cases of (3).

The primary difference between them is that, while Dalton's measure is in the utility space Atkinson's measure is in the income space. Dalton's measure represents the relative shortfall in social welfare from that maximally achievable, while Atkinson's represents the extent of "waste" in national income compared to the national income required with a distribution of income which is more efficient in welfare terms. The two measures thus appear complementary to each other, and have their analogues in measurements of consumer surplus. However, Atkinson's index can behave anomalously just because it is framed in terms of incomes rather than the quantity of more fundamental significance: utility.

To see this, recall that income as measured in the index is real income, so that a transformation $y \to cy$ corresponds to a magnification of income by a factor c. If real incomes are thus magnified (by a factor $c > 1$) then there is no doubt that the levels of all individual incomes have increased, but whether inequality has increased or decreased is by no means evident. Income variations are then stretched out over a wider scale, but utility variations can well be compressed into a narrower scale, because of satiation of utility with increasing income. This difference is reflected in the behaviour of the Dalton and Atkinson indices, as we shall see.

The utility function (6) is unique in that scale changes in income produce scale changes in utility, so that an index insensitive to scale changes in utility will also be unaffected by scale changes in income. The utility function (8) satiates faster, and indices based on this choice will not have the scale invariance property (7). In this, utility function (8) is perhaps more realistic than the power-law (6), in that function (8) satiates

A BROADER MODEL OF MAN   33

strongly enough that utility has a finite limit as income increases. We shall calculate the Dalton and Atkinson indices on the basis of this particular utility function.

For the sake of concreteness, consider an income distribution in the population of the F-form

$$\lambda(y) = \frac{1}{c^n \, \Gamma(n)} \, e^{-y/c} \, y^{n-1} \tag{9}$$

so that c measures scale of income, and n measures "peakedness" of the distribution. If we also assume $\gamma \neq 1$ in (8), we find that

$$E(y) = nc$$
$$EU(y) = 1 - (1 + c)^{-n}$$
$$y_A = n \log (1 + c)$$

so that

$$F_D = \frac{1 - (1 + c)^{-n}}{1 - e^{-nc}} \tag{10}$$

$$F_A = \frac{\log (1 + c)}{c} \tag{11}$$

As c increases from unity, one gets the contradictory indications that F_D increases, and F_A decreases. In fact, as $c \to \infty$ then F_D and F_A tend respectively to the extreme values 1 and 0. One has $F_D \to 1$ because, as c increases, ultimately all the population receives the same (maximal) utility, and utility is then uniformly distributed. One has $F_A \to 0$ because the fixed income that gives one the same (near-maximal) utility as does the distributed income is on average small relative to the average of the distributed income.

It seems strange that an index should indicate *maximal* inequality precisely in a situation where an arbitrarily large proportion of the population receives a utility arbitrarily near the maximal possible. The trouble is, that F_A is expressed in terms of income, rather than the more meaningful quantity, utility.

These conclusions are not specific to the distribution (9) and the utility function (8). They persist qualitatively for virtually any income distribution, and for any utility function which satiates faster than a power law, i.e. for which "elasticity" $\dfrac{y}{U} \dfrac{dU}{dy}$ decreases with increasing income.

The conclusion is, then, that the two indices respond oppositely to a uniform magnification c in the income scale if utility satiates faster than a power law. One can argue as to which effect one might expect for moderate values of c, but, as evident from above, there is no doubt that it is the Atkinson index whose behaviour is unacceptable for large c.

DYNAMIC MEASURES OF INEQUALITY

We now turn to the construction of a dynamic index.

We shall set the dynamic situation in discrete time t $(= 0,1,2,...)$. Individuals will be considered as moving between income classes labelled $j = 1,2,...,m$; the income in class j being z_j. The class of a particular individual at time t will be denoted $x(t)$ and his income by $y(t)$ (so that $y(t) = Z_{x(t)}$). We shall suppose that motion of different individuals between classes is independent, and described by a time-homogeneous Markov process with transition matrix P. We shall also define the s-step transition probability

$$P^{(s)}_{jk} = P(x(s) = k \mid x(o) = j)$$

The initial distribution over classes (at time t = 0) will be denoted by the distribution vector $a = (a_j)$ and the equilibrium distribution of the Markov chain (if this is unique) by $\pi = (\pi_j)$.

We have spoken of the movement of an individual between classes. In some cases the process will refer to movement over generations, so it is not the individual that moves, but rather his son who enters an income class perhaps different from that of his father. Rather than speaking of an "individual" one should perhaps then speak of a "line". One partially identifies the individuals of a line, insofar as one assumes that future utility (i.e. good fortune accruing to later members of a line) has a positive value even for the present (i.e. that the current representative of the line enjoys the fortune of his successors to some degree). With this understanding, we shall continue to speak of an individual, rather than of a line.

One may, or may not, assume that the Markov process governing transitions is irreducible. It will be irreducible if there is enough mixing between classes that the probability of ultimately reaching any given class from any other is positive. In this case the equilibrium distribution is independent of initial conditions, and is unique. But, if some classes can never be reached from certain starting points, then this is very pertinent to prospects and to the equality of incomes in the future. We cannot, then, exclude this case.

SOME PROPOSALS FOR A DYNAMIC INDEX

A dynamic index should take account of future income, as well as of current income. That is, it should give weight to prospects, as well as to current state. It should make sense whether the process starts from equilibrium (i.e. $a = \pi$) or whether it does not.

Proposal 1. One could calculate $F(y(s))$, where F is some particular static index, as explained in the first section. That is, one simply calculates a static measure inequality for the income distribution at some future time s. However, this is a purely one-point calculation, and takes no account of the fact that the mobility of an individual can give him equalising experience of both good and bad fortune over time. If the process is irreducible, then the index will tend to that appropriate to the equilibrium distribution as s increases.

Proposal 2.   Calculate the expected income $\bar{y}(s)$ of an individual after time s has elapsed, conditional on his initial income class $x(0)$, and take $F(\bar{y}(s))$ as a possible index. The conditional expectation

$$\bar{y}(s) = E[y(s) \mid x(o)]$$

is still a random variable, because it depends upon the initial state, which is random with distribution a.

This measure does take some account of the tendency to equalisation of long-term prospects offered by a model in which there is mobility between classes. If the process is irreducible then $\bar{y}(s)$ will converge to the equilibrium expected income $\Sigma \pi_u z_u$ as s increases, independent of starting point. Correspondingly, the index will tend to unity, indicating complete equalisation of long-term prospects. If the process is reducible, then the index will tend to a smaller value, measuring inequality between the ergodic classes.

In fact, one will wish to strike a balance between measuring inequality of current income distribution, and that of long-term expectations, and so would use a time-averaged index

$$F(\bar{y}(s), r) = \sum_{s=o}^{\infty} (1 - r)r_s F(y(s))$$

where r is an appropriately chosen discount factor.

However, $F(\bar{y}(s))$ and its time-averaged versions exhibit the drawback that they depend only on the conditional expected value over the time-path, and fluctuations around this time path are averaged out before the index is calculated. Account is taken of the statistical variation of the starting point only, whose effect becomes smaller (even vanishing) as s is increased.

Proposal 3.   If the index is to depend upon the actual income path over the period 0 to τ, then a natural suggestion would be to calculate the discounted value of total income over the horizon 0 to τ, and then calculate the inequality index of the discounted income stream. That is, the dynamic index would be then of the form

$$F_{\beta} = I(\sum^{\tau} \beta^s y(s)) \qquad (12)$$

for an appropriate static index I and discount factor β. So, time-averaging is achieved by discounting the actual income stream, rather than the indices of the expected values of that stream. In the authors' view this proposal provides the most appropriate dynamic measure of inequality, in that it takes account of the retained identity of an individual or line over time, by formation of the discounted total income for that individual, and yet also takes account of all statistical variation in this quantity. Note that we may well have $\tau = \infty$.

These suggestions are not without their precedents. Shorrocks[6] has suggested calculating an inequality index based on integrated income over a period. Weizsäcker[7] has taken the view that income is not easily transferred in time, and so has integrated *utility* of current income for an individual over a period, calculated the 'equivalent income' corresponding to average utility, and then calculated an inequality index (over individuals) for the equivalent incomes thus derived. The validity of this approach is strongly dependent on the notion that income is localised in time, yields its utility then, and is not easily transferred through time (by means, for example, of savings or dissavings). Furthermore, the whole notion of an equivalent income is open to the type of criticism expressed in our discussion of the Atkinson index.

Conceptually our approach is much like Shorrocks' developed simultaneously and independently of ours. Our major contributions over and above Shorrocks' are in the computational formulae, given below, which permit easy empirical evaluation, and in the decomposition procedures which permit numerical attribution of different structural sources of inequality.

COMPUTATION OF THE INDEX F_D

Denote the discounted total income $\sum_0^\tau \beta^s y(s)$ by Y. One then wishes to calculate I(Y) and, in the course of this, to calculate expressions such as EU(Y) and EY, if one is using indices based on utility.

In fact,

$$E(\exp(-\gamma Y)) = \sum_{j_0} \sum_{j_1} \dots \sum_{j_t} a_{j_0} \exp(-\gamma Z_{j_0}) \prod_{s=0}^{t-1} P_{j_s j_s+1} \exp(-\gamma \beta^s Z_{j+1})$$

$$= a^1 D_0 P D_1 P D_2 P D_3 \dots P D_t 1$$

where D_s is the diagonal matrix with jth entry $\exp(-\gamma \beta s z_j)$.

For a utility such as

$$U(Y) = 1 - e^{-\gamma Y} + \lambda Y$$

one has then all the components needed to calculate the dynamic version of the Dalton index (2)

$$F_D(Y) = \frac{1 - E(e^{-\gamma Y}) \rightarrow \lambda EY}{1 - e^{-\gamma EY} + \lambda EY} \qquad (14)$$

for a suitable range of values the discount factor β. The corresponding expression for the dynamic version of the Atkinson index would be

$$F_A(Y) = \frac{Y_A}{EY} \qquad (15)$$

---

[6] A. F. SHORROCKS, "Income Inequality and Income Mobility", to appear, *Journal of Economic Theory*.

[7] C. C. V. WEIZSÄCKER, "Annual Income, Lifetime Income and Other Income Concepts in Measuring Income Distribution", Discussion paper, Bellagio, 1977.

where y_A is the solution of

$$e^{-\gamma Y_A} - {}^-\gamma Y_A = E(e^{-\gamma Y}) - \lambda EY \tag{16}$$

In the case $\lambda = 0$ (16) has the solution

$$Y_A = -\frac{1}{\gamma} \log E(e^{-\gamma Y})$$

so that

$$F_A(Y) = \frac{\log E(e^{-\gamma Y})}{\gamma EY} \tag{17}$$

In other cases (16) must be solved for Y_A numerically.

AN INEQUALITY INDEX FOR TOTAL LIFE INCOME

If the period of interest is the lifetime of a single individual, then the natural dynamic index is $F(Y_L)$, where Y_L is the total life income of the individual. Lifetime naturally defines a finite (but random) future, so that there is no need to discount.

However, Y_L shows statistical variations for two reasons: because income history over life will vary between individuals, and because length of life will vary. It is only the first source of variation which is relevant for an inequality index; one would wish to eliminate the second.

To this end, consider a situation in which any individual still alive at age t is given *the average income for individuals of age t*; let the total life income under these circumstances be denoted $\tilde{Y}_L$. The quantity $\tilde{Y}_L$ is still a random variable, insofar as individuals have different lifespans, but variations of income history during life have been eliminated.

Plainly

$$E(\tilde{Y}_L) = E(Y_L)$$

and

$$EU(Y_L) \leqslant EU(\tilde{Y}_L) \leqslant U(EY_L)$$

An index

$$F = \frac{EU(Y_L)}{U(EY_L)} \tag{18}$$

(or, more generally, an index

$$F = \frac{\phi(EU(Y_L))}{\phi(U(EY_L))} \tag{19}$$

where ϕ is a function having the properties (i)-(iv) applying to equation (3), measures inequality due to both sources: variation of income history, and of life-span. However, the index

$$\tilde{F} = \frac{EU(Y_L)}{EU(\tilde{Y}_L)} \tag{20}$$

(or its variant analogous to (19)) measures inequality due only to variation of income history; it takes the value unity if all individuals have the same income history during life. This is the index we propose.

The factorisation

$$\frac{EU(Y_L)}{U(EY_L)} = \frac{EU(Y_L)}{EU(\tilde{Y}_L)} \frac{EU(\tilde{Y}_L)}{U(EY_L)} \tag{21}$$

corresponds to a decomposition of the index (18) into the product of two indices, one reflecting variation in income history alone, the other reflecting variation in life-span alone. This is the type of decomposition referred to on page 5.

When it comes to calculation of $\tilde{F}$, one must have a model for the joint statistical variation of life and income. The simplest would be a Markov model, in which the fact of survival to age $t+1$ from age t, and size of income at age $t+1$, are conditioned only by income at age t (and, of course, the supposition of survival to age t). We would define then,

$P + (Y_k/Y_j)$ = probability that an individual, alive at age t, and then enjoying income level y_j, survives to age $t+1$ and then enjoys income level y_k.

Let the matrix with $P + (Y_k/Y_j)$ as jk^{th} element be denoted P_t. The probability that an individual survives at least to age t is then

$$P_t = A'P_0 P_1 \dots P_{t-1} 1$$

where a is the vector describing the distribution over income classes at birth. The average income for individuals alive at age t is

$$Y(t) = \frac{A'P_0 P_1 \dots P_{t-1} Y}{A'P_0 P_1 \dots P_{t-1} 1}$$

where y is the vector with j^{th} element y_j. The average total income over life is

$$EY_L = \sum_{t=0}^{\infty} A'P_0 P_1 \dots P_{t-1} Y$$

The average utility with "standardised" income histories is

$$EU(\tilde{Y}_L) = \sum_{t=1}^{\infty} (P_t - P_{t+1}) U(\sum_{s=0}^{\infty} Y(s))$$

with $P_0 = 1$ by convention.

As in the previous section, the calculation of $EU(Y_L)$ is forbidding for any case except linear or exponential utility functions.

For the exponential case, define D as the diagonal matrix with entry $\exp(-\gamma Y_i)$ at the jth diagonal place. Then

$$E(1 - e_{sgYL})$$

$$= A' [1 \to DP_0 + DP_0 DP_1 + DP_0 DP_1 DP_2 + \dots] (I - D) 1$$

APPLICATION OF THE INDICES

The numerical results of the study are illustrative. Better data, specifically collected for dynamic income mobility analyses, is required to reach firm substantive conclusions.

THE DATA

To our knowledge, there exist no studies of intergenerational income-mobility and only two usable occupational-mobility studies — that of Glass[8] for Great Britain and of Duncan and Blau[9] for the United States. In addition, there exists one intragenerational income-mobility study, for the United States, carried out by Schiller[10], based on the 15 year income history of a sample of 75,000 individuals covering all income deciles. Results from this study are analyzed separately, and serve to indicate the rough magnitude of biases stemming from the use of occupational-mobility data.

The Glass and Duncan and Blau occupational-mobility studies, which are roughly comparable as between the two countries, are used for the basic applications of the index. Both studies refer to the intergenerational and intragenerational occupational mobility of male employees as of 1960. For our purposes, the occupational mobility data had to be converted into income-mobility data. This was done by using Census information on average male wages by occupational category, a procedure which, by ignoring dispersion of wages within occupations, understates static inequality.

Nevertheless, despite apparent comparability between the two studies, variations in demographic, statistical and economic conditions result in intercountry differences which reflect more than inherent contrasts in pure mobility patterns. For example, the actual time period implicit in the intergenerational mobility information is undefined and may differ as between the two countries. There are differences in degree of occupational disaggregation and coverage of nominally similar occupational categories. Comparability is also affected by intercountry differences in family size, life expectancy, work cycle and business cycle. Fathers with more than one surviving son are oversampled to a different degree in both countries; sons are represented at different stages in their working-life cycles; and the same calendar year need not represent the same stage in the business cycles of the two countries.

The Glass and Duncan and Blau data also falls short of the ideal because in both countries the occupational mobility information does not cover important segments of the population. Female employees are omitted, thereby biassing the mobility information for the lower tail of the

---

    [8] D. V. GLASS, *Social Mobility in Britain* (Routledge and Kegan, 1967).
    [9] P. M. BLAU and O. D. DUNCAN, *The American Occupational Structure* (Wiley, 1967).
    [10] B. R. SCHILLER, "Relative Earnings Mobility in the United States" (mimeographed, 1976).

income distribution of those employed. More important, the unemployed are excluded entirely. The above omissions result in substantial understatement of income inequality (though not necessarily of income-mobility) in both countries. In addition, this tendency to understate inequality in both countries was reinforced by our conversion technique from occupational into income-mobility. The use of *average* wages in each occupational category omits the contributions to static inequality of variance around the average. Income other than wages — self-employment and property income of all types, which is more variable and has greater dispersion than wage income, is also not considered in the conversion. On the other hand, the use of individuals rather than households as the basic sampling unit for income tends to overstate income (and mobility?) inequality.

These caveats must be borne in mind in interpreting the empirical results.

CHOICE OF PARAMETERS

To evaluate the indices, one must choose values for γ and β.

Two considerations guided our choice of γ: the need to achieve comparability among countries; and the degree of compression of the measurement scale when income differentials are converted into utility differentials. Naturally, the higher γ, the steeper the utility function, and hence the less the degree of compression of the income scale; also, the lower the utility of the average income. When γ is set equal to the inverse of the mean income, the utility of the mean income becomes the same (.632) in both countries. This is in accord with empirical studies of subjective evaluations of the utility of income across countries[11] which suggest that households assign the same utility to the mean income of each country. In addition, this choice of γ leads to a virtually identical and quite reasonable compression factor (1.65 in Great Britain and 1.60 in the United States). In Great Britain, where the ratio of wages of the top decile of employed males to the bottom decile is 2.9 (less than in Mainland China!), the corresponding utility ratio becomes 1.8. The analogous compression for the United States is from 4.3 for incomes to 2.7 for utilities. Thus, both criteria are satisfied when γ is set equal to the inverse of mean income. Other values for γ are given in Tables 1-4 of the Appendix. As to the intergenerational weight factor, β, values between .1 and .9 were all tried; but the most relevant values for the Judeo-Christian cultures appear to us (on purely introspective grounds) to be somewhere between one third and one half.

RESULTS

Tables 1-4 summarize the results. They confirm only some of our a priori expectations. Static inequality is larger in the United States than in

———
[11] B. M. S. VAN PRAAG, T. GOEDHART and A. KAPTEYN, "The Poverty Line in the European Community: First Results of a Pilot Survey" (Economics Institute of Leyden University Report 77.04, 1977), (memeographed).

Great Britain. But the absolute contribution of mobility to inequality reduction is the same and the relative reduction in inequality due to mobility is actually larger in Great Britain than in the United States. In addition, the numerical magnitudes of all effects are surprisingly small.

At the preferred values of γ and using the Dalton index, static inequality leads to a social welfare level which is only 4.7% less than the maximum attainable with the same total product in the United States, and 3.7% less than the maximum in Great Britain; the corresponding numbers using the Atkinson index are larger: 8.9% in the United States versus 6.4% in Great Britain. But regardless which index is used, the absolute difference in welfare losses due to inequality between the two countries is only one or two percentage points. The relative difference is, of course, much larger. There would be a 30% reduction in social welfare losses from inequality were the United States to achieve a static level of equality comparable to that of Great Britain. Given the substantial differences in economic and social structures between the two countries, the smallness of the absolute effect is rather surprising.

The reduction in inequality due to dynamic influences naturally varies with the discount rate. In the relevant range ($\beta = .3$ and $\beta = .5$), the absolute contribution of male mobility to inequality reduction is virtually identical in both countries — about 1.4 percentage points with $\beta = .4$ and using the Dalton index. The precise numbers, and even the directions of the dynamic effects, vary with the formula chosen. While the Dalton dynamic index always indicates an increase in equality due to mobility the Atkinson index sometimes shows an apparent decrease (e.g. in the U.S. for $\beta = .4$ and $\beta = .000250$). But for reasons indicated earlier, we do not place much weight on the results using the Atkinson index. For example, when all expected utilities are identical (for Great Britain, when $\gamma = .00164$, $\beta = 1.0$, in the tenth period) the Atkinson index has a value of .9139, indicating that a further 8.6% increase in social welfare could be obtained from still further equalisation.

In percentage terms, the contribution of social mobility to inequality reduction is more dramatic. With $\beta = .4$ and using $1 - F_D$, the asymptotic welfare gain due to social mobility is 30% in the United States and 39% in Great Britain. In one generation, the percentage reductions in welfare losses under the same assumptions are between 12 and 17 percent in the United States, depending on the mobility concept used, and 22% in Great Britain. Thus, interestingly enough, the calculations suggest that social mobility will induce a greater degree of equalization, sooner, in Great Britain than in the United States even with the same relative weight, β, placed on future generations.

The contribution of intragenerational mobility to inequality reduction are slightly larger than those of intergenerational mobility.

SENSITIVITY ANALYSES

1. *Choice of parameter*

As might be expected, the results do vary with the choice of values for γ and β, but they are not overly sensitive to that choice. Both the Atkinson and the Dalton dynamic indices decrease with γ, but at a declining rate. For $\gamma = .00001$ the elasticity of the index with respect to γ is $.000513$; for $\gamma = .001$, the elasticity is $-.00199$. The Atkinson index is slightly more sensitive to γ than the Dalton index, and its elasticity declines more rapidly. The sensitivity of both indices to γ declines over time.

The behaviour of the index when β increases differs as between the Dalton and the Atkinson dynamic indices. And the difference illustrates the deficiencies of the Atkinson index. For the Dalton index, the higher β, the larger the index (i.e. the closer the index to perfect equality). With $\beta = 1.$, the index eventually goes to unity as sufficiently high levels of expected income are reached so that the expected utilities are all near maximal levels and differences among them become insignificant. In the second period, the elasticity of the Dalton index rises from $-.002236$ (for $\beta = .1$, in Great Britain, $\gamma = .00153$) to $-.0081$ as β increases from $.1$ to $.9$; by the fifth period the elasticity of the index with respect to β is almost constant over the same range. For the Atkinson index, for small β, $\leq .2$, the index rises as β goes up. But as β increases above $.5$ the index goes *down* when mobility is first introduced and rises thereafter. With high β, the asymptotic value of the index declines below the initial, static, value despite substantial equalisation in the expected utilities. Indeed, with $\beta = 1.$, the index attains a value of $.91349$ despite the fact that all expected utilities are identical! This behaviour of the Atkinson index appears to us unreasonable.

2. *Choice of static index*

For small values of γ, $\leq .0001$, when the utility function is quite flat, the two indices are numerically quite close. But as γ rises, the indices diverge and the Atkinson index falls below the Dalton index, indicating less equality. The difference is the more pronounced the higher the expected income, the greater the curvature of the utility function, and the larger the income range covered by the index.

For reasons indicated above, we favour the Dalton based index and place most weight on results obtained with it.

3. *The form of the utility function*

Even though it becomes quite difficult to calculate the dynamic index with non-exponential forms of the utility function, we did evaluate the static index with a different functional form. If we assume a log normal distribution of the utility function with the actual mean and standard deviation, as suggested by van Praag and Kapteyn[12] for cross national com-

---

[12] *Ibidem.*

parisons, the static Dalton index for Great Britain is .99594. This is quite close to the value of the index corresponding to $\gamma = .0001$. Thus, the closeness of our index to perfect equality is not an artifact due to our choice of utility function. Other plausible utility functions would yield quite similar results.

BIASES INTRODUCED BY THE USE OF OCCUPATIONAL MOBILITY DATA

As might be expected, the use of occupational mobility data substantially understates utility gains possible through income equalisation. The index based on Schiller's data, which measure income mobility directly, suggests that an 11% increase in social welfare could be obtained by complete static income equalisation (see Table 4), whereas the corresponding figure based on the Duncan and Blau data is only 4.7%. The Atkinson based index leads to even more dramatic conclusions: about 18% for the Schiller data, as compared to approximately 9%. The equalising effects of mobility are, however, quite similar in relative terms using either data source. The Schiller index for the second period with $\beta = .4$ indicates a 12% decline in inequality due to dynamic effects. This relative decline is precisely equal to that obtained from the Duncan and Blau data. The absolute asymptotic decline is, of course, much larger with the Schiller data: 3.14 percentage points as compared to 1.4. Thus the biases due to omissions in data coverage and due to the use of average wages for converting occupational mobility data into income mobility lead to quite substantial underestimation of not only potential welfare gains from equalisation in the distribution of income but also in the absolute contribution of income mobility to social welfare.

DISCUSSION OF RESULTS

In this paper we provide an operational approach for evaluating the contribution of income mobility, both within and across generations, to equalisation in the distribution of income. The actual magnitudes we estimate vary with the weight placed on the future as well as with the curvature of the utility function. At the preferred value for γ, and with β between one third and a half, mobility takes society between a third and four-tenth of the way towards complete equalisation of utility prospects in ten periods in both Great Britain and the United States. With $\beta \geqslant .7$, it goes virtually all the way. Thus, unless one essentially disregards the welfare of future generations, mobility considerations go a fair share of the way towards offsetting the effects upon social welfare of static inequality in the long run. And even in a single period, the relative contribution of mobility to inequality reduction is substantial (of the order of one fifth).

The absolute losses in social welfare due to inequality in male wages only, and the absolute gains in social welfare due to wage mobility appear rather small in both Great Britain and the United States. But these losses (and gains) represent only about one half of the total welfare change arising from income inequality, as the comparison between the Duncan and Blau and Schiller results indicate. This comparison suggests that there is much more improvement in welfare to be had by a combination of equalising non-wage and wage income and reducing male-female wage-income differentials. (These are the major omissions from the Duncan-Blau data which are included in the Schiller data).

In any case, in assessing the numerical magnitude of calculated welfare effects one should compare them with those arising from other sources of malfunctioning of the economy: allocative inefficiency, unemployment, and low growth. When that is done, it is apparent that compared to other static welfare losses, that arising from income inequality is as large. The various numerical estimates of output (and hence potential welfare) losses due to allocative inefficiency depend, of course, on the assumptions made with respect to elasticities of substitution in production and consumption, and on the size and nature of the initial distortions. Nevertheless, the upper limit of the usual range of estimates in developed economies places the potential gains from efficient full-employment reallocations at no more than about two percent. And the losses due to unemployment of factors have been estimated for developed economies to average about five percent in the sixties and eight percent in the seventies. Thus, if anything, the welfare losses from income inequality appear to outweigh them.

The only real issue is to what extent welfare gains through redistribution might damage growth prospects through possible adverse changes in savings and in work incentives. The empirical evidence on this score is inconclusive and confounded by issues such as: would an equalising redistribution increase the rate of growth of demand, thereby permitting fuller utilisation of factors, especially capital? Would it raise the rate of accumulation of human capital, thereby substituting higher accumulation of one form of capital for another? Would redistribution change the structure of demand so that growth more in accord with inherent comparative advantage is possible? What effect would redistribution have on rates of innovation and technical change? How would an equalising redistribution affect the adverse externalities of growth?

No one knows the answers to these questions. Our estimates shed some light on potential tradeoffs by indicating the upper limits on welfare gains to society attainable through redistribution. They also shed light on a further potential three-way tradeoff: that between higher static inequality, higher economic growth rate, and higher income mobility. They suggest that this particular tradeoff is likely to be quite small since differences in social stratification and economic performance as large as those between the United States and Great Britain in the sixties led to quite similar social welfare gains through dynamic income prospect equalisation.

Table 1

DYNAMIC MOBILITY INDICES: GREAT BRITAIN, $\alpha = \dfrac{1}{\text{Mean income}} = $ .00153

	Dalton Index F_D				Atkinson Index F_A		
β	Period 1	Period 2	Period 5	Period 10	Period 11	Period 2	Period 5	Period 10
1.	.96297	96594	.96638	.96638	.93595	.93744	.93782	.93782
.2	.96297	.96810	.96973	.96975	.93595	.93777	.93910	.93912
.3	.96297	.96974	.97321	.97323	.93595	.93728	.93990	.94009
.4	.96297	.97105	.97685	.97731	.93595	.93622	.94014	.94066
.5	.96297	.97215	.98064	.98188	.93595	.93476	.93962	.94109
.6	.96297	.97311	.98447	.98704	.93595	.93301	.93801	.94121
.7	.96297	.97400	.98823	.99239	.93595	.93106	.93500	.94047
.8	.96297	.97484	.99174	.99688	.93595	.92897	.93033	.93534
.9	.96297	.97565	.99478	.99907	.93595	.92680	.92393	.92805
1.0	.96297	.97646	.99713	1.0000	.93595	.92457	.91590	.91349

Source: Indices Computed from Glass data, using formulae given in text.

Table 2

DYNAMIC MOBILITY INDICES, UNITED STATES $\alpha = \dfrac{1}{\text{Mean income}} = $ .000202 $\beta = .4$

	Dalton Index F_D				Atkinson Index F_A			
	Period 1	Period 2	Period 5	Period 10	Period 1	Period 2	Period 5	Period 10
Father to First Job	.95262	.95929	.96603	.96666	.91147	.90296	.90508	.90578
First job to 1962	.95236	.96037	.96764	.96776	.91007	.90188	.90492	.90500
Father to Present	.95262	.95825	.96628	.96635	.91147	.90292	.90545	.90570

Source: Indices Computed from Duncan and Blau data, using formulae given in text.

Table 3

DYNAMIC MOBILITY INDICES, SENSITIVITY TO α – GREAT BRITAIN, $\beta = .3$

	Dalton Index F_D				Atkinson Index F_A		
α	Period 1	Period 2	Period 5	Period 10	Period 11	Period 2	Period 5	Period 10
.00001	.99947	.99946	.99949	.99950	.99947	.99946	.99948	.99950
.00005	.99739	.99736	.99746	.99747	.99735	.99730	.99740	.99741
.00010	.99492	.99489	.99510	.99511	.99475	.99467	.99487	.99488
.00050	.97947	.98042	.98156	.98163	.97582	.97575	.97668	.97573
.00100	.96846	.97186	.97417	.97426	.95614	.95655	.95829	.95838
.00153	.96297	.96974	.97321	.97323	.93595	.93728	.93990	.94009

Source: Indices Computed from Glass data, using formulae given in the text.

Table 4

DYNAMIC MOBILITY INDICES, UNITED STATES FIVE YEAR MOBILITY,

$$\alpha = \frac{1}{\text{Mean income}} = .000250$$

	Dalton Index F_D					Atkinson Index F_A		
β	Period 1	Period 2	Period 5	Period 10	Period 11	Period 2	Period 5	Period 10
.1	.88550	.89128	.89247	.89247	.82167	.82229	.82318	.82318
.2	.88550	.89508	.89958	.89963	.82167	.82014	.82325	.82331
.3	.88550	.89758	.90728	.90767	.82167	.81603	.82199	.82237
.4	.88550	.89925	.91579	.91735	.82167	.81051	.81901	.82057
.5	.88550	.90039	.92507	.92936	.82167	.80397	.81351	.81780
.6	.88550	.9012	.93134	.94297	.82167	.79669	.80854	.81496
.7	.88550	.91985	.96359	.97650	.82167	.79078	.79925	.81264
.8	.88550	.92129	.97482	.99049	.82167	.78444	.78483	.80279
.9	.88550	.92558	.98958	.99815	.82167		.76507	.77359

Source: Indices Computed from Schiller data, using formulae given in the text.

[16]

Some Dynamic Aspects of Rural Poverty in India

Irma Adelman
K Subbarao
Prem Vashishtha

Studies on income distribution have tended to be point observations and throw little light on longer-term movements in relative inequality. Analysis of movement in poverty ratios on the basis of data on rural households collected by the NCAER for three years between 1968 and 1971, using probability models, have led the authors of the paper to conclude that long-term trends are divergent for different states. For seven states—Assam, Jammu and Kashmir, Kerala, Madhya Pradesh, Punjab, Rajasthan and Tamil Nadu—a reduction in poverty ratios can be reasonably expected, while for Bihar, Orissa and Maharashtra, the converse holds true.

The analysis, the authors conclude, suggests that a two-pronged strategy combining technical improvements in agricultural production, along with greater absorption of rural labour into non-agricultural activity like the food-for-work programme offers the greatest probability for reduction of rural poverty in India.

STUDIES of rural poverty in India have generally concentrated on the static aspects of income or expenditure inequality (Bardhan and Srinivasan, 1974). Some of the recent studies estimated the past trends in the rural poverty ratio as well as the trends in the Gini ratios for different Indian states (Ahluwalia, 1978; Gupta, *et al*, 1983). The insights into the static aspects of poverty provided by these studies can be enriched by dynamic perspectives based on the mobility patterns of households from one income class to another over time and the underlying causal nexus behind such income mobility. This paper makes an attempt in this direction. It generates the long-run income distributions implicit in the observed income mobility patterns of rural households during 1968-1971. It then compares the long-run income distributions toward which different states of India are tending with the prevailing income distributions and with past income distribution and poverty trends.

DATA

The study is based on survey data collected by the National Council of Applied Economic Research (NCAER), known as the All India Rural Income Survey (ARIS) for the years 1968-69, 1969-70, and 1970-71. This Survey collected information on rural household incomes from the same set of rural households in each of three consecutive years.

The survey was based on a sample of 4,118 rural households selected in 1968-69 according to a multistage stratified probability sample design so as to provide a representative cross-section of households from high-, middle-, and low-income groups in rural areas.[1] These households were then reinterviewed in a second (1969-70) and a third (1970-71) round.

METHODOLOGY

Since the income information in the ARIS was collected from the same households at three points in time, it can be used to estimate a Markov household income mobility matrix. The typical element in this matrix, P, represents the probability, p_{ij}, that a household which has an income in range i at time t will have an income in range

j at time (t+1). We shall refer to p_{ij} as a transition probability. The transition probabilities, p_{ij}, were estimated as the proportion of households in the ARIS which moved from income range i to income range j between a pair of years. Three income mobility matrices were constructed from the ARIS data: one from 1968-69 to 1969-70, one for 1969-70 to 1970-71, and one for 1968-69 to 1970-71. The Markov model assumes that the p_{ij} s are conditioned only on the household's position in the current period, are constant, and independent of the history of how the household got to its present income position. Both assumptions are, of course, approximations. Since the data permitted the construction of three different matrices, P, we shall be in a position to test the first assumption but not the second.

The application of income mobility matrices to studies of income dynamics has a long history (for a literature summary, see Shorrocks, 1979; Adelman and Whitte, 1980). But the present data set is the first data set which permits the application of this theory to a developing country.

The income mobility matrix can be used to study the probable future income dynamics. If we take S to be a vector portraying the size distribution of income at time t, then, under the above constancy assumptions, the size distribution of income at (t+1), S_{t+1}, will be given by:

(1) $\quad S_{t+1} = S_t \cdot P$.

If the income mobility matrix, P, is ergodic (i e, if one can get to any state from any other state in P in a finite number of steps),[2] then a unique equilibrium size distribution of income exists and that distribution is independent of the initial size distribution of income.

The equilibrium size distribution of income, S_e, which describes the long-run tendencies of the system, can be found by noting that since the equilibrium distribution must be stationary we must have:

(2) $\quad S_e = S_e P$,

or

(3) $\quad S_e(I-P) = 0$.

Therefore, S_e must be the eigenvector cor-

responding to the largest eigenvalue of P.

We calculate the vector, S_e, for each Indian state and compare them with the current size distributions. The vector, S_e, also provides a reasonable test of the constancy of P. Given two matrices, P_1 and P_2, applying to two different time periods in the same state, a reasonable test of constancy would be given by the Euclidian distance between S_{e1} and S_{e2}. This distance can vary between 0 and $\sqrt{2}$. For all states except Karnataka, the Euclidian distance is quite small. In Karnataka, however, the expected direction of the change in poverty ratio differs among the three matrices. We, therefore, reject the constancy assumption for Karnataka but accept it for all other states.

INITIAL AND LONG-RUN DISTRIBUTIONS: A COMPARISON

The income mobility matrices and the final (long-run) income distributions for the 15 Indian states are presented in the Appendix.[3] Using equation (3), we computed the long-run and initial Gini ratios and the proportion of population below the poverty line (poverty ratio) for different states.

Following earlier approaches (Bardhan and Srinivasan, 1974; Ahluwalia, 1978), the poverty line adopted by us represents a minimum income of Rs 15 per capita at 1960-61 prices. Bardhan (1970) has shown that a consumer expenditure level of Rs 15 in 1960-61 at rural prices corresponds to Rs 20 per person at all-India 1960-61 prices. Since then, the norm of Rs 15 per capita at 1960-61 prices has been used by researchers for defining the poverty line for rural India. Although this norm was meant to represent a nutritionally minimum specified consumption bundle, it may be misleading to interpret the poverty line to indicate the extent of malnutrition (Sukhatme, 1978). Nevertheless, as Ahluwalia points out, this level is indicative of "an extremely low level of living" (*op cit*, p 7).

Summaries of the results pertaining to the initial and long-run Gini ratios and to the poverty ratios are presented in Tables 1 and 2 along with the past trends observed by Ahluwalia. It is interesting to ask how fast the "long-run" distribution would be attained if the income mobility matrices were to

Economic and Political Weekly Vol XX, No 39
Review of Agriculture, September 28, 1985

A-103

remain constant. To answer this question we computed the 10th and 20th powers of the income mobility matrix, P. For all but four states, at least one of the transition probability matrices converges to the equilibrium vector within 10 years. The remaining four—Jammu and Kashmir, Kerala, Tamil Nadu and West Bengal—converge to equilibrium in 20 years. One would not, of course, expect the income mobility matrices to remain constant over time. Nevertheless, these results suggest that the tendencies we discuss are, in some sense, medium-run tendencies. Also, to the extent that the tendencies we describe did not materialise, there is some indication of nonconstancy in the income mobility matrices.

CONCENTRATION

In general, the coefficients of concentration of income estimated by us from the NCAER data are higher than the corresponding estimates for the concentration of consumption expenditure based on the National Sample Survey (NSS) data (Table 2). It is, of course, reasonable to expect the Gini ratios of *income* to be larger than the Gini ratios of *consumption expenditure*. There are also conceptual and sampling design differences between the two surveys which tend to show higher concentration in the NCAER data. Bardhan (1970) points out that (1) the NSS sample, though much larger than the NCAER sample, under-represents the very rich and (2) the NSS procedure of valuation of home-grown and market pruchases of cereal stocks shows less inequality in consumption than does the NCAER procedure. Finally, our initial concentration coefficients apply to 1968-1971 rather than to 1968-1974. Our primary interest, however, is in the direction of change rather than in the absolute

magnitudes of the Gini ratios.

The long-run Gini ratios for all states except Gujarat are lower than the initial ratios, and the direction of change is in conformity with past trends except for Kerala (Table 2). Yet, the welfare implications of the decline in relative inequality are ambiguous in all cases, except Punjab (including Haryana) and Bihar, because the initial and long-run Lorenz curves intersect. Furthermore, in 8 out of 13 states, they intersect in the bottom two decile range.

The cases of Punjab and Bihar require comment. Both states show declining concentration. In the case of Punjab, the long-run poverty ratio also declines along with a fall in the Gini ratio (Table 2). In Bihar, however, the long-run poverty ratio rises explosively from the already high initial level of 55.3 per cent to 77.7 per cent, so that the decline in relative inequality in the long-run is merely indicative of the prospective increasing immiserisation of the vast majority of the population of the state.[4]

POVERTY RATIOS

Bihar is not the only state to show a long-run rise in the poverty ratio. The long-run poverty ratios are higher than the initial levels in Gujarat, Maharashtra and Orissa (Table 1). In all other states the long-run poverty ratios are lower than the initial ratios. But despite this, the long-run poverty ratio may be expected to exceed 50 per cent in Maharashtra, Bihar and Orissa and to be about 40 per cent in Madhya Pradesh.

It is interesting to compare the direction of change in the poverty ratio from the initial to the final (long-run) level derived from our study with the direction of change between 1957-58 and 1960-61 and between 1968-69 and 1973-74 based on past trends estimated

by Ahluwalia (1978). Our long-run results suggest a continuation of past trends estimated by Ahluwalia in seven states. A continued reduction in the poverty ratio is implicit in the mobility patterns of Andhra Pradesh, Kerala, Punjab (including Haryana) and Tamil Nadu, and a continued rise in poverty in Bihar, Gujarat, and Orissa. In other states, while Ahluwalia's past trends show a rise in the poverty ratio for Assam, Madhya Pradesh, Rajasthan, Uttar Pradesh, and West Bengal, or long-run direction of change suggests a reduction in the ratio. In Maharashtra, past trends show a small reduction, but the long-run direction of change indicates a substantial rise in the poverty ratio.

In order to explore the inter-state differences in the long-run dynamics underlying the poverty ratios, we arranged the states in descending order of these ratios at the initial and the long-run situations (Table 3).

At the initial situation, the following states fall in the high poverty zone: Bihar and Orissa in the east, Madhya Pradesh in central India, Tamil Nadu in the south, and Jammu and Kashmir in the north. Only Punjab falls in the low poverty zone while the rest are in the middle. In the long-run situation, the eastern states of Bihar and Orissa show the least dynamism and continue to be in the high poverty zone along with Maharashtra. Assam and Uttar Pradesh join Punjab in the low poverty zone in the long-run.[5]

In the following section, we further explore the inter-state disparities in the long-run dynamics relating to reductions in relative inequality and the levels of absolute poverty.

LOGIT ANALYSIS

What are the systematic bases for predicting whether the poverty ratio in a state may be expected to increase or diminish? To answer this question we perform a multinomial logit analysis on the states grouped by similarity in the expected long-run changes in poverty ratios implicit in their past income dynamics. We exclude Karnataka from this analysis since the income mobility matrices in this state did not pass the test of constancy over time. Each remaining state appears as three observations, except for Bihar and Jammu and Kashmir, which appear each as two observations, since in each of these states one income mobility matrix was non-ergodic. Thus, we are left with 40 observations. These 40 observations are classified into three groups: (1) where long-run poverty is increasing substantially by more than 15 percentage points (consisting of Bihar and Maharashtra); (2) where the change in poverty is small, less than five percentage points in either direction (comprising of Andhra Pradesh, Gujarat, Orissa, Uttar Pradesh and West Bengal); and (3) where the long-run decrease in poverty is expected to be large, over 20 per cent of

TABLE 1: PAST TRENDS AND EXPECTED LONG-RUN BEHAVIOUR OF POVERTY RATIO IN INDIAN STATES

State	Past Trends in Poverty Ratio Computed from Ahluwalia's Study			Long-Run Expected Behaviour of Poverty Derived from Present Study		
	Average for:		Direction of Change	Initial (1968-69 to 1970-71)	Long-Run	Direction of Change
	1957-58 to 1960-61	1968-69 to 1973-74				
Andhra Pradesh	50.8	42.7	−	40.2	37.3	−
Assam	28.3	40.6	+	30.9	9.8	−
Bihar	52.3	58.9	+	55.3	77.7	+
Gujarat	36.6	40.7	+	32.8	36.9	+
Jammu and Kashmir	a			53.8	28.0	−
Karnataka	43.1	51.0	+	42.5	43.0	+
Kerala	59.9	58.6	−	36.5	27.6	−
Madhya Pradesh	49.3	53.7	+	56.6	40.8	−
Maharashtra	51.5	50.4	−	49.9	66.5	+
Orissa	64.1	64.7	+	51.1	54.0	+
Punjab (including Haryana)	23.7	23.5	−	11.4	4.0	−
Rajasthan	32.9	37.7	+	44.0	27.7	−
Tamil Nadu	62.0	55.6	−	57.8	37.5	−
Uttar Pradesh	42.3	44.8	+	22.6	19.8	−
West Bengal	54.7	70.3	+	41.1	36.2	−
All India	48.0	50.1	+	44.0	31.7	−

Note: a Blanks indicate no data available.
Source: Past trends computed from Ahluwalia (1978); others are based on present study.

ECONOMIC AND POLITICAL WEEKLY

Review of Agriculture   September 1985

the base year poverty ratio. This last group includes both states in which the absolute decline in poverty is expected to be large (over 15 percentage points) such as Assam, Jammu and Kashmir, Madhya Pradesh,

Rajasthan, and Tamil Nadu and states in which there is a substantial decline from an already relatively low base (Kerala and Punjab).

The N-chotomous logit model provides a

framework for estimating the probabilities that, in a given state, the proportion of households that is in poverty will be increasing, staying constant, or decreasing. In this model, the dependent variable is the probability that a specific state will fall in one particular long-run poverty group out of k groups. The probability that state i is in poverty group h is assumed to be a random function of a vector of coefficients, α, and a vector of attributes, X. Let

$$Y_i = X_i \, \alpha + \varepsilon_i$$

and assume that the ith state is assigned to group h if Y_i lies between the values a_{h-1} and a_h, that there are k states, and that ε_i is distributed in a standard logistic density function. Then the *a priori* probability that state i is in poverty group h, $P(Y_i = h)$, is given by

$$P(Y_i = h) = \frac{e^{X_i \alpha_i}}{\sum\limits_{k=1}^{K} e^{X_i \alpha_k}}.$$

The model was estimated by maximum likelihood method. The results of the estimation yield two classification functions—one estimating the probability that a given observation falls in Group 2 and the other estimating the probability that it falls in Group 3. (The probability that it falls in Group 1 can be derived from the other two probabilities and is not estimated independently.) Several different classification functions were estimated. We were limited to four independent variables or less by the fact that one group, Group 1, has only five observations. To derive the classification functions, we proceeded as follows. We first used step-wise discriminant analysis to select the best two variables for the logistic function and then estimated the logistic function for all three-variable functions, adding the remaining n−2 variables one at a time. Having selected the best three-variable logit function, we then added a fourth variable to it, again, adding one of the remaining n−3 variables one at a time. The criterion we used for "best" in this process was that the subset of variables selected yield the classification functions which result in the smallest number of misclassifications.

The best logistic functions comprise only three variables. They perform remarkably well in producing the original assignment of states into three groups by expected poverty performance. The two functions succeed in classifying all but three observations correctly. The incorrectly classified observations are Jammu and Kashmir and Maharashtra, both in 1968-69, and Gujarat in 1969-70. Maharashtra in 1968-69 appears to have shared the characteristics of states in which poverty is increasing, Jammu and Kashmir in 1968-69 was more akin to states with little change in poverty, and Gujarat in 1969-70 was closer to states in which poverty is

TABLE 2: PAST TRENDS AND LONG-RUN EXPECTED BEHAVIOUR OF RELATIVE INEQUALITY IN INDIAN STATES

State	Past Trends in the Gini Ratio of Rural Consumer Expenditure from Ahluwalia's Study			Expected Long-Run Behaviour of Gini Ratios of Rural Income Derived from Present Study			
	Average for:		Direction of Change[a]	Initial (1968-69 to 1970-71)	Long-Run	Direction of Change	Remarks: Do the Initial and Long-Run Lorenz Curves Intersect?
	1957-58 to 1960-61	1968-69 to 1973-74					
Andhra Pradesh	0.32	0.29	−	0.47	0.40	−	Yes, at top decile
Assam	0.27	0.21	−	0.31	0.21	−	Yes, at top decile
Bihar	0.37	0.28	−	0.46	0.30	−	No
Gujarat	0.30	0.27	−	0.42	0.43	+	Yes, at several places
Jammu and Kashmir	b			0.40	0.35	−	Yes, at several places
Karnataka	0.33	0.30	−	0.46	0.44	−	Yes, at top and bottom deciles
Kerala	0.34	0.36	+	0.44	0.38	−	Yes, at bottom decile
Madhya Pradesh	0.33	0.31	−	0.43	0.37	−	Yes, at bottom decile
Maharashtra	0.29	0.28	−	0.54	0.39	−	Yes, at several places
Orissa	0.34	0.30	−	0.46	0.36	−	Yes, at top and bottom deciles
Punjab (including Haryana)	0.33	0.29	−	0.38	0.32	−	No
Rajasthan	0.36	0.35	−	0.47	0.39	−	Yes, at top and bottom deciles
Tamil Nadu	0.32	0.28	−	0.48	0.36	−	Yes, at second decile from bottom
Uttar Pradesh	0.30	0.28	−	0.41	0.38	−	Yes, at several places
West Bengal	0.33	0.29	−	0.43	0.38	−	Yes, at bottom decile
All India	0.33	0.29	−	0.47	0.42	−	Yes, at top and bottom deciles

Notes: a Ahluwalia does not report whether or not the Lorenz curves intersect.
    b Blanks indicate no data available.
Source: Past trends computed from Ahluwalia (1978); others derived from present study.

TABLE 3: RANKING OF STATES IN DESCENDING ORDER OF POVERTY AT THE INITIAL AND LONG-RUN SITUATIONS

High > 50 Per Cent	Medium 20-50 Per Cent	Low < 20 Per Cent
	Initial Situation	
Tamil Nadu	Maharashtra	Punjab (including Haryana)
Madhya Pradesh	Rajasthan	
Bihar	Karnataka	
Jammu and Kashmir	West Bengal	
Orissa	Andhra Pradesh	
	Kerala	
	Gujarat	
	Assam	
	Uttar Pradesh	
	Long-Run Situation	
Bihar	Madhya Pradesh	Uttar Pradesh
Maharashtra	Tamil Nadu	Assam
Orissa	Andhra Pradesh	Punjab (including Haryana)
	Gujarat	
	West Bengal	
	Jammu and Kashmir	
	Rajasthan	
	Kerala	

Source: Derived from Table 1.

declining rapidly. But since no state was consistently misclassified, these misclassifications appear to be more or less random deviations. The mean probability of states in each group belonging to the groups in which they were originally classified is high: 0.59 for Group 1, 0.67 for Group 2, and 0.81 for Group 3.

The list of potential variables is reproduced in Table 4. The best classification functions are given by

$$Y_2 = .827\ X_1 + .0079\ X_2 - .0175\ X_3$$
$$\quad\quad (.240)\quad\quad (.0032)\quad\quad (.011)$$

$$Y_3 = 2.42\ X_1 + .137\ X_2 - .108\ X_3$$
$$\quad\quad (1.12)\quad\quad (.088)\quad\quad (.072)$$

where X_1 is our index of rainfall, X_2 is the change in the rate of foodgrain production, and X_3 is the proportion of agricultural landless labour in the rural population.

By far the most significant variable conditioning poverty performance in rural India appears to be the extent of rainfall.[6] Its F ratio is 6.5; the next closest variable has an F ratio of 3.9. This finding is consistent with econometric analysis of supply responsiveness of Indian farmers based on all India time series (Lahiri, 1983). Lahiri found that the supply elasticity of rice is quite sensitive to rainfall, albeit in a non-linear manner. In contrast, the estimated price elasticity of Indian rice supply functions in Lahiri's study turned out to be fairly low and the expectations of farmers static. Studies on aggregate supply response show that the magnitude of the supply elasticity of irrigation variable is three times that of the price (terms of trade) variable (Krishna, 1983). These studies, therefore, imply a paucity of policy levers on the supply side other than those which affect agricultural productivity directly, namely, rainfall and irrigation. In addition, agronomic studies (for a summary, see Dastane, 1970) indicate that the new high yielding varieties are more dependent on rainfall than traditional varieties.

The second variable associated with poverty reduction is the growth in foodgrain production. Its F ratio, after rainfall is included, becomes 3.9. The association of a decrease in poverty with greater food production is consistent with the finding that agricultural workers are net buyers of rice in India. Periods of high production, in which prices are relatively low and demand for rural labour high, should, therefore, benefit the very poor by raising both their nominal and real incomes.

The final variable associated with poverty reduction is the per cent of agricultural workers in the total population. Its F ratio, once both prior variables are included, is 4.2. The larger the percentage of agricultural labour, the less poverty reduction. This finding is consistent with the labour surplus theory of Lewis as well as with the labour market studies of Bardhan and Rudra summarised in Bardhan (1984).

CONCLUSION

The present analysis adds a dynamic dimension to the discussion of poverty trends by calculating the long-run dynamics implicit in the household income mobility of a stratified sample of rural Indian households between 1968-69 and 1970-71.

The trends implicit in the data, if continued, give cause for optimism. The analysis suggests that seven states—Assam, Jammu and Kashmir, Kerala, Madhya Pradesh, Punjab, Rajasthan and Tamil Nadu—are likely to experience reduction in the poverty ratio. There are only three states falling in the long-run high poverty range—the predominantly rainfed Bihar and Orissa in the east, and the predominantly millet-growing Maharashtra. This is not surprising inasmuch as the constraints to growth faced by the two eastern states are well known and formidable: high density of population and heavy pressure of population on the agricultural sector; low and weather-induced fluc-

A-106

TABLE 4: VARIABLES INCLUDED IN THE STUDY

Serial and State Number	NSAC	AG NDP	Agri Lab	SCH Caste	Literacy	Infra	GDP PC	FGRT	Rainfall	IRRI Ratio	ΔIRRI Ratio	ΔAGR Prod	ΔFood Grains	ΔNDP	ΔFood Price Index	Grouping Variable Code
									1968-69 to 1969-70							
1 Andhra Pradesh	1.8	46.00	33.35	17.10	29.90	88	1,002	1.68	3	30.79	5.6	11.0	8.0	9.0	5.6	2
2 Assam	1.2	50.00	8.45	17.20	43.10	88	866	2.36	3	21.20	-14.4	-1.5	-8.7	3.0	-14.4	2
3 Bihar	1.1	46.00	30.35	22.90	26.00	100	735	1.92	1	24.77	9.5	-0.5	-15.5	23.5	9.5	1
4 Gujarat	2.7	36.00	19.19	20.80	43.80	121	1,452	3.56	1	12.46	7.1	19.5	36.2	17.0	7.1	3
5 Jammu and Kashmir	1.8	44.00	22.50	21.50	36.20	100	1,189	2.00	0	38.22	5.7	6.0	-4.5	5.0	5.7	3
6 Kerala	2.0	49.00	27.60	9.60	69.20	147	968	1.39	3	20.43	3.7	2.0	-13.3	6.0	3.7	3
7 Madhya Pradesh	2.3	27.00	20.96	33.10	27.80	61	896	1.67	1	7.15	6.9	8.0	3.3	4.0	6.9	1
8 Maharashtra	2.8	57.00	31.50	11.90	47.40	117	1,639	1.77	1	8.32	3.6	-3.0	-3.5	2.0	3.6	2
9 Orissa	1.7	54.00	23.14	38.20	34.10	80	857	1.19	2	17.55	-2.1	1.2	-7.4	8.0	-2.1	3
10 Punjab	2.5	56.00	17.19	24.70	40.70	207	1,900	6.50	3	73.72	1.0	11.0	20.8	8.0	1.0	3
11 Rajasthan	2.9	56.00	4.83	27.90	24.10	70	925	2.97	3	16.39	8.9	26.0	18.4	4.0	8.9	2
12 Tamil Nadu	1.3	32.00	32.44	18.60	45.80	142	1,036	1.83	2	45.54	8.9	12.0	15.1	8.0	8.9	2
13 Uttar Pradesh	1.1	51.00	14.74	21.20	27.40	113	916	2.79	3	34.24	11.5	10.0	7.7	7.0	11.5	3
14 West Bengal	1.6	35.00	33.67	25.60	40.90	144	1,313	2.72	2	21.82	-1.4	14.0	2.3	4.0	-1.4	2
									1969-70 to 1970-71							
15 Andhra Pradesh	1.8	46.0	33.35	17.10	29.90	88	1,002	1.68	3	30.79	-6.3	10.0	0.1	6.0	-6.3	2
16 Assam	1.2	50.00	8.45	17.20	43.10	68	866	2.36	3	21.20	10.4	5.0	0.9	2.0	10.4	2
17 Gujarat	2.7	36.00	19.19	20.80	43.80	121	1,452	3.56	1	12.46	0.5	35.8	37.8	25.0	0.5	3
18 Jammu and Kashmir	1.8	44.00	22.50	21.50	36.20	100	1,189	2.00	0	38.22	4.2	-8.0	-18.3	1.0	4.2	3
19 Kerala	2.0	41.00	27.60	9.60	69.20	147	968	1.39	3	20.43	6.7	3.0	6.5	4.0	6.7	3
20 Madhya Pradesh	2.3	49.00	20.96	33.10	27.80	61	898	1.67	3	7.15	-5.9	9.0	11.8	3.0	-5.9	2
21 Maharashtra	2.8	27.00	31.50	11.90	47.40	117	1,637	1.77	1	8.32	5.0	-15.0	-19.1	3.0	5.0	3
22 Orissa	1.7	57.00	23.14	38.20	34.10	80	857	1.19	1	17.55	-1.3	0.9	1.4	3.0	-1.3	1
23 Punjab	2.5	54.00	17.19	24.70	40.70	207	1,900	6.50	2	73.72	-2.8	4.0	3.3	4.0	-2.8	3
24 Rajasthan	2.9	56.00	4.83	27.90	24.10	70	925	2.97	2	16.39	-17.7	15.0	86.1	14.0	-17.7	3
25 Tamil Nadu	1.3	32.00	32.44	18.60	45.80	142	1,036	1.83	3	45.54	-13.1	11.0	11.7	8.0	-13.1	3
26 Uttar Pradesh	1.1	51.00	14.74	21.20	27.40	113	916	2.79	3	34.24	-10.3	9.0	11.6	5.0	-10.3	2
27 West Bengal	1.6	35.00	33.67	25.60	40.90	144	1,313	2.72	2	21.82	3.7	6.0	1.8	0.0	3.7	2
									1968-69 to 1970-71							
28 Andhra Pradesh	1.8	46.00	33.35	17.10	29.90	88	1,002	1.68	3	30.79	-0.6	23.0	8.2	15.0	-0.6	2
29 Assam	1.2	50.00	8.45	17.20	43.10	88	866	2.36	3	21.20	-3.6	4.0	-11.7	5.0	-3.6	2
30 Bihar	1.1	46.00	30.35	22.90	26.00	100	735	1.92	1	24.77	11.0	17.0	-11.2	40.0	11.0	1
31 Gujarat	2.7	36.00	19.19	20.80	43.80	121	1,452	3.56	1	12.46	7.6	62.3	87.7	46.0	7.6	3
32 Kerala	2.0	41.00	27.60	9.60	69.20	147	968	1.39	3	20.43	10.6	5.0	-7.7	8.0	10.6	3
33 Madhya Pradesh	2.3	49.00	20.96	33.10	27.80	61	896	1.67	3	7.15	0.9	18.0	15.4	6.0	0.9	2
34 Maharashtra	2.8	27.00	31.50	11.90	47.40	117	1,637	1.77	1	8.32	8.9	-18.0	-21.9	5.0	8.9	3
35 Orissa	1.7	57.00	23.14	38.20	34.10	80	857	1.19	1	17.55	-3.4	2.0	-6.1	11.0	-3.4	1
36 Punjab	2.5	54.00	17.19	24.70	40.70	207	1,900	6.50	2	73.72	-1.9	15.0	24.9	23.0	-1.9	3
37 Rajasthan	2.9	56.00	4.83	27.90	24.10	70	925	2.97	2	16.39	-8.1	45.0	120.4	14.0	-8.1	3
38 Tamil Nadu	1.3	32.00	32.44	18.60	45.80	142	1,036	1.83	3	45.54	-3.8	24.0	28.6	12.0	-3.8	2
39 Uttar Pradesh	1.1	51.00	14.74	21.20	27.40	113	916	2.79	3	34.24	1.0	20.0	20.1	12.0	1.0	2
40 West Bengal	1.6	35.00	33.67	25.60	40.90	144	1,313	2.72	2	21.82	3.7	20.0	4.6	4.0	3.7	2

Notes: NSAC = Net area sown per cultivator (1971); AGNDP = Agriculture's contribution to net domestic product (1970-71); Agrilab = Proportion of agricultural labour population to rural population; Sch Caste = Proportion of scheduled caste population to rural population; Literacy = Rate of literacy (per cent); Infra = Index of infrastructure (computed by the Centre for Monitoring Indian Economy, Bombay); GDPPC = Gross domestic product per capita (1970-71); FGRT = Linear growth rate of foodgrains output; Rainfall = Dummy variable derived as follows: 0 = States with bad rainfall in all three relevant years; 1 = States with bad rainfall in one year and bad rainfall in two years and bad rainfall in one year; 3 = States with good rainfall in all three years; A shortfall of more than 25 per cent from normal rainfall is regarded as bad rainfall. However, states which received rainfall more than 2,000 mm (irrespective of departure from normal rainfall) are classified as having had "good rainfall"; Irri Ratio = Gross irrigated area as a per cent of gross cropped area, averaged for three years; ΔIrri Ratio = Per cent change in the gross irrigated area under cultivation; ΔAgr Prod = Per cent change in the index of agricultural production; ΔFoodgrains = Per cent change in the output of foodgrains; ΔNDP = Per cent change in the net domestic product at current prices; ΔFood Price Index = Per cent change in the index of staple foods consumed by agricultural labourers; Grouping Variable Code: 1 = Deteriorating states, 2 = states with small change, and 3 = states with large improvement.

Review of Agriculture September 1985

ECONOMIC AND POLITICAL WEEKLY

APPENDIX TABLE 1: ANDHRA PRADESH

Income Class	Income Mobility Matrix								Long-Run Size Distribution of Income
	Income Class								Per Cent of Population Computed from:
	1	2	3	4	5	6	7	8	
	1968-69 to 1969-70								
1	0.354	0.305	0.146	0.085	0.073	0.012	0.012	0.012	.21708
2	0.246	0.393	0.197	0.131	0.016	0.0	0.016	0.0	.34135
3	0.100	0.400	0.300	0.050	0.125	0.0	0.025	0.0	.20550
4	0.241	0.207	0.172	0.207	0.069	0.034	0.069	0.0	.12104
5	0.083	0.417	0.250	0.167	0.0	0.083	0.0	0.0	.06463
6	0.077	0.231	0.308	0.385	0.0	0.0	0.0	0.0	.01578
7	0.0	0.091	0.091	0.182	0.364	0.091	0.0	0.182	.02224
8	0.0	0.083	0.083	0.125	0.083	0.125	0.042	0.458	.01237
	1969-70 to 1970-71								
1	0.386	0.421	0.123	0.018	0.018	0.0	0.018	0.018	.21611
2	0.329	0.402	0.122	0.061	0.0	0.037	0.037	0.012	.28678
3	0.098	0.294	0.333	0.157	0.039	0.0	0.059	0.020	.14587
4	0.200	0.171	0.200	0.257	0.086	0.029	0.029	0.029	.11986
5	0.0	0.150	0.250	0.200	0.250	0.0	0.050	0.100	.04703
6	0.0	0.286	0.0	0.429	0.0	0.0	0.143	0.143	.03458
7	0.0	0.0	0.0	0.500	0.0	0.500	0.0	0.0	.04132
8	0.0	0.0	0.0	0.0	0.143	0.0	0.071	0.786	.10845
	1968-69 to 1970-71								
1	0.317	0.415	0.122	0.073	0.049	0.0	0.024	0.0	.23321
2	0.279	0.410	0.164	0.066	0.0	0.033	0.033	0.016	.32359
3	0.225	0.275	0.225	0.175	0.075	0.0	0.0	0.025	.17522
4	0.172	0.207	0.241	0.207	0.069	0.069	0.034	0.0	.11666
5	0.083	0.417	0.250	0.083	0.0	0.0	0.083	0.083	.04316
6	0.231	0.154	0.462	0.077	0.0	0.0	0.0	0.077	.02580
7	0.0	0.0	0.091	0.182	0.182	0.091	0.273	0.182	.03797
8	0.0	0.0	0.0	0.250	0.083	0.083	0.083	0.500	.04439

Source: Computed from National Council of Applied Economic Research Survey.

APPENDIX TABLE 2: ASSAM

Income Class	Income Mobility Matrix								Long-Run Size Distribution of Income
	Income Class								Per Cent of Population Computed from:
	1	2	3	4	5	6	7	8	
	1968-69 to 1969-70								
1	0.207	0.586	0.069	0.138	0.0	0.0	0.0	0.0	.02414
2	0.063	0.417	0.292	0.167	0.063	0.0	0.0	0.0	.14832
3	0.0	0.195	0.317	0.366	0.073	0.049	0.0	0.0	.24359
4	0.0	0.048	0.381	0.286	0.095	0.095	0.048	0.048	.23051
5	0.077	0.0	0.154	0.154	0.077	0.385	0.0	0.154	.12837
6	0.0	0.125	0.125	0.250	0.125	0.250	0.125	0.0	.11094
7	0.0	0.0	0.0	0.0	0.667	0.0	0.333	0.0	.08338
8	0.0	0.0	0.0	0.0	0.0	0.0	1.000	0.0	.03074
	1969-70 to 1970-71								
1	0.100	0.800	0.100	0.0	0.0	0.0	0.0	0.0	.02098
2	0.043	0.617	0.277	0.043	0.021	0.0	0.0	0.0	.31038
3	0.0	0.200	0.550	0.225	0.025	0.0	0.0	0.0	.37492
4	0.027	0.108	0.324	0.432	0.027	0.027	0.054	0.0	.21007
5	0.0	0.0	0.250	0.417	0.250	0.083	0.0	0.0	.04325
6	0.0	0.0	0.091	0.182	0.273	0.273	0.091	0.091	.02006
7	0.0	0.250	0.0	0.0	0.250	0.250	0.250	0.0	.01757
8	0.0	0.0	0.0	0.0	0.333	0.333	0.0	0.333	.00276
	1968-69 to 1970-71								
1	0.069	0.724	0.172	0.034	0.0	0.0	0.0	0.0	.00649
2	0.042	0.396	0.375	0.167	0.0	0.021	0.0	0.0	.14507
3	0.0	0.146	0.341	0.341	0.098	0.024	0.049	0.0	.34571
4	0.0	0.0	0.429	0.429	0.095	0.048	0.0	0.0	.27726
5	0.0	0.231	0.154	0.077	0.308	0.154	0.0	0.077	.10643
6	0.0	0.125	0.375	0.125	0.0	0.125	0.125	0.125	.06238
7	0.0	0.0	0.333	0.0	0.333	0.333	0.0	0.0	.04066
8	0.0	0.0	0.0	0.0	0.0	0.0	1.000	0.0	.01600

Source: Computed from National Council of Applied Economic Research Survey.

ECONOMIC AND POLITICAL WEEKLY   Review of Agriculture   September 1985

APPENDIX TABLE 3: BIHAR

Income Class	Income Mobility Matrix								Long-Run Size Distribution of Income
	Income Class								Per Cent of Population
	1	2	3	4	5	6	7	8	Computed from:
	1968-69 to 1969-70								
1	0.745	0.194	0.051	0.0	0.0	0.010	0.0	0.0	.65890
2	0.545	0.364	0.061	0.0	0.030	0.0	0.0	0.0	.23537
3	0.389	0.222	0.222	0.056	0.0	0.0	0.111	0.0	.06783
4	0.294	0.353	0.176	0.059	0.0	0.0	0.059	0.059	.00757
5	0.800	0.0	0.100	0.0	0.0	0.0	0.100	0.0	.00970
6	0.125	0.125	0.250	0.0	0.250	0.125	0.125	0.0	.00933
7	0.214	0.286	0.0	0.286	0.0	0.143	0.0	0.071	.01012
8	0.0	0.200	0.200	0.400	0.200	0.0	0.0	0.0	.00117
	1969-70 to 1970-71								
1	0.696	0.226	0.052	0.009	0.017	0.0	0.0	0.0	a
2	0.404	0.426	0.085	0.085	0.0	0.0	0.0	0.0	
3	0.167	0.389	0.389	0.056	0.0	0.0	0.0	0.0	
4	0.125	0.250	0.625	0.0	0.0	0.0	0.0	0.0	
5	0.0	0.500	0.0	0.250	0.0	0.250	0.0	0.0	
6	0.0	0.250	0.250	0.250	0.250	0.0	0.0	0.0	
7	0.0	0.0	0.200	0.200	0.400	0.200	0.0	0.0	
8	0.0	0.0	0.0	0.0	0.0	0.0	0.0	1.000	
	1968-69 to 1970-71								
1	0.724	0.214	0.051	0.010	0.0	0.0	0.0	0.0	.58312
2	0.455	0.333	0.061	0.121	0.030	0.0	0.0	0.0	.26774
3	0.222	0.389	0.278	0.0	0.056	0.056	0.0	0.0	.08248
4	0.294	0.353	0.176	0.059	0.059	0.0	0.0	0.059	.04316
5	0.500	0.200	0.200	0.100	0.0	0.0	0.0	0.0	.01587
6	0.0	0.500	0.250	0.125	0.125	0.0	0.0	0.0	.00509
7	0.214	0.429	0.143	0.071	0.071	0.0	0.0	0.071	.0
8	0.0	0.200	0.600	0.0	0.0	0.200	0.0	0.0	.00255

Note: a The transition matrix is nonergodic.
Source: Computed from National Council of Applied Economic Research Survey.

APPENDIX TABLE 4: GUJARAT

Income Class	Income Mobility Matrix								Long-Run Size Distribution of Income
	Income Class								Per Cent of Population
	1	2	3	4	5	6	7	8	Computed from:
	1968-69 to 1969-70								
1	0.493	0.384	0.082	0.041	0.0	0.0	0.0	0.0	.24017
2	0.232	0.326	0.211	0.147	0.021	0.032	0.011	0.021	.29328
3	0.162	0.311	0.189	0.149	0.068	0.054	0.041	0.027	.16885
4	0.063	0.219	0.250	0.250	0.094	0.031	0.0	0.094	.13629
5	0.174	0.174	0.130	0.261	0.130	0.043	0.087	0.0	.05284
6	0.056	0.167	0.222	0.111	0.167	0.056	0.056	0.167	.03794
7	0.0	0.133	0.067	0.067	0.200	0.267	0.133	0.133	.02428
8	0.143	0.095	0.095	0.095	0.095	0.095	0.095	0.286	.04634
	1969-70 to 1970-71								
1	0.475	0.262	0.113	0.063	0.063	0.0	0.012	0.012	.17390
2	0.280	0.310	0.210	0.110	0.040	0.030	0.020	0.0	.20325
3	0.121	0.276	0.259	0.138	0.103	0.017	0.034	0.052	.18917
4	0.043	0.213	0.298	0.128	0.149	0.064	0.043	0.064	.11819
5	0.0	0.0	0.143	0.286	0.190	0.095	0.0	0.286	.10251
6	0.0	0.125	0.250	0.188	0.125	0.125	0.125	0.063	.06034
7	0.0	0.091	0.0	0.091	0.364	0.0	0.091	0.364	.03505
8	0.056	0.056	0.111	0.0	0.056	0.222	0.056	0.444	.11759
	1968-69 to 1970-71								
1	0.575	0.274	0.096	0.014	0.027	0.014	0.0	0.0	.21033
2	0.253	0.253	0.253	0.137	0.032	0.042	0.011	0.021	.22787
3	0.068	0.338	0.270	0.095	0.149	0.041	0.014	0.027	.18972
4	0.094	0.156	0.281	0.188	0.094	0.063	0.031	0.094	.11585
5	0.043	0.130	0.217	0.174	0.217	0.087	0.087	0.043	.09869
6	0.0	0.056	0.0	0.056	0.111	0.111	0.278	0.389	.04474
7	0.0	0.0	0.200	0.333	0.267	0.0	0.0	0.200	.03337
8	0.048	0.190	0.0	0.143	0.143	0.048	0.048	0.381	.07943

Source: Computed from National Council of Applied Economic Research Survey.

Review of Agriculture September 1985   ECONOMIC AND POLITICAL WEEKLY

APPENDIX TABLE 5: JAMMU AND KASHMIR

Income Class[a]	Income Mobility Matrix[a]							Long-Run Size Distribution of Income
	Income Class							Per Cent of Population
	1	2	3	4	5	6	7 8	Computed from:
	1968-69 to 1969-70							
1	0.233	0.467	0.200	0.100	0.0	0.0	0.0	.06671
2	0.0	0.400	0.300	0.200	0.0	0.100	0.0	.29354
3	0.083	0.250	0.417	0.167	0.0	0.0	0.083	.28961
4	0.167	0.0	0.333	0.167	0.167	0.0	0.167	.16209
5	0.0	0.250	0.500	0.250	0.0	0.0	0.0	.02701
6	0.0	0.0	0.0	0.500	0.0	0.0	0.500	.02935
7} 8	0.0	0.500	0.0	0.0	0.0	0.0	0.500	.13167
	1969-70 to 1970-71							
1	0.444	0.444	0.0	0.111	0.0	0.0	0.0	.16148
2	0.217	0.304	0.261	0.087	0.087	0.0	0.043	.33298
3	0.0	0.611	0.167	0.056	0.167	0.0	0.0	.24743
4	0.200	0.100	0.200	0.300	0.100	0.0	0.100	.08663
5	0.0	0.0	1.000	0.0	0.0	0.0	0.0	.07885
6	0.0	0.0	0.0	1.000	0.0	0.0	0.0	.0
7} 8	0.0	0.0	0.250	0.0	0.0	0.0	0.750	.09263
	1968-69 to 1970-71							
1	0.333	0.367	0.133	0.033	0.100	0.0	0.033	b
2	0.0	0.500	0.200	0.300	0.0	0.0	0.0	
3	0.083	0.250	0.417	0.250	0.0	0.0	0.0	
4	0.0	0.167	0.333	0.0	0.333	0.0	0.167	
5	0.0	0.750	0.0	0.250	0.0	0.0	0.00	
6	0.0	0.0	0.0	0.0	0.500	0.0	0.500	
7	0.0	0.0	0.0	0.0	0.0	0.0	1.000	
8								

Notes: a Groups 7 and 8 were aggregated to produce an ergodic matrix.
    b Blanks indicate the transition matrix is nonergodic.
Source: Computed from National Council of Applied Economic Research Survey.

APPENDIX TABLE 6: KERALA

Income Class	Income Mobility Matrix								Long-Run Size Distribution of Income
	Income Class								Per Cent of Population
	1	2	3	4	5	6	7	8	Computed from:
	1968-69 to 1969-70								
1	0.482	0.373	0.060	0.060	0.0	0.024	0.0	0.0	.21927
2	0.362	0.449	0.130	0.029	0.014	0.0	0.014	0.0	.26749
3	0.043	0.261	0.217	0.174	0.174	0.0	0.087	0.043	.11660
4	0.063	0.188	0.156	0.156	0.125	0.125	0.156	0.031	.10304
5	0.0	0.138	0.172	0.138	0.207	0.172	0.069	0.103	.08704
6	0.0	0.0	0.056	0.278	0.222	0.0	0.222	0.222	.05755
7	0.063	0.0	0.063	0.125	0.188	0.250	0.188	0.125	.08282
8	0.0	0.056	0.056	0.111	0.056	0.056	0.278	0.389	.06619
	1969-70 to 1970-71								
1	0.543	0.329	0.114	0.014	0.0	0.0	0.0	0.0	.05441
2	0.118	0.494	0.294	0.059	0.012	0.012	0.012	0.0	.15596
3	0.027	0.189	0.459	0.216	0.054	0.027	0.027	0.0	.24148
4	0.0	0.030	0.303	0.242	0.121	0.091	0.182	0.030	.13084
5	0.0	0.074	0.222	0.185	0.370	0.074	0.074	0.0	.15357
6	0.0	0.0	0.0	0.0	0.375	0.250	0.250	0.125	.07843
7	0.0	0.0	0.042	0.042	0.292	0.208	0.333	0.083	.11205
8	0.0	0.0	0.0	0.053	0.053	0.053	0.158	0.684	.07326
	1968-69 to 1970-71								
1	0.373	0.325	0.253	0.012	0.012	0.024	0.0	0.0	.08322
2	0.232	0.464	0.217	0.043	0.014	0.014	0.014	0.0	.17428
3	0.022	0.196	0.304	0.130	0.196	0.065	0.043	0.043	.19679
4	0.0	0.156	0.188	0.281	0.125	0.125	0.125	0.0	.11800
5	0.0	0.0	0.241	0.172	0.207	0.103	0.103	0.172	.13847
6	0.0	0.056	0.056	0.167	0.278	0.056	0.333	0.056	.07078
7	0.063	0.0	0.063	0.125	0.188	0.125	0.188	0.250	.11918
8	0.0	0.056	0.111	0.0	0.111	0.056	0.333	0.333	.09927

Source: Computed from National Council of Applied Economic Research Survey.

A-110

ECONOMIC AND POLITICAL WEEKLY   Review of Agriculture   September 1985

APPENDIX TABLE 7: MADHYA PRADESH

Income Class	Income Mobility Matrix								Long-Run Size Distribution of Income
	Income Class								Per Cent of Population Computed from:
	1	2	3	4	5	6	7	8	
	1968-69 to 1969-70								
1	0.446	0.353	0.109	0.043	0.033	0.005	0.0	0.011	.13548
2	0.215	0.366	0.226	0.075	0.043	0.054	0.022	0.0	.23785
3	0.061	0.286	0.184	0.102	0.143	0.061	0.143	0.020	.15933
4	0.068	0.176	0.382	0.176	0.029	0.029	0.059	0.059	.09202
5	0.0	0.231	0.0	0.154	0.308	0.154	0.0	0.154	.11432
6	0.0	0.111	0.333	0.0	0.111	0.222	0.111	0.111	.07935
7	0.0	0.0	0.0	0.125	0.250	0.125	0.375	0.125	.09654
8	0.071	0.071	0.0	0.071	0.071	0.071	0.214	0.429	.08510
	1969-70 to 1970-71								
1	0.376	0.523	0.083	0.009	0.009	0.0	0.0	0.0	.12476
2	0.210	0.452	0.210	0.097	0.016	0.016	0.0	0.0	.29696
3	0.030	0.227	0.303	0.333	0.076	0.030	0.0	0.0	.20342
4	0.067	0.300	0.267	0.133	0.067	0.033	0.100	0.033	.14106
5	0.0	0.115	0.308	0.192	0.115	0.192	0.077	0.0	.05654
6	0.0	0.063	0.125	0.188	0.250	0.063	0.250	0.063	.04061
7	0.0	0.0	0.167	0.111	0.167	0.111	0.278	0.167	.05473
8	0.0	0.0	0.0	0.0	0.0	0.067	0.133	0.800	.08193
	1968-69 to 1970-71								
1	0.293	0.446	0.130	0.082	0.016	0.011	0.011	0.011	.08461
2	0.129	0.355	0.269	0.151	0.032	0.032	0.032	0.0	.25328
3	0.041	0.265	0.286	0.143	0.122	0.082	0.041	0.020	.20702
4	0.029	0.206	0.265	0.265	0.059	0.029	0.118	0.029	.13694
5	0.0	0.154	0.0	0.154	0.385	0.077	0.0	0.231	.08088
6	0.0	0.222	0.111	0.222	0.111	0.111	0.111	0.111	.06143
7	0.0	0.125	0.250	0.0	0.0	0.250	0.250	0.125	.07346
8	0.143	0.071	0.071	0.0	0.0	0.0	0.143	0.571	.10238

Source: Computed from National Council of Applied Economic Research Survey.

APPENDIX TABLE 8: MAHARASHTRA

Income Class	Income Mobility Matrix								Long-Run Size Distribution of Income
	Income Class								Per Cent of Population Computed from:
	1	2	3	4	5	6	7	8	
	1968-69 to 1969-70								
1	0.424	0.404	0.121	0.020	0.030	0.0	0.0	0.0	.21658
2	0.273	0.455	0.121	0.061	0.030	0.030	0.015	0.015	.30577
3	0.184	0.342	0.105	0.184	0.079	0.053	0.026	0.026	.15170
4	0.050	0.250	0.300	0.150	0.050	0.050	0.0	0.150	.08937
5	0.0	0.0	0.182	0.182	0.091	0.091	0.273	0.182	.04231
6	0.0	0.0	0.143	0.286	0.143	0.0	0.143	0.286	.04336
7	0.0	0.143	0.143	0.143	0.0	0.0	0.0	0.571	.03525
8	0.077	0.0	0.231	0.0	0.0	0.154	0.077	0.462	.11566
	1969-70 to 1970-71								
1	0.638	0.290	0.058	0.014	0.0	0.0	0.0	0.0	.33126
2	0.292	0.404	0.191	0.090	0.022	0.0	0.0	0.0	.33153
3	0.108	0.351	0.378	0.108	0.0	0.054	0.0	0.0	.17565
4	0.048	0.333	0.238	0.190	0.048	0.0	0.143	0.0	.08789
5	0.0	0.091	0.091	0.273	0.182	0.091	0.273	0.0	.01422
6	0.0	0.0	0.125	0.375	0.0	0.125	0.0	0.375	.02130
7	0.0	0.429	0.0	0.143	0.0	0.286	0.143	0.0	.02125
8	0.0	0.0	0.105	0.158	0.0	0.105	0.105	0.526	.01690
	1968-69 to 1970-71								
1	0.444	0.364	0.121	0.020	0.020	0.010	0.020	0.0	.26022
2	0.288	0.364	0.212	0.091	0.015	0.015	0.0	0.015	.29955
3	0.263	0.289	0.184	0.079	0.026	0.053	0.053	0.053	.17847
4	0.100	0.250	0.200	0.300	0.050	0.0	0.100	0.0	.11372
5	0.0	0.091	0.182	0.455	0.0	0.182	0.091	0.0	.02018
6	0.0	0.143	0.143	0.143	0.0	0.286	0.286	0.0	.02832
7	0.0	0.143	0.286	0.143	0.0	0.0	0.0	0.429	.03595
8	0.0	0.077	0.154	0.231	0.0	0.0	0.0	0.538	.06361

Source: Computed from National Council of Applied Economic Research Survey.

APPENDIX TABLE 9: KARNATAKA

Income Class	Income Mobility Matrix								Long-Run Size Distribution of Income
	Income Class								Per Cent of Population Computed from:
	1	2	3	4	5	6	7	8	
	1968-69 to 1969-70								
1	0.414	0.356	0.057	0.023	0.046	0.057	0.023	0.023	.07504
2	0.147	0.333	0.227	0.053	0.067	0.053	0.080	0.040	.15253
3	0.023	0.205	0.159	0.205	0.091	0.045	0.091	0.182	.12892
4	0.040	0.200	0.160	0.240	0.080	0.120	0.040	0.120	.17606
5	0.0	0.0	0.077	0.154	0.154	0.308	0.154	0.154	.14715
6	0.091	0.0	0.091	0.455	0.273	0.0	0.091	0.0	.12814
7	0.0	0.067	0.133	0.0	0.333	0.133	0.0	0.333	.07532
8	0.0	0.071	0.071	0.143	0.214	0.286	0.071	0.143	.11686
	1969-70 to 1970-71								
1	0.700	0.260	0.040	0.0	0.0	0.0	0.0	0.0	.49390
2	0.333	0.486	0.167	0.0	0.014	0.0	0.0	0.0	.35119
3	0.237	0.342	0.316	0.053	0.026	0.026	0.0	0.0	.12419
4	0.100	0.367	0.233	0.133	0.067	0.067	0.033	0.0	.01137
5	0.036	0.286	0.214	0.179	0.071	0.071	0.036	0.107	.01085
6	0.0	0.292	0.208	0.125	0.167	0.0	0.083	0.125	.00496
7	0.059	0.353	0.176	0.235	0.176	0.0	0.0	0.0	.00151
8	0.040	0.160	0.200	0.200	0.040	0.080	0.160	0.120	.00204
	1968-69 to 1970-71								
1	0.540	0.287	0.115	0.023	0.023	0.0	0.011	0.0	.26391
2	0.240	0.453	0.213	0.027	0.040	0.027	0.0	0.0	.36300
3	0.136	0.341	0.182	0.114	0.091	0.045	0.0	0.091	.18491
4	0.080	0.320	0.320	0.080	0.0	0.0	0.080	0.120	.06770
5	0.077	0.385	0.231	0.154	0.0	0.0	0.154	0.0	.04666
6	0.0	0.455	0.0	0.273	0.182	0.091	0.0	0.0	.02435
7	0.0	0.133	0.333	0.267	0.133	0.0	0.067	0.067	.02109
8	0.0	0.214	0.143	0.214	0.071	0.143	0.143	0.071	.02838

Source: Computed from National Council of Applied Economic Research Survey.

APPENDIX TABLE 10: ORISSA

Income Class	Income Mobility Matrix								Long-Run Size Distribution of Income
	Income Class								Per Cent of Population Computed from:
	1	2	3	4	5	6	7	8	
	1968-69 to 1969-70								
1	0.613	0.300	0.038	0.025	0.0	0.012	0.0	0.012	.17656
2	0.229	0.542	0.188	0.021	0.0	0.0	0.0	0.021	.42543
3	0.048	0.571	0.190	0.190	0.0	0.0	0.0	0.0	.16655
4	0.0	0.211	0.474	0.263	0.0	0.0	0.053	0.0	.07591
5	0.182	0.091	0.091	0.364	0.182	0.091	0.0	0.0	.00961
6	0.0	0.0	0.143	0.571	0.143	0.0	0.143	0.0	.00433
7	0.0	0.0	0.500	0.0	0.500	0.0	0.0	0.0	.01448
8	0.0	0.0	0.0	0.091	0.0	0.0	0.364	0.545	.02714
	1969-70 to 1970-71								
1	0.714	0.270	0.016	0.0	0.0	0.0	0.0	0.0	.42736
2	0.999	0.463	0.209	0.015	0.015	0.0	0.0	0.0	.33427
3	0.179	0.429	0.214	0.107	0.036	0.036	0.0	0.0	.12500
4	0.0	0.286	0.190	0.286	0.143	0.048	0.048	0.0	.03753
5	0.0	0.0	0.500	0.0	0.0	0.250	0.0	0.250	.07160
6	0.0	0.0	0.0	0.0	0.0	0.0	0.500	0.500	.01904
7	0.0	0.0	0.333	0.333	0.0	0.167	0.167	0.0	.01691
8	0.0	0.0	0.0	0.125	0.125	0.250	0.125	0.375	.02230
	1968-69 to 1970-71								
1	0.575	0.288	0.075	0.025	0.012	0.0	0.012	0.012	.36857
2	0.292	0.417	0.208	0.063	0.0	0.0	0.0	0.021	.35731
3	0.238	0.429	0.190	0.048	0.095	0.0	0.0	0.0	.15497
4	0.105	0.474	0.158	0.158	0.053	0.053	0.0	0.0	.05375
5	0.182	0.273	0.182	0.0	0.091	0.182	0.091	0.0	.02610
6	0.0	0.286	0.286	0.143	0.0	0.0	0.143	0.143	.01218
7	0.500	0.0	0.500	0.0	0.0	0.0	0.0	0.0	.01025
8	0.0	0.0	0.091	0.273	0.091	0.273	0.091	0.182	.01687

Source: Computed from National Council of Applied Economic Research Survey.

ECONOMIC AND POLITICAL WEEKLY   Review of Agriculture September 1985

APPENDIX TABLE 11: PUNJAB (INCLUDING HARYANA)

Income Class	Income Mobility Matrix								Long-Run Size Distribution of Income
	Income Class								Per Cent of Population
	1	2	3	4	5	6	7	8	Computed from:
	1968-69 to 1969-70								
1	0.214	0.286	0.286	0.071	0.071	0.0	0.071	0.0	.01276
2	0.0	0.500	0.208	0.125	0.0	0.0	0.083	0.083	.11725
3	0.0	0.226	0.290	0.161	0.226	0.032	0.032	0.032	.11753
4	0.0	0.067	0.067	0.167	0.200	0.133	0.233	0.133	.16376
5	0.0	0.095	0.143	0.143	0.238	0.238	0.048	0.095	.11835
6	0.0	0.063	0.0	0.188	0.063	0.250	0.313	0.125	.10010
7	0.0	0.0	0.083	0.208	0.125	0.042	0.167	0.375	.14963
8	0.045	0.0	0.068	0.159	0.023	0.068	0.159	0.477	.22060
	1969-70 to 1970-71								
1	0.0	0.200	0.400	0.0	0.0	0.0	0.400	0.0	.00859
2	0.214	0.393	0.321	0.036	0.0	0.036	0.0	0.0	.04010
3	0.0	0.143	0.429	0.179	0.071	0.036	0.071	0.071	.15841
4	0.0	0.0	0.219	0.281	0.344	0.0	0.0	0.156	.17424
5	0.0	0.0	0.125	0.292	0.125	0.125	0.250	0.083	.13328
6	0.0	0.0	0.011	0.056	0.222	0.167	0.333	0.111	.07098
7	0.0	0.0	0.071	0.250	0.107	0.143	0.250	0.179	.16145
8	0.0	0.0	0.0	0.049	0.049	0.049	0.195	0.659	.25296
	1968-69 to 1970-71								
1	0.0	0.357	0.429	0.143	0.0	0.071	0.0	0.0	.01725
2	0.167	0.208	0.375	0.042	0.042	0.0	0.042	0.125	.04711
3	0.065	0.129	0.226	0.097	0.161	0.097	0.194	0.032	.14571
4	0.0	0.033	0.133	0.200	0.233	0.067	0.200	0.133	.16867
5	0.0	0.048	0.238	0.143	0.190	0.190	0.143	0.048	.14104
6	0.0	0.0	0.188	0.313	0.063	0.063	0.188	0.188	.07397
7	0.0	0.0	0.042	0.208	0.167	0.0	0.250	0.333	.17297
8	0.0	0.0	0.045	0.159	0.068	0.068	0.136	0.523	.23328

Source: Computed from National Council of Applied Economic Research Survey.

APPENDIX TABLE 12: RAJASTHAN

Income Class	Income Mobility Matrix								Long-Run Size Distribution of Income
	Income Class								Per Cent of Population
	1	2	3	4	5	6	7	8	Computed from:
	1968-69 to 1969-70								
1	0.291	0.298	0.172	0.113	0.073	0.026	0.013	0.013	.17711
2	0.295	0.263	0.232	0.084	0.042	0.032	0.042	0.011	.22226
3	0.157	0.181	0.250	0.208	0.056	0.014	0.069	0.056	.21464
4	0.103	0.205	0.256	0.128	0.205	0.026	0.026	0.051	.14051
5	0.080	0.080	0.320	0.200	0.080	0.040	0.120	0.080	.08459
6	0.071	0.286	0.143	0.214	0.0	0.071	0.071	0.143	.04269
7	0.0	0.300	0.100	0.150	0.100	0.200	0.150	0.0	.06481
8	0.0	0.094	0.063	0.063	0.156	0.094	0.219	0.313	.05339
	1969-70 to 1970-71								
1	0.363	0.319	0.176	0.099	0.011	0.033	0.0	0.0	.13689
2	0.151	0.358	0.302	0.085	0.057	0.009	0.019	0.019	.27776
3	0.089	0.267	0.300	0.133	0.089	0.067	0.033	0.022	.22852
4	0.138	0.276	0.138	0.121	0.086	0.086	0.121	0.034	.13100
5	0.0	0.250	0.278	0.194	0.083	0.0	0.083	0.111	.07138
6	0.0	0.333	0.167	0.167	0.111	0.0	0.111	0.111	.03571
7	0.077	0.038	0.154	0.308	0.077	0.038	0.155	0.192	.05327
8	0.043	0.087	0.0	0.174	0.130	0.0	0.130	0.435	.06547
	1968-69 to 1970-71								
1	0.232	0.298	0.258	0.099	0.060	0.020	0.013	0.020	.12966
2	0.211	0.368	0.221	0.063	0.053	0.032	0.042	0.011	.28153
3	0.097	0.333	0.181	0.181	0.028	0.083	0.056	0.042	.21880
4	0.077	0.231	0.333	0.154	0.077	0.0	0.077	0.051	.13982
5	0.080	0.120	0.200	0.280	0.160	0.040	0.0	0.120	.06558
6	0.0	0.214	0.214	0.143	0.071	0.143	0.143	0.071	.04128
7	0.050	0.250	0.150	0.200	0.050	0.050	0.150	0.100	.06126
8	0.0	0.031	0.094	0.188	0.156	0.0	0.156	0.375	.06207

Source: Computed from National Council of Applied Economic Research Survey.

Review of Agriculture September 1985

APPENDIX TABLE 13: TAMIL NADU

Income Class	Income Mobility Matrix								Long-Run Size Distribution of Income
	Income Class								Per Cent of Population Computed from:
	1	2	3	4	5	6	7	8	
	1968-69 to 1969-70								
1	0.583	0.294	0.092	0.018	0.0	0.0	0.006	0.006	.27638
2	0.316	0.430	0.165	0.025	0.038	0.0	0.013	0.013	.23865
3	0.129	0.226	0.226	0.161	0.097	0.032	0.097	0.032	.13087
4	0.100	0.250	0.100	0.050	0.250	0.100	0.0	0.150	.06435
5	0.100	0.100	0.200	0.300	0.100	0.0	0.0	0.200	.05667
6	0.0	0.091	0.091	0.182	0.0	0.182	0.0	0.455	.03574
7	0.167	0.0	0.0	0.083	0.083	0.167	0.250	0.250	.06476
8	0.0	0.0	0.118	0.0	0.059	0.059	0.235	0.529	.13257
	1969-70 to 1970-71								
1	0.612	0.341	0.023	0.0	0.015	0.0	0.008	0.0	.09334
2	0.188	0.552	0.177	0.031	0.031	0.0	0.021	0.0	.18221
3	0.024	0.286	0.333	0.190	0.071	0.024	0.048	0.024	.08472
4	0.0	0.059	0.176	0.294	0.176	0.059	0.059	0.176	.07586
5	0.0	0.0	0.0	0.286	0.143	0.071	0.357	0.143	.06301
6	0.0	0.0	0.125	0.0	0.0	0.125	0.250	0.500	.06925
7	0.0	0.083	0.0	0.0	0.0	0.250	0.250	0.417	.08873
8	0.0	0.040	0.0	0.040	0.080	0.080	0.040	0.720	.34288
	1968-69 to 1970-71								
1	0.454	0.442	0.043	0.018	0.018	0.006	0.018	0.0	.08780
2	0.241	0.367	0.228	0.076	0.025	0.025	0.013	0.025	.12238
3	0.065	0.258	0.258	0.161	0.065	0.032	0.097	0.065	.07338
4	0.050	0.100	0.200	0.100	0.250	0.0	0.100	0.200	.09281
5	0.200	0.0	0.0	0.100	0.100	0.200	0.200	0.200	.04567
6	0.0	0.0	0.091	0.182	0.182	0.0	0.091	0.455	.04650
7	0.0	0.083	0.0	0.0	0.0	0.250	0.167	0.500	.12546
8	0.0	0.0	0.0	0.118	0.0	0.0	0.176	0.706	.40601

Source: Computed from National Council of Applied Economic Research Survey.

APPENDIX TABLE 14: UTTAR PRADESH

Income Class	Income Mobility Matrix								Long-Run Size Distribution of Income
	Income Class								Per Cent of Population Computed from:
	1	2	3	4	5	6	7	8	
	1968-69 to 1969-70								
1	0.259	0.321	0.160	0.148	0.062	0.012	0.0	0.037	.09802
2	0.151	0.381	0.230	0.087	0.063	0.040	0.024	0.024	.25969
3	0.100	0.355	0.236	0.118	0.073	0.073	0.027	0.018	.22946
4	0.051	0.190	0.316	0.165	0.114	0.051	0.063	0.051	.14351
5	0.0	0.130	0.196	0.217	0.174	0.065	0.087	0.130	.08756
6	0.033	0.033	0.300	0.200	0.100	0.067	0.167	0.100	.06681
7	0.017	0.100	0.200	0.250	0.100	0.150	0.117	0.067	.06044
8	0.0	0.019	0.093	0.148	0.074	0.222	0.241	0.204	.05451
	1969-70 to 1970-71								
1	0.158	0.561	0.193	0.070	0.018	0.0	0.0	0.0	.04186
2	0.120	0.408	0.331	0.049	0.056	0.028	0.007	0.0	.18683
3	0.024	0.252	0.331	0.205	0.087	0.024	0.047	0.031	.21216
4	0.060	0.107	0.190	0.238	0.119	0.119	0.071	0.095	.13225
5	0.0	0.091	0.164	0.200	0.127	0.164	0.109	0.145	.09482
6	0.0	0.022	0.111	0.156	0.156	0.133	0.178	0.244	.08149
7	0.0	0.050	0.050	0.150	0.175	0.125	0.100	0.350	.09027
8	0.0	0.028	0.111	0.0	0.056	0.111	0.222	0.472	.16032
	1968-69 to 1970-71								
1	0.099	0.346	0.235	0.148	0.074	0.037	0.025	0.037	.05607
2	0.079	0.357	0.270	0.119	0.079	0.048	0.032	0.016	.22742
3	0.091	0.245	0.300	0.127	0.073	0.073	0.064	0.027	.23257
4	0.025	0.203	0.215	0.241	0.101	0.101	0.076	0.038	.13760
5	0.022	0.152	0.239	0.109	0.065	0.065	0.152	0.196	.09098
6	0.067	0.200	0.100	0.200	0.200	0.0	0.033	0.200	.07060
7	0.017	0.167	0.183	0.100	0.133	0.117	0.083	0.200	.07072
8	0.0	0.019	0.148	0.074	0.074	0.111	0.130	0.444	.11404

Source: Computed from National Council of Applied Economic Research Survey.

ECONOMIC AND POLITICAL WEEKLY   Review of Agriculture   September 1985

APPENDIX TABLE 15: WEST BENGAL

Income Class	Income Mobility Matrix								Long-Run Size Distribution of Income
	Income Class								Per Cent of Population
	1	2	3	4	5	6	7	8	Computed from:
	1968-69 to 1969-70								
1	0.526	0.316	0.105	0.018	0.018	0.018	0.0	0.0	.22928
2	0.274	0.484	0.194	0.016	0.0	0.0	0.032	0.0	.30337
3	0.130	0.304	0.239	0.239	0.043	0.043	0.0	0.0	.19493
4	0.0	0.150	0.350	0.250	0.200	0.0	0.050	0.0	.11069
5	0.0	0.100	0.200	0.200	0.400	0.100	0.0	0.0	.08245
6	0.0	0.0	0.250	0.250	0.250	0.250	0.0	0.0	.04094
7	0.0	0.0	0.0	0.0	0.125	0.250	0.500	0.125	.03064
8	0.0	0.0	0.0	0.100	0.100	0.300	0.0	0.500	.00769
	1969-70 to 1970-71								
1	0.434	0.302	0.132	0.113	0.019	0.0	0.0	0.0	.15333
2	0.258	0.318	0.227	0.121	0.030	0.030	0.0	0.015	.22100
3	0.051	0.410	0.282	0.103	0.103	0.0	0.051	0.0	.21863
4	0.045	0.0	0.318	0.273	0.136	0.091	0.045	0.091	.19377
5	0.071	0.071	0.143	0.429	0.071	0.143	0.071	0.0	.06822
6	0.0	0.200	0.100	0.200	0.100	0.100	0.0	0.300	.04914
7	0.143	0.0	0.0	0.429	0.0	0.0	0.286	0.143	.03485
8	0.0	0.0	0.167	0.333	0.0	0.167	0.0	0.333	.06105
	1968-69 to 1970-71								
1	0.404	0.316	0.175	0.070	0.035	0.0	0.0	0.0	.15320
2	0.210	0.403	0.210	0.097	0.032	0.032	0.0	0.016	.23032
3	0.152	0.152	0.239	0.261	0.130	0.022	0.022	0.022	.20579
4	0.0	0.200	0.200	0.200	0.100	0.050	0.150	0.100	.20201
5	0.100	0.100	0.400	0.200	0.0	0.200	0.0	0.0	.05985
6	0.0	0.250	0.250	0.500	0.0	0.0	0.0	0.0	.04547
7	0.125	0.0	0.0	0.375	0.0	0.125	0.250	0.125	.04636
8	0.0	0.0	0.100	0.400	0.0	0.100	0.0	0.400	.05700

Source: Computed from National Council of Applied Economic Research Survey.

APPENDIX TABLE 16: ALL INDIA

Income Class	Income Mobility Matrix								Long-Run Size Distribution of Income
	Income Class								Per Cent of Population
	1	2	3	4	5	6	7	8	Computed from:
	1968-69 to 1969-70								
1	0.529	0.285	0.092	0.046	0.024	0.011	0.005	0.008	.20778
2	0.236	0.392	0.198	0.076	0.036	0.023	0.024	0.014	.25288
3	0.105	0.288	0.227	0.168	0.088	0.039	0.052	0.033	.17281
4	0.076	0.187	0.258	0.180	0.113	0.057	0.066	0.064	.12096
5	0.076	0.120	0.175	0.191	0.155	0.120	0.072	0.092	.07497
6	0.034	0.091	0.176	0.233	0.119	0.091	0.131	0.125	.05185
7	0.033	0.098	0.107	0.144	0.167	0.153	0.140	0.158	.05509
8	0.025	0.046	0.079	0.111	0.079	0.125	0.175	0.361	.06365
	1969-70 to 1970-71								
1	0.598	0.284	0.073	0.025	0.012	0.003	0.004	0.002	.20347
2	0.222	0.427	0.228	0.066	0.028	0.014	0.009	0.004	.26227
3	0.070	0.286	0.333	0.169	0.068	0.026	0.029	0.018	.19266
4	0.068	0.171	0.237	0.221	0.115	0.062	0.070	0.056	.11623
5	0.007	0.114	0.199	0.232	0.152	0.101	0.101	0.094	.06460
6	0.0	0.108	0.127	0.157	0.167	0.108	0.162	0.172	.04002
7	0.019	0.070	0.089	0.182	0.150	0.131	0.178	0.182	.04834
8	0.012	0.035	0.055	0.074	0.063	0.086	0.133	0.541	.07241
	1968-69 to 1970-71								
1	0.477	0.307	0.121	0.045	0.025	0.009	0.010	0.007	.17175
2	0.206	0.372	0.235	0.096	0.033	0.027	0.017	0.014	.25401
3	0.105	0.266	0.256	0.149	0.095	0.052	0.045	0.033	.19862
4	0.061	0.199	0.241	0.208	0.102	0.052	0.083	0.054	.12691
5	0.064	0.155	0.203	0.159	0.131	0.096	0.088	0.104	.07181
6	0.028	0.165	0.153	0.176	0.125	0.063	0.136	0.153	.04524
7	0.037	0.121	0.153	0.153	0.121	0.084	0.126	0.205	.05466
8	0.011	0.046	0.089	0.146	0.075	0.071	0.129	0.432	.07700

Source: Computed from National Council of Applied Economic Research Survey.
Notes to Appendix: The income classes (per capita) are: (1) 0-150; (2) 151-250; (3) 251-350; (4) 351-450; (5) 451-550; (6) 551-650; (7) 651-850; (8) 851 and above.
All incomes are at 1960-61 prices (deflated by consumer price index for agricultural labourers state-wide). Poverty line adopted: Rs 180 per capita.

Review of Agriculture   September 1985

ECONOMIC AND POLITICAL WEEKLY

tuations in yields (incomes); a technological lag super-imposed on unfavourable structural conditions (Subbrao, 1984). As for Maharashtra, it is well known that a viable dry-farming technology for millets is yet to evolve.

It is always risky to derive policy conclusions from statistical associations. However, for what they are worth, the results suggest that a two-prong strategy, which combines improvements in agricultural production with greater labour absorption of the rural work force outside agriculture, would yield the largest probability for the greatest poverty reduction in rural India. This is essentially the strategy suggested by Mellor (1976) for India and other less-developed countries and by Adelman (1984) for most second-tier less developed countries. The prevailing anti-poverty policy package in India which focuses on generating non-agricultural employment for rural labour through measures such as assisting the landless with income generating non-land assets, food-for-work programmes, etc, is also consistent with our findings.

Notes

[The authors wish to thank I Z Bhatty, Director General, NCAER, for permission to use ARIS data and Raj Bhatia, M A Gandhi and Connie Cartwright for their help in computer programming.]

1 For further details relating to the sample design and data procedures of the Survey, see the National Council of Applied Economic Research (1975).
2 We applied ergodicity tests to the income mobility matrices described by our data and, after suitable aggregation of income ranges, all but the matrices for years 1969-70 to 1970-71 for Bihar and 1968-69 to 1970-71 for Jammu and Kashmir were found to be ergodic.
3 Before generating the income mobility matrices, we converted incomes at current prices to the base year 1968-69 using the state specific Consumer Price Index for Agricultural Labourers (CPIAL) as deflators following Bardhan (1970) and Ahluwalia (1978). The use of base-weighted indices for deflation is subject to the limitation that arises from its inability to reflect the impact of changing relative prices upon the commodity composition of consumption. Yet, the CPIAL deflators are probably the best available *at the state level* and were used by previous writers.
4 A recent district-level analysis of household data for 1978-79 shows the inequality ratio to be higher in Ludhiana (Punjab) than in Gaya (Bihar), but the poverty index (headcount ratio and also the Sen's index) to be much lower in the former than in the latter (Vashishtha, 1985).
5 The location of Uttar Pradesh in the medium poverty at the initial and low poverty in the long run by our results is a surprise and could presumably be due to oversampling of households from the western Uttar Pradesh in the

NCAER data set used by us. This region is highly developed and adjacent to the richer states of Punjab and Haryana. Any study of long-run dynamics for this large state as a whole is difficult owing to extremely wide intra-regional inequality in this state.
6 Using the same data set, Nugent and Walther (1982) conducted a decomposition analysis of the Gini ratio, and noted the dominant role of good weather in reducing relative income inequality. They, however, did not examine the role of weather on the income profile of poverty households as such.

References

Adelman, Irma, 'Beyond Export-led Growth' *World Development*, Vol 12, No 9, (1984), pp 937-950.
Adelman, Irma and Whitte, Peter, 'Static and Dynamic Indices of Income Inequality',*Can J Develop Stud*, Vol 1 (1980), pp 27-46.
Ahluwalia, M S, 'Rural Poverty and Agricultural Performance in India', *J Develop Stud*, Vol 14, No 3, (1978), pp 298-323.
Bardhan, P 'On the Minimum Level of Living and the Rural Poor', *Indian Economic Review*, Vol 5 (New Series), No 1, (1970), pp 129-136.
—, "Land Labour and Rural Poverty: Essays in Development Economics", New York: Columbia Press, 1984.
Bardhan, P and Srinivasan, T N, "Poverty and Income Distribution in India", Calcutta, India: Statistical Publishing House, 1974.
Dastane, N G, "Review of Work Done on Water Requirements of Crops in India", Poona, India: Navasharat Prakashan, 1970.
Gupta, S P, Singh, Padam and Datta, K L, 'Measurement of Poverty: A Development Index' in *Regional Dimensions of India's*

Economic Development, Planning Commission, Government of India, and State Planning Board, Uttar Pradesh, Lucknow (1983).
Krishna, Raj, 'Some Aspects of Agricultural Growth, Price Policy and Equity in Developing Countries', *Food Research Institute Studies*, Vol 18, No 3, 1982, pp 219-260.
Lahiri, A K, "Rainfall and Supply Response: A Study of Rice in India", mimeographed, Delhi School of Economics, April, 1983.
Mellor, J W, 'The New Economics of Growth: A Strategt for India and the Developing World", New York: Twentieth Century Fund, 1976.
National Council of Applied Economic Research: Changes in Rural Income in India, Delhi, 1975.
Nugent, J B and Walther, R J, 'Short-run Changes in Rural Income Inequality: A Decomposition Analysis', *The Journal of Development Studeis*, Vol 18, No 2, January, 1982, pp 239-269.
Shorrocks, A, 'Income Inequality and Income Mobility', *J Econ Theory*, Vol 19(2), (December 1978), pp 376-393.
Subbarao, K, "Price and Non-Price Policies in the Design of Rural Development Strategy for India's Eastern States", mimeographed, Institute of Economic Growth, Delhi, 1984.
Sukhatme, P V, 'Assessment of Adequacy of Diets of Different Income Levels' *Economic and Political Weekly*, Special Number, Vol 13, Nos 32 and 33, August 1978, pp 1373-1385.
Vashishtha, Prem, "Household Income and Its Disposition—A Micro Level Study" (A Comparative Analysis of Saving and Investment Behaviour), mimeo, National Council of Applied Economic Research, New Delhi, February 1985.

17

IRMA ADELMAN

United Nations

Strategies for
Equitable Growth

Growth has meant immiserization for the poor in most developing countries—but not in all. There is a pattern of development in which the majority can share the benefits.

The political problem of mankind is to combine three things: economic efficiency, social justice, and individual liberty.

—J. M. KEYNES
Essays in Persuasion (1926)

Economic development usually occurs at the expense of the poor. That is the sad conclusion that emerges from an examination of noncommunist countries over the period from 1957 to 1968. Of forty-three underdeveloped countries studied, only five combined economic growth with increasing equity. Nor is the picture one of short-run phenomena; even in the long run, the prospect for increasing human welfare through conventional development programs is questionable.

Bleak as these findings may be, they can help us map out those strategies that will—and those that will not—promote both equity and economic growth in underdeveloped countries.

The typical pattern of growth

In exploring the nature of economic growth, we related social and economic changes in the developing countries to two important dimensions of social equity: political participation and income distribution.

With regard to political participation, perhaps the principal lesson suggested by our study is that an increase in participation is by no means an automatic

IRMA ADELMAN is Professor of Economics at the University of Maryland. This article is based on *Economic Growth and Social Equity in Developing Countries.* by Professors Adelman and Cynthia Taft Morris (Stanford University Press, 1973).

consequence of economic progress. True, the early stages of social mobilization and economic modernization generate pressures for political and administrative change. But if these pressures are to be translated into viable forms of political participation, the groups advocating change must be incorporated into the existing power structure. Mechanisms must be developed that allow these groups to share the political and economic power once belonging to the elite, and these mechanisms must be fair enough to be generally acceptable.

Obviously, the transformation of political power is fraught with conflict and is often violent. Frequently, the process only results in authoritarianism which may postpone indefinitely the development of equitable forms of political participation.

With regard to income, our findings indicate that more egalitarian income distributions are characteristic of two extremes: the severely underdeveloped nations and the economically most advanced. Between these extremes, higher rates of industrialization, faster increases in agricultural productivity and steeper rates of growth all tend (at least up to a point) to worsen income inequality. When graphed, this relationship appears asymmetrically U-shaped.

The beneficiaries of economic development vary with the level of development of the particular country. In the typical case, as economic growth begins with the expansion of a narrow modern sector in a subsistence agrarian economy, the income share of the poorest 60 percent of the population declines significantly, as does that of the middle 20 percent; but the income share of the top 5 percent increases strikingly. The path toward sustained economic growth is eventually blocked unless the country is sufficiently large, or redistributive policies sufficiently vigorous, to generate an internal market for growth.

Once countries move successfully beyond the stage of sharply dualistic growth (where the modern sector is isolated from the traditional agrarian sector), the enlarged base for economic growth primarily benefits the middle income receiver. The position of the poorest 40 percent typically worsens in both relative and absolute terms. In those countries where higher levels of development have been attained and where the capacity for more broadly based economic growth has been established, the poorest segments of the population typically benefit from economic growth only when widespread efforts are made to improve health, education, housing and other aspects of human welfare.

To reach the relatively unusual state where equity and economic development are both increasing, a country must be in the top half of the group we would already consider the most advanced of the developing nations. Indeed, in the absence of domestic policy aimed specifically at redirecting the benefits of growth, a nation must attain a level of development corresponding to that which exists in the socioeconomically most developed of the underdeveloped countries (Argentina, Chile, Taiwan, Israel) before the income distribution becomes even as equal as it is in countries that have undergone virtually no development (Dahomey, Chad, Niger).

The economic processes underlying these observations (admittedly somewhat oversimplified) can be described in three general cases. The distinguishing characteristics are the speed and type of economic development. In the first case, GNP expands slowly, too slowly to generate the necessary conditions for equitable growth. And the growth that does occur is capital intensive: new production processes rely on machinery and technology rather than on the skills of labor. In the second case, growth is sufficiently rapid—usually 5.5 percent or better—the base is sufficiently broad and the country is at least moderately developed. But the capital-intensive nature of growth leads to a deterioration in the incomes of the poor and speeds the accumulation of assets by a relatively small number of owners. In the third case, GNP expands at a rate of 5.5 percent or more, the expansion is labor intensive and growth is equitable.

What separates the first two cases is the rate of growth, since in both cases growth is capital intensive. When such growth is fast, its effects on the poor are intensified and the income gap between urban and rural areas widens. Growth may be sharply dualistic, stressing a narrow modern sector to the exclusion of the traditional agrarian economy, or it may be more broadly based. As long as it is capital intensive, it reduces the incomes of the poor. Capital-intensive development is characterized by changes in product mix and technology within both agricultural and nonagricultural sectors, rapid expansion of the urban industrial sector, a continued high rate of population increase, migration to the cities, lack of upward social mobility and inflation. Capital-intensive methods are adopted because owners of large-scale enterprises can easily and cheaply obtain capital abroad and because entrepreneurs often prefer to use advanced technologies.

Industrialization that is capital intensive does not

generate sufficient employment to absorb the labor force released by higher agricultural productivity and the related structural reorganization of agriculture. The eviction of tenant farmers and the other measures of land consolidation create a new agricultural proletariat that roams the countryside. Moreover, those tenants, subsistence farmers and other small farmers who remain cannot take full advantage of modern methods and cannot expand production as much as can the owners of plantations or large mechanized farms. Overall, agricultural output expands. Taken together with the lack of responsiveness to lower prices that typifies demand for many agricultural products, the increased food supplies weaken agricultural prices and the real income of the subsistence agricultural producers and small farmers tends to fall.

In the industrial sector, mechanization displaces artisans and cottage workers in both urban and rural areas. Where cheap manufactures are permitted to flood domestic markets, the destruction of handicraft industries further reduces incomes and increases unemployment among the poor of both areas. Moreover, the conventional policy of erecting tariff barriers to encourage the domestic manufacture of import goods causes inflation which erodes the wage gains of those who are employed.

In the third type of development, economic growth promotes equity. If labor can be absorbed into high-productivity employment at a pace faster than the growth rate of the urban proletariat, then wage rates and employment for both unskilled and semiskilled workers will tend to rise faster than GNP. Wage differentials in industry will tend to narrow, since skilled and white-collar wage rates will not rise so fast. The consequent shift of the distribution of money income toward the lower 40 percent of the population will then raise the demand for agricultural products. This rise in demand will more than offset the consequences of an expanded supply. The differential between urban and rural incomes then shrinks, both because of the increase in actual or effective demand and because of the continued outward migration from agriculture. Finally, if the industrialization process is export oriented, domestic prices for light consumer goods need not rise above international levels and gains in money income will not be so completely eroded. In short, once increases in productive employment begin to exceed additions to the labor force, economic growth begins to benefit the poor.

A word of caution. Our observations have taken

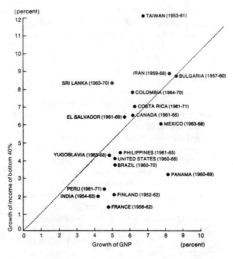

Points above the forty-five degree line mark cases where incomes of the poor have grown faster than overall GNP. In general, GNP must grow by at least 5.5 percent for growth to be equitable.

Source: H. Chenery, J. Duloy, and Richard Jolly, "Redistribution with Growth: An Approach to Policy," International Bank for Reconstruction and Development, August 1973.

account of various technical problems that we do not intend to dwell on here. The reader should be aware, however, that caveats are in order concerning the reliability of the available data (particularly with respect to income distribution); the suitability of extrapolating social and economic relationships characteristic of one period to a future period; the omission from consideration of potentially relevant social and economic forces; and errors in measurement. Nonetheless, though the recent case-study evidence is of necessity sketchy, the similarity of the experiences of several countries and the findings of our analyses support the conclusions presented above.

The politics of equitable growth

The major unresolved questions posed by equity-oriented development economics are these: Is equitable growth possible under the political and social arrangements existing in most developing countries? If not, what social and economic framework is most conducive to equitable economic growth? Neither question can be answered unequivocally, and I shall not speculate on the answers. But the following thoughts may be helpful in developing solutions:

—Greater political participation, that favorite remedy of Western democracy for making equitable economic growth politically possible, does not appear to redistribute income to the poor. To the extent that it is effective at all, it tends to redistribute income from the upper toward the middle income groups.

—Greater government ownership of productive enterprise, that favorite remedy of the socialist world, also does not appear to redistribute income to the poor. It dramatically reduces the income share of the upper 5 percent, but the benefit of the redistribution redounds to the next quintile in the income scale. It also tends to reduce growth relative to the free enterprise rate, thus providing less to redistribute.

In the economic arena, there appears to be an uncomfortable trade-off between freedom of action and equity in income distribution. Such a conflict is evident in Yugoslavia, for example, where inequalities in income distribution started reasserting themselves with disconcerting rapidity after the adoption of decentralization and a more liberal economic policy. My guess is that an inherent propensity of human nature is at work here.

A quite different view of human nature is held by most radical social scientists today. They believe that the conflict between equity and growth is rooted not in human nature, but rather in the system. Observing the pervasive social and political forces opposing equitable growth within and among nations, they conclude that radical political change is necessary before equitable growth can be attempted. This conclusion leads many to infer that the economics of equitable growth is irrelevant: it is only the politics of redistribution that matters.

Personally, I am convinced that, whatever the definition of radical political change and whatever its merits, the inference that only political change matters does not follow. Leaders of most socialist countries are clearly quite serious about economic policy for equitable growth. Also, the failure of Salvador Allende to combine democratic growth with massive redistribution in Chile resulted from plain economic mismanagement in the wake of major redistributive efforts.

The existence of a handful of successful equitable-growth countries in the noncommunist world (Israel, Japan, South Korea, Singapore, Taiwan) suggests that the radical argument for fundamental political change is also not universally applicable. Clearly, in many developing countries the political power of conservative forces (such as traditional elites, expatriates and international corporations) must be significantly weakened before growth with social justice can become a national goal. However, in others, it is just barely possible that the political and intellectual leaderships may have (or may be made to have) a change of heart once they realize that the trickle-down policy of economic development does not effectively improve the welfare of the poor.

The reason that the political climate is so important is that the redistribution of assets—and of the opportunities for asset accumulation—is a necessary first step for the initiation of equitable growth. The reallocation of both wealth and the opportunity to accumulate wealth has been an actual precondition in all successful equitable-growth countries to date. But in these cases the redistribution has been followed up by a host of policies designed to maintain the value of the redistributed assets. Poor economic management or excessively slow growth rates have invariably negated redistributive efforts, both by causing a drastic fall in the value of the redistributed assets (witness the host of abortive land reforms and enterprise nationalizations) and by providing unforeseen and undesirable windfall profits for the upper

United Nations/L. Groseclose

20 percent of the population.

How much growth is necessary?

Our analysis suggests that the relationship between the rate of economic growth and the change in the share of income accruing to the poorest 40 percent of the population is rather complicated:

—Per capita GNP growth below 3.5 percent in real terms (which exclude the effects of price changes) tends to be associated with declines in the share of income of the poor. At current rates of population growth, this puts the minimum required growth rate of real GNP at around 5.5 percent. If GNP grows faster than this minimum, equitable growth can occur sooner.

—Higher rates of growth are necessary *but not sufficient* for substantial improvements in the share of income received by the poor. High growth rates tend to benefit the poorest 40 percent of the population only when accompanied by a strategy emphasizing educational development, and only when the growth pursued is not sharply dualistic, that is, when it does not stress the modern industrial sector to the exclusion of the traditional agrarian sector. (Panama, Mexico and the Middle Eastern oil economies fail to meet either of these requirements.)

As we indicated, empirical estimates suggest that the minimum rate of growth required for equitable development is 5.5 percent. But we can arrive at a similar number by a simpler approach. Consider the

arithmetic. In the average developing country, urban population growth (natural increase plus immigration) is currently about 4 percent per year. The industrial sectors of these countries absorb new labor at about half the rate of growth of industrial output. Thus an 8 percent annual increase in industrial production is necessary just to keep pace. Output in the industrial sector typically grows about 25 percent faster than overall GNP. Therefore, the 8 percent rise in industrial production means that GNP must grow by over 6 percent for equitable growth to be possible.

The 6 percent figure is simply a rule of thumb. If the process of industrialization is labor intensive, if the differential between industrial and total growth is greater than 25 percent, or if urban population growth is slower than 4 percent, then the critical GNP growth rate will be less than 6 percent.

Examples of equitable growth

The results of our statistical analysis suggest that equitable growth requires a major reorientation of development strategies. The most hopeful redirection would be to stress the development of human skills. It is significant that all five noncommunist countries that have successfully combined accelerated growth with improvements in the share of income accruing to the poor (Israel, Japan, South Korea, Singapore and Taiwan) have followed a strategy consistent with this human development goal. Each has stressed export-oriented growth based on labor- and skill-intensive products. That is, they have all adopted strategies that coordinate a major investment in raising the general educational level with subsequent creation of productive employment opportunities.

In Korea, for example, the educational level of the population in 1964 was approximately three times that of the average country at its level of per capita GNP; at the same time, high school graduates were competing for jobs as municipal street sweepers, and the Minister of Education was fired for allowing too large an enrollment in universities. Despite the disaffection and political unrest implied by this abundance of educated people, there followed six years of very rapid growth. Real GNP expanded at an average rate of 10 percent per year and an unusually high share of that growth came from the increasing production of labor-intensive products. By 1970 unemployment had fallen from 7.7 percent to 4.5 per-

cent. Real wages of unskilled and skilled workers were rising at an average annual rate of 20 percent in manufacturing and 12 percent in agriculture. These spectacular results were achieved only after the education and training phase was well advanced, and they were accomplished by an economic development program which involved two major elements. First, the conventional policy of stressing replacement of imports with domestically manufactured goods was abandoned. In its place came the strategy of manufacturing goods for export. Second, Korea restructured its pricing system, a program that entailed a dramatic increase in the real cost of capital, a significant currency devaluation and a substantial dismantling of the quantitative restrictions on trade.

In assessing the success of the Korean experience, it must be emphasized that the improvement in education preceding the growth phase involved universal primary education as well as improvements in secondary schools and higher levels of education. In addition, the educational system was converted from an essentially classical one to an American-type system. In this process the educational pyramid was broadened substantially, and the curricula were directed toward the acquisition of basic skills.

Similar changes in education also took place in Japan and, to a lesser extent, in Taiwan. A comparable policy typified Jewish Palestine (and hence Israel). Singapore, Israel and Taiwan acquired much of their skilled and semiskilled labor through immigration. All three of these nations maintained and improved their people's skills, a policy which permitted subsequent equity-oriented growth. Their educational program stands in sharp contrast to that of India, where the educational pyramid is quite narrow and the content remains largely classical.

Thus all countries whose development process has successfully combined equity with growth have followed the same sequence: a massive buildup of human skills and talents followed by a growth strategy which made intensive use of those talents as industrialization accelerated.

Policies that don't work

With this background in mind, we can now turn to a discussion of policy. First, a word about those policies that don't work. Our findings identify a number of instruments that are relatively unimportant for improving income distribution, though they appear to be unimportant only if applied in isolation. When included in a policy package which is part and parcel of the ideal development strategy, these instruments might not be ineffective.

Increases in the relative importance of direct taxation produced insignificant results. Recent studies of Latin America tend to confirm this finding. They show that neither tax structures nor government expenditure patterns typically favor a larger share for the poorest groups in the population. The reasons are complex, but one factor probably is that the politically powerful usually stand in the way of effective progressivity. Also, tax agencies are poorly developed and unevenly administered.

Financial institutions are also less important mechanisms for favorable redistribution than one might expect. This finding is consistent with John Gurley's hypothesis that the functioning of financial systems is closely tied to the power structure of an underdeveloped country. In the absence of changes in that structure, financial institutions operate inequitably.

The relative unimportance of agricultural structure and technology is rather striking. With respect to land reform, the reason is probably that redistribution of land favors higher incomes for the agricultural poor only when supported by measures to maintain the productivity of the redistributed assets, supportive measures which are often not carried out.

Improvements in agricultural productivity also do not appear to be as significant as expected. This result, which is consistent with the findings of those who studied the green revolution, suggests that the adoption of improved techniques and the spread of new seeds and fertilizers tend to benefit the middle income and rich farmers, rather than the poor. In fact, as mentioned earlier, productivity increases that are concentrated on the larger farms can undermine the position of small farmers by reducing agricultural product prices, putting pressure on tenancy and restricting access to credit and other resources. Thus, government policies should stress both rural development and technology rather than technological innovation alone.

Industrialization, too, is less important in our results than one might expect. Short-term rates of change in the degree of industrialization are not significantly associated with any particular trend in income distribution. But in those countries having successively higher levels of industrial technology, the relationship between technological advance and share of income received by the poorest 60 percent of the population is U-shaped: the least and most advanced states of technology are associated with the most egalitarian income distribution. Between these two poles, increases in technology correspond—at least up to a point—to declines in the share of income accruing to the poor. This finding is consistent with the hypothesis advanced by Simon Kuznets and with our discussion regarding the impact of the early stages of industrialization in the currently advanced nations. The finding suggests that policies promoting industrialization are likely to worsen income distribution until a very high level of development is reached unless these are combined with policies emphasizing educational development.

Strategies for equitable growth

For countries at the lowest level of development, such as the sub-Saharan African nations, the policy implications of our results are rather depressing. No policies emerge as effective instruments for systematically improving the position of the poor. The usual alternative to the extreme inequality associated with expatriate domination of an underdeveloped nation appears to be stagnation. Neither the expulsion of expatriates nor indigenous revolution appears likely to lead to economic growth, probably because of the very limited institutional and administrative capabilities found in these countries.

For countries at intermediate and higher levels of development, the prognosis is more hopeful. Improvements in areas such as education and health, increased direct government control of enterprise and economic programs and increased stress on diversified manufacturing for the export market are strategies that can result in more equitable income distribution. But even for these countries, such policies appear more likely to benefit the middle income groups than to raise living standards of the poorest two quintiles, unless direct government action is taken.

A policy maker committed to equitable growth must decide whether his nation has the potential for growth above the 5.5 percent minimum in the foreseeable future. If it does, he should first attempt to create the appropriate preconditions for equitable development. The only proven way to do so is to follow the example of the five successful countries: reduce the vast disparities in wealth (particularly in land ownership); redistribute access to further wealth by imposing controls over the use of capital; and invest in a massive and broad-based educational effort. This approach will generally lead to a decade or so

of relatively slow GNP growth, political instability, social tension and unrest.

Once the investment in human talents has taken place, the subsequent acceleration of growth can be just if the strategies for development stress the productive use of those human talents. That will occur only if proper attention is paid to economic policy. In small countries, the effort will have to be export oriented; in large countries, policy can be aimed at satisfying domestic demand, particularly when a more equitable growth pattern generates a mass market.

If the policy maker does not believe that his country can achieve the 5.5 percent rate within a reasonable time (and, realistically speaking, there are a significant number of countries for which this will be the case), then he must make an explicit choice between equity and growth. The only policy I can see that is appropriate under these conditions is one which directly transfers income to the poor. This redistribution would further reduce the already slow growth rate, a reduction that by itself would improve equity, or at least slow the rate of its deterioration.

A word of caution: in deciding whether rapid growth potential exists, past economic performance may not be a reliable guide. During the 1950s, for example, South Korea was generally known in international circles as the hellhole of foreign assistance. Even in the early 1960s, there was nothing in the performance of the economy to suggest that spectacular growth was just around the corner.

Toward growth with justice

To achieve equitable growth, two extreme strategies are theoretically possible: grow now, redistribute and educate later; or, redistribute and educate now, grow later. The former strategy is the one that has typically been followed in developed noncommunist economies, except for the United States, Japan and possibly Brazil. The redistribute-first strategy is the one followed by the successful equitable-growth countries in the past two decades.

I am convinced that for equitable growth to become prevalent there must be a deliberate application of the redistribute-and-educate-first strategy on a wide scale. My argument is a practical one: there is selective but consistent evidence that it can work and significant evidence that the opposite strategy does not work on anything resembling an acceptable time scale. Once the slower growth phase is passed, the transition to a stage of relatively high development can be accomplished in short order. In the five countries considered, the first phase lasted about a decade. In another decade and a half, once economic incentives were restructured to permit an export-oriented industrialization that employed the new skills of the population, rapid economic growth became almost self-sustaining.

The past, of course, is not necessarily a reliable guide to the future. Some may object that the generally discouraging relationship of equity to growth may be merely the result of generally poor but readily rectified packages of economic policies. In this view, a restructuring of relative prices, use of improved technologies and a better balance between domestically oriented and export-oriented development strategies would suffice to permit future growth to be equitable. Unfortunately, however, to date the real world offers no evidence of equitable growth without the preconditions described in this article.

Some may also dismiss the success stories as special cases, asserting that these are small nations with nonrepresentative cultural traditions and attitudes, helped by unusually large per capita infusions of foreign aid and subjected to exceptional challenges that strengthened the governments and made economic viability a major condition for national survival. Special cases they are, but five successful cases are certainly more encouraging than none, and the consistency of their experiences surely weakens the "uniqueness" argument.

There is also evidence that the entire package— resource redistribution, massive education and labor-intensive growth policies—must be adopted in that sequence to achieve rapid success. Incomplete versions of this program, such as land reform alone or education without labor-intensive growth, have not worked. For the advanced countries which followed a grow-first pattern, economic development did eventually benefit the poor, but the time it took to do so was much longer (roughly two or more generations) than in our five successful cases.

In conclusion, I believe that our analysis, in combination with other empirical evidence, leads inescapably to the position that a major reorientation of development strategies is required to achieve growth with equity. Marginal adjustments of current strategies will not work.

18

World Development, 1976, Vol. 4, No. 7, pp. 561–582. Pergamon Press. Printed in Great Britain.

Policies for Equitable Growth

IRMA ADELMAN

University of Maryland

CYNTHIA TAFT MORRIS

The American University

SHERMAN ROBINSON

Princeton University

1. INTRODUCTION

After two decades of concern with the problem of raising *per capita* GNP in low-income developing countries, the development community of the 1970s has shifted its focus to the challenge of increasing the equity of the distribution of income. The shift proved to be dramatically needed as the empirical studies of the distribution of the benefits from economic growth showed that the expected trickle-down was not taking place. More serious, a number of studies indicated a systematic worsening, both relative and absolute, in the position of the poorest stratum of income recipients.

In this paper, we attempt to summarize our insights with respect to anti-poverty policy in developing countries. These insights were gained in the course of three different major research projects focused upon the relationship between the various facets of modernization and relative and absolute poverty. The first is a cross-section statistical study of the sources of differences among countries in the relative income shares of the poorest 60% of households.[1] The second is a historical analysis of processes and initial conditions leading to extreme poverty in 24 countries in the middle of the nineteenth century.[2] The third is a modelling effort for the South Korean economy used as a laboratory to explore the probable efficacy of a large variety of major, but non-revolutionary strategies, policies, and programmes for the alleviation of poverty in the medium run.[3]

The present paper is organized as follows. The next three sections are devoted to brief summaries of the methodology and principal findings of each study. Our summary of the cross-section study is quite brief since the results have already been published. The final section draws the policy implications emerging from the three-pronged attack.

2. ADELMAN-MORRIS CROSS-SECTION STUDY

Our cross-section study of economic growth and social equity relates interactions among economic and social structure and change to the distribution of income as measured by the income shares of the poorest 60%, the middle 20%, and the upper 5% of the population. The data are for the period 1957–68 for 43 underdeveloped countries. They include a wide range of measures of economic structure and institutions and social and political characteristics potentially relevant to poverty.

The statistical analysis attempts to assess the relative importance of 35 independent variables in explaining inter-country differences in

1. Irma Adelman and Cynthia Taft Morris, *Economic Growth and Social Equity in Developing Countries* (Stanford, Calif.: Stanford University Press, 1973).

2. Irma Adelman and Cynthia Taft Morris, 'A typology of poverty in 1850', in *Essays in Honour of Bert Hoselitz*, ed. by Manning Nash (forthcoming).

3. Irma Adelman and Sherman Robinson, *Income Distribution Policies in Developing Countries* (Stanford University Press, forthcoming).

patterns of income distribution. The analysis selects the independent variable which splits the sample into two sub-groups between which the largest difference in scores on the independent variable is obtained. For example, country scores on the share of income of the poorest 60% can be split into two groups, the variance between which accounts for 28% of the total variance, by the independent variable 'socio-economic dualism'; no other candidate variable accounts for as high a proportion of the total variance. Each of the groups obtained in this way is then treated as a 'parent' group and the 'best' partition together with the 'best' independent variable obtained. The process is stopped when no variable can be found that yields a reduction of variance between group means significant at the 5% level. A leading characteristic of the technique is that it permits the selection of different independent variables for different portions of the data.

The results of the study suggest a set of hypotheses regarding the dynamics of economic development and income distribution. The generalizations which follow assume that in its growth path a typical underdeveloped country will embody the average characteristics of the groups of countries which are associated with successive levels of development.

The relationship between levels of economic development and the equity of income distribution is shown to be asymmetrically U-shaped, with more egalitarian income distributions being characteristic of both extreme economic underdevelopment and high levels of economic development. Between these extremes, however, the relationship is, for the most part, inverse: up to a point, higher rates of industrialization, faster increases in agricultural productivity, and higher rates of growth all tend to shift the income distribution in favour of the higher-income groups and against the low-income groups.

The beneficiaries of economic development, as well as the processes by which the poor are penalized by economic development, vary with the level of development of the country. At the lowest level of development, as economic growth begins in a subsistence agrarian economy through the expansion of a narrow modern sector, inequality in the distribution of income typically increases greatly, the income share of the poorest 60% declines significantly, as does that of the middle 20%, and the income share of the top 5% increases strikingly. In these countries the path toward sustained economic growth is eventually blocked unless either the country is sufficiently large or

redistributive policies are sufficiently important to generate an internal market for growth.

Once countries move successfully beyond the stage of sharply dualistic growth, the middle-income receivers are the primary beneficiaries of the widening of the base for the economic growth which follows. The position of the poorest 40% typically worsens both relatively and absolutely, even where a transition from sharply dualistic growth to more broadly based economic growth is accomplished. Where relatively high levels of development have been attained and the capacity for more broadly based economic growth has been established, the poorest segments of the population still typically benefit from economic growth only where widespread efforts are made to improve the human resource base.

Finally, it should be noted that, in order to reach the relatively small positively correlated portion of the equity-level-of-economic-development curve, a country must be among the upper half of those underdeveloped countries at the highest level of development. Indeed, in the absence of domestic policy action aimed specifically at redirecting the benefits of growth, a nation must attain a level of development corresponding to that which exists among the socio-economically most developed of the underdeveloped countries (Argentina, Chile, Taiwan, Israel) before the income distribution tends to become as even as it is in countries that have undergone virtually no economic development (e.g. Dahomey, Chad, Niger).

Perhaps the most interesting policy findings of the study were the negative ones – the paucity of potentially relevant influences that proved to have systematic relationships to variations in shares. As Table 1 shows, the ineffective influences include most of the conventional economic variables as well as most of the social variables which economists stress. Among these are increases in agricultural productivity, changes in degree of industrialization, rate of growth of population, and improvements in tax systems and financial institutions. The unimportance of these variables is reconfirmed by the results of the Adelman-Robinson policy experiments for Korea.

The important economic instruments are quite few. Nor are policies to change them easily designed and carried out. Furthermore, they benefit primarily the middle class. Increasing the rate of economic growth and accelerating modernization have complex consequences that depend upon the stage of economic development; faster growth can

Table 1. *Summary of results of Adelman-Morris cross-section study of influences on the distribution of income*

	Direction of relationship*			Frequency of significance		
	Bottom 60%	Middle 20%	Top 5%	Bottom 60%	Middle 20%	Top 5%
Potentially effective						
Rate of improvement in human resources	+	+	—	1	2	1
Direct government economic activity	+	o	—	1	o	3
Socio-economic dualism	—	—	+	1	1	1
Potential for economic development	—	+	o	1	2	o
Per capita GNP	—	o	—	2	o	1
Strength of labour movement	—	+	—	1	1	1
Moderately effective						
Abundance of natural resources	—**	o	+	1	o	1
Factor scores on level of socio-economic development	o	+	o	o	2	o
Structure of foreign trade	+	+	o	1	1	o
Importance of indigenous middle class	o	+	—	o	1	1
Character of agricultural organization	o	+	o	1	1	o
Political participation	o	+	—	o	1	1
Political strength of traditional elite	—	o	+	1	o	o
Level of modernization of industry	o	+	o	1	1	1
Literacy	o	+	o	o	1	1
Degree of cultural and ethnic homogeneity	—	o	o	1	o	o
Leadership commitment to economic development	o	—	o	o	1	o
Effectiveness of financial institutions	o	—	o	o	1	o
Urbanization	o	+	o	o	1	o
Not effective						
Adequacy of physical overhead capital	o		o			o
Rate of population growth	o		o			o
Total population	o		o			o
Level of modernization of agricultural techniques						
Improvements in agricultural productivity						
Change in degree of industrialization						
Size of the traditional agricultural sector						
Rate of growth of per capita GNP						
Level of effectiveness of tax system						
Improvements in the tax system						
Improvements in the effectiveness of financial institutions						
Country size and orientation of development strategy						
Extent of social mobility						
Type of colonial experience						
Length of experience with self-government						
Political strength of the military						

* Where a variable is significant at more than one split in a single analysis, the sign refers to the first split.

** This sign is incorrectly stated to be positive in the footnote to Fig. 1, p. 163 of *Economic Growth and Social Equity in Developing Countries.*

achieve a more equal income distribution only at the highest stage characteristic of developing countries. Even then, a favourable impact on distribution is likely only when growth is achieved through a broadly based strategy predicated upon both the wide spread and application of educational skills. At all levels, increased access to the acquisition of middle-level skills and professional training contributes to improving the income distribution through its favourable impact on the share of the middle quintile. Policies tending to reduce dualism by widening the base for economic growth are conducive to income equality, benefiting particularly the middle-income groups. The distributional effects of a large government role in industrial production are favourable to lower- as well as middle-income recipients. To implement a major spread of education together with effective use of the increased stock of human capital in a labour- and skill-intensive growth strategy, and at the same time to achieve a significant reduction in dualism and a marked change in the role of the government, requires in most countries a fundamental reorientation of development policies. The required changes are likely to be so far-reaching that they imply a radical transformation of power relationships and economic and social structures.

3. ADELMAN-MORRIS HISTORICAL ANALYSIS

Our analysis of economic growth and impoverishment in the middle of the nineteenth century applies the techniques for the development of 'soft' data to gain insight into the historical impacts of economic change on the structure and extent of poverty. A typology of the structure of poverty is constructed for 1850 for 24 countries, and the nine 'types' which emerge are ranked by the probable extent of extreme poverty. The nature and ranking of the types is then used to develop hypotheses regarding the historical processes generating poverty. The year 1850 was selected in order to focus on the impact on the poor of the early stages of commercialization and industrialization. The sample consists of countries of widely different levels of development. The countries selected are those where some significant aggregate economic change occurred between 1850 and 1914 for which adequate materials appeared to be accessible.

The concept of poverty applied is that of extreme material poverty. The extremely poor are defined to include three overlapping cate-

gories: (1) those who were starving or destitute; (2) those whose food consumption was marked by recurrent inadequacy of their staple food and infrequent consumption of meat, fish, dairy products, and pulses; and (3) those subject to very poor health conditions as indicated by extreme overcrowding, unusually high mortality rates, or disease. The 'poverty-line' dividing the extremely poor from the rest of the population, while above the level of near starvation and destitution, lies below a rigorously determined level of adequacy of diet and living conditions.

The sorts of historical data which permit the identification of the major groups in poverty are extremely various: overt signs of destitution and famine; data on poor relief; data (usually qualitative or impressionistic) on unemployment, vagrancy, begging; descriptive evidence on food consumption; information on the prevalence of land holdings insufficient to support a family; crude estimates of the relative importance of selected occupational groups; indirect indications of undernourishment and malnutrition; and information on extreme overcrowding or the health hazards of housing, water, and sanitation.

The final typology of the structure of poverty is summarized in Table 2. Each 'type' is listed together with a brief indication of its main features in the first column and the countries composing it in the second column. The third column summarizes structural conditions or processes associated with extreme poverty for each country. The fourth column shows the probable ranking of the types by overall extent of extreme poverty with the lowest number assigned to the type with the least extreme poverty and the highest number to that with the most. The final column gives the principal sources of information. Since our main interest is in the impact of industrialization and commercialization on poverty, we ordered the types initially by level of industrialization as judged primarily by the relative importance of the factory sector. The five types in which industrialization was negligible were ordered by extent of commercialization.

An overview of the typology suggests the following generalizations about variations in the structure and extent of poverty in the middle of the nineteenth century.

The comparative abundance of agricultural resources and the nature of institutions for landholding and cultivation differentiated between the extremes of widespread poverty. Poverty was most widespread in India and China (Type G) where . parcellized holdings combined with pressure of population on resources with given technology. Poverty was next most widespread in Types H (Russia, Egypt, Turkey, and Brazil) and D (Italy and Spain) where high rates of appropriation of product existed either because of cultivation by some form of servile or bonded labour or because land ownership was highly concentrated with cultivation by small-scale tenants or landless labourers. Poverty was least widespread in the relatively resource-abundant newly settled countries where internal frontiers were still expanding and the distribution of land was comparatively egalitarian (Type C). In the non-commercial economy of Burma (Type I), abundance of land compared with population, and pre-industrial village and extended family institutions for social security combined to hold extreme poverty to a minimum.

In countries of the middle range (Types A, B, E, and F) extreme poverty was greatest where economic or demographic change had been widespread or very rapid. In the non-industrial countries of Scandinavia (Type E), surges of population growth in the absence of sufficient growth of employment led to large numbers of landless unemployed labourers. In the industrially advanced countries of Belgium and Great Britain (Type A) widespread and rapid economic change was associated with major failures to absorb surplus population into the expanding sectors of the economy. In contrast, in Germany, France and Switzerland (Type B) industrialization had proceeded more slowly with more frequent location of factories in rural areas. In Japan (Type F), commercialization of agriculture had spread slowly over a period of many decades and population growth rates were low.

Several major hypotheses emerge from our historical study of the processes that generate poverty. First, the inherited constraints on economic structure that most affect the incidence of poverty in low-level agricultural economies are the abundance of accessible agricultural resources relative to population and the nature and structure of landholding institutions. Second, the relationship between the level of economic development and the extent of poverty is complex and non-linear with extreme poverty possible both at very low and at higher levels of development. Third, any kind of structural change such as industrialization or commercialization tends to increase poverty among the poorest members of the population. Furthermore, in the early stages of development, the increase in poverty tends to be quite large unless the change is sufficiently slow and

of such a kind that the population whose activities are displaced or marginalized can be reabsorbed into expanding sectors of the economy. Our study suggests the hypothesis that both rapid commercialization and rapid industrialization systematically depressed the standard of living of the poorest stratum of the population in the early part of the nineteenth century. Finally, the structure and processes of economic activity matter most in determining the incidence of poverty; the structures of production, the market sector, and the labour force; the processes of technical change, commercialization, and population growth. We will discuss each of these hypotheses in turn.

First, our comparative analysis of poverty in 1850 reinforces the proposition that the constraints on economic structure contributing most to widespread poverty in overwhelmingly agricultural economies in the nineteenth century were the comparative scarcity of agricultural resources and the institutions of land ownership and cultivation. Where population was dense relative to available resources (for example China and India), increases in population and long lags in the adaptations of population growth to the level of economic opportunity contributed to widespread poverty and recurrent food shortages.

Landholding institutions also affected the structure of poverty. Two kinds of landholding institutions were particularly unfavourable. Extreme concentration of landownership with small-scale tenant cultivation (as in Spain and Italy) or large-scale cultivation by servile labour (as in Brazil and Russia) led to high rates of appropriation by landowners and extreme poverty among agriculturalists. Widespread poverty also occurred with small-scale peasant ownership where population pressed hard against resources and customary or legal constraints on the subdivision of holdings were weak. In India, China, and parts of Belgium and southwest Germany, for example, the incidence of poverty was closely associated with population density and parcellization of small independent landholdings.

Second, our study suggests that the relationship between the extent of poverty and the level of economic development is complex. At the lowest level of economic development there was the most widespread extreme poverty. It was characterized by either unfavourable resource–population endowments or exploitative landholding institutions. At the highest level of development extreme poverty was much less widespread. However, within the group of high-level countries the incidence of

566   Table 2. *A typology of poverty in 1850*

Type of Country	Brief Description of Type	Countries in Group (a)	Structural Influences and Processes Contributing to Poverty in Individual Countries (b)
A	Rapidly industrializing and most advanced industrially; major population displacements	Belgium	Dis 1, Dis 2, Dis 4, Ag 1 (weak), Ag 3(weak), Ag 4, Ag 7, Ag 8(weak), Urb 2, Urb 3(weak)
		England	Dis 1, Dis 2, Dis 4(weak), Ag 8(weak), Urb 2, Urb 3(weak)
B	More slowly industrializing countries; moderate displacements of population	Germany	Ag 1(weak), Ag 2(weak), Ag 4(weak), Dis 2(weak) Urb 2(weak), Urb 3(weak)
		France	Dis 2(weak), Urb 2(weak), Urb 3(weak)
		Switzerland	Dis 2(weak), Urb 2(weak), Urb 3(weak)
C	Newly settled countries; scarcity of agricultural labour; poverty concentrated among urban immigrants	(U.S.A.)	Urb 2, Urb 4, Ag 2(weak), Ag 4(weak), Ag 5(weak), Dis 1(weak)
		Australia	Urb 2, Urb 4
		(New Zealand) (E)	Urb 2, Urb 4, Ag 2
		Canada	Ag 2(weak), Urb 4
D	Extreme concentration of land ownership; major region of dense population; low product per worker	Italy	Ag 1(weak), Ag 2, Ag 4, Ag 6, Ag 8, Dis 1
		Spain	Ag 1(weak), Ag 2, Ag 4, Ag 6, Ag 8, Urb 1, Dis 1
E	Small-scale independent cultivation; rapid population growth in presence of expansion of employment opportunities; resource population ratio not unfavourable	Norway Sweden Denmark (F)	Dis 1, Dis 4, Urb 1, Ag 8
F	Slowly commercializing; considerable disintegration of feudal-type economy; dense stable population; moderate displacements of population	Japan	Dis 1, Ag 2, Ag 3(weak), Ag 6(weak), Ag 8(weak)
G	Dense population; parcellized holdings by independent peasants; low product per worker	India	Ag 1, Ag 2, Ag 3, Ag 4, Dis 3
		China	Ag 1, Ag 2, Ag 3, Ag 4, Viol 1
H	High rate of appropriation of product; serf, bonded or slave labour; low product per worker	Russia	Ag 2, Ag 3, Ag 4, Ag 5, Ag 6
		(Brazil)	Ag 2, Ag 3(weak), Ag 5, Ag 6
		Egypt	Ag 2, Ag 3, Ag 4, Ag 5, Ag 6
		Turkey (Asian)	Ag 2, Ag 3, Ag 4, Ag 5, Ag 6, Viol 1, Dis 3(weak)
I	Favourable resource population ratio; stable population; pre-industrial institutions of social insurance	Burma	Ag 1(weak), Ag 2(weak)
Unclassified		Argentina	Ag 2, Ag 6
		Netherlands	Ag 2(weak), Dis 1(weak), Urb 1, Urb 2, Urb 3(weak)

Rank of Type on Extent of Poverty (c)	Major Sources of Country Information (d)	Country
5	Dechesne (1932); Chlepner (1956); Baudhuin (1928–29); Ducpétiaux (1850).	Belgium
	Chambers and Mingay (1966); Clapham (1939); Engels (1844); Lyons (1976); Usher (1920); Caird (1851); Mayhew (1860–61); Redford (1964).	England
3½	Hamerow (1969); Wunderlich (1961); Kuczynski (1945).	Germany
	Bogart (1942); Clapham (1921); Levasseur (1904).	France
	Rappard (1914); Schwiezerische Ges. fur Statistiek (1964); Wittman (1963).	Switzerland
2	Bidwell and Falconer (1925); Gray (1925); Jones (1960); Ware (1964); Lebergott (1964); Fogel (1975); Woodman (1966).	(U.S.A.)
	Coghlan (1918); Griffin (1970); Shaw (1946).	Australia
	Condliffe (1930); Simkin (1951); Sutch (1969); Thomson (1859).	(New Zealand)
	Easterbrook and Aitken (1956); Firestone (1960); Tucker (1936).	Canada
7	Clough (1964); Eckaus (1961); Seton-Watson (1946); Schmidt (1939).	Italy
	Brenan (1943); Carr (1966); Vives (1969); Merin (1938); Higgins (1886); Livi-Bacci (1968).	Spain
6	Drake (1969); Hovde (1943); Janson (1931); Lieberman (1970); Nielson (1928); Youngson (1959); Montgomery (1939); Soltow (1965).	Norway Sweden Denmark
3½	Honjo (1965); Smith (1959); Tsuchiya (1937); Hanley and Yamamura (1971); Yamamura (1973).	Japan
9	Davis (1951); Blyn (1966); Bhatia (1967); Gadgil (1942); Singh (1965); Digby (1901).	India
	Fairbank, Eckstein, and Yang (1960); Hou (1963); Tawney (1932); Perkins (1969); Condliffe (1932); Mallory (1926).	China
8	Lyashchenko (1949); Tugan-Baranovsky (1907); Tuma (1965); Mavor (1925); Haxthausen (1847–48); Tourgueneff (1847).	Russia
	Graham (1968); Prado (1967); Stein (1957); Conrad (1972).	Brazil
	Baer (1959); Dicey (1881); Nahas (1901); Owen (1969).	Egypt
	Mukdim (1935); Hershlag (1964); Issawi (1966); Mordimann (1878).	Turkey
1	Furnivall (1931); Hliang (1964); Tun Wai (1961).	Burma
–	Diaz Alejandro (1970); Scobie (1964).	Argentina
–	Brugmans (1961); Jonge (1968); Baasch (1927); Kemper (1850).	Netherlands

(See notes overleaf)

(a)   Countries in parentheses are in some significant respect anomalous for their type; see text for explanation.
(b)   The symbols representing structural influences and processes contributing to poverty in individual countries
      are as follows:

Dis 1: displacement of small agriculturalists because of agricultural commercialization
Dis 2: displacement of craft workers because of domestic industrialization
Dis 3: displacement of craft workers because of foreign imports
Dis 4: unemployment or underemployment because of surge in population growth greater than growth
in employment opportunities
Urb 1: overcrowding of urban informal sector
Urb 2: cyclical unemployment
Urb 3: factory wages below subsistence
Urb 4: urban foreign immigrants
Ag 1: pressure of population on agricultural resources
Ag 2: low productivity per worker in agriculture
Ag 3: natural disasters
Ag 4: parcellization of cultivating units
Ag 5: slavery/serf labour/*de facto* bonded labour
Ag 6: exploitative landholding institutions
Ag 7: agricultural indebtedness associated with commercialization of agriculture
Ag 8: wages of agricultural labourers below subsistence
Viol 1: domestic violence

Note that the structural influences and processes are not mutually exclusive. 'Weak' in parentheses indicates that
the influence in question contributes to the poverty of relatively few or affects only a single region. The
omission of an influence does not indicate that it was not present, only that it does not appear to have operated
strongly enough to cause extreme poverty. Influences probably affecting less than 1% of the population are not
cited.

(c)   For discussion of empirical bases for the ranking, see text.
(d)   See bibliography in Adelman and Morris, 'A typology of poverty', for full references.
(e)   Inadequacy of empirical evidence leaves *serious* doubt about the extent of extreme poverty in this country.
(f)   Overall extent of extreme poverty less than characteristic of type.

extreme poverty was greater in the most industrialized countries where economic change had
been most rapid and pervasive. Within the
group of agricultural economies (above the
lowest level) which were undergoing significant
commercialization, variations in the incidence
of extreme poverty were accounted for by
constraints posed by land institutions and the
rapidity of economic or demographic change
rather than the level of economic development.

Third, the present analysis suggests strongly
the proposition that all kinds of structural
change hurt the poor. A leading hypothesis
emerging from our study is that during the first
half of the nineteenth century, the spread of
mechanized techniques and the spread of
markets in agriculture systematically increased
poverty among the poorest segments of society.
The salient features of comparative experience
during that period suggest the following model
of the key interactions contributing to
increased poverty. The extent of increased
poverty depended on the nature, strength and
pattern (regional and sectoral) of two processes
associated with structural change: first, the
process of displacement of one set of economic
activities by another as a result of monetization
or technological change; and second, the

process of expansion associated with the introduction of new economic activities. The impact
of structural change on poverty depended upon
the net balance of the two processes. Interacting with these processes were national and
regional patterns of population growth and
migration.

The process of displacement rarely meant
that the outmoded activities disappeared
immediately. Rather, the people engaged in
such activities were forced through competition
with the newer activities to accept reduced
earnings or reduced employment. The earnings
of rural handicraft workers in both Belgium and
Great Britain declined steadily after the
Napoleonic Wars as they faced the cheaper
products and rising output of the factory
sector. In all countries, the commercialization
of agriculture had reduced possibilities for small
agriculturalists to obtain a livelihood; enclosures had taken away the use of common lands
on which they depended for their livelihood;
rising land values and rents had squeezed small
tenants; and the shift to production for the
market had led to indebtedness and dispossession of smallholders without the resources to
survive market fluctuations. The people
engaged in the increasingly marginal activities

had joined the permanent wage-earning class or the permanently unemployed only when faced with eviction or incomes below an irreducible minimum.

The processes of expansion associated with the introduction of new economic activities provided for increased employment in both new activities and selected older ones. Factories provided employment directly to only a small proportion of the total labour force in the industrializing countries of northern Europe in 1850. Furthermore, the demand for factory labour was mainly for women and children. Employment had also expanded in related activities such as mining, forestry, and certain handicrafts not yet threatened by mechanization. The demand for unskilled weavers had increased greatly for a time as a result of the mechanization of spinning in England and Switzerland, for example, at the beginning of the nineteenth century. Where commercialization of agriculture had favoured the growth of large-scale farming, the demand for agricultural labourers increased substantially (for example in the north of England, northeast Germany, Normandy, Flanders and the Po Valley). Commercialization had also provided increased profits and employment to those peasant families with sufficient resources and skills to produce successfully for the market.

Sectoral and regional patterns of displacement, absorption, and population growth mattered greatly. The segmented nature of labour markets implied that labour shortages in particular regions or industries did not cancel out surpluses elsewhere. Institutional, social, and cultural forces limiting geographic mobility thus contributed to an unfavourable net balance of the processes of displacement and absorption. Strong preferences for rural ways of living had led many agriculturalists and rural handicraft workers to accept declining earnings rather than leave their small plots of land. Legal impediments to mobility (for example the English Settlement Laws), had aggravated regional labour surpluses. Cultural barriers to mobility, such as those posed by Flemish reluctance to move to French Belgium, had intensified unemployment among farmers whose activities had been displaced or marginalized by technical change and commercialization. As a result, the detailed net balances, industry by industry and region by region, rather than national balances, determined both the pattern and extent of overall impoverishment associated with structural change.

In the more industrialized countries, cyclical unemployment and fluctuations in prices contributed significantly to poverty. Recurrent unemployment depressed the living standards of urban industrial workers, while price fluctuations contributed to indebtedness and loss of land in agricultural areas.

The extent of imbalance in the labour market was strongly affected by the acceleration of population growth that had occurred during the latter half of the eighteenth century in many countries and regions. The sources of the spurt in population lay in processes that took place as far back as the seventeenth century: improvements in diet related to the spread of new crops, lowered death rates due to mild disease prevention and the lessened impact of wars and domestic violence, and some increases in fertility associated with the weakening of traditional social checks to population growth. The impact of population growth on the extent of extreme poverty operated through its effect on the net balances of the processes of displacement and absorption. Migration, both internal and external, had operated to mitigate the unfavourable effects of segmentation of labour markets, but at that time had generally been insufficient to reduce significantly the net national balance through the evening out of regional imbalances. The pace, distribution and structure of economic change in turn affected population growth. Where economic change had proceeded slowly, adaptation of population change was possible, and adaptive changes had taken place in some countries and regions. Rapid and pervasive change rendered unlikely adaptive responses of fertility rates to the rate of expansion of economic opportunities. As a result, while rapid economic change meant increased possibilities for absorbing an expanding labour force, the net impact of more rapid growth was mostly negative because the failure of adaptive population responses more than counterbalanced its positive effects.

Thus, the nature and extent of structural change together with its rapidity and pattern determined both the incidence and characteristics of poverty in the mid-nineteenth century. The critical features whose interrelationships accounted for the incidence of economic change on the poor were the rapidity, breadth and spread of economic change, landholdings and landholding institutions, and past patterns of population growth. We found no automatic trickle down to the poorest segments of the population of the benefits of industrialization. On the contrary, economic growth appears to have worked systematically to reduce their levels of living even where average standards of living of workers rose (as in Great Britain between 1800 and 1850).

In summary, the lessons of economic change suggested by our comparative study of the first half of the nineteenth century are that: (1) any kind of structural change in underdeveloped countries is achieved through processes of net displacement tending to lower the living standards of the poorest members of the society; (2) there is no automatic mechanism ensuring that expanding economic activities will be either appropriate or adequate to reabsorb the population displaced or threatened by structural change; (3) the faster the structural change, the more likely the processes of displacement are to swamp the processes of absorption and result in a marked deterioration in the living standards of the poorest members of the economy; and (4) the impact of economic change on poverty depends critically on the nature of social structure and social responses to economic change. These include social constraints on population growth, the response of fertility and migration rates to changing economic opportunities, legal and customary barriers to the subdivision of land, arrangements for land tenure and holding, and the strength of extended family protection of the unemployed and underemployed.

4. ADELMAN-ROBINSON KOREAN MODEL OF INCOME DISTRIBUTION

The model is designed to provide a laboratory within which one can explore the potential impact of standard economic policy instruments and programmes intended to improve the relative and absolute incomes of the poor. The model traces out both the direct and indirect influences upon the distribution of income. Its structure is set by the nature of the major economic forces determining the distribution of income in the relatively short run and of the major policy instruments which could affect it.

The model is in the tradition of economy-wide planning models. It has as its primary focus the modelling of the distribution of income, but it also includes all the components of more traditional planning models as well as some monetary elements typical of macro-models. Its distinguishing features are: (1) it solves for prices endogenously in both factor and product markets; (2) its solution is based on achieving a measure of consistency among the results of individual optimizing behaviour by a large number of actors (households, firms);

(3) it incorporates income distribution, monetary phenomena, and foreign trade; (4) it is dynamic, with imperfect inter-temporal consistency; and (5) it allows for varying principles of market clearing and institutional behaviour.

The model operates by simulating the operation of factor and product markets with profit-maximizing firms and utility-maximizing households. Although it is broadly in the neo-classical tradition, it has a number of disequilibrium, non-neoclassical features. The overall model consists of a static within-period adjustment model linked to a dynamic inter-temporal model. Within each period, the degree of adjustment is constrained by the existence of capital in place of a specific type; by the immobility of the self-employed both in agriculture and in urban production; by rigidities in wage structures; and by government constraints on firm behaviour, especially in the foreign trade sector. Between periods, some degree of flexibility is provided by capital accumulation, population growth, migration, changes in the amount of self-employment, and changes in the size structure of production. Nevertheless, the ability of the economy to achieve full Walrasian equilibrium remains severely constrained.

The model is quite comprehensive in its degree of 'closure', i.e. the number of features of the economy which are endogenous and mutually consistent. The model explicitly goes from endogenously determined factor payments and employment to household incomes, with savings and expenditure decisions being modelled at the household level. The overall size distribution of household incomes is determined by explicit aggregation. Accounting consistency is maintained among: (1) household, firm, government, and trade accounts; (2) national income accounts; (3) input-output accounts; (4) the national product accounts and (5) the labour force and the number of households.

The model's focus on policy experiments led to its design in as flexible a manner as possible. The model incorporates optimizing responses by firms and households to a wide range of policy instruments such as indirect tax rates, direct tax rates, tariffs, interest rates, and monetary variables. Furthermore, the model is capable of portraying a variety of institutional principles in the operation of credit markets and factor markets, the degree of monopoly, and even the objective functions of firms.

A summary description of the overall model follows. For each period, the computation of the model is decomposed into three stages. The Stage I model describes the contracts made between firms and the financial markets to spend funds on investment goods. Stage II describes how factor and product markets reach an equilibrium constrained by the investment commitments undertaken in Stage I and by various institutional rigidities imposed by foreign trade and by the operation of product and labour markets. Stage III serves to generate the expectations on which Stage I decisions are based, some of the rules of its operation (e.g. the credit regime), and to 'age' the model economy. Stage II is the major simultaneous core of the model, and represents the basic static portion of the model, used for comparative-statics experiments. Stages I and III are used only in the dynamic analysis.

Stage I models the loanable funds market. Producers form their demands for loanable funds on the basis of expected sales and expected prices of inputs. Credit is then rationed either by setting an interest rate and allowing the market to clear at that rate or by setting a target rate of expansion of credit and allowing the rate of interest to adjust in order to clear the loanable funds market. The output of Stage I is the allocation of loanable funds among firms and sectors, and an overall injection of credit into the economy. Stage I is diagrammed in Fig. 1.

The Stage II model is a general equilibrium model in that prices or supplies are assumed to adjust so as to clear all markets, subject to various constraints that prevent the economy from fully adjusting by means of pure market mechanisms. Furthermore, money enters in the Stage II model in an essential way.

The Stage II model is itself subdivided into a number of parts representing different computational phases: supply, demand, wage, income and price determination. The output of this is 'actual' production, employment, prices, wages and income distribution for the period. Figs. 2 and 3 portray the basic model structure. In Fig. 2, the product and labour markets are pictured. The treatment of traded goods is especially important. Imports and exports which compete on the world market are assumed to sell domestically at the world price plus a fixed tariff (or subsidy). For these goods, imports and exports are determined residually after calculating domestic supply and demand at the fixed prices. For protected goods or non-traded goods, we assume that the domestic markets are insulated from the rest of the world and prices are determined so as to clear them.

Fig. 3 shows the income accounts and especially the steps in translating the functional distribution into the household distribution. There are 15 different socio-economic categories of income recipients for whom the model determines income, taxes, allocation to household groups, transfers, savings, and consumption expenditure. For each category, a within-group distribution is calculated by summing the 15 different group distributions.

The Stage II model reaches its solution by means of a tatonnement process which stimulates market behaviour. However, in both Stages I and II, no actual transactions take place until the solution of each stage is reached. Thus, the capital stock of firms is altered only at the end of Stage I; factors are hired, production takes place, and income is earned and spent only at the end of Stage II.

The Stage III model consists of a set of functions which update the relevant variables and formulate expectations which enter into the Stage I model for the next period. Stage III

Table 3. *Stage III model summary*

Stage II Output	Stage III Model components	Stage III Output
Factor payments	Population growth	Expectations parameters
Product prices	Education/skill	for Stage I
Production	Exchange rate	Factor supplies
Employment	Expected prices	Technological and
Functional dist.	Expected sales	behavioural parameters
Household dist.	Household para-	
	meters	
	Govt. parameters	
	Trade parameters	
	Firm parameters	
	Technological	
	change	
	Migration	

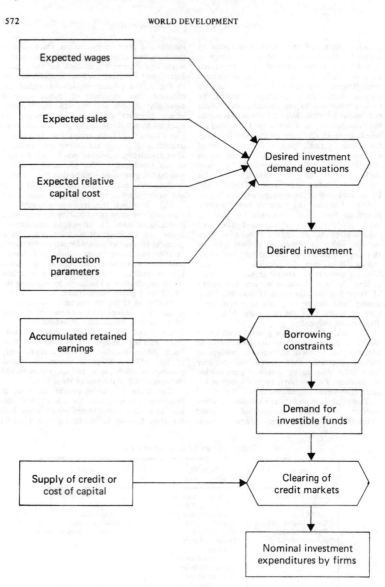

Figure 1. *Stage I: Determination of investment*

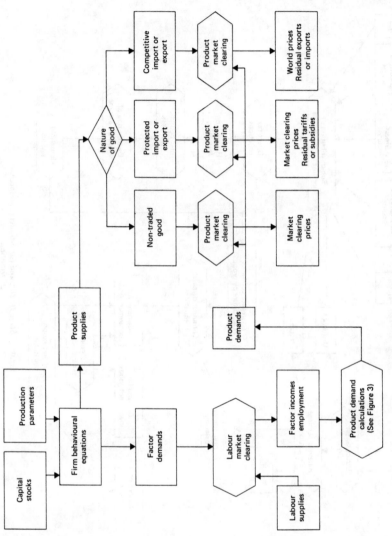

Figure 2. *Determination of wages, employment, prices, and profits*

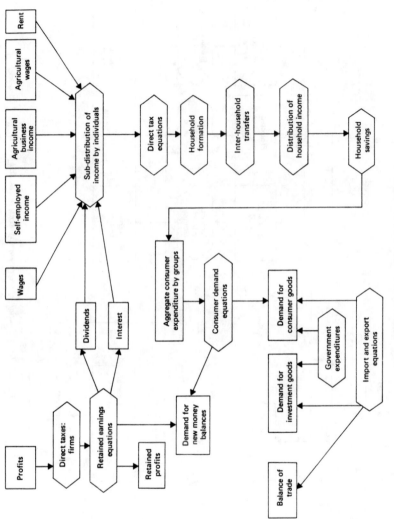

Figure 3. *Stage II: Demand for products and income distribution*

can be seen as consisting of a collection of sub-models which specify all the dynamic adjustments and inter-temporal linkages for the overall model (Table 3). Our relatively short time horizon has led us to specify a fairly simple set of Stage III functions. A number of variables such as population growth are simply assumed to grow at an exogenously specified rate. Rural—urban migration is explicitly modelled as a function of only rural—urban income differentials, with an upper limit on the possible annual rate of migration. In general, there are no interactions among the various sub-models and each is specified as a self-contained set of functions.

In each period, the three stages are solved serially. Variables which are assumed fixed in Stage I are allowed to vary in Stage II. Thus the overall model distinguishes between expectations and realizations. In the third stage, the differences between expectations and realizations are incorporated into the forecast functions for the expected variables with which calculations are made in the periods subsequent to the first. In fact the overall dynamic model represents a kind of 'lurching equilibrium' which, it is hoped, represents a more realistic specification of actual growth than would be provided by some inter-temporally efficient equilibrium growth model.

Conclusions based on policy experiments

We now turn to a discussion of the major implications of the model. The major conclusion from the policy experiments is that the time path of the size distribution of income is exceedingly stable. Under a great variety of experiments, many of which involve quite sizable interventions, there is a marked tendency to return to the basic-path distribution. Even when the policy or programme is sustained over time, it is quite rare that, after 10 years, there is more than a 5% change in the Gini coefficient, or that a percentile's share is altered by more than 20%. Most single-policy interventions, with the exception of transfers, even when quite large, do not have lasting effects. Even transfer policies, while to some extent effective, are potentially of quite limited scope in most less developed countries. Only when a sufficient number of different interventions are applied simultaneously so that there is, in effect, a change in development strategy — are more sizable or lasting effects possible. These results support the position that struc-

tural change is required to affect inequality and that equity objectives must shape the choice of basic development strategy if they are to be met.

The stability of the size distribution is associated in our experiments with relative instability in factor shares and in the functional distribution of income. This instability indicates that the relative position of various socio-economic groups is very sensitive to the choice of economic policy. By appropriate choice of instruments, it is easy to favour or discriminate against particular groups. The relative degrees of poverty and wealth in the economy as a whole are little affected, but the composition of the poor and wealthy groups changes dramatically.

Partial analyses are rarely indicative of the ultimate effects of policy interventions once their impact is allowed to permeate throughout the system. Particular instruments or policies often have different effects than expected. Not only orders of magnitude but also directions of effects are often different. Also, the effects of policy or programme combinations are rarely equal to the sum of the effects of their individual components, indicating that inter-action effects among policies are significant.

Our results underscore the importance of the agricultural terms of trade and of the extent of rural—urban migration for anti-poverty policy. In contrast, they indicate that such often advocated changes as the promotion of small-scale industry, and changes in the labour intensity of technology in manufacturing, unless part of a wider package, are either ineffective or effective for reasons which are different from the grounds on which they are usually advocated. Population policy has relatively little effect on the size distribution of household incomes over the medium time period considered. Indeed, population policies which result in relatively less labour in urban areas tend to deteriorate the distribution of income.

Of the possible instruments for policy intervention to improve the size distribution of income, the agricultural terms of trade are particularly crucial. An increase in the terms of trade raises the incomes of small farmers and, to a lesser extent, landless labour, and injures urban groups, including the urban poor. Overall, however, even though the incomes of rich farmers are raised more than proportionately and the urban poor are hurt, the net reduction in poverty is significant. Policy actions are required to maintain the agricultural terms of trade, as the terms of trade have a natural tendency to worsen with growth.

Rural—urban migration can affect poverty significantly. In general, the incomes of the urban poor are much higher than the incomes of the rural poor, so that one would expect migration to alleviate overall poverty. However, there clearly can be too much migration, creating a Marxian 'reserve army' of the would-be employed and thereby keeping unskilled urban wages at subsistence. If, in addition, agricultural output falls due to out-migration, food prices will rise, raising the cost of living and further impoverishing urban workers.

As expected, choice of trade policies has a significant impact on poverty and equity. However, it is not the direct effects of trade policy on the urban sector that matter — that impact is rapidly dissipated throughout the economy — rather it is the impact of trade policy on the agricultural terms of trade and upon rural—urban migration that provides the major influences of trade upon poverty and equity. For example had Korea followed an import substitution strategy rather than a labour-intensive export expansion policy, our experiments indicate that the resultant deterioration of the agricultural terms of trade would have produced a significantly poorer size distribution of income and significantly greater poverty than were actually experienced. By contrast, a stronger labour-intensive export promotion package would have had some beneficial effects, the most important of which would have been felt ultimately through trickle-down to the poor farmers.

As for population policy, we found that a reduction in rural population reduces poverty by decreasing the agricultural labour force. It leads to an increase in average land holdings through reductions in the number of farm households and also results in a more intensive use of labour. In contrast, reducing the urban population leads to increases in overall poverty by restricting the supply of urban goods, thus causing their prices to rise, and by lowering the demand for food products, thus causing their prices to fall. The consequence is deterioration in the agricultural terms of trade. The negative effect of urban population reduction can be mitigated by induced increases in migration to replace the lost urban labour and act as a substitute for direct reduction in rural population.

Perhaps the most frequently proposed anti-poverty measure is that of direct transfers to the poor. Two different types of transfer programme were tried: (1) direct income transfers and (2) price subsidies for consumption of necessities (food, housing, and medical care) for both rural and urban poverty groups. Both types of transfer policies help the specific target groups and have the least leakage and market distortion effects of any of our experiments. The effects of the price subsidy programme, however, are somewhat eroded over time because, as incomes rise, the share spent on necessities falls. The more important problem with transfer programmes, however, is that the effects last only as long as the programme is in effect and therefore, if such programmes are to be the major tool of anti-poverty policy, society must be committed to persistently large welfare budgets and to the resulting dualistic society.

The choice of an appropriate development strategy can lead to major improvements in the share and absolute incomes of the poor, given appropriate initial conditions. The difference to the poor between following a labour-intensive export strategy and an import-substitution strategy can be major and lasting. In the presence of reasonably equitable distribution of land ownership and tenure arrangements and widespread ownership of human capital, a labour-intensive export strategy contributes significantly to a more egalitarian distribution of income. Even with such a strategy and favourable initial conditions, however, a systematic tendency for the deterioration in the share of income accruing to the poor appears to be built into the operation of rapidly growing economic systems. To avoid the impact of such deterioration is quite difficult and requires further pervasive reorientation of policy.

To explore the nature of desirable reorientations of policy imposed over and above the basic development strategy, dynamic policy experiments for both rural and urban target groups were carried out. For each sector, packages were investigated containing social development programmes, production and employment programmes, and programmes involving varying degrees of institutional change. Policy experiments with both rural and urban packages showed that the overall programme is considerably more effective than the sum of its components. In general, the ultimate impact of the packages is determined largely by the extent and nature of indirect leakage effects, which, in turn, are strongly influenced by interactions among the component sets of programmes.

Of the individual rural development packages, programmes to promote increases in agricultural production are not an unqualified blessing. They are ineffective in reducing poverty and improving the distribution after import substitution possibilities in food are exhausted. They then tend to worsen the position of the rural poor and improve the lot of urban groups, including the urban poor, unless effective price stabilization policies are implemented. In general, who gains from the rural policy packages depends largely on what happens to the terms of trade. If they turn against agriculture enough, the results are a transfer or trickle-up to the urban groups. Rural groups gain only if special policies are implemented to prevent the terms of trade from deteriorating too much. Rural public works lead to substantial improvement in the real incomes of the poor, especially landless rural labour, and are a moderately effective policy. Land reform, which redistributes land to small farmers, is very effective, both reducing poverty and narrowing the distribution within the rural sector. Rural cooperatives – which market the crop, subsidize agricultural inputs, and provide low cost credit – have some beneficial effects and represent a moderately effective programme. Of the individual policy packages, land reform has the most effect on the relative distribution and raises the incomes of the poor by almost as much as rural public works.

The implementation of a rural development strategy (including production, public works, cooperatives, social development, and price stabilization programmes) is very effective in alleviating poverty and improving the distribution. Under the rural development strategy which includes land reform, the number of people living in poverty is reduced to about one quarter of the number in the basic run by the final year. The rural strategy without land reform is less beneficial (there are 20% more households living in poverty than in the package with land reform), although it is still very effective.

The individual urban programmes are all at most moderately effective in reducing poverty and changing the overall distribution. They do, however, exhibit a certain amount of synergism such that the combination of several urban programmes is more effective than the sum of the separate components. The moderately effective individual urban packages are a public works programme in housing construction and transportation, and a programme to intensify the promotion of labour-intensive and export industries. However, these programmes are successful in alleviating poverty not because of their effect on urban wages and employment but rather through their influence on rural poverty via changes in the terms of trade. A

number of programmes were ineffective in reducing overall poverty and improving the relative distribution: consumption subsidies to urban working groups, the promotion of small-scale industries, and the adoption of labour-intensive technology (by changes in the production functions). Some programmes were harmful. A programme to reduce the rate of growth of the urban population (and hence the urban labour force) increased the amount of poverty and worsened the overall distribution. A programme to nationalize large-scale manufacturing industry also increased the degree of poverty, largely because it resulted in lower productivity in the nationalized firms, less manufacturing output overall, and hence drove up the relative price of manufactures. The resulting decline in the agricultural terms of trade lowered rural incomes and so increased poverty.

Despite the largely disappointing nature of the individual urban programmes, an urban development strategy combining public works and the promotion of labour-intensive industries is effective in reducing poverty and improving the distribution. Its effectiveness, however, is not nearly so great as the overall rural strategies and is due largely to indirect effects which improve the agricultural terms of trade and so allow the benefits to leak across to the rural poor. This trickle-down effect is more pronounced with time and, if allowed to operate, would continue to have favourable effects even after the experimental period.

Our experience with the separate rural and urban packages led us rather quickly to examine combined rural–urban packages. We sought an integrated and balanced approach which would affect all sectors of the economy and ensure that leakages to urban groups of rural programmes are more than counter-balanced by leakages to rural groups of urban programmes (because most of the poor are rural).

Two large across-the-board policy packages were considered in our policy experiments: a 'market socialism' package (Package A) and a 'reform capitalism' package (Package B). Package A was intended to represent a package of policies similar to those frequently adopted in non-communist socialist countries. Package A emphasizes land reform, nationalization of large-scale industry, and import substitution, in addition to programmes of social development, urban and rural public works, rural cooperatives, and industrial decentralization.

Package B, on the other hand, was intended to illustrate what a capitalist economy could do if it were sufficiently motivated by the goal of poverty alleviation to undertake significant alterations in the structure of its society. This reform capitalism package includes the same programmes of social development, urban and rural public works, rural cooperatives, and industrial decentralization that appear in Package A. However, instead of an import-substitution strategy, there is an emphasis on promotion of labour-intensive exports. And, in preference to land reform, Package B introduces rural marketing boards and improvements in agricultural productivity. There is no analogue to Package A's nationalization programme.

Both Packages A and B were effective. By the end of the decade, in spite of leakages to the rich in Package B and a decline in the growth rate in Package A, all seven of the lowest income deciles of the society remained better off in absolute terms than they were without any policy package at all. The trade-offs between the two approaches are the familiar ones. The market socialist package leads to better and improving distribution but deteriorating output performance relative to the unperturbed time path of the economy. The reform capitalism package shows evidence of deterioration of the distributional gains over time and of acceleration of production growth. By the end of the decade, everyone (including the lowest decile) is better off with the reform capitalism package than with the market socialism package in absolute terms. However, the seven lowest income deciles are still better off under the socialist package than in the basic dynamic solution, which has no significant anti-poverty measures.

On the whole, our results underscore the difficulties of effective policy interventions to improve the distribution of income. They emphasize the magnitude of the policy effort necessary to avoid rapid erosion of benefits. Since individual programmes tend to be considerably less effective than packages of programmes, and the benefits of most single-pronged interventions rapidly trickle up, a big-push balanced strategy appears to be best. However, a successful big push requires major government intervention and large implicit and explicit economic transfers. Therefore, the implementation of a successful anti-poverty programme would entail either a change in the ideology of the ruling classes towards explicit egalitarian concerns or a certain degree of centralization of authority in order to over-come resistance by the rich, or, most likely, a combination of both. The problem would then remain of reducing the power of the centralized authority once its basic job is done.

5. POLICY IMPLICATIONS OF THE THREE STUDIES

The present section is devoted to distilling the combined implications for policy emerging from the three studies. To avoid lengthy discussion, the results are summarized in tabular form. Table 4 lists the major hypotheses concerning the relationships between various economic processes and the distribution of income, especially the share of income to the poor. For each variable or influence the nature of the interaction with income distribution is described; an indication of the studies on which the description is based is given; and the reasons for the impact on income distribution, as we understand them are summarized. Table 5 lists in similar manner the major policy conclusions about economic influences which emerge from only one study.

All three studies, while utterly different in methodology and in the settings in which the relationships between poverty and growth are investigated, lead to a remarkably consistent and reinforcing set of policy conclusions. As is apparent from Table 4, the results of each study tend to be confirmed and illuminated by those of the other studies, not only in general terms, but in specific detail. Since the tables are self-explanatory, we will concentrate here on an elaboration of only the principal conclusions of our work.

A leading conclusion of our studies is that intervention to improve the distribution of income is extremely difficult. The Adelman-Robinson model emphasized the stability of the size distribution of income in the face of policy interventions and the ephemeral nature and inefficacy of most single-pronged anti-poverty programmes. The cross-section study indicated how few potentially effective policy instruments there were and the difficulties which their very nature posed for efforts at purposive change. The historical study showed the systemic character of the dynamic processes that worked to the detriment of the very poor in the middle of the nineteenth century. The irreversibility of detrimental impacts implied that a remarkably long time was usually required before initially unfavourable effects were counter-balanced.

All our studies emphasize that, in a given configuration of structural conditions, it is strategy and process which determine the impacts of economic change on the poor. The historical study indicated that countries sharing a particular mix of poverty also shared a set of historical processes of change. The cross-section study stressed the need for certain critical

Table 4. *Hypotheses generated by more than one study concerning the impact of economic processes on income distribution*

Variable or influence	Nature of impact and studies by which generated	Reasons for impact
Per capita GNP and level of socio-economic development	Relative share of poorest 60% of population shows U-shaped relationship to per capita GNP (A–M). Relationship between absolute per capita income and income distribution complex; very large differences in development levels positively related to both average income and reduction in poverty; but rapid growth tends to increase poverty even where average income rises (Hist and A–M).	At very low levels of development small number of growth points leads to concentration of benefits of economic change in hands of oligarchy of merchants, industrialists, and plantation owners; indirect effects of economic change tend to hurt the very poor by displacing and marginalizing their activities; only beyond a threshold determined by extent and spread of expansion of economic opportunities is trickle-down sufficient to raise average incomes of urban wage earners and agricultural labourers; even then, reductions in extreme poverty take place very slowly because of the segmented nature of the labour market and lack of adaptability of human skills.
Short-term rate of growth of per capita GNP	No simple association with the distribution of income; structure and composition of the increase in income, not average degree of income change, determines impact (A–M and A–R).	Nature, extent, and rapidity of *structural* change govern the direction and magnitude of the net balance of the processes of displacement, absorption, and social adaptation.
Economic innovations	At low and medium levels of development net impact of structural change of any kind on the poor systematically unfavourable even where average incomes rise.	Poor do not have resources and skills to take advantage of expanding economic opportunities; the operation of product and factor markets tends to marginalize their earnings or displace their skills; once skills permanently marginalized or products displaced, the poor lack human and financial capital for adaptation.
Socio-economic dualism	Sharply dualistic growth favours the rich and harms the relative and absolute position of the poor more than lesser degrees of dualism (whether at very low or higher levels of development).	Concentration of growth in limited sectors or regions, in the presence of segmented labour markets characteristic of underdeveloped countries, aggravates displacement and marginalization of skills, thus contributing to pools of surplus labour.
Natural resources	A favourable ratio of agricultural land to population with prevalence of family-size holdings restricts extreme poverty; an abundance of natural resources is associated with extreme concentration of income (A–M and Hist).	Availability of reserve of unappropriated agricultural land restricts numbers of extremely poor; presence of abundance of natural resources fosters exploitation and the appropriation of the benefits by small elites, foreign and indigenous
Rate of population growth	Past patterns of population growth important determinant of resource-population ratios and thus a key initial condition determining extent of extreme poverty (Hist and A–M). In medium run, population growth affects significantly net balance of processes of displacement and absorption (Hist and A–R). In short run, population growth of little significance to the income distribution (A–R and A–M).	Extremely long lag (50 years or more) before changes in rate of growth of population affect extent of extreme poverty significantly; medium-run effects depend on interaction of population and migration and are subject to threshold effect with respect to resource abundance.

(continued overleaf)

Variable or influence	Nature of impact and studies by which generated	Reasons for impact
Rural–urban migration	Rural–urban migration reduces rural poverty and increases urban poverty; up to a point, it reduces overall poverty (Hist and A–R).	In labour market reduces urban wages or increases urban unemployment, while decreasing rural underemployment or increasing wages of agricultural labour; in commodity markets it shifts the terms of trade in favour of agriculture, thus favouring the more numerous and poorer rural low-income groups; extremely rapid migration leads unfavourable impact on the urban poor to dominate favourable rural effects.
Education	Wide spread of education and literacy associated with larger share of income to middle quintile; no systematic association with other features of income distribution (A–M and A–R).	Spreads ownership of human capital; narrows distribution of wage income; increases rural–urban migration, thereby shifting population to higher income areas and improving agricultural terms of trade.
Land tenure and holdings	Impact of change on the poor critically dependent on distribution of land ownership; prevalence of subsistence farming where land abundant is favourable to distribution of income; parcellization of land or marked concentration of ownership with cultivation by either landless labourers or subsistence tenants contribute directly to poverty; widespread owner-operation of commercial farms favourable to distribution of income, although may not help the very poor (A–M and Hist).	Concentrated ownership where cultivators face lack of alternative employments permits high rate of appropriation of surplus product; opening up of new opportunities in presence of unequal abilities to respond widens inequality; processes conducive to dispossession or marginalization tend to be irreversible.
Modernization of agricultural techniques	Increases in agricultural productivity tend to worsen the position of the rural poor, while benefiting better-off farmers and the urban poor (A–R and Hist). No significant cross-sectional relationship.	Access to complementary resources (held only by better-off farmers) necessary for adoption of improvements; increases in output worsen terms of trade, harming rural poor and benefiting urban poor; lack of cross-sectional relationship due to interdependence between impact of agricultural technology and land tenure.
Size of subsistence agricultural sector	Total absence of commercialization of agriculture favourable to distribution of income (Hist). Among countries with some commercialization, no systematic relationship between commercialization and distribution of income (Hist and A–M).	Impact on the distribution of income of commercialization of agriculture dependent on land tenure and concentration of ownership; also dependent on course of terms of trade; short-term and medium- or long-term impacts may diverge, depending on demand and supply elasticities.
Trade and industrialization strategy	More diversified labour-intensive exports associated with larger share of income to both the poor and the middle classes (A–M and A–R).	Improves agricultural terms of trade and increases absorption of rural–urban migration.

Variable or influence	Nature of impact and studies by which generated	Reasons for impact
Level and change in industrialization	U-shaped relationship evident in cross-section and historical study; major differences in level of industrialization negatively associated with extent of poverty, but among more industrialized countries, poverty greater in those at higher levels which industrialized most rapidly (A–M and Hist).	Relationship complicated: interdependence between level and rate and threshold effect. See text for discussion.
Market socialism	Reduces share of income of top 5%; increases share of next 15% (A–M and A–R). Reduces overall growth rate and overall mean incomes, but relative and absolute incomes of lowest 70% higher in medium run (A–R).	Reduces profits and interest accruing to top 5%; increases technocrat and bureaucrat incomes; given nationalized firms which less dynamic, absolute gains to the poor evident in medium run eventually eroded, but distributional gains increase.
Effectiveness of and improvements in financial institutions	No systematic association with income shares of the poor even though important for growth (A–M and A–R).	Spread of financial institutions even in rural areas tends to benefit primarily those who are better-off; improved access to credit for poor farmers only beneficial when combined with improved access to technology and knowledge; increases in investment, even in small-scale industry, tend to work through their impact on economic growth (relationship of latter to income distribution complex).
Effectiveness of and improvements in tax systems	No systematic association with distribution in cross section (A–M). Little impact in model (A–R).	Structure of tax system influences who is poor and rich rather than how many; tax base sufficiently low so that little scope for impact.

transformations of economies and societies which could not be brought about without changes in the process and strategy of growth. The Korea model policy experiments showed that, as long as policy interventions were tacked onto a given strategy which remained unchanged, the distribution of income tended to revert to the pattern it would have had in the absence of the interventions.

In addition, complicated interactions are evident in our studies between the impact of policy changes, on the one hand, and the initial conditions describing the socio-economic structure upon which the policies impinge, on the other. Successful anti-poverty policy does not merely entail choosing the right development strategy. Initial conditions must also be appropriate. The critical thresholds for successful policy interventions relate to the distribution of ownership of certain assets – those which enter the production functions of the newly expanding activities. In the cross-section results the

existence of thresholds with respect to initial conditions is suggested by the fact that some variables proved important only when countries had achieved minimal levels of education and spread of economic modernization. The historical study showed that the impact of processes of change on the poor depended upon the particular complex of initial conditions. Within complexes there were some possibilities for substitution among conditions; in addition, there were interactions among processes, on the one hand, and initial conditions, on the other.

A further important conclusion of our work is that unbalanced growth strategies are bad for the poor. In the Korea model the dissipation of the benefits from programmes with a single focus was larger and more rapid than from programmes with multiple foci. In the cross-section study, sharply dualistic growth led to a worsening of the income distribution. Historically, the concentration of growth in either a few sectors or a few regions had backwash effects that accentuated new overall displacements arising from commercialization and industrialization.

A final conclusion emerging from our studies is that a systems or general equilibrium approach is required in order to design a strategy which predictably improves the position of the poor in the medium term. Both the historical and the modelling studies emphasize the importance of indirect effects and dynamic interactions. Not infrequently, the indirect effects of an initial impact of change swamp the direct effects and even reverse their direction. Thus, both studies reinforce the need for a careful systems-wide analysis of the impact of potential policy actions. Taken together, the cross-section, historical, and modelling studies underline the great difficulty which planners face in finding policy instruments or programmes which are effective in achieving more equitable paths of economic growth.

Table 5. *Major hypotheses generated by only one study concerning the impact of economic processes on income distribution*

Hypotheses	Study	Reasons for importance
Agricultural terms of trade critical determinant of distribution of income	A – R	Inelasticity of demand and supply leads to price changes; methodology of other studies does not provide test.
Size distribution quite insensitive to major changes in the functional distribution of income	A – R	High variance of earnings within functional distribution; socio-economic composition of deciles varied and overlapping; functional not measured in other studies.
Functional distribution very sensitive to economic policy	A – R	Economic change is both accomplished by and affects people in their functional capacities as producers; therefore most economic change and economic policies impinge directly upon socio-economic rather than income groups.
Import substitution strategy worsens distribution of income	A – R	Deteriorates agricultural terms of trade substantially; not measured in other studies.
The impact on the poor of structural change is determined by the detailed net balances of the processes of displacement, absorption, and labour force redistribution.	Hist	Innovation entails both substitutions for and complementarities with existing economic activities; the substitutions tend to both displace and absorb workers; complementary activities expand; segmentation of markets prevents evening out of unemployment and labour shortages; even within a given market no automatic balancing of expansionary and contractionary influences in either short or medium run because of socially-induced rigidities and lack of adaptability of skills.

19

Chapter 1

A Poverty-Focused Approach to Development Policy

Irma Adelman

The definition of poverty adopted in this essay is one of abject poverty—a poverty level so severe that it stunts the attainment of human potential. In 1980, 880 million people (22 per cent of the world population) lived below that level. This estimate of the extent of poverty is based on a poverty line specified in terms of the income level required to purchase a nutritional level minimally adequate for calorie replacement at average levels of activity. The World Bank suggests setting the standard at an annual per capita income of U.S. $50 of 1960 purchasing power. There can be little argument that a reduction in the number of people living in such a state of absolute deprivation should be a major objective of economic development and of development assistance. Indeed, many (including myself) would say that this should be the prime objective of economic development.

In this essay, I shall pretend that the removal of absolute deprivation is the accepted priority goal of economic development and shall summarize my understanding of what the pursuit of this goal implies for the design of development policy within developing countries. I shall here leave aside the political problems associated with the adoption of such an approach as well as its foreign assistance implications. With respect to internal politics, I shall assume that a coalition of interests exists that accords high priority to the goal of eradicating absolute deprivation. With respect to foreign

49

assistance, I shall assume the existence of an international consensus that foreign aid ought to aim at supporting policies, financing programs, and establishing an international environment that will enable developing countries to pursue the goal of poverty alleviation effectively. These assumptions will allow me to concentrate upon *what developing countries themselves can and must do to reduce their poverty problems.*

The approach to poverty alleviation that I shall advocate is a productivity-oriented approach that aims to raise the incomes of the poor by increasing both their productivity and their access to productivity-enhancing assets. I will not advocate an alternative, transfer-oriented approach, whereby the goods and services required for subsistence are delivered to the poor *directly*, for several reasons:

(1) A direct-transfer approach becomes less effective over time, since its benefits, even when the transfer continues unabated, tend to be dissipated into higher prices and into other leakages.[1]

(2) It is beyond the fiscal capacities of virtually all developing countries.

(3) It needs to be maintained forever.

(4) It does not allow for a more differentiated approach to enable the poor to decide on their consumption patterns according to their own priorities as defined by their own circumstances and cultures.

To be appropriate, policy must be rooted in the "stylized facts" of the problem that it seeks to address. Before discussing policy, I shall therefore summarize the stylized facts concerning poverty and income distribution that have been learned from the research of the past decade.

The Theory of Poverty: Lessons of a Decade

The Structure of Poverty

In developing countries, poverty is overwhelmingly a *rural* phenomenon. In most developing countries, the great majority of the poorest 40 per cent of the population is engaged in agricultural pursuits. The landless and the nearly landless are the poorest of the poor. In urban areas, the majority of the poor are unskilled workers in the service sector; but even they are generally richer than the rural poor. Workers in the manufacturing sector, whether skilled or unskilled, are part of the richest 20–40 per cent of the population. Thus unskilled labor is the major asset owned by the poor, and what determines the course of poverty is the state of demand for and the productivity of their labor.

The Course of Income Distribution During the Development Process

What happens to poverty over time is determined by the rate at which total income grows and by changes in the share of the poor in that income. If the share of income accruing to the poor declines more rapidly than overall income rises, the poor lose from growth; otherwise, they gain. Just *how* the income share of the poor changes with economic development is, therefore, critical to understanding the poverty problem and its alleviation.

The initial phases of the development process, during which a mostly agrarian economy starts industrialization, are almost inevitably marked by substantial increases in the inequality of income distribution. The shares of the poorest fifth, two-fifths, and three-fifths of the population all decrease sharply—thanks to the introduction of a small high-income island in a large low-income sea.

Subsequent phases of the development process are marked by an increase in the share of the population involved in the modern high-income sector of the economy, an increase in the income gap between the high-income and the low-income sectors of the economy, and increases in inequality within both the high-income and the low-income sectors. The shift in population from the low- to the high-income sectors is a force working for reductions in inequality; on the other hand, the increases in mean income differentials among sectors and the widening of income dispersion within sectors are factors making for greater inequality. Overall, the tendency is for inequality to increase, at least for a while. Various simulations have suggested that this increase in inequality will tend to continue until at least half of the population is in the high-income sector.

There is no *automatic* tendency for the distribution of income to improve as countries enter the last phase of their transition to the status of industrial countries. Whether inequality does or does not increase depends upon the policies that countries follow. In particular, it depends upon the extent to which the policies adopted narrow the income gap between the sectors, the extent to which they decrease the dispersion of income within the modern sector, and the relative speed of absorption into the modern sector. Thus, the plot of the income share accruing to the poorest, as a function of development, can be either U-shaped, as hypothesized by Simon Kuznets from a comparison of a sample of developed with mid- to high-income developing countries,[2] or J-shaped, depending on the nature of development strategies chosen.[3]

Trends in the Size Distribution of Income and Poverty

The trends in inequality during the past two decades are consistent with the stylized facts described above. Table 1 presents summary data on the course of the concentration of income and on the poverty ratio from 1960 to 1980 in groups of non-communist less developed countries. The figures in the table were calculated by estimating how the shape of the size distributions in the rural and urban sectors of each country varies with the country's structural characteristics and level of development. These rural and urban distributions were aggregated numerically to produce a single size distribution for each country. The individual country distributions were then again aggregated numerically to produce a single distribution for geopolitical regions. Within a given group of countries, each individual was treated as if he were a citizen of that group.[4] The numbers labeled Gini coefficients are measures of the degree of concentration of the size distribution of income. A higher figure indicates greater inequality.

The figures in the table indicate that, between 1960 and 1980, income inequality in the entire group of non-communist developing countries increased substantially; but separate groups of countries were subject to different trends in income concentration. Income concentration increased quite markedly in the group of low-income non-communist countries and in the group of oil-exporting countries, and it decreased significantly in the middle-income, non-oil-exporting countries. As indicated by the poverty-ratio figures, on the other hand, the amount of absolute poverty (defined as previously indicated) declined. Despite the overall increase in inequality, the percentage of population falling below the poverty level (held fixed in real purchasing power) declined by a third between 1960 and 1980.

To see how much of these trends can be attributed to within-country inequality and how much to inter-country inequality, two experiments were performed. In the third and fourth columns of the table, per capita income in each country was set equal to the average income in the world; the only source of inequality in these columns is, therefore, inequality in the size distribution of income *within* each country. In the fifth and sixth columns, the opposite

Table 1. Trends in Income Distribution and Poverty, 1960–1980

	Overall		Eliminating Inter-Country Inequality[a]		Eliminating Within-Country Inequality[a]	
	1960	1980	1960	1980	1960	1980
Income Distribution *(Gini coefficient[b])*						
All non-communist developing countries	.544	.602	.450	.468	.333	.404
Low-income	.407	.450	.383	.427	.113	.118
Middle-income, non-oil	.603	.569	.548	.514	.267	.251
Oil-exporting	.575	.612	.491	.503	.328	.375
Poverty *(poverty ratio[c]—percentages)*						
All non-communist developing countries	46.8	30.1	5.2	0.9	8.8	3.5
World	39.8	22.4	9.9	1.6	6.3	2.0

[a] The sum of the only-within and only-between country inequalities does not add up to the overall total because of inter-correlations between the two.

[b] The numbers labeled Gini coefficients are measures of the degree of concentration of the size distribution of income. A higher figure indicates greater inequality.

[c] Percentage of population falling below the poverty level (held fixed in real purchasing power). The definition of absolute poverty adopted for these calculations is that of the World Bank: an annual per capita income of less than U.S. $50 (1960). National currencies were converted into dollars using the Kravis purchasing power parity index for 1975.

Source: Irma Adelman, "The World Distribution of Income," Working Paper, Department of Agricultural Economics (University of California, Berkeley: August 1984).

54 A POVERTY-FOCUSED APPROACH TO DEVELOPMENT

experiment was performed; each individual in each country was assumed to have a per capita income equal to the country average. Therefore the only source of inequality in the fifth and sixth columns is inequality among countries. The sum of only within-country and only inter-country inequalities exceeds overall inequality because, in all subgroups, countries at the upper and lower extremes of the group had less inequality than countries in the middle (i.e., within-country inequality was negatively correlated with inter-country inequality).

It is clear from these experiments that both within-country inequality and inter-country inequality are important contributors to overall developing-country inequality. Within-country inequality is more important than inter-country inequality in explaining total developing-country inequality; but reductions in *either* source of inequality can make important contributions to poverty reduction. The poverty-ratio lines of Table 1 show that if either of the two forms of inequality could be eliminated (admittedly an extreme assumption), absolute poverty would virtually disappear.

Both within-country inequality and inter-country inequality in the non-communist developing countries increased between 1960 and 1980, but the greater disparities were those generated *within* countries. The dispersion of growth rates among non-communist developing countries also increased, since the middle-income countries grew considerably more rapidly than the low-income countries, and the dispersion in growth rates among the oil-exporting countries went up as well.

Efforts to reduce developing-country poverty therefore must focus both on more participatory growth processes within developing countries and on accelerating the growth rates of the poorer countries.

Policies and Programs Aimed at Reducing Income Inequality Within Developing Countries

How the poor fare during the course of economic development depends on how the distribution of assets, the institutions for asset accumulation, and the institutions for access to markets by the poor all interact with the development strategies chosen.

Chief among assets whose distribution has a significant impact on income distribution and poverty are land and education. The effects of economic change on the poor are critically dependent on land tenure conditions and the size distribution of landholdings. Poverty is greatest where land is divided into many small holdings and where there is a marked concentration of landownership coupled with cultivation by either landless labor or subsistence tenants. In contrast, where commercial farm owners supply most of their own labor, the rural distribution of income is in general more equal, and productivity increases may well improve the distribution of income. Concentration of landownership under circumstances in which small cultivators and landless workers lack alternative employment opportunities permits large landowners to pay low wages and to charge high rents. In addition, these tenurial conditions also increase the probability that innovations that raise average income and productivity in agriculture will have negative consequences for the poor. The opening up of new commercial or technological opportunities to populations with unequal abilities to respond to them widens inequality. Increasing the productivity of land when subsistence farmers and the landless cannot take advantage of that increasing productivity—because of limited access to credit or technologically superior inputs—tends to make for the marginalization of subsistence farmers and small tenants and may even lead to their eviction and dispossession. (An exception to this generalization occurs in the rare circumstances when the increase in the demand for hired labor is sufficiently large to overcome the fall in net income from farming that arises from the price decreases and rent increases that accompany the rise in productivity on larger farms.)

Turning to education's impact on income distribution, a broader incidence of education and literacy is associated with a larger share of income accruing to the middle group of income recipients but, at least initially, may not help the very poor. Increases in education spread the ownership of human capital and reduce inequalities in wage income. They also increase the rate of rural-urban migration—thereby augmenting the share of population that is employed in the higher-income sector and improving the agricultural terms of trade by raising urban demand for food while reducing its supply.

Institutions in factor and product markets are important determinants of how development affects the poor. Structural change associated with development gives rise to processes that simultaneously increase the absorption of some labor and other factors, displace labor and other factors, and generate geographic and sectoral reallocations of employment of labor and other factors. How these processes of absorption, displacement, and labor-force redistribution "net out" in their effect on the poor depends upon the institutional structure of factor and product markets. Segmentation of markets leaves some regions and sectors with labor gluts and others with shortages. Even without market segmentation, socially induced rigidities, the lack of relevant skills, or the absence of capital and information may in the short- or medium-run prevent the poor from escaping the contractionary influences to which they are exposed and finding expansionary ones elsewhere.

If one takes the initial distribution of assets and the structure of institutions as given, the major determinant of the course of income inequality and poverty becomes the overall development strategy chosen. The development strategy defines the basic thrust of economic policy. It combines a definition of policy targets (e.g., export expansion) with an identification of policy instruments (e.g., devaluation or export subsidies). Each strategy is associated with a specific configuration of the structure of production and a particular pattern of factor use. It is the development strategy that determines the pre-tax, pre-transfer (i.e., the primary) distribution of income. It governs the speed of absorption of labor into the modern sector, the extent of the income gap that develops between the modern and the traditional sectors, and the degree of income inequality within sectors.

The primary policy for helping absorption into the modern sectors is to adopt *labor-intensive* modes of expansion in those sectors. The labor intensity of growth can, in principle, be changed either by expanding the share of labor-intensive products and sectors in total employment or by increasing the labor intensity of production of a given mix of outputs (i.e., by appropriate technology). Of the two, the first process appears to be the more effective. Artificial shifts away from best-practice technology for a given factor mix reduce the amount of output obtainable from a given amount of resources. This approach is therefore less effective than shifting the mix of output toward sectors requiring a mix of resources that corresponds more closely to the basic factor endowments of the labor-abundant economies of the developing countries.

Once the choice of development strategy has jelled, policies and programs aimed at changing the primary distribution of income can accomplish very little.[5] This is true of both transfer programs and poverty-oriented projects. The size distribution of income tends to be quite stable around the trend established by the basic choice of development strategy. Following any intervention, even one sustained over time, the size distribution of income tends to return to the pre-intervention distribution. Only large, well-designed, complementary packages of anti-poverty policies and programs can change the primary distribution of income somewhat; but, to be effective, they must essentially amount to a gradual change in the overall development strategy.

Types of Anti-Poverty Policy

If one includes among the "assets" of the poor their personal capacities, trained or otherwise, their incomes consist of the value of the services of the assets owned by them that are sold on the market. In a very basic sense, then, the poverty problem is one of too small a quantity of assets, too low a volume of market sales, and/or too low a market price.

Poverty-focused approaches to policy therefore consist of measures to accomplish one or more of the following policy targets: 1) increase the quantity of assets owned by the poor, 2) increase the volume of their market sales, and 3) increase the prices of the services they sell. The general approaches that have been advocated to achieve a non-immiserating growth process can be grouped under these three headings.

Asset-Oriented Approaches

The quantity of assets owned by the poor can be increased either by redistributing assets to them (e.g., through land reform) or by creating institutions for their preferential access to opportunities for accumulation of further assets (e.g., through subsidized credit or wider access to primary education). Elsewhere I have argued for redistributing land and for tilting new educational opportunities toward the poor.[6] And in the famous World Bank/Sussex study of the middle 1970s, Hollis Chenery and his colleagues emphasized the second strategy, i.e., of concentrating asset *increments* on the poor— primarily on grounds of political feasibility.[7]

My own position is based on the experiences of the non-communist newly industrializing countries, notably Korea and Taiwan, that have successfully combined no deterioration in the relative incomes of the poor with accelerated growth. These examples lead me to advocate 1) tenurial reform in agriculture *before* implementation of policies designed to improve the productivity of agriculture, and 2) massive investments in education *before* rapid industrialization.

My rationale for this sequence, which I have called "redistribution before growth," is twofold: First, a better distribution of the major asset whose productivity is about to be improved, together with more equal access to markets and to opportunities for improving the productivity of that major asset, will obviously diminish the adverse effects of unequal asset distribution on income distribution. Second, the redistributed asset is not as valuable before improvements in productivity as it is after. Redistribution with full compensation would therefore be possible, at least in principle. I have argued, therefore, for the establishment of an internationally financed land-reform fund to: 1) help countries interested in implementing land reform design the reform; and 2) provide international guarantees for the nationally issued industrial and commodity bonds used to compensate the landlords whose land is redistributed.

Chenery's recommendations are more modest. In an approach he calls "redistribution with growth," he advocates differentially allocating a larger share of the proceeds of economic growth to asset accumulation by the poor. If, for example, the growth rate is 6 per cent per year, one-third of the growth (or 2 per cent of GNP) should be devoted to investment in assets owned by the poor or in assets that are complementary to assets owned by the poor. Examples of such investments would be: nutrition, health, and education programs for the poor; investment in irrigation facilities for land owned by the poor; or investment in credit programs or input subsidies aimed at subsistence farmers.

Demand-Generating Strategies

How much of the assets owned by the poor can be monetized on the market depends largely on the development strategy chosen and on the institutions for access to factor markets by the poor. Since the assets owned by the poor consist largely of unskilled labor, development strategies that increase the absolute and relative demand for unskilled labor, coupled with institutions that enhance labor mobility and access to jobs by the poor, are the ones that benefit the poor the most.

Two strategies look promising along these lines: 1) reliance upon export-oriented growth in labor-intensive manufactures and 2) reliance upon agricultural-development-led industrialization. I shall argue that, during the coming decade, the second strategy looks more promising for most developing countries that do not yet have an established position in international markets.

Once institutional conditions that permit reallocations of the labor power of the poor to higher productivity pursuits have been established by education, by removal of barriers to migration, and by dismantling of discrimination in hiring, equitable growth requires that subsequent increases in the rate of economic growth be achieved through measures that stress rapid growth in high-productivity, labor-intensive sectors and activities. An effective anti-poverty strategy must therefore increase the rate of growth of output of high-productivity, labor-intensive sectors and assure that the poor have access to the jobs so created.

The most labor-intensive sectors in any economy are agriculture, light manufacturing, and some types of services, especially construction (many services are skill-intensive rather than labor-intensive); but these are not necessarily the high-productivity, labor-intensive sectors. Generally, labor-intensive manufacturing is a (relatively) high-productivity sector in developing countries. That is, although output per worker is lower than it would be for more capital-intensive modes of producing the same product, it is generally higher than in most of agriculture and labor-intensive services. Policies that focus on labor-intensive growth in different sectors are therefore quite different, depending upon which sectors they stress.

Strategies that emphasize employment growth in manufacturing must focus primarily on *generating* demand for the output of the labor-intensive industries. In smaller nations, this implies that development will have to be oriented toward export markets. The small countries that follow this approach must therefore adopt a strategy of export-led growth and tailor their price and non-price incentives to be compatible with such an approach. In large countries, industrialization can be oriented toward the domestic market, particularly when the distribution of income is not too skewed.[8]

By contrast, a strategy that focuses on agriculture or on services can appeal to *existing* demand but must concentrate on increasing the productivity of labor in these sectors. There are no known technologies for increasing the productivity of purely labor-intensive services. The choice, therefore, is between a labor-intensive manufacturing strategy, on the one hand, and an agricultural strategy on the other. Bhagwati as well as Solis and Montemayor in this volume espouse the first of these, while Mellor advocates the second.

The choice between the two strategies depends on two factors: 1) the size of the direct and indirect employment multipliers that result from expanding either labor-intensive manufacturing or agriculture, and 2) comparison of the cost and feasibility of entering export markets with the cost and feasibility of increasing agricultural productivity.

Simulations with the two alternative strategies in a price- and wage-endogenous multi-sectoral model of the Republic of Korea

60   A POVERTY-FOCUSED APPROACH TO DEVELOPMENT

indicate that both strategies can be effective in achieving higher growth and a better distribution of income. However, they also indicate that during periods of low growth in world demand for labor-intensive manufactured exports (which is likely to characterize the rest of the 1980s), the agricultural strategy is more effective. In such conditions, this strategy results in less inequality and poverty, as well as in a higher rate of growth and a better balance of payments.

The basic reasons for the superiority of the agricultural strategy—which Mellor emphasizes in an "agriculture-and employment-led" strategy—are: 1) agriculture is much more labor-intensive than even labor-intensive manufacturing; 2) land-augmenting increases in agricultural productivity generate increases in demand for the labor of the landless—the poorest of the poor; 3) increases in agricultural incomes generate high leakages into demand for labor-intensive manufactures on the consumption side and for manufactured inputs on the production side; 4) expansion in agricultural production is less import-intensive than an equivalent increase in manufacturing production; 5) increases in agricultural output with "good-practice," developing-country technology are less capital-intensive than increases in manufacturing; and 6) the agricultural infrastructure required to increase agricultural productivity (roads, irrigation, and drainage facilities) has a high labor-output ratio.

It should be noted, however, that, to be effective, both strategies have certain institutional and asset-distribution prerequisites. The labor-intensive growth strategy in manufacturing requires a wide distribution of education and low barriers to access to jobs by the poor. The agricultural strategy requires that tenurial conditions in agriculture not be too unfavorable and that small farmers be assured access to the complementary resources (particularly credit and water) that they need to improve agricultural yields.

Both strategies also have implications for price policies. The trade-oriented strategy requires a price policy that does not discriminate against exports by means of an overvalued exchange rate and tariffs. The agricultural strategy requires a price policy that enables farmers to capture some of the benefits from improvements in agricultural productivity. The latter, therefore, implies a terms-of-trade policy that divides the income benefits of increased output more equitably between urban and rural groups.

Price-Increasing Policies

Price-increasing policies can operate through factor or commodity markets, and/or they can increase the productivity of the assets owned by the poor.

Price-increasing policies that operate through *factor markets* must raise the wages of the poor. The labor-intensive growth strategies discussed above can therefore also be wage-increasing policies, since an increase in the demand for labor can either raise the quantity of labor sold or raise the wage rate (or both); but the effects of these policies upon the wages of the poor depend critically on *how the labor market operates*. If the barriers to access to jobs by the poor are low and the amount of unemployment and underemployment is small, an increase in the demand for labor will raise the wage rate of the poor. On the other hand, if there are institutional or economic barriers (for example, obstacles to migration) to an increase in the quantity of labor that can be bought from the poor, an increase in the demand for labor can augment the wage rate of the non-poor while leaving the wage rate of the poor largely unchanged and having only a second-round effect on the employment of the poor. The effects of demand-increasing strategies on the price of labor, therefore, depend critically on the institutional organization of the labor market.

Price-increasing policies that operate through *commodity markets* must raise the prices of the goods produced with the labor of the poor. Since the poor are mostly rural, an increase in the relative price of agricultural output (i.e., an increase in the agricultural terms of trade) will tend to benefit the poor. This is true even though such an increase (if not counteracted by price subsidies for urban consumers) will tend to reduce the real wages of the urban poor—for the urban poor, poor as they are, generally are richer than the rural poor. An increase in the agricultural terms of trade will also tend to benefit landless workers, even though they are net buyers of agricultural produce, by increasing the demand for their labor. This is so because, given the usual employment elasticities in developing-country agriculture, the employment effect raises the entire income of landless labor more or less in proportion to the increase in agricultural prices, whereas the food-price effect reduces only that fraction of their income that the landless spend on purchased food.

Productivity-Increasing Policies

Another way to increase the price of the major asset owned by the poor—their labor—is to increase its productivity. This can be done through 1) upgrading the quality of labor through investment in human capital; 2) increasing the amount of complementary assets employed by the poor (e.g., land or capital); or 3) introducing productivity-enhancing technical change (e.g., land-intensive innovations in agriculture).

Human Capital Investments. Direct investments in the poor are desirable in and of themselves, as part of providing the poor with the minimal bundle of goods necessary to open up their access to opportunities for a full life. However, the discussion that follows will focus only on how such investments can affect the *productivity* of the poor, thereby enabling them to earn higher incomes, which in turn would permit them at some future date to purchase the minimal bundle of goods on the market with their own earnings.

Investments in the nutrition, education, and health of the poor not only increase their welfare directly, but also enhance their capacities for productive labor. Much of the employment of the poor is physical labor. Not infrequently, the market wage that the poor are paid is not even sufficient to allow them to purchase enough food to replace the calories used in earning that wage.[10] Such wage labor therefore results in exposing the poor to higher morbidity and mortality and to higher health hazards than if they had remained unemployed. Consequently it is not surprising that the productivity of the poor, when employed, remains low. In such circumstances, nutrition supplements or higher wages can raise the productivity of the poor.

Investments in the education of the poor—through adult literacy campaigns and increases in the availability of primary education in rural areas and in other places where the poor reside—spread the ownership of human capital. They qualify the poor for more productive jobs and narrow the distribution of wage income. They also increase the rate of rural-urban migration, thereby providing the poor with access to higher-income employment opportunities and raising the agricultural terms of trade. Primary education of females also tends to reduce population growth.

Although the availability of basic health care for the poor—through mobile clinics, "barefoot doctors," investment in environmental sanitation, potable water, and training in food preparation practices and elementary hygiene—raises the well-being of the poor, there is little evidence of significant direct links with productivity. Better health does, however, increase school attendance and learning while in school. It also raises the efficiency of transforming nutritional intake into caloric output and, therefore, substantially reduces malnutrition. Thus, from a productivity point of view, the contributions of investments in better health are mostly indirect, in that they raise the effectiveness of other productivity-enhancing investments in the poor.

Complementary Resources and Land-Augmenting Investments. The primary causes of rural poverty of the rural poor are the meager amount of land that they have to till with their own labor combined with a low demand for hired labor by large cultivators. The most effective productivity improvements for raising the incomes of the rural poor are therefore land-augmenting investments and innovations. Examples of land-augmenting innovations are: irrigation and drainage facilities, which, by allowing water control, may permit multiple cropping; improved seed, which by itself can triple the yield per acre; and fertilizer. These types of investments and innovations stretch the yields from whatever land the poor cultivate, and they significantly raise demand for hired labor by larger farmers.

To be most effective, however, these innovations and investments require making complementary resources available to the poor. For even when the more productive technologies are scale-neutral—as they are in the case of the high-yielding varieties of wheat and rice—the poor are not able to take advantage of these innovations because they do not have access to water, credit, improved seed, the wherewithal with which to buy fertilizer, or the technological know-how disseminated by extension. At least in the early stages of the diffusion of such innovations, productivity-increasing innovations tend to have two opposite effects on the rural poor: They increase the demand for wage labor, since the land-augmenting innovations are all quite labor-intensive; but they also reduce the price of the marketable surplus of small cultivators, since the increase in output from the larger farms generates an increase in overall supply in the face of inelastic demand. Large farmers benefit, since they can increase their sales—but the small ones lose, since they are not able to take advantage of the yield-increasing innovations. Therefore the net impact of agricultural innovations upon the rural poor depends, at least in the early stages, on the share of income that they derive from farming as opposed to wage labor.

64   A POVERTY-FOCUSED APPROACH TO DEVELOPMENT

The negative effects of the yield-enhancing innovations upon the nearly landless discussed above could be avoided if institutions were developed to provide them with access to the complementary resources with which they, too, could shift to more productive technologies. Small farmers need agricultural extension, improved seed and fertilizer, better irrigation and drainage facilities, and, most of all, credit.

Conclusion

Several points emerge from this review of findings derived from the experience with development, poverty, and income distribution over the past decade and a half.

1. Validated strategies, policies, and programs for poverty alleviation do exist. Indeed, there has been substantial progress toward the achievement of this goal between 1960 and 1980 in the non-communist developing countries as a group despite the fact that the distribution of income has become substantially more unequal.

2. Strategies for poverty alleviation are not compatible with just any kind of economic growth. They entail particular kinds of economic growth.

3. Approaches to poverty alleviation require the implementation of mutually consistent and reinforcing multifaceted programs. The most effective approaches entail a combination of several elements: asset-oriented policies that are supported by institutions designed to facilitate the poor's access to jobs; investments that enhance the productivity of assets that the poor possess and can sell; and development strategies that generate a rapid increase in the demand for unskilled labor.

4. More than one method exists to achieve each element of the package described above. The choice among instruments needs to be tailored to each country's particular initial conditions, resource base, size, asset distribution, institutional structure, and sociopolitical configuration—as well as to the external conditions and trends that the country faces at any point in time.

5. Choices among poverty-alleviation packages and programs are inherently *political*. A critical aspect of the political choice among competing goals and instrumentalities is the time dimension.

6. The sequence in which different policy interventions are taken up is important: The most effective approach to poverty

alleviation entails implementing asset-oriented policies and institutional changes designed to give the poor access to high-productivity jobs *before*, not after, shifting development strategies. If that is done, there is no "trade-off" between growth promotion and poverty alleviation. The same development strategy is then optimal for both goals.

7. Which strategy and which set of policies is most effective for a given country is likely to change over time—as changes take place both in the initial conditions within each country and in the economic and political environment in which the country operates.

8. With all of this in view, two strategies appear to promise the poor the most: 1) reliance upon export-oriented growth in labor-intensive manufactures and 2) reliance upon agricultural-development-led industrialization. During the coming decade—likely to be one of low growth in world demand for labor-intensive manufactured exports—the agriculture-led approach is likely to deliver more in terms of less inequality and poverty, a higher growth rate, and a better balance of payments.

Notes

[1] Irma Adelman and Sherman Robinson, *Income Distribution Policy in Developing Countries: A Case Study of Korea* (Stanford: Stanford University Press and Oxford University Press, 1978), pp. 148–151.

[2] Simon Kuznets, "Economic Growth and Income Inequality, "*American Economic Review*, Vol. 45, No. 1 (March 1955), pp. 1–28.

[3] Irma Adelman and Cynthia Taft Morris, *Economic Growth and Social Equity in Developing Countries* (Stanford: Stanford University Press, 1973); Gary S. Fields, *Poverty, Inequality, and Development* (Cambridge: Cambridge University Press, 1980).

[4] For a fuller explanation of this method, see Irma Adelman, *The World Distribution of Income*, Working Paper No. 346, Department of Agricultural and Resource Economics, University of California, Berkeley, August 1984.

[5] Adelman and Robinson, *A Case Study of Korea*, op. cit.; Frank J. Lysy and Lance Taylor, *Models of Growth and Distribution for Brazil* (Cambridge: Oxford University Press, 1980).

[6] See Irma Adelman, "Beyond Export-Led Growth," *World Development*, Vol. 12, No. 9 (September 1984), pp. 937–49.

[7] Hollis Chenery, et al., *Redistribution With Growth* (Cambridge: Oxford University Press, 1974).

[8] A. de Janvry and Elizabeth Sadoulet, "Social Articulation as a Condition for Equitable Growth," *Journal of Development Economics*, Vol. 13 No. 3 (December 1983), pp. 275–304.

[9] Irma Adelman, *Redistribution Before Growth—A Strategy for Developing Countries* (The Hague: Martinus Nijhof, 1978).

[10] Gerry B. Rodgers, "A Conceptualization of Poverty in Rural India," *World Development*, Vol. 4, No. 4 (April 1976), pp. 261–76.

20

Journal of Development Economics 34 (1991) 25–55. North-Holland

Food security policy in a stochastic world*

Irma Adelman and Peter Berck

University of California, Berkeley, CA 94720, USA

Received November 1987, final version received February 1989

Abstract: Food security may be increased by variance-reducing strategies, by food aid, or by development strategies. This paper uses a Korea CGE model, subjected to random fluctuation in world-prices and domestic food productivity, to evaluate these policies. We find that poverty-reducing development strategies are the most food-security strategies.

1. Introduction

Malnutrition in developing countries is a serious policy concern in international agencies and within developing countries themselves. There is agreement that malnutrition is widespread but little agreement where the best cures might lie. Some analysts and policymakers advocate variance-reducing policies and focus on decreasing international price instability or export-receipt instability. Others see the remedies as lying in reducing national food-supply shortages and advocate some form of food-aid or food-staple R&D. Still others view malnutrition as an acute manifestation of a poverty problem and hold that malnutrition is best tackled by choosing poverty-reducing development strategies.

Which view is most correct? In the present paper we 'implement' variants of all these diverse approaches in a common model representing a poor, food-deficit country that is very dependent on international trade. We expose the model-economy to a common set of stochastic shocks arising from fluctuations in domestic food supplies and international prices, implement each policy or strategy in turn, and compare the food security, household welfare, and macroeconomic results. Our results support the poverty-reduction approach to tackling malnutrition, although they indicate that the choice among approaches depends on the country's risk aversion. International interventions we find least effective and sometimes downright

*The authors would like to thank Kathryn Gordon for her assistance in the early stages of a food-security analysis [Adelman, Berck and Gordon (1983)] which led to the present project. This is Giannini Foundation Paper no. 934.

harmful. Our results thus in part support current orthodoxy and in part conflict with it.

There is no agreed-upon definition of the term 'food-security' even though much has been written on the subject and many different policy proposals have been made to address the issue. While all authors view food security as a condition in which there is less world hunger, some authors implicitly define it as stability in world grain prices; others, as availability of ample world grain supplies; others, as self-sufficiency in food; and still others as availability of foreign exchange to meet food-import requirements. We accept the definition of food-security offered by Reutlinger and Knapp (1980) – that it represents a condition in which the probability of a country's citizens falling below a minimal level of food consumption is quite low. Aside from the conceptual problems inherent in defining minimal nutritional standards, common to all food-security analyses, this approach requires evaluating the probability of below-subsistence food consumption for all population groups in the economy as a function of international and domestic conditions. For each population group, this probability is clearly related to both the group's mean food consumption and to the variance of its food consumption.

The major current policy proposals for attaining food-security fall into several categories, which can be viewed as affecting either the variance in food prices or the mean real incomes of consumers in developing countries. More specifically, the proposals are: (1) The accumulation of buffer stocks aimed at stabilizing the world price of wheat [Reutlinger (1976), Cochrane and Danin (1976)]. Critics have pointed out that price stabilization policies benefit producers at the expense of consumers [Waugh (1944), Oi (1961), Turnovsky (1978), Turnovsky, Shalit and Schmitz (1980), and Dunn and Heien (1982)]; that trade policies with respect to agricultural products [Bigman and Reutlinger (1979)] or improved market information services [Scandizzo, Hazell and Anderson (1983)] are more potent than buffer stock policies in stabilizing countries' food supplies; and that stabilization schemes which take up existing supplies will generate a transfer from producers to consumers and have small overall benefits, if any [Newbery and Stiglitz (1981)]. (2) The accumulation of stocks aimed at ensuring supply availability [Bailey, Kurish and Rojko (1974), Eaton et al. (1976), Johnson and Sumner (1976), and Sarris, Abbot and Taylor (1977)]. Critics have pointed out that commodity storage schemes actually accentuate variability in production and are most effective in eliminating the incidence of high consumption rather than in reducing shortfalls in consumption [Wright and Williams (1982)]. (3) An international insurance scheme to cover higher-than-trend food-import bills [Johnson (1978), Konandreas, Huddleston and Ramangkura (1978) and the Brandt Commission (1980)]. Critics have pointed out that import-expenditure data may provide a wholly misleading picture of a country's need for assistance and that as a consequence the program is likely to fail in the objective of stabilizing food consumption levels [Green and Kirkpatrick (1982)]. (4) Food-aid by developed countries [Mellor (1980) and Lane (1980)]. Critics point out that food-aid does not tend to reach the neediest [Lele (1971)], that the income of the poor needs to be raised so that they can benefit from food aid [Berg (1980)] and that it tends to generate negative production incentives which need to be countered by specific policies [Hall (1980), Gavan and Chandrasekar (1979), Rogers, Srivastava and Heady (1972), Lane (1980) and Mellor (1980)] if food-aid is not to result in worse rather than better nutrition for the neediest. (5) Price-subsidy schemes to consumers [Reutlinger and Selowsky (1976), Ahmed (1979), Kumar (1979), George (1979), Perrin and Scobie (1981)] or production subsidy schemes to producers [Barker and Hayami (1976), and Hayami (1977)]. Critics point out that this policy is expensive if not limited to well defined target groups [Berg (1980)] and administratively demanding and open to evasion if limited to well defined target groups [Lele (1971)], and that it leads to a decrease in the competitiveness of export industries when financed through inflation [Schneider (1985)]. (6) Self-sufficiency in food [Lappe (1978)]. Critics point out that this policy may result in higher food-prices than can be obtained by specializing according to comparative advantage and importing food [Falcon (1984)] and that the degree of optimality of food-self-sufficiency policies depends on the country's degree of risk aversion [Sarris (1985)]. (7) Agricultural development [Mellor (1976) and Adelman (1984)]. Critics indicate that this policy requires a high rate of return to investment in agriculture to be effective, and that the inelasticity of demand for agricultural products implies that there are definite limits beyond which this policy cannot be pursued without reducing the incomes of farmers, who constitute a large share of the poor. And (8) Raising the income of the poor [Berg (1980), Pinstrup-Andersen and Caicedo (1978), Streeten (1985), and Sen (1981)]. Critics indicate that, when achieved through income transfers, this is expensive and needs to be maintained forever and that, when achieved through productivity and through patterns of growth which enhance demand for unskilled labor, this approach requires changes in development strategies which may generate political opposition and take time to implement.

Thus, the proposals for achieving food security are numerous, and cogent criticisms have been advanced against each and every proposal. With rare exceptions, the empirical evaluations of these policy proposals have been carried out in a partial equilibrium framework and analyze the effectiveness of food-security programs only at the national level. They do not trace out how the interaction of demand and supply responses within the economy mediates the impacts of shocks at the national level upon the incomes of the various groups within the country and upon the prices of the commodities they consume. This paper implements a model that describes how this mediation occurs for a poor, chronic food-deficit country.

Our analysis adds several elements to previous models: (1) In previous models, shocks in production and/or international prices affect consumer-demand only through the prices consumers face, not their incomes; (2) In most previous models, the shocks to food prices are independent of other shocks to the economy (i.e., there is no correlation among shocks); (3) We use an interdependent model with a great many substitution possibilities to translate shocks in international prices and domestic production into shocks on the food-consumptions and real incomes of consumers; and (4) We disaggregate consumers into eight socioeconomic classes distinguished by ownership and access to factors of production and by whether they are net suppliers or demanders of food. Within each class we further disaggregate households by income levels.

The next section describes the methodology of our study. Section 3 presents the results of six simulated food-security policies for the South Korea of 1968.

The Korea of 1968 was a rapidly growing but very poor country. Its per capita income was around 170 1968 dollars, converted at the official exchange rate. It was an open economy with a very large trade deficit; exports were 15 percent of gross domestic product (GDP), and the trade deficit accounted for 10 percent of GDP. About half of its labor force was employed in agriculture, only 15 percent in manufacturing, and the rest in services. It was a consistent food-deficit country; in 1968 its cereal imports accounted for about 11 percent of its total consumption. Thus, in static terms, the Korea of our study is a typical small, poor, open, negative balance-of-trade, large food-deficit country.

2. The methodology

Agricultural output, internal and international terms of trade, oil prices, and the world-price of food are all subject to random fluctuations. Random shocks to international markets or agricultural production in turn affect consumers through their effects on consumer-incomes and consumption-prices. We describe the shocks at a national level in terms of a multivariate probability distribution. The probability distribution of international prices and domestic food production is then transformed into a probability distribution of incomes and prices for each of several groups of consumers by means of a computable general equilibrium (CGE) model. Finally, food-security and welfare-measures are computed for each consumer-group from the distribution of incomes and prices and used to evaluate the policies.

The remainder of this section describes: (1) The choice of international shocks and the construction of their variance–covariance matrix; (2) The use of CGE model to transform the probability distribution of these shocks into a probability distribution of prices and incomes; and (3) The indicators used to evaluate food-security and welfare.

2.1. The shocks

In this model we analyze shocks to food-security arising from four different sources: variations in domestic production of cereals due to factors such as weather; changes in the international price of cereal imports; changes in the prices of domestic exports, which affect the economy's ability to import food; and changes in energy-prices, which affect both the economy's ability to import food and its ability to import inputs, like fertilizer, used to grow food. This section describes the derivation of the shocks in these variables.

For food-security analysis, the systematic changes in time series (from, for instance, growth) need to be separated from the changes induced by random shocks that a food-security program might reduce. Our method of modelling the shocks was to consider the values of the variables that could be predicted two-years ahead and treat the difference between the predictions and the actual values as the shocks. We chose two-years ahead rather than one-year ahead because food stocks have a major impact on food prices, and food stocks adjust slowly. As a result, the random variations from changes in the food system do not fully work themselves out within a single year, and one-year-ahead forecasts badly underestimate the variability to which shocks expose the economy.

The four variables (food production, international cereal prices, domestic export prices, and oil prices) are each normalized so that their 1968 value is unity. The normalized values are then regressed (using Zellner's seemingly unrelated regressions technique) over the period 1963 to 1978 on their own twice-lagged value, a constant term, the year squared, and the year. All equations except the grain equation fit with an R^2 of better than 90 percent and have significant coefficients on all but the lagged variables. The grain-equation has no significant coefficients and an R^2 of only 7 percent. Thus, most of the actual variability in oil prices, export prices, and agricultural production appears systemic while most of the variability in world-grain-prices appears random. The variance–covariance matrix of residuals from these equations is taken as the true variance–covariance matrix of the shocks.

Table 1 gives the correlation matrix and standard errors of the shocks. World-grain-prices have the largest standard error, about one-third of its trend value. Export prices and food-production have the least variation, about 8 percent of trend. The off-diagonal elements indicate that the correlations among shocks are important: the correlation between export prices and the price of oil is 0.88 so that high (low) foreign-exchange earnings are likely to offset a high (low) energy-import bill. On the other hand,

Table 1

Correlations and standard errors of shocks.[a]

| | Correlations | | | |
	World grain prices	Export prices	Oil prices	Food production
World grain prices	1.00	−0.20	0.04	−0.61
Export prices	−0.20	1.00	0.88	0.30
Oil prices	0.04	0.88	1.00	0.35
Food production	−0.61	0.30	0.35	1.00
Standard errors	0.33	0.08	0.24	0.08

[a]Standard errors are percent of mean.

Source: Computed

domestic food production and world-food-prices are negatively correlated (−0.61) so that bad harvests coincide with high world-prices, clearly reinforcing any food-shortfall. The other correlations are of much lower magnitude and are positive with one exception – an R^2 of −0.20 between domestic food-production and world-grain-prices.

The shocks themselves are constructed by drawing 100 quadruples of price-shocks from a multivariate t distribution with five degrees of freedom and the estimated variance–covariance matrix. A t distribution was used because it has relatively fat tails, and our sample period (1963–1978) included many observations, such as the formation of an OPEC cartel, that would have been poorly represented by a normal distribution. A check of the histograms of the shocks shows significant probability of shocks as great as a doubling or halving of oil or grain-prices and reasonable agreement with the historical data. Since our reported results are averaged over the 100 trials, our reported statistics are subject to the central limit theorem, and increasing the number of replications to, say, 1,000 would increase accuracy by only a factor of three while it would impose impossible computational burden.

2.2. Mapping the external shocks into domestic income and price variations

These 100 quadruples of shocks were then applied to a CGE model one at a time. The CGE model was used to translate the shocks into the means and variances of group-incomes and of consumer-good prices. This model is well suited to the analysis of food-security issues since it translates shortfalls in domestic food-production or rises in the price of food-imports into changes in food-consumption by each class of consuming households, especially the poor. In our model, a rise in the price of food-imports affects not only domestic food-prices and domestic food-production but also the real incomes of all consumers. It also changes the exchange rate and, therefore, other imports and exports. This chain links international and domestic food-security policies to each class food-consumption and enables us to trace through precisely how food-security policies affect the nutritional status of the poor and near poor in each class. By contrast, most other food-security analyses evaluate food-security policies solely by their effects on the overall supply of grain at the national level and do not consider how these policies affect the ability of the poor to partake of the national supply of food.

The CGE model we use consists of an economy-wide, simultaneous, multisectoral model that solves endogeneously not only for quantities but also for prices [for detailed descriptions of the model, see Adelman and Robinson (1978) and Dervis, de Melo and Robinson (1982). We use the stripped-down version of the CGE model contained in Dervis, de Melo and Robinson, but with many consumers.] The core of the model consists of the reconciliation of potential demand and supply imbalances in factor and commodity markets by price adjustments, which simulate the workings of labor, commodities, and foreign-exchange markets. The model solves for: wages, profits, product-prices, and the exchange rate; sectoral production, import, export, employment, consumption, and investment; and the flow of funds, gross national product, and balance-of-payments accounts as well as the functional distribution and the size distributions of income to households. The model is pretty neoclassical in that all prices except for world prices are flexible and the equilibrium is a full-employment equilibrium of all factors.

The technological and behavioral functions in the model incorporate substitution possibilities among factors in production and among commodities in final demand. Production technology is represented by fixed input–output coefficients for intermediate goods and constant elasticity of substitution (CES) functions for labor and capital. In the factor markets, labor-demand arises from the profit-maximizing behavior of producers. The supply of labor is disaggregated by skill type. It is assumed fixed within a given period, and only its sectoral allocation is allowed to vary. Farmers and service workers are immobile within each period though mobile between periods. Small farmers in 'our' Korea are both land and income poor, but not destitute. They average less than 3/4-acre plots and devote about 50 percent of their expenditures to food purchases. Agricultural proprietors are owner-operators with less than 2-acre plots. On the average, their incomes are only 25 percent higher than those of small farmers. Hired farm-labor is mobile between rural and urban employment as marginal workers. The model determines market-clearing wages and the sectoral allocation of skilled and unskilled workers.

The demand for commodities is responsive to relative price and income variations. The price-responsiveness arises because of the use of linear expenditure system (LES) consumption functions and because of the trade specification which induces price-sensitive substitution among imports and domestic production. The incomes of consumers are determined in the factor markets after subtracting taxes. The demand for commodities by sector is evaluated from these incomes and the exogenously specified savings rates and government consumption functions. Output-prices that clear commodity-markets are then calculated by comparing demand and supply. They determine relative prices. To fix absolute prices we set the wholesale price level as numeraire and use a Cambridge-K money demand equation together with a fixed money supply to calculate the wholesale price level.

Imports and domestic production in a given sector are not considered to be either perfect substitutes or complete complements; rather, there is an elasticity of substitution among them which lies between zero and unity. The balance of trade determines the net demand for foreign exchange. The exchange rate adjusts so as to maintain a predetermined level of foreign capital inflow.

Several closure rules are possible for the model. The one we chose is the one which gives maximum intermediate-run sensitivity to balance-of-payments fluctuations arising in international markets. In it, investment absorbs the full brunt of the adjustment since investment is forced to adjust directly to the enlarged or diminished supply of domestic plus foreign savings.

To provide the counterfactual for the evaluation of the policy alternatives proposed to achieve food-security, this CGE model was run 100 times, once for each of the previously computed combinations of shocks. The factor-incomes for each group, their food-consumptions, and the prices of consumption-goods were then used to determine the welfare and degree of food-security enjoyed by each decile in each group in the base solution. For this purpose, distributions of income within each consumer group were applied to calculate the distributions of consumption in each household-category and to compute the percent of households in each group falling below a specific nutritional intake.

The base-solution indicates that the mapping of external shocks on internal price-fluctuations is contractionary. Substitution effects through international trade and through changes in domestic production and consumption results in a standard error of domestic grain-prices which is only 36 percent of the standard error of world grain-prices and in a variance in manufactured food-prices which is only about 5 percent of the standard error of world grain-prices. On the other hand, the variance in the world-prices of Korean exports is reflected in the variance of domestic prices of the export sector, manufactured consumer-good prices is 72 percent of that of Korean export prices on world markets. And shocks in the world price of oil are almost fully reflected in the domestic price of intermediates (the standard error of intermediate-good prices is 93 percent of that in the world price of oil) since substitution possibilities for intermediate goods are more limited:

the trade-substitution elasticities are smaller, and the input–output nature of intermediate-input technology limits substitution effects for intermediates to changes in the composition of output. In addition, the variance in world-prices is also transmitted to sectors not directly affected by shocks; the standard error in their prices is about the same as that of export prices.

2.3. The evaluation of food-security policies

The food-security policies are evaluated by their effects on nutritional status as well as by their effects on overall welfare. The measures of nutritional status we have chosen are the percent of households in each household group that are below their recommended caloric intake and the group's per capita calorie deficit. The deficit is the average number of calories by which the malnourished fall short of their minimal caloric need. Since one of the purposes of stabilization policies is to eliminate extreme outcomes, we also evaluated these policies by calculating the percent of time a severe food shortfall could be expected. Bigman (1982) provides a nice discussion of the merits of these food-security indicators as welfare measures.

The welfare measure we have chosen for each group is the expected equivalent variation for the consumer with the mean income of his group. Consider an initial allocation called 'the base' and a proposed food security policy called 'the policy'. The equivalent variation is the amount of money one would have to pay a consumer in the base to make him as well off as he would be if the policy were implemented. The CGE model uses a linear-expenditure system (LES) to represent consumers. Let $v(y,p)$ be the ordinal indirect utility function associated with that demand system. For a LES, $v(y,p)$ can be written as: $v=(y-m'p)\prod p_i^{\alpha_i}$ where y is income, p is the vector of p_i prices, m is the 'subsistence bundle' vector, and α_i's are the marginal shares of income spent on goods i. Of course, any monotone transformation of v will also give the same demands but will have a different coefficient of risk aversion. Let expected utility be

$$EU = E\left[\frac{v^{1-\beta}}{1-\beta}\right],\qquad\qquad (1)$$

where the expectation is taken over the 100 replicates. Then, the coefficient of absolute risk aversion to income change is β/v and R, the coefficient of relative risk aversion, is $\beta y/v$. Thus, EU has decreasing absolute risk aversion and increasing, and asymptotically constant, relative risk aversion. For the cases we will consider, the value of the subsistence bundle is approximately half of mean group-income, and the product of the prices to the powers α_i in the base is nearly one. Thus, β is approximately $1/2R$. In what follows we chose R as four and β as two.

3. Food-security policies

The policies selected for evaluation are: a price stabilization policy; a food import bill insurance scheme; food aid; a food price subsidy scheme; a food self-sufficiency policy implemented by productivity-enhancing investments in agriculture; and a standard development strategy – export expansion. These six policies break into three natural groupings: (1) insurance schemes to reduce variance in food prices, (2) lowering food prices, and (3) development strategies to raise income.

To maintain comparability among food-security programs, we calibrate the experiments so that the increase in the budget deficit incurred for each food-security policy is the same ($20 million) and that deficit is financed by foreign donations. The two variance-reducing policies required only this amount of financing and little other commitment from domestic policy-makers. Thus these would be the easiest policies to implement. The next set of food security policies, the food-price reducing experiments (food-aid and a food-price subsidy), both require a domestic policy action costing $20 million. In food aid, that sum is used to import food while in the two-price scheme, it is used to finance the difference between producer and consumer prices. The final programs, development strategies, change investment and trade incentives and are most committing of all. Again they have budget costs of $20 million. Twenty million dollars is 180 won per capita which is 0.4 percent of GDP. We compare the results of the implementation of each food-security policy with the base, which contains no food-security program. To see whether the relative and absolute effectiveness of food-security policies depends on the magnitude we chose for the program, we also implemented the policies with each component (tariff rates changes, growth rates changes, tax changes, etc.) increased by 50 percent. These enhanced policies increase the country's aid-compensated budget deficit to $30 million. We report the expenditure-multipliers for each program in a final table.

For each of these six policies, we compute the calories consumed by each decile of each class of consumers and identify the percentage of consumers in each class whose average daily caloric intake over the year is less than 90 percent of the FAO norm for Korea of 2,200 [United Nations (1973)]. For shorthand purposes, we refer to the percentage of households whose annual average daily calorie intake falls below 90 percent of the norm as the percent malnourished, though we recognize that daily variations in intake and adaptations in activity levels probably result in better nutritional and health status than this average would suggest. The percentages we calculate are higher than those one would get by looking at the mean per capita food supply available to the country or at the average calorie intake of an average member of each class of consumers. But we believe that our calculations offer a more valid picture of the likelihood of below-norm food intake in each population group and in the country as a whole. In any case, the ranking of the policies by their effects on food security is unaffected by the choice of cutoff point.

Table 2 summarizes the macro variables for the six policy alternatives considered as a percent of the base in the absence of shocks. The import-price stabilization and the trade-balance stabilization policies affect only the variances of the shocks and are, therefore, omitted from this table since they leave the means under these policies the same as in the base. Tables 3–5 summarize the food-security implications of these policies.

The first point to emerge from these calculations is that none of the policies considered achieve very much in terms of cutting the percentage malnourished. The differences among policies in their effects on the average expected food-deficit (defined as the average food-deficit over all 100 shocks) is somewhat more pronounced, but the maximum effect is only 6 percent above the least effective policy. The least effective policies are those that operated only on the variances of the shocks; the most effective are those that raise the mean-incomes of the poverty-groups by appropriate changes in development strategy. We now turn to detailed analyses of each policy.

Import-price stabilization policy. The first experiment we consider is an import-price stabilization scheme. Grain is purchased and stored in years when grain prices are cheap and released when grain prices reach a preset release price. The benefits of the buffer-stock are a lessening of the variability in grain-prices, while the costs are the operating costs (less operating revenues) of the buffer stock. In a very different model, Reutlinger (1980) performed a similar stabilization experiment, which he summarized in the form of a table. The table gives the frequency of food-shortfalls as a function of the amount of grain in storage. Reutlinger also stated the storage costs so, by assuming a log-normal distribution, we were able to convert his numbers to a table giving the cost of the program as a function of the percent-reduction in the variance. An expenditure of \$20 million reduces the variance in world grain-prices by 56.7 percent.

In our experiment, the buffer-stock policy is modeled by approximately halving the variance in world food prices by a mean-preserving spread. Although the variance in world prices was reduced by somewhat more than one-half, the variance in domestic food prices predicted by the CGE was reduced by only 31.2 percent. Similarly, the experiment reduced the covariances between food prices and other prices and incomes. These reductions in the variance of domestic prices were not as great as the reduction in the

I. Adelman and P. Berck, Food security policy

Table 2

Macroeconomic indicators for food security.

	GDP[a]	Consumption[a]	Investment[a]	Exchange rate	Price level	Wages[a]	Capital rental rate[a]	International terms of trade	Agricultural output[a]	Agricultural consumption[a]	Agricultural net imports[a]	Agricultural prices	Agricultural terms of trade
Base	1,620	1,406	408	0.277	100.2	105.7	9.61	100	668	379	60.4	1.04	1.066
						Percent of base							
Food aid	100.0	100.1	96.1	101.8	100.3	100.0	101.9	103.8	100.0	101.8	111.9	97.5	95.7
Grain price subsidies	99.9	100.0	94.6	101.4	99.8	100.2	100.2	103.9	100.0	101.0	111.1	99.3	99.0
Agricultural development	104.3	103.3	100.7	108.7	99.8	105.5	96.7	103.8	105.1	104.3	95.2	101.3	99.5
Export-led growth	101.9	103.8	97.6	107.9	99.8	104.8	93.1	103.7	101.6	99.8	110.2	107.0	109.2

[a]Denotes constant prices, billions of won.
Source: Computed.

Table 3

Measures of food security.[a]

	Base	World price stabilization	Food import insurance	Food aid	Grain price subsidy	Agricultural development	Export-led growth
Percent malnourished							
Small farmers	55.88	55.76	55.91	58.13	56.08	53.23	52.48
Marginal laborers	84.56	85.24	84.51	84.09	85.4	82.12	84.60
Organized labor	13.71	13.56	13.69	12.03	12.6	12.40	15.79
Service labor	20.40	20.42	20.07	18.99	20.4	18.46	20.83
Total population	36.88	36.81	36.81	37.34	36.86	34.79	35.70
Average daily calorie deficit per malnourished person[a]							
Small farmers	340	338	341	352	340	327	322
Marginal laborers	525	527	524	523	528	495	518
Organized labor	143	143	143	143	138	128	138
Service labor	200	199	199	200	198	188	193

[a]The deficit is measured from 1,930 calories, which is already 10 percent below the norm of 2,200; averages over the 100 replicates.

variance of world prices because of the supply and demand responses of the model.

World-price stabilization policies change mean real incomes vary little (see table 4). Producers gain a very small amount in expected real income, while consumers loose between 1 and 4 percent. But the effects on the variances of real incomes are quite marked. The variances of farmer incomes are reduced by about 40 percent, and urban groups have their income-variances cut by anywhere from 30 percent for service workers to 60 percent for organized labor and 56 percent for marginal workers. Nevertheless, the expected food-security of the economy, as viewed from the perspective of the malnourished, changes very little as a result of the price stabilization. Averaging over the shocks, there is virtually no change in the expected food-deficit, or the expected percentage malnourished. The basic point is that, when the group means are close to subsistence, and one averages over the shocks, reducing the variance around the mean changes the probability of below-norm food intake very little.

Another way of viewing the effects of stabilizing prices would be to ask about the probability that a group's food-intake deficit is 25 percent greater than its mean value. For small farmers, for example, the price stabilization policy reduces the probability of such an extreme food shortfall from 7 to 2 percent. As a result, the small farmers are willing to pay about 4 percent of

Table 4

Mean and variance of real above subsistence income for seven institutions and seven policies.[a]

Institution	Small farmers		Marginal labor		Organized labor		Service labor		Agricultural proprieters		Agricultural capitalists		Industrial capitalists	
	Mean	Variance	Mean	Variance	Mean	Variance	Mean	Variance	Mean	Variance	Mean	Variance	Mean	Variance
Base	4.40	1.11	3.27	0.09	8.63	17.30	7.93	2.69	5.40	1.67	19.78	9.19	50.56	119.00
World price stabilization	4.41	0.70	3.25	0.04	8.28	6.79	7.86	1.87	5.43	1.06	19.75	6.48	50.80	96.79
Food import insurance	4.38	1.12	3.27	0.08	8.51	14.63	8.03	2.73	5.38	1.70	19.75	7.94	51.34	130.89
Food aid	4.07	0.84	3.26	0.10	9.20	17.24	8.32	2.36	5.00	1.26	19.63	10.37	53.79	117.44
Grain price subsidies	4.34	0.30	3.24	0.12	8.50	8.81	7.74	0.78	5.37	0.44	19.80	10.04	50.46	36.90
Agricultural development	4.78	1.11	3.66	0.27	9.90	29.51	8.97	3.23	5.90	1.69	21.94	13.81	52.80	130.82
Export-led growth	5.13	1.03	3.55	0.11	8.34	18.46	8.29	3.15	6.32	1.59	22.05	10.11	51.06	161.60

[a]Income is average for each group across the 100 replicates, and the variance is also across the 100 replicates.
Source: Computed.

I. Adelman and P. Berck, Food security policy

Table 5

Expected equivalent variation for seven policies (percentage of income).

Institution Policy	Small farmers	Marginal laborers	Organized laborers	Service laborers	Agricultural proprietors	Agricultural capitalists	Industrial capitalists
World price stabilization	4.08	−0.25	0.48	0.21	4.09	0.50	1.55
Food import insurance	−0.77	−0.05	−0.03	0.67	−0.75	0.07	0.95
Food aid	−2.41	−0.34	4.63	3.02	−2.40	−0.69	4.00
Grain price subsidies	4.05	−0.76	3.04	0.24	4.05	0.03	2.38
Agricultural development	5.08	6.24	5.73	7.09	5.13	8.19	3.43
Export-led growth	11.04	4.66	−3.24	2.09	12.00	9.3	0.41

Source: Computed; average across the 100 replicates of equivalent variation.

their income for the reduced variance in their food-intake (see table 5, which lists the equivalent variations for all the experiments and socioeconomic groups) even though their expected food-deficit is virtually unchanged.

Consumers benefit less than producers from the stabilization – a familiar result; they trade off small losses in mean income for substantial reductions in income variance. Indeed, marginal workers would actually have to be compensated for the existence of a stabilization program to the tune of 0.25 percent of their income. Other urban groups still feel somewhat better off: They would be willing to pay between 0.21 percent of their income (service workers) to 1.5 percent (industrial capitalists) for world-price stabilization. If the cost of the price stabilization program were to be passed on to the households in the form of increased taxes, it would amount to four-tenths of a percent of their incomes; everyone except for marginal and service-workers would be willing to pay this insurance cost.

Food-import insurance.   The second policy we consider is a food-import-bill insurance program. In this program a foreign guarantor pays the Korean government 55 percent of the amount of foreign exchange by which the food import bill exceeds its trend value at a cost of $20 million in our experiments. This is a version of the International Monetary Fund (IMF) food facility. The current IMF program is based on an average of export receipts and food-import-bill variations, but it has been argued [Green and Kirkpatrick, (1982)] that a pure food-import-bill insurance scheme would be superior to the existing program. The insurance policy paid off in 50 percent of our Monte Carlo replicates.

A policy of this sort has several problems. Since governments can most certainly influence the food-import bill by their agricultural policies and the foreign guarantor can only imperfectly estimate the country's expected insurance payments, the government has an incentive to increase its food-import bill. This moral hazard exists in all import-bill insurance schemes. Similarly, imperfect ability to rate risk will result in adverse selection of countries to participate in the program. Finally, on the national level, the program has the problem of not paying off precisely when the extra income would be most useful for averting starvation: a high food-import bill happens in our replicates much more frequently as an outcome of high national income and high demand than it does as a consequence of crop-failure. The first two problems are not captured in this model while the third is.

The experiments indicate that this is not a good policy due to the inverse correlation of insurance payouts with situations of low food consumption and due to the relatively high price of insurance were it to be charged at its fair actuarial value. Table 4 indicates that the food-import-bill insurance policy is dominated by the price stabilization policy for food producers: it generates a higher variance and a lower mean for them. It is not dominated for urban consumer groups since for them it has a slightly higher mean and a much higher variance. However, the poor lose in expectation terms from food-import-bill insurance, as indicated by the fact (see table 5) that they would have to be compensated for participating in the scheme anywhere from 0.77 percent of their income for small farmers to 0.05 percent for marginal workers, even in the absence of increased taxes to pay for the insurance scheme. No wonder there are very few countries that make use of the IMF food-financing facility in practice!

Food aid.   The next experiment is a food-aid program, such as was available under PL 480. The policy was implemented in the model by increasing the net imports of food by 10 percent (or $20 million) and simultaneously raising the foreign capital inflow by $20 million. The net result is to give the country $20 million worth of imports for free. This is a policy of direct appeal to farmers in developed countries, and one that has great intuitive appeal, but it is a food-security disaster. The total expected food-deficit is the highest of any policy, 3 percent higher than in the base. Food aid makes all farmers (both small farmers and other farmers) very much poorer. Agricultural prices fall about 3 percent. Agricultural terms of trade are about 11 percent lower and expected overall farmer incomes are 9 percent lower. The expected percent of small farmers that are malnourished is 4 percent higher than the base percentage, and they would require a compensation of about 2.5 percent of their income in order to be as well off in expectation terms as they were in the base. Overall food grain consumption in the economy does go up, but only by 1 percent. Urban workers other than marginal workers were better off than in the base since they have both a higher mean and a lower variance in incomes.

Grain-price subsidies.   Most developing-country governments that are concerned with poverty tend to subsidize the price of grain to consumers, maintaining a dual-price policy. Korea instituted such a policy in 1972. We modeled this dual-price policy by fixing the consumption price of grain below its equilibrium price and placing a value-added tax rebate on grain. The value of the rebate was $20 milion. Price was fixed 0.8 percent below equilibrium, an amount calculated so that the sum of the effects of fixed price and tax rebate leaves farm income at nearly its level in the base policy and costs $20 million. Since at least $20 million worth of food is imported in all the random replicates,[1] this policy could be financed by a gift in food rather than money. Therefore, one can interpret this policy as food aid plus compensation to the farm sector. Scaling the policy to cost only $20 million

---

[1]Hall (1980) argues Brazil financed its two-price policy with subsidized grain from the U.S. PL 480 program, a very similar policy to the one discussed here.

makes the variance reducing effects of the policy its most prominent part. Below, we will comment on a much more ambitious policy along these lines.

This experiment has two main macro effects. It raises the consumption of grains somewhat (by 1 percent) and it increases the domestic supply of grains through imports, even though the relative price in domestic currency of imported grain has risen substantially. The import-increase (of 11 percent) is required to satisfy the increase in domestic demand in the face of a virtually fixed domestic supply and is financed by decreasing other imports, through a devaluation (of 1.5 percent). There is no discernible change in GDP.

The program's effects on real incomes are slight; most groups experience a small decline in their incomes, ranging from 0.2 percent for industrial capitalists to 2.4 percent for service labor. But there is a very substantial decrease in the variance of all real incomes (the variance is cut by between a factor of 3.85 for agricultural proprietors to a factor of 2 for organized labor), except for marginal workers and agricultural capitalists, who find their variance increased by 33 and 9 percent, respectively. The result is that, except for marginal workers, all groups benefit under this policy. The largest welfare increase is to small farmers and agricultural proprietors (by about 4 percent). In the urban sector, the poor benefit less than the rich not only in absolute terms but also in proportion to their incomes. Indeed, the poorest urban workers actually lose. This is ironic since these policies are usually instituted to benefit the urban poor. By contrast, in the rural sectors, the poorer farmers benefit proportionately more than agricultural capitalists. As a food security policy, the grain-price subsidy scheme accomplishes very little (see table 3). The overall percent malnourished and the overall calorie deficit are virtually the same as in the base. There is some slight reshuffling of the incidence of poverty: small farmers and organized labor are a relatively smaller proportion of the malnourished population while marginal labor is a larger percentage.

The trivial scale of this two-price policy leads us to experiment with two-price policies of much larger scale. The experiment was to drop consumer prices to 95 percent of their value in the base and, as before, to use a value-added tax rebate to leave farmers with nearly their base real-mean incomes. The cost above the $20 million of aid, $173 million, was financed by a value-added tax on all non-food sectors. Thus, comparing this experiment to the other experiments is an exercise in balanced budget rather than differential incidence. At this scale, a two-price policy leaves only 34.92 percent of the population malnourished, which is the best performance of any of the policies examined in this study.

Changes in development strategies. The last two food-security policies consist of changes in development strategy. They are modeled by reallo-cations of the economy's capital stock, induced changes in sectoral productivities, and changes in the tariff structure. Unlike the stabilization and insurance policies, these trade and investment policies affect mean incomes as well as affecting variances.

In modeling these experiments, we always reallocated 6 percentage points of total investment away from the service sector. In the base, service-sector investment absorbed 70 percent of total investment and had the lowest rate of return. (Its rate of return was about 40 percent of that in agriculture, 46 percent of that in intermediate manufacturing, and a third of that in consumer-goods and machinery production). As a result, any reallocation of invesetment away from services improves the total factor productivity of the economy and sets up the potential for large welfare gains. The different development strategies have larger distributional effects than do the food-security policies discussed earlier. They distribute the welfare gains and losses differently and represent different mean–variance trade-offs for different groups in the economy.

Agricultural development. The first reallocation of the economy's capital stock represents an agricultural-development-led-industrialization strategy in which agricultural productivity is increased by increased investment in agriculture [ADLI, see Adelman (1984)]. The increased investment could take the form of increased infrastructure such as irrigation programs or land consolidation or terracing. A policy of rural development implemented by increased agricultural invesetment was followed by Korea between 1972 and 1978. In the experiment we reallocated 6 percentage points more of total investment to agriculture, bringing its share of total investment up to 13 percent; increased productivity in agriculture by 2.5 percent; and reduced all tariffs and subsidies in the economy by two-thirds. The extent of reduction in trade incentive distortions was set by the requirement that the loss in tariff revenues plus the reduction in subsidy payments cost exactly $20 million. This reduction in tariffs and subsidies brought trade incentives very close to neutral: the ratio of the effective protection rate on imports to the effective protection rate on exports dropped from 1.08 to 1.03.

We calculated the increase in agricultural productivity induced by the increase in investment in agriculture assumed for this experiment by fitting an agricultural production function to Korean data for 1962 to 1978. To estimate the productivity-enhancement effect of investment in the agricultural sector, it is necessary to disentangle the output-increase due to more capital from the productivity-enhancing effects of infrastructure investment. This requires fitting a production function of the form

$$X_{at} = A^{\rho(K_t)} K_t^{\alpha_1} M_t^{\alpha_2} L_t^{\alpha_3} G_t^{\alpha_4},$$

where

X_{at} = gross agricultural output,
$A^{\rho(K_t)}$ = technical progress that is agricultural capital-stock related,
K_t = agricultural capital stock,
M_t = intermediate inputs, mostly fertilizer,
L_t = agricultural labor,
G_t = agricultural land, and
t = a time subscript.

It was impossible to estimate this production function econometrically because of multicollinearity problems between the two forms in which capital enters the production function. Instead, we estimated a double log production function of the form

$$\log X_{at} = -19.6 + 0.06 \log M_t + 3.52 \log L_t + 0.55 \log K_t + 0.85 \log G_t;$$
$$\quad (21.4)\ (0.07) \quad\quad (4.15) \quad\quad (0.26) \quad\quad (1.05)$$

$$R^2 = 0.87.$$

We then decomposed the coefficient of 0.55 on the capital stock into two components as follows: we set the output–increase due to more capital being used in production equal to the CGE-exponent of capital in the production function of the primary sector (0.17) estimated from the share of capital in value added in the base year. We then attributed the difference between this CGE-exponent and 0.55 (i.e., 0.38) to the productivity-enhancement effect. Finally, to get the increase in productivity due to the agricultural-development program, we multiplied 0.38 by the percentage increase in agricultural capital stock due to the program (6.58 percent). This yielded the assumed productivity-increase of 2.5 percent.

Comparing the results of the agricultural-development strategy with the base, we find substantial differences in consumption, GNP and reductions in the percentage malnourished (tables 2 and 3). The strategy improves the domestic production of grain (by 5 percent). Farmers gain from the improvement in agricultural productivity (total real value added in agriculture rises by 4.8 percent); and the urban groups, especially the urban poor, gain as well. The expected mean income of marginal workers is about 12 percent higher, and the mean incomes of organized labor and service workers are 15 to 13 percent higher. This is a wage-goods strategy. Furthermore, real wages rise by 5.5 percent, while the real rate of return on capital drops by 7 percent.

This policy achieves the most in terms of food-security of all policies considered. The food-security of the economy decreases by 6 percent, the total food deficit is reduced by 10 percent, and both urban and rural groups experience an increase in their food security. The equivalent variation (see table 5) is about 5 percent for farmers, 8 percent for agricultural capitalists, 7 percent for urban service workers, 6 percent for organized labor, and 3 percent for industrial capitalists. Table 5 indicates that agricultural development is the preferred food-security policy for all urban groups, even organized labor, but that rural groups prefer export-led growth.

Export-led growth. The export-expansion strategy was modeled in an analogous fashion to agricultural development. For the export-promotion program, the investment shares in food-processing and in light consumer-goods were increased by 6 percentage points each, with corresponding reductions in the share of investment in services. Tariffs and subsidies were cut by two-thirds, at a fiscal cost of $20 million, as in the agricultural development experiment. At the same time, the productivity of capital in these sectors was increased by 3 percent to simulate the effects of international competition on efficiency.

This increase in productivity was estimated from sectoral regression equations for Korea in Chenery, Robinson, and Syrquin (1986, p. 304) for 1960 to 1977. In these regressions, they decomposed sectoral total factor-productivity increases into productivity change due to import substitution and productivity change due to increases in the share of sectoral output exported. We aggregated their sectors to correspond to our sectors by using shares in value added, looked at the increase in the share of output of consumer goods and processsed foods exported under initial versions of the export-led growth experiment, and then multiplied the aggregated regression coefficients relating to export shares by the change in the share of exports occurring in our export-led growth experiment to obtain estimates of the export-induced change in total factor productivity. We then looked at the change in the share of exports produced by the experiment to check whether the share assumed for the calculation and the share yielded by the experiment were the same and then repeated the procedure until the two numbers converged (only two iterations were required). This procedure yielded a rate of export-induced increase in total factor productivity of approximately 3 percent in both the processed-food and light consumer-goods sectors.

The export-promotion strategy is both a good growth-strategy and a good food-security strategy for the economy (tables 2, 3 and 4). But it is not as good on either count as agricultural development. In macroeconomic terms, export-led growth achieves less GDP growth and less investment than agricultural development. Real wages and real capital rental rates are both lower. Overall consumption is the same but food consumption is significantly less than with agricultural development, and food imports are substantially higher and food production smaller. The price level is the same, but food prices are very significantly higher. Export-led growth therefore also achieves less overall food security than does agricultural development. In terms of overall food security, agricultural development is a superior strategy since it reduces the expected food deficit for all groups most and decreases the percent malnourished (by 3 percent) more than export-led growth.

Agricultural terms of trade are almost 10 percent higher with export-led growth than with agricultural development. Farmers therefore fare much better than do urban groups under this strategy; more of the incidence of malnutrition is shifted towards urban groups. Export-led growth has better mean–variance properties than agricultural development for farmers and both lower mean and lower variance for the urban poor. As a result, farmers would prefer export-led growth to agricultural development and urban groups would prefer agricultural development to export-led growth (table 5).

3.1. The mean–variance frontier

Agents whose utility can be represented as a function of the mean and variance of their instantaneous utility will only select policies on the mean–variance frontier. The frontier is the set of policies that have maximal mean for given variance. Since the six policies and the base case affect different groups differently, there is no guarantee that any policy is mean–variance efficient for all the groups. In the case of the policies considered here, there appears to be a dichotomy between rural and urban groups as to which policies are mean–variance efficient.

The agricultural development policy is the most efficient high-mean, high-variance policy for all non-farm households except industrial capitalists who prefer food aid. Agricultural development is thus the preferred high-risk choice for the overwhelming majority of the urban sector. The agricultural development policy is high risk because it increases the quantity of food that is subject to random shocks in food production. The high-variance, high-mean policy preferred by rural groups is export-led growth. For farmers it leads to higher mean income and lower variance than does agricultural development. Agricultural terms of trade for farmers are 10 percent higher under export-led growth, which raises urban demand for grain without increasing domestic production. It has lower income-variance because there is smaller domestic grain-production that is subject to production shocks.

At the low end of the mean–variance frontier there are two candidate policies that are mean–variance efficient: the dual-price policy and world-price stabilization. Both policies achieve extremely low variances in above-subsistence incomes by reducing the variance in grain prices, either by operating on domestic grain-prices or on world-prices. The dual-price policy is the most efficient low-variance choice for farm households, for service sector workers, and for industrial capitalists. For other households deriving their incomes from manufacturing and for agricultural capitalists, world-price stabilization is the most efficient low-risk choice.

Moving to moderate-mean, moderate-variance policies, there is little consistency among different groups about efficient policies. There is, however, a general tendency to rely on world-market-oriented measures for mean–variance-efficient moderate-risk food-security programs. World-price stabilization is the efficient moderate-risk policy for the rural sector; workers in the service sector find both world-price stabilization and food-aid mean–variance efficient; organized labor would choose food-aid as mean–variance efficient for moderate degrees of risk aversion; marginal labor would select export-led growth; and moderately risk-averse agricultural capitalists would choose grain-price subsidies.

Finally, some programs are dominated for all degrees of risk aversion: The base and import insurance are mean–variance inefficient for all groups and under all degrees of risk aversion.

Thus, except for dominated policies, the choice of which food-security program to pursue will clearly depend on the degree of risk aversion of the society and upon the political influence of rural versus urban groups. With our assumed, relatively low degree of risk-aversion, the high-mean, high-variance, agricultural-development-led-industrialization policy is clearly the policy preferred by the overwhelming majority of the urban population as indicated by the equivalent-variation calculations of table 5. By the same token, export-led growth is the high-mean, high-variance policy of choice for the rural population.

If the population (or its government) were extremely risk averse, there is about an even split between those that would prefer world price stabilization and those that would prefer the dual-price policy as the low-risk mean–variance efficient policy, with the majority of the rural population preferring the two-price policy. It is interesting to note that most developing-country governments have instituted some form of dual-price policy while only a few have pursued agricultural development programs. This may imply that most less-developed-country governments have high degrees of risk aversion rather than that they have an urban bias, as argued by Lipton (1977), though the two propositions are clearly not mutually exclusive. On the contrary, urban bias would lead governments with higher risk-tolerance to favor agricultural development.

3.2. Multipliers

To check the sensitivity of our results to the choice of program magnitude, we estimated program multipliers (table 6). To compute the multipliers, we increased the program magnitudes for each component (e.g., taxes, tariffs, foreign aid, etc.) of all the food-security experiments by 50 percent and reran the 100 replicates with the same random shock samples as for the $20 million experiments. We reproduce results for the effects on the percent

Table 6

Impact multipliers.

	World price stabilization	Food import insurance	Food aid	Grain price subsidy	Agricultural development	Export-led growth
Percentage change in percent malnourished						
Small farmers	−0.23	0.08	0.33	−0.26	−0.41	0.17
Marginal laborers	0.36	−0.13	−0.03	−0.35	0.28	0.17
Organized labor	0.00	−0.78	−1.15	−1.78	1.94	3.4
Service workers	0.21	−1.04	−0.02	−1.14	−1.14	3.4
Total population	−0.10	−0.13	0.09	−0.67	−0.23	0.76
Percentage change in calorie deficit						
Total	−0.40	−0.13	−0.03	−0.47	−0.24	0.75

Source: Computed as the percent change from the policies costing $20 million to those costing $30 million.

malnourished and the food deficit in table 6. For each food-security program and each group, the entries in the table indicate the percentage change from the $20 million program induced by the 50 percent increase in the program.

The table indicates that at a larger scale grain-price subsidy, agricultural development, and world-price stabilization would all become relatively more attractive policies, while export-led growth would become significantly worse.

4. Conclusions

How efficient are the food-security policies analyzed? An unrealistic but idealized standard of comparison would be how much calorie-deficit reduction could be accomplished with a 'frictionless' $20 million program. Visualize a program in which $20 million is spent to increase the calorie-availability of the poorest third of the population; and assume that the program is perfectly targeted, costlessly implemented, and has no indirect effects on prices or quantities. Such a program would represent a 3 percent increase in the availability of processed and unprocessed food to the poor and would cut the average daily calorie-deficit of the malnourished by between one fourth and one eighths, depending on the group. None of the food-security programs modeled accomplish nearly as much. The most effective food-deficit reduction programs cut the average calorie deficit by only 3 percent – 12 percent of the 'frictionless' program. Actual programs thus have substantial leakages to the non-poor, significant indirect effects mostly through prices, and large implementation costs. These combine to greatly reduce the expected effectiveness of all food-security programs relative to this, unrealizable, ideal program.

To maintain comparability among programs, we calibrated all programs to a $20 million cost and examined their food-security effects one year after implementation. The programs are feasible, but moderate in size. However, our multiplier calculations indicate that a 50 percent increase in the cost of the programs does not generate a dramatic change in effectiveness.

Among the food-security programs we examined, we found that the best food-security policies are those that are implementable at the national level. The international policies considered in our experiment – grain-price stabilization, food-import insurance, and food aid – achieve less in terms of food-security than do the national policies and strategies. Price stabilization of grains is useful in reducing the incidence of catastrophic outcomes and many groups would be willing to pay for this policy, but it has virtually no effect on decreasing the percentage of malnourished or the food deficit on the average. The other international food-security policies impoverish domestic farmers and reduce their production incentives. In addition, IMF-type food-import-bill insurance schemes have perverse effects, paying off in periods of national prosperity and not paying off in periods of crop failure. Finally, in the absence of measures to counteract the adverse effects of food aid on the incomes of farmers, food aid is an overall food-security disaster, though it does help a few urban groups.

Agricultural development and export-led growth are the most effective approaches to reductions in expected malnutrition. In our simulations, agricultural development dominates export-led growth as a food-security strategy. Both strategies generate growth in GNP realtive to the base, though agricultural development generates higher GNP-growth. Both strategies generate substantially higher mean incomes and higher income variances than the base. And both strategies diffuse income growth in their sector to producers in the complementary sector. But agricultural development leads to the lowest percent malnourished. Furthermore, agricultural development increases food consumption and releases foreign exchange for the import of machinery and intermediate inputs so that it helps the export-drive of the manufacturing sector. By contrast, export-led growth induces an increase in the price of grains, a decrease in overall grain consumption and an increase in net imports of grain.

Our simulations indicate that the choice among food-security measures is sensitive to the risk-aversion of the population or of its government. Agricultural development is the preferred high-risk choice of the overwhelming majority of the urban population, and export-led growth is the preferred rural strategy, while price-stabilization policies (national or international) are the preferred low-risk choices. International measures come into their own only as moderate-risk, moderate-income programs, but they achieve very little decrease in average expected malnutrition.

Also, group preferences among policies differ among groups. The dichotomy among net food sellers and net food buyers tends to run across our results, though it is not as simple as all that since the policies have both direct and indirect effects on prices and incomes.

How general are the conclusions of our simulations? The results of the simulations were generated by considering how international and agricultural production shocks affect a model economy. They, therefore, reflect the economy's exposure to shock and the institutional rules of the game portrayed in the model. Less open economies, or oil or primary-exporting economies, will face different shock-covariance matrices. Similarly, rigidities in factor or commodity markets will accentuate income-shocks and transmit them through either enhanced price or quantity-fluctuations. Our experiments, which assumed a flexibly adjusting economy, thus overstate the mitigating effects that substitution would have upon adjustment to shock in an economy with greater rigidities. The covariance of internal prices with international price or demand-fluctuations will be greater in a more rigid economy. Stabilization policies may then accomplish more in terms of food-security. Furthermore, the fixed, or less flexibly adjusting, factors will bear a larger fraction of the adjustment cost and experience greater variances in incomes. Differences in program-incidence may be magnified. In our experiments, we allowed only marginal workers to migrate between rural and urban occupations and did not allow for compensating changes in urban–rural remittances. These would tend to reduce, though not eliminate, the dichotomy between how different food-security programs affect rural and urban groups in the short run. In addition, our model was a flexible-wage model. A fixed-wage economy would allocate the incidence of an external shock differently among wage earners and capitalists in a given sector and would change the distribution of income among workers (the employed versus the unemployed) in response to shocks but would have very little effect on the urban–rural allocation of malnutrition and on the overall extent of malnutrition [Adelman and Robinson (1988)]. Our economy had no sharecropping and no tenancy, only owner-operators with different plot sizes and different degrees of reliance on hired labor. Shocks, therefore, tended to affect all farm operators in the same way. In economies with more varied tenancy structures, there would be greater differences in the impact of shocks on different types of farmers. The risk-sharing properties of different farming systems would be different.

Before drawing definitive conclusions, it would, therefore, be desirable to experiment with alternative institutional specifications and redo the food-security simulations for different types of economies. We, nevertheless, believe that the group-specific results of our simulations, which describe how different individual groups are affected by individual programs, are probably qualitatively generalizable. We suspect that for most poor, food-deficit economies, the relative ranking of food-security policies for individual groups would not differ much from ours. We therefore think that our results offer a qualitatively good basis for extrapolating to economies with different compositions of poverty, different relative income levels, and different exposures to shocks by appropriate reaggregation.

In particular, we believe that the relative ranking of national versus international food-security policies and of income-stabilization versus mean-income-growth food-security policies are quite robust since the reasons for effectiveness or ineffectiveness of most programs are rather fundamental. Thus, import-bill-stabilization fails because it provides ineffective insurance to any country – large or small, open or closed, rigid or flexible – that can and will use increased income to purchase food. Price-stabilization does not reduce malnutrition much in other studies [Reutlinger (1976)] geared to less open economies. More fundamentally, stabilization policies achieve a higher probability of being close to the mean in food intake; if that intake is inadequate, they are a prescription for malnutrition with increased certainty. These conclusions are unlikely to depend much on the type of country or model. On the other hand, for a two-price system or for food-aid, it matters a great deal what the tenancy arrangements are. Because Korea was a land of small owner-operators, it was possible to run a two-price system that neutralized some of the losses to the potentially malnourished small farmers. For much the same reason, uncompensated food-aid hurt this group of poor and hence increased food-insecurity. Developing nations with very different tenancy arrangements could expect different food-security results from such policies, but our experiment may well be the best case for both of these policies. Finally, the major result of our simulation experiment – that development strategies that raise the rates of growth of the incomes of the poor constitute the most effective approach to reducing malnutrition in the long run – is extremely unlikely to be affected by model-specification or exposure to shock.

But how robust is the relative ranking of agricultural vs. export-led growth as food-security strategies? We must ask this question since export-led growth, though dominated in our experiments by agricultural development for the majority of the population which is urban, was a close second-best policy to agricultural development. Clearly, the relative ranking of the two strategies must depend on their relative potential for raising the incomes of the poor and on their relative riskiness. Among newly industrializing countries, the potential for industrial development is more uniform than the potential for agricultural development. The inherent short-run potential of agriculture for productivity improvement and the riskiness of agriculture is likely to vary significantly among countries with different topographies and land-densities, degrees of institutional responsiveness to market incentives in agriculture, size distributions of landholdings, and levels of rural education.

Furthermore, successful agricultural development requires maintaining a delicate balance among: the growth of productivity of the agricultural sector; the composition of output of the agricultural sector, especially as between food-grains and feed-grains; and the growth in urban incomes, and hence level and composition of demand for food of the non-agricultural sector. Agricultural develoment can fail as a food-security strategy in the medium run, if the growth of agricultural productivity is too fast relative to the rates of growth of the non-agricultural sectors plus either agricultural import-replacement or agricultural exports. On the other hand, if agricultural development is too slow, it can pose a major bottleneck for industrial development. What matters for the success of both the industrial and the agricultural food-security strategies is the balance between the growth of the two sectors in the medium run.

In the medium run, it is possible to improve agricultural productivity faster than the growth in urban demand plus net import-replacement. This did not happen in our experiment with agricultural development because of the way the productivity estimates came out and because of the large share of agricultural imports in the base year. In our experiments, the rate of growth of productivity of agriculture in the agricultural development experiment was slower than the rate of growth of industrial productivity, but applied to a much larger base.

The relationships we estimated are, however, not limited to Korea alone. De Janvry and Sadoulet (1986) provide general evidence concerning the changing relationships between agricultural growth, growth in overall GNP, and international trade in less-developed countries. Their estimates suggest that countries start with low growth in agriculture, relying on agricultural exports for both industrialization and GNP growth. They then start industrializing, and they neglect and tax agriculture. The result is that the slow growth in agricultural output becomes a binding constraint on industrial growth. At this point, most newly industrializing developing countries start engaging in serious efforts to improve agricultural productivity. They then first go through an import-substitution phase (the Korea of our experiment) and, if they continue the agricultural strategy, they next move to a second agricultural-export phase (e.g., Indonesia). Then, with continued urban-income growth, there is a shift in the composition of demand towards animal proteins. This, in turn, entails a vastly enhanced demand for feed-grains and increased pressures for improvement in the productivity of the agricultural sector. At this point, countries again turn to importing either feed-grains or food-grains or both (e.g., Mexico). So, in the long run, there can't be too much improvement in agricultural productivity if cropping patterns are flexible, and there is worldwide evidence that they are.

In sum, the case for agricultural development as a preferred food-security strategy appears strong, especially for the newly industrializing countries and the least-developed countries. But it is not likely to be universal. What is likely to be universal is that the primary hope for a poor food-deficit country to achieve food-security is to grow out of it through development strategies that raise the rates of growth of the incomes of the poor. Other food-security measures should be viewed as stop-gap measures, worth implementing only till the right type of growth takes hold.

References

Adelman, I., 1984, Beyond export-led growth, World Development 12, no. 9, 11–35.

Adelman, I., P. Berck and K. Gordon, 1983, Food security: A mean variance approach, Working paper no. 251 (Department of Agricultural and Resource Economics, University of California, Berkeley, CA).

Adelman, I. and S. Robinson, 1978, Income distribution policies in developing countries (Stanford University Press, Standford, CA).

Adelman, I. and S. Robinson, 1988, Macroeconomic adjustment and income distribution: Alternative models applied to two economies, Journal of Development Economics 29, no. 1, 23–44.

Ahmed, R., 1979, Foodgrains supply distribution, and consumption policies within a dual pricing mechanism: A case study of Bangladesh, Research report no. 8 (International Food Policy Research Institute, Washington, DC).

Bailey, W.R., F.A. Kurish and A.S. Rojko, 1974, Grain stocks, issues and alternatives – A progress report (U.S. and World Food Security, U.S. Congress, Senate, Committee on Agriculture and Forestry, 93rd Congress, 2nd Session, Washington, DC).

Barker, R. and Y. Hayami, 1976, Price support vs. input subsidy for food self-sufficiency in developing countries, American Journal of Agricultural Economics 58, 617–638.

Berg, A., 1980, A strategy to reduce malnutrition, Finance and Development 17, no. 1, 23–26.

Bigman, D., 1982, Coping with hunger: Towards a system of food security and price stabilization (Ballinger, Cambridge, MA).

Bigman, D. and S. Reutlinger, 1979, National and international policies toward food security and price stabilization, American Economic Review 69, 159–163.

Brandt Commission, 1980, North-South: A programme for survival (M.I.T. Press, London).

Chenery, H.G., S. Robinson and M. Syrquin, 1986, Industrialization and growth (Oxford University Press, New York).

Cochrane, W. and Y. Danin, 1976, Reserve grain models and the world, 1975–1985, in: Analysis of grain reserves, a proceedings, Economic Research Service report no. 634 (U.S. Department of Agriculture and the National Science Foundation, Washington, DC).

De Janvry, Alain and Elisabeth Sadoulet, 1987, Agricultural policy and general equilibrium, American Journal of Agricultural Economics 69, no. 2, 230–246.

Dervis, K., J. de Melo and S. Robinson, 1982, General equilibrium models for development policy (Cambridge University Press, New York).

Dunn, J. and D.M. Heien, 1982, The gains from price stabilization: A quantitative assessment, American Journal of Agricultural Economics 64, no. 3, 578–580.

Eaton, D., W.S. Steel, J.L. Coho and C.S. Revelle, 1976, The Joseph problem: How large a grain reserve? Mimeo. (Department of Geography and Environmental Engineering, Baltimore, MD).

Falcon, W., 1984, Recent food policy lessons from developing countries, American Journal of Agricultural Economics 66, no. 2, 180–185.

Gavan, J.D. and I.S. Chandrasekar, 1979, The impact of public food grain distribution on food consumption and welfare in Sri Lanka, Research report no. 13 (IFPRI, Washington, DC).

George, P.S., 1979, Public distribution of food grains in Kerala – Income distribution implications and effectiveness, Research report no. 7 (IFPRI, Washington, DC).

Green, C.J. and C.H. Kirkpatrick, 1982, The IMF's food financing facility, Journal of World Trade Law 18, no. 2, 265–273.

Hall, L.L., 1980, Evaluating effects of PL 480, Wheat imports on Brazil's grain sector, American Journal of Agricultural Economics 62, 14–28.

Hayami, Y., 1977, Price incentives vs. irrigation investment to achieve food self-sufficiency in the Philippines, American Journal of Agricultural Economics 59, 717–721.

Johnson, D.G., 1978, Increase stability of grain supplies in developing countries: Optimal carryovers and insurance, World Development 4, 977–987.

Johnson, D.G. and D. Sumner, 1976, An optimization approach to grain reserves for developing countries, in: D.J. Eaton and W. Scott, eds., Analysis of grain reserves: A proceedings, Economic Research Service report no. 634 (U.S. Department of Agriculture, Washington, DC).

Konandreas, P., B. Huddleston and V. Ramangkura, 1978, Food security: An insurance approach, Research report no. 4 (IFPRI, Washington, DC).

Kumar, S.K., 1979, Impact of subsidized rice on food consumption and nutrition in Kerala, Research report no. 5 (IFPRI, Washington, DC).

Lane, S., 1980, The contribution of food aid to nutrition, American Journal of Agricultural Economics 62, no. 5, 984–987.

Lappe, F.M., 1978, Food first: Beyond the myth of scarcity (Ballantine Books, New York).

Lele, U., 1971, Food grain marketing in India (Cornell University Press, Ithaca, NY).

Lipton, M., 1977, Why poor people stay poor (Temple Smith, London).

Mellor, J.W., 1976, The new economics of growth (Cornell University Press, Ithaca, NY).

Mellor, J.W., 1980, Food aid and nutrition, American Journal of Agricultural Economics 62, no. 5, 979–983.

Newbery, D.M.G. and J.E. Stiglitz, 1981, The theory of commodity price stabilization (Oxford University Press, Oxford).

Oi, W.Y., 1961, The desirability of price instability under perfect competition, Econometrica 29, 58–64.

Perrin, R.K. and G.M. Scobie, 1981, Market intervention policies for increasing the consumption of nutrients by low income households, American Journal of Agricultural Economics 63, no. 1, 73–82.

Pinstrup-Andersen, P. and E. Caicedo, 1978, The potential impact of changes in income distribution on food demand and human nutrition, American Journal of Agricultural Economics 60, 402–415.

Reutlinger, S., 1976, A simulation model for evaluating worldwide buffer stocks of wheat, American Journal of Agricultural Economics 58, 1–12.

Reutlinger, S. and K. Knapp, 1980, Food security in food deficit countries, World Bank staff working paper no. 393 (World Bank, Washington, DC).

Reutlinger, S. and M. Selowsky, 1976, Malnutrition and poverty: Magnitude and policy options (Johns Hopkins University Press, Baltimore, MD).

Rodgers, K.D., U.K. Srivastava and E.O. Heady, 1972, Modified price, production, and income impacts of food aid under market differentiation distribution, American Journal of Agricultural Economics 54, 201–208.

Sarris, A.H., 1985, Food security and agricultural production strategies and risk in Egypt, Journal of Development Economics, 85–111.

Sarris, A.H., P.C. Abbot and L. Taylor, 1977, Grain reserves, emergency relief and food aid, Mimeo. (Overseas Development Council, Washington, DC).

Scandizzo, P.L., P.R.B. Hazell and J.R. Anderson, 1983, Producer's price expectations and the gains from price stabilization, Review of Marketing in Agricultural Economics 51, no. 2, 93–107.

Schneider, R.R., 1985, Food subsidies: A multiple price model, International Monetary Fund Staff paper 32, no. 2, 289–316.

Sen, A., 1981, Poverty and Famines (Oxford University Press, Oxford).

Streeten, P.P., 1985, First things first (Oxford University Press, Oxford).

Turnovsky, S.J., 1978, The distribution of welfare gains from price stabilization: A survey of some theoretical issues, in: F.O. Adams and S.A. Klein, eds., Stabilizing world commodity markets (Heath, Lexington, MA), 119–148.

Turnovsky, S.J., H. Shalit and A. Schmitz, 1980, Consumer's surplus, price instability and consumer welfare, Econometrica 48, 135–152.

United Nations, Food and Agricultural Organization, 1973, Energy and protein requirements, Report of a joint FAO/WIHO Ad Hoc Expert Committee (FAO, Rome).

Waugh, F.V., 1944, Does the consumer benefit from price instability, Quarterly Journal of Economics 58, 603–614.

Wright, B.D. and J.C. Williams, 1982, The economic role of commodity storage, Economic Journal 92, no. 367, 596–614.

Name index

Economists of the Twentieth Century

Monetarism and Macroeconomic Policy
Thomas Mayer

Studies in Fiscal Federalism
Wallace E. Oates

The World Economy in Perspective
Essays in International Trade and European Integration
Herbert Giersch

Towards a New Economics
Critical Essays on Ecology, Distribution and Other Themes
Kenneth E. Boulding

Studies in Positive and Normative Economics
Martin J. Bailey

The Collected Essays of Richard E. Quandt (2 volumes)
Richard E. Quandt

International Trade Theory and Policy
Selected Essays of W. Max Corden
W. Max Corden

Organization and Technology in Capitalist Development
William Lazonick

Studies in Human Capital
Collected Essays of Jacob Mincer, Volume 1
Jacob Mincer

Studies in Labor Supply
Collected Essays of Jacob Mincer, Volume 2
Jacob Mincer

Macroeconomics and Economic Policy
The Selected Essays of Assar Lindbeck, Volume I
Assar Lindbeck

The Welfare State
The Selected Essays of Assar Lindbeck, Volume II
Assar Lindbeck

Classical Economics, Public Expenditure and Growth
Walter Eltis

Money, Interest Rates and Inflation
Frederic S. Mishkin

The Public Choice Approach to Politics
Dennis C. Mueller

The Liberal Economic Order
Volume I Essays on International Economics
Volume II Money, Cycles and Related Themes
Gottfried Haberler
Edited by Anthony Y.C. Koo

Economic Growth and Business Cycles
Prices and the Process of Cyclical Development
Paolo Sylos Labini

International Adjustment, Money and Trade
Theory and Measurement for Economic Policy, Volume I
Herbert G. Grubel

International Capital and Service Flows
Theory and Measurement for Economic Policy, Volume II
Herbert G. Grubel

Unintended Effects of Government Policies
Theory and Measurement for Economic Policy, Volume III
Herbert G. Grubel

The Economics of Competitive Enterprise
Selected Essays of P.W.S. Andrews
Edited by Frederic S. Lee and Peter E. Earl

The Repressed Economy
Causes, Consequences, Reform
Deepak Lal

Economic Theory and Market Socialism
Selected Essays of Oskar Lange
Edited by Tadeusz Kowalik

Trade, Development and Political Economy
Selected Essays of Ronald Findlay
Ronald Findlay

General Equilibrium Theory
The Collected Essays of Takashi Negishi, Volume I
Takashi Negishi

The History of Economics
The Collected Essays of Takashi Negishi, Volume II
Takashi Negishi

Studies in Econometric Theory
The Collected Essays of Takeshi Amemiya
Takeshi Amemiya

Exchange Rates and the Monetary System
Selected Essays of Peter B. Kenen
Peter B. Kenen

Econometric Methods and Applications (2 volumes)
G.S. Maddala

National Accounting and Economic Theory
The Collected Papers of Dan Usher, Volume I
Dan Usher

Welfare Economics and Public Finance
The Collected Papers of Dan Usher, Volume II
Dan Usher

Economic Theory and Capitalist Society
The Selected Essays of Shigeto Tsuru, Volume I
Shigeto Tsuru

Methodology, Money and the Firm
The Collected Essays of D.P. O'Brien (2 volumes)
D.P. O'Brien

Economic Theory and Financial Policy
The Selected Essays of Jacques J. Polak (2 volumes)
Jacques J. Polak

Sturdy Econometrics
Edward E. Leamer

The Emergence of Economic Ideas
Essays in the History of Economics
Nathan Rosenberg

Productivity Change, Public Goods and Transaction Costs
Essays at the Boundaries of Microeconomics
Yoram Barzel

Reflections on Economic Development
The Selected Essays of Michael P. Todaro
Michael P. Todaro

The Economic Development of Modern Japan
The Selected Essays of Shigeto Tsuru, Volume II
Shigeto Tsuru

Money, Credit and Policy
Allan H. Meltzer

Macroeconomics and Monetary Theory
The Selected Essays of Meghnad Desai, Volume I
Meghnad Desai

Poverty, Famine and Economic Development
The Selected Essays of Meghnad Desai, Volume II
Meghnad Desai